HIDDEN®

Southern California

"Excellent."
—*Chicago Tribune*

"A handy paperback."
—*Los Angeles Times*

"A complete guidebook!"
—*San Diego Tribune*

"Breezy and informative."
—*Fresno Bee*

"Covers it all from the obvious to the obscure."
—*San Antonio Express-News*

"A fast-paced, extraordinarily comprehensive, highly readable
guidebook to Southern California."
—*Books of the Southwest*

"This book is superb and is recommended for the seasoned or neophyte
traveler to the area."
—*St. Louis Post-Dispatch*

"A sure-fire clue to a good travel book is if it includes the word 'hidden'
in the title and is written by Ray Riegert."
—*Toronto Sun*

HIDDEN®
Southern California

Including Los Angeles, Hollywood, San Diego, Santa Barbara, and Palm Springs

Ray Riegert

NINTH EDITION

Ulysses Press®
BERKELEY, CALIFORNIA

Published by:
ULYSSES PRESS
P.O. Box 3440
Berkeley, CA 94703
www.ulyssespress.com

ISSN 1522-1180
ISBN 1-56975-403-9

Printed in Canada by Transcontinental Printing

20 19 18 17 16 15 14 13 12 11 10

UPDATE AUTHOR: Ellen Clark
EDITORIAL DIRECTOR: Leslie Henriques
MANAGING EDITOR: Claire Chun
PROJECT DIRECTOR: Laura Brancella
COPY EDITOR: Lily Chou
EDITORIAL ASSOCIATES: Kate Allen, Kaori Takee
TYPESETTERS: Steven Schwartz, Lisa Kester, James Meetze
CARTOGRAPHY: Pease Press
HIDDEN BOOKS DESIGN: Sarah Levin
COVER DESIGN: Sarah Levin, Leslie Henriques
INDEXER: Sayre Van Young
COVER PHOTOGRAPHY: Larry Ulrich (Channel Islands)
ILLUSTRATOR: Tim Carroll

Distributed in the United States by Publishers Group West
and in Canada by Raincoast Books

The author and publisher have made every effort to ensure the
accuracy of information contained in *Hidden Southern California*,
but can accept no liability for any loss, injury, or inconvenience
sustained by any traveler as a result of information or advice
contained in this guide.

For my mother

Acknowledgments

If publishing a book is comparable to sailing a boat, the vessel I captain is a cross between *The Good Ship Lollipop* and a *Ship of Fools.* Surprisingly, during the voyage, no one mutinied.

My wife and co-publisher Leslie Henriques is primarily responsible for keeping the project on course. She worked indefatigably on every phase and shares equally in any credit that may be forthcoming.

Claire Chun also weathered the storms, proving that it's really quite easy to simultaneously research a chapter, type notes, and supervise a production team. Laura Brancella worked ably and conscientiously as project director. Thanks as well to Lily Chou for her work with the red pencil.

Tim Carroll created the illustrations, and the cover was nicely designed by Sarah Levin and Leslie. Kate Allen helped with research and production. Sayre Van Young turned out another in a long line of professionally rendered indexes.

To all of them I want to extend a large, warm, and heartfelt thank you.

*

Ulysses Press would like to thank the following readers who took the time to write in with suggestions that were incorporated into this new edition of *Hidden Southern California*:

Ellen T. Herman of Berkeley Heights, NJ; Carolina Cristancho of Kailua, HI; Dana Clark of Oakland, CA; Manon and Kurt Weise of Hollywood, Fl; Deanna and Andrew Olsen of San Francisco, CA; Jolie Kaytes of Moscow, ID; Omri Sitton via e-mail.

What's Hidden?

At different points throughout this book, you'll find special listings marked with a hidden symbol:

◄ HIDDEN

This means that you have come upon a place off the beaten tourist track, a spot that will carry you a step closer to the local people and natural environment of Southern California.

The goal of this guide is to lead you beyond the realm of everyday tourist facilities. While we include traditional sightseeing listings and popular attractions, we also offer alternative sights and adventure activities. Instead of filling this guide with reviews of standard hotels and chain restaurants, we concentrate on one-of-a-kind places and locally owned establishments.

Our authors seek out locales that are popular with residents but usually overlooked by visitors. Some are more hidden than others (and are marked accordingly), but all the listings in this book are intended to help you discover the true nature of Southern California and put you on the path of adventure.

Write to us!

If in your travels you discover a spot that captures the spirit of Southern California, or if you live in the region and have a favorite place to share, or if you just feel like expressing your views, write to us and we'll pass your note along to the author.

We can't guarantee that the author will add your personal find to the next edition, but if the writer does use the suggestion, we'll acknowledge you in the credits and send you a free copy of the new edition.

ULYSSES PRESS
P.O. Box 3440
Berkeley, CA 94703
E-mail: readermail@ulyssespress.com

Contents

Maps

OUTDOOR ADVENTURE SYMBOLS

The following symbols accompany national, state and regional park listings, as well as beach descriptions throughout the text.

Camping

Hiking

Biking

Horseback Riding

Downhill Skiing

Cross-country Skiing

Swimming

Snorkeling

Surfing

Waterskiing

Windsurfing

Canoeing or Kayaking

Boating

Boat Ramps

Fishing

ONE

Southern California

"The lands of the sun," according to an old Spanish proverb, "expand the soul." In the iconography of American life, sunshine is synonymous with Southern California. Life here is lived outdoors. Since the turn of the 20th century the region has been cast as the country's Mediterranean shoreline, picturesque and leisurely.

A land without water resources and lacking natural harbors, it has built its reputation on climate. Warm winters and cool summers, ocean breezes and desert warmth, have created a civilization whose foremost symbol is the palm tree.

Geographically Southern California is a place apart, a domain that the historian Carey McWilliams termed "an island on the land." Bounded by the Tehachapis to the north and the Sierra Nevada to the east, it is vast but solitary.

Constituting only half a state, Southern California is broader and more diverse than most nations are. Its western border nuzzles the Pacific; the interior is a region of piedmont and plain, once given over to cattle ranching and citrus cultivation, but presently being developed into one continuous megalopolis; to the east lies the desert, wind-burnished domain of piñon and palm, Joshua trees and juniper.

Southern California, paradoxically, is a desert facing an ocean. It's a region that has everything—luxurious beaches, dynamic cities, desolate sand dunes, and bald mountains. The highest peak in the contiguous United States rests here just 60 miles from the lowest point.

To capture this diversity in a guidebook, to confine the grandeur of the place within the pages of a single volume, is to square the circle. Los Angeles alone deserves several texts. Here it is covered in two sections—Chapter Two, which extends from Downtown to Hollywood, then out to the San Gabriel and San Fernando valleys; and Chapter Three, which combs the L.A. coastline from Long Beach to Malibu.

Chapter Four is dedicated to Orange County, ranging from the Pacific resorts of Newport Beach and Laguna Beach to theme parks such as Disneyland and

Knott's Berry Farm. Then, in a stubborn attempt to find something still "hidden" in this sprawling suburb, it ventures out to the Santa Ana Mountains. San Diego, from city to coast to Mt. Palomar, is the subject of Chapter Five. The Central Coast, Chapter Six, sweeps from Ventura north to Santa Barbara and San Simeon, taking in Ojai and San Luis Obispo along the way.

The California desert is the subject of Chapters Seven and Eight, with the former devoted to the Inland Empire, Palm Springs, and the Sonora Desert, and the latter covering the central Mojave Desert, Death Valley, and the Sierra Nevada. General information on how, where, when, and why to visit Southern California appears in the chapter you are reading.

Throughout the book I have tried to convey a specific sense of place, providing information on hotels, restaurants, and sightseeing spots, then carrying you several strides farther to the beaches, parks, trails, and unknown locales that make adventuring in Southern California high sport. Although the region's hidden realms are rapidly falling to the advance of suburbia, the soul of the place prevails.

What remains hidden in Southern California, underlying every aspect of its outward reality, is the mythology of the region. Southern California is a picture in your mind. Envision an orange—plump, round, and spilling over with the promise of good health—and you think of Southern California. Conversely, if you visualize an automobile, L.A.'s smog-shrouded freeways will occur just as naturally. Think of political conservatism—the presidencies of Richard Nixon and Ronald Reagan—and the nation's southwestern corner will flash to the fore. Or conjure a picture of Mexican culture, saturated with romantic imagery, and your daydreams will lead inevitably to the far edge of the Sunbelt.

To tour Southern California is to experience déjà vu. Regardless of your place of origin, the area exists, through the medium of film, somewhere in the psyche. More than being inseparable, myth and reality in the Southland feed on one another. Many times during my explorations I felt as if I were leading both of us back through our own pasts, to locations not yet real, but already behind us.

The first time I saw Southern California I was 18 years old, hitchhiking down the coast to Mexico. A child of the television age, I had grown up on the East Coast believing that major cities were lined with palm trees, the Wild West began in the Mojave and ended in the Sierra Nevada, and that all oceans resembled the Pacific. To kids like me all across the country, the architecture of Southern California represented the building styles of the world and the people of the Southland portrayed populations everywhere. I was hitchhiking along Memory Lane.

For all of us, Hollywood has elevated Southern California to a metaphor for living. The attributes that initially attracted movie makers to Los Angeles—its Italian climate, diverse geography, and leisurely pace—are precisely the features that Hollywood projects onto movie screens and television sets around the globe. It is the greatest act of cultural feedback in history. And it continues today.

To provide you with an unclouded picture, I have included historical information and factual details throughout the text in the hope that you can draw from them substantive ideas for planning and executing a trip. Regardless, you'll find in the end that truth in Southern California is built on a foundation of fiction. The region is living out its own legend. Follow my specific directions to a particular address and you'll discover that the romance rather than the reality of the place sweeps you along. It is the spirit of Southern California that entices and enthralls us all, holding us prisoners in paradise as long as we wish.

Any place the size of Southern California is bound to have several different climates. When it is also a region that ranges from seashore to desert to mountains and climbs from below sea level to over 14,000 feet, the problem is compounded.

When to Go

SEASONS

In Southern California you can surf and ski in the same day. Temperatures sometimes vary 40° between the beaches and the mountains. In the desert the mercury can fluctuate this drastically in a single location: a balmy 70° day can give way to a 30° night.

Along the Pacific and on the coastal plain, where most visitors concentrate, the weather corresponds to a Mediterranean climate with mild temperatures year-round. Because the coastal

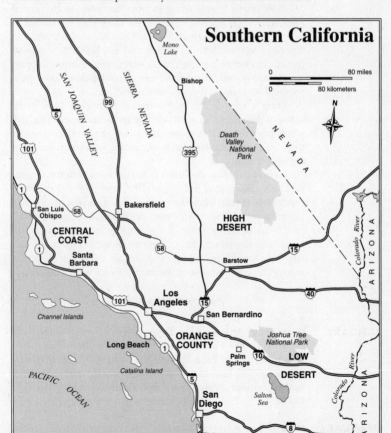

Southern California

fog creates a natural form of air conditioning and insulation, the mercury rarely drops below 40° or rises above 80°. September and October are the hottest months, and December and January the coolest. In Los Angeles the average temperature is 75° during the warm period and about 50° in mid-winter.

More kiwi fruit grows in California than in its native New Zealand.

Spring and particularly autumn are ideal times to visit. Winter is the rainy season, which extends from November to March, with the heaviest showers from December to February. During the rest of the year there is almost no rain. Summer is the peak tourist season, when large crowds can present problems. Like spring, it's also a period of frequent fog; during the morning and evening, fog banks from offshore blanket the coast, burning off around midday.

Most winter storms sweep in from the north, so the annual rainfall averages and the length of the rainy season diminish as you go south. Santa Barbara receives 17 inches of rain a year, Los Angeles averages about 15 inches, and San Diego gets only 10 inches. The ocean air also creates significant moisture, keeping the average humidity around 65 percent and making some areas seem colder than the thermometer would indicate.

Smog is heaviest during August and September. Then in the autumn, the Santa Ana winds kick up out of the desert. Hot, dry winds from the northeast, they sometimes reach velocities of 35 to 50 miles per hour, blowing sand, fanning forest fires, and making people edgy.

It's no secret that the desert is hot in the summer, with temperatures often rising well above 100°. Spring is a particularly pretty time to visit, when the weather is cool and the wildflowers are in bloom. Autumn and winter are also quite pleasant.

The mountains are cold in winter, cool during spring and autumn, and surprisingly hot in summer. You can expect less precipitation than there is along the coast, but the higher elevations receive sufficient snow to make them popular winter ski areas.

CALENDAR OF EVENTS

JANUARY   **Greater Los Angeles**   The Tournament of Roses Parade kicks off the Rose Bowl game in Pasadena on New Year's Day.
Low Desert   The Palm Springs International Film Festival features over 200 films from 60 countries. Celebrities and pros gather in Palm Springs for the annual Bob Hope Desert Chrysler Golf Classic.

FEBRUARY   **Greater Los Angeles**   Chinese New Year celebrations snake through L.A.'s Chinatown.

San Diego Mardi Gras festivities take to the streets in San Diego's historic Gaslamp Quarter.

Low Desert The **Riverside County Fair & National Date Festival** at Indio Fairgrounds features camel races and a diaper derby. The **Frank Sinatra Invitational**, a premiere celebrity and amateur golfing event, is a crowd pleaser.

Orange County Newport Beach hosts the **Toshiba Senior Golf Classic**. In Dana Point, the **Festival of the Whales** features a concert series, sporting competitions, sand castle workshops, and a street fair. The **Fiesta de las Golondrinas** welcomes the swallows back to San Juan Capistrano.

San Diego San Diego's Gaslamp Quarter block party celebrates **St. Patrick's Day** with music and entertainment.

Low Desert Palm Springs hosts **The Nabisco Championship** LPGA **Golf Tournament.** Borrego Springs holds a **Circle of Arts** art show and sale.

MARCH

Greater Los Angeles **Easter Sunrise Services** are marked at the famed Hollywood Bowl. In Little Tokyo **Buddha's Birthday** is celebrated; along nearby Olvera Street the **Blessing of the Animals**, a Mexican tradition, is re-enacted. In Palmdale the **Lilac Festival** signals the advent of spring.

Los Angeles Coast Race car buffs train their binoculars on the **Toyota Grand Prix** in Long Beach.

San Diego **Motorcars on MainStreet** in Coronado features 150 pre-1972 automobiles.

Low Desert The **Peg-Leg Liars Contest,** a tall-tale competition, takes place in Borrego Springs. Hemet's **Ramona Pageant** depicts Early California history with American Indian rituals, music, and dance.

APRIL

Greater Los Angeles Dancers, revelers, and mariachi bands around Olvera Street and East Los Angeles mark **Cinco de Mayo**, the festival celebrating the Battle of Puebla in the French-Mexican War. The UCLA **Mardi Gras** offers games, entertainment, and food.

San Diego Carlsbad hosts the first of the semiannual **Village Faire** with hundreds of arts-and-crafts booths, rides, and countless foodstands. Old Town celebrates **Cinco de Mayo** with mariachis, traditional Mexican folk dancers, food, and displays.

Central Coast Ventura observes the **Ventura Chamber Music Festival** with a series of chamber music concerts situated in various historic landmarks.

High Desert A parade, steer-roping contest, barbecues, and crafts displays mark the **Mule Day Celebration** in Bishop on Memorial Day weekend.

MAY

JUNE

Greater Los Angeles **Gay Pride Week** is celebrated here by a parade through West Hollywood.

San Diego Balboa Park hosts the **The Old Globe Shakespeare Festival**, a series of five plays performed at three theaters in the park.

Central Coast Near Santa Barbara, Santa Maria's **Elk's Rodeo and Parade** offers a glimpse of ranch life, complete with calf roping and bronco-riding. The **Ojai Music Festival**, at the end of May or beginning of June, includes concerts of classical and new music.

JULY

Greater Los Angeles The **Hollywood Bowl Summer Festival** explodes with a Fourth of July concert.

Los Angeles Coast Every Thursday evening from July through August the **Santa Monica Pier Twilight Dance Series** features a variety of live music from reggae to Western swing. Surfers hang ten at the **International Surf and Health Festival** on Hermosa, Manhattan, Torrance, and Redondo beaches.

Orange County The **Art-A-Fair Festival**, one of Southern California's most notable events, occurs in Laguna Beach. The popular and prestigious **Festival of Arts/Pageant of Masters** opens in Laguna Beach.

Low Desert Big Bear Lake remembers **Old Miners Days** with week-long festivities featuring a chili cook-off, parades, and dances from the end of July to the beginning of August.

AUGUST

Greater Los Angeles The three-day **Long Beach Jazz Festival** brings together some of the world's best jazz performers.

San Diego Crowds in costume liven up San Diego's 20 miles of coastline during the **Midnight Madness Fun Bicycle Run.** Chamber music concerts, lectures, and workshops are all part of the three-week **SummerFest La Jolla.**

Central Coast Santa Barbara rounds up everyone for a rodeo, open-air food markets, a children's parade, a historical parade, and live entertainment at the five-day-long **Old Spanish Days.**

SEPTEMBER

Greater Los Angeles **Los Angeles County Fair**, the nation's largest county fair, offers music, food, carnival rides, livestock competitions, and just about everything else you can imagine.

San Diego **Old Town Fiestas Patrias** celebrates the Hispanic heritage with food, crafts, music, and dance.

Central Coast Ojai applauds **Mexican Independence Day** with a grand fiesta. Solvang celebrates **Danish Days** with food, music, and dance.

OCTOBER

Los Angeles More than 150 free events are featured in the **Los Angeles County–Wide Arts Open House**, including jazz, classical, and rock concerts.

San Diego   In the San Diego area, the **La Mesa Oktoberfest** features Bavarian bands, beer gardens, and arts and crafts.
Central Coast   Morro Bay hosts the **Harbor Festival**, which includes food and wine tastings, maritime exhibits, entertainment, and arts and crafts.

Greater Los Angeles   Santa arrives early at the **Hollywood Christmas Parade** and is joined by television and movie stars. In Pasadena, the rollicking **Doo Dah Parade** parodies the city's staid Rose Parade.
San Diego   Carlsbad hosts the year's second **Village Faire** (see May listing).
High Desert   The **Death Valley Annual Encampment** honors desert pioneers with gold-panning contests, liars' competitions, and historical programs.

NOVEMBER

During December   Several coastal communities, including Marina del Rey, Naples, Huntington Beach, and San Diego, mark the season with **Christmas Boat Parades**. Los Angeles, San Luis Obispo, San Diego, and other Southland cities celebrate the Mexican yuletide with **Las Posadas**.

DECEMBER

Several agencies provide free information to travelers. The **California Office of Tourism** will help guide you to areas throughout the state. ~ 801 K Street, Suite 1600, Sacramento, CA 95814; 800-862-2543; www.visitcalifornia.com. You'll find information at the **Los Angeles Visitors and Convention Bureau**. ~ 333 South Hope Street, 18th floor, Los Angeles, CA 90071; 213-624-7300; www.visitlanow.com. The **Anaheim/Orange County Visitors and Convention Bureau** can be useful. ~ 800 West Katella Avenue, Anaheim, CA 92803; 714-765-8888, 888-598-3200; www.anaheimoc.org. In San Diego the **San Diego Convention and Visitors Bureau** might be a good source. ~ 401 B Street, Suite 1400, San Diego, CA 92101; 619-236-1212; www.sandiego.org. The **Palm Springs Bureau of Tourism** can assist travelers. ~ 777 North Palm Canyon Drive, Palm Springs, CA 92262; 760-778-8415, 800-927-7256; www.palm-springs.org. Also consult local chambers of commerce and information centers, which are mentioned in the area chapters.

▼▼▼▼▼▼▼▼▼▼
Before You Go

VISITORS CENTERS

There are two important guidelines when deciding what to take on a trip. The first is as true for Los Angeles and Southern California as anywhere in the world—pack light. Dress styles here are relatively informal unless you're planning to spend all of your time in Beverly Hills (in which case you should pack an Armani suit and a Dior dress!). Otherwise, try to keep it casual. The airlines allow two suitcases and a carry-on bag.

PACKING

The second rule is to prepare for temperature variations. While day-time temperatures often hover in the mid-70s, evenings can bring on temperatures as low as 30°, especially in Death Valley. A warm sweater and jacket are absolute necessities year-round, in addition to shorts and T-shirts. Pack a raincoat if you're planning to visit from December to February. And if you're traveling in the high mountains in winter, carry cold-weather clothing. Drinking water, flashlights, blankets, and extra gas are essential requirements when you're traveling long distances with very few amenities along the way.

LODGING

Overnight accommodations in Southern California are as varied as the region itself. They range from highrise hotels and neon motels to hostels and bed-and-breakfast inns. Check through the various regional chapters and you're bound to find something to fit your budget and taste.

Southern California is an extremely popular area, particularly in summer, and facilities fill up quickly—reserve well in advance.

The neon motels offer bland facilities at low prices and are excellent if you're economizing or don't plan to spend much time in the room. Larger hotels often lack intimacy, but provide such conveniences as restaurants and shops in the lobby. My personal preference is for historic hotels, those slightly faded classics that offer charm and tradition at moderate cost. Bed-and-breakfast inns present an opportunity to stay in a homelike setting. Like hostels, they are an excellent way to meet fellow travelers; unlike hostels, Southern California's country inns are quite expensive.

To help you decide on a place to stay, I've organized the accommodations not only by area but also according to price (prices listed are for double occupancy during the high season; prices may decrease in low season). *Budget* hotels generally are less than $60 per night for two people; the rooms are clean and comfortable, but not luxurious. The *moderately* priced hotels run $60 to $120 and provide larger rooms, plusher furniture, and more attractive surroundings. At a *deluxe* hotel you can expect to spend between $120 and $175 double. You'll check into a spacious, well-appointed room with all modern facilities; downstairs the lobby will be a fashionable affair, usually with a restaurant, lounge, and cluster of shops. If you want to spend your time (and money) in the city's very finest hotels, try an *ultra-deluxe* facility, which will include all the amenities and cost more than $175.

DINING

It seems as if Southern California has more restaurants than people, particularly in Los Angeles. To establish a pattern for this parade of dining places, I've organized them according to location and cost. Restaurants listed in this book offer lunch and dinner unless otherwise noted.

Within a particular chapter, the restaurants are categorized geographically, with each restaurant entry describing the establishment as budget, moderate, deluxe, or ultra-deluxe in price. Dinner entrées at *budget* restaurants usually cost $9 or less. The ambience is informal café-style and the crowd is often a local one. *Moderately* priced restaurants range between $9 and $18 at dinner and offer pleasant surroundings, a more varied menu, and a slower pace. *Deluxe* establishments tab their entrées above $18, featuring sophisticated cuisines, plush decor, and more personalized service. *Ultra-deluxe* dining rooms, where $25 will only get you started, are gourmet gathering places in which cooking (one hopes) is a fine art form and service is a way of life.

Breakfast and lunch menus vary less in price from restaurant to restaurant. Even deluxe kitchens usually offer light breakfasts and lunch sandwiches, which place them within a few dollars of their budget-minded competitors. These early meals can be a good time to test expensive restaurants.

Visiting Southern California with kids can be a real adventure, and if properly planned, a truly enjoyable one. To ensure that your trip will feature the joy, rather than the strain, of parenthood, remember a few important guidelines.

TRAVELING WITH CHILDREN

Use a travel agent to help with arrangements; they can reserve spacious bulkhead seats on airlines and determine which flights are least crowded. Also plan to bring everything you need on board—diapers, food, toys, and extra clothes for kids and parents alike. If the trip to Southern California involves a long journey, plan to relax and do very little during the first few days.

Always allow extra time for getting places. Book reservations well in advance and make sure the hotel has the extra crib, cot, or bed you require. It's smart to ask for a room at the end of the hall to cut down on noise. Be aware that many bed-and-breakfast inns do not allow children.

Most towns have stores that carry diapers, food, and other essentials; in cities and larger towns, 7-11 stores are sometimes open all night (check the Yellow Pages for addresses). Hotels often provide access to babysitters, or check the Yellow Pages for state licensed and bonded babysitting agencies. A first-aid kit is always a good idea. Consult with your pediatrician for special medicines and dosages for colds and diarrhea.

Finding activities to interest children in Southern California couldn't be easier. Especially helpful in deciding on the day's outing is the "Calendar" section of the Sunday *Los Angeles Times*.

Traveling solo grants an independence and freedom different from that of traveling with a partner, but single travelers are more vulnerable to crime and should take additional precautions.

WOMEN TRAVELING ALONE

It is better not to let strangers know you are traveling alone or where you are staying or planning to travel. It's unwise to hitchhike and probably best to avoid inexpensive accommodations on the outskirts of town; the money saved does not outweigh the risk. Bed and breakfasts, youth hostels, and YWCAs are generally your safest bet for lodging, and they also foster an environment ideal for bonding with fellow travelers.

The more rural areas are somewhat safer, but at the same time, women traveling alone are considered something of an anomaly outside the big cities. It's best to avoid accommodations at motels in industrial areas or other places where there is no real neighborhood after dark. When requesting reservations at hotels and motels, ask for rooms near the elevator or facing a central courtyard rather than find yourself in a remote location. For more hints, get a copy of *Safety and Security for Women Who Travel* (Travelers Tales).

Keep all valuables well-hidden and clutch cameras and purses tightly. Avoid late-night treks or strolls through undesirable parts of town, but if you find yourself in this situation, continue walking with a confident air until you reach a safe haven. A fierce scowl never hurts.

These hints should by no means deter you from seeking out adventure. Wherever you go, stay alert, use your common sense and trust your instincts. If you are hassled or threatened in some way, never be afraid to call for assistance. It's also a good idea to carry change for a phone call and to know a number to call in case of emergency. Several Southern California communities offer women's resource centers, referral numbers, and health centers. In the Los Angeles, Orange County, and Ventura County areas, consult the **Women's Yellow Pages.** ~ 818-995-6646; www.referral-guide.com. Feminist bookstores are also good sources of information.

GAY & LESBIAN TRAVELERS

Although Southern California is often known for its social and political conservatism, the tolerance that accompanies the booming entertainment industry makes certain areas inviting and exciting for gay and lesbian travelers. Southern California's largest gay area is centered in and around the city of West Hollywood. It is estimated that about one-third of the city's population of 35,000 is gay and lesbian, a fact that makes West Hollywood one of the most gay-friendly municipalities in the country. The city's first mayor was lesbian; other gays have since filled that rotating position, and many councilmembers have also been gay. On and near Santa Monica Boulevard, the main drag through the city's gay commercial district, you'll find hotels, shops, restaurants, and nightclubs catering to gay and lesbian travelers. (See "West Hollywood Gay Scene" in Chapter Two.)

Farther south, San Diego's Hillcrest district is the focus of that city's gay scene, with guesthouses, stores, and cafés. (See "Hillcrest & San Diego Gay Scene" in Chapter Five; for information on services aimed at gay travelers, see "Gay-friendly travel" in the index.)

An oasis in more ways than one, Palm Springs beckons to the gay or lesbian traveler from the heart of the desert. While the resort town may be more famous as the home of the late Sonny Bono, the city's former Republican mayor, and the spring break destination of rowdy college students, it's also the locale of **The Nabisco Championship** LPGA **Golf Tournament**, a sort of unofficial lesbian annual event drawing thousands of women to the desert resort each March. (See "Palm Springs Gay Scene" in Chapter Seven.)

> West Hollywood was the first city in the nation to boast a gay city government.

One of the best places to get plugged into the Southern California LGBT scene is **A Different Light Bookstore**. Besides stocking hundreds of titles appealing to gay and lesbian readers, A Different Light hosts readings and other community events. It's also the place to pick up copies of local publications, most of which are free (see below). ~ 8853 Santa Monica Boulevard, West Hollywood; 310-854-6601; www.adlbooks.com. Pick up a copy of *i*N magazine, which comes out twice a month—almost as often as the average Sunset Strip pedestrian—and covers the goings-on for men in L.A. County. ~ 8235 Santa Monica Boulevard, Suite 306, West Hollywood; 323-848-2200; www.inmagla.com. Also look for the biweekly *Frontiers Magazine*; it's full of movie, theater, and club reviews that cover the area between San Francisco and San Diego. ~ 5657 Wilshire Boulevard, Los Angeles, CA 90036; 323-848-2222; www.frontiersnewsmagazine.com. Women may consult *Lesbian News*, a monthly publication based in L.A. that covers the Southern California entertainment scene. Along with reviews, interviews, health, and travel, the magazine has a comprehensive club guide and calendar of events. ~ P.O. Box 55, Torrance, CA 90507; 800-458-9888; www.lesbiannews.com.

In San Diego, get a copy of *Gay & Lesbian Times*, a weekly publication with local and world news, business, sports, weather, and arts sections. It also contains a calendar of events, and a directory of gay-friendly businesses and establishments. ~ 1730 Monroe Avenue, San Diego; 619-299-6397; www.gaylesbiantimes.com. **The Lesbian Gay Bisexual and Transgender Community Center** offers referrals for those seeking drop-in counseling, mental health services, or support groups—or stop by on Tuesday nights for bingo. Closed Sunday. ~ 3909 Centre Street, San Diego; 619-692-2077; www.thecentersd.org.

In Palm Springs, look for the bimonthly *MEGA-Scene* for worldwide and local gay news. It also has maps that come in handy when you're attempting to visit all the highlights within the folds of its entertainment guide. ~ 611 South Palm Canyon Drive #7-B, Palm Springs; 760-327-5178; www.megasceneps.com. *The Bottom Line*, a bimonthly magazine, publishes a detailed roster of desert eateries, bars, hotels, and nightspots that gay travelers will find essential. It also includes reviews of movies, books, and theater. ~ 312 North Palm Canyon Drive, Palm Springs; 760-323-0552; www.psbottomline.com. For information on gay-oriented events, entertainment, and activities, order the free *Palm Springs Gay & Lesbian Guide*. ~ 800-347-7746; www.palm-springs.org.

SENIOR TRAVELERS   Southern California is ideal for older vacationers. The mild climate makes touring in the off-season possible, helping to cut down on expenses. Many museums, theaters, restaurants, and hotels have senior discounts (with a driver's license, Medicare card, or other age-identifying card). Ask your travel agent when booking reservations.

The AARP offers members travel discounts and provides referrals for escorted tours. ~ 3200 East Carson Street, Lakewood, CA 90712; 562-496-2277, 800-424-3410; www.aarp.org. For those 55 or over, **Elderhostel** provides educational programs in California. ~ 11 Avenue de Lafayette, Boston, MA 02111; 877-426-8056; www.elderhostel.org.

Be extra careful about health matters. Bring along any medications you ordinarily use, together with the prescriptions for obtaining more. Consider carrying a medical record with you—including your medical history and current medical status as well as your doctor's name, phone number, and address. Also be sure to confirm that your insurance covers you away from home.

DISABLED TRAVELERS   California stands at the forefront of social reform for travelers with disabilities. During the past decade, the state has responded with a series of progressive legislative measures to the needs of the blind, wheelchair-bound, and others.

There are also agencies in Southern California assisting persons with disabilities. For tips and information about the Los Angeles area, contact the **Westside Center for Independent Living**. ~ 12901 Venice Boulevard, Los Angeles; 310-390-3611; www.wcil.org. In the San Diego area, try the **Access Center**. ~ 1295 University Avenue, Suite 10, San Diego; 619-293-3500; www.accesscentersd.org.

There are numerous national organizations offering general information. Among these are:

The **Society for Accessible Travel & Hospitality** (SATH). ~ 347 5th Avenue #610, New York, NY 10016; 212-447-7284; www.sath.org.

Flying Wheels Travel. ~ 143 West Bridge Street, P.O. Box 382, Owatonna, MN 55060; 507-451-5005; www.flyingwheelstravel. com.

Travelin' Talk, a network of people and organizations, also provides assistance. ~ P.O. Box 1796, Wheat Ridge, CO 80034; 303-232-2979; www.travelintalk.net.

Access-Able Travel Source has worldwide information online. ~ 303-232-2979; www.access-able.com.

Or consult the comprehensive guidebook, *Access to the World—A Travel Guide for the Handicapped*, by Louise Weiss (Henry Holt & Company, Inc.).

Be sure to check in advance when making room reservations. Many hotels and motels have facilities for travelers in wheelchairs.

The Department of Motor Vehicles provides special parking permits for the disabled (check the phone book for the nearest location). Many local bus lines and other public transit facilities are wheelchair accessible.

Passports and Visas Most foreign visitors need a passport and tourist visa to enter the United States. Contact your nearest U.S. Embassy or Consulate well in advance to obtain a visa and to check on any other entry requirements.

FOREIGN TRAVELERS

Customs Requirements Foreign travelers are allowed to carry in the following: 200 cigarettes (1 carton), 50 cigars, or 2 kilograms (4.4 pounds) of smoking tobacco; one liter of alcohol for personal use only (you must be 21 years of age to bring in alcohol); and US$100 worth of duty-free gifts that can include an additional quantity of 100 cigars (except Cuban cigars). You may bring in any amount of currency, but must fill out a form if you bring in over US$10,000. Carry any 90-day supply of prescription drugs in clearly marked containers. (You may have to produce a written prescription or doctor's statement for the custom's officer.) Meat or meat products, seeds, plants, fruits, and narcotics are not allowed to be brought into the United States. Contact the **United States Customs and Border Protection** for further information. ~ 1300 Pennsylvania Avenue NW, Washington, DC 20229; 202-927-1770; www.cbp.gov.

California receives a quarter of all overseas tourism to the U.S., with 7 million international travelers visiting each year. Most foreign travelers are from Japan, the U.K., Germany, France, and Australia.

Driving If you plan to rent a car, an international driver's license should be obtained before arriving in the United States. Some car rental agencies require both a foreign license and an international driver's license. Many also require a lessee to be at least 25 years of age; all require a major credit card. Remember: Seat belts are mandatory for the driver and all passengers. Children

Text continued on page 16.

California
Microclimates

What the weather's like in Southern California depends on where you are at the moment. More than almost anyplace else in America, this region is a patchwork quilt of "microclimates," where the weather in small, specific places may have little to do with the overall weather pattern.

California basks in what meteorologists and gardeners know as a Mediterranean climate zone, which is found nowhere else in the United States and in only four other regions on earth. Besides California and the Mediterranean Basin, these regions are southern and western Australia, central Chile, and the western cape of South Africa. The characteristics of this climate zone are cool, wet winters and summer drought—the result of an endless tug-of-war between ocean moisture and inland desert dryness. It is the opposite of the subtropical climate of Florida and the Caribbean, where winters are dry and summers are rainy.

But in Southern California, the climate situation is complicated by mountains. Climbing 1000 feet in elevation can mean a temperature drop of from five to nine degrees. That's why in downtown Los Angeles snow is a once-in-a-lifetime event, while 30 miles away at Mount Baldy Ski Area on 10,064-foot Mount San Antonio, several feet of snow stay on the ground all winter. Farther east, the snowcap never completely melts from the top of 14,495-foot Mount Whitney, even in midsummer, and the temperature rarely rises above freezing for more than a few hours, while 30 miles away in Death Valley, the thermometer often hits 100° on the first day of spring.

Clouds tend to build up over mountain ranges as air currents carry coastal moisture to higher altitudes, where it condenses. As a result, most rain and snow fall in the coastal ranges and the Sierra Nevada, feeding the reservoirs and aqueduct that supply drinking water to Los Angeles. By the time the air currents reach the east side of the mountains, the moisture is gone and the resulting "rain shadow" has created the Mohave and Colorado deserts, some of the most arid land on the continent.

Another effect of the mountains is to help create air inversions, especially in the winter months, filling the coastal valleys of the Los Angeles metropolitan area with morning fog—and air pollution. Because of this phenomenon, smog was first noticed in L.A. almost 20 years before automotive air pollution was recognized as a problem in other American cities. Although L.A. air quality has been improving gradually since the early 1990s, it remains one of the major factors affecting Southern California's climate.

The diversity of Southern California's microclimates is most obvious in its vegetation. A characteristic of Mediterranean climate zones is that plants can thrive during the winter but face the challenge of surviving the heat and drought of summer. In coastal valleys, including Los Angeles and San Diego, flowers bloom throughout the winter and most trees don't lose their leaves; tropical plants that can't tolerate frost, such as palms and banana plants, do well, as do tropical cacti.

In the coastal mountains, live oak grows at relatively low elevations, giving way higher up to pines and other evergreens that can survive freezing winters. The sparse vegetation in the desert east of the mountains is made up of highly drought-resistant plants. Even cacti are uncommon, and vegetation is limited to almost leafless species such as Joshua trees and ocotillo. Yet the desert is not as sterile as it appears. If you have the good fortune to visit the Mojave Desert during a wet spring—an event that happens about once every five years—you'll see a spectacular display of wildflowers.

California's unusual and diverse climate enables farmers to produce crops that will not grow elsewhere in the United States. All Mediterranean foods thrive: California produces 90 percent of the nation's grapes, 99 percent of the olives, and 100 percent of the dates, figs, and artichokes. When it comes to nuts, California is the only state that produces almonds and the only place outside Iran that grows pistachios. (While Iranian pistachios are dyed red, California's are left their natural tan color so buyers can tell the difference.) Due to these microclimates, residents of and visitors to California are able to see, taste, and experience an international array of things—all in one place.

under age 5 or 40 pounds should be in the back seat in approved child safety restraints.

Currency United States money is based on the dollar. Bills generally come in denominations of $1, $5, $10, $20, $50, and $100. Every dollar is divided into 100 cents. Coins are the penny (1 cent), nickel (5 cents), dime (10 cents), and quarter (25 cents). Half-dollar and dollar coins are rarely used, as are $2 bills. You may not use foreign currency to purchase goods and services in the United States. Consider buying traveler's checks in dollar amounts. You may also use credit cards affiliated with an American company such as Interbank, Barclay Card, Visa, and American Express.

Electricity and Electronics Electric outlets use currents of 110 volts, 60 cycles. For appliances made for other electrical systems, you need a transformer or other adapter. Travelers who use laptop computers for telecommunication should be aware that modem configurations for U.S. telephone systems may be different from their European counterparts. Similarly, the U.S. format for videotapes is different from that in Europe; National Park Service visitors centers and other stores that sell souvenir videos often have them available in European format on request.

Weights and Measurements The United States uses the English system of weights and measures. American units and their metric equivalents are: 1 inch = 2.5 centimeters; 1 foot (12 inches) = 0.3 meter; 1 yard (3 feet) = 0.9 meter; 1 mile (5280 feet) = 1.6 kilometers; 1 ounce = 28 grams; 1 pound (16 ounces) = 0.45 kilogram; 1 quart (liquid) = 0.9 liter.

Outdoor Adventures

CAMPING

The state government oversees 277 camping facilities. Amenities at each campground vary, but there is a day-use fee of $4–$14 per vehicle. Campsites range from about $11 up to $25 (a little less in the off season). For a complete listing of all state-run campgrounds, send for *California Escapes*, published by the **California Department of Parks and Recreation**.)~ P.O. Box 942896, Sacramento, CA 94296; 916-653-6995; www.parks.ca.gov. For campground reservations call 800-444-7275. Note: At press time, the State of California's new parking, day-use, and camping rates (due to go into effect July 2004) were still unknown. They are slated to go up, and in some cases, double. Many county and city facilities are also expected to follow suit.

For general information on National Park campgrounds, contact the **National Park Service**. ~ Western Information Center, Fort Mason, Building 201, San Francisco, CA 94123; 415-561-4700; www.nps.gov or www.nps.gov/goga. To reserve a National Park campsite call the individual park directly or call 800-365-2267. In addition, the National Park Service offers a **National Parks**

Pass, which costs $50 and admits you and your family to all national parks for a year from date of issue. Just keep in mind that other fees, such as boating and camping, may not be waived.

Reservations for **U.S. Forest Service** campsites must be made by calling the National Forest Reservation System at 800-280-2267. A fee is charged at these facilities and the length of stay varies from forest to forest. It's best to reserve in advance, though many forests keep some sites open to be filled daily on a first-come, first-served basis. For more information contact the National Forest Service's regional office in the Bay Area. ~ 1323 Club Drive, Mare Island, Vallejo, CA 94592; 707-562-8737; www.fs.fed.us/r5.

Southern California also offers numerous municipal, county, and private facilities. See the "Beaches & Parks" sections in each area chapter for the locations of these campgrounds.

Wilderness Permits   For camping and hiking in the wilderness and primitive areas of national forests, a wilderness permit is required. Permits are largely free and are issued for a specific period of time, which varies according to the wilderness area. Information is available through the **U.S. Forest Service.** ~ 1323 Club Drive, Mare Island, Vallejo, CA 94592; 707-562-8737; www.fs.fed.us/r5. You can obtain permits from ranger stations and regional information centers, as described in the "Beaches & Parks" sections in each area chapter.

PERMITS

The largest state park in California? Anza–Borrego, at 600,000 acres. The smallest? Watts Towers (yes, an official park!) at .11 acre.

Boating Permits   Permits, which cost from $2 to $15 and can usually be applied for up to 60 days in advance, are required for independent rafting or kayaking on most popular whitewater rivers. There is no central agency to process permit applications. Different rivers, and sometimes different stretches of the same river, are administered by various forest service or state park ranger stations or river conservancy groups. For information, contact American Whitewater. ~ 1424 Fenwick Lane, Silver Spring, MD 20910; 866-262-8429; www. americanwhitewater.org, e-mail info@amwhitewater.org.

For current information on the fishing season and state license fees, contact the **California Department of Fish and Game.** ~ 1416 9th Street, Sacramento, CA 95814; 916-653-7664; www.dfg.ca.gov.

FISHING

TWO

Greater Los Angeles

Naturally it began as fiction. California, according to the old Spanish novel, was a mythical island populated by Amazons and filled with gold, a place "very near to the terrestrial paradise." The man who set off to pursue this dream was Juan Rodríguez Cabrillo. The year was 1542 and Cabrillo, a Portuguese navigator in the employ of the Spanish crown, sailed north from Mexico, pressing forward the boundaries of empire.

Failing to find either royalty or gilded cities, Cabrillo discovered a land that, in the contrary course of its history, produced kings of industries not yet invented and cities wealthy beyond the imagining of even the conquistadors. California is a mythical land indeed, with a cultural capital called Los Angeles.

If California is the land of dreams, L.A. is the dream factory, that worldly workshop where the impossible takes form. Since its founding as a pueblo in 1781, the city has continually recast itself as a promised land, health haven, agricultural paradise, movie capital, and world financial center.

The second-largest city in the country, it rests in a bowl surrounded by five mountain ranges and an ocean and holds within its ambit sandy beaches, tawny hills, and wind-ruffled deserts. At night from the air Los Angeles is a massive gridwork an illuminated checkerboard extending from the ink-colored Pacific to the dark fringe of the mountains.

The religious dream of this "city of angels" began way back in 1769 when Padre Junípero Serra and Gaspar de Portolá ventured north from Mexico to establish the first of California's 21 missions. Two years later Mission San Gabriel Archangel was founded several miles from Los Angeles.

The first settlers comprised a mixed bag of Spaniards, Indians, mestizos, and blacks, among them a surprising number of women and children. They planted vines, olives, and grains, and spent 50 years expanding their population to 700.

Today, with a census numbering almost four million urban dwellers and nearly ten million throughout Los Angeles County, it remains a multicultural city. In Los Angeles minorities have become the majority. Over 80 different languages are spoken in the schools. Neighborhoods are given over to Latinos, blacks, Chinese, Japanese, Koreans, Jews, Laotians, Filipinos, and Armenians. There are gay communities and nouveau riche neighborhoods, not to mention personality sects such as low riders, Valley girls, punks, and hippies.

One group that never became part of this sun-baked melting pot were the Indians. For American Indians, Padre Serra's dream of a New World became a nightmare. Before the advent of Westerners, as many as 300,000 indigenous people populated California. Around Los Angeles the Gabrieleños held sway.

Like other groups west of the Sierra Nevada they were hunter-gatherers, exploiting the boundless resources of the ocean, picking wild plants, and stalking local prey. Primitive by comparison with the agricultural tribes of the American Southwest, they fashioned dome-shaped dwellings from wooden poles and woven grasses.

The conquistadors eventually overcame American Indian resistance, forcibly converting these native spiritualists to Catholicism and pressing them into slavery. Eventually American Indians built a chain of missions that formed the backbone of the Spanish empire and broke the back of the tribal nations. While their slaves were dying in terrible numbers, the Spanish, dangerously overextended, fell plague to problems throughout the empire. Finally, in 1821 Mexico declared its independence and seized California from Spain.

Then in 1846 American settlers, with assistance from the United States government, fomented the Bear Flag Revolt. That summer Captain John C. Fremont pursued Governor Pío Pico from Los Angeles south to San Juan Capistrano, forcing the Mexican official to flee across the border. Finally in February 1848, at a home in the San Fernando Valley, a treaty was signed and the Stars and Stripes flew over California.

Latinos, who were driven from Los Angeles, now number close to 50 percent of the population and represent the largest concentration of Mexicans outside Mexico. The countryside they departed was a region of ranchos, land grants often measuring 75 square miles, which were used for cattle ranching.

The metropolis they now inhabit is the world's seventh largest city. Once a pastoral realm of caballeros and señoritas, greater metropolitan L.A. now leads the nation in aerospace, boasts one of the country's largest concentrations of high-tech industries and possesses the fastest growing major port in the country.

Disparagingly referred to as the "cow counties" by Northern Californians in the 19th century, metropolitan L.A. is a megalopolis unified by a convoluted freeway system—a congeries of cloverleafs, overpasses, and eight-lane speedways that lies snarled with traffic much of the day.

A distinctly Western city, it has grown *out* toward the open range, not *up* within tightly defined perimeters. A collection of suburbs in search of a city, it has broken all the rules, leading urban experts to describe Los Angeles as a series of constellations creating a metropolitan galaxy. A schizophrenic among cities, it is comprised of many facets, many cities. In fact, there are 88 incorporated cities in Los Angeles County, as well as 1500 miles of freeways and 19,000 miles of surface streets.

To simplify matters, the urban quiltwork is divided in this chapter into eight geographic sections. Creating an arc around central *Downtown* is *Greater Los Angeles*, an expansive area that sweeps from Inglewood to East Los Angeles, then north to Silver Lake. The *Wilshire District* forms a narrow corridor along Wilshire Boulevard, running west from Downtown toward the ocean. *Hollywood* and *Beverly Hills* require little introduction; both border the *Westside*, an upscale area comprised of Westwood and Bel Air. To the northeast, bounded by mountains and desert, lies the *San Gabriel Valley*, whose cultural center is Pasadena. Northwest of Los Angeles is the *San Fernando Valley*.

This entire territory is a region with unhealthy air, healthy crime statistics, and one of the highest divorce rates in the world. Known for traffic and smog, Los Angeles is cleaning up its act, steadily improving its air quality to more breathable levels. Still, it ranks as the third most polluted area in the country. In L.A. the proverbial silver lining in every cloud may be just that—a layer of airborne metal.

Little more than a century ago this mega-city was a tough Western town. The population totaled less than 3000 but L.A. still managed to average a murder a day. By the time the transcontinental railroad connected California with the rest of the country in 1869, Southern California's economy trailed far behind its northern counterpart.

During the 1870s the South began to rise. The Southern Pacific railroad linked San Pedro and Santa Monica with interior valleys where citrus cultivation was flourishing. Southern California's rich agriculture and salubrious climate led to a "health rush." Magazines and newspapers romanticized the region's history and beauty; one writer proclaimed that "if the Pilgrim fathers had landed on the Pacific Coast instead of the Atlantic, little old New York wouldn't be on the map."

Santa Monica became a fashionable resort town and the port of San Pedro expanded exponentially, making Los Angeles a major shipping point. Around the turn of the 19th century Henry Huntington, nephew of railroad baron Collis P. Huntington, established the Pacific Electric Railway Company and created a series of land booms by extending his red trolley lines in all directions.

When oil was discovered early in the 20th century, Southern California also became a prime drilling region. Oil wells sprang up along Huntington Beach, Long Beach, and San Pedro, adding to coastal coffers while destroying the aesthetics of the shore. The Signal Hill field in Long Beach, tapped by Shell Oil in the 1920s, turned out to be the richest oil deposit in the world and Los Angeles became the largest oil port.

Little wonder that by 1925, flush with petroleum just as the age of the automobile was shifting into gear, Los Angeles became the most motor-conscious city in the world. The Pacific Coast Highway was completed during the 1930s, "auto camps" and "tourist cabins" mushroomed, and motorists began exploring Southern California in unprecedented numbers.

This burgeoning city, with its back to the desert, had already solved its water problems in 1913 when the Los Angeles Aqueduct, bleeding water from the distant Owens Valley, was completed. An engineering marvel, stretching almost 250 miles from the Sierra Nevada, the controversial pipeline supplied enough water to enable Los Angeles to annex the entire San Fernando Valley.

Ironically, the semi-arid Los Angeles Basin was once underwater. Built by volcanic activity, the geologic area is so young that the Palos Verdes Peninsula was a chain of offshore islands just one million years ago. Earthquakes still rattle the

Three-day Weekend

Discovering the Many Faces of L.A.

The greater Los Angeles area has such an abundance of attractions that not even most locals have seen them all. You can find virtually anything you want here, and we urge you to browse thoroughly through Chapters Two, Three, and Four of *Hidden Southern California* to customize a tour that will fit your interests. For an introductory look at some classic highlights of L.A., try the following.

DAY 1 • Start your visit with a look at old-time Hollywood. Check out the hand-, foot-, and nose-prints in the sidewalk in front of **Mann's Chinese Theatre** (page 78) and stargaze your way along at least a part of the **Walk of Fame** (page 75). Then head for the **Hollywood Entertainment Museum** (page 79) for an interactive look at filmmaking's first century.

• Join the **Paramount Studios** (page 74) tour—the only authentic studio tour left in Hollywood. Next, drive down Santa Monica Boulevard to **Beverly Hills** to see old-time movie stars' mansions (see the Scenic Drive on pages 108–109) and window-shop on Rodeo Drive. In the evening, attend a film screening at the **Egyptian Theatre** (page 78).

DAY 2 • Sample the Los Angeles art scene. While there are several outstanding art museums, none can really rival the exquisite collections at the hilltop **Getty Center** (page 117) or the **Norton Simon Museum** (page 139) in Pasadena. If you prefer your art a little folksier, drive to Watts to see the **Watts Towers** (page 47), the neighboring arts center, and **Farmer John's Pig Mural** (page 47).

Day 3 • Search out L.A.'s ethnic diversity, starting as the city did—at **Olvera Street** (page 38) and the nearby **Grand Central Public Market** (page 33).

• Head over to **Chinatown** (page 42), stroll along North Spring Street and visit the **Kong Chow Temple**.

• Drive to **Exposition Park** (page 43) to visit the **California African American Museum**.

• Dine on Japanese delights in **Little Tokyo** (page 36), then consider seeing a show at the **Japan America Theatre** (page 38).

region with disturbing frequency. The last colossal quake was back in the 1850s when almost every building in Los Angeles collapsed. More recently, major earthquakes rocked the San Fernando Valley in 1971 and 1994. Though property damage was high, the loss of life—fortunately—was not.

Perhaps with an eye to earthquakes, not to mention Southern California's flaky reputation, architect Frank Lloyd Wright developed a theory of "continental tilt" by which all the loose nuts slid into Hollywood. Its penchant for health, fitness, and glamour have always rendered L.A.'s hold on reality a bit shaky, but it is the city's appeal to religious sects that has particularly added to its aura of unreality.

The first book printed in Los Angeles was a religious tract by a heretical Scotsman. Aimee Semple McPherson preached her Four Square Gospel here in the 1920s and other groups have included everything from the Theosophists and Krishnamurtis to the Mankind United and Mighty I Am movements. Televangelism is now big business throughout the area and Hollywood serves as headquarters for Scientology.

In the end L.A. is a city that one comes to love or scorn. Or perhaps to love and scorn. It is either Tinseltown or the Big Orange, Smogville or the City of Angels. To some it is the Rome of the West, a megalopolis whose economic might renders it an imperial power. To others Los Angeles is the American Athens, an international center for cinema, music, and art.

Culturally speaking, the sun rises in the west. L.A., quirky but creative, sets the trends for the entire nation. It has been admired and self-admiring for so long that the city has swallowed its own story, become a reflection of its mythology. Beautifully crazed, pulsing with electric energy, Los Angeles is living its own dream.

Downtown

Contrary to the opinion of Los Angeles bashers, the city does indeed possess a center. Ever since the town was settled in 1781, the focus of the community has been near Olvera Street and the Civic Center, along the Los Angeles River.

While there's barely enough water in the river these days to cause a ripple, the Downtown district is inundated with people. About 20,000 people live in this vital neighborhood and more than 200,000 commuters arrive daily. Adding to the smog and congestion, they also make Downtown the center for politics, finance, and culture.

SIGHTS   To help you navigate around this urban core, I've divided the district into several sections: Olvera Street, Chinatown, the Civic Center, Central Downtown (which includes the financial district), and Little Tokyo. In exploring each neighborhood, remember that the DASH shuttle, a purple-striped minibus, serves most of Downtown for just 25 cents a ride. Downtown is also served by the **Metro Red Line**, Los Angeles' first subway. Starting at Union Station, the line runs between Union Station and MacArthur Park, at the corner of Wilshire and Alvarado boulevards.

CIVIC CENTER   Art and politics have always been odd bedfellows, but they make a cozy couple around the Los Angeles Civic

Center. Here an impressive group of government buildings combines with an array of museums to create a complex well worth touring.

The centerpiece of the ensemble is **City Hall,** a vintage 1928 building. Rendered famous by the old *Dragnet* television show, this pyramid-topped edifice is also a frequent backdrop in many contemporary movies. The tile-and-marble rotunda on the third floor is a study in governmental architecture. But the most impressive feature is the **observation deck** on the 27th floor, from

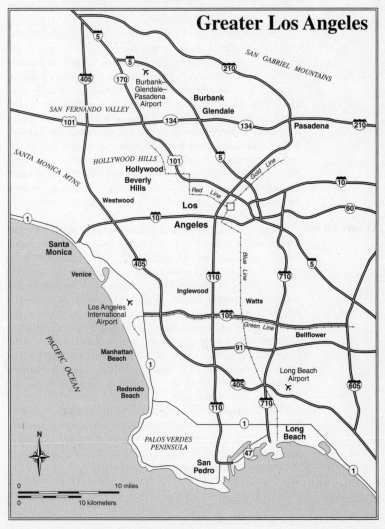

Greater Los Angeles

which you can enjoy a 360-degree view of Los Angeles' smog banks. ~ 200 North Spring Street; 213-978-1995; www.lacity.org.

Those who report on City Hall reside across the street at the **Los Angeles Times Building**. One of the nation's largest and finest newspapers, the *Times* sits in a classic 1935 moderne-style building to which latter day architects, in a fit of ego and insanity, added a glass box monstrosity that appears to be devouring the original. The older structure, housing the newspaper, is open to guided tours; the glass accretion contains corporate offices. Call ahead for times. Closed Saturday and Sunday. ~ 145 South Spring Street; 213-237-3178; www.latimes.com.

The **Performing Arts Center of Los Angeles**, locally know as the **Music Center**, is one of the three largest performing-arts centers in the nation and welcomes more than 1.3 million people a year to its performances. Gathered into one stunningly designed complex are the **Dorothy Chandler Pavilion**, a marble-and-black-glass music hall that hosts the opera and symphony; the **Mark Taper Forum**, a world-renowned theater that presents contemporary and experimental drama; and the **Ahmanson Theatre**, a 2000-seat auditorium where touring Broadway plays are staged. Not to be outdone, the visual arts are represented by a pulsating fountain with more than 100 rhythmically timed streams. Guided tours are available. ~ 135 North Grand Avenue, between 1st and Temple streets; 213-972-7211; www.musiccenter.org, e-mail general@musiccenter.org.

Designed by architect extraordinaire Frank Gehry, the latest entertainment venue to hit the Downtown area is the much talked about **Walt Disney Concert Hall**. While the curving stainless-steel structure looks more like a piece of sculpture than the home of the Los Angeles Philharmonic, don't be fooled—the acoustics are state of the art. The 3.6-acre complex's main auditorium is a 2265-seat, wood-paneled space where the audience surrounds the orchestra platform, creating a visually intimate and musically exciting experience. Outside, stairs curl around the building's curves, which open out into secluded garden areas shadowed by neighboring high-rise office buildings, a great place for a picnic lunch on a sunny day. ~ 111 South Grand Avenue; 323-850-2000; wdch.laphil.com.

The **Museum of Contemporary Art**, affectionately dubbed "the MOCA," is an ultramodern showplace designed by Japanese architect Arata Isozaki. It's an exotic mix of red sandstone and pyramidal skylights with a sunken courtyard. The galleries consist of expansive open spaces displaying a variety of traveling exhibits and the works of Mark Rothko, Robert Rauschenberg, Jackson Pollock, and others. Closed Tuesday and Wednesday. Admission. ~ 250 South Grand Avenue; 213-626-6222, fax 213-620-8674; www.moca.org.

CENTRAL DOWNTOWN While social classes may be miles apart culturally, their neighborhoods often stand shoulder to shoulder. Midway between the Los Angeles centers of political and financial power sits **Broadway**, a vibrant Latino shopping district. This, not Olvera Street, is where today's Mexican population shops. A cross between New York's 42nd Street and the boulevards of Mexico City, this multiblock strip is crowded with cut-rate clothing stores, swap meets, pawn shops, and stands selling pizza by the slice.

Start at the South 300 block and wander uptown.

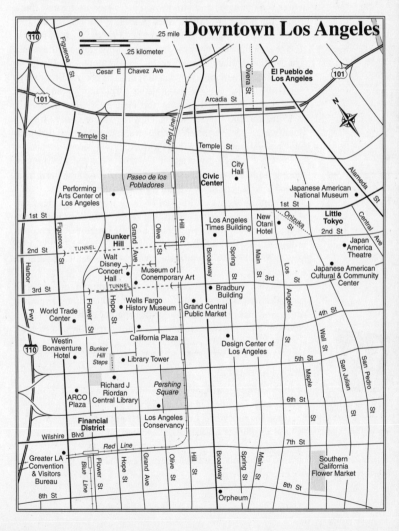

Downtown Los Angeles

The **Bradbury Building** across the street from Grand Central Public Market (see "Food, Flowers, and More") has undergone a massive restoration. The interior of this National Historic Landmark features an extraordinary courtyard illuminated by a skylight, as well as wrought-iron grillwork and winding stairs surrounding an open-cage elevator. Add flourishes of marble and brick to finish off this 1893 masterpiece. Access granted to ground floor only. ~ 304 South Broadway; 213-626-1893, fax 213-626-2945.

During the 1940s Broadway was the city's Great White Way, where stars mingled and Hollywood premiered its greatest films. Today the boulevard's diminished glory is evident in the old theaters between 3rd and Olympic streets. Once the pride of the studios that built them, they are now in varying stages of disrepair. **The Million Dollar Theater**, where movie mogul Sid Grauman began as a showman, is now a church. ~ 307 South Broadway.

Also of note are the magnificent **Orpheum**, at 842 South Broadway, a 2000-seat Spanish and French Gothic hybrid built in 1926, and the **United Artists Theatre**, situated on 933 South Broadway, a 1927 Spanish Gothic structure with murals depicting Charlie Chaplin and Mary Pickford, now restored for service as Dr. Gene Scott's Los Angeles University Cathedral. Many of these grande dames currently show Spanish-language films from noon 'til night, but most will allow you to glance inside.

Recapturing part of this past is the nearby **Los Angeles Conservancy**, a preservation group that on Saturday conducts tours of the theaters and other places of historic interest. Reservations required. Fee. ~ 523 West 6th Street, Suite 826; 213-623-2489, fax 213-623-3909; www.laconservancy.org, e-mail info@laconservancy.org.

A multimillion-dollar renovation of Downtown's main public park, **Pershing Square**, transformed what had become a rundown refuge for transients into a colorful urban construction of pink columns, a purple water tower, and yellow structures. Low walls

AUTHOR FAVORITE

Grand Performances at California Plaza offers a full summer schedule (June through October) of free outdoor entertainment in the Water Court. You can see everything from solo artists in dance, music, and theater to fully staged opera, Shakespeare, and hula performances. This venue is one of L.A.'s most exciting performance spaces, featuring international artists. ~ 350 South Grand Avenue; 213-687-2190; www.grandperformances.org.

and benches provide places to rest and enjoy occasional enter-tainment or an alfresco lunch of sandwiches from a concession stand. ~ Bounded by Olive, Hill, 5th, and 6th streets; www.la parks.org/pershingsquare/pershing.htm.

If Broadway was once the Great White Way, **Spring Street** was once the Wall Street of the West. Like its theatrical counterpart, this faded financial district is now the venue of historians and sentimentalists. ~ Between 4th and 7th streets. The former **Pacific Coast Stock Exchange**, a 1930 masterpiece of moderne architec-ture, has been closed. ~ 618 South Spring Street. Among the other hallowed halls of finance is the **Design Center of Los Angeles**, a 1928 building with tile murals and zigzag facade. ~ 433 South Spring Street. Another worthy stop is the **Banco Popular**, a 1903 beaux-arts office building. ~ 354 South Spring Street.

Today the focus of finance has shifted to a highrise district between Grand Avenue, Figueroa Street, 3rd Street, and 8th Street.

The **Water Court at California Plaza** is a pleasant oasis amid the towers of glass and steel. Surrounded by shops and restaurants, this space centers around the "Water Feature," an elaborate combination of water jets and cascades that converts to a perfor-mance space during the summer months. ~ 350 South Grand Avenue; 213-687-2190.

◄ HIDDEN

At the beginning of the 20th century, Bunker Hill was a res-idential neighborhood of Victorian homes and residential hotels. A funicular, or cable, railway called **Angels Flight** connected Bunker Hill with the commercial district that lay below on 3rd and Hill streets. For a quarter, you can ride the "world's short-est railway" up or down the steep incline between Hill and Olive streets. The ride may last less than a minute, but it's a long reach back into Los Angeles history. Temporarily closed for renovations; call ahead for availability. ~ Water Court at California Plaza, and Hill Street at 4th Street; 213-626-1901.

◄ HIDDEN

One of the focal points of Bunker Hill is the city's tallest building, **Library Tower** (formerly known as First Interstate World Center), which rises 74 stories. For some reason, the developers did not include an observation deck, so unless you've got busi-ness in the tower, the lobby is about as far as you'll get. But that's worth a peek. ~ 633 West 5th Street.

◄ HIDDEN

Next door to the Library Tower are the bottom of **Bunker Hill Steps**. This monumental stairway leads from 5th Street to Hope Street. Water from a fountain at the top of the stairs cas-cades down a narrow channel to a small pool at the foot of the steps. Terrace landings relieve the climb, as do food and bever-age kiosks along the way.

At the top of the steps, walk to the corner of Hope and 4th streets to the sleek **Stuart M. Ketchum** YMCA and take a stroll

◄ HIDDEN

through the sculpture courtyard wrapped around three sides of the modern building. On a clear day the view to the northeast, of the San Gabriel Mountains, is stunning. ~ 401 South Hope Street.

If you survive the Bunker Hill Steps (or even if you opt for the escalators), cross 4th Street to the **Wells Fargo History Museum**, where you can view displays re-creating more than a century of Western history. Closed weekends. ~ 333 South Grand Avenue; 213-253-7166, fax 213-680-2269; www.wellsfargohistory.com.

The **World Trade Center**, another architectural extravaganza, looms nearby. Closed weekends. ~ 350 South Figueroa Street.

At **ARCO Plaza**, a twin-tower, 52-story behemoth, you'll encounter the **MTA** (Metropolitan Transportation Authority, Level C), where you can obtain route maps of the city's largest transportation agency. ~ Flower Street between 5th and 6th streets; 213-626-4455; www.mta.net.

Amid all these elite and expensive office buildings, one structure stands forth like a visitor from the future. Its five mirror-glass cylinders resembling a space station with legs, the **Westin Bonaventure Hotel** is easily the city's most imaginative skyscraper. Because of its unique design, together with an interior of reflecting pools and bubble elevators, the 1976 building is a favorite backdrop for sci-fi movies. ~ 404 South Figueroa Street; 213-624-1000, fax 213-612-4800; www.westin.com.

Across the street from this symbol of tomorrow stands an emblem of the past. The **Richard J. Riordan Central Library**, built in the 1920s, incorporates Egyptian, Roman, and Byzantine elements into a beaux-arts design. The most striking feature of all is the pyramid tower inlaid with colorful tile patterns. In 1986, fire gutted the interior and the city closed the library for repairs—and expansion. Seven years later, it reopened its doors, doubling the floor space with the addition of a new wing and a one-and-a-half-acre garden atop the parking garage—an oasis of greenery replete with five fountains. It is now the third largest central library in the nation. ~ 630 West 5th Street; 213-228-7000; www.lapl.org, e-mail phoneref@lapl.org.

HIDDEN ►

After a stint at Universal CityWalk, the **Museum of Neon Art** (MONA) has settled once again in downtown Los Angeles. In addition to its gallery of neon and electric-media art, the museum still maintains an outdoor exhibition of historic neon signs that now decorate building exteriors at Universal CityWalk. MONA also conducts guided Saturday-night bus tours of neon landmarks in the city, only given March through October. Closed Monday and Tuesday. Admission. ~ 501 West Olympic Boulevard at Hope Street; 213-489-9918, fax 213-489-9932; www. neonmona.org, e-mail info@neonmona.org.

The **Greater Los Angeles Convention & Visitors Bureau** is the city's main information center. There you'll find maps, leaflets, and a friendly staff to help point the way through this urban maze. Closed Sunday. ~ 685 South Figueroa Street; 213-689-8822, 800-228-2452, fax 213-624-1992; www.lacvb.com.

Hotel Stillwell, a competitively priced hostelry, offers 232 rooms in a vintage 1920 building. The lobby is decorated with Asian wall-hangings, matching the hotel's Indian restaurant. Each guest room has been refurbished with pastel colors, trim carpeting, and modern furniture throughout. ~ 838 South Grand Avenue; 213-627-1151, 800-553-4774, fax 213-622-8940; www.stillwell-la.com, e-mail hstillwell@aol.com. MODERATE.

LODGING

In the reasonable price range it's hard to top the **Figueroa Hotel.** A 1926 Spanish-style building, it offers a beautiful lobby with tile floor and hand-painted ceiling. The palm-fringed courtyard contains a swimming pool, jacuzzi, and lounge. The rooms are very large, adequately furnished, and decorated with wallhangings. Tile baths add a touch of class to this very appealing establishment. A lobby café is located on the premises. ~ 939 South Figueroa Street; 213-627-8971, 800-421-9092, fax 213-689-0305; www.figueroahotel.com. MODERATE TO DELUXE.

The city that today has a scandalously deficient transit system once possessed the finest electric trolley network in the world.

What can you say about a place that became a landmark as soon as it was built? To call the **Westin Bonaventure Hotel** ultramodern would belittle the structure. "Post Future" is a more appropriate tag. Its dark glass silos rise 35 stories from the street like a way station on the road to the 21st century. Within are five levels of shops, 1354 rooms, more than 15 restaurants, and a revolving cocktail lounge. The atrium lobby features reflecting pools, glass-shaft elevators, and lattice skylights. Considering all this, the guest rooms seem almost an afterthought; because of the building's configuration they are small and pie-shaped but offer good views of the surrounding financial district. ~ 404 South Figueroa Street; 213-624-1000, 800-228-3000, fax 213-612-4800; www.westin.com. ULTRA-DELUXE.

The past rests safely ensconced a few blocks distant at **The Millennium Biltmore Hotel.** Here the glamour and elegance of the Roaring '20s endure in a grand lobby replete with stately pilasters and floor-to-ceiling mirrors. A classic in the tradition of grande-dame hotels, the Biltmore conveys an Old World ambience with hand-oiled wood panels, frescoes, and ornamental molding. Its gourmet restaurants and sumptuous lounges reflect the rich Spanish–Italian Renaissance style that makes this 683-room hostelry a kind of museum for overnight guests. The bedrooms are moderately sized, adorned with contemporary artworks and provided with traditional French furniture. Among the other amenities is an elegant health club with swimming pool, jacuzzi, and sauna. ~ 506 South Grand Avenue; 213-612-1575, 800-245-8673, fax 213-612-1545; www.thebiltmore.com. ULTRA-DELUXE.

Located downtown is the European-style **Hilton Checkers Hotel**. This 188-room luxury hostelry originally opened in 1927 as the Mayflower Hotel. Its impressive modeled art stone facade of two carved ships, the *Mayflower* and the *Santa Maria*, made it one of the most strikingly beautiful buildings of its time. A massive renovation has restored it beyond its original elegance into one of the swankier hotels in town. Posh rooms come complete with original artwork, marble bathrooms, and three telephones. A gourmet restaurant, comfortable lounge, library, and rooftop spa make Checkers well worth the price tag. ~ 535 South Grand Avenue; 213-624-0000, 800-423-5798, fax 213-626-9906; www.hiltoncheckers.com. ULTRA-DELUXE.

The tasteful and contemporary 17-story **Omni Los Angeles Hotel at California Plaza**, is perched on Bunker Hill next to California Plaza's one-and-a-half-acre Watercourt (check out the dancing waters). Sunlight streams through the lobby's glass walls, creating a bright, open atmosphere. The 443 guest rooms are large, comfortably furnished, and decorated in Asian and neo-classical themes. Guests can also enjoy the health club that has a sauna, hot tub, and an outdoor swimming pool. ~ 251 South Olive Street; 213-617-3300, 800-843-6664, fax 213-617-3399; www.omnihotels.com. ULTRA-DELUXE.

DINING

To dine in the true style of Mexico the place to go is not a restaurant at all. **Grand Central Public Market**, a block-long produce market, features stands selling Mexican finger foods. Tacos, tostadas, and burritos are only part of the fare. Try the *chile rojo* (pork in red chile sauce), *machaca* (shredded beef), and *lengua* (tongue). If you're really daring there's *rellena* (blood sausage), *buche* (hog maws), and *tripas* (intestines). ¡Mucho gusto! ~ 317 South Broadway; 213-624-2378, fax 213-624-9496; www.grandcentralsquare.com. BUDGET.

You might recognize Casey's Bar and Grill from episodes of "Murder, She Wrote" or the movie *Mulholland Falls*.

Another funky but fabulous low-priced eating place is **Clifton's Brookdale Cafeteria**, a kind of steam-tray vistarama. The second floor of this cavernous place displays illuminated photos of California's sightseeing spots. The ground floor resembles a redwood forest, with tree trunks bolted to the walls, fake rocks stacked on the floor, and a waterfall tumbling through a cement funnel. It's a scene you cannot afford to miss. Breakfast, lunch, and dinner are served. ~ 648 South Broadway; 213-627-1673, fax 213-629-1329. BUDGET.

Completely subterranean, **Casey's Bar and Grill** is one of those marvelous old dining lounges with dark paneling, trophy cases, a 50-foot mahogany bar and graying photographs. One room displays antique song sheets, another is covered with sports photos; my personal favorite is the back room, where you can request a private booth with curtain. Lunch consists of hamburgers, sandwiches, and entrées such as Dublin broil (steak with mushrooms, spinach, and mashed potatoes). For dinner there are pasta dishes, fish and chips, barbecued ribs and crab-stuffed salmon. Bottoms up! Closed Saturday during the day and Sunday. ~ 613 South Grand Avenue; 213-629-2353, fax 213-629-5922. MODERATE.

Gill's Cuisine of India, set in the lobby of the 1920-era Hotel Stillwell, conveys an air of South Asia. Indian fabrics adorn the walls, complementing a menu of chicken masala, tandoori shrimp, lamb vindaloo, and curry dishes. There's also a buffet-style lunch (Monday through Friday). Closed Sunday. ~ 838 South Grand Avenue; 213-623-1050, 800-553-4774, fax 213-622-8940; www. gillsindiancuisine.com. BUDGET.

Part of the ever-growing dynasty of California French bistros and cafés presided over by the inventive Joachim and Christine Splichal (of Patina fame) are Cafe Pinot and Patinette at MOCA. **Cafe Pinot**, set next to Macguire Gardens behind the Central Library, is a downtown oasis of fine bistro-style dining and sophistication. You can't go wrong with the rôti chicken and Pinot fries, especially sitting in the garden. No lunch on weekends. ~ 700 West 5th Street; 213-239-6500, fax 213-239-6514; www. patinagroup.com. ULTRA-DELUXE.

Tucked below street level in the courtyard of MOCA is **Patinette**, a stylish little eatery where you step up to the counter, order a green-bean salad with artichokes, tomatoes, and Black Forest ham, or smoked turkey on dark wheat bread, then take a seat outside under the umbrellas. It's a great place to stop for a cappuccino or espresso, or a glass of wine. Lunch only, but open until 8 p.m. on Thursday. Closed Monday. ~ 250 South Grand Avenue; 213-626-1178, fax 213-626-0773. BUDGET TO MODERATE.

The Original Pantry, short on looks but long on soul, has been serving meals 24 hours a day since 1924 without missing a beat. When forced to relocate in 1950, they prepared lunch in the old building and served dinner at the new place. It simply consists of a counter with metal stools and a formica dining area decorated with grease-stained paintings. The cuisine is a culinary answer to heavy metal—ham hocks, navy bean soup, standing rib roast, sirloin tips with noodles, and roast pork. ~ 877 South Figueroa Street; 213-972-9279, fax 213-972-0187. BUDGET.

◄ HIDDEN

Elegance 24 hours a day? In a restaurant on wheels? Somehow all-night restaurants conjure visions of truck-stop dives, but at **Pacific Dining Car** 'round-the-clock service is provided in dark wood surroundings. Modeled after an old-style railroad dining car, with plush booths and outsized plate-glass windows, this destination has been a Los Angeles landmark since 1921. The cuisine is well-heeled all-American: breakfast includes eggs Benedict and eggs Sardou, and the dinner menu features lobster and some of the best steaks in the city. The Dining Car offers a complimentary shuttle to the Performing Arts Center and the Staples Center. ~ 1310 West 6th Street; 213-483-6000, fax 213-483-4545; www.pacificdiningcar.com, e-mail pdc@pacificdiningcar.com. ULTRA-DELUXE.

SHOPPING   At the **Atlantic Richfield Shopping Center** 55 shops and restaurants create one of the largest subterranean shopping centers in the country. ~ ARCO Plaza, 5th and Flower streets.

In a space age linkup, this mall connects via glass footbridge with the **Westin Bonaventure Shopping Gallery**, where numerous other stores, located on three levels, surround the Bonaventure's vaulting atrium lobby. ~ 404 South Figueroa Street.

Macy's Plaza lies at the heart of the downtown shopping hub and features a galleria of specialty shops as well as a Macy's department store. ~ 750 West 7th Street; 213-624-2891.

A charming European-style center, **7 + Fig at Ernst & Young Plaza** has dozens of shops and restaurants in an open-air setting. With an emphasis on fashion, the mall is highlighted by stores such as **Ann Taylor** (213-629-2818). ~ 735 South Figueroa Street; 213-955-7150.

The city's old jewelry district still houses a variety of shops selling goods at competitive prices. ~ Hill Street between 6th and 7th streets. Historic **St. Vincent Jewelry Center** is reputed to be the world's largest jewelry outlet, covering an entire square block. ~ 650 South Hill Street; 213-629-2124. Here and at the **International Jewelry Center**, another mammoth complex, you'll find items in every price range, from ten dollars to ten thousand. Closed Sunday. ~ 550 South Hill Street; 213-624-3201.

As in many urban areas, warehouses and industrial districts around Los Angeles have become home to young artists seeking low rents. Among the galleries that have resulted is **Cirrus Gallery**, where contemporary works by West Coast artists are displayed. Closed Sunday and Monday. ~ 542 South Alameda Street; 213-680-3473; www.cirrusgallery.com. **L.A. Artcore** is a nonprofit artists' organization where you'll find outstanding contemporary works. Closed Monday and Tuesday. ~ 120 Judge John Aiso (North San Pedro Street); 213-617-3274; www.laartcore.org.

The former Theater District, which served as Los Angeles' Great White Way during the 1930s, is now the main shopping district for the Latino community. Today, discount clothing, luggage, and electronic stores line this crowded boulevard. Latino sounds and the spicy aroma of Mexican food fills the air. ~

Food, Flowers, and More

Perhaps because of its long Spanish and Mexican heritage, Los Angeles has more public markets than almost any other city in the country. Here's a sampling of the best.

Grand Central Public Market is a fresh food bazaar in the tradition of Mexico's *mercados*. More than 50 fruit stalls, vegetable stands, butchers, and fresh fish shops line the aisles; juice stands dispense dozens of flavors; and vendors sell light meals. More than 30,000 people pass through every day, making it one of the city's most vital scenes. ~ 317 South Broadway; 213-624-2378, fax 213-624-9496.

The life of the barrio is evident at **El Mercado**, an indoor market crowded with shoppers and filled with the strains of Spanish songs. Clothing shops, fresh food markets, and stores sell everything from cowboy boots to Spanish-language videos. The signs are bilingual and the clientele represents a marvelous multicultural mix. ~ 3425 East 1st Street; 323-268-3451, 800-434-5273, fax 323-768-3295.

Back in 1934 local farmers created a market where they could congregate and sell their goods. Today the **Farmers Market** is an open-air labyrinth of stalls, shops, and grocery stands. Tables overflow with vegetables, fruits, meats, poultry, fish, cheeses, and baked goods—a total of over 120 outlets. Stop by for groceries, gifts, and finger foods or simply to catch Los Angeles at its relaxed and informal best. ~ 6333 West 3rd Street; 323-933-9211, fax 323-549-2145; www.farmersmarketla.com.

At the **Produce Market**, the bounty from California's interior valleys goes on the block every morning. The place is a beehive of business, a fascinating area where the farm meets the city. You can purchase produce by the lug or bushel. Even if a box of lettuce doesn't sound like the perfect souvenir from your L.A. sojourn, plan to visit these early-morning markets. Burly truckers, out-of-town farmers, and Latino workers are all part of this urban tableau. Closed Sunday. ~ Central Avenue and 7th Street; www.citymarketla.com.

For a view of blue-collar L.A., depart central downtown for the **Flower District**. Here, huge warehouses are filled with flowers and potted plants in one of the region's most amazing floral displays. There are Southern California proteas, New Zealand calla lilies, Dutch lilacs, Columbian roses, and French tulips. ~ Wall Street between 7th and 8th streets. Within the Flower District is the **Southern California Flower Market**, where wholesale flower merchants line an entire block and the air is redolent with fragrant merchandise. Closed Sunday. ~ 742 Maple Avenue; 213-627-2482.

Broadway between 3rd and 10th streets. The **Old Globe Theater**, once a legitimate theater, has been converted into a swap meet. ~ 744 South Broadway.

You can literally shop until you drop in Los Angeles' bustling **Garment District**. Known as a major manufacturing center since the 1930s, the district today lies concentrated along Los Angeles Street between 4th and 10th streets.

Academy Award Clothes stocks thousands of quality men's suits, as well as casual and sportswear at very reasonable prices. Closed Sunday. ~ 821 South Los Angeles Street; 213-622-9125.

The Garment District does not begin and end on Los Angeles Street, but rather extends along side streets and down alleyways. A bargain hunter's delight, **The Alley** is part and parcel of this busy neighborhood. Boxes, bins, and mannequins line the two-block-long alleyway where hawkers and vendors vie for your attention. ~ Located between Santee Street and Maple Avenue.

Consider **Bell of California**, which displays a beautiful selection of silks, cottons, linens, and more for ladies and juniors. Happy hunting! ~ 220 East Pico Boulevard; 213-748-5716.

Located nearby, **Basket World & Supply II** is floor to ceiling with baskets (sold at wholesale, even to retail buyers). Be forewarned: They are only open from 6 a.m. to 11:30 a.m. Closed Sunday. ~ 739 Wall Street; 213-689-0111. **Nuts To You** has been selling nuts to the public in the same location since early in the 20th century. Closed Sunday. ~ 901 South San Pedro Street; 213-627-8855.

NIGHTLIFE Its dual role as music center of the United States and film capital of the world makes Los Angeles one very hot entertainment destination. There are nightclubs frequented by Hollywood stars, movie theaters premiering major films, and dancehalls headlining top musicians from local recording studios. With so much talent concentrated in one city, the performing arts also flourish. Attending the theater in Los Angeles often means seeing a famous movie star playing the lead in a new drama.

The **Public Rush ticket program** at the Mark Taper Forum gives you a great deal on same-day performances. Two hours before curtain, canceled reservations and remaining tickets are released at $12 per ticket on a first-come, first-served basis. If spontaneity and the risk of disappointment aren't for you, then visit the theater box office or call for reservations. Public Rush purchases are cash only. Not available for Saturday evenings and Sunday matinees. ~ 213-628-2772.

A lovely place for evening cocktails, **BonaVista** offers a revolving 360° panorama of the city from the 34th floor of the Westin Bonaventure Hotel. One floor up, **L.A. Prime**, a New York–style steakhouse, also sports a tremendous although nonrevolv-

ing view. ~ 404 South Figueroa Street; 213-624-1000; www.
westin.com/bonaventure.

The **Grand Avenue Bar** offers 13 TV screens broadcasting
sports events in the stately Biltmore Hotel. For a more upscale
scene, check the hotel's **Rendezvous Court**. ~ 506 South Grand
Avenue; 213-624-1011; www.millenniumhotels.com.

Located a block away from the Biltmore, **Casey's Bar and
Grill** may well be the most popular downtown bar. A comfortable Irish-style pub filled with sports memorabilia, it draws business people on weekdays until 10 p.m. ~ 613 South Grand Avenue; 213-629-2353.

Brightly painted terra-cotta warrior priests welcome guests to
The Mayan Nightclub. Here a young and fashionable crowd
dances to deejay tunes and live salsa bands in a
grandiose Mayan tomb on Friday and Saturday.
Cover. ~ 1038 South Hill Street; 213-746-4287;
www.clubmayan.com.

> To find out what's happen-
> ing all over town, check
> out the "Calendar" sec-
> tion in the *Los Angeles
> Times*, the *L.A. Weekly*,
> and *Los Angeles* mag-
> azine.

The most prestigious performing arts complex on
the West Coast, the **Performing Arts Center of Los
Angeles County** consists of four major theaters located
within a massive, white marble plaza. The elegant **Dorothy Chandler Pavilion**, home to the Los Angeles Opera,
is a spectacular 3200-seat facility. The concert hall also
hosts performances by the Joffrey Ballet and American Ballet
Theatre. The 2000-seat **Ahmanson Theatre** presents classic dramas and comedies as well as West Coast premieres like *Phantom
of the Opera*. The more intimate 760-seat **Mark Taper Forum** is
ideal for contemporary dramatic and musical performances. The
resident Center Theater Group, associated with the Ahmanson
Theatre and the Mark Taper Forum, is committed to the development of new works and artists and has produced such award-
winning plays as *Zoot Suit*, *Children of a Lesser God*, and *The
Shadow Box*. ~ 135 North Grand Avenue; 213-972-7211; www.
musiccenter.org, e-mail general@musiccenter.org.

Across the street, the Frank Gehry–designed **Walt Disney
Concert Hall** hosts the Los Angeles Philharmonic and Master
Chorale. ~ 111 South Grand Avenue; 323-850-2000; wdch.la
phil.com.

The 6700-seat **Shrine Auditorium and Expo Center** hosts
major musical events, including classical, opera, jazz, pop, rock,
and ethnic folk music presentations. ~ 665 West Jefferson Boulevard; 213-749-5123. For same-day tickets, you'll need to go to
the Shrine ticket booth.

The **Staples Center**, L.A.'s latest major sports and entertainment venue, takes up 900,000 square feet in Downtown's south
end and cost a staggering $375 million to build. Three home
teams, the Lakers, the Clippers, and the Kings, play to crowds of

up to 20,000. ~ 1111 South Figueroa Street; 213-742-7340; www.staplescenter.com.

Tickets for performances at the Dorothy Chandler Pavilion, the Ahmanson, the Mark Taper Forum, the Shrine, and the Staples Center are available through **Ticketmaster**. ~ 213-480-3232; www.ticketmaster.com.

Little Tokyo

It's frequently noted that most Japanese Americans live elsewhere in the city—only about 700 people of Japanese descent still live in this historic neighborhood bounded by Los Angeles Street, Central Avenue, 1st Street, and 3rd Street. But Little Tokyo, which is adjacent to the central downtown district, is still the symbolic heart and soul of the Japanese-American community in Los Angeles.

SIGHTS

At the heart of the district is the **Japanese American Cultural and Community Center**, a stoic plate-glass-and-poured-concrete structure designed by Buckminster Fuller and Isamu Noguchi. The complex, which houses dozens of Asian organizations, faces a spacious brick-paved courtyard. The expansive Cultural Room boasts an authentic Japanese tea room, displays of calligraphy, *ikebana*, and other traditional arts, and hosts lectures and demonstrations. ~ 244 South San Pedro Street; 213-628-2725, fax 213-617-8576; www.jaccc.org, e-mail jaccc@jaccc.org.

> Little Tokyo is a busy shopping district centered along 1st Street between Main Street and Alameda Boulevard.

Part of the Japanese American Cultural and Community Center, the **Japan America Theatre** is an important showcase for kabuki theater, Asian music, and other performing arts. ~ 244 South San Pedro Street; 213-680-3700, fax 213-617-8576; www.jaccc.org, e-mail info@jaccc.org.

Follow the brick paving stones from the cultural center through **Japanese Village Plaza**, a two-block shopping mall adorned with fountains and sculptures. At the end of the plaza stands Little Tokyo's tile-roofed **fire tower**, an ornamental but practical structure that has become a local landmark.

Another cultural gathering place is the lovely **Higashi Honganji Buddhist Temple**. With its traditional tile roof, the temple represents Japanese architecture adapted to a Western cityscape. Call before visiting. ~ 505 East 3rd Street; 213-626-4200, fax 213-626-6850; www.hhbt-la.org, e-mail info@hhbt-la.org.

HIDDEN ►

On the day the **Japanese American National Museum** opened in 1992, riots were breaking out across L.A. as news of the acquittal of the policemen charged in Rodney King's beating became known. The violence overshadowed the opening of a museum dedicated to improving the "understanding and appreciation for America's ethnic and cultural diversity." The JANM, housed in a restored Buddhist temple, is a gem. Through changing exhibits, it presents the Japanese-American experience as an integral part of the nation's heritage. The National Museum houses the largest and most thoroughly documented collection of Japanese-American artifacts in the world. It offers a slew of history and art exhibitions, an expansive resource and research center, family programs, and video presentations. Closed Monday. Admission. ~ 369 East 1st Street; 213-625-0414, 800-461-5266, fax 213-625-1770; www.janm.org.

On the third floor of the New Otani Hotel & Garden is an authentic **Japanese garden**, where you can stroll along tranquil pathways, next to a stream and cascades of water. At night, the lighted towers of downtown form a magical backdrop. ~ 120 South Los Angeles Street; 213-629-1200, 800-421-8795; www.newotani.com.

◄ HIDDEN

Catering largely to an international clientele, the **New Otani Hotel & Garden** is a 434-room extravaganza with restaurants, shops, lounges, spa, and a tranquil half-acre Japanese "garden in the sky." The hotel offers small rooms, many decorated in traditional Japanese style with shoji screens. Standard guest accommodations are painted in pastel hues and decorated with ultramodern furniture in curvilinear designs. Finest feature of all is the lobby, a vaulted-ceiling affair with a skylight and an eye-catching sculpture. ~ 120 South Los Angeles Street; 213-629-1200, 800-421-8795; www.newotani.com, e-mail laotani@aol.com. ULTRA-DELUXE.

LODGING

Suehiro Café offers a Japanese menu in an American-style setting, complete with blue vinyl booths and counter service. You will find such Japanese standards as chicken teriyaki, tempura, and sukiyaki. ~ 337 East 1st Street; 213-626-9132. BUDGET TO MODERATE.

DINING

Japanese Village Plaza, right in the heart of the neighborhood, is a commercial expression of the sights, sounds, smells, and flavors of Japan. Enter at the site of the Fire Tower, a traditional fireman's lookout facing 1st Street, and walk the Plaza's winding brick pathways while browsing its tile-roofed shops. One such store, **Mikawaya Sweet Shop** (213-613-0611), tempts you with subtle Japanese candies. ~ 333 South Alameda Street.

SHOPPING

Just beyond the Plaza, **Bun-ka Do** offers an interesting collection of Japanese art objects, records, and books. ~ 340 East 1st Street; 213-625-1122.

Weller Court, a modern tri-level shopping arcade, boasts among its tenants **Kinokuniya Book Store of America** (213-687-4480, 800-595-2726), a branch of Japan's largest bookstore featuring a complete selection of books on Japan. ~ At Onizuka and 2nd streets.

Conveniently, Weller Court is connected via walking bridges to the **New Otani Hotel Shopping Arcade**, where a series of specialty shops showcase everything from fine jewelry to tourist trinkets. ~ 110 South Los Angeles Street.

Patterned after a Japanese department store, Little Tokyo Square is an array of small shops and restaurants on two floors clustered around a large grocery, **Mitsuwa**. The fresh fish counter is a key feature but it's overshadowed by the 40-foot-long refrigerator case of ready-to-eat sushi. You would be hard pressed to find any signs in English in either of the two Hello Kitty shops in the Square. ~ 333 South Alameda Street; 213-687-6699.

NIGHTLIFE   The **Genji Bar** at the New Otani Hotel is a Japanese karaoke bar in the heart of Little Tokyo. ~ 120 South Los Angeles Street; 213-253-9255.

Housed in the Japanese American Cultural and Community Center in Little Tokyo, the **Japan America Theatre** presents traditional and contemporary Japanese productions. Performances include Grand Kabuki, Bugaku, and Noh dramas, and Japanese-American plays. In addition, Western dance troupes and chamber orchestras are sometimes featured. ~ 244 South San Pedro Street; 213-680-3700, fax 213-617-8576; www.jaccc.org, e-mail jaccc@jaccc.org.

▼▼▼▼▼▼▼▼▼▼
Olvera Street

Olvera Street is commonly, but erroneously, called the birthplace of Los Angeles. The actual 1781 founding site was moved to its present Olvera Street location after a flood in 1815. Olvera Street is, however, the oldest surviving section of the city, featuring 27 historic buildings, some dating from the early 19th century. It's about as close to a Mexican village as you can get without actually crossing the border. Stalls sell all sorts of Mexican-made goodies, from *huaraches* (Mexican sandals) to *piñatas*. Restaurants specialize in spicy Mexican dishes, and tortillas are made by hand.

SIGHTS   Start your visit to Olvera Street at the **visitors center**, which provides maps, brochures, and walking tours. It's located in one of the pueblo's vintage buildings, an 1887 brick-faced Victorian called the Sepulveda House. Walking tours are offered Tuesday through Saturday mornings; two-hour bus tours of historic Los Angeles begin here on the third Wednesday of every month. Closed Sunday. ~ 622 North Main Street; 213-628-1274, fax 213-485-8238.

Heart of hearts is the **Plaza**, a tree-shaded courtyard adorned with statues and highlighted by a wrought-iron bandstand. A colorful gathering place, it's a frequent site for fiestas and open-air concerts. ~ North Main and Los Angeles streets.

Anchoring one corner of the plaza is **Firehouse No. 1**, Los Angeles' original fire station. Built in 1884, the brick structure served the fire department for little more than a decade, after which it became a saloon, boarding house, and store. Today it's a miniature museum filled with horse-drawn fire wagons, old-time helmets, and an ample inventory of memories. ~ 134 Paseo de la Plaza.

The plaza's most prestigious building, **Pico House** was built in 1870 by Pío Pico, the last Mexican governor of California. Italianate in style, it represented the grandest hotel of its era. Today it houses art and historical exhibits celebrating Latino culture. ~ Paseo de la Plaza and North Main Street.

Old Plaza Church, first dedicated as a church in 1822, also faces the square. The city's oldest Catholic church, it is unassum-

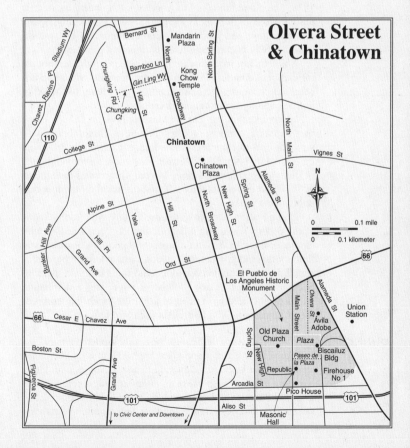

Olvera Street & Chinatown

ing from the outside but displays an interior that is a study in wrought iron and gold leaf. Murals cover the ceiling of the diminutive chapel and a collection of religious canvases adorns the altar. ~ 535 North Main Street.

Mexicans with more worldly matters in mind gather in large crowds outside the **Biscailuz Building**, a whitewashed structure decorated with brightly hued murals by Leo Politi, El Pueblo's resident artist for over 30 years. It serves as the main office for El Pueblo de Los Angeles. ~ 125 Paseo de la Plaza, northeast corner of the plaza.

For the full flavor of Spanish California, wander down **Olvera Street**. Lined with *puestos* (stands) selling Mexican handicrafts, it provides a window into Mexican culture. The brick-paved alleyway is also one of the West's first pedestrian shopping malls.

Among the antique buildings bordering this narrow corridor is the **Ávila Adobe**, a classic mud-brick house constructed around 1818. The oldest house in Los Angeles, it has undergone numerous incarnations, serving as a private residence, boarding house, and restaurant and surviving several earthquakes. Today it's a museum, fully restored and filled with period pieces.

A nearby historical marker points out the vital water source for early Los Angeles. **La Zanja Madre**, the mother ditch, channeled the precious waters of the Los Angeles River to the fledgling community for more than a century.

Located just off the plaza is **Masonic Hall**, an 1858 building that houses a museum of Masonic Order memorabilia. With wrought-iron balcony and ornate facade it follows an Italianate design. ~ 416½ North Main Street. Even more elaborate, though of later vintage, the neighboring **Merced Theatre** was constructed in 1870 and represents the city's first theatrical center. It is currently under repair.

Union Station, just across the street from Ávila Adobe, is one of the country's great train depots, and has been a Los Angeles landmark since 1939. With a Spanish-Mexican exterior, the station is a cavernous structure boasting marble floors, a beam ceiling 52 feet high, arched corridors, and walls of inlaid tile. Embodying the romance and promise of travel, it is a destination with a distinct identity, a point of departure for the far fringes of the imagination. ~ 800 North Alameda Street.

DINING   Olvera Street, where the Spanish originally located the pueblo of Los Angeles, is still a prime place for Mexican food. Tiny **taco stands** line this brick-paved alley. Little more than open-air kitchens, they dispense fresh Mexican dishes at budget prices. You'll also find bakeries and candy stands, where old Mexican ladies sell *churros* (Mexican donuts) and candied squash. BUDGET.

La Golondrina provides something more formal. Set in the historic Pelanconi House, an 1850s-era home built of fired brick, it features an open-air patio and a dining room with stone fireplace and *viga* ceiling. The bill of fare includes a standard selection of tacos, tostadas, and enchiladas as well as specialties such as fajitas and crab-meat enchiladas. ~ 17 West Olvera Street; 213-628-4349, fax 213-687-0800. MODERATE.

Across from Union Station, midway between Olvera Street and Chinatown, stands one of the city's most famous cafeterias. **Philippe The Original** has been around since 1908, serving pork, beef, turkey, and lamb sandwiches in a French-dip style. With sawdust on the floors and memories tacked to the walls, this antique eatery still serves ten-cent cups of coffee. Open for breakfast, lunch, and dinner. ~ 1001 North Alameda Street; 213-628-3781, fax 213-628-1812; www.philippes.com, e-mail philippe@philippes.com. BUDGET.

◀ HIDDEN

Historic **Olvera Street**, the site of Los Angeles' original pueblo, is the setting for a traditional Mexican marketplace. Its brick-paved walkways are lined with shops and stalls selling Mexican artworks and handicrafts. **Casa de Sousa** sells Mexican Indian folk art and Ecuadorean clothing, and also operates as a coffee house. Stroll the plaza, where restaurants serve homemade *maza* (cornmeal) tortillas, fresh tropical fruits, and tempting *nopales* (fresh diced cactus candies). ~ 19 West Olvera Street; 213-626-7076; e-mail casadesouza@hotmail.com.

SHOPPING

Mariachi music and margaritas draw Angelenos and outlanders alike to **La Golondrina**. You can sit by the fireplace or out on the patio of this historic adobe building. ~ 17 Olvera Street; 213-628-4349.

NIGHTLIFE

THE LAST OF THE BUNCH

Take a short drive up North Main Street and discover **San Antonio Winery**, the last of a disappearing breed. Years ago vineyards dotted the San Gabriel foothills, but Los Angeles' phenomenal urbanization steadily displaced them. Somehow this family-operated facility remained, situated surprisingly close to the center of the city. Today second- and third-generation members of the Riboli clan lead tasting tours through the vintage 1917 building. ~ 737 Lamar Street; 323-223-1401, fax 323-221-7261; www.sanantoniowinery.com, e-mail wineshop@sanantonio winery.com.

Chinatown

Back in 1870, when the Chinese population numbered perhaps 200, "Orientals" were sequestered in a rundown neighborhood southeast of the original plaza. As that area was torn down during the 1930s to build Union Station, they moved in increasing numbers to modern-day Chinatown, a multi-block neighborhood that has become the cultural and commercial center for Chinese residents throughout the city.

SIGHTS

For an authentic view, stroll the **600 block of North Spring Street** past the herb shops and fresh fish stores. Here local residents buy goat meat and fresh produce and choose from among the racks of roast ducks that hang forlornly in store windows.

HIDDEN ▶

Don't miss **Kong Chow Benevolent Association and Temple,** a tiny chapel tucked away on the second floor of an unassuming building. Crowded with elderly Chinese, the place is heavy with incense and handwoven tapestries. Gilded altars and bas-relief figures add a touch of the exotic. Closed Monday. ~ 931 North Broadway; 213-626-1955.

The commercial heart of the district lies along Broadway and Hill Street, with stores lining both boulevards for several blocks. Connecting these two thoroughfares is **Central Plaza** (Gin Ling Way), a two-block-long pedestrian mall. Traditional gates with swirling outlines mark the entranceways to this enclave. Figures of animals and ceremonial fish adorn the buildings and dragons breathe fire from the rooftops.

LODGING

An 80-room establishment, the **Metro Plaza Hotel** is close to Union Station and across the street from the historic Olvera Street complex. This four-story hostelry offers rooms and suites decorated in a contemporary style. Downstairs you'll find a small lobby with two sitting rooms. ~ 711 North Main Street; 213-680-0200, 800-223-2223; www.metroplazahotel.com, e-mail res@metroplazahotel.com. MODERATE.

DINING

Chinese Friends Restaurant is a postage-stamp eatery with plastic chairs, Chinese-style paintings of birds and flowers. In addition to the standard selection of shrimp, pork, and vegetable dishes they offer several unusual specials such as hot-and-sour chicken. There's little else to note except one salient point: the place is inevitably crowded with Chinese. Closed Tuesday. ~ 984 North Broadway; 213-626-1837. BUDGET TO MODERATE.

One of Chinatown's dim sum dining rooms, **Ocean Seafood** is a voluminous second-floor establishment. The dim sum service, in which you choose finger foods from passing carts, is only during lunch. At dinner there's a comprehensive Cantonese menu. With its fragile lamps and molded woodwork, Ocean Seafood has established a solid reputation for good food in sumptuous surroundings. No dinner. ~ 747 North Broadway; 213-687-3088, fax 213-687-8549. MODERATE.

The heart of Chinatown, where local Chinese shop at food emporiums, markets, and cookware stores, rests along **North Spring Street**. **SHOPPING**

Ornate Chinese-style roofs in reds and greens adorn **Chinatown Plaza,** the focal point of Chinatown. Along this promenade, well-stocked gift shops offer everything from imported trinkets to very fine, very ancient antiques and artworks. ~ 900 block of North Broadway.

Walk through the Plaza, then cross Hill Street, and you'll discover a treasure trove of antique stores dotting Chung King Road. **Fong's** carries a fine array of Chinese antique pieces. Closed Monday. ~ 943 Chung King Road; 213-626-5904. For beautiful screens and antique teapots, check out **The Jade Tree**. ~ 957 Chung King Road; 213-624-3521.

> On Thursday from 3 to 7 p.m., the Chinatown Farmer's Market sells a wide assortment of exotic Asian goods. ~ 727 North Hill Street.

The smell alone will lure you into the **Phoenix Bakery**. A Chinatown institution since 1938, this Asian-style bakery prepares whimsical confections that seem inevitably to attract a long line to its door. ~ 969 North Broadway; 213-628-4642.

Mandarin Plaza is a "modern" pedestrian mall, that houses **Asian Craft Imports** (213-626-5386), an imaginative shop filled with a large selection of import gift items. ~ 970 North Broadway.

Home to impressive architecture, major museums, an athletic palace, and one of the city's fine universities, the Exposition Park area lies just southwest of downtown Los Angeles. Whatever your interests, you'll find more than enough outdoor and indoor activities to entice you in and around Exposition Park. After dark, this is not the safest area in the city; confine your exploration to daylight hours and the main attractions.

Exposition Park Area

Minutes from Los Angeles' ultramodern downtown, where real estate sells by the square foot, sits the spacious, Romanesque campus of the **University of Southern California**. Lined with sycamore and maple trees, this red-brick-and-ivy enclave boasts a park-like setting filled with historic buildings. The movie location for everything from *The Hunchback of Notre Dame* to *The Graduate*, the campus is an ideal spot for a stroll. **SIGHTS**

Among the many features of the USC campus is the **Fisher Gallery**, with an excellent collection of European and New World art from the 15th century to the present. Closed Sunday and Monday, summer, and school holidays. ~ 213-740-4561; www.usc.edu/fishergallery. Also on campus is the **Hancock Memorial Museum**, which features rooms that were removed from the Villa de Medici–inspired 1907 Hancock Mansion and rebuilt here. In addition to the architecture, you will view the original furniture that accompanied the move. Open by appointment. ~ 213-740-5144; e-mail melindah@usc.edu.

Famous for its football team, USC has produced four Heisman trophy winners and more than 100 All-Americans. Although the school has received a lot of flack in the past for focusing on sports rather than academics, today this 28,000-student university boasts a slew of professional schools, including a well-established film program. ~ Bounded by Jefferson Boulevard, Vermont Avenue, Exposition Boulevard, and Figueroa Street; 213-740-2311.

EXPOSITION PARK This multiblock extravaganza is long on exposition and short on park. There *is* an enchanting **sunken garden** with a fountain, gazebos, and almost 20,000 rose bushes representing nearly 200 varieties of roses. Otherwise the park blooms with museums and sports arenas. ~ Bounded by Exposition Boulevard, Vermont Avenue, Martin Luther King, Jr. Boulevard, and Figueroa Street.

The **California Science Center** is one of those hands-on, great-for-kids-of-all-ages complexes. Its halls contain over 100 exhibits devoted to health and economics and displays demonstrating everything from simple laws of science to the latest advances in high technology. ~ Exposition Park; 213-744-7400; www.californiasciencetheater.org, e-mail 4info@cscmail.org.

In the Science Center's **Air and Space Gallery** there are exhibits explaining the principles of aerodynamics as well as planes, jets, and space capsules suspended from the ceiling in mock flight. Climbing a catwalk-like series of staircases, you'll have a bird's-eye view of a 1920 glider, an Air Force T-38, an F-20 Tiger Shark, and a Gemini II spacecraft. ~ 700 State Drive, Exposition Park.

Also at the Science Center, an **IMAX Theater**, with a seven-story-high screen, takes viewers on film adventures of stunning, you-are-there realism. Several different films are screened daily. You might find yourself cruising with whales, sledding through Alaska, or grazing with African wildlife. Call ahead for schedule. Admission. ~ Exposition Park; 213-744-7400; www.californiasciencetheater.org, e-mail 4info@cscmail.org.

The **Natural History Museum of Los Angeles County** is a world (and an afternoon) unto itself. Among the three-dozen galleries are rock and gem displays; dioramas of bears, wolves, and bison; set pieces from the American past, including a cut-away Conestoga wagon demonstrating life on the frontier; and, of course, the dinosaur skeletons required of every self-respecting natural history museum. If this is not enough, the museum con-

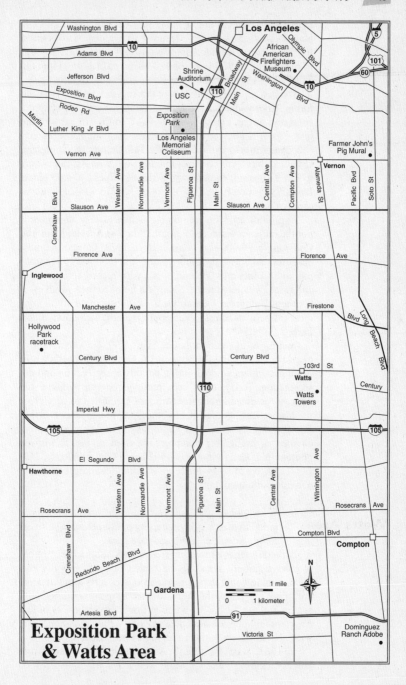

Exposition Park & Watts Area

tains bird specimens and a "discovery center" where kids can play scientist; the insect zoo features 30 live displays of critters from around the world. Admission (except on the first Tuesday of the month). ~ 900 Exposition Boulevard; 213-763-3466, fax 213-743-4843; www.nhm.org, e-mail info@nhm.org.

Prettiest of all the buildings in this museum park is the **California African American Museum** with its glass-roofed sculpture court and bright, airy galleries. Devoted to the art, culture, and history of African Americans west of the Mississippi, the primary collection features artifacts from the 18th century to the present. Other exhibits focus on topics ranging from West African culture to Ella Fitzgerald. Closed Sunday through Tuesday. ~ 600 State Drive, Exposition Park; 213-744-7432, fax 213-744-2050; www.caam.ca.gov.

Exposition Park's most notable architectural achievement is not the museum buildings, but rather the **Los Angeles Memorial Coliseum**, a 96,000-seat arena built in 1923. One of the most beautiful stadiums in the country, site of the 1932 and 1984 Olympics, the Coliseum is a classic arena with arched entranceways and rainbow-colored seats. Today it is home to the University of Southern California football team, and hosts a variety of concerts and performances. ~ 3939 South Figueroa Street, Exposition Park; 213-748-6131.

Just north of the park is Fire Station 30, one of two segregated fire stations in L.A. between 1924 and 1955. This is where black firefighters worked during periods of segregation and desegregation. Today it has been proudly restored to house the **African American Firefighter Museum**. Dedicated to preserving the history and heritage of Los Angeles' African-American firemen (known today as "Old Stentorians"), the museum displays all sorts of firefighting paraphernalia from engines to historic photographs. Call for hours. ~ 1401 South Central Avenue; 213-744-1730, fax 213-744-1731; www.aaffmuseum.org, e-mail aaffmuseum@affmuseum.org.

HIDDEN ▶

▼▼▼▼▼▼▼▼▼▼

Watts Area

Watts, one of L.A.'s poorest neighborhoods with a reputation to match, is known for two divergent things: an eccentric artistic creation and race riots.

A fantasy series of twisting steel towers adorned with pieces of colored pottery, sea shells, and other cast-off items is about the last thing you'd expect to see in this poverty-stricken area. Still, over the years, the Watts Towers have survived not only neglect and vandalism, but a pull-test ordered by the City of Los Angeles that approximated the force of a 120-mile-an-hour gale wind. Needless to say, the Towers remained standing.

In 1965, Watts became the scene of the devastating Watts race riots, during which 43 people were killed and 4000 arrested.

Today, Watts is still one of L.A.'s poorest areas, filled with blocks of decrepit bungalows and bisected by Southern Pacific railroad tracks. Yet artists from local communities and visitors from around the world come here to take inspiration from the beauty of one immigrant's artistic achievement. And while you're in the neighborhood, stop and explore some off-the-beaten-path sights of L.A.'s urban industrial areas.

SIGHTS

◄ HIDDEN

One of the seven wonders of Los Angeles is located northeast of Watts in the industrial town of Vernon, where **Farmer John's Pig Mural** covers an entire city block. Probably the biggest mural you'll ever see, it's also one of the funniest, picturing hundreds of pigs running through open fields. This idyllic landscape, in the midst of miles of factories, was begun in 1957 by a movie-industry artist named Les Grimes. For years Grimes gave everything to the project and ultimately lost his life, falling from a scaffold while working on the mural. His legacy is a romping, rollicking, technicolor creation. ~ 3049 East Vernon Avenue, Vernon.

After priming your eyes with this porcine art, head down to L.A.'s legendary folk-art wonder, also the result of an individual artist with an uncommon vision—**Watts Towers**. Fashioned by Simon Rodia over a three-decade period, these delicate, curving towers, inlaid with *objets trouvés*, rise nearly 100 feet. Encrusted with tile shards, stones, and more than 70,000 sea shells, they form a work of unsettling beauty. After five years of being untended and vandalized, the towers were purchased by a group of volunteers, who set up a committee to oversee their maintenance. ~ 1765 East 107th Street, in Simon Rodia State Historic Park, Watts.

> After half a lifetime of work Simon Rodia finished the Watts Towers in 1954, gave the property to a neighbor, and left Los Angeles, never to visit his towers again.

The **Watts Towers Arts Center** next door features a rotating series of exhibits by artists in the black and Asian community. Tours of the towers are available through the Arts Center. Call ahead for times. Admission. Closed Monday. ~ 1727 East 107th Street, Watts; 213-847-4646, fax 323-564-7030.

◄ HIDDEN

Continuing farther south, Los Angeles' industrial district also contains some of California's early creations. The **Dominguez Ranch Adobe,** in the heavy-metal town of Compton, is an 18th-century Spanish rancho and historic museum. The grounds of this sprawling hacienda are landscaped with lovely flower and cactus gardens. The museum features the original furniture and effects of the Dominguez family, the Spanish dons who first built a home here in 1826 (the land itself was the first land grant decreed by the King of Spain in 1784). Guided tours are conducted from 9 to 11 a.m. Tuesday and Thursday and 1 to 3 p.m. Wednesday. It is open on the first and last Sunday of the month from 1 to 3 p.m. ~ 18127 South Alameda Street, Compton;

310-631-5981, fax 310-631-3518; e-mail dominguezadobe@com cast.net.

When you've had your fill of history and art, head up to **Hollywood Park,** one of the Southland's great tracks, where you'll find thoroughbred racing from the end of April until the end of July, and again in November and December. Beautifully laid out, the track features a landscape complete with palm trees, lagoon, and children's play area. Closed Monday and Tuesday. Admission. ~ 1050 South Prairie Avenue, Inglewood; 310-419-1500; www. hollywoodpark.com.

▼▼▼▼▼▼▼▼▼▼▼▼▼
East Los Angeles

The spirit of Mexico is alive and shimmering in the *barrio* of East L.A. With a population that is 90 percent Latino, this sprawling neighborhood represents the country's largest concentration of Hispanics. Originally settling Los Angeles in the 18th century, Mexicans emigrated en masse following the Mexican Revolution of 1910.

Today Latinos make up the largest population group in the city, flexing political muscle and demonstrating cultural pride. As playwright Luis Valdez explains, "No Statue of Liberty ever greeted our arrival in this country. We did not in fact come to the United States at all. The United States came to us."

SIGHTS

Cesar Chavez Avenue (Brooklyn Avenue), a major thoroughfare in the Boyle Heights district, represents "Little Mexico," a region rich in Mexican restaurants, candy stores, and family shops. If Cesar Chavez Avenue is the heart of the *barrio*, **Whittier Boulevard** is the spine, a neon ganglion charged with electric color. It is here that a guy goes to show off his girl, his car, and himself. Lined with discount stores, *taquerías*, and auto body shops, Whittier is the Sunset Strip of East L.A.

Of course the full flavor of the Chicano community is found among the murals that decorate the streets of East Los Angeles.

◆◆

THE HEARTBEAT OF A COMMUNITY

Many of the muralists decorating East Los Angeles' streets started at **Plaza de la Raza.** This Chicano cultural center is intimately involved in the artistic life of the community, sponsoring classes in dance, music, theater, and visual arts. For visitors there's a variety of regularly scheduled events. Closed Sunday and from December 14 through January 4. ~ 3540 North Mission Road; 323-223-2475, fax 323-223-1804; www.plazadelaraza.org, e-mail admin@plazaraza.org. Adjacent to the cultural center, **Lincoln Park** features a lake and tree-studded picnic area.

Exotic in design, vibrant with color, they are a vital representation of the inner life of the *barrio*, a freeform expression of the Mexican people and their 400-year residence in the United States.

A spectacular series of murals adorn the walls of the **Estrada Courts Housing Project**. Here dozens of bright-hued images capture the full sweep of Latin history. ~ Olympic Boulevard between Grande Vista Avenue and Lorena Street.

◄ HIDDEN

Two other buildings also provide a panoramic image of Mexican history. In a succession of panels, the **First Street Store** recreates prehistoric Mexican society, then progresses through the Aztec area to modern times. ~ 3640 East 1st Street. With a series of surreal tile murals, the nearby **Pan American Bank** carries the saga into the future, portraying Latinos in the post-atomic age. ~ 3626 East 1st Street.

Another color-soaked mural, painted in 1983, **"El Corrido de Boyle Heights"** ("The Ballad of Boyle Heights") captures the community at work and play, with the family, and on the road. A succession of overlapping scenes, it's an anecdotal expression of the *barrio*, done with a flair unique to Chicano culture. ~ Corner of Cesar Chavez Avenue (Brooklyn Avenue) and Soto Street.

Mexican restaurants are on parade at **El Mercado**, a two-story indoor market adorned with tile floors and colorful murals. Along the mezzanine of this Spanish emporium are chili bars, taco stands, seafood restaurants, and cafés from south of the border. Adding to your dining pleasure, Mexican bands perform love songs and ballads. ~ 3425 East 1st Street; 323-268-3451. BUDGET TO MODERATE.

DINING

The greatest of all East L.A.'s Mexican restaurants is **El Tepeyac Café**, a hole-in-the-wall with so much soul people migrate across the city to feast on its legendary burritos. Consisting of a small dining room with take-out window and side patio, the place serves everything—*machaca*, tacos, steak *picado*, enchiladas, *chile colorado*, *huevos con chorizo*, and so on. The food is delicious, and the portions are overwhelming. Breakfast, lunch, and dinner are served. Closed Tuesday. ~ 812 North Evergreen Avenue; 323-268-1960. BUDGET.

For neighborhood shopping in an ethnic environment, just traverse the Macy Street Bridge over the Los Angeles River and enter East Los Angeles. Affectionately known as "Little Mexico," the area around Cesar Chavez Avenue (Brooklyn Avenue) is chockablock with restaurants, markets, bridal shops, and toy stores. **El Mercado** is an enclosed marketplace filled with shops and stalls. Vendors here sell cowboy boots and Mexican blankets, restaurants serve up tacos *de cabeza* and strolling mariachis create an atmosphere of Old Mexico. ~ 3425 East 1st Street.

SHOPPING

NIGHTLIFE The **Margo Albert Theatre**, part of the Plaza de la Raza arts center, hosts drama, music, and dance programs that relate to Mexican culture. ~ 3540 North Mission Road; 323-223-2475.

The East L.A. theater scene is dominated by the **Bilingual Foundation of the Arts**, which presents plays in English and Spanish. ~ 421 North Avenue 19; 323-225-4044; www.bfatheatre.org.

▼▼▼▼▼▼▼▼▼▼▼▼▼▼▼
Echo Park–Silver Lake

Set along sloping hillsides and separated by parks and eucalyptus groves are several suburban neighborhoods. Once a favored spot among Yang-Na Indians, this hill-and-dale district is now inhabited by an intriguing mix of blue- and white-collar workers. While the areas around Elysian and Echo parks have become Latino neighborhoods, the heights above Silver Lake are given over to professionals, including a significant gay population. In fact, together with West Hollywood, Silver Lake has emerged as one of Los Angeles' major centers of gay culture. With its curving mountain roads, tile-topped houses, jogging paths, and city vistas, this last neighborhood is also popular with artists.

SIGHTS For the outdoor-minded, 575-acre **Elysian Park**, the city's second largest park, is a forested region of rolling hills and peaceful glens. There are picnic areas, meadows planted with exotic palm trees, and numerous nature trails offering views of central Los Angeles and the San Gabriel Valley, as well as basketball, volleyball, and tennis courts. For the sports-minded, the park contains 56,000-seat **Dodger Stadium**, home of the Los Angeles Dodgers. ~ Located near the intersection of Routes 110 and 5; 323-224-1500, fax 323-224-1269; www.dodgers.com.

Nearby, **Echo Park** features a palm-fringed lake complete with footbridge and ducks. There are rental boats (213-847-8524) for exploring the fountain and lotus flowers, which highlight this 15-acre body of water. The lake is stocked with trout and catfish; fishing is allowed, although you need a license. There's also a playground. ~ Glendale Boulevard and Echo Park Avenue; 213-250-3578, fax 213-250-8946.

That circular structure with the imposing white columns across the street is **Angelus Temple**. Modeled after London's Royal Albert Hall, it served the congregation of spiritualist Aimee Semple McPherson during the 1920s and 1930s. Open Sunday and Thursday. ~ 1100 Glendale Boulevard; 213-484-1100; www.angelus temple.org.

The nearby neighborhood of **Angelino Heights** was the city's first suburb, built during the 1880s on a hill overlooking Downtown and connected to the business district by cable car. Today the once elegant borough, ragged along the edges, still retains vestiges of its glory days. Foremost is the **1300 block of Carroll Avenue**, where a string of gingerbread Victorians have been gussied up in the fashion of the Gay Nineties. Representing Los Angeles' largest concentration of Victorian houses, the street is an outdoor museum lined with turrets, gables, and fanciful woodwork.

Another noteworthy housing colony surrounds the reservoir at **Silver Lake**. Built after World War II, the homes are generally of stucco construction. Since they cover nearby hills, the best way to tour the neighborhood is by winding through the labyrinth of narrow streets that ascends from the lake. ~ Silver Lake Boulevard.

Of architectural note is the row of houses on the **2200 block of East Silver Lake Boulevard**. Designed by Austrian architect Richard Neutra, they are stucco-and-plate-glass structures representative of the International style. Neutra's homes are currently the rage, and Silver Lake real-estate prices have gone sky-high because of the large concentration of such homes. The area is inhabited by young showbiz types, record and TV execs, writers, artists, and musicians who pay premium prices for these mid-20th-century modern homes.

Sunset Boulevard, particularly around Echo Park and Silver Lake, is a veritable restaurant row. Traveling northeast on this famous street you'll come upon restaurants of every ethnic persuasion.

DINING

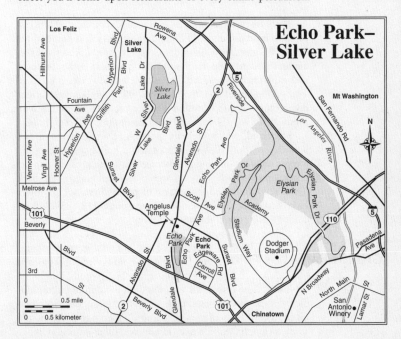

Taix French Restaurant is a huge, common-denominator restaurant serving French country cuisine in several dining rooms. The lunch and dinner *cartes* include roast pork, trout almondine, roast duck, and lamb chops. The interior is attractive, if crowded. There's musical entertainment Wednesday through Saturday. ~ 1911 West Sunset Boulevard; 213-484-1265, fax 213-484-0041; www.taixfrench.com. MODERATE TO DELUXE.

Burrito King serves superb *frijoles*, as well as a memorable *machaca* burrito consisting of shredded tender beef mixed with sautéed onions and green peppers. Open 'til 1 a.m. for late-night feasts. ~ 2823 Hyperion Avenue; 323-663-9378. BUDGET.

If you like spicy Caribbean flavor in food and atmosphere, make your way over to **Cha Cha Cha**. It's in a rundown East Hollywood neighborhood, but don't let that put you off. A valet will look after your car, and a hip crowd, fired up on *camarones negros*, *sopes*, *empanadas*, and jerk chicken pizza, will hold your attention. ~ 656 North Virgil Avenue; 323-664-7723, fax 323-660-0449. MODERATE.

NIGHTLIFE The Bavarian-style **Red Lion Tavern**, a friendly German rathskeller, serves lagers in two-liter boots. The German bartenders occasionally initiate impromptu sing-alongs, especially after games at nearby Dodger Stadium. ~ 2366 Glendale Boulevard; 323-662-5337.

There are two small theaters of note in Silver Lake. The **Knightsbridge Theatre**, built in 1927 as a movie palace, is home of the National American Shakespeare Company (they have a sister theater in Pasadena). It performs the Bard's work in both traditional and experimental productions, as well as showcases other classics. ~ 1944 Riverside Drive; 323-667-0955; www.knightsbridge theatre.com. The **Celebration Theatre** presents gay and lesbian productions. ~ 7051 Santa Monica Boulevard; 323-957-1884.

Spaceland, which presents mostly live alternative and pop with the occasional deejay night of jungle, house, and techno, has a reputation for offering the surprise big-name artist and sometimes eliminating the cover charge. There's a lounge in the back if you're in the mood for a game of pool. Cover. ~ 1717 Silver Lake Boulevard; 323-661-4380 reservations, 213-833-2843 recorded info; www.clubspaceland.com.

Griffith Park–Los Feliz

Every great city boasts a great city park, and Los Angeles is no exception. Set astride 4000 acres in the Hollywood Hills in the city's northeast corner, Griffith Park is the nation's largest municipal park. Golf courses, miles of hiking trails, pony rides, tennis courts, a display of miniature trains, a merry-go-round, a museum, an amphitheater, a planetarium, and other attractions make the park one of the most popular places in town on warm, sunny days. Los Feliz, the neighborhood on the surrounding slopes, has long appealed to artists, architects, movie stars, and writers.

GRIFFITH PARK   There are three main entrances to the park off Los Feliz Boulevard. Fern Dell Drive, on the park's western edge near Western Avenue, winds past a children's playground and a popular picnic area. Vermont Avenue leads directly to the outdoor Greek Theater amphitheater and then to Observation Drive, which leads to the observatory. At the eastern edge, near Route 5, Griffith Park Drive is the most direct route to the merry-go-round, the zoo, the Gene Autry Western Heritage Museum, and Travel Town.

SIGHTS

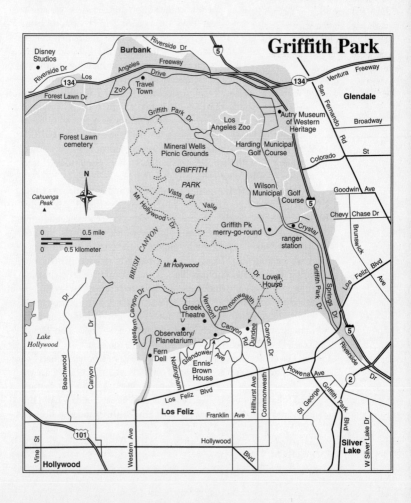

Standing above the urban fray at the southern end of the park is the **Griffith Observatory and Planetarium**, a copper-domed beauty that perfectly represents the public-monument architecture of the 1930s. With its bas-reliefs and interior murals, this eerie site also resembles a kind of interplanetary temple. In fact it has been the setting for numerous science fiction films such as *When Worlds Collide* (1951). The Observatory's most famous appearance, however, was in *Rebel Without a Cause* (1955) when James Dean was confronted by the neighborhood gang.

Apart from a movie setting, the Observatory, which is closed through 2005 for major renovations, will feature a high-tech planetarium theater and astronomy exhibits complete with telescopes. A lot of people come simply for the view, which on clear days (in Los Angeles?) extends from the Hollywood Hills to the Pacific. A temporary satellite facility near the L.A. zoo offers mini-planetarium shows, a meteorite exhibit, and a telescopic viewing of the moon and planets at night. Call for details. ~ 2800 East Observatory Road; 323-664-1191, fax 323-663-4323; www.griffithobs.org, e-mail info@griffithobs.org.

Local bird species nest in Fern Dell, a shady glade in Griffith Park with a spring-fed stream. The picnic tables lining the dell create an inviting spot to while away an afternoon. ~ Western Canyon Road.

Toward the southern edge of the park, you'll see the **Griffith Park & Southern Railroad**, a miniature train ride. In the winter, you can ride with Santa. A nearby track offers **pony rides** (closed Monday). Admission. ~ 323-664-6788.

The **ranger station** will provide maps and information while directing you across the street to the **merry-go-round**, a beautiful 1926-vintage carousel. The merry-go-round is open weekends only.

Featuring real life versions of these whirling animals, the **Los Angeles Zoo** is among the highlights of the park. Over 1200 animals inhabit this 113-acre facility, many in environments simulating their natural habitats. The African exhibit houses elephants, rhinos, zebras, and monkeys; Eurasia is represented by tigers; there are jaguars from South America as well as kangaroos and koalas from Australia. Check out its sea lion exhibit slated for inauguration in summer 2004. Admission. ~ 5333 Zoo Drive; 323-644-6400, fax 323-662-9786; www.lazoo.org.

The adjacent **Adventure Island** is where newborn animals are bottle-fed. You can see the baby animals in an exhibition area.

Travel Town is a transportation museum featuring a train yard full of cabooses, steam engines, and passenger cars from the glory days of the railroad. The exhibit also includes a fleet of 1920-era fire trucks and old milk wagons. For the kids there are narrow-gauge train rides (fee). ~ 5200 West Zoo Drive; 323-662-5874.

For Hollywood's version of American history, there's the **Autry Museum of Western Heritage**, located inside the park. The focus here is both on Westerns and the West, and you will see Billy the Kid's gun and Wyatt Earp's badge. There are displays of saloons and stagecoaches, silver saddles, and ivory-handled six-shooters, plus paintings, photos, and film clips of all your favorite stars, kids. Its nine galleries feature art by Frederic Remington and Thomas Moran. Closed Monday. Admission. ~ 4700 Western Heritage Way; 323-667-2000, fax 323-660-5721; www.autry-museum.org.

High on a slope overlooking Los Angeles stands the **Ennis-Brown House**, a squarerigged, Mayan temple–style home designed by Frank Lloyd Wright in 1924. You need a reservation to visit. Closed Sunday. Admission. ~ 2655 Glendower Avenue, Los Feliz; 323-660-0607; www.ennisbrownhouse.org, e-mail ennisbrn@ primenet.com.

The Ennis-Brown mansion resides in the same neighborhood as the **Lovell House**, a prime example of Richard Neutra's International style of architecture, circa 1929. ~ 4616 Dundee Drive, Los Feliz.

Hillhurst Avenue is the Los Feliz area's restaurant row. The Los Feliz edition of the perennially popular chain, **Louise's Trattoria**, offers a patio for alfresco dining on California pizzas (try the sausage), salads, homemade pastas (the penne bolognese is simple but satisfying), lasagne, and chicken entrées. Reliable and affordable. ~ 4500 Los Feliz Boulevard at Hillhurst Avenue; 323-667-0777. MODERATE.

DINING

The tiny, storefront **Trattoria Farfalla** has received its fair share of praise over the years for simple, but terrific, Italian cooking and reasonable prices. Try tagliolini with shrimp, garlic, and olive oil, and *insalata farfalla* of romaine and radicchio atop crisp pizza bread. The place is always crowded, so if you're uncomfortable dining almost intimately with strangers, skip it. ~ 1978 Hillhurst Avenue; 323-661-7365, fax 323-661-5956. MODERATE.

Capriccio on Vermont is located toward the eastern edge of Griffith Park. This little storefront restaurant spills out onto the wide corner sidewalk on warm evenings, creating a scene reminiscent of Rome or Paris. Try any of the pastas—spaghetti *del mare*, for example, or Antonio chicken in a light, creamy tomato sauce. Dinner only. ~ 1757 North Vermont Avenue; 323-662-5900, fax 323-465-2638. MODERATE.

You can browse the stacks or snuggle up in a reading chair at **Skylight Books** in Los Feliz. This marvelous facility has an extensive selection of foreign and American literature as well as literary periodicals. They also produce a variety of discussions with

SHOPPING

and readings by local authors, artists, and community leaders. ~ 1818 North Vermont Avenue; 323-660-1175; www.skylight books.com, e-mail skylightbooks@earthlink.net.

NIGHTLIFE   The giant 6000-seat **Greek Theatre**, nestled in the rolling hills of Griffith Park, is patterned after a classical Greek amphitheater. The entertainment in this enchanting spot ranges from stellar jazz, classical, pop, and rock music to dance and dramatic performances. Bring a sweater and picnic. ~ 2700 North Vermont Avenue; 323-665-1927; www.nederlander.com/greekbo.html.

Get into the Latin swing of things at **La Fogata**, a sizzling Colombian restaurant and nightclub. Cover. ~ 3000 Los Feliz Boulevard; 323-664-2955.

There's live entertainment every night at **The Derby**, starting between 9:30 and 10:30 p.m. and ranging from rockabilly bands to tap dancing. Call 323-769-5105 for entertainment information. This contemporary club (featuring an oval bar that appeared in *Mildred Pierce*) also offers swing dance lessons Wednesday through Saturday, from 8 to 9 p.m. Cover. ~ 4500 Los Feliz Boulevard at Hillhurst Avenue; 323-663-8979; www.the-derby.com.

North Vermont Avenue, between Hollywood Boulevard and Franklin Avenue, offers some nightlife possibilities. For film offerings in the neighborhood, look to the **Los Feliz Theater**. ~ 1822 North Vermont Avenue at Franklin Avenue; 323-664-2169. **The Dresden**, a stately brick-and-stained-glass restaurant, hosts an elegant piano bar. ~ 1760 North Vermont Avenue; 323-665-4294; www.thedresden.com.

▼▼▼▼▼▼▼▼▼▼▼▼▼▼▼
Mt. Washington Area

If an entire neighborhood could qualify as an outdoor museum, the Mt. Washington district would probably charge admission. Here within a few blocks are several picture-book expressions of desert culture.

SIGHTS   The **Lummis House**, or El Alisal, is the work of one man, Charles Fletcher Lummis, whose life is inextricably bound to the history of the region. Though born in the Northeast, Lummis fell in love with the Southwest, devoting his life to defending the region's Indian tribes and promoting local arts and crafts. A writer and magazine editor, he built this stone house himself, carving the doors by hand and even embedding photographs from his South American travels in the windows where the sun still shines through them. Surrounded by a "waterwise" garden, the house is an excellent example of turn-of-the-20th-century Southwestern sensibilities. Closed Monday through Thursday. ~ 200 East Avenue 43; 323-222-0546, fax 323-222-0771; www.social history.org, e-mail hssc@socialhistory.org.

Perhaps Charles Lummis' most important role was as founder of the **Southwest Museum**. Set in a Mission-style structure over- ◄ HIDDEN
looking downtown Los Angeles, this important facility contains exquisite jewelry, basketry, weaving, and other handicrafts from Pueblo Indian tribes. California's Indians are represented by their petroglyphs, pottery, weapons, and decorative beadwork. In fact, the museum has so expanded its collection since Lummis' day that the current theme focuses more on American Indians in general than on the Southwest. There are bead cradle boards, a tepee, and leather clothing hand-painted by Plains Indians; totem poles and artifacts from the Pacific Northwest tribes; and an excellent research library. Changing exhibits present the work of contemporary American Indian artists. Closed Monday. Admission. ~ 234 Museum Drive; 323-221-2164, fax 323-224-8223; www.southwestmuseum.org, e-mail info@southwestmuseum.org.

The Lummis House was contructed using stone from the nearby arroyo.

That antique neighborhood on the other side of the Pasadena Freeway is **Heritage Square Museum**, an open-air, living history museum with a collection of historic buildings. Several impressive Victorian buildings, a Methodist church, and the old Palms Railroad Depot are located here. There's also an exhibition area, guided tours, and rotating exhibits. Open Friday (though access to buildings is restricted) through Sunday, and select holiday Mondays. Admission. ~ 3800 Homer Street; 626-449-0193, fax 626-304-9652; www.heritagesquare.org, e-mail director@heritagesquare.org.

There are hundreds, perhaps thousands of reasons to visit Los Angeles. But could any be as important as a Richard Nixon

Whittier–El Monte Area

pilgrimage? Think about it, a sacred visit to the hometown of the only president who ever resigned from office, "Tricky Dick" himself, the first national leader ever compelled to assure the American public that "I am not a crook."

Anyone who has ever heard a maudlin Nixon speech knows   **SIGHTS**
Whittier, where the 37th President of the United States was raised, schooled, and elected to Congress. The **Whittier Chamber of Commerce** is a source of information. Closed weekends. ~ 8158 Painter Avenue, Whittier; 562-698-9554, fax 562-693-2700; www.whittierchamber.com, e-mail carol@whittierchamber.com.

Among the highlights are **East Whittier Elementary School** (Whittier Boulevard and Gunn Avenue); **Whittier High School** (Philadelphia Street and Pierce Avenue), where young Richard graduated in 1930; and the Spanish-style campus of **Whittier**

College (Painter Avenue and Philadelphia Street), from which he received his diploma four years later.

The **Whittier Museum and Historical Society** has displays on local history from the 1800s and early 1900s. Permanent exhibits include "Main Street in the 1890s," complete with shop windows, and a replica of the original 1905 "Old Red Car" in the children's room. Here, kids play with turn-of-the-20th-century typewriters, telephones, and clothes. There is also a retrospective on Richard Nixon's life, as well as temporary exhibits. The museum is open to the public on Saturday and Sunday. ~ 6755 Newlin Avenue, Whittier; 562-945-3871, fax 562-945-9106; www.whittiermuseum.org, e-mail info@whittiermuseum.org.

Richard Nixon married Pat Ryan in 1940; after the future President was elected to Congress in 1946, the **Nixon residence** became a modest, low-slung stucco house. Interestingly, none of these places acknowledge the Watergate President. Not to worry, for those of us who remain true believers, each location is an immortal shrine. ~ 14033 Honeysuckle Lane.

The Nixon family store was converted into a gas station, but the **Pat Ryan Nixon House**, where the future First Lady lived when she met her husband, still stands. ~ 13513 Terrace Place.

Of course the true pilgrimage is to the **Richard Nixon Presidential Library and Birthplace,** several miles southeast of Whittier in Yorba Linda. Here you'll find the 900-square-foot home (that "made up in love what it lacked in size") where Nixon was born "on the coldest day of one of the coldest winters in California history." Also here are the garden and gravesite. The library itself, with barely a book to be seen, is a marvelous succession of movies, interactive videos, and touch-screen presentations that rewrite American history in a fashion that would make even a novelist blush. Admission. ~ 18001 Yorba Linda Boulevard, Yorba Linda; 714-993-3393, 800-872-8865, fax 714-528-0544; www. nixonlibrary.org.

Another famous politician, who eventually died in poverty, made his home nearby. **Pío Pico State Historic Park** contains the 22-room adobe house built by Pío Pico, the last governor of California under Mexican rule, and one of the wealthiest men in Southern California. Surrounded today by freeways and railroad tracks, the home was once a vibrant center of life during the 19th century. Call for guided tour and times. Closed Monday and Tuesday. ~ 6003 Pioneer Boulevard, Whittier; 562-695-1217, fax 562-693-1503.

A natural island in a sea of commerce, **Whittier Narrows Nature Center** is a 419-acre preserve near the San Gabriel and Rio Hondo rivers. Over 290 bird species have been sighted within this quiltwork of rivers, lakes, and open fields. To help you get back

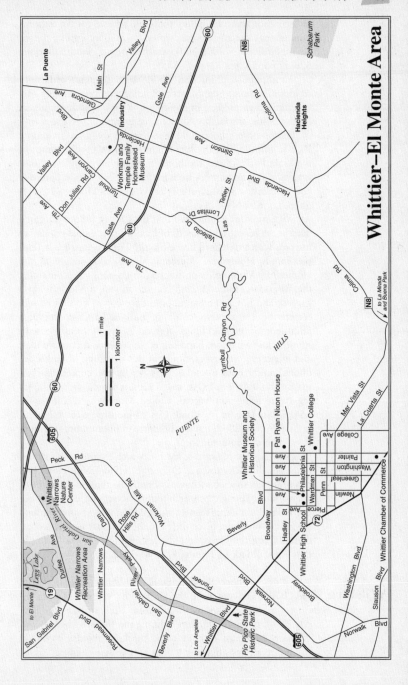

Whittier–El Monte Area

to the basics, there are nature trails and an interpretive center; a museum has live animals on display. On Sunday, sign up for the 8 a.m. birdwalk. ~ 1000 North Durfee Avenue, South El Monte; 626-575-5523, fax 626-443-5359.

Another point of interest, the **El Monte Museum of History** resides in a classic Spanish-style building that was actually part of a 1936 WPA project. In addition to a typical 19th-century El Monte home, the facility contains representations of the town's old general store, school, and barber shop, as well as an art gallery. Rich in historic lore, the surrounding area was the terminus of the Santa Fe Trail; as a result, the museum has countless photographs, maps, and diaries from the pioneer era. Closed Saturday and Monday. ~ 3150 North Tyler Avenue, El Monte; 626-444-3813, fax 626-444-8142.

Who could have imagined that the City of Industry, located deep in the industrial outlands of Los Angeles, would remember its roots with a tree-lined historic park? **The Workman and Temple Family Homestead Museum,** also known simply as the Homestead Museum, is an impressive six-acre site, containing the Workman House (a 19th-century adobe), a Victorian-style gazebo, and El Campo Santo, one of the county's oldest private cemeteries. The centerpiece of the park is La Casa Nueva, a 1920s-era Spanish Colonial Revival mansion complete with stained-glass windows, hand-carved ornaments, decorative tiles, and intricate iron fittings. Tours of this intriguing complex are offered on the hour from 1 p.m. to 4 p.m. and concentrate primarily on the 1840s, 1870s, and 1920s, when the various buildings were being constructed. Closed Monday and Tuesday. ~ 15415 East Don Julian Road, City of Industry; 626-968-8492, fax 626-968-2048; www.homesteadmuseum.org, e-mail info@homesteadmuseum.org.

HIDDEN ▶ Carrying you forward to the tacky architecture of the 1950s, in the equally tacky town of La Puente, is **The Donut Hole.** This drive-through snack bar consists of two structures in the shape of giant donuts. Though these architectural accretions look more like overinflated truck tires than anything edible, visitors drive through the first donut hole, place their orders, then exit via the second donut. Open until midnight for late-night munchies. ~ 15300 East Amar Road, La Puente; 626-968-2912.

▼▼▼▼▼▼▼▼▼▼▼▼
Wilshire District

Though Wilshire Boulevard actually extends from Downtown to the Pacific, the Wilshire District encompasses the stretch from Downtown to the Beverly Hills city limits. Developed during the 1890s by H. Gaylord Wilshire, a socialist with an ironic knack for making money in real estate, it was originally a tony area whose buildings exhibited some of the most creative and elaborate architectural features of the day. As the affluent moved west, the area deteriorated, many of these architectural wonders fell into disrepair, and a seedy element moved in.

Today the area is home to an assortment of ethnic groups and, since the 1990s, an on-going revitalization effort has been working to return the area to at least some semblance of its former glory. Not surprisingly, the farther west and closer to Beverly Hills one travels, the better the neighborhood.

WESTLAKE/MACARTHUR PARK   Several stately Victorians, built in the 19th century when the Westlake district was a wealthy neighborhood, remain along the **800 and 1000 blocks of South Bonnie Brae Street**. Particularly dramatic are the Queen Anne confection at 818 and the onion-domed house next door.

SIGHTS

MacArthur Park, a 32-acre greensward bisected by Wilshire Boulevard, is one of Los Angeles' oldest parks. Today the place has become a gathering place for local immigrants, who enjoy the shady picnic areas, playground, and snack bar. Home to more than 80 plant species, the park's central feature is a small lake complete with fountain, boat rental, and palm-fringed island inhabited by ducks. ~ Alvarado Street between 6th and 7th streets.

An art deco masterpiece built in 1929, for decades the **Bullocks Wilshire** building housed a high-end Los Angeles department store chain. Today this stunning copper-sided tower, where wealthy Angelino grandmothers used to take their granddaughters to lunch in the "Tea Room," is occupied by Southwestern University School of Law. ~ 3050 Wilshire Boulevard; 213-738-8240, fax 213-738-1205.

The Asian answer to gentrification is evident in **Koreatown**, a burgeoning neighborhood that has redefined the Wilshire District. Colorful storefronts, refurbished cottages, and Korean calligraphy have transformed the entire area into a unique enclave. ~ Centered between 4th Street and Olympic Boulevard, Western Avenue, and Vermont Avenue.

An art-deco masterpiece, the Wiltern Center is a towering building with wings flaring from either side. Built in 1931, it is covered in green terra cotta. ~ 3780 Wilshire Boulevard.

In fact, if you take a long drive down Pico Boulevard or Olympic Boulevard from the Harbor Freeway (Route 110) to Fairfax Avenue, you'll pass through a succession of **ethnic neighborhoods** including Indonesian, Japanese, Taiwanese, Vietnamese, and Thai sections.

LARCHMONT VILLAGE   Within spitting distance of El Royale, the apartment building on Rossmore Avenue where Mae West lived, is a bit of small-town charm called **Larchmont Village**.

Despite the contemporary trappings of yuppification—Starbucks, for example—there's a homey sense of family, traditional as well as alternative, along this lovely, tree-lined street of small shops and restaurants. ~ Larchmont Boulevard, between 1st Street and Beverly Boulevard.

From Larchmont Village, it's a short few blocks to **South Wilton Place**, a historical district of modest California bungalows dating from the early part of the 20th century. ~ South Wilton Place at Beverly Boulevard.

HANCOCK PARK/LA BREA AVENUE   The residential architecture of **Hancock Park** includes posh estates once owned by the Crocker, Huntington, and Doheny families. Developed during the 1920s, this well-tended neighborhood contains a variety of architectural styles. With wide boulevards and manicured lawns, it's a perfect place for a Sunday drive (even on a Tuesday). ~ Between Wilshire Boulevard and Melrose Avenue, centered around the Wilshire Country Club.

One of the highlights of the district, politically if not architecturally, is the **Getty House**. A 1921 Tudor home with leaded-glass windows and slate roof, it is the official residence of the mayor of Los Angeles. ~ 605 South Irving Boulevard.

HIDDEN ►   **MID-CITY**   St. Elmo Village marks another breed of neighborhood entirely. Here a complex of cottages has been transformed into a kind of creative art center. The simple bungalows are painted primary colors and adorned with murals and sculptures. Containing private residences and art studios, the settlement is luxuriously landscaped. Some houses are open to the public. ~ 4830 St. Elmo Drive; 323-931-3409, fax 323-931-2065; www. stelmovillage.org, e-mail stelmovillage@earthlink.net.

MIRACLE MILE/MUSEUM ROW   Back in the 1920s and 1930s the showcase for commercial architecture rested along the **Miracle Mile**. That was when an enterprising developer turned the area into a classy corridor for shops and businesses. The magnificent art-deco towers that lined the strip still survive, particularly between the 5200 and 5500 blocks of Wilshire, but Wilshire's early glory has faded as the area has changed from popular to historic. ~ Wilshire Boulevard between La Brea and Fairfax avenues.

The West's largest museum is a multibuilding complex with an international art collection. Providing a thumbnail tour of the entire history of art, the **Los Angeles County Museum of Art** ranges from pre-Columbian gold objects and African masks to post–World War II minimalist works. Stops along the way include sculpture, paintings, and stained-glass windows from the Middle Ages; a Renaissance gallery featuring Rembrandt and other Masters; Impressionist paintings by Cézanne, Gauguin, and Monet; and early-20th-century creations by Magritte, Chagall,

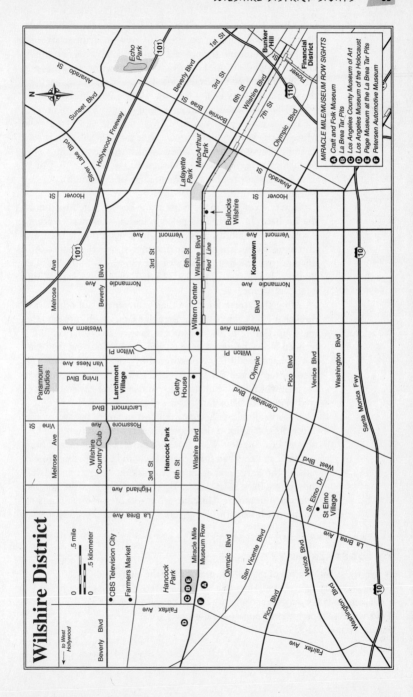

Wilshire District

to West
Hollywood

0   .5 mile

0   .5 kilometer

N

MIRACLE MILE/MUSEUM ROW SIGHTS

Ⓐ Craft and Folk Museum
Ⓑ La Brea Tar Pits
Ⓒ Los Angeles County Museum of Art
Ⓓ Los Angeles Museum of the Holocaust
Ⓔ Page Museum at the La Brea Tar Pits
Ⓕ Petersen Automotive Museum

and Miró. The Pavilion for Japanese Art houses the well-known Shin'enkan collection of paintings, as well as Japanese screens, scrolls, ceramics, and sculpture. The entire complex is beautifully laid out around a central courtyard adorned with terra-cotta pillars and four-tiered waterfall. Closed Wednesday. Admission (free the second Tuesday of the month). ~ 5905 Wilshire Boulevard; 323-857-6000; www.lacma.org, e-mail publicinfo@lacma.org.

Dedicated to works created by hand, the **Craft and Folk Museum** draws its exhibits from a wide range of subjects, showcasing objects such as the handcrafted furniture of Sam Aloof, mechanical toys, and masks of Mexico. Closed Monday and Tuesday. Admission (free the first Wednesday of the month). ~ 5814 Wilshire Boulevard; 323-937-4230.

Beauty gives way to the beast at the nearby **Page Museum at the La Brea Tar Pits**. This paleontological showplace features displays of mammoths, mastodons, and ground sloths. There are also extinct camels, ancient horses, and ancestral condors. Admission (free the first Tuesday of the month). ~ 5801 Wilshire Boulevard; 323-934-7243, fax 323-933-3974; www.tarpits.org, e-mail info@nhm.org.

Altogether, there are more than 200 varieties of other creatures that fell victim to the **La Brea Tar Pits**, which surround the museum. Dating to the Pleistocene Era, these oozing oil pools trapped birds, mammals, insects, and reptiles, creating fossil deposits that are still being discovered by scientists. Indians once used the tar to caulk boats and roofs. Today you can wander past the pits, which bubble menacingly with methane gas and lie covered in globs of black tar.

Wilshire Boulevard, conceived in the emerging age of the automobile as a linear downtown, is part of the automotive history of Los Angeles. Wide store windows were set close to the sidewalk and street so their contents could be easily seen from a passing car. Large rear entrances to parking lots accommodated the automobile. So it's an altogether appropriate site for the **Petersen Automotive Museum**, which devotes its four floors to automotive history through a series of dioramas, rotating special

OY TOGETHER NOW

A favorite gathering place of the Jewish community is the intersection of Fairfax and Oakwood avenues. Here one corner supports a mural depicting Jewish life in Los Angeles and another corner contains **Above the Fold**, which sells periodicals from around the world. ~ 370 North Fairfax Avenue; 323-935-8525.

exhibits of cars, and art related to the automobile. There's also a children's Discovery Center to keep the little ones occupied. Closed Monday. Admission. ~ 6060 Wilshire Boulevard; 323-930-2277, fax 323-930-6642; www.petersen.org, e-mail info@petersen.org.

Still retaining its luster and heritage is **Carthay Circle**, a cluster of small 1930s-era homes. This antique neighborhood is shaped more like a triangle than a circle. The Spanish stucco and art-deco homes create an island surrounded by streets streaming with traffic. ~ Bounded by Fairfax Avenue and Wilshire and San Vicente boulevards.

L.A.'s vernacular architecture is alive and well at **Tail O' The Pup**, a hot dog stand shaped like (what else?) a hot dog. Created in 1945, the hot dog stands in humorous contrast to its well-heeled neighbors. ~ 329 North San Vicente Boulevard; 310-652-4517.

◄ HIDDEN

The oldest holocaust museum in the United States, the **Los Angeles Museum of the Holocaust** is filled with images from the Nazi extermination camps. The ovens of Buchenwald, the gas chambers of Auschwitz, and skeletal figures from other camps are captured in terrifying detail. The photos portray masses being executed; tiny children, their hands in the air, surrounded by storm troopers; and a mother being shot while clutching a child in her arms. Many of the docents are Holocaust survivors with personal stories to recount as they lead visitors through these harrowing halls. Closed Saturday. ~ 6006 Wilshire Boulevard; 323-761-8170, fax 323-761-8174; www.lamuseumoftheholocaust.org, e-mail rjagoda@jewishla.org.

◄ HIDDEN

Nearby, **Fairfax Avenue** is the center of the city's Jewish community. Since World War II this middle-class neighborhood has been a local capital for Los Angeles Semites. Filled with delicatessens, bakeries, and kosher grocery stores, it is occupied by Orthodox, Hasidic, and Reform Jews. ~ Located between Beverly Boulevard and Melrose Avenue.

Once a small gathering place for local farmers to sell their goods, today's **Farmers Market** has grown to house over 100 stalls, shops, and stands featuring fresh produce, meats, and baked goods.

The Grove, a distinctly more urban annex, features additional shopping and dining, as well as a movie complex (this is L.A., after all). A replica of the old Los Angeles Red Car trolley ferries visitors between the Market and The Grove. ~ 6333 West 3rd Street; 323-933-9211, fax 323-549-2145; www.farmersmarketla.com, e-mail info@farmersmarketla.com.

You'll have to travel a couple of miles south, to Culver City, to experience one of the most original museums Los Angeles County has to offer. The **Museum of Jurassic Technology** is idio-

◄ HIDDEN

syncratic, to say the least. It had been flying under the radar since its inception in the early '90s until the museum's curator and founder, David Wilson, received a MacArthur Grant in 2001. Nothing about the plain front of the nondescript building would give you any hint as to the wonders within. Without insider information or a tip from one of the cognoscente, it's doubtful anyone would venture inside. Every exhibit here, no matter how odd, is substantiated with "authentic" and thorough scholarship, yet the museum constantly challenges one's perception of the credibility of its displays, blurring the line between fantasy and reality with a huge degree of whimsy. Along with the permanent collection, there are changing exhibits, such as microscopic still lifes constructed entirely out of the scales of butterflies and diatoms. Closed Monday through Wednesday. ~ 9341 Venice Boulevard, Culver City; 310-836-6131, fax 310-287-2267; www.mjt.org, e-mail mjt@mjt.org.

LODGING   **Best Western, The Mayfair Hotel,** located on the fringes of the Downtown district, is a 295-room hostelry. Built in 1927 and beautifully refurbished, it offers a touch of luxury at a price lower than the five-star hotels. There's a restaurant and lounge as well as an attractive skylit lobby. The guest rooms are average size and feature contemporary furnishings, textured wallpaper, and pastel color schemes. ~ 1256 West 7th Street; 213-484-9789, 800-821-8682, fax 213-484-2769; www.mayfairla.com, e-mail mayfair @mayfairla.com. MODERATE.

In the Beverly, Wilshire and 3rd Street neighborhood, the **Beverly Plaza Hotel** is a charming boutique hotel with 98 rooms. It offers a fitness center, two saunas, and a pool. Perhaps its most appealing feature is the location, which is within walking distance of shopping and good restaurants. ~ 8384 West 3rd Street; 323-658-6600; www.beverlyplazahotel.com, e-mail info@beverly plazahotel.com. DELUXE.

A refurbished 1920s-era art-deco building, the **Wilshire Royale Howard Johnson Plaza Hotel** has been transformed into a contemporary 200-room facility. The lobby is a beamed-ceiling affair with piano, fresh flowers, and upholstered armchairs. Rooms have tile baths and standard furnishings. Restaurant, lounge, pool, and spa are additional facilities. This historic hotel is an excellent choice. ~ 2619 Wilshire Boulevard; 213-387-5311, 800-421-8072, fax 213-380-8174; www.hojola.com, e-mail ho jola@hojola.com DELUXE.

Wilshire Crest Inn is one of those terribly modern hotels with track lighting, black trim, and fabric wall coverings. The 33 rooms, built around an interior courtyard, are done in oak and furnished with platform beds. The color scheme, naturally, is pastel. There's a dining room where continental breakfast is served and a sitting area complete with potted plants and trimly upholstered armchairs. The hotel is conveniently located near Wilshire Boulevard in the Fairfax district. ~ 6301 Orange Street; 323-936-5131, 800-654-9951, fax 323-936-2013. MODERATE.

WESTLAKE/MACARTHUR PARK   The coming of the Metrorail to   **DINING**
MacArthur Park revived the fortunes of long-loved **Langer's**. For hungry central-city office workers, their beloved pastrami sandwiches are now just a quick subway ride away. Closed Sunday. ~ 704 South Alvarado Street; 213-483-8050, fax 213-483-7171. BUDGET TO MODERATE.

The reason for the balcony at **La Fonda** becomes stirringly evident every evening when Los Camperos strike up a Spanish song. One of the city's best mariachi bands, they lure dinner guests by the dozens to this hacienda-style restaurant. In addition to the sound of Los Camperos, diners enjoy the flavor of Veracruz-style shrimp, steak *picado*, chicken flautas, and *chile verde*. Dinner only. Closed Monday. ~ 2501 Wilshire Boulevard; 213-380-5055, fax 213-386-2569. MODERATE TO DELUXE.

Also consider **La Fonda Antioqueña,** a Columbian restaurant that comes recommended by a former Consul General of Colombia. Here you will discover about 15 different platters, each prepared with South American flair. This intriguing ethnic restaurant offers everything from fish, chicken, beef, and pork dishes to liver and tongue. For an adventure in south-of-the-border dining, La Fonda Antioqueña is the place. ~ 4903 Melrose Avenue; 323-957-5164. MODERATE.

The interior of **Casa Carnitas** is tiny but overwhelming. Colorful as an old mission chapel, the walls are covered with murals portraying Mayan warriors. Naturally, the food is Yucatecan and includes a variety of beef, chicken, and shrimp dishes prepared with tasty *ranchera* sauce. Considering the imaginative decor and low prices, Casa Carnitas is an excellent find. ~ 4067 West Beverly Boulevard; 323-667-9953. BUDGET.

Tommy's Hamburgers is a Los Angeles landmark. In fact at   ◄ *HIDDEN*
last count there were 23 such landmarks. But the original Tommy's,

THE WURST IS THE BEST

L.A.'s best known delicatessen lies at the heart of the Jewish neighborhood around Fairfax Avenue. **Canter's,** a casual 24-hour restaurant and bar, doubles as local landmark and ethnic cultural center. As you might have guessed, lox and bagels, hot pastrami, corned beef, and matzo ball soup are the order of the day. ~ 419 North Fairfax Avenue; 323-651-2030, fax 323-651-4835. BUDGET TO MODERATE.

dating back to 1946, is at 2575 West Beverly Boulevard. Here you can enjoy "while you watch" service as they prepare hamburgers, hot dogs, and tamales before your hungry eyes. Open 24 hours, this is the place where they give you paper towels instead of napkins and still charge cheap prices. (Ain't L.A. amazing?) ~ 2575 West Beverly Boulevard; 213-389-9060; www.originaltommys.com. BUDGET.

One of Koreatown's best restaurants is a multiroom complex named **Dong Il Jang**. The place contains several dining rooms as well as a sushi bar, each decorated with bamboo screens and Asian statuary. The Korean dinners include *maewoon tahng* (spicy codfish casserole), *kalbi* (marinated ribs), and *jun bok juk* (abalone porridge). A complete offering of Japanese dishes is also presented. ~ 3455 West 8th Street; 213-383-5757. MODERATE TO DELUXE.

LARCHMONT VILLAGE   Very popular with neighborhood regulars, **La Luna** offers a quiet, atmospheric spot for a low-key meal of grilled vegetables topped with goat cheese, spaghetti *misto funghi* (wild mushrooms and garlic–white wine sauce), risotto *frutti di mare*, *vitello* (veal), *pollo* (chicken), or thin-crust pizza. No lunch on Sunday. ~ 113 North Larchmont Boulevard; 323-962-2130, fax 310-962-4816. MODERATE TO ULTRA-DELUXE.

HIDDEN ▶

Well-known for its Thai cuisine, **Chan Dara** is a modern restaurant with a mirrored bar and brass-rail dining room. The specialties vary from spicy barbecue to vegetable entrées. Patio dining is available. ~ 310 North Larchmont Boulevard; 323-467-1052; www.chandara.com, e-mail chandarett@loop.com. MODERATE.

HANCOCK PARK/LA BREA AVENUE   **Campanile**, something of a foodie shrine for years now, offers what is probably the best contemporary American cooking in the city. Mark Peel and Nancy Silverton are nearly cult heroes—he for his rustic originality in turning out grilled meats and fish, aromatic soups, and zesty veg-

AUTHOR FAVORITE

A restaurant inside a flower shop is unique enough, but it's the clever concoctions, healthfully prepared, that account for the popularity of **Flora Kitchen**. Sandwiches and salads are the specialties, with ingredients such as olive tapenade, roasted peppers, fresh herbs, buffalo mozzarella, and fresh ahi tuna. They do breakfast, lunch, and dinner as well as cappuccino and espresso. Flora also does a booming gourmet takeout business, and you can pick up fresh flowers at the same time. They have beer and wine as well. Only brunch is served on Sunday. ~ 460 South La Brea Boulevard; 323-931-9900, fax 323-938-7941. MODERATE.

etables, she for her unmatched skill at baking great breads and desserts. The setting is quite lovely, too—a glass-roofed court-yard with a tiled fountain. Dinner and Saturday and Sunday brunch served. ~ 624 South La Brea Avenue; 323-938-1447; www.campanilerestaurant.com, e-mail campanile@campanile restaurant.com. DELUXE TO ULTRA-DELUXE.

The **Sonora Café** is a Southwestern restaurant decorated with earth tones and *viga* ceilings. The patio in front is covered with wrought-iron latticework. Lunch and dinner include fajitas, duck tamales, chicken tostadas, and blue-corn enchiladas. There are also fresh fish and steak dishes. Outdoor seating with a view of the city skyline is available. No lunch on weekends. ~ 180 South La Brea Avenue; 323-857-1800, fax 323-857-1601; www.sonora cafe.com. MODERATE TO DELUXE.

FAIRFAX DISTRICT Eclectic Asian delicacies are served up at **Buddha's Belly**, a simple feng shui–ed restaurant. Even the tra-ditional foods come with a twist, such as fried rice with caramel-ized garlic cloves and Japanese salad dressing that tingles with chiles. Diners can watch all the action in the wide-open kitchen from either tables or the counter. No lunch on Sunday. ~ 7475 Beverly Boulevard; 323 931-8588. BUDGET.   ◄ HIDDEN

The **Authentic Cafe** is truly trendy, but the food merits its pop-ularity. Its eclectic array is really tasty: try the designer pizzas, Szechuan fire dumplings, wood-grilled Yucatán chicken, or *chi-laquiles*. There's a full bar and weekend brunch. Closed Monday. ~ 7605 Beverly Boulevard; 323-939-4626, fax 323-931-7929; www.authenticcafe.com, e-mail authcafe@earthlink.net. MODER-ATE TO DELUXE.

Farmers Market, a sprawling open-air collection of vendor stands, is a good spot to visit and an even better place to eat. The takeout stands lining each corridor dispense burritos, egg rolls, jambalaya, corned beef, hot dogs, crêpes, and every other type of ethnic food imaginable. Simply order at the counter, then find a table in the sun. ~ 6333 West 3rd Street; 323-933-9211, fax 323-954-4229; www.farmersmarketla.com, e-mail farmersmarketla.com. BUDGET TO MODERATE.

Also in the Farmers Market area are two critically acclaimed ethnic restaurants. **Sofi Greek Restaurant** is a family-run Greek restaurant with a potful of grandmother's recipes. Open for lunch and dinner, they serve moussaka in the dining room or out on the patio. No lunch on Sunday. ~ 8030¾ West 3rd Street; 323-651-0346, fax 323-651-0347. MODERATE TO DELUXE.

SOUTH OF WILSHIRE Favored among savvy locals, **Rosalind's West African Cuisine** serves plantains, yam balls, and *akara* (deep-ried black-eyed peas). Main courses include Niger-style goat (sautéed with African herbs and spices), sautéed beef with onions   ◄ HIDDEN and herbs, and groundnut stew (with nuts, beef, chicken, and spices). Enhancing the exotic cuisine is a complete wall mural depicting a waterfall on the Nile river. ~ 1044 South Fairfax Avenue; 323-936-2486, fax 323-936-1997. MODERATE.

SHOPPING   The city's burgeoning **Koreatown** is a warren of small shops and markets, each brightly painted in the calligraphy of the East. While many sell Korean foodstuffs and cater to local clientele, each provides a small glimpse into the life of this energetic community. ~ Centered between 4th Street and Olympic, Western, and Vermont avenues.

A spate of art galleries and restaurants attracts shoppers along **La Brea Avenue**. **Jan Baum Gallery** presents national and international contemporary art exhibits. Closed Sunday and Monday. ~ 170 South La Brea Avenue; 323-932-0170; www.janbaum.com. **Jack Rutberg Fine Arts** features modern paintings, drawings, sculptures, original prints, and museum-quality collectibles. Closed Sunday and Monday. ~ 357 North La Brea Avenue; 323-938-5222.

The La Brea corridor, as the area between Wilshire Boulevard and Melrose Avenue is called, is home to a collection of innovative galleries.

Along Wilshire Boulevard, stop in at the gift shop at the **Los Angeles County Museum of Art**, where you'll find art books, photographic items, and graphic reproductions. Closed Wednesday. ~ 5905 Wilshire Boulevard; 323-857-6146.

Nearby Fairfax Avenue, the center of L.A.'s Jewish community, is a neighborhood steeped in religious tradition and filled with delis, bakeries, and kosher grocery stores. **Canter's**, with its sumptuous baked goods and delicious sandwiches, is by far the most popular deli in the district. ~ 419 North Fairfax Avenue; 323-651-2030.

NIGHTLIFE   The Mexican food may be good at **El Cholo**, but the famed margaritas really draw the crowds to this lively bar scene. ~ 1121 South Western Avenue; 323-734-2773; www.elcholocafe.com.

Tom Bergin's, a traditional Irish pub dating to the 1930s, was voted one of the top 100 bars in the United States by *Esquire* magazine. Judging from the 7500 patron-inscribed shamrocks mounted on the wood-paneled walls, the regular crowd confirms *Esquire*'s vote. ~ 840 South Fairfax Avenue; 323-936-7151; www.tombergins.com.

The **Wiltern Theatre** opened its doors in 1931 as a Warner Brothers movie house. Now restored to its art-deco splendor, the terra-cotta structure is a center for the performing arts. Rock and classical music, drama, and opera programs are regularly scheduled. ~ 3790 Wilshire Boulevard; 213-380-5005.

A beautiful 1927 Renaissance-style building, the **Wilshire Ebell Theatre** is the setting for television specials and live theater, opera, and dance presentations. ~ 4401 West 8th Street; 323-939-1128; www.ebellla.com.

You'll want to jump and jive at the **Atlas Supper Club**, a snazzy supper club showcasing jazz, swing, salsa, and cabaret acts. Cover on Friday and Saturday, and for special events. ~ 3760 Wilshire Boulevard; 213-380-8400.

The **Los Angeles County Museum of Art** (LACMA) presents an ongoing series of outdoor jazz concerts on Friday evenings (free), film screenings on Friday and Saturday evenings (admission), and Sunday afternoon music concerts (free). ~ 5905 Wilshire Boulevard; 323-857-6000; www.lacma.org, e-mail publicinfo@lacma.org.

Hollywood

It was farm country when Horace and Daeida Wilcox first moved to Cahuenga Valley. Originally part of the Rancho La Brea land grant, the dusty hills lay planted in bell peppers, watermelons, and citrus trees. Then in 1887 Horace had a brainstorm: he subdivided the family farm, Daeida christened the spread "Hollywood," and they put lots on the market for $150 an acre.

By 1910, the cow town's population had grown to 4000 god-fearing, middle-class souls. Like the Wilcoxes, they were staid and sober folk, drawn predominantly from Midwestern stock.

Then came the deluge. The fledgling movie industry—attracted by warm weather and natural locations and conspiring to avoid the royalties levied by Thomas Edison's East Coast company for use of his moving-picture inventions—began relocating to Hollywood. The first studio arrived in 1911. Two years later the trio of Jesse Lasky, Samuel Goldfish (later Goldwyn), and Cecil B. De Mille set up shop. De Mille soon began shooting *Squaw Man*, the first full-length motion picture, in a barn on the corner of Selma Avenue and Vine Street.

The townsfolk termed these studios "gypsy camps" and posted signs declaring, "No dogs, No actors." Movie people were Easterners, morally suspect and in many cases Jewish, defining characteristics guaranteed to stir unease among the local Protestant majority.

But if there is no stopping progress, it is simply impossible to halt a tidal wave. During the 1920s the movie industry became a billion-dollar business, with Hollywood its capital. Picture palaces mushroomed along Hollywood Boulevard beside glamorous restaurants and majestic hotels, and by 1930 the population totaled 150,000.

Hollywood's glory days lasted until the 1960s, when development gave way to decline. The boulevard of dreams became a byway for bikers; Chevys with hydraulic lifters replaced limousines; punks with flaming hair supplanted platinum starlets; and movie studios moved to the San Fernando Valley. Prostitutes worked side streets, leaving the major thoroughfares to hawkers, hustlers, and Hollywood visionaries.

Today sizable Latino, Asian, African-American, and Armenian populations have created ethnic neighborhoods and the commercial districts are slowly being refurbished

A considerable redevelopment effort has resulted in cleaner streets and sidewalks, particularly along Hollywood Boulevard. Enough new palm and jacaranda trees have been planted to satisfy preconceived images, new "old Hollywood" light fixtures installed, and private security patrols ensure the safety of (and even answer questions for) Hollywood tourists.

Regardless of the changes, seemingly in spite of itself, the place remains Hollywood, tawdry and tragic, with all its myth and magic. The town that F. Scott Fitzgerald said "can be understood . . . only dimly and in flashes" is still an odd amalgam of truth and tinsel, promise and impossibility, conjuring images of big studios and bright stars.

SIGHTS   **CENTRAL HOLLYWOOD**   It was 1918 when Aline Barnsdall, an enchantingly eccentric oil heiress, purchased an entire hill in Hollywood, planted the 36 acres with olive trees and christened the spot Olive Hill. She next hired Frank Lloyd Wright to design a family home and adjoining arts center. Olive Hill subsequently became **Barnsdall Park**, an aerie studded with olive and conifer trees, from which visitors can survey the entire sweep of Hollywood. ~ 4800 Hollywood Boulevard.

Wright's masterwork became **Hollyhock House**, a sprawling 6200-square-foot home that represents his California Romanza style. Constructed of poured concrete and stucco, the house incorporates a geometric motif based on the hollyhock, Aline Barnsdall's favorite flower. Closed for renovations until spring 2004. ~ Barnsdall Park; 323-913-4157.

Wright also designed the **Barnsdall Arts Center Gallery,** where adult art classes are taught. Call for hours. ~ Barnsdall Park; 323-644-6295.

The nearby **Municipal Art Gallery**, a gray concrete structure built in 1971, offers changing exhibits of Southern California contemporary artwork. While the focus is regional, nearly every arts and crafts medium is represented. Closed Monday and Tuesday. ~ Barnsdall Park; 323-644-6269.

Also part of the Barnsdall Park art complex, the **Junior Arts Center** offers classes for young people. Be sure to see the Hollywood mural that covers an outside wall of this building. Call for hours. ~ Barnsdall Park; 213-485-4474, fax 213-485-7456.

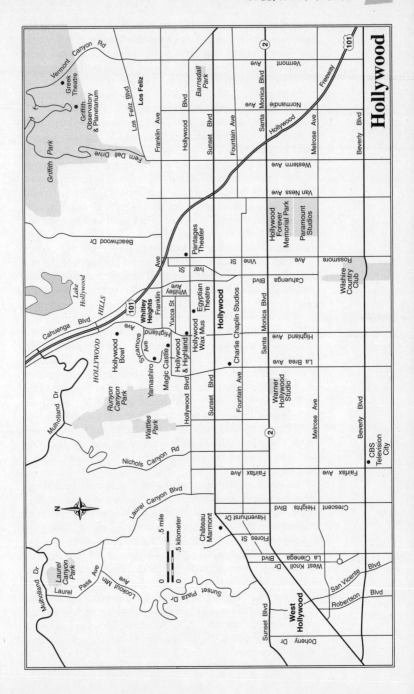

Hollywood

Not so very long ago, the public wasn't allowed behind the famous wrought-iron gate at **Paramount Studios**. A subject for countless newsreels and Hollywood movies, the portal's most memorable appearance was in *Sunset Boulevard* (1950) when Erich von Stroheim drove Gloria Swanson onto the lot for her tragic encounter with Cecil B. De Mille. (See "Hollywood in Action" for more about studio tours.)

Established during the silent era, Paramount signed stars such as Rudolph Valentino and Clara Bow in the 1920s, Gary Cooper and Marlene Dietrich during the 1930s, and later headlined Bob Hope and Bing Crosby. Today the studio creates TV shows such as "Frasier" and "Charmed," as well as produces blockbuster movies. Unfortunately, with the events of September 11, 2001, the studio and lot remain closed to the public. Tickets to show tapings are still available, though (323-956-1777). Closed weekends. Admission. ~ 5555 Melrose Avenue; 323-956-1777; www.paramount.com, e-mail info@pde.paramount.com.

Many of these same legends lie buried just north of the studio in **Hollywood Forever Memorial Park**. Surrounded by high walls and shaded with palm trees, the 60-acre greensward is a kind of museum park crowded with Greek statues, Egyptian temples, and Roman memorials. Marble urns and obelisks adorn the place, and the Paramount water tower rises above the south wall.

Paramount is the last of the great studios to remain in Hollywood.

Along the eastern side of the cemetery, Rudolph Valentino rests in Cathedral Mausoleum, crypt number 1205; Peter Finch is across the aisle in number 1224. Around the nearby pond are the graves of Tyrone Power, Marion Davies, Adolphe Menjou, and the double tomb of Cecil B. De Mille and his wife, Constance Adam De Mille. Next to the Cathedral Mausoleum, a staircase leads to the reflecting pool and tomb of Douglas Fairbanks. ~ 6000 Santa Monica Boulevard.

No one can quite figure how Movieland's most famous address became so prominent. Most of the action occurred elsewhere, but somehow the corner of **Hollywood and Vine** has come to symbolize Hollywood. But Hollywood is good at making the most of fables, so new "skytracker" lights at each of the four corners create an archway of light above the vaunted intersection.

Maybe it's the many radio studios that lined the thoroughfare during the 1930s, or perhaps because the **Pantages Theater** is just down the street. One of the nation's finest art-deco theaters, the Pantages was built in 1930, with a vaulted-ceiling lobby and a monumental auditorium. ~ 6233 Hollywood Boulevard; 323-468-1770, fax 323-468-1718; www.nederlander.com, e-mail concerts@nederlander.com.

Gazing down on all the commotion is the **Capitol Records Building**, a building you have seen in countless photographs. Resembling a squadron of flying saucers piggy-backed on one another, the 13-story structure was actually designed to look like a stack of records with a stylus protruding from the top. ~ 1750 Vine Street.

In a tribute to the great studios once occupying the area, **Home Savings of America** adorned its facade with the names of hundreds of stars and added a tile mural depicting the most noteworthy. The interior contains a marvelous stained-glass window with scenes from Hollywood's early movies. ~ 1500 North Vine Street.

Above Hollywood Boulevard, the **1800 block of North Ivar Street** is lined with apartment buildings reflecting the architecture of the 1920s and 1930s. Nathaniel West lived in the mock-Tudor **Parua Sed Apartments** at #1817 in 1935. Here he wrote screenplays and began work on his great Hollywood novel *The Day of the Locust*. The Mediterranean-style **Alto Nido Apartments** were the fictional home of the down-and-out screenwriter played by William Holden in *Sunset Boulevard*. ~ 1851 North Ivar Street.

Eschewing nostalgia, **Los Angeles Contemporary Exhibitions** (LACE), a nonprofit fine-arts center, works with artists to produce and present work in all mediums. Closed Monday and Tuesday; open late on Friday nights. ~ 6522 Hollywood Boulevard; 323-957-1777, fax 323-956-1777; www.artleak.org, e-mail info@artleak.org.

During the halcyon days of the 1920s, as silent movies gave way to talkies, Hollywood Boulevard was door-to-door with mansions. **The Janes House**, one of the last of this long-vanished breed, is a Queen Anne Victorian complete with turret, gable, and stained-glass windows. This architectural grande belle rests at the end of a plastic shopping mall. Closed Sunday. ~ 6541 Hollywood Boulevard.

Today, Hollywood Boulevard has been taken over by taco vendors, cut-rate video stores, T-shirt and wig shops, and souvenir stands. More like New York's 42nd Street than the Great White Way, it's a cheap strip where photo galleries take tourists' pictures next to cardboard cutouts of stars.

Throughout this area—extending for two and a half miles along Hollywood Boulevard from Gower Street to La Brea Boulevard and on Vine Street between Sunset Boulevard and Yucca Street—is the **Walk of Fame**, of star-studded terrazzo, commemorating notables from the film, television, radio, theater, and music industries. The names of more than 2230 legends appear on brass-rimmed stars embedded in the glittery sidewalk. Among the stars most frequently sought out by visitors are Marilyn Monroe at 6774 Hollywood Boulevard, James Dean at 1719

Text continued on page 78.

Hollywood
in Action

The tram is filled with innocent people, a random collection of folks from all walks, some with little kids in tow. Suddenly it is blasted by aliens and hijacked onto a giant spaceship. As the Cyclons prepare to destroy the tram, a laser battle of galactic proportions breaks out.

Escaping one peril, the passengers cross a collapsing wooden bridge, dodge a flash flood and are swept up in an avalanche. This is all child's play compared to the next adventure, when the tram crosses the Brooklyn Bridge with flames erupting, sirens screaming, and King Kong clinging to the trembling girders.

Sound like Hollywood? Actually it's **Universal Studios Hollywood**, a Disneyesque introduction to one of the nation's biggest motion picture and TV facilities. Founded in 1912 when Carl Laemmle, a Bavarian immigrant, converted a chicken farm into a production lot for silent films, Universal is a mammoth 415-acre complex complete with 36 sound stages, a 15-story administration building, and a staff of more than 10,000 filmmakers. Admission. ~ 100 Universal City Plaza, Universal City; 818-508-9600, fax 818-622-0407; www.universal studios.com.

More like an amusement park than an authentic studio tour, Universal offers visitors an ersatz introduction to Hollywood. The tram passes the locations for classic films such as *My Little Chickadee* (1940) and *The Sting* (1973) and explores the backlot with its street sets of Europe, Texas, New York, and Mexico. If Hollywood is one step away from reality, the Universal Tour is two steps. It's a staging of a staging, a Hollywood version of Hollywood.

Among the most exciting rides at this movie-studio-cum-theme-park are "Jurassic Park—The Ride," "Shrek 4-D," "Back to the Future," "E.T. Adventure," "Revenge of the Mummy—The Ride," "Van Helsing: Fortress Dracula," and "Terminator2: 3D," based on some of

Universal's most popular films. Be prepared for long lines! However, a new service, once offered only to movie stars and public figures, is available—for a steep price. The VIP Experience offers guests a "private tour" of Universal aboard a 15-seat trolley. Walk through props and costume shops, peek inside sound stages and enjoy side-door admittance to the park's signature rides and attractions. But this doesn't come cheaply; expect to pay a pretty penny for one of the limited daily spots on the VIP trolley.

The **NBC Studio Tour** provides a similar view of the television industry. Though only 70 minutes long (in contrast to Universal's half-day extravaganza), it takes guests onto the set of Jay Leno's "Tonight Show" and offers glimpses at other sound stages in use. The wardrobe area, set-construction shop, and make-up room are also on the itinerary. Closed Saturday in winter and Sunday year-round. Admission. ~ 3000 West Alameda Avenue, Burbank; 818-840-3537, fax 818-840-3065; www.nbci.com.

The **Warner Brothers Studios**, by contrast, takes you behind the scenes to see the day-to-day activities of a multimedia complex. It's also home to the Warner Brothers Museum, where memorabilia from the 75-year history of the studio is displayed, including an Oscar awarded for creating Hollywood's first talkie movie, *The Jazz Singer*. No children under the age of eight allowed; tours are mostly technical and educational and change daily. Closed weekends. Admission. ~ 4301 West Olive Avenue, Burbank; 818-954-1744, fax 818-954-2089; www.wbstudiotour.com, e-mail studiotour@warnerbros.com.

Dozens of television programs are taped in Los Angeles. The prime production season runs from August through March. For information on tickets call: **Audiences Unlimited** (818-506-0067); **Paramount Guest Relations** (323-956-1777); **NBC-TV** (818-840-4444).

That's Hollywood!

Vine Street, John Lennon at 1750 Vine Street, and Elvis Presley at 7080 Hollywood Boulevard. If you've just got to know where your favorite star's star is located, call the **Hollywood Chamber of Commerce**. The Chamber of Commerce also can tell you when the next ceremony will take place to honor a celebrity with a sidewalk star. Closed weekends. ~ 323-469-8311, fax 323-469-2805; www.hollywoodchamber.net, www.explore hollywood.com.

> The pride of Hollywood, the Walk of Fame is the only walkway in Los Angeles to be washed several times weekly.

The perfect expression of this high-camp neighborhood is **Frederick's of Hollywood**, a lingerie shop located in an outrageous battleship gray-and-pink art-deco building. With a naughty reputation and a selection of undergarments that leave nothing to the imagination, Frederick's is one of those places we visit in spite of ourselves. Be sure to make your way to the back of the store and visit **Frederick's of Hollywood Lingerie Museum**, rich in Hollywood's version of cultural treasures. On display are a tassels-and-leather bustier from Madonna, the bra Marilyn Monroe wore in *Let's Make Love*, a more modest (but autographed) 32B from Cher, and celebrity undergarments worn by such icons as Mae West and Zsa Zsa Gabor. ~ 6608 Hollywood Boulevard; 323-466-8506, fax 323-464-5149; www.fredericks.com.

The nonprofit film preservation group American Cinematheque had recently agreed to purchase the abandoned **Egyptian Theatre** from the city for a $1 token payment when a 1994 earthquake knocked 40-foot holes in its walls. Earthquake insurance provided seed money for the $13 million restoration of the venerable theater where Cecil B. De Mille's *The Ten Commandments* premiered. Today, with 616 seats instead of the original 2071, the theater presents nightly film retrospectives and a Saturday-and-Sunday afternoon 55-minute history of filmmaking entitled *Forever Hollywood*. ~ 6712 Hollywood Boulevard; 323-466-3456; www.egyptiantheatre.com.

Then there's the **Hollywood Wax Museum**, a melancholy place where you can "see your favorite stars in living wax." Here they are—Marilyn Monroe and Elvis Presley, Clint Eastwood, Sylvester Stallone and the "Governator" (Arnold Schwarzenegger) —looking just as they would three days after rigor mortis set in, that classic grin or sneer frozen forevermore into a candle with arms. Admission. ~ 6767 Hollywood Boulevard; 323-462-8860, fax 323-462-3993; www.hollywoodwax.com, e-mail contact@ hollywoodwaxmuseum.com.

Built by Sid Grauman in 1927, **Mann's Chinese Theatre** is a fabulous movie palace, fashioned in a kind of Oriental Baroque style with pagoda roof, stone guard dogs, metal towers, Asian masks, and beautiful bas-reliefs. The interior is equally as lavish with its ornate columns, murals, and Asian vases.

Though the architecture is splendid, the theater is actually known for its sidewalk. Embedded in the cement forecourt are the handprints and footprints of Hollywood's greatest stars. Elizabeth Taylor, Harrison Ford, Susan Sarandon, and Denzel Washington have left their signatures in this grandest of all autograph collections. Not every celebrity simply signed and stepped, however: there are also cement images of Jimmy Durante's nose, Betty Grable's leg, Harpo Marx's harp, and the webbed feet of Donald Duck. ~ 6925 Hollywood Boulevard; 323-464-6266, fax 323-463-0879; www.manntheatres.com.

Butting up against the theater is **Hollywood & Highland**—a mega-entertainment center chock full of restaurants and shops. The Kodak Theatre stands at the heart of the complex and hosts plays, musical performances and the Academy Awards. Also located here is the **Hollywood Visitors Center**. (See "Hooray for Hollywood!" feature in this chapter.) ~ 6801 Hollywood Boulevard; 323-467-6412.

◄ HIDDEN

Hollywood's been around for 80 years, but until the **Hollywood Entertainment Museum** came on the scene in 1996, there had never been a museum dedicated solely to the history, technology, and artifacts of Hollywood and the entertainment arts. The central gallery is a rotunda, where a multimedia presentation about Hollywood is shown at intervals throughout the day. Radiating from the rotunda are interactive displays employing interactive computers, video clips, and a few special effects. Visitors can actually step onto the bridge of the U.S.S. *Enterprise*, one of the sets from the television series "Star Trek." Then it's on to the set of "Cheers," whose cast members carved their names into the bar as a farewell when the show ended. Closed Wednesday from Labor Day to Memorial Day. Admission. ~ 7021 Hollywood Boulevard; 323-465-7900; www.hollywoodmuseum.com, e-mail info@hollywoodmuseum.com.

Despite numerous incarnations, including the most recent as headquarters for Jim Henson Studios, the **Charlie Chaplin Studios** have weathered the years relatively unchanged, except for the statue of Kermit the Frog that proudly adorns the entryway. This row of Tudor cottages, built by Chaplin in 1918, housed the star's sound stage, dressing rooms, carpentry shop, and stables. The studios currently screen silent movies. ~ 1416 North La Brea Avenue.

HOLLYWOOD HILLS The lower slopes of the enchanting Santa Monica Mountains contain some of Los Angeles' most fashionable addresses. These rugged foothills, divorced from the glitter of Hollywood by serpentine roads, provide a pricey escape valve from the pressures of Tinseltown. But for those with a car and an afternoon, it costs no more to explore Hollywood's vaunted upcountry than to browse Beverly Hills' Rodeo Drive.

Beachwood Canyon, one of the town's prettiest residential areas, is a V-shaped valley with 1920s- and 1930s-era homes on either side. First developed as "Hollywoodland" by *Los Angeles Times* publisher Harry Chandler, the neighborhood is now popular with screenwriters. When Chandler broke ground, he hoped to create an urban utopia "above the traffic congestion, smoke, fog, and poisonous gas fumes of the lowlands." (It seems that even in the 1920s, long before Los Angeles had a name for it, the city suffered from smog.) ~ Beachwood Drive.

To advertise "Hollywoodland" the developer erected a huge sign on the hillside. Eventually "land" was removed, the fixture was refurbished, and Chandler's billboard became the **Hollywood Sign,** a 45-foot-tall, 450-foot-long landmark that is now the foremost symbol of Movieland. (Head up Beachwood Drive toward the sign and you'll pass through the stone entrance gates of Hollywoodland at Westshire Drive. Be forewarned: hiking up to the sign can earn you a hefty ticket.) The corner of Gower Street and Sunset Boulevard provides a picture-perfect view of the sign.

HIDDEN ▶   Los Angeles has little space for idyllic retreats. One of the city's more placid places is **Lake Hollywood,** a forest-framed reservoir created by the Mulholland Dam. Popular with hikers and joggers, the lake is surrounded by a chain-link fence but still offers splendid views. The reservoir was built in 1925 by Water Commissioner William Mulholland as part of Los Angeles' scandalous water program. Scenes from *Chinatown* (1974), the movie that exposed the civic corruption behind Mulholland's project, were shot around the lake. ~ Southern entrance is at Weidlake Drive; northern entrance is at Lake Hollywood Drive.

HIDDEN ▶   For stars living in **Whitley Heights** during the 1920s, life was much like it is in Beverly Hills today. This hilltop neighborhood, with its tile-roofed Mediterranean homes, was the premier residential area for the silent-movie set. Rudolph Valentino lived here, and later stars included Gloria Swanson, Bette Davis, and Janet Gaynor. Today the realm is as unspoiled as it was when H. J. Whitley, a Los Angeles developer with an eye to Europe, first built his "Italian hilltown." To explore the landmark neighborhood, drive up Whitley Avenue to Whitley Terrace and Wedgewood Place, following all three streets as they spiral around the hilltop.

One of Hollywood's most enduring symbols is the **Hollywood Bowl,** a concrete band shell built in 1929. Situated in a sylvan glade called Daisy Dell, the concert hall is an amphitheater within an amphitheater, surrounded by a circle of wooded hills. ~ 2301 North Highland Avenue; 323-850-2000, fax 213-972-7560; www.hollywoodbowl.org.

The Los Angeles Philharmonic performs here and a regular series of concerts is presented. Many movies have used the shell as a backdrop, including *Anchors Aweigh* and the 1937 version of *A Star Is Born*.

The **Hollywood Bowl Museum** presents a fine exhibit of the   ◄ HIDDEN
Bowl's fascinating 75-year history. Display drawers can be opened for a look at vintage programs or letters written by the likes of Aaron Copland and Eugene Ormandy. Listening stations are set up with headphones so you can listen to an 80-year-old recording of soprano Amelita Galli-Curci, a superstar of her day, singing "Caro Nome" from Verdi's *Rigoletto*; or the first open-air recording, made in 1928 of Tchaikovsky's Adagio from *Sleeping Beauty*; or recordings of other artists who've appeared at the Bowl, including Ella Fitzgerald and Paul McCartney. Closed Sunday and Monday. ~ 2301 North Highland Avenue; 323-850-2058, fax 213-972-7560; www.hollywoodbowl.org, e-mail museum@laphil.org.

A part of Hollywood's history stands just across the street. Back in 1913, a young director named Cecil B. De Mille found a farm town called Hollywood with a horse barn he could use as a studio. The barn, a kind of woodframe keepsake, moved around with De Mille over the years, seeing use as an office, a set, and even a gymnasium for stars like Gary Cooper and Kirk Douglas. It was here that Paramount Pictures was born. Eventually moved to its present site, the historic building became the **Hollywood Heritage Museum**, a showplace dedicated to the era of silent films and containing a replica of De Mille's original office. Open weekends only. Admission. ~ 2100 North Highland Avenue; 323-874-2276, fax 323-789-7281.

If that French Renaissance mansion above Hollywood Boulevard begins to levitate, you'll know the residents are busy at work. The **Magic Castle**, built in 1909, is "the only club in the world devoted to magicians and lovers of magic." Once a private estate, the club now plays host to the Academy of Magical Arts, a members-only organization that includes many of the town's top tricksters. ~ 7001 Franklin Avenue; www.magiccastle.com.

Farther up the hill lies another dream house, a magnificent replica of a Japanese palace called **Yamashiro**. Built of cedar and

◆◆

TOWERING LEGENDS

The **sculpture** at the intersection of Hollywood and La Brea boulevards defies simple characterization. It's a gleaming, 30-foot-high gazebo supported at each corner by a statue of a Hollywood legend (Dolores del Rio, Anna May Wong, Mae West, and Dorothy Dandridge) and crowned with what is supposed to be Marilyn Monroe but looks more like an angel atop the Eiffel Tower. Check it out.

teak in 1911, the former estate is presently a restaurant complete with ceremonial gardens and a 600-year-old pagoda. Of the many films shot here perhaps the most famous was *Sayonara* (1958), in which Yamashiro was cast as the American Officers' Club. ~ 1999 North Sycamore Avenue; 323-466-5125, fax 323-462-4523; www.yamashirorestaurant.com, e-mail marketing@yamashiro restaurant.com.

From here it's an easy jaunt up Outpost Drive through **Outpost Estates**. Another of Hollywood's picture-perfect neighborhoods, this residential canyon was developed during the 1920s by a creative contractor who placed the utilities underground and built Mediterranean-style homes. The result is a lovely, tree-shaded community, an unpretentious version of Beverly Hills.

HIDDEN ►

Tucked into a narrow canyon lies **Wattles Park**, part of the old Gurdon Wattles Estate, a 49-acre preserve. While the Wattles Mansion and formal gardens can be viewed by appointment only, the adjacent park is open on a regular basis. A pond, palm grove, and teahouse occupy the property. ~ 1850 North Curson Avenue; 323-874-4005; www.hollywoodheritage.org.

Château Marmont is a brooding presence amid the glitter. Constructed around 1929 in the pattern of a Norman castle, the place has numbered James Dean, Bob Dylan, and Robert DeNiro among its guests. With its petite gardens, imposing colonnade, and arched-window lobby, the hotel is a study in European elegance. Little wonder it is still favored by Hollywood stars as a hometown hideaway. ~ 8221 Sunset Boulevard; 323-656-1010.

The real spirit of the Hollywood Hills resides in the deep canyons that climb from Hollywood Boulevard into the Santa Monica Mountains. **Nichols Canyon**, a chaparral-coated valley adorned with million-dollar homes, represents one of the toniest parts of town. A narrow two-lane road winds through dense forest to bald heights. ~ Nichols Canyon Road.

Possessing the same cachet and even greater fame, **Laurel Canyon** became known as a hippie hideaway during the 1960s. With its sinuous side streets and modest bungalows, the wooded vale has a decidedly rustic atmosphere. ~ Laurel Canyon Boulevard.

Both Nichols and Laurel canyons rise sharply into the mountains, eventually reaching the rim of Los Angeles, a 50-mile-long road called **Mulholland Drive**, which extends from Hollywood to Malibu. Tracing a course along the ridge of the Santa Monicas, Mulholland is a spectacularly beautiful road, curving through forests and glades, climbing along sharp precipices, and offering magnificent views of the Los Angeles Basin and San Fernando Valley.

LODGING

The **Hollywood Celebrity Hotel** occupies a 1930s art-deco building located just above Hollywood Boulevard. The 40 guest rooms are nicely refurbished, furnished in neo-deco style and decorated in a Hollywood motif. The rooms are quite spacious and a continental breakfast is included in the rate. There's a sitting room off the lobby. ~ 1775 Orchid Avenue; 323-850-6464, 800-222-7090, fax 323-850-7667; www.hotelcelebrity.com. MODERATE.

The **Orchid Suites Hotel** a few doors down is another 40-unit facility. Lacking the character of its neighbor, it substitutes space and amenities for personality. Every room is a suite and includes a kitchen or kitchenette; there's also an outdoor heated pool. Rooms are fashioned in contemporary style. The building itself is a bland, modern stucco. Reservations strongly recommended. ~ 1753 North Orchid Avenue; 323-874-9678, 800-537-3052, fax 323-874-5246; www.orchidsuites.com, e-mail info@orchidsuites. com. MODERATE.

Hollywood Boulevard is one of several strips lined with motels. Representative of the species is the **Hollywood Premiere Motel**. This L-shaped building contains standard rooms. There's also an outdoor pool open seasonally. ~ 5333 Hollywood Boulevard; 323-466-1691. BUDGET.

One of Hollywood's best bargains is found at the **Magic Castle Hotel**, a 44-unit establishment next to the famed Magic Castle, a private club for magicians. Suites with fully equipped kitchens are priced moderately and decorated in cool cream tones. They are quite spacious and well maintained. A pool and sundeck are a bonus. ~ 7025 Franklin Avenue; 323-851-0800, 800-741-4915; www.magiccastlehotel.com, e-mail info@magic hotel.com. MODERATE.

Coral Sands Motel is a 58-unit establishment serving the gay community. The guest rooms look out on a central courtyard with pool, jacuzzi, sauna, and exercise area. Each is carpeted wall-to-wall and sentimentally furnished with standard appointments.

AUTHOR FAVORITE

The traditional Hollywood hideaway is **Château Marmont**, a Norman-style castle built in 1929. Once favored by Jean Harlow and Howard Hughes, the hotel still lures Hollywood luminaries such as Robert DeNiro, Dustin Hoffman, and Diane Keaton. They come for the privacy and quirky charm of the place, which offers rooms, suites, bungalows, and cottages. Around its beautifully maintained grounds are flower gardens, shade trees, and a heated swimming pool. More than anything, the Marmont possesses cachet, as if the hotel itself were a celebrity, holding within its cloistered lobby a thousand tales of Hollywood. ~ 8221 Sunset Boulevard; 323-656-1010, 800-242-8328, fax 323-655-5311; www.chateaumarmont. com. ULTRA-DELUXE.

Continental breakfast is included in the price. Gay-friendly. ~ 1730 North Western Avenue; 323-467-5141, 800-421-3650, fax 323-467-4683; www.coralsands-la.com, e-mail info@coralsands-la.com. BUDGET TO MODERATE.

It's as much a part of Hollywood as the Academy Awards. In fact, the very first Oscars were presented at the **Hollywood Roosevelt Hotel**. Built in 1927, the Spanish Revival building has been completely refurbished and now offers 302 rooms, a restaurant, lounges, and a palm-studded courtyard with pool and hot tub. Priced below many of the city's five-star hotels, this classic caravansary has many features of the finest hostelries. The lobby is a recessed-ceiling affair with colonnades and hand-painted beams. Guest rooms are historic and luxurious. ~ 7000 Hollywood Boulevard; 323-466-7000, 800-950-7667, fax 323-469-7006; www.hollywoodroosevelt.com, e-mail sales@hollywoodroosevelt.com. ULTRA-DELUXE.

DINING

Jitlada is one of those great ethnic restaurants that L.A. likes to tuck away in minimalls. Just a funky little café, it serves an array of Thai dishes; the most notable are seafood entrées such as squid, mussels, and scallops. Closed Monday. ~ 5233 Sunset Boulevard; 323-667-9809, fax 323-663-3104. BUDGET TO MODERATE.

The best of France and California meet in **Patina**—beautiful, intimate, expensive, and worth it. Housed in the Walt Disney Concert Hall, its specialties include shrimp with mashed potatoes and potato truffle chips and peppered tournedos of tuna with Chinese vegetables and ponzu sauce. Try the chocolate plate for dessert. Dinner is served daily; lunch is served on Friday only. ~ 141 South Grand Avenue; 213-972-3331; www.patinagroup.com, e-mail patina@patinagroup.com. DELUXE TO ULTRA-DELUXE.

HIDDEN ►

The Hollywood address for righteous soul food is **Roscoe's House of Chicken & Waffles**, a tiny wood-slat café with overhead fans and an easy atmosphere. Ask for an "Oscar" and they'll bring chicken wings and grits; "E-Z Ed's Special" is a chicken liver omelette; and a "Lord Harvey" is a half chicken smothered in gravy and onions. Very hip. ~ 1514 North Gower Street; 323-466-7453, fax 323-962-0278. MODERATE.

La Poubelle means "garbage pail," but it is anything but. This small candlelit restaurant serves up delicate French and Italian cuisine with a style (and a local following) all its own. ~ 5907 Franklin Avenue; 323-465-0807, fax 323-465-0471. MODERATE TO DELUXE.

Popular with entertainers from nearby studios, **Pinot Hollywood and Martini Lounge** is the last word in sleek. From the brick patio with topiary trees and peaked skylight to the pullman booths and green-glass shades, the place is designed with a delicate touch. The American regional cuisine menu changes weekly and offers

Hooray for Hollywood!

Hollywood & Highland is the latest evidence that Hollywood is coming into a renaissance. An enormous entertainment, shopping, and dining complex, **Hollywood & Highland** is part mall, part theater, and part street scene. Mann's Chinese Theater is here, as is the Kodak Theater (the new home of the Academy Awards), the Grand Ballroom (an upscale venue for catered parties, run by L.A.'s favorite chef, Wolfgang Puck), and a six-screen multiplex cinema. The shopping area features many of the usual suspects (Banana Republic, the Gap) alongside boutiques offering everything from diamonds to blue jeans. The restaurants range from chains like California Pizza Kitchen (323-460-2080) to unique, upscale spots like The Grill on Hollywood (323-856-5530).

This huge outdoor mall dominates the neighborhood and displays a completely different aspect depending on the angle from which you approach it. Coming down Highland Avenue from the north, the enormous four-story Babylonian Arch is the first thing to catch your eye. Its size is impressive, but most arresting is its diagonal positioning. If you enter through the arch, towering above you are two 20-foot pedestals with a life-size elephant sculpture atop each one. Cruising along Hollywood Boulevard traveling east or west, the wraparound, fully animated billboard at the top of the building will make you think you're in the Ginza in Tokyo or Times Square in New York. (The effect is most successful after dark, of course.) Approaching this $615 million dollar extravaganza from underneath, you rise out of the metro station to Hollywood Boulevard, the glittering sidewalk embedded with the names of entertainment stars. The whole complex offers something that's been missing in Hollywood for a long time: glamour. ~ Hollywood Boulevard and Highland Avenue; 323-467-6412; www.hollywoodandhighland.com.

If you like it so much here that you want to stay, you can book a room at the **Renaissance Hollywood Hotel**. With its cool curves and white mirrored facade, this 22-story hostelry evokes the sleek modern design of '50s L.A. Inside, the 637 rooms and suites are appointed in classic '50s fashion, complete with Eames-style chairs and a muted green and yellow color scheme. Amenities include a terrace-top pool and bar, a fitness center, and a restaurant serving eclectic California cuisine. ~ 1755 North Highland Avenue; 323-856-1200, fax 323-856-1205; www.renaissance hollywood.com. ULTRA-DELUXE.

fresh fish, pasta, pizza, assorted steaks, chops, and chicken for lunch and dinner. No lunch on Saturday. Closed Sunday. ~ 1448 North Gower Street; 323-461-8800; www.patinagroup.com, e-mail hollywood@patinagroup.com. DELUXE.

A cozy Hollywood bungalow has been converted into the fine little restaurant **Off Vine**, known for turning out an eclectic menu of pasta, chicken, and fish. Nothing fancy, but always satisfying. Look for the shark in the roof. ~ 6263 Leland Way, just south of Sunset Boulevard; 323-962-1900, fax 323-962-1969; www.off vine.com. MODERATE TO DELUXE.

Hollywood's oldest restaurant, **Musso & Frank's Grill** is a 1919 original with dark paneling, murals, and red leather booths. A bar and open grill create a clubby atmosphere that reflects the eatery's long tradition. Among the American-style dishes are cracked crab, fresh clams, sea bass, prime rib, roast lamb, plus assorted steaks and chops. Closed Sunday and Monday. ~ 6667 Hollywood Boulevard; 323-467-7788, fax 323-467-3360. MODERATE TO ULTRA-DELUXE.

HIDDEN ►   **Pink's Famous Chili Dogs** is a popular takeout stand that serves hamburgers and tamales. But at Pink's, not ordering a dog slapped with sauce is nearly sacrilegious. For the meat-free among us, vegan dogs are also available. ~ 709 North La Brea Avenue; 323-931-4223, fax 323-935-7465; www.pinkshollywood.com. BUDGET.

The fish they serve at **Seafood Village** are not only fresh, they are right there in the display cases of the adjacent market. This nondescript café features several dozen fish dishes plus about a dozen meat entrées; ask about their daily specials. Red snapper, orange roughy, rex sole, sea bass, shark steak, calamari, fried oysters, scallops, shrimp, Alaskan king crab, and Maine lobsters are only some of the offerings. ~ 5732 Melrose Avenue; 323-463-8090. MODERATE.

The celebrity photos covering every inch of **Formosa Cafe** tell a tale of Hollywood that reaches back to the 1940s. This crowded café, originally fashioned from a streetcar, has seen more stars than heaven. Over the years they've poured in from the surrounding studios, leaving autographs and memories. Today you'll find a Chinese restaurant serving dinners, a kind of museum with meals. Dinner only; open super-late. ~ 7156 Santa Monica Boulevard; 323-850-9050. BUDGET.

Hollywood's prettiest restaurant is a re-created Japanese palace called **Yamashiro**. Set in the hills overlooking Los Angeles, the mansion was built earlier in the century, modeled after an estate in the high mountains of Japan, and trimmed with ornamental gardens. Dine here and you are surrounded by hand-carved columns, *shoji* screens, and Asian statuary. The courtyard garden contains a waterfall, koi pond, and miniature trees. For dinner they serve a complete Japanese menu as well as Western-style entrées. Dinner only. ~ 1999.North Sycamore Avenue; 323-466-5125. DELUXE TO ULTRA-DELUXE.

SHOPPING

Nowhere is the nostalgic heartbeat of Hollywood more evident than along Hollywood Boulevard's Walk of Fame. Most tourist attractions revolve around **Mann's Chinese Theatre**, where the souvenir shops, poster studios, T-shirt stores, and postcard vendors are packed tight as a crowd on opening night. ~ 6925 Hollywood Boulevard; 323-461-3331.

Head over to **Supply Sergeant** and stock up on military and camping gear. A favorite among survivalists, bargain hunters, and pink-coiffed punks, this civilian commissary has everything from the subtle to the bizarre. ~ 6664 Hollywood Boulevard; 323-463-4730.

Hollywood Boulevard probably has more bookstores than movie theaters. **Larry Edmunds Bookshop** claims to have the world's largest collection of books and memorabilia on cinema and theater. Closed Sunday. ~ 6644 Hollywood Boulevard; 323-463-3273.

Universal News Agency, reputedly the country's oldest outdoor newsstand, has newspapers and magazines from around the world. ~ 1655 North Las Palmas Avenue; 323-467-3850.

Frederick Mellinger started a tiny mail-order company in 1946 based on the philosophy that "fashion may change but sex appeal is always in style." Today, **Frederick's of Hollywood**, strikingly set in a grey-and-pink art-deco building, continues to entice and enrage onlookers with its fantasy lingerie. ~ 6608 Hollywood Boulevard; 323-466-8506; www.fredericks.com.

The bold exterior of **Soap Plant/Wacko/La Luz de Jesus** hints at the crazy collection of gift items and books within this store. The wild interior is jam-packed with wacky toys and keepsakes, L.A. style. ~ 4633 Hollywood Boulevard; 323-663-0122; www.soapplant.com.

A bigger-than-life mural of Marilyn Monroe marks **Cinema Collectors**. Selling film and television collectibles from every period, they have over 18,000 movie posters and thousands of photos. Closed Sunday. ~ 1507 Wilcox Avenue; 323-461-6516.

If Hollywood glamour seems in short supply along the streets of the motion picture capital, a bit of it can be found at the **Cinema Glamour Shop**. Gowns, furs, and other wardrobe items are donated by stars like Julie Andrews, Florence Henderson, and Bob Newhart. You might find a black beaded dress designed by Oleg Cassini ($85), a red Alfred Nipon suit ($125), a white mink jacket ($400), or an original Ferre gown ($95). Closed weekends. ~ 343 North La Brea Avenue; 323-936-9060, fax 323-634-3868.

◄ *HIDDEN*

NIGHTLIFE Reminiscent of the 1930s, the Hollywood Roosevelt Hotel's deco-style **Feinstein's at the Cinegrill** is putting glamour back into Hollywood nightlife. Crème de la crème cabaret entertainers perform here in an intimate, sophisticated atmosphere. Cover. ~ 7000 Hollywood Boulevard; 323-466-7000.

The intimate L-shaped room of the **Gardenia Club** is an ever-popular supper club venue for cabaret entertainers. You don't have to have dinner to attend the show, but sometimes that's the only way to guarantee seating. Reservations required. Cover. ~ 7066 Santa Monica Boulevard; 323-467-7444.

Following a $6 million remodel, Pacific's **El Capitan Theatre** has been returned to its early glory as one of Hollywood's classic theaters. Opened in 1926, the El Capitan is part of the "Cinema District," an eight-block section along Hollywood Boulevard filled with historic landmarks, including several vintage theaters. If you're going to the movies, this is the place! ~ 6838 Hollywood Boulevard; 800-347-6396, www.elcapitantickets.com.

The Palace also has a colorful history dating back to 1927. Today the luxurious complex showcases popular names in rock and jazz, as well as deejay dance nights. Several bars, dancefloors, a restaurant, and an open courtyard add to the luxury. Cover. ~ 1735 North Vine Street; 323-462-3000; www.hollywoodpalace. com, e-mail hpinfo@hollywoodpalace.com.

For sunset panoramas, nothing quite matches **Yamashiro**. Set in a Japanese palace, the lounge overlooks gracious Asian gardens from a perch in the Hollywood Hills. ~ 1999 North Sycamore Avenue; 323-466-5125.

THEATER Theater in Hollywood varies from tiny storefront establishments to famous stages. In a city filled with actors, the playhouses inevitably are loaded with talent. Professionals from local television and movie studios continually hone their skills on stage, and the area's "equity-waiver" theaters provide an opportunity to see these veterans perform at affordable prices.

The **Hollywood Arts Council** publishes *Discover Hollywood*, calendar listings of all Hollywood theaters. The free, bi-annual publication is available at the Hollywood Visitors Center, or by mailing $2 (postage) to the Council at P.O. Box 931056, Hollywood, CA 90093. ~ 323-462-2355; www.discoverhollywood.com.

To secure tickets for productions, call ticket agencies to charge by phone. Major ticket agencies include **Ticketmaster** (213-480-3232), **Goodtime Tickets** (323-464-7383), and **Murray's Tickets** (323-234-0123). Or contact the theater directly; day-of-the-event tickets are frequently available for as much as 50 percent off. **Theater LA**'s website offers same-day half-price tickets by using your credit card and paying a service charge for each ticket. ~ www.theatrela.org.

Pantages Theatre, one of Hollywood's largest playhouses, presents major productions, including Broadway musicals. Closed Monday. ~ 6233 Hollywood Boulevard; 323-468-1770; www.nederlander.com, e-mail concerts@nederlander.com.

The refurbished **James Doolittle Theatre**, built in 1926, features top shows from Broadway and London. ~ 1615 North Vine Street. Tickets are available through Telecharge, 800-447-7400.

Tucked into a hard-to-find space behind the Egyptian Theatre and down a side street is the **Egyptian Arena Theatre**, home of the Grace Players, one of the better equity-waiver theaters. They offer acting workshops and an irregular season of plays—both original works and classics. ~ 1625 North Las Palmas Avenue; 323-464-1222.

◄ HIDDEN

The John Anson Ford Theatre, an outdoor amphitheater, produces jazz, dance, and family programs from June through September. They also house an indoor 87-seat theater that mounts new plays November through April. Closed Monday in summer, Monday and Tuesday in winter. ~ 2580 Cahuenga Boulevard East; 323-461-3673, fax 323-464-1158; www.fordamphitheater.com.

The **Henry Fonda Theatre** also hosts dramatic and musical performances. ~ 6126 Hollywood Boulevard; 323-468-1770; www.henryfondatheater.com.

The Hollywood Bowl is one of the world's largest natural amphitheaters.

Seating 18,000, the **Hollywood Bowl** dates back to the 1920s. The concert shell hosts the Los Angeles Philharmonic and features top-bill pop, jazz, and classical concerts. Bring a cushion, sweater, and picnic, and come join the festivities in this park-like setting. ~ 2301 North Highland Avenue; 323-850-2000; www.hollywoodbowl.org.

The **Hollywood Palladium**, which once headlined the swing bands of the '40s, now features new wave, rock, international, and Latin groups. ~ 6215 Sunset Boulevard; 323-962-7600.

West Hollywood

West Hollywood has always been a bastion of the unconventional and the cutting edge. But since the city was incorporated in 1983, West Hollywood has commanded the lion's share of attention when it comes to all things alternative in Los Angeles—lifestyles, fashion, art and design, entertainment. Progressive, ultra-image conscious (it markets itself as "The Creative City"), a bit impudent, West Hollywood is charged with an energy not found anywhere else in Los Angeles.

The rest of the world began to notice West Hollywood back in the booming 1980s, when hip clothing boutiques started opening up on a rather dingy stretch of Melrose Avenue. Innovative eateries and galleries followed, and Melrose became *the* retail mecca. Trendiness is fleeting, of course, and Melrose's glam appeal has faded slightly, but West Hollywood's star is still on the rise. For such a small city—1.8 square miles—West Hollywood lays claim to the highest concentration of top-rated restaurants in Los Angeles. Its art galleries exhibit Warhol and Ruscha as well as emerging Caribbean artists. Celebrities from Bette Davis to Jim Morrison to Jerry Seinfeld have called the city home at one time or another. Today, its population of about 35,000 is a dynamic, if curious, mix of gays and lesbians, Russian immigrants, and retirees. And while street parking in West Hollywood is a nightmare, there's something undeniably appealing about this remarkable little city that appeals to just about everybody.

SIGHTS   Technically, not all of **Melrose Avenue** is in West Hollywood. But that's being picky. The Melrose attitude—cutting-edge, irreverent, haute-hip, trashy—has always been in keeping with the free-wheeling spirit of West Hollywood. A possible signal that things had changed on Melrose was the coming of Starbucks; latex was out and latté was in. But there's still enough of an edge to this street to make it worth a detour (if you can find a parking space). ~ Between La Brea and Fairfax avenues.

The tone of Melrose changes as you move westward, past Fairfax and La Cienega, where very high-end decorator showrooms and fine-art galleries are located. If you need a landmark to lead you through this tony part of town, consider a whale. The "Blue Whale," to be precise; that's the nickname for the blue-glass monstrosity on Melrose Avenue and San Vicente Boulevard. Formally known as the **Pacific Design Center**, it's a mammoth mall catering to the interior design industry. Since opening in 1975, it has spawned a Green Whale next door. Rumor has it that Moby Blue is pregnant with a Red Whale, due sometime in the next couple of years. Closed weekends. ~ 8687 Melrose Avenue; 310-657-0800, fax 310-652-8576; www.pacificdesigncenter.com.

Also located in the Pacific Design Center is the **West Hollywood Convention and Visitors Bureau**. ~ 8687 Melrose Avenue; 310-289-2525, 800-368-6020; www.visitwesthollywood.com, e-mail whcvb@visitwesthollywood.com.

The concentration of designer studios and galleries has given a collective moniker—the **Avenues of Art and Design**—to several streets in this area, among them Robertson Boulevard, Almont Drive, and Melrose Avenue. Periodically (every four to eight weeks) several of the galleries host a Saturday evening reception, when a dozen or more are open to the public. Wine, fruit, and cheese are served, and people stroll from one gallery to another. Call the West Hollywood Convention and Visitors Bureau for information about dates for the Saturday night group receptions.

~ 310-289-2525, 800-368-6020; www.visitwesthollywood.com,
e-mail whcvb@visitwesthollywood.com.

With as much as one-third of the population thought to be
gay and lesbian, West Hollywood is often represented as a "gay
city." Of course, the gay and lesbian presence there is a driving
force, economically and politically. One of the largest parades in
California, the Gay Pride Parade and Festival, takes place every
June in West Hollywood, drawing hundreds of thousands of cel-
ebrants. **Santa Monica Boulevard**, between La Cienega Boulevard and Robertson Boulevard, is the core of the gay community
in West Hollywood. This is where you'll find restaurants, bars
and nightclubs, retail stores, and other businesses catering to gay
and lesbian clientele. (For more information on the gay scene, see
"West Hollywood Gay Scene" in this chapter.)

The scene is quite different along **Sunset Boulevard**, which
hugs the base of the Hollywood Hills as it snakes through West
Hollywood. Known as the Sunset Strip along this stretch, the
boulevard really comes alive at night, a pattern that has been re-
peating itself for decades. During the 1930s and 1940s, the sec-

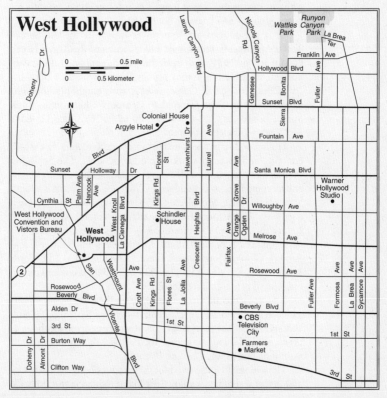

tion between Crescent Heights Boulevard and Doheny Drive formed the fabled **Sunset Strip**. Center of Los Angeles night action, it was an avenue of dreams, housing nightclubs like Ciro's, the Trocadero, Mocombo, and the Clover Club. As picture magazines of the times illustrated, starlets bedecked with diamonds emerged from limousines with their leading men. During the 1950s, Ed "Kookie" Byrnes immortalized the street on the television show "77 Sunset Strip."

Today, the two-mile strip is chockablock with the offices of agents, movie producers, personal managers, and music executives. The street's most artistic achievement is the parade of **vanity boards** that captivate the eye with their colors and bold conception. These outsize billboards, advertising the latest movie and record releases, represent the work of the region's finest sign painters and designers. Often done in three dimensions, with lights and trompe l'oeil devices, they create an outdoor art gallery.

An artist with equal vision was at work here in 1936. That's when architect Robert Derrah built the **Crossroads of the World**. Designed as an oceanliner sailing across Sunset Boulevard, the prow of this proud ship is topped by a tower complete with rotating globe. ~ 6671 Sunset Boulevard.

That streamlined art-deco tower nearby is the old Sunset Tower Apartments, refurbished and rechristened the **Argyle Hotel**. Completed in 1931, this moderne palace contained 46 luxury apartments, leased to luminaries like Errol Flynn, the Gabor sisters, Zasu Pitts, Clark Gable, and Howard Hughes (who seems to have slept in more places than George Washington). ~ 8358 Sunset Boulevard; 323-654-7100, 800-225-2637, fax 323-654-9287; www.argylehotel.com.

Hollywood might be noted for its art-deco towers, but it also contains architectural works by other schools. The **Schindler House**, a house-studio with concrete walls, sliding canvas doors, and sleeping lofts, was designed by Viennese draftsman Rudolph Schindler in 1921. Modeled on a desert camp, the house has been a gathering place for avant-garde architects ever since. The MAK Center for Art and Architecture hosts exhibitions, lectures, and performances here and offers docent tours on Saturday and Sunday. Closed Monday and Tuesday. Admission. ~ 835 North Kings Road; 323-651-1510, fax 323-651-2340; www.makcenter.org, e-mail office@makcenter.org.

F. Scott Fitzgerald fans will want to see the garden court apartments at 1401 North Laurel Avenue where the Roaring '20s novelist spent the final years of his life. Recovering from alcoholism, his career in decline, the author worked here on a film script and his unfinished novel, *The Last Tycoon*.

The **Colonial House** two blocks away was home to celebrities and fictional characters alike. Bette Davis resided in the red brick building, as did Carole Lombard and her husband, William Powell. They were joined, in the imagination of Hollywood novelist Budd Schulberg, by Sammy Glick, the overly ambitious protagonist in *What Makes Sammy Run?* ~1416 North Havenhurst Drive.

The **Nelson House**, where the entire family lived during the 1950s, was used as the model for their TV home on "The Ozzie and Harriet Show." Harriet sold the house several years after Ozzie died in 1975. ~ 1822 Camino Palermo Drive.

The **Los Angeles Conservancy** offers 12 different walking tours of Los Angeles, including Angeline Heights and Highland Park. Tours are held on Saturday at 10 a.m. Reservations required. Fee. ~ 523 West 6th Street, Suite 826, Los Angeles; 213-623-2489, fax 213-623-3909; www.laconservancy.org.

LODGING

Several streamlined and ultramodern hotels are located within a ten-block radius here in West Hollywood. The hallmark of the Mondrian, Bel Âge, Le Parc, Summerfield Suites, and Veladon hotels is the artwork, which hangs seemingly everywhere—in the lobby, public areas, corridors, and guest rooms. You can expect ultramodern furnishings, creative appointments, and personal service at each address.

Ian Schrager spent a fortune renovating his **Mondrian** hotel, transforming a rather dated, cliched property into a surreal temple of contemporary urban style, not to mention attitude. Light, white, and luminescent, the Mondrian sports the "simple chic" look of designer Philippe Starck, who handled the renovation. The hotel's Sky Bar has become the West Hollywood spot to see and be seen. ~ 8440 Sunset Boulevard; 323-650-8999, 800-525-8029, fax 323-650-5215; www.ianschragerhotels.com. ULTRA-DELUXE.

Somewhat more offbeat is the **Wyndham Bel Âge Hotel**. This all-suite hotel offers similar amenities in a complex that is positively laden with artwork. On the rooftop are a pool, jacuzzi, and exercise area. ~ 1020 North San Vicente Boulevard; 310-854-1111, 800-996-3426, fax 310-854-0926; www.wyndham.com. ULTRA-DELUXE.

AUTHOR FAVORITE

The elegant **Argyle Hotel**, once the St. James Club, treats guests to an upper-crust club atmosphere. Completed in 1931 as Sunset Towers and now restored to its art-deco magnificence, the Club once was home to screen luminaries from nearby studios. There are 64 beautifully appointed rooms and an on-site restaurant. ~ 8358 Sunset Boulevard; 323-654-7100, 800-225-2637, fax 323-654-9287; www.argylehotel.com. ULTRA-DELUXE.

Located in a quiet residential neighborhood, **Le Parc Suite Hotel De Luxe** offers 154 studio and one-bedroom rooms with a number of amenities. Among the facilities are a restaurant, bar, swimming pool, and gym. ~ 733 West Knoll Drive; 310-855-8888, 800-578-4837, fax 310-659-7812; www.leparcsuites.com, e-mail leparcres@aol.com. ULTRA-DELUXE.

Summerfield Suites Hotel features 111 suites with a kitchen, fireplace, and balcony. This establishment also has a rooftop garden with pool, spa, city views, and a café that serves a complimentary breakfast buffet. ~ 1000 Westmount Drive; 310-657-7400, 800-949-6326, fax 310-854-6744; www.summerfieldsuites.com. ULTRA-DELUXE.

Valadon Hotel offers similar accommodations. Among the amenities are laundry facilities and 24-hour room service. You'll find a pool, jacuzzi, and exercise area on the rooftop. ~ 8822 Cynthia Street; 310-854-1114, 800-835-7997, fax 310-657-2623; www.valadonhotel.com. ULTRA-DELUXE.

Another chic Hollywood resting spot, the **Sunset Marquis Hotel and Villas** is a Mediterranean-style hotel frequented by beautiful people with big purses. Guest rooms surround a terrace pool, creating a tropical ambience enhanced by pastel colors and potted plants. The rooms are furnished in contemporary style and range from standard facilities to lavish villas. High in snob appeal, the hotel offers complete amenities. ~ 1200 North Alta Loma Road; 310-657-1333, 800-858-9758, fax 310-652-5300; www.sunsetmarquishotel.com, e-mail reservations@sunsetmarquis hotel.com. ULTRA-DELUXE.

DINING

A mixed bag these days, Melrose Avenue is where you'll find designer fashion boutiques sitting alongside cheap T-shirt outlets, used clothing shops, and specialty stores selling whoopie cushions. Vestiges of the avenue's former glory remain in its excellent restaurants, tucked amid fast-food eateries and theme diners.

AUTHOR FAVORITE

Duke's is an old favorite watering hole, especially popular with music industry figures. A crowded coffee shop bedecked with posters, it also attracts West Hollywood's underground population. People with purple hair pile into the communal tables, order meatloaf or Chinese vegetables, and settle down for the day. That's what makes Duke's Duke's: it's a scene, a flash, a slice of unreality. A colorful breakfast stop, it features dozens of omelette selections; also hamburgers, sandwiches, diet plates, and a few American dinners. No dinner on weekends. ~ 8909 Sunset Boulevard; 310-652-3100. BUDGET

The **Moustache Café** was one of the early signs that Melrose was becoming a prominent dining area. Its large enclosed patio is heated on those chilly L.A. evenings Angelenos call winter and Easterners enjoy in short-sleeve shirts. The cuisine is French Continental, featuring striped bass, rack of lamb, and all the other usual suspects. For many, the highlight of the menu is the chocolate soufflé: order yours when you first sit down—it takes about 20 minutes. ~ 8155 Melrose Avenue; 323-651-2111. MODERATE TO DELUXE.

Angeli Caffe/Pizzeria is the archetypal Melrose address. Its high-tech interior is a medley of flying buttresses, wood-slat ceilings, exposed ducts, and whitewashed walls. The menu matches this cutting-edge design with pizza, pasta, calzone, and daily fresh fish specials. No lunch on weekends. ~ 7274 Melrose Avenue; 323-936-9086, fax 323-938-9873. MODERATE.

Try **Tommy Tang's** when next you have an inclination for Thai food and/or sushi. Here you'll find a full sushi bar and an ever-changing gallery of artwork that reflects the trendy crowd. The food is delicious, the portions are small. Happily, everyone is rich. No dinner on Monday. ~ 7313 Melrose Avenue; 323-937-5733, fax 323-937-5781; www.tommytangs.net. MODERATE.

Modern art and pastel walls are also standard issue in the neighborhood's best Chinese restaurant. **Genghis Cohen** serves gourmet dishes to an appreciative crowd at its multiroom complex off Melrose Avenue. Not your ordinary Asian restaurant, specialties here are "scallops on fire," candied shrimp, garlic catfish, soft-shelled shrimp, and "no-name" duck. ~ 740 North Fairfax Avenue; 323-653-0640, fax 323-653-0701. MODERATE TO ULTRA-DELUXE.

When you tire of the tinsel along Melrose Avenue you can always retreat to **Noura Café**, one of the street's few down-home restaurants. Here the food is Middle Eastern with a Mediterranean touch. Just order shish kebab, falafel, grape leaves, or salad at the counter, then enjoy it in a comfortable dining room or out on the patio. For a few dollars more, you can opt for table service. ~ 8479 Melrose Avenue; 323-651-4581, fax 323-651-1375. BUDGET TO MODERATE.

Dominick's has a long history of being a Hollywood hotspot. But even though it's a supper club with fine food, the emphasis is the casual trendy atmosphere that attracts the rock crowd. Dinner only. Closed Sunday. ~ 8715 Beverly Boulevard; 310-652-7272. MODERATE TO DELUXE.

Hugo's is a great café for brunch (try one of the pasta or egg dishes). The menu also offers sandwiches and soups. Alfresco dining is available, as is an herb and tea room. ~ 8401 Santa Monica Boulevard; 323-654-3993, fax 323-654-4089; www.hugo restaurant.com. MODERATE.

At **La Boheme,** dining on Cal-French specialties takes on theatrical grandeur under a soaring ceiling and next to an oversized fireplace. The seared ahi with wasabi mashed potatoes is a popular starter. As for entrées, the potato-wrapped halibut with yellow tomato coulis is just one of the possibilities. Dinner only. ~ 8400 Santa Monica Boulevard; 323-848-2360, fax 323-848-9447; www.laboheme-la.com, e-mail boheme-losangeles@global-dining. co.jp. MODERATE TO ULTRA-DELUXE.

Tucked into a cozy storefront space is **Cynthia's,** an altogether delightful spot to dine on updated American comfort food like fried chicken and dumplings, meatloaf, and spicy corn chowder. No lunch on weekends. ~ 8370 West 3rd Street; 323-658-7851, fax 323-658-7535; e-mail cynthiasrestaurant@hotmail.com. MODERATE TO ULTRA-DELUXE.

HIDDEN ▶   **Barney's Beanery** is the only place around where you can shoot pool while eating chili, burritos, pizza, ribs, and hamburgers. Or where you can choose from nearly 300 varieties of beer. A dive with character, Barney's has rainbow-colored booths, license plates on the ceiling, and road sign decor. Native funk at low prices. ~ 8447 Santa Monica Boulevard; 323-654-2287, fax 323-654-5123. BUDGET TO MODERATE.

For lunch or weekend brunch, the **Sunset Plaza** stretch of Sunset Boulevard offers several restaurants with sidewalk cafés. ~ 8500–8700 blocks of Sunset Boulevard, between La Cienega and San Vicente boulevards.

L'Orangerie possesses all the pretensions you would expect from one of Los Angeles' finest, most expensive French restaurants. The building has the look of a château, with imposing arches and finials atop the roof. The dining areas are appointed with oil paintings and outsized wall sconces; fresh flowers and the scent of money proliferate. Food, decor, service—all are the finest. The *foie gras* and seafood are flown in fresh from France. Life, or dinner at least, doesn't get much better than this classic French restaurant. Reservations are required (as are jackets for men). Dinner only. Closed Monday. ~ 903 North La Cienega Boulevard; 310-652-9770, fax 310-652-8870; www.lorangerie. com, e-mail lorangerie@lorangerie.com. ULTRA-DELUXE.

SHOPPING   The section of Sunset Boulevard between Crescent Heights Boulevard and Doheny Drive, commonly known as Sunset Strip, is marked by creatively designed billboards announcing the latest Hollywood releases. Amid this skein of signs is a series of star-studded cartoon characters signaling the way to **Dudley Do-Right's Emporium**. Jay Ward's cartoon characters come to life at this Bullwinkle enthusiast's mecca. Closed Sunday, Monday, Wednesday, and Friday. ~ 8200 Sunset Boulevard; 323-656-6550.

Sunset Plaza, a two-block cluster of shops located on Sunset Boulevard between Sunset Plaza Drive and Sherbourne Drive, offers some of the most luxurious shopping on the Strip.

Book Soup, a small but special bookstore, offers a top-notch selection of art books, classic literature, current fiction, and international magazines. ~ 8818 Sunset Boulevard; 310-659-3110; www.booksoup.com.

Step over to **Aahs!** for a selection of greeting cards, informal gifts, and crazy toys. ~ 8878 Sunset Boulevard; 310-657-4221.

Don't worry, you won't miss **Aida's Flowers.** If the festive mural doesn't catch your eye, the character on the corner (dressed as Santa, the Easter Bunny, or Uncle Sam) will flag you down. Once inside, if you dare to enter, you'll find flowers, cards, produce, and piano music in an exotic setting. ~ 1261 North La Brea Avenue; 323-876-6482.

Gallery 825 is a great place to discover the up and coming while they are still down and out.

Ultramodern shoppers make a beeline for **Melrose Avenue.** West Hollywood's proving ground for innovative style, Melrose is the smartest street in all L.A., a multi-block mélange of signature boutiques, fresh cuisine restaurants, and heartthrob nightspots. Peopled by visionaries and voluptuaries, it's sleek, fast, and very, very chic. Shops and galleries, with names as trendy as their concepts, come and go with tidal regularity in this super-heated environment. ~ Between Sycamore Avenue and Ogden Drive.

Of course the most futuristic element of all is the past. At **Chic-A-Boom,** the "Mother Lode" of vintage retail, you'll find such shards of American history as a Davy Crockett lamp, a drugstore display from the '50s, toys from the '60s and '70s, vintage *TV Guides*, a huge selection of rock-and-roll posters, plus movie memorabilia. Closed Sunday. ~ 6817 Melrose Avenue; 323-931-7441.

Off The Wall is known for "weird stuff" and unusual 20th-century antiques. You can also pick up some of your favorite vintage advertising signs. Closed Sunday. ~ 7325 Melrose Avenue; 323-930-1185; www.offthewallantiques.com.

Occupying an entire block, **Ron Herman/Fred Segal** is a series of stores within stores. Seeming to specialize in everything, this consumer labyrinth has clothes for men, women, and children, plus lingerie, luggage, shoes, electronic gear, and cosmetics. There's even a café at hand when you tire of browsing or simply become lost. ~ 8100 Melrose Avenue; 323-651-3342.

Gemini GEL is one of the country's top art publishers. Producing limited-edition prints and sculptures, it features two display galleries. Open Saturday by appointment; closed Sunday. ~ 8365 Melrose Avenue; 323-651-0513; www.geminigel.com.

The Bodhi Tree Bookstore is *the* place for books on mysticism, metaphysics, nature, health, and religion. Behind the main store, The Used Book Ranch displays used books as well as herbs, teas, and homeopathic remedies. ~ 8585 Melrose Avenue; 310-659-1733; www.bodhitree.com.

The Beverly Center, a neon-laced shopping mall, features signature clothing stores, world-class restaurants, and a multiplex entertainment center. Exterior glass-enclosed elevators move shoppers quickly through this eight-story complex. ~ 8500 Beverly Boulevard; 310-854-0070; www.beverlycenter.com.

Clustered nearby around Robertson Boulevard are several prestigious art galleries. Margo Leavin Gallery houses an impressive collection of contemporary American and European art. Closed Sunday and Monday. ~ 812 North Robertson Boulevard; 310-273-0603.

HIDDEN ► For free travel advice, browse through Traveler's Bookcase, a friendly bookstore for people on the move. Here you'll discover a collection of hard-to-find regional titles as well as literature for the new breed of adventure traveler. Take a sojourn on one of the plush couches and flip through a few vacations. ~ 8375 West 3rd Street; 323-655-0575; www.travelbooks.com.

Next door is Cook's Library, a speciality bookstore crammed with cookbooks and other food-related literature. Closed Sunday. ~ 8373 West 3rd Street; 323-655-3141.

Another constellation of galleries lies along the 600-to-800-block stretch of North La Cienega Boulevard. Most venerable of all these art centers is Gallery 825, which showcases talents from the Los Angeles Art Association. Gallery 825 also offers lectures and workshops. Closed Sunday and Monday. ~ 825 North La Cienega Boulevard; 310-652-8272; www.laaa.org.

NIGHTLIFE The level of talent at the Comedy Store is evident from the celebrity signatures covering the building's black exterior and photo-lined interior. The Main Room features the best comedians, the Original Room showcases new talent, and the Belly Room presents a wide range of alternative comics. Cover. ~ 8433 Sunset Boulevard; 323-656-6225; www.thecomedystore.com.

The ultrahip Skybar at the Mondrian hotel features great views for those who want to see and be seen. Reservations required. ~ 8440 Sunset Boulevard; 323-650-8999.

Two long-standing rock clubs dominate Sunset Strip. Whisky A Go Go features live music on a nightly basis. Cover. ~ 8901 Sunset Boulevard; 310-652-4202; www.whiskyagogo.com. The Roxy Theater headlines known rock-and-roll and alternative rock performers in an art deco–style room. Cover. ~ 9009 Sunset Boulevard; 310-276-2222.

Another of Hollywood's jazz clubs, **Catalina Bar & Grill** draws a relaxed crowd and features name performers. Cover. ~ 6725 Sunset Boulevard; 323-466-2210; www.catalinajazzclub.com.

The Key Club joined the Strip's club lineup in 1997, with a two-level venue for rock, jazz, country, and blues acts. Its in-house restaurant overlooks the stage. Twenty-one and over. Cover. ~ 9039 Sunset Boulevard; 310-274-5800.

Live music at **1020** starts around 7 p.m., Friday and Saturday. ~ In the Wyndham Bel Âge Hotel, 1020 North San Vicente Boulevard; 310-358-7776.

One mainstay in Hollywood nightlife is the coffeehouse. With plump armchairs, weatherbeaten tables and walls covered by contemporary art, the **Insomnia Cafe** serves cappuccino and desserts until the wee hours of the morning. ~ 7286 Beverly Boulevard; 323-931-4943.

The Hard Rock Cafe, a wildly popular gathering place in the Beverly Center, features the loud music and rock memorabilia decor for which this nightclub chain is renowned. ~ 8600 Beverly Boulevard; 310-276-7605; www.hardrock.com.

The **Coronet Theatre** presents comedies, musicals, and occasional dramas. The resident nonprofit theater company, Playwrights' Kitchen Ensemble, hosts an array of interesting workshops. ~ 366 North La Cienega Boulevard; 310-657-7377; www.coronet-theatre.com.

The Gig Hollywood headlines live bands seven nights a week: blues, R&B, surf, funk. Settle down in one of the big cushy couches and imagine yourself in your own living room. Twenty-one and over. Cover. ~ 7302 Melrose Avenue; 323-936-4440; www.liveatthegig.com.

There are often as many comedians in the bar as on stage at the **Improv**. This spacious brick-walled club, patterned after the

AUTHOR FAVORITE

If you haven't been to the **House of Blues**, you're missing out on one of the best nightspots around. This establishment combines a Delta-inspired restaurant with a live music club. The specialty is blues, although other musical traditions from reggae to rock are also featured. Buddy Guy and Paul Simon have played here as well as Al Green and Melissa Etheridge. The walls at this nightspot are adorned with the portraits of legendary bluesmen including Stevie Ray Vaughan, Robert Johnson, and Albert King. Gospel brunch on Sunday gets the day off to a rousing start. Cover. ~ 8430 Sunset Boulevard; reservations 323-848-5123, box office 323-848-5100; www.hob.com.

New York original, draws top-name comics such as Drew Carey, as well as local talent. Cover. ~ 8162 Melrose Avenue; 323-651-2583; www.improv.com.

THEATER Small theaters and local playwrights make sections of West Hollywood the Off-Broadway of the West. Dozens of talented companies perform regularly on these less-known but equally entertaining stages:

The **Coast Playhouse** specializes in original musicals and new dramas. ~ 8325 Santa Monica Boulevard; 323-650-8507. A replica of the British original, the **Globe Playhouse** stages Shakespearean plays in addition to other dramas of historical significance. ~ 1107 North Kings Road; 323-654-5623. The **Matrix Theatre Company** is home to Joseph Stern's award-winning troupe, Actors for Themselves. ~ 7657 Melrose Avenue; 323-852-1445. Comedy and improvisation top the bill at the **Groundling Theatre**. ~ 7307 Melrose Avenue; 323-934-9700.

West Hollywood Gay Scene

West Hollywood did not mysteriously blossom overnight into a gay mecca after the city was incorporated in 1983. Decades ago, gay bars and other establishments that ran the risk of being raided by the Los Angeles Police Department found a more tolerant environment outside the city limits and established themselves in the unincorporated area of West Hollywood. Naturally, many gay men and lesbians settled in, too. Artists, designers, and actors were also drawn to West Hollywood, which helped establish the area's reputation for creativity.

In 1983, residents of the district championed their own destiny and voted to incorporate the City of West Hollywood. Today, few places in the country are as gay-friendly as West Hollywood, and for many gay and lesbian visitors to Southern California, the city has become a destination in its own right.

LODGING The **Grove Guesthouse** offers just one bright and airy cottage decorated with contemporary leather furniture and high ceilings. There's a distinct home-away-from-home atmosphere here, complete with a pre-stocked pantry from which to create your own meals. As a guest, you have pool and hot tub privileges as well. Hopefully, the oranges on the tree out back will be ready for plucking. Reservations required. ~ 1325 North Orange Grove Avenue; 323-876-7778, 888-524-7683, fax 323-876-0890; www.groveguesthouse.com, e-mail info@groveguesthouse.com. ULTRA-DELUXE.

Located right in the heart of West Hollywood, the **Holloway Motel** is a haven for gays and lesbians. The 22 units are comfortably furnished; suites have full kitchens. ~ 8465 Santa Monica Boulevard; 323-654-2454, 888-654-6400; www.hollowaymotel. com. MODERATE.

Centrally located, the **Ramada West Hollywood** offers classy lodging within its art-deco exterior. Straights and gays alike can be found relaxing on the sundeck and around the heated pool. Rooms are appointed in pastels and contemporary furniture. Suites come equipped with kitchens, wet bars, and sleeping lofts. ~ 8585 Santa Monica Boulevard; 310-652-6400, 800-845-8585, fax 310-652-2135; www.ramadawh.com, e-mail info@ramadawh.com. DELUXE TO ULTRA-DELUXE.

> Santa Monica Boulevard, between La Cienega and Robertson boulevards, offers a slew of restaurants, bars, and shops catering to a mainly gay and lesbian clientele.

The gay bed-and-breakfast scene is well served by **San Vicente Inn Resort**. This 28-unit complex features an attractive tropical courtyard and a clothing-optional pool, hot tub, and sauna. Rooms and suites may have kitchenettes and shared baths. An expanded breakfast is served poolside. ~ 845 North San Vicente Boulevard; 310-854-6915; e-mail info desk@sanvicenteinn.com. MODERATE TO ULTRA-DELUXE.

Upon entering **Le Montrose**, guests will be greeted by friendly attendants along with fresh fruit and mineral water. The posh, art nouveau accommodations consist of fireplaces and Nintendo sets; some include full kitchens and balconies. This all-suite hotel also makes it easy to keep fit while traveling. There's a pool, a hot tub, a fully equipped fitness center, free bike use, and a rooftop tennis court with tennis instructors to help you perfect your serve. Afterward, schedule an appointment with the on-staff masseuse to work out those knots. Cookies and milk await guests at check-out time. ~ 900 Hammond Street; 310-855-1115, 800-776-0666, fax 310-657-9192; www.lemontrose.com, e-mail frontdesk@lemontrose.com. ULTRA-DELUXE.

DINING

Located inside the French Quarter Market Place is the **French Quarter Restaurant**, festooned with hanging plants among wrought-iron appointments. Breakfast is served all day for those who don't feel like having one of the many choices of sandwiches, steaks, and pasta dishes. Specialties include braised pot roast, glazed King salmon, and blackened chicken penne. Its late hours also make it a great nightspot. Breakfast, lunch, and dinner are served daily. ~ 7985 Santa Monica Boulevard; 323-654-0898, fax 323-656-7898. MODERATE.

Basix Café is always busy, from morning to night, serving fresh-baked muffins and rolls, as well as sandwiches, grilled chicken, salads, and pastas. It's located on a busy corner, so its sidewalk tables are always a good spot to sit to see and be seen.

~ 8333 Santa Monica Boulevard at Flores Street; 323-848-2460, fax 323-848-2462. MODERATE.

Around the corner is **Marix Tex-Mex**. Margaritas by the pitcher, pretty good Tex-Mex food, and an infectiously festive atmosphere guarantee there's always a wait to get in. ~ 1108 North Flores Street; 323-656-8800. MODERATE.

At **Benvenuto**, dine inside in a warm, cheerful trattoria or outside on the narrow, tented patio. Chicken sausage lasagne, risotto, pizza, and traditional pasta dishes are generally well prepared. An occasional celebrity sighting (Rosie O'Donnell, for example) adds to the fun. No lunch on Monday, Saturday and Sunday. ~ 8512 Santa Monica Boulevard at La Cienega Boulevard; 310-659-8635, fax 310-659-8638. MODERATE.

A large gay crowd shows up for Argentine tantalizers at the **Tango Grill**—authenticity furnished courtesy of the owner, who's from Buenos Aires. The brick walls, Mexican tile floors, and wooden tables do much for the South American atmosphere, and diners may choose to take their sizzling dishes out on the patio under large umbrellas. Chicken, seafood, beef, and vegetables are marinated in special blends of citrus juice and garlic. ~ 8807 Santa Monica Boulevard; 310-659-3663. BUDGET TO MODERATE.

More upscale but equally popular with West Hollywood's gay population is **Café D'Etoile**. The cuisine here is a Continental mix of pasta, steak, chicken, and roast pork dishes, and the decor is a mix of antique furniture and contemporary artwork. ~ 8941½ Santa Monica Boulevard; 310-278-1011. MODERATE TO DELUXE.

You'll find sandwiches, salads, burgers, chicken, and pastas prepared in a variety of ways at **The Abbey**. Although the regulars tend to be gay men, lesbians and straight couples frequently come to chat over coffee and a huge assortment of desserts and martinis (which, by the way, outnumber the regular menu). Out-

AUTHOR FAVORITE

Mark's serves elegant California cuisine in a casual, contemporary setting. Along with tasty entrées such as grilled rare ahi with sesame-ginger sauce, there are Maryland crab cakes with corn purée and tomato-basil sauce, and turkey-vegetable potstickers. Advance reservations are the smart way to go on "half-price Mondays." Dinner only; Sunday brunch. ~ 861 North La Cienega Boulevard; 310-652-5252, fax 310-652-0295; www.marksrestaurant.com, e-mail marksresla@aol.com. MODERATE TO DELUXE.

door seating is available. Open for breakfast, lunch, and dinner. ~ 692 North Robertson Boulevard; 310-289-8410, fax 310-289-8429. BUDGET TO MODERATE.

Not only is **A Different Light** a "full service gay and lesbian bookstore," it also serves as a focal point for West Hollywood's gay population, complete with community bulletin board and an ongoing schedule of events. ~ 8853 Santa Monica Boulevard; 310-854-6601.

SHOPPING

Specializing in erotica, **The Pleasure Chest** offers an unparalleled array of leather goods, lingerie, latex clothing, novelties, and gay literature. ~ 7733 Santa Monica Boulevard; 323-650-1022; www.nocost.com.

Two former clubs (and $2 million) created **Ultra Suede at the Factory**, a 15,000-square-foot danceclub. Plush couches in the back lounge are a good resting spot away from the exuberance of the dancefloor. Discotheque inspired, the driving beat at this happening place favors music from the past few decades, particularly the '80s and '90s. Open Wednesday, Friday, and Saturday. ~ 661 Robertson Boulevard; 310-659-4551; www.factorynightclub.com/ultra-suede.htm.

NIGHTLIFE

The Abbey is another popular gay hangout. ~ 692 North Robertson Boulevard; 310-289-8410.

A neighborhood bar located in the heart of West Hollywood, **Mother Lode** is ideal for those looking for a cozy place to hang out and have a stout or two. Nightly deejays spin tunes ranging from rock-and-roll to dance music; ironically, there's no dancefloor to let loose on. But the crowd, which mainly consists of gay men, doesn't seem to mind. Sunday and Thursday also features karaoke. ~ 8944 Santa Monica Boulevard; 310-659-9700.

Rage Restaurant and Bar is a spacious all-gay dance club that spills onto the sidewalk; inside there are outrageous videos plus sounds ranging from house and high-energy music to alternative rock. Cover Tuesday/Wednesday and Thursday/Friday. ~ 8911 Santa Monica Boulevard; 310-652-7055.

It is primarily gay men who frequent **Micky's**, a West Hollywood nightspot that offers dancing to a deejay video. Occasional cover. ~ 8857 Santa Monica Boulevard; 310-657-1176; www.mickys.com.

The Palms is the oldest women's bar in Los Angeles. It features pool playing, a dancefloor, music videos, a deejay and something going on every night of the week. Cover. ~ 8572 Santa Monica Boulevard; 310-652-6188.

Beverly Hills

Back in 1844 a Spanish woman named Maria Rita Valdez acquired controlling interest over 4500 acres of sagebrush and tumbleweed. Luckily she spent only $17.50 on the transaction. The land was of little worth. Even by the turn of the 20th century it consisted only of lima bean fields, sheep meadows, and a few isolated farmhouses. Plans for wheat cultivation, oil drilling, and a community of German immigrants failed.

Finally in 1912 a group of entrepreneurs, struggling to sell this barren real estate, happened on the idea of building a big hotel to publicize their new housing development. Happily, the fledgling movie industry was already attracting people to neighboring Hollywood and the Beverly Hills Hotel became a rendezvous for rising stars.

Then in 1920, when the undisputed King and Queen of Hollywood, Douglas Fairbanks and Mary Pickford, built their palace on a hill above the hotel, the community's future was secure. Within a few years Gloria Swanson, Charlie Chaplin, Rudolph Valentino, Buster Keaton, John Barrymore, and Will Rogers were neighbors. The dusty farmland, now a town named Beverly Hills, had finally blossomed.

It's a rags-to-riches town with a lot of Horatio Alger stories to tell. The world capital of wealth and glamour, Beverly Hills is a place in which driving a BMW makes you a second-class citizen and where the million-dollar houses are in the poorer part of town. The community with more gardeners per capita than any other United States city, Beverly Hills is one of the few spots outside Texas where flaunting your money is still considered good taste. A facelift here is as common as a haircut and many of the residents look like they've been embalmed for the past 30 years.

Still, it's Beverly Hills. The town has style, history, and an indomitable sense of magic. It's a void that became a constellation; a place where everyone—whether in movies, television, clothes design, or business—is a star.

SIGHTS

It seems only fitting that the gateway to this posh preserve should be along **Santa Monica Boulevard**, a greenbelt with an exotic array of plant life. Each block of this blooming corridor is alive with a variety of vegetation. Trees are closely pruned, shrubs carefully shaped, and the flowers are planted in a succession of colorful beds. Most impressive of all is the landscape of cactus and succulents between Camden and Bedford drives. ~ Between Doheny Drive and Wilshire Boulevard.

Rising near the center of the promenade is **Beverly Hills City Hall,** a Spanish Baroque structure capped with a tile cupola. The foyer of this 1932 building has a recessed ceiling with scroll or-

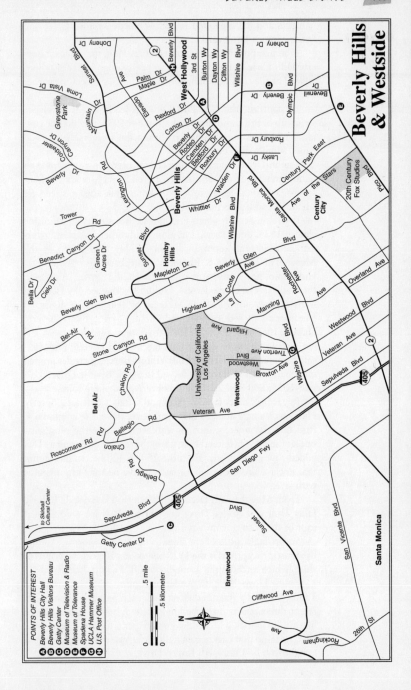

Beverly Hills & Westside

POINTS OF INTEREST
Ⓐ Beverly Hills City Hall
Ⓑ Beverly Hills Visitors Bureau
Ⓒ Getty Center
Ⓓ Museum of Television & Radio
Ⓔ Museum of Tolerance
Ⓛ Spadena House
Ⓛ UCLA Hammer Museum
Ⓗ U.S. Post Office

naments and hand-painted panels. ~ North Rexford Drive and Santa Monica Boulevard.

A contemporary commentary on City Hall, the adjacent **Beverly Hills Civic Center** features a stepped design in Spanish deco style. The tile trim and palm landscape further reflect the earlier building.

By contrast, the **U.S. Post Office** is an Italian Renaissance structure of brick and terra cotta. Built in 1933, the interior contains WPA-type murals popular during the Depression. ~ 9300 Santa Monica Boulevard.

Canon Drive, another horticultural corridor, is a parade of palms stretching for four blocks between Santa Monica and Sunset boulevards. The 80-foot trees lining this august street are Mexican and California sand palms.

If you missed President Franklin D. Roosevelt's first fireside chat in 1933, don't despair. It, along with other events of historical and cultural importance, can be seen and heard at the **Museum of Television & Radio.** You can access over 100,000 TV and radio programs from the '20s to the '90s. This sleek, three-story, classic-modernist building, designed by Richard Meier, is the outpost of the Museum of Television & Radio in Manhattan. Closed Monday and Tuesday. ~ 465 North Beverly Drive; 310-786-1000, fax 310-786-1086; www.mtr.org.

To help find your way around the winding streets of this hillside community, the **Beverly Hills Visitors Bureau** provides printed information. Closed weekends. ~ 239 South Beverly Drive; 310-248-1015, 800-345-2210; www.beverlyhillsbehere.com.

Regardless of its famous faces and stately residences, Beverly Hills has a single address that symbolizes the entire community. **Rodeo Drive,** where wannabes walk with the wealthy, represents one of the most fashionable strips in the world of shopping. This gilded row extends only from the 200 to 400 block, but within that enclave are shops whose names have become synonymous with style.

From May through December, catch the classic-style **Beverly Hills Trolley** at Rodeo Drive and Dayton Way for a docent-led tour of the posh downtown area. Fee. ~ 310-285-2438.

Surprisingly, little of the architecture is noteworthy. Among the artistic exceptions is the 1928 beaux-arts **Regent Beverly Wilshire,** which anchors the avenue. ~ 9500 Wilshire Boulevard.

Frank Lloyd Wright's **Anderton Court,** created during the 1950s, projects a fractured effect with each part angling in a different direction, as if the building were about to split in pieces like a child's block pile. Holding it together is a Guggenheim-type circular ramp that curves past multiple levels of shops to a jagged metal tower. ~ 332 North Rodeo Drive.

Just beyond the commercial district stands the **O'Neill House**, an art nouveau confection reminiscent of the work of Spanish architect Antonio Gaudi. ~ 507 North Rodeo Drive.

For years Hollywood's chief gossip factory was the **Beverly Hills Hotel**, a pink Mission Revival building dating to 1912. During the 1930s the hotel's Polo Lounge attracted Darryl Zanuck, Will Rogers, and other polo enthusiasts. Later its private bungalows became trysting places for celebrities. Howard Hughes, Marilyn Monroe, and Sophia Loren rented them. John Lennon and Yoko Ono holed up for a week here, and Elizabeth Taylor and Richard Burton made love and war. Today the hotel's manicured grounds are tropically landscaped and well worth visiting, even when the stars are not out. ~ 9641 Sunset Boulevard; 310-276-2251, 800-283-8885, fax 310-281-2905; www.thebeverlyhills hotel.com, e-mail sales@beverlyhillshotel.com.

> Marilyn Monroe reportedly entertained John and Robert Kennedy in a very private bungalow at the Beverly Hills Hotel.

The most famous homes in Beverly Hills may be those of the stars, but its most intriguing residence is the **Spadena House**. Built in 1921 as a movie set and office, this "Witch's House" resembles something out of a fairy tale. Its sharp peaked roof, mullioned windows, and cobweb ambience evoke images of Hansel and Gretel. ~ 516 Walden Drive.

By calling in advance you can tour the **Virginia Robinson Gardens**, a six-acre estate landscaped with king palm trees and a variety of gardens. The home here, which is part of the tour, is the oldest house in Beverly Hills, a 1911 Mediterranean Revival structure. Open Tuesday through Friday, by appointment only. Admission. ~ 310-276-5367, fax 310-276-5352.

Greystone Park is the site of a 55-room English Tudor manor built during the 1920s by oil tycoon Edward L. Doheny. Although the house is closed to the public, visitors can stroll through the 18-acre grounds and perhaps take in a summer concert and occasional theater performance (June through September). ~ 905 Loma Vista Drive; 310-550-4654, fax 310-858-9238; www.beverlyhills.org.

LODGING

Despite its standing as one of the wealthiest communities in the nation, Beverly Hills offers at least one low-cost lodging facility. The **Beverly Terrace Hotel** is a 39-unit facility, with accommodations typical of motel digs. Among the amenities are a pool and a restaurant that serves lunch and dinner. The choice location is less than a block from Melrose Avenue. Continental breakfast and free parking are included. ~ 469 North Doheny Drive; 310-274-8141, 800-842-6401, fax 310-385-1998; www. beverlyterracehotel.com, e-mail bthotel@aol.com. MODERATE.

Text continued on page 110.

Hollywood Legends

The favorite sport in Beverly Hills has always been stargazing. Synonymous with glamour, wealth, and fame, the town has been home to actors since the era of silent films. In fact, the best way to trace Hollywood's past is by driving through Beverly Hills.

LOVE—HOLLYWOOD STYLE   Starting at the intersection of Rodeo Drive and Santa Monica Boulevard, drive nine blocks northwest on Santa Monica to North Palm Drive and turn left. That Elizabethan cottage on your right at 508 North Palm Drive was home to **Marilyn Monroe and Joe DiMaggio** in 1954 during their stormy marriage. The couple moved in around April, but by September, when Marilyn was filming *The Seven Year Itch,* the tumultuous tie had already been broken. Continue two blocks up Palm, turn left on Elevado Avenue and then right on North Maple Drive, to see the home of a couple who had a happier and far more enduring marriage. If **George Burns and Gracie Allen**'s place at 720 North Maple Drive looks familiar, that's because a model of the home was used for their 1950s TV show.

TAYLOR–TODD MANSION   Beverly Hills is nothing if not the story of marriages. The bond between **Elizabeth Taylor and Mike Todd** ended tragically in 1958 when Todd's plane crashed over New Mexico. The couple was occupying the Mediterranean-style mansion at 1330 Schuyler Road when the movie producer died. To find it, from George and Gracie's house continue a block north on Maple to Sunset Boulevard; turn right, go two blocks to Hillcrest and make a U-turn to go west on Sunset; take the next right onto Mountain Drive. Take the next right onto Schuyler Road, which skirts **Greystone Park** (page 107); turn right onto Doheny Road, then left to get back on Schuyler. The Taylor-Todd mansion is at Schuyler and Cerrocrest Drive.

LANA'S LOVE NEST   **Lana Turner**'s relationship with mobster Johnny Stompanato didn't last long, either. It seems that after Stompanato threatened Turner's life during a heated argument, her daughter Cheryl Crane stabbed him to death in their prim Colonial house at 730 North Bedford Drive. The even more heated trial that followed drew tremendous press coverage and exposed secrets of the star's love life. To see the scene of the crime, after driving back down the hill to Sunset Boulevard, turn right and drive four blocks west to Beverly Drive. Turn left, drive one block south past Will Rogers Park, and turn right onto Lomitas Avenue. Three blocks down, turn left on Bedford Drive, where the Lana Turner house is on your left in the middle of the block.

NORTH ROXBURY DRIVE   Continue to the end of the block, turn left on Elevado Avenue, then left again at the next block to drive up North Roxbury Drive, a residential street trimmed with trees and lined with 1930s-era estates that celebrities once called home. **Marlene Dietrich** lived in the squarish, art-deco mansion at 822. **Jimmy Stewart** set up residence in the brick Tudor house just across Sunset at 918, while **Lucille Ball** lived at 1000 and **Jack Benny** lived next door at 1002. Benny's brick Colonial home, like Burns and Allen's house, was sometimes filmed in his television show.

CITIZENS HEARST AND GARBO   Continue north on Roxbury Drive as it curves around to the right and becomes Hartford Way. At 1700 Lexington Road, where Hartford and Lexington intersect, is the mansion that newspaper baron William Randolph Hearst purchased during the 1920s for his mistress, **Marion Davies**. Later in the decade **Greta Garbo** and her parrot, four cats, and a chow chow moved into the neighborhood at 1027 Chevy Chase Drive. To get there, backtrack one block on Hartford to Benedict Canyon Drive, turn right, drive one block, and turn left.

TOWER ROAD AND GREEN ACRES   One block farther north on Benedict Canyon Drive, veer right onto Tower Road, which also saw its share of stars. **Juliet Prowse** lived behind the mullioned windows at 1136; **Arthur Rubinstein** occupied 1139; and actor **Spencer Tracy** called 1158 Tower Road home. Two blocks farther north on Benedict Canyon Drive, turn left on Greenacres Drive, where Green Acres, the estate of silent film comedian **Harold Lloyd** at 1740 Green Acres Place, has been reduced to a mere five acres. When Lloyd moved here in 1928 the grounds included 20 acres and were planted with 12 gardens, each following a different theme. The house he occupied until his death in 1971 has 44 rooms, including 26 bathrooms.

FALCON LAIR   Continuing up Benedict Canyon Road, take the second left onto Cielo Drive and follow it to Bella Drive, then turn left and look for the mansion at 1436, where **Rudolph Valentino** sought seclusion from his adoring fans in 1925 by moving here to Falcon Lair (named for his movie *The Hooded Falcon*), a magnificent mansion appointed with Renaissance art, oriental carpets, and medieval armor. Little did the young actor realize when he finally found his retreat that he would die from ulcers the next year.

Located within easy walking distance of Rodeo Drive and Century City, **The Peninsula Beverly Hills** sets the tone for your stay with its light, cream-colored lobby where large windows look out on gardens and a fountain by day and crystal chandeliers cast a soft glow after dark. The 196 guest rooms feature marble baths, French doors, king-size beds, overstuffed chairs, and armoires containing satellite TVs. Guests for whom money is truly no object can opt for one of the 16 villa suites, some with private spas, terraces, and fireplaces. ~ 9882 South Santa Monica Boulevard; 310-551-2888, 800-462-7899, fax 310-788-2319; www.peninsula.com, e-mail pbh@peninsula.com. ULTRA-DELUXE.

HIDDEN ►

Comprising two former apartment houses and the late Beverly Carlton Hotel, whose guest register included such industry legends as Mae West and Marilyn Monroe, the **Avalon Hotel** is one of the hippest and hottest places to stay in Beverly Hills. The mid-20th-century architecture, complete with kidney-shaped pool, cries retro chic. The 86 rooms, suites, and studios are also coolly decorated, and outfitted with VCRs, CD players, and fax machines; a number have private balconies. ~ 9400 West Olympic Boulevard; 310-277-5221, 800-535-4715, fax 310-277-4928; www.avalonbeverlyhills.com. DELUXE.

On a knoll overlooking Beverly Hills is the **Loews Beverly Hills Hotel,** a 12-story building with 137 rooms. The hotel offers a range of amenities including an outdoor swimming pool, health club, and restaurant. The lobby has an airy feel with a front desk inlaid with onyx and mother of pearl. ~ 1224 South Beverwil Drive; 310-277-2800, 800-421-3212, fax 310-277-5470; www.loewshotels.com. ULTRA-DELUXE.

An intimate and stylish alternative is **Maison 140**. A brick Colonial-style structure, it was once owned by silent film star Lillian Gish. Today, each of the 45 guest rooms is furnished in Asian and French vintage style; all have private baths, cable TV, and mini-refrigerators. Add a friendly staff and a comfortable lobby to round out this fine small Beverly Hills hotel. ~ 140 South Lasky Drive; 310-281-4000, 800-432-5444, fax 310-281-4001; www.maison140.com. DELUXE TO ULTRA-DELUXE.

The Mosaic Hotel is an elegant boutique hostelry on a residential street just off Wilshire Boulevard. Rooms are outfitted with king beds, warm wood furniture, plush bedding and marble bathrooms, as well as amenities such as robes, hairdryers, CD players and internet connection; some have private decks that overlook the pool surrounded by lush foliage. You'll also find an exercise room as well as a bar. Breakfast, lunch and dinner are served in the restaurant. ~ 125 South Spalding Drive; 310-278-0303, 800-463-4466, fax 310-278-1728; www.mosaichotel.com, e-mail reservations@mosaichotel.com. ULTRA-DELUXE.

Small and elegant, **Raffles L'Ermitage** is tucked away on a quiet tree-lined street. Only the discreet sign reveals that it's a hotel. A rooftop garden terrace with a 360-degree view has a heated pool and private cabanas for guests' use. Although Raffles L'Ermitage is expensive, you're not dollared to death. ~ 9291 Burton Way; 310-278-3344, 800-800-2113, fax 310-278-8247; www.lermitage hotel.com. ULTRA-DELUXE.

The Regent Beverly Wilshire Hotel, a 1928 beaux-arts building, is another grand old hotel in Beverly Hills. Located at the foot of Rodeo Drive, this landmark features a Wilshire wing with 147 rooms and suites and an adjacent Beverly wing, built during the 1970s. Guest rooms in the Wilshire wing are quite spacious, designed with flair, and possess the character that makes this a great hotel. The 248 rooms and suites in the newer wing are decorated in a Southern California contemporary style. Both sections draw on a full line of amenities, including shops, restaurants, lounges, fitness center, and pool. ~ 9500 Wilshire Boulevard; 310-275-5200, 800-427-4354, fax 310-274-2851; www.fourseasons.com. ULTRA-DELUXE.

DINING

The place to nosh in Beverly Hills is **Nate 'n' Al Deli**, a traditional delicatessen with a complete assortment of kosher dishes. There are bagels, sandwiches on rye and pumpernickel, and a smoked fish plate that includes lox, cod, and whitefish. ~ 414 North Beverly Drive; 310-274-0101, fax 310-274-0485. MODERATE.

With an exterior that looks like a shiny chrome Airstream trailer and an interior full of turquoise- and apricot-colored formica and vinyl, the kitschily retro **Airstream Diner** is about the last place you'd expect to find in Beverly Hills. Diners perch on garden gnome–supported stools, wolfing down such over-the-

AUTHOR FAVORITE

Most Beverly Hills restaurants are places to be seen; **Kate Mantílini** is a place to see. A kind of *Star Wars* diner, this 21st-century rendezvous is an artwork in steel and tile. Jagged edges and angular beams are everywhere; a boxing mural covers an entire wall; and in the center a sundial/skylight rises from floor to dome. For dinner there's rotisserie chicken, meatloaf, lamb shank, frogs' legs, a half dozen steaks, and fresh fish daily. Open for breakfast, lunch, and dinner on weekdays; brunch, lunch, and dinner only on weekends. ~ 9101 Wilshire Boulevard; 310-278-3699, fax 310-273-0863; www.gardensonglendon.com. MODERATE TO ULTRA-DELUXE.

top creations as the Hunka, Hunka Burnin' Love pancakes that come with peanut butter, chocolate chips, and bananas, drizzled with carmel sauce. Kids can make their own peanut-butter-and-jelly sandwiches, and meatloaf takes on a new meaning when covered in cumin ketchup. ~ 9601 Santa Monica Boulevard; 310-550-8883. BUDGET TO MODERATE.

Owned and frequented by celebrities, minimalist in decor, **Maple Drive** has emerged as one of Beverly Hills' top trysts. Here you can dine on a number of American/Continental tidbits while catching the flash and dance of Hollywood on parade. There's live jazz Tuesday through Saturday nights, and a jazz brunch on Sunday. No lunch on Saturday. ~ 345 North Maple Drive; 310-274-9800; www.mapledriverestaurant.com, e-mail info@maple driverestaurant.com. DELUXE TO ULTRA-DELUXE.

Gourmet food, chic surroundings, and beautiful people combine to make **Prego** a popular rendezvous. This Italian trattoria serves pizza, pasta, and several entrées. Among the pizzas are calzones, folded pizzas with smoked mozzarella, and stracchino cheese pizzas. Pasta dishes include *fusilli con luganega* (corkscrew noodles with sausage); entrées feature Italian sausage, veal chops, and fresh fish. The kitchen is open to view and the decor consists of modern artwork along brick walls, track lights, and hardwood trim. No lunch on Sunday. ~ 362 North Camden Drive; 310-277-7346, fax 310-858-7879; www.spectrumfoods.com. MODERATE TO DELUXE.

Ranking among Los Angeles' finest restaurants, **La Scala** is an intimate and well-appointed dining room. Upholstered booths add to an elegant interior where oil paintings are combined with decorative plates. The gourmets and celebrities frequenting this address also come for the excellent Italian cuisine. Among the entrées are spaghetti *alla* cognac, filet mignon, and fresh fish dishes. Closed Sunday. ~ 434 North Canon Drive; 310-275-0579, fax 310-246-9099. MODERATE TO ULTRA-DELUXE.

Spago owner and celebrity chef Wolfgang Puck helped originate California cuisine.

With the possible exception of Berkeley's Chez Panisse, **Spago** is California's most famous restaurant. Spago's incarnation in Beverly Hills, just north of Wilshire Boulevard, offers many of the original restaurant's signature dishes like smoked salmon pizza, but also a slate of new entrées. You can enjoy selections from their daily-changing menu while dining on the open-air patio. No lunch Sunday. ~ 176 North Canon Drive; 310-385-0880. DELUXE TO ULTRA-DELUXE.

SHOPPING Without doubt, the capital of consumerism is Beverly Hills. In the mythic order of things, this gilded neighborhood is a kind of shopper's heaven, where everything sparkles just out of reach.

Often the fun of shopping in Beverly Hills (especially if you're on a budget) is in the people watching.

At the heart of the capital lies the "golden triangle," an exclusive shopping district bounded by Wilshire Boulevard, Rexford Drive, and Santa Monica Boulevard. The heart within the heart is, you guessed it, **Rodeo Drive**. World-famous designer showcases like Gucci, Van Clef and Arpels, Cartier, Louis Vuitton, Giorgio, and Ralph Lauren are part of the scenery on Rodeo Drive. Some are soooo exclusive they open only by appointment.

The breathtaking etchings of Rembrandt are among the rare selections at **Galerie Michael**. ~ 430 North Rodeo Drive; 310-273-3377; www.galeriemichael.com.

The **Rodeo Collection** houses designer boutiques that carry Stephanie Anais and Thalian designs. ~ 421 North Rodeo Drive; 310-858-7580.

The **Barakat** collection of jewelry features an amazing combination of Old World antiquities spanning the globe. This magnificent shop also holds an extensive pre-Columbian art collection. Even the catalog is a collector's item. Closed Sunday. ~ 405 North Rodeo Drive; 310-859-8408; www.barakatgallery.com.

Among the town's chic spots is **Giorgio Armani Boutique**, home of Giorgio perfume and an array of haute couture. ~ 436 North Rodeo Drive; 310-271-5555.

Frances Klein Antique & Estate Jewelry could be the world's most exclusive mom-and-pop store; and there may be enough fine jewelry here to make it the world's first mom-and-pop museum. Closed Sunday. ~ 310 North Rodeo Drive; 310-273-0155.

Tiffany & Co. continues to awe and inspire. ~ 210 North Rodeo Drive; 310-273-8880.

Two Rodeo is a $200-million cobblestone mall featuring about two dozen shops. Built along three levels, it's a brass-door-and-antique-street-lamp promenade reminiscent of a European boulevard. ~ Corner of Rodeo Drive and Wilshire Boulevard.

Beverly Hills supports several dozen art galleries, many located along Rodeo Drive. Most galleries stay open until 10 p.m.

Some of the country's most famous department stores line Wilshire Boulevard between the 9600 and 9900 blocks. **Neiman Marcus** (310-550-5900) and **Saks Fifth Avenue** (310-247-9419) are only part of this elite company.

"Little" Santa Monica Boulevard has less formal, less expensive shops, such as **Susanna**, which features custom-made haute-couture designs for day and evening wear. Closed Sunday. ~ 9647 Little Santa Monica Boulevard; 310-276-7510.

South Robertson Boulevard is home to dozens of small boutiques. At **Lisa Kline**, you can browse through an array of vintage and new clothing for women. ~ 136 South Robertson Boulevard; 310-246-0907.

NIGHTLIFE   Rub elbows with hollywood stars and celebrities of the moment at **The Lounge**. Every Wednesday through Saturday, deejays spin lively tunes to the delight of the crowd. Cover. ~ 9077 Santa Monica Boulevard; 310-888-8811.

At the late-night drinking and dancing Beverly Hills elite goes to **Joya**. This classy dance place really rocks on Wednesday nights and weekends, when a deejay plays everything from hip-hop to R&B. Closed Monday. ~ 242 North Beverly Boulevard; 310-274-4440, fax 310-274-2611.

▼▼▼▼▼▼▼▼▼▼▼▼

Westside   Like Horace Greeley's proverbial pioneer, wealth in Los Angeles has gone west. With its elite country clubs and walled estates, the Westside has developed since the mid-20th century into the city's golden ghetto. Cultural diversity is defined here not so much by race and class as by whether one is already rich or simply striving to be. Business mavens from Bel Air whiz along in Maseratis and co-eds buzz by in battered Toyotas.

At UCLA in Westwood, more than 35,000 students are squeezed into one of the most valuable real-estate districts in the nation. While this campus town is an odd mix of blocky apartment buildings and mundane office towers, Bel Air and Brentwood are exclusive colonies marked by manicured lawns and lofty mansions.

Nearby Century City, a former film studio, has been transformed into a futuristic city with plazas, greenswards, and vaulting highrises. Culver City, the self-proclaimed "Motion Picture Capital of the World" that produced more than half the movies released in the United States during the 1930s and 1940s, still clings to its aging glory with several studios.

SIGHTS   **CENTURY CITY**   If Beverly Hills is the ultimate in residential communities, Century City represents the final word in business centers. Bland as a three-piece suit, this 180-acre highrise heaven is built of office towers and broad boulevards.

The **Century Plaza Hotel** is a twin-tower city in itself, an over 700-room hotel that vies with Century City's other metal-and-glass palaces for prominence.

What today is a corporate version of Las Vegas was once the fabled backlot of 20th Century Fox. While the studio still holds ground in part of the city, it has lost the glamour of its glory days and is closed to the public.

WESTWOOD   To students everywhere, Westwood is the scholastic capital of California. Home to UCLA, one of the largest universities in the country, the town was little more than ranch land in the early 20th century. Originally developed during the 1920s as a Mediterranean-style complex with shops and restaurants,

Westwood boomed when UCLA opened in 1929. Now, with highrises continually springing up along Wilshire Boulevard, it's a major commercial center.

A sense of the old Westwood pervades **Westwood Village**, near the university. Here you can stroll past a succession of shops, many located in 1920s-era buildings of brick and wood. The Village's true identity, however, is revealed on Friday and Saturday nights when major movies are previewed and the place becomes a world of bumper people, with traffic gridlocked and crowds milling everywhere. ~ Centered around Westwood Boulevard.

Of Westwood's countless movie houses, the most inventive by far is **Mann's Village Theatre**, with its lofty tower and Spanish Moderne design. Built in 1931, the landmark features elevated pillars, ornamental scrollwork, and a free-standing box office. ~ 961 Broxton Avenue; 310-208-5576. The proximity of the 1937 **Mann's Bruin Theatre** across the street makes this the city's busiest crosswalk. ~ 948 Broxton Avenue; 310-208-8998.

Just across Le Conte Avenue from this cinema center lies the UCLA **Campus,** an impressive 419-acre enclave. A true multiversity, UCLA has 13 libraries and boasts over 70 separate departments. The grounds are a labyrinth of grand staircases and brick walkways leading past over 100 buildings that (as on most major campuses) constitute an architectural hodge-podge. Next door to classic structures are blocky metal-and-glass highrises reflective of the Bauhaus movement; modern masterpieces stand cheek-by-jowl with utilitarian monstrosities. ~ 310-825-4321, fax 310-206-8460; www.ucla.edu.

To navigate this enormous tree-shaded campus, hop on the **Campus Express,** a campus shuttle service. ~ 310-206-2908.

Ackerman Student Union represents the center of campus activity. **Kerckhoff Hall** next door is the only Gothic-style building on campus, a brick imitation of King Edward VII's Westminster chapel.

TEACHING PEACE

The consequences of intolerance are the focus of the **Museum of Tolerance**. Here enlightening displays reveal the terrible impact of prejudice throughout history; from Nazi Germany to segregation in America. The center utilizes modern multimedia techniques to create stunning audio, visual, and interactive presentations. Computers quiz observers about social justice and responsible citizenship. Holocaust survivors speak daily of their experiences. Closed Saturday. Admission. ~ 9786 West Pico Boulevard; 310-553-8403, 800-900-9036, fax 310-553-4521; www.museumoftolerance.com.

The geographic center of UCLA lies along the quadrangle at the top of **Janss Steps.** Anchoring the corners of the quad are the school's original buildings, magnificent Italian Romanesque structures dating to 1929. **Royce Hall,** a cloister-like building with twin towers and loggia, contains a public auditorium. The **Fowler Museum of Cultural History,** located next to Royce Hall, offers a changing series of exhibitions on world arts and cultures. Closed Monday and Tuesday. ~ 310-825-4361, fax 310-206-7007; www.fowler.ucla.edu, e-mail fowlerws@arts.ucla.edu.

Powell Hall across the rectangle is an ornate, gargoyled Moorish masterwork housing the UCLA **Film and Television Archive Research and Study Center.** This important cultural resource, known as the second largest film and TV archive in the country, has a collection of over 220,000 movies and television shows dating as far back as the silent film era. With advance notice, visitors can view many of the archive films at no charge (as long as they're working on a specific research project). Closed weekends. ~ 310-206-5388, fax 310-206-5392; www.cinema.ucla.edu, e-mail arsc@ucla.edu.

Prettiest place on the entire campus is the **Franklin Murphy Sculpture Garden,** a five-acre park planted with jacaranda trees. Among the more than 70 artworks adorning this greensward are pieces by Arp, Calder, Matisse, Moore, and Rodin. ~ Located near the University Research Library.

Because of its reputation as a university town, Westwood's beautiful residential areas are frequently overlooked. Explore the neighborhood just west of campus and you'll discover the **Tischler House,** a contemporary home designed by Austrian architect Rudolph Schindler in 1949. With a geometric layout and plate-glass prow, the home is like a ship moored in a hillside port. ~ 175 South Greenfield Avenue.

The **Strathmore Apartments,** located several blocks away, were built by Schindler's Viennese colleague, Richard Neutra, in 1937. Among the former tenants of this glass-and-stucco court were Orson Welles and Clifford Odets. ~ 11005 Strathmore Drive.

AUTHOR FAVORITE

The **Mildred Mathias Botanical Garden,** an enchanted spot in the southeastern corner of the UCLA campus, displays nearly 4000 plant species within its eight-acre domain. Focusing on tropical and subtropical vegetation, the glade is filled with lilies and rhododendrons, palms, and cactus. Visits to the **Hannah Carter Japanese Garden,** a Kyoto-style rock garden with teahouse and footbridges, can be arranged through the visitors center. It's about a mile from campus in Bel Air.

Nearby you'll encounter the UCLA **Hammer Museum**, which features lithographs and sculptures by Honoré Daumier as well as paintings by Rembrandt, Van Gogh, Monet, Cassatt, and Chagall. The Hammer also features contemporary artists in all visual media. Closed Monday. Admission. ~ 10899 Wilshire Boulevard; 310-443-7000, fax 310-443-7099; www.hammer.ucla.edu, e-mail hammerinfo@arts.ucla.edu.

In the same building as the Hammer Museum, you'll find the **Grunwald Center for the Graphic Arts**. Dedicated to "works on paper," the collection contains more than 35,000 prints, drawings, and photos. There are works by Dürer, Cézanne, Toulouse-Lautrec, and Picasso, as well as contemporary artists such as June Wayne and Carlos Almaraz. Open by appointment only; closed weekends. ~ 310-443-7076, fax 310-443-7099; www.hammer.ucla.edu.

Tucked away, ironically, behind the Avco cinema complex on Wilshire Boulevard in Westwood is **Pierce Brothers Westwood Village Memorial Park**. This small cemetery is the final resting place for an impressive number of Hollywood legends, including Marilyn Monroe, Dean Martin, Natalie Wood, Burt Lancaster, Peggy Lee, Walter Matthau, and Jack Lemmon. ~ 1218 Glendon Avenue; 310-474-1579.

◄ HIDDEN

BEL AIR AND BRENTWOOD   Beverly Hills, at least the flatland section, seems downright middle-class in comparison with the palatial estates hidden in the hills of Bel Air and Brentwood. Besides posh movie-star homes, these hills also contain two important cultural institutions.

High on a hilltop in the Santa Monica Mountains, the **Getty Center** resembles some kind of postmodern fortress. And with its own freeway exit, to boot. The Getty Center commands attention, like a castle on a hill, a white, gleaming presence on the landscape. Visitors arrive via trams to the Arrival Plaza and continue by foot up the steps to the Entrance Hall—a series of five pavilions connected by glass walkways that provide views of the surrounding hillsides. Visitors can make up their own route through the museum and view the Getty's superb collection of pre-20th-century European sculpture and paintings, French decorative arts, European master drawings, illuminated manuscripts, and photography. Painting galleries on the upper floors have skylights whose louvers admit natural light, approximating the conditions under which pictures were painted and exhibited before the advent of electricity. Closed Monday and major holidays. Parking fee, $5. ~ 1200 Getty Center Drive; 310-440-7300, fax 310-440-7760; www.getty.edu.

The **Skirball Cultural Center** presents a range of visual, literary and performing arts focused on the Jewish Experience. The museum displays include exhibits on the Torah and the Jewish holy days. The archaeology of the Middle East is also represented in a series of artifacts. One imaginative exhibit features simulated dig sites as well as a cut-away that shows how different strata of a hill contain remnants from earlier and earlier civilizations. Closed Monday. Admission. ~ 2701 North Sepulveda Boulevard; 310-440-4500, fax 310-440-4595; www.skirball.org, e-mail info@skirball.org.

Developed during the 1920s by an entrepreneur with a sense of elegance, Bel Air was originally subdivided into plots of several acres, guaranteeing that only the wealthy would need apply. At first even movie people, many of whom were Jewish, were excluded from this elite area. Then during the Depression, with other businesses dying while Hollywood flourished, Bel Air's greed proved stronger than its bigotry. Movie stars began moving in en masse and by the 1940s were rapidly becoming the area's most notable residents.

Shirley Temple's house is next door to the former home of O. J. Simpson. If you slow down for some innocent sightseeing, you may get a ticket for causing congestion.

Humphrey Bogart and Lauren Bacall, who met on the set of *To Have and Have Not* in 1944, settled down together in a brick Colonial house in Bel Air. Bogey was 25 years older than Bacall, but they became one of America's most legendary couples, starring together in *The Big Sleep* (1946), *Dark Passage* (1947), and *Key Largo* (1948). ~ 232 South Mapleton Drive.

The stone mansion at 750 Bel Air Road served for eight seasons as the **"Beverly Hillbillies" House**. This French estate was the prime-time home for one of television's oddest families.

A real-life family, **Judy Garland** and her mother, lived in the red brick house located at 1231 Stone Canyon Road. The childhood star of *The Wizard of Oz* built the place in 1940, equipping it with a badminton court, pinball machines, and her own top-floor suite.

One of Hollywood's most infamous families, **Joan Crawford** and her *Mommie Dearest* daughter Christina, lived in the sprawling Brentwood house at 426 North Bristol Avenue. Crawford moved here in 1929 with her first husband, Douglas Fairbanks, Jr., divorced him in 1934, and went on to marry three more husbands while raising four adopted children. Following the death of her last husband she sold the place in 1959.

A far happier child lived just one block away. During the 1930s **Shirley Temple** and her family moved into the Brentwood mansion at 209 North Rockingham Road. The young actress had already blossomed into the country's archetypal little girl, destined to play the curly-haired beauty in over 20 films and then to become, incongruously, a right-wing politician as an adult.

Cowboys may be buried on Boot Hill, but movie stars are interred in a site overlooking the MGM studios. The celebrities in **Holy Cross Cemetery** have one thing in common—they were all Catholic. Rosalind Russell of *Auntie Mame* fame is here along with Bing Crosby, Jimmy Durante, and Charles Boyer. Bela Lugosi rests nearby; the most macabre tombstone, however, is that of Sharon Tate Polanski and her unborn son Paul, murdered in 1969 by the Charles Manson gang. (Rosalind Russell's grave is marked by the large crucifix near the center of the park; most of the other resting places are near the "grotto" to the left of the entrance.) ~ 5835 West Slauson Avenue, Culver City.

Just one block from the UCLA campus, the **Hotel Claremont** has 53 rooms. These are plain, clean accommodations that share a large lobby. ~ 1044 Tiverton Avenue, Westwood; 310-208-5957, 800-266-5957, fax 310-208-2386. BUDGET.

LODGING

The **Royal Palace Westwood** next door offers 36 guest rooms, many with kitchens. These units are also well maintained and feature private patios. ~ 1052 Tiverton Avenue, Westwood; 310-208-6677, 800-631-0100, fax 310-824-3732; www.royalpalace westwood.com, e-mail lahotels@earthlink.net. MODERATE.

Nearby **Hilgard House Hotel** is a spiffy brick building with 47 rooms and six suites. Accommodations in this three-story structure are furnished with facsimile antiques, plushly carpeted, and attractively decorated with wall hangings; many come equipped with jacuzzi tubs. A complimentary continental breakfast is included. ~ 927 Hilgard Avenue, Westwood; 310-208-3945, 800-826-3934, fax 310-208-1972; www.hilgardhouse.com, e-mail reservations@hilgardhouse.com. DELUXE.

Directly across the street, but a big step uptown, stands the **W Los Angeles**, a 16-floor, all-suite hotel. There are restaurants and lounges steps away from a sumptuous lobby, two pools set in a landscaped garden, plus a complete work-out facility. ~ 930 Hilgard Avenue, Westwood; 310-208-8765, 877-946-8357, fax 310-824-0355; www.whotels.com. ULTRA-DELUXE.

Hotel Del Capri is a bright, cozy complex complete with two tiers of guest rooms encircling a pool terrace, and more suites and rooms in an adjoining tower. The lobby and many of the 79 guest rooms contain modern curvilinear furniture. Many of the tile bathrooms include jacuzzi bathtubs; continental breakfast is served in your room or out by the pool; all suites have kitchenettes; all the beds are adjustable. In sum, a very attractive establishment. ~ 10587 Wilshire Boulevard, West Los Angeles; 310-474-3511, 800-444-6835, fax 310-470-9999; www.hoteldelcapri. com. DELUXE.

Los Angeles' most Eden-like address lies in a forested canyon surrounded by peach and apricot trees. A classic country inn, the

Hotel Bel-Air is an exclusive 91-room complex and private haven for show business celebrities and European royalty. The 1920s Mission-style buildings are shaded by a luxuriant garden of silk floss trees and redwoods. A stream tumbles through the property, creating small waterfalls and a pool with swans. All around is a mazework of archways and footbridges, colonnades, and fountains. Numbering among the nation's finest hotels, the Bel-Air also provides an oval swimming pool, a gym, a gourmet restaurant, a lounge, and a patio terrace. ~ 701 Stone Canyon Road, Bel Air; 310-472-1211, 800-648-4097, fax 310-476-5890; www.hotelbelair.com, e-mail info@hotelbelair.com. ULTRA-DELUXE.

DINING

Sepi's Giant Submarines makes the best submarine sandwiches on the West Side. Half a sandwich is a meal for most humans. ~ 10968 Le Conte Avenue, Westwood; 310-208-7171. BUDGET.

Farther out on Westwood Boulevard, proceeding south from the UCLA campus, there is a string of ethnic restaurants worth trying. **La Bruschetta** serves high Italian cuisine. This gourmet address is filled along several walls with wine racks. Vibrant artwork of recent vintage decorates the place. No lunch on weekends. ~ 1621 Westwood Boulevard, Westwood; 310-477-1052. MODERATE TO DELUXE.

The flavor is Persian at **Shamshiry Restaurant,** a pleasant restaurant with latticework booths and hanging plants. The shish kebab and other Middle Eastern dishes, served at lunch and dinner, are reasonably priced. ~ 1712 Westwood Boulevard, Westwood; 310-474-1410, fax 310-474-3396. MODERATE.

Enjoy *tandoori* chicken and a host of curry dishes prepared in **India's Oven**. It isn't the Taj Mahal—at lunch and dinner you'll dine from plastic plates, but at these prices, who can complain? Closed Monday. ~ 11645 Wilshire Boulevard, Westwood; 310-207-5522, fax 310-820-1467. BUDGET TO MODERATE.

For standard old American fare, head farther out to **The Apple Pan,** a clapboard cottage that contains a single U-shaped counter. Renowned for great burgers, The Apple Pan also serves sandwiches (as in ham, Swiss cheese, and tuna salad) and pies (as in apple, berry, and pecan). Closed Monday. ~ 10801 West Pico Boulevard, West Los Angeles; 310-475-3585. BUDGET.

HIDDEN ►

Mr. Cecil's California Ribs is one of the last places you'd expect to find on the Westside. The exterior looks like a cartoon character–festooned moonshiner's still, and the food is heart stopping. Still, the unadorned barbecued St. Louis baby back and beef ribs are delicious, as are the grilled corn, hushpuppies, and cole slaw that accompany them. ~ 12244 West Pico Boulevard, West Los Angeles; 310-442-1550. BUDGET.

HIDDEN ►

You may have to wait for a table at **La Serenata Gourmet**. This cheery Mexican eatery specializes in fresh fish and gorditas—cornmeal pockets filled with shrimp. ~ 10924 Pico Boulevard, West Los Angeles; 310-441-9667. BUDGET TO MODERATE.

Commercial establishments are rare in residential Bel Air. Finding a restaurant with reasonable prices is even more challenging, especially as you ascend the hills—the farther you climb, the higher the prices become.

At **Four Oaks Restaurant** you encounter a French restaurant that's comfortable and understated. This intimate dining room is illuminated through skylights and features a brick patio for dining alfresco. The constantly evolving fare consists of organically grown ingredients prepared in a modern French-American style. Reservations recommended. Closed Monday. ~ 2181 North Beverly Glen Boulevard, Bel Air; 310-470-2265, 877-804-2788, fax 310-475-5492; www.four oaksrestaurant.com. DELUXE TO ULTRA-DELUXE.

You'll find cafeterias at Ackerman Student Union (310-825-2311) and the North Campus Student Center (310-206-0720). The food will fill your stomach without emptying your purse; beyond that I guarantee nothing. ~ BUDGET.

The restaurant at the Hotel Bel-Air—**The Restaurant**—is so low-key it doesn't even have a name. This is no glitzy, glamorous monument to gastronomy. At the end of a graceful arcade in the hotel's Mission-style main building, its understated decor soothes diners who settle into comfortable Queen Anne chairs. A menu of topnotch Continental/American food caters to the worldly, well-heeled patron looking for a traditional meal in a comfortable atmosphere. Breakfast, lunch, and dinner are served, with brunch on Sunday. ~ 701 Stone Canyon Road, Bel Air; 310-472-1211, 800-648-4097, fax 310-476-5890; www.hotelbelair.com. ULTRA-DELUXE.

SHOPPING

Over in Century City, where broad boulevards and highrise buildings rest on the former lot of 20th Century Fox, there's a 100-store mall complete with boutiques, markets, crafts shops, and international food pavilions. **Westfield Shoppingtown Century City** sprawls across 18 acres, counting among its more glamorous addresses Louis Vuitton, Coach, Kenneth Cole, Tiffany & Co. and the Metropolitan Museum of Art Store. ~ 10250 Santa Monica Boulevard, Century City; 310-553-5300.

Westwood might house UCLA, but this highrise city is a far cry from the typical campus town. Among its cosmopolitan attributes is a shopping district large enough to wear a hole in any shopper's shoes (and purse). **Westwood Village**, adjacent to UCLA, is the Westside's premier shopping and entertainment district. Designed with the pedestrian in mind, "the village" is frequented by college crowds and fashionable Westside residents alike. Student-oriented shops devoted to books, clothes, and accessories combine with cafés and first-run movie theaters to keep the district hopping day and night. ~ Westwood Boulevard.

Bookstores, of course, are a Westwood specialty. Large chain stores and small specialty shops proliferate throughout the neighborhood. Browse the 2000 to 2300 blocks of Westwood Boulevard, affectionately known as "Booksellers Row."

Westside Pavilion, an urban mall designed by the architects of the 1984 Olympics, is a glass atrium affair that spans Westwood Boulevard and contains over 100 shops. Department stores anchor this triple-tiered mall. ~ 10800 West Pico Boulevard, West Los Angeles; 310-474-6255; www.westsidepavilion.com.

Boys and girls with dreams of the great outdoors can chart a course to **Adventure 16, Inc**. Catering to the wilderness enthusiast, this shop can outfit you for rock climbing and backpacking. The inventory for adventurers includes clothing, camping equipment, luggage, and travel gear. ~ 11161 West Pico Boulevard, West Los Angeles; 310-473-4574; www.adventure16.com.

Not far from Westwood, in a hillside setting complete with country estates, lies the town of Brentwood. Commercial establishments in this well-heeled community center around San Vicente Boulevard, a beautiful tree-lined street. **P. J. London** is Brentwood's ultimate resale shop, offering designer clothes handed down from wealthy Westside and Malibu residents. ~ 11661 San Vicente Boulevard; 310-826-4649; www.pjlondon.com. **Brentwood Country Mart**, a village-style shopping complex, features several dozen stores. Closed Sunday. ~ 26th Street and San Vicente Boulevard; 310-395-6714. **del Mano Gallery** displays three-dimensional artwork and fine crafts by American artists. Here you'll find a beautiful collection of ceramics, blown glass, and other media. Closed Monday. ~ 11981 San Vicente Boulevard; 310-476-8508; www.delmano.com.

Shopping in Culver City, on the other hand, centers around **Fox Hills Mall**, a modern, 140-store center anchored by large department stores. ~ Slauson Avenue and Sepulveda Boulevard; 310-390-5073. There are more dads than lads at **Allied Model Trains**, a toy wonderland and replica of the Los Angeles Union Station that's filled with every type of model train imaginable. Closed Sunday except in December. ~ 4411 South Sepulveda Boulevard; 310-313-9353; www.alliedmodeltrains.com.

AUTHOR FAVORITE

One of the largest independent bookstores in the city, **Dutton's Brentwood** is a bibliophile's dream come true (not to mention lovers of CDs and CD-ROMs). The store features a café, and has one of the best selections of greeting cards around. ~ 11975 San Vicente Boulevard, Brentwood; 310-476-6263, 800-388-8667; www.duttonsbrentwood.com.

Westchester Faire Antique Mall, a massive marketplace, houses about 70 shops selling antiques, collectibles, and jewelry. ~ 8655 South Sepulveda Boulevard, Westchester; 310-670-4000. **The Place and Company**, one of the best resale stores in the city, carries a large selection of top-designer fashions. Closed Sunday. ~ 8820 South Sepulveda Boulevard, Westchester; 310-645-1539.

Westwood Village, located at the heart of Westwood a few strides from the UCLA campus, bubbles with nighttime activity. Students and moviegoers crowd the sidewalks and spill into the streets. While many are headed to the first-run movie theaters for which this college town is known, some frequent the local clubs.

NIGHTLIFE

Geffen Playhouse, a 500-seat Egyptian-style "event theater," produces classic plays and often showcases world premieres. ~ 10886 Le Conte Avenue, Westwood; 310-208-5454; www.gef fenplayhouse.com.

The **UCLA Center for the Performing Arts** holds performances on campus. ~ 405 Hilgard Avenue, Westwood; 310-825-4401; www.cto.ucla.edu.

The "equity-waiver" **Odyssey Theatre** offers avant-garde productions by a variety of playwrights. ~ 2055 South Sepulveda Boulevard, West Los Angeles; 310-477-2055.

San Francisco Saloon and Grill is a small, intimate bar. Wood paneling, historic photos of San Francisco, and comfortable surroundings create a sense of intimacy. ~ 11501 West Pico Boulevard, West Los Angeles; 310-478-0152.

A formerly 1950s-type dive, the **Arsenal Restaurant & Lounge** has been remodeled and reinvented as a hip nightspot. Divided into three rooms (a happening bar, a cozy red-boothed dining room, and an open-air "smoking" patio), the music is loud—there's a deejay on the weekends—and the crowd youngish and lively. ~ 12012 West Pico Boulevard, West Los Angeles; 310-575-5511.

◄ HIDDEN

Hidden in a forested Bel Air canyon, **The Bar** at the Hotel Bel-Air is the perfect place for an intimate cocktail. Piano music from this wood-paneled den wafts onto the patio and out across the garden, waterfall, and pond. ~ 701 Stone Canyon Road, Bel Air; 310-472-1211, fax 310-476-5890; www.hotelbelair.com.

San Fernando Valley

Sprawling across 220 square miles and containing a population of more than 1.3 million suburbanites, the San Fernando Valley is an inland version of Los Angeles. This mirror image across the mountains, known simply as "The Valley," is a smog-shrouded gridwork of tract homes and shopping malls, a kind of stucco version of the American Dream. The dream was disturbed in January

1994 when a devastating 6.8 earthquake rolled through the region, but today life has returned to normal.

Bounded by the Santa Monica Mountains to the south and the San Gabriels on the east, The Valley first entered the history books in 1796 when Spanish padres established the San Fernando Mission, an isolated outpost which became a cultural center for the *ranchos* that soon sprang up between the mountains.

If you're lucky a film crew will be shooting a commercial, a television show, or even a movie while you're visiting Paramount Ranch.

During the 1870s, when the Spanish land grants were subdivided and the railroad entered the area, the San Fernando region enjoyed its first boom. But the major escalation in population and real-estate prices came early the next century during one of the biggest scandals in Los Angeles history.

When Los Angeles. voters passed a $1.5 million bond issue in 1905 to buy water-rich land in the distant Owens Valley, they believed they were bringing water to their own parched city. In fact much of this liquid gold poured into the San Fernando Valley, filling the coffers of a cabal of civic leaders who bought up surrounding orange groves and transformed them into housing developments.

In 1914, when Universal turned a 230-acre chicken ranch into a world-acclaimed movie studio, The Valley found a home industry. With its stark mountains and open spaces, the place proved an ideal location for filming Westerns. Columbia, Warner Brothers, and other television and movie studios eventually arrived, as the San Fernando Valley began rivaling that celluloid center on the far side of the Hollywood Hills.

By the post–World War II era, the aerospace industry had landed in The Valley, adding money and glamour to an area fast becoming a kind of promised land for the middle class. With its checkerboard lawns and prefab houses, the place is now the West Coast answer to middle America, with parents who commute to Los Angeles and kids who commute to the nearest shopping mall.

SIGHTS   **UNIVERSAL CITY** Universal Citywalk is a two-block-long pedestrian mall that connects the Universal Studios Hollywood theme park (see "Hollywood in Action") and Amphitheater to the Cineplex Odeon movie theaters. Although the emphasis is on shops and restaurants, you can stroll down the middle of this "city street" and enjoy a collection of vintage neon signs and wacky, eclectic architecture. Street performers entertain visitors nightly, and in the central court, children enjoy darting in and out of jets of water shooting up from the sidewalk fountain. ~ 100 Universal Center Drive, Universal City; 818-622-4455, fax 818-622-0407; www.universalstudios.com.

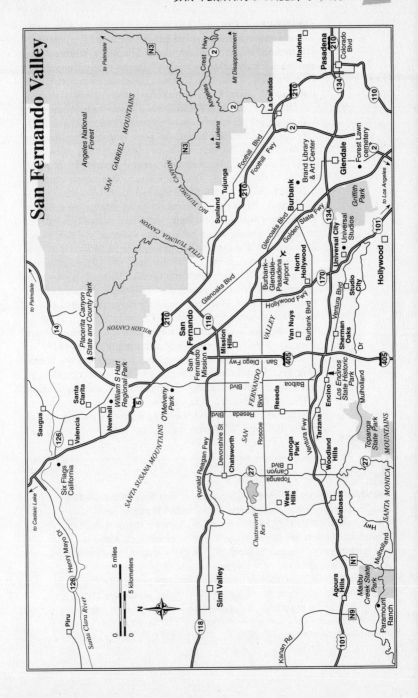

San Fernando Valley

VENTURA BOULEVARD   Only in the San Fernando Valley could a single street define an entire geographic area. Running from east to west along the southern edge of The Valley, Ventura Boulevard parallels the Santa Monica Mountains as it passes through Universal City, Studio City, Sherman Oaks, and Encino, then continues to the distant towns of Calabasas and Agoura.

Along the way you'll encounter a house called **Campo de Cahuenga**, a 1923 re-creation of a building constructed in 1845. Of little architectural interest, the place is noteworthy because the treaty ending the Mexican War in California was signed here by Lt. Col. John C. Fremont and General Andrés Pico in 1847. Closed to the public. ~ 3919 Lankershim Boulevard, Universal City; 818-763-7651, fax 818-756-9963.

Several phases of San Fernando Valley life are preserved at **Los Encinos State Historic Park**. This five-acre facility is studded with orange trees, which covered the valley at the turn of the 20th century. The De La Osa Adobe, built in 1850 and utilized as a resting place along El Camino Real, is a squat eight-room ranch house. Nearby stands the Garnier Building, a two-story limestone residence constructed in 1872 after the fashion of a French farmhouse. However, the buildings that serve as a visitors center and museum remain closed. With its duck pond and shaded lawns, the park is a choice spot for a picnic. Closed Monday and Tuesday. ~ 16756 Moorpark Street, Encino; 818-784-4849.

Making these old houses seem like youngsters is the **Encino Oak Tree**. With branches spreading 150 feet and a trunk eight feet thick, this magnificent specimen dates back about 1000 years. ~ Ventura Boulevard and Louise Avenue, Encino.

Farther out in The Valley lies the town of Calabasas, which prides itself on a Wild West heritage but looks suspiciously like

sights

AUTHOR FAVORITE

Among the finest of California's missions, **San Fernando Mission** has been beautifully restored and reconstructed. Exploring the gardens and courtyards of this 1797 institution, visitors encounter the workshops of weavers, blacksmiths, and carpenters, as well as an excellent collection of altar furnishings and religious oil paintings. One of the chapels, rebuilt after an earthquake, is decorated with trompe l'oeil murals while another is literally covered with gilded appointments, as if God were somehow more receptive to baroque icons. At the rear of this complex lies the site that best symbolizes the experience of the neophyte Indians who struggled and suffered here—the cemetery. Admission. ~ 15151 San Fernando Mission Boulevard, Mission Hills; 818-361-0186, fax 818-361-3276.

surrounding suburban towns. It does possess a few remnants from its romantic past, including the **Leonis Adobe,** an 1844 mud-brick house that was expanded around 1879 into a stately two-story home with porches on both levels. This Monterey-style beauty stands beside the **Plummer House,** an antique Victorian home. There's also an 1880s-era Victorian rose garden. Closed Monday and Tuesday. Admission. ~ 23537 Calabasas Road, Calabasas; 818-222-6511, fax 818-222-0862; www.loomis adobemuseum.org, e-mail leonisadobe@aol.com.

An ersatz but enchanting version of the Old West awaits at **Paramount Ranch,** a 750-acre park that once served as the film location for Westerns. Paramount owned the spread for two decades beginning in the 1920s, using it as a set for *Broken Lullaby* (1932) with Lionel Barrymore, *Thunder Below* (1932) with Tallulah Bankhead, and *Adventures of Marco Polo* (1937), the Samuel Goldwyn extravaganza that included a fortress, elephants, and 2000 horses. During the heyday of TV Westerns in the 1950s, the property was a location for "The Cisco Kid," "Bat Masterson," and "Have Gun, Will Travel."

Today you can hike around the ranch, past the rolling meadows, willow-lined streams, grassy hillsides, and rocky heights that made it such an ideal set. "Paramount Ranch" still stands, a collection of falsefront buildings that change their signs depending on what's being filmed. ~ In Santa Monica Mountains National Recreation Area; 805-370-2301, fax 805-370-1850; www.nps. gov/samo.

Orcutt Ranch Horticultural Center, once a private estate, is now a 24-acre historical monument in full bloom. You'll see a ranch house (not open to the public), rose gardens, and citrus orchards. You can wander through the oak groves, enjoying a vision of the San Fernando Valley before the advent of suburbia. ~ 23600 Roscoe Boulevard, West Hills; 818-346-7449, fax 818-346-0376.

NORTH SAN FERNANDO VALLEY The **Tujunga Wash Mural,**   ◄ *HIDDEN* one of the Southland's local wonders, is reputedly the world's longest mural. Extending for one-half mile along the wall of a flood control channel, it portrays the history of California from prehistoric times to the present. Bright-hued panels capture the era of American Indians and early Spanish explorers, the advent of movies, and the terrors of World War II. ~ On Coldwater Canyon Boulevard between Burbank Boulevard and Oxnard Street, North Hollywood.

In Mission Hills stands Los Angeles' second oldest house. Built before 1834 by mission Indians, the **Andrés Pico Adobe** is a prime example of Spanish architecture. Possessing both beauty and strength, it's a simple rectangular structure with a luxurious courtyard. ~ 10940 Sepulveda Boulevard, Mission Hills.

Just in case you thought Los Angeles County was entirely urban, there are 350 acres of oak forest and native chaparral at **Placerita Canyon State and County Park**. A stream runs through the property and there are hiking trails and a nature center. ~ 19152 Placerita Canyon Road, Newhall; 661-259-7721, fax 661-254-1426; www.placerita.org.

Over at **William S. Hart Regional Park** there's another 260-acre spread once owned by a great star of silent Westerns. A Shakespearean actor who turned to cinema—starring in his last feature, *Tumbleweeds*, in 1925—William S. Hart left his mansion and estate to the movie-going public.

While much of the property is wild, open to hikers and explorers, the most alluring features are the buildings. The old ranch house, once Hart's office, contains photos of friends and mementos from his career. The central feature is Hart's home, a 22-room Spanish hacienda filled with guns, cowboy paintings, and collectibles from the early West. ~ 24151 North San Fernando Road, Newhall; 661-259-0855, fax 661-253-2170.

HIDDEN ► California's haunting history of earthquakes is evident at **Vasquez Rocks County Park**, where faulting action has compressed, folded, and twisted giant slabs of sandstone. Tilted to 50° angles and rising 150 feet, these angular blocks create a setting that has been used for countless Westerns as well as science fiction films such as *Star Trek* (1979) and *Star Wars* (1977).

Tataviam Indians first lived among these natural rock formations over 4000 years ago. During the 1870s the infamous bandito Tiburcio Vasquez hid amid the caves and outcroppings to elude sheriff's deputies. A kind of Mexican Robin Hood, Vasquez gave his name to the rocks when he shot it out with lawmen here and escaped, only to be captured and hanged later. ~ Escondido Road, northeast of Newhall off Route 14; 661-268-0840, fax 661-268-1343.

To explore this parched and rocky terrain further, head up into **Bouquet Canyon** (Bouquet Canyon Road), a curving, lightly wooded valley with hiking trails and picnic areas. **San Francisquito Canyon** (San Francisquito Canyon Road) is a river-carved valley that parallels Bouquet Canyon. Back in 1928 the Saint Francis Dam collapsed, inundating this quiet canyon and killing more than 400 people in one of the worst natural disasters in United States history. Today it's a placid mountain valley providing ample opportunities to wander. Like Bouquet Canyon it lies outside Saugus near a region appropriately tagged Canyon Country.

Six Flags California encompasses Six Flags Magic Mountain, a quintessential roller-coaster park, and Six Flags Hurricane Harbor, a family-oriented water park featuring water slides and a wave pool. Though adjacent to one another, Magic Mountain and Hurricane Harbor are separate parks with their own entrances and admission fees, not to mention distinct personalities.

Spreading across 260 acres and featuring more than 100 rides, shows, and attractions, *Six Flags Magic Mountain* is an entertainment center featuring everything from picnic areas to danceclubs to super-thrill rides. Take for instance "Superman the Escape." It's an exceptional adventure-filled ride that accelerates from 0 to 100 miles per hour in seven seconds and rockets up a 41-story tower, then freefalls back down. "Viper," a 188-foot-high megacoaster, takes you on three vertical loops, plus a boomerang and corkscrew, all experienced at 70 miles per hour. The newest addition "Scream" offers seven 360-degree inversions while fearless riders are strapped into flying chairs or bottomless trains. At a speed of 65-miles-per-hour and a length of 4000 feet, it's a ride that's sure to thrill and chill the heartiest of coaster fans. There are also gentler rides for small children, such as the classic 1912 carousel.

> At one point during the Superman the Escape ride, you'll experience 4.5 Gs before you go into weightlessness for six and a half seconds.

Hurricane Harbor is a fantasy entertainment environment of lost lagoons and pirate coves that was designed with children in mind; one attraction doesn't even allow adults. Of the five themed areas there's "Castaway Cove," a large water play area with slides, waterfalls, and swings. On a raft, you can float along on the "River Cruise," a 1300-foot-long lazy river that surrounds Castaway Cove and Shipwreck Shores. A wave pool called "Forgotten Sea" generates two-foot waves and is up to six feet deep. "Taboo Tower," with a 325-foot enclosed spiraling slide, is one of the four water slides in Hurricane Harbor. Call ahead to check their schedule (Hurricane Harbor is open May through September). Admission. ~ 26101 Magic Mountain Parkway, Valencia; 661-255-4100, fax 661-255-4817.

GLENDALE AND BURBANK   The portal to the land of the living, some say, is through the gates of death. In the San Fernando Valley that would be **Forest Lawn**, one of the most spectacular cemeteries in the world.

Within the courtyards of this hillside retreat are replicas of Michelangelo's "David," Ghiberti's "Baptism of Jesus," and a mosaic of John Trumbull's painting "The Signing of the Declaration of Independence." There are also re-creations of a 10th-century English church and another from 14th-century Scotland. The museum houses a collection consisting of every coin mentioned in the Bible. "The Crucifixion," the nation's largest religious painting, a tableau 195 feet long and 45 feet high, is also on display.

Death has never been prouder or had more for which to be prideful. On the one hand, Forest Lawn is quite beautiful, a parkland of the dead with grassy slopes and forested knolls, a garden planted with tombstones. On the other, it is tasteless, a theme park of the dead where the rich are buried amid all the pomp their heirs can muster. ~ 1712 South Glendale Avenue, Glendale; 818-241-4151, fax 323-551-5073.

HIDDEN ►   The **Casa Adobe de San Rafael** is a single-story, mud-brick home built in the 19th century. Once occupied by the Los Angeles County Sheriff, the hacienda's chief feature is the grounds, which are trimly landscaped and covered with shade trees. The house itself is furnished in Early California style. ~ 1330 Dorothy Drive, Glendale.

Situated in the foothills overlooking Glendale is the **Brand Library & Art Center**. Neither the library nor the galleries are exceptional, but both are located in **El Miradero**, a unique 1904 mansion modeled after the East Indian Pavilion of the 1893 Columbian World Exposition. With bulbous towers, crenelated archways, and minarets, the building is Saracenic in concept, combining Spanish, Moorish, and Indian motifs. The grounds also include a spacious park with nature trails and picnic areas as well as "The Doctor's House," a heavily ornamented 1890 Queen Anne Eastlake Victorian. Closed Sunday and Monday. ~ 1601 West Mountain Street, Glendale; 818-548-2051, fax 818-548-5079.

Blinded by the glitz and glamour of Tinsel Town, most visitors overlook the unassuming, Ozzie-and-Harriet suburb of **Burbank**, located in the San Fernando Valley about ten miles north of downtown Los Angeles. This is, however, where the majority of "Hollywood" films and television shows are shot—NBC, Warner Bros., and Walt Disney Productions all have studios here (see "Hollywood in Action" earlier in this chapter for information on studio tours). With this in mind, keep an eye open if you spend time here: having lunch at an eatery near the studios or browsing through a local bookstore might just lead to a chance spotting of a star from "ER" or "Will & Grace" taking a breather between tapings.

LODGING   Universal City, the center for tours of Universal Studio, is big on highrise hotels. Among the most luxurious is the **Universal City Hilton and Towers**, a 24-story steel-and-glass structure overlooking the San Fernando Valley. Guest rooms are contemporary in decor and feature plate-glass views of the surrounding city. Among the amenities are one restaurant, two lounges, shops, a pool, a jacuzzi, and a exercise room. ~ 555 Universal Terrace Parkway, Universal City; 818-506-2500, 800-445-8667, fax 818-509-2058. DELUXE TO ULTRA-DELUXE.

The **Coast Anabelle Hotel** offers a fresh look reminiscent of a posh European-style hostelry. Designed to accommodate visitors to the nearby NBC and Warner Bros. studios, its 47 guest rooms and suites are traditionally furnished in warm color schemes. The staff, which seems to almost outnumber the guests, prides itself on friendliness. ~ 2011 West Olive Avenue, Burbank; 818-845-7800, 800-633-1144, fax 818-845-0054; www.coasthotels. com. DELUXE.

A subtle charm pervades the atmosphere at **Sportsmen's Lodge Hotel**. Hidden within this English country–style establishment are gardens with waterfalls and foot-bridges, as well as a swan-filled lagoon. The interior courtyard contains an Olympic-sized swimming pool and the lobby features shops, restaurants, and a pub. Numbering about 200 rooms (each with private patio and room service), the hotel is worth its price. ~ 12825 Ventura Boulevard, Studio City; 818-769-4700, 800-821-8511; www.sl hotel.com, e-mail information@slhotel.com. DELUXE TO ULTRA-DELUXE.

Ventura Boulevard, a major thoroughfare in The Valley, is chockablock with motels. Passing through Sherman Oaks, Encino, and Tarzana, you'll find a multitude of possibilities. Among the more upscale motels is **St. George Motor Inn**, a 57-unit, mock-Tudor facility. Microwaves and refrigerators are in every room, and a pool and spa are on the premises. ~ 19454 Ventura Boulevard, Tarzana; 818-345-6911, 800-845-8919, fax 818-996-2955; www.stgeorgemotorinn.com, e-mail stgeorge@aol. com. MODERATE.

Adding to the Valley's hospitality industry is the 15-story **Woodland Hills Hilton**. The updated art-deco look extends from the lobby to the 325 guest rooms and suites. Suites offer wet bars; other amenities include a restaurant and sports bar. ~ 6360 Canoga Avenue, Woodland Hills; 818-595-1000, 800-922-2400, fax 818-595-1003, www.woodlandhills.hilton.com. ULTRA-DELUXE.

SLUMBER IN STYLE

The Safari Inn is that rarest of creatures, a motel with soul. In fact this 55-room facility also possesses a pool, restaurant, and lounge. The film location for several movies, it offers rooms and suites decorated in high '50s style. The amenities and accoutrements here are definitely a step above those of a roadside motel. ~ 1911 West Olive Avenue, Burbank; 818-845-8586, 800-633-1144, fax 818-845-0054; www.coasthotels.com. MODERATE.

DINING

One of Southern California's great restaurant strips, Ventura Boulevard stretches for miles along the southern rim of The Valley, offering fine kitchens all along the route.

The decor at **Teru Sushi** is as inviting as the cuisine. Hand-painted walls and carved figures combine with slat booths and a long dark wood sushi bar. The sushi menu includes several dozen varieties; they also serve a selection of traditional dishes. There is a beautiful garden dining area with a koi pond. No lunch on Saturday and Sunday. ~ 11940 Ventura Boulevard, Studio City; 818-763-6201, fax 818-763-5016; www.terusushi.com. DELUXE TO ULTRA-DELUXE.

For Belgian cuisine and charming intimacy try **Mon Grenier**. With a name that translates as "my attic," this whimsical dining room has a solid reputation for fine cuisine. Entrées include pepper steak, crispy duck, tenderloin of ostrich, and salmon in crust. Dinner only. Closed Sunday. ~ 18040 Ventura Boulevard, Encino; 818-344-8060, fax 818-993-9634; e-mail mongrenier18040@aol.com. DELUXE TO ULTRA-DELUXE.

The **Sagebrush Cantina** is a sprawling restaurant and bar with ample patio space. In addition to an assortment of Mexican dishes they feature steak, salads, and seafood. ~ 23527 Calabasas Road, Calabasas; 818-222-6062, fax 818-222-6053. BUDGET TO DELUXE.

Way up in the Santa Monica Mountains, that rocky spine separating the San Fernando Valley from the ocean, you'll uncover a rare find at **Saddle Peak Lodge**. A true country lodge, this antique building is constructed of logs lashed together with leather straps. Flintlocks and trophy heads adorn the walls and leather upholstered chairs surround a stone fireplace. Open for dinner and Sunday brunch, the restaurant offers a varied assortment from roasted elk tenderloin to grilled duck. If you have the time, it merits the mountain drive. Closed Monday and Tuesday. ~ 419 Cold Canyon Road, Calabasas; 818-222-3888, fax 818-222-1054; www.saddlepeaklodge.com, e-mail spl@saddlepeaklodge.com. ULTRA-DELUXE.

AUTHOR FAVORITE

All the critics agree that the food at **Anajak Thai** is outstanding. The menu features more than four dozen noodle, curry, beef, and chicken dishes. Small and comfortable, the restaurant is painted mauve and decorated with white latticework and Asian art. No lunch on Saturday and Sunday. Closed Monday. ~ 14704 Ventura Boulevard, Sherman Oaks; 818-501-4201, fax 818-501-7623. BUDGET.

Over at **Delhi Palace** you can dine on affordable Indian cuisine. Cloth napkins and Asian decor are part of the bargain at this excellent restaurant. The dishes include lamb curry, chicken *tandoori*, and many vegetarian dishes. ~ 22323 Sherman Way, Canoga Park; 818-992-0913, fax 818-992-0944. BUDGET TO DELUXE.

If meat seems inappropriate just **Follow Your Heart** to a vegetarian restaurant and natural foods market popular with folks from miles around. Specialties at this gathering place include stir-fry, deep-dish pizza, nutburgers, black bean and tofu tacos, and steamed organic vegetables. Open for breakfast, lunch, and dinner. ~ 21825 Sherman Way, Canoga Park; 818-348-3240, fax 818-348-1509; www.followyourheart.com. BUDGET TO MODERATE.

Ask anyone in the Valley where to go for downhome cooking and they will tell you **Dr. Hogly Wogly's Tyler Texas Bar-B-Que**. It's just a regular old café that happens to serve delicious brisket of beef and stick-to-the-ribs ribs. Dinner comes with half a loaf of home-baked bread and your choice of baked beans, cole slaw, potato salad, or macaroni salad. Chow down! ~ 8136 Sepulveda Boulevard, Van Nuys; 818-780-6701. MODERATE TO DELUXE.

◀ HIDDEN

Another conversation piece is the **94th Aero Squadron**, a wildly imaginative establishment obliquely modeled after a World War I aviation headquarters in France. The building resembles a provincial French farmhouse, but it's surrounded by charred airplanes and other artifacts of war. The interior is a sandbagged warren with wings and propellers dangling from the ceiling. The cuisine, which somehow seems irrelevant, is American. Prime rib, Cajun shrimp, and "farmhouse" chicken are regulars on the menu. There's also Saturday and Sunday brunch. ~ 16320 Raymer Avenue, Van Nuys; 818-994-7437, fax 818-994-0442. MODERATE TO DELUXE.

A small Japanese restaurant, **Aoba**, contains a sushi bar and fewer than a dozen tables. The menu offers a standard array of Japanese dishes, including teriyaki entrées, tempura specials, and, of course, sushi. ~ 239 North Brand Boulevard, Glendale; 818-247-9789, fax 818-247-9486. MODERATE.

Out in "The Valley," shopping is such popular sport that the area has bred a new species—"mallies"—who inhabit the shopping malls from the moment the stores open until the second they close.

SHOPPING

VENTURA BOULEVARD   Cities blend into one another on Ventura Boulevard, the busy east–west corridor that stretches across the entire southern rim of the San Fernando Valley. Shops line every point along the thoroughfare, with only subtle distinctions marking changes in locale. Start in Studio City and you'll find your credit cards still working in Sherman Oaks, Encino, Tarzana, and points west.

Traders of Studio City may not look like a pawnshop, but a hock shop it is. You'll find everything from bangles to cameras at this secondhand store. Closed Sunday. ~ 12238 Ventura Boulevard, Studio City; 818-985-6136.

Strange as it may sound here in Shopperland, there are no department stores at **Encino Town Center** and **Plaza de Oro**. These multitiered plazas provide for more relaxed shopping. Within these open-air facilities are several novel stores offering everything from clothing to chocolate, as well as the Valley's only cinema offering foreign films. ~ 17200 and 17171 Ventura Boulevard, Encino.

Specializing in 19th-century works, **Charles Hecht Gallery** offers a museum-quality selection of impressionist paintings. This exemplary gallery also features work by other artistic schools. Closed Monday. ~ 18584 Ventura Boulevard, Tarzana; 818-881-3218; www.hechtgalleries.com.

Out in the Western-style town of Calabasas, a two-block shopping area offers a chance to browse. Wander **Calabasas Road** and you'll discover a variety of small, one-of-a-kind shops.

GLENDALE AND BURBANK   Glendale shopping centers around the **Glendale Galleria**, a mammoth 240-store complex anchored by such heavies as **Macy's** (818-240-8411) and **Nordstrom** (818-502-9922). A host of apparel stores, specialty shops, knickknack stores, and restaurants offer variety, if not imagination. ~ Central Avenue and Broadway, Glendale.

If it happens to be the first Sunday of the month, add the **Glendale Civic Auditorium** to your list of must-see addresses. That's when more than 80 antique dealers gather to sell their wares. Admission. ~ 1401 North Verdugo Road, Glendale; 818-548-2147; www.ci.glendale.ca.us.

A promised land for browsers is **Glendale Costumes**, which rents over 60,000 costumes from the tights of Renaissance dandies to the tights of Batman. Closed Sunday and Monday. ~ 746 West Doran Street, Glendale; 818-244-1161.

Burbank is not really geared to shopping, with the exception of San Fernando Boulevard between San Jose and Tujunga avenues. Home to several used bookstores, the area includes **Movie World**, which adds volumes about movies to its inventory of books. ~ 212 North San Fernando Boulevard, Burbank; 818-846-0459.

For New Age titles consider stopping in at the **Psychic Eye Book Store**. Decorated with crystals and Asian statuary, it carries volumes on metaphysics, palmistry, numerology, and the occult. ~ 1011 West Olive Avenue, Burbank; 818-845-8831; www.pebooks.com.

NIGHTLIFE   **UNIVERSAL CITY**   The **Lobby Bar** at the Universal City Hilton and Towers represents a choice piano bar. ~ 555 Universal Terrace Parkway, Universal City; 818-506-2500.

The **Baked Potato** serves up contemporary jazz and blues every night. If you want to rub shoulders with L.A. music heavies, this is the place. It's also the place to sample one of 21 different kinds of baked spuds. Cover. ~ 3787 Cahuenga West Boulevard, Studio City; 818-980-1615; www.thebakedpotato.com.

VENTURA BOULEVARD   Representative of the gay scene in The Valley are four Studio City clubs. **Oil Can Harry's** is a country-and-western club that offers dance lessons on Tuesday and Thursday, open dancing on Friday, and retro disco dancing on Saturday. ~ 11502 Ventura Boulevard, Studio City; 818-760-9749.

Apache Territory is the area's most popular gay disco. Occasional cover. ~ 11608 Ventura Boulevard, Studio City; 818-506-0404.

The outdoor patio and country atmosphere at **Sagebrush Cantina** draw steady crowds. Here you can sip margaritas, linger after sunset and, on weekends, work out on the sawdust floors to rock bands. ~ 23527 Calabasas Road, Calabasas; 818-222-6062.

NORTH SAN FERNANDO VALLEY   The Valley is a prime place for jazz. For live jazz nightly, try **The Money Tree**, located just outside of Burbank. ~ 10149 Riverside Drive, Toluca Lake; 818-752-8383.

Norah's Place is an altogether different experience. This lively Bolivian supper club serves up tango music. In between sets by the resident band the dancefloor fills with dancers moving to merengue, cumbia, and salsa tunes on Saturday nights. Closed Monday and Tuesday. Cover. ~ 5667 Lankershim Boulevard, North Hollywood; 818-980-6900.

GLENDALE AND BURBANK   **Jax Bar & Grill**, with its brass elephants and local clientele, is a supper club where notable jazz musicians headline nightly. ~ 339 North Brand Boulevard, Glendale; 818-500-1604.

For sophisticated entertainment there's the **Glendale Centre Theatre**, which presents musicals and comedies. ~ 324 North Orange Street, Glendale; 818-244-8481; www.glendalecentre theatre.com.

AUTHOR FAVORITE

The **L.A. Connection Comedy Theatre** developed a unique comedy concept several years back. They show camp film classics with house comedians ad-libbing the dialogue. Other shows include regular audience participation improvisation. Closed Monday through Wednesday. Cover. ~ 13442 Ventura Boulevard, Sherman Oaks; 818-784-1868; www.laconnectioncomedy.com.

The **Third Stage** is a comedy and improv venue. Closed Monday. ~ 2811 West Magnolia Boulevard, Burbank; 818-842-4755; www.thirdstage.org.

Colony Theatre Company hosts classic dramas, musicals, comedies, and new plays. ~ 555 North 3rd Street, Burbank; 818-558-7000; www.colonytheatre.org.

Named after Shirley Temple, **Dimples** is a showcase for fledgling singers. Dance music alternates every half hour with musical auditions. Sing for your drinks while pursuing those dreams of stardom! ~ 3413 West Olive Avenue, Burbank; 818-842-2336.

PARKS

CASTAIC LAKE RECREATION AREA Set at the foot of the Castaic Mountains, two manmade lakes are surrounded by rugged slopes. The countryside—covered with chemise, sage, and chaparral—is stark but beautiful. Along the upper lake, which carves a V in the hills, are facilities for picnicking, boating, and waterskiing; there are fishing boat and waverunner rentals. Swimming is good in the lagoon. Castaic is filled with bass, trout, and bluegill. Other facilities are restrooms, picnic areas, and playgrounds. Day-use fee, $6 per vehicle. ~ Access to Castaic Lake is at 32132 Castaic Drive, Castaic; 661-257-4050, fax 661-257-3759; www.castaiclake.com.

▼▼▼▼▼▼▼▼▼▼
Pasadena Area

Tucked between the Downtown district and the lofty San Gabriel Mountains lies the San Gabriel Valley. Extending east from the San Fernando Valley toward San Bernardino, this former orange-growing empire has developed into a suburban realm noted for its wealth, botanic gardens, and smog.

Back in 1771, when 14 soldiers, two priests, and several mule drivers founded a mission in San Gabriel, they laid claim to an outpost that controlled the entire countryside, including Los Angeles Pueblo. The priests became land barons as the region was divided into vineyards, cattle ranches, and olive groves. In the mid-19th century American settlers further transformed the valley into an oasis of lemon and orange trees.

By the late 19th century Pasadena was supplanting San Gabriel as the cultural heart of the San Gabriel Valley. Boasting an ideal climate, it billed itself as a health lover's paradise and became a celebrated resort area. Its tree-trimmed boulevards were lined with beaux-arts, Mediterranean, Italian Renaissance, and Victorian houses, making the town a kind of open-air architectural museum.

Eventually visitors became residents, hotels were converted to apartments, and by the mid-20th century paradise became suburbia. In the process, Pasadena's overweening wealth and stubborn sense of tradition left the town with a reputation for stodgy

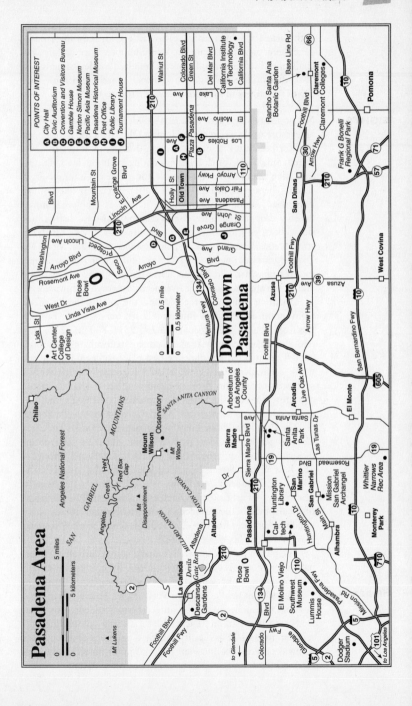

Pasadena Area

0 —— 5 miles
0 —— 5 kilometers

Mt Lukens ▲

SAN GABRIEL MOUNTAINS

Angeles National Forest

Angeles Crest Hwy

Red Box Gap

Mt Disappointment ▲

Mt Wilson ▲

Mount Wilson Observatory

SANTA ANITA CANYON

Chilao

MILLARD CANYON

EATON CANYON

Devils Gate Res

La Cañada

Altadena

Descanso Gardens

Foothill Blvd

Foothill Fwy

to Glendale ←

Glendale Fwy

Colorado Blvd

Rose Bowl ⊙

Pasadena

Cal-tech ●

El Molino Viejo

Southwest Museum ●

Lummis House ●

to Los Angeles →

Dodger Stadium ●

Mission Rd

Pasadena Fwy

Huntington Library ●

San Marino

Huntington Dr

Mission San Gabriel Archangel ●

San Gabriel

Alhambra

Main St

Rosemead Blvd

Monterey Park

Arboretum of Los Angeles County

Sierra Madre Blvd

Sierra Madre

Santa Anita Park

Arcadia

Live Oak Ave

Santa Anita Ave

Las Tunas Dr

El Monte

Whittier Narrows Rec Area

San Bernardino Fwy

Foothill Blvd

Foothill Fwy

Azusa

Azusa Ave

Arrow Hwy

San Dimas

Arrow Hwy

Claremont

Claremont Colleges

Base Line Rd

Rancho Santa Ana Botanic Garden

Foothill Blvd

West Covina

Pomona

Frank G Bonelli Regional Park

Arrow Hwy

Downtown Pasadena

Art Center College of Design ●

Lida St

Linda Vista Ave

West Dr

Rosemont Ave

Rose Bowl ◯

Arroyo Blvd

Seco

Arroyo Blvd

Washington Ave

Lincoln Ave

Prospect Blvd

Lincoln Ave

Orange Grove Blvd

Mountain St

Blvd

Walnut St

Colorado Blvd

Del Mar Blvd

Green St

California Blvd

California Institute of Technology

Lake Ave

El Molino Ave

Los Robles

Plaza Pasadena

Old Town

Holly St

Fair Oaks Ave

Pasadena Ave

Grand Ave

Orange Grove Ave

St John Ave

Arroyo Pkwy

Arroyo Blvd

Colorado Blvd

Ventura Fwy

0 —— 0.5 mile
0 —— 0.5 kilometer

conservatism. The Beach Boys captured the sense of the place with their 1964 hit record, "The Little Old Lady from Pasadena." But in recent years the world-famous Rose Parade was challenged by the annual Doo Dah Parade, a motley gathering of "briefcase drill teams" and "lawnmower marching groups" that leaves the streets of Old Town abuzz late into the night.

SIGHTS

Not so many years ago, Pasadena's **Old Town** historic core was an eyesore of decaying old buildings. Old Town today has been transformed into one of the liveliest districts in Southern California. Small-scale brick buildings dating from the late 19th century have been renovated and now house cafés, restaurants, and shops. The arrival of high-profile national retailers like Pottery Barn, Gap, Williams-Sonoma, and Barnes & Noble has introduced a shopping-mall feel to this charming historic district. But sidewalk cafés and plenty of pedestrians create a very satisfying street scene. Plenty of parking helps draw crowds, too. Most Old Town businesses open around 11 a.m. and remain open well into the evening, when Old Town is at its liveliest. ~ Bordered by Holly and Green streets, Pasadena Avenue, and Arroyo Parkway.

Orienting visitors to the old and the new is the **Pasadena Convention and Visitors Bureau**. Closed Sunday. ~ 171 South Los Robles Avenue, Pasadena; 626-795-9311, 800-307-7977, fax 626-795-9656; www.pasadenacal.com, e-mail cub@pasadenacal.com. They will tell you that the best place to begin touring the town is **Pasadena City Hall**, a 1925 Baroque building with a spectacular tile dome. A prime example of the city's classical architecture, the edifice features a colonnaded courtyard with fountain and formal gardens. ~ 100 North Garfield Avenue, Pasadena.

The **Pasadena Public Library**, completed two years later, is a Renaissance-style building with sufficient palm trees and red roof tiles to create a quintessentially Southern California setting. ~ 285 East Walnut Street, Pasadena; 626-744-4052, fax 626-585-8396. The **Pasadena Post Office** is a 1913 Italian Renaissance beauty. ~ 281 East Colorado Boulevard, Pasadena. Another point of local pride is the **Pasadena Civic Auditorium**, an attractive building that dates from 1932. ~ 300 East Green Street, Pasadena; 626-449-7360, fax 626-395-7132.

The public sector can never compete with its private counterpart when money is concerned. Pasadena displays its real wealth on the west side of town, where civic gives way to civilian.

HIDDEN ►

First stop at the **Pacific Asia Museum**, a Chinese palace–style building originally owned by an eccentric Pasadena art dealer. Dedicated to Asian and Pacific Island art and culture, the museum showcases 18th-century Japanese paintings and Southeast Asian ceramics. The museum boasts 15,000 objects in its permanent collection and an 8000-volume research library. Take time to contemplate the Chinese garden and koi fish pond in the courtyard. Closed Monday and Tuesday. Admission. ~ 46 North Los Robles Avenue, Pasadena; 626-449-2742, fax 626-449-2754; www.pacasiamuseum.org, e-mail info@pacificasiamuseum.org.

Then drive out Colorado Boulevard, route of the Rose Parade held every New Year's Day, to the **Norton Simon Museum**. Housed in this odd edifice, which looks more like it was planned by a camera maker than an architect, is one of the finest collections of European and Asian art in the country.

Touring the Simon's 38 galleries and picturesque gardens is like striding through time and space. The works span 2000 years, traveling from ancient India and Southeast Asia to the world of contemporary art. The Old Masters are represented by Rembrandt, Rubens, and Raphael. There are Goya etchings, 17th-century watercolors, and pieces by Cézanne and Van Gogh. Closed Tuesday. ~ 411 West Colorado Boulevard, Pasadena; 626-449-6840, fax 626-796-4978; www.nortonsimon.org, e-mail art@nortonsimon.org.

> Even the gardens at the Norton Simon Museum are landscaped with 19th- and 20th-century sculptures by Rodin and Henry Moore.

Art on a grander scale is evident at the **Colorado Street Bridge**, an antique causeway arching high above an arroyo. ~ Colorado Boulevard west of Orange Grove Boulevard, Pasadena. Not far from this engineering wonder, the old Wrigley mansion, a splendid Italian Renaissance–style estate, now serves as the **Tournament House**, headquarters of the Rose Bowl game and Rose Parade. The house itself captures the spirit of its early years. Guided tours are available every Thursday from February through August. Situated on four princely acres, the gardens are open daily. ~ 391 South Orange Grove Boulevard, Pasadena; 626-449-4100, fax 626-449-9066; www.tournamentofroses. com, e-mail rosepr@earthlink.net.

Another estate with meaning is the imposing 1906 edifice of the Fenyes Mansion that plays host to the **Pasadena Historical Museum**. Containing furnishings and keepsakes from Pasadena's early days, this beaux-arts house with an Edwardian interior was once home to the Finnish Consul. As a result the museum expresses a second theme: Finland, represented on the grounds, a facsimile 16th-century farmhouse, and an exhibit of Finnish folk art. There's also a lovely garden on-site. Docent-guided tours are offered Wednesday afternoon. Closed Monday and Tuesday. Admission. ~ 470 West Walnut Street, Pasadena; 626-577-1660, fax 626-577-1662; www.pasadenahistory.com.

Humbling all these estates is **The Gamble House**, jewel of Pasadena, a Craftsman-style bungalow designed by the famous architectural firm of Greene & Greene in 1908. Heavily influ-

◄ HIDDEN

enced by such Japanese innovations as overhanging roofs and pagoda flourishes, the wood shingle home is a warm blend of hand-rubbed teak and Tiffany glass. Built for the Cincinnati-based Gamble (as in Procter & Gamble) family, the house displays crafted woodwork and the original furnishings. A veritable neighborhood of these elegantly understated Greene & Greene bungalows lines the **Arroyo Terrace** loop next to The Gamble House. Closed Monday through Wednesday; afternoon tours offered Thursday through Sunday. The bookstore is open daily. Admission. ~ 4 Westmoreland Place, Pasadena; 626-793-3334, fax 626-577-7547; gamblehouse.usc.edu, e-mail gamblehs@usc.edu.

To continue the architectural tour, follow nearby **Prospect Boulevard** and **Prospect Crescent** along their tree-lined courses. The neighborhood entranceway and several local structures were designed by Charles and Henry Greene, the brothers who fashioned the Gamble House. Another architect, one Frank Lloyd Wright, enters the picture at **La Miniatura** (the Millard House), an unusual assemblage of crosses and concrete blocks resembling a pre-Columbian tower. ~ 645 Prospect Crescent.

Grandest of all the area's architectural achievements is the **Rose Bowl**. Built in 1922, this 92,542-seat stadium is the home of UCLA's football team and the site of the New Year's Day clash between the Big Ten and the Pac-10. ~ 1001 Rose Bowl Drive, Pasadena; 626-577-3100, fax 626-405-0992; www.rosebowl stadium.com.

The future greats of the art world reside up the hill at the **Art Center College of Design**. An excellent school of art and design, the college has galleries displaying work by both students and established artists. It also rests on 175 hillside acres that provide marvelous views of Pasadena and the San Gabriel Mountains. ~ 1700 Lida Street, Pasadena; 626-396-2200, fax 626-795-0578; www.artcenter.edu.

Students with a more scientific bent are cracking the books at **Caltech**, an internationally renowned science and engineering school whose faculty and alumni have won 30 Nobel Prizes and whose faculty once included Richard Feynman. These hallowed halls, in case you were wondering, were modeled after a Spanish Colonial style. There are campus tours Monday through Friday. ~ California Institute of Technology Visitors Center, 315 South Hill Avenue, Pasadena; 626-395-6327; www.caltech.edu, e-mail www@caltech.edu.

HIDDEN ►

El Molino Viejo, the Old Mill, represents a vital part of the area's Spanish tradition. Built in 1816 by Indians from San Gabriel Mission, it was Southern California's first water-powered grist mill. Only the millstones remain from the actual mill, but the building, an adobe beauty with red-tile roof, is still intact. With its courtyard setting and flowering fruit trees, the place is thoroughly enchanting. Down in the basement you'll find a working scale model of the mill's machinery. Closed Monday. ~ 1120 Old Mill Road, San Marino; 626-449-5458.

One of the Southland's most spectacular complexes and certainly the premier attraction in the San Gabriel Valley is the **Huntington Library, Art Collections, and Botanical Gardens**. This incredible cultural preserve was once presided over by a single individual, Henry E. Huntington (1850–1927), a shrewd tycoon who made a killing in railroads and real estate, then consolidated his fortune by marrying the widow of his equally rich uncle.

The focal point of Huntington's 207-acre aesthetic preserve, the **Huntington Gallery**, was originally his home. Today the mansion is dedicated to 18th- and 19th-century English and French art and houses one of the finest collections of its kind in the country. Gainsborough's "Blue Boy" is here, as well as paintings by Turner and Van Dyck, tapestries, porcelains, and furniture. Another gallery contains Renaissance paintings and French sculpture from the 18th century; the **Virginia Steele Scott Gallery of American Art,** housed in an enchanting building, traces American painting from 1730 to the mid-1900s.

Moving from oil to ink, and from mansion to mansion, the **Huntington Library** contains one of the world's finest collections of rare British and American manuscripts and first editions. the exhibit includes a Gutenberg bible, the Ellesmere Chaucer (a handpainted manuscript dating from 1410), classics such as Ovid's *Metamorphosis* and Milton's *Paradise Lost*, and latter-day works by James Joyce and Henry James. The Founding Fathers are present with original manuscripts by Washington, Franklin, and Jefferson; and the American Renaissance is evident in the literary works of such classic authors as Poe, Hawthorne, and Twain.

> The Huntington Library's collection of rare books represents nine centuries of literature!

This describes only some of the *buildings* on the property! There are also the grounds, a heavenly labyrinth of gardens ranging from a verdant jungle setting to the austerely elegant **Desert garden**. Rolling lawns are adorned with Italian statuary and bordered by plots of roses and camellias. The **Shakespeare garden** is filled with plants mentioned by the playwright; the **Japanese garden** features an arched bridge, koi pond, and 19th-century house. All are part of the amazing legacy of a philanthropist with a vision equal to his wealth. Closed Monday. Admission. ~ 1151 Oxford Road, San Marino; 626-405-2100; www.huntington. org, e-mail publicinfo@huntington.org.

EASTERN SAN GABRIEL VALLEY Fourth in California's historic chain of missions, **Mission San Gabriel Archangel** is an oasis in an urban setting. Built in 1771, the church is fashioned from cut stone, brick, and mortar. Its buttressed walls and vaulted roof indicate Moorish influences and lend a fortress-like quality, but inside the sanctuary peace reigns: the grounds are covered in cactus gardens and grape arbors and flanked by a cemetery. The chapel features an 18th-century altar built in Mexico City as well as colorful statues from Spain. The winery next door was once the largest in California. Admission. ~ 428 South Mission Drive, San Gabriel; 626-457-3048, fax 626-282-5308; www. sangabrielmission.org, e-mail sgmission@aol.com.

> The Rancho Santa Ana Botanic Garden boasts the largest collection of native California plants in the world.

Rarely does a racecourse represent a work of art, but **Santa Anita Park**, built in 1934, is one of the country's most beautiful tracks. Surrounded by landscaped gardens and ornamented with wrought-iron fixtures, the clubhouse is a local landmark. Added to the aesthetics is another unique attraction: the family-oriented park, featuring picnic areas and playgrounds and offering free admission to children accompanied by parents. During the morning from 7:30 to 9:30 the public is admitted free and, during race season, visitors can take a guided tour on weekends and watch the horses work out. Thoroughbred racing season is from October to mid-November and from Christmas through April. Admission. ~ 285 West Huntington Drive, Arcadia; 626-574-7223, fax 626-445-4202; www.santaanita.com.

The **Arboretum of Los Angeles County** located across the street may be the most photographed location in the world. Everything from Tarzan movies to Bing Crosby's *Road to Singapore* to television's "Fantasy Island" has been filmed in this 127-acre garden. With plants from every corner of the globe, it has portrayed Hawaii, Burma, Africa, Samoa, and Devil's Island. Wander past the duck pond, tropical greenhouse, fountain, and waterfall and you'll be retracing the steps of Humphrey Bogart, Cary Grant, Ingrid Bergman, and Dustin Hoffman.

The history of the surrounding region, captured in several historic structures still standing on the grounds, long precedes the movies. There are **wickiups** similar to those of the original Gabrieleño Indians, who used the local spring-fed pond as a watering hole. Representing the Spanish era is the **Hugo Reid Adobe**, an 1840 structure built with over 3000 mud bricks. Crudely furnished in 19th-century Mexican fashion, the adobe dates to the days when the area was part of a huge Mexican land grant. E. J. "Lucky" Baldwin, the silver-mining magnate who helped introduce horse racing to Southern California, bought the ranch in 1875, and built a **Queen Anne Cottage**. His castle-in-the-sky dream house, painted white with red stripes and topped by a bell tower, is a gingerbread Victorian. The interior, decorated in period style, is a masterwork of hardwoods and crystal, stained glass and marble. Admission. ~ 301 North Baldwin Avenue,

Arcadia; 626-821-3222, fax 626-445-1217; www.arboretum.org, e-mail comments@arboretum.org.

Also part of this never-ending complex is the **Santa Anita Depot**. Built in 1890, it's a classic brick train station filled with equipment and memorabilia from the great age of railroads. Open Sunday, Tuesday, and Wednesday. Admission. ~ 301 North Baldwin Avenue, Arcadia; 626-821-3222, fax 626-445-1217.

In the trim little town of Claremont, near the foothills of the San Gabriel Mountains, you can tour another idyllic enclave. The **Claremont Colleges**, a collection of six independent colleges, including the famous Harvey Mudd engineering school, form a continuous campus studded with shade trees. There are walking tours of turn-of-the-20th-century buildings and strolls through pretty parks. ~ From Route 10 take the Indian Hill Boulevard North exit; go right on 1st Street; go left on College Avenue, Claremont; 909-621-8000.

Several hundred yards closer to the mountains lies the **Rancho**   ◄ *HIDDEN*
Santa Ana Botanic Garden. This enchanting 86-acre preserve is dedicated to native desert plants, coastal vegetation, wildflowers, and woodlands. Wandering its nature trails is like touring a miniature version of natural California. A particularly pretty time to visit is during spring when the California poppies are in bloom. Be sure to visit the garden shop. ~ 1500 North College Avenue, Claremont; 909-625-8767, fax 909-626-7670; www.rsabg.org.

SAN GABRIEL MOUNTAINS   Eaton Canyon, set in the foothills, is a 190-acre park laced with hiking trails that traverse an arroyo and four different plant communities. Sufficiently close to the ocean and mountains to support flora from both regions, the park is a mix of coastal sage scrub, chaparral, oak woodland, and riparian vegetation. Trails meander through the park and lead deep into the adjacent Angeles National Forest. In 1993 about half of Eaton Canyon, including the interpretive center, burned in a fire. Since then, the park has built a new Nature Center, and a fire ecology trail shows the amazing regeneration of foothill flora. ~ 626-398-5420, fax 626-398-5422; www.ecnca.org.

Another of the region's botanic preserves, **Descanso Gardens**   ◄ *HIDDEN*
stretches across 160 acres at the foot of the San Gabriel Mountains. This former estate has one of the largest camellia gardens in the world, numbering over 60,000 plants, as well as a rose garden where droves of the species' strains are cultivated. There is also a Japanese teahouse and garden, a section devoted to native California plants, and iris and lilac gardens. An art gallery showcases a changing roster of local art. Unifying this restful hideaway is a tumbling stream that meanders through an oak forest past bird preserves and duck ponds. Admission. ~ 1418 Descanso Drive, La Cañada; 818-952-4401, fax 818-952-1238; www.descanso.com.

To fully explore the San Gabriel Mountains, follow the Angeles Crest Highway (Route 2) in its sinuous course upward from La Cañada. With their sharp-faced cliffs and granite outcroppings, the San Gabriels form a natural barrier between the Los Angeles Basin and the Mojave Desert. Embodied in the 693,000-acre **Angeles National Forest**, these dry, semi-barren mountains are a mix of high chaparral, pine forest, and rocky terrain. Hiking trails crisscross the heights and wildflowers bloom in spring.

A side road from Route 2 leads to 5710-foot **Mount Wilson**, from which you can gaze across the entire expanse of Los Angeles to the Pacific. **Mount Wilson Observatory**, the region's most famous landmark, supports a 100-inch reflecting telescope used by Edwin Hubble in his formulation of the Big Bang theory of the expanding universe. Today the telescope can be seen through an observation window. There's also a museum here. ~ 626-793-3100, fax 626-793-4570; www.mtwilson.edu.

For complete information on the mountains and the Angeles National Forest, stop by the **Chilao Visitors Center**. Located on Route 2 about 14 miles past the turnoff for Mount Wilson, this small facility has its own nature center and two miles of self-guided nature trails. Closed Tuesday; call for changing hours. ~ 626-796-5541.

LODGING

Motel row in Pasadena lies along Colorado Boulevard, route of the famous Rose Parade. **Pasadena Central Travelodge**, a 53-unit stucco complex, is typical of the accommodations. It offers standard rooms with cinderblock walls, stall showers, wall-to-wall carpeting, and other basic amenities. ~ 2131 East Colorado Boulevard, Pasadena; 626-796-3121, 800-578-7878, fax 626-793-4713. BUDGET.

The revered 1907 **Ritz-Carlton Huntington Hotel & Spa** is situated on 23 manicured acres. This 392-room hotel combines modern amenities with the style and charm of another era. There's an Olympic-size swimming pool (reputed to be the first in California) to exercise in, a spa to relax in, or you can wander the hotel's Japanese and Horseshoe gardens. If you are seeking Old World elegance, this is the address. ~ 1401 South Oak Knoll Avenue, Pasadena; 626-568-3900, 800-241-3333, fax 626-568-1842; www.ritzcarlton.com. ULTRA-DELUXE.

DINING

HIDDEN ►

For a great buy, try **Burger Continental**, a congested and crazy café where you order at the counter, then dine indoors or on a patio. Portions are bountiful and the prices ridiculously low. But it's not only the huge, low-priced menu that keeps this establishment packed—the belly dancing shows also draw crowds, Thursday through Sunday evening and at Sunday brunch. In addition to hamburgers they serve steaks, seafood, sandwiches, and an enticing array of Middle Eastern dishes. Breakfast, lunch, and dinner are served daily. ~ 535 South Lake Avenue, Pasadena; 626-792-6634, fax 626-792-8520; www.burgercontinental.com, e-mail mail@burgercontinental.com. BUDGET TO MODERATE.

You can people watch from the sidewalk dining area while feasting on delectable dishes at the **Crocodile Café**. Try the Chinese pot stickers to start. The Cobb salad is also very tasty. Inside seating is a little noisy, but the food makes up for it. Highly recommended. ~ 140 South Lake Avenue, Pasadena; 626-449-9900, fax 626-449-6968. BUDGET TO MODERATE.

Tucked away in an art-deco building on a side street, **Bistro 45** is a gathering spot for Pasadena's "elegancia." The airy high-tech atmosphere, pastel walls, and contemporary art match the handsomely presented French (with just a dash of Californian) cuisine. The menu includes roasted chicken with fresh herbs and garlic, grilled ahi, and grilled beef tenderloin. No lunch on weekends. Closed Monday. ~ 45 South Mentor Avenue, Pasadena; 626-792-2535, fax 626-792-2676; www.bistro45.com. DELUXE TO ULTRA-DELUXE.

Specializing in Mandarin and Szechuan cuisine, **Panda Inn** is a dimly lit restaurant with Chinese prints. The spicy Szechuan dishes include hot braised shrimp, sweet and pungent chicken, spicy bean curd, and twice-cooked pork. There are also chow mein, egg foo yung, and noodle entrées, as well as a full inventory of Mandarin-style beef, fowl, seafood, and vegetable dishes. ~ 3488 East Foothill Boulevard, Pasadena; 626-793-7300, fax 626-793-2781; www.pandainn.com. MODERATE.

Don't be fooled by the unpretentious decor and reasonable prices. **Akbar Cuisine of India** serves traditional and creative   ◄ HIDDEN
Indian dishes such as ginger-marinated lamb chops and mint chicken kabobs. ~ 44 North Fair Oaks Boulevard, Pasadena; 626-440-0309, fax 626-577-9919; www.akbarcuisineofindia. com. BUDGET.

AUTHOR FAVORITE

If you are the former head chef at L'Orangerie and the person who replaced Wolfgang Puck at Les Anges when he left to open Spago, you can rightfully name your restaurant after yourself. That is exactly what Hideo "Shiro" Yamashiro did. **Restaurant Shiro** combines French and Asian influences to produce an everchanging menu that might include lamb chops marinated in mint and garlic, scallops in ginger and lime sauce, and steamed whitefish with capers. Dinner only. Closed Monday and Tuesday. ~ 1505 Mission Street, South Pasadena; 626-799-4774. MODERATE TO ULTRA-DELUXE.

Any town as wealthy and prone to gentrification as Pasadena is bound to have numerous California-cuisine cafés. One of note is **Parkway Grill**, a brick-wall-and-bare-beam restaurant decorated with track lights and stained glass. The antique bar is hardwood; the kitchen, *naturalement*, sits in the center of the complex, completely open to view. The chefs prepare gourmet pizza and pasta dishes such as black linguini with popcorn shrimp, spicy Thai tagliatelle and forest mushroom ravioli. Entrées include catfish in lime-soy sauce, mesquite-grilled filet mignon, and oak oven–roasted garlic chicken with goat cheese, potato purée and fig chutney. No lunch Saturday or Sunday. ~ 510 South Arroyo Parkway, Pasadena; 626-795-1001, fax 626-796-6221. DELUXE TO ULTRA-DELUXE.

Italian food is hot in Pasadena. There's always an exuberant and bustling crowd in Old Town's popular *ristorantes*.

For alfresco dining, be sure to delve into the pleasures of **Sorriso**. Decorated with a stunning art collection, this trattoria-style eatery serves authentic Italian cuisine. Try their delicious *linguine saporose* (linguine served with a zesty tomato sauce and lightly breaded pan-fried calamari and shrimp). The food is outstanding, and the ambience is *molto* Italian. ~ 168 West Colorado Boulevard, Pasadena; 626-793-2233, fax 626-796-8392; www.sorrisopasadena.com. MODERATE TO DELUXE.

At **Mi Píace**, the cuisine is exquisite. Try their chicken lasagne with a sweet pepper cream sauce, and you'll be very *contento*. The airy interior is further enhanced by simple pine-colored chairs, a wrought-iron bar, and fresh flowers. ~ 25 East Colorado Boulevard, Pasadena; 626-795-3131. MODERATE.

Regional Italian cuisine is the name of the game at **Il Fornaio**. Will it be Tuscany, Sicily, or Sardinia? The menu changes monthly, but there are always wood-fired pizzas and mesquite-grilled steaks, chicken, and seafood. With its white marble floors, a fashionable bar, and sleek, contemporary Italian feel, this eatery comes highly praised. Patio dining is also available. ~ Located on the northwest corner of Colorado Boulevard and Fairoaks Avenue, Pasadena; 626-683-9797, fax 626-683-0789; www.ilfornaio.com. DELUXE.

East conquers West at **Chez Sateau**, where a Japanese chef prepares French meals with special flair. The frosted-glass-and-private-booth dining room features a menu that changes seasonally, including specialties such as rack of lamb. Filling out the *carte* are outlandish desserts like soufflés and crêpes suzettes. No lunch on Saturday. Closed Monday. ~ 850 South Baldwin Avenue, Arcadia; 626-446-8806, fax 626-446-0402. MODERATE TO DELUXE.

Way up in the San Gabriel Mountains, where Angeles National Forest creates an ideal retreat, you'll find **Newcomb's Ranch Inn**. This remote restaurant, set in a rustic wooden building, serves an

HIDDEN ▶

array of American dishes, burgers, and sandwiches. Little more than a log diner, it's a welcome sight for anyone wandering the mountains. Open for breakfast, lunch, and dinner. ~ Route 2, Chilao; 626-440-1001; www.newcombsranch.com. BUDGET.

Shopping in the San Gabriel Valley centers around Pasadena. **South Lake Avenue**, the oldest and once the most prestigious shopping district in town, had its origins in 1947 when Bullocks department store opened for business. Today the venerable establishment has been replaced by **Macy's**. ~ 626-792-0211.

SHOPPING

Stop by **The Colonnade**, a small arcade that houses **Kokila's Boutique**. At this shop you'll find natural fiber fashions for women. ~ 626-584-1157. Closed Sunday. **Burlington Arcade**, modeled after the one in London, is another elegant gallery of specialty shops. ~ 380 South Lake Avenue, Pasadena.

Just west of South Lake Avenue, visit a charming group of English-style cottages. One is the **Rose Tree Cottage**, where you can browse for fine British imports or enjoy afternoon tea in a traditional setting. Reservations for tea should be made one week in advance. Closed Monday. ~ 828 East California Boulevard, Pasadena; 626-793-3337; www.rosetreecottage.com.

Touted as the world's largest swap meet, the Rose Bowl Flea Market is held on the second Sunday of each month. You'll find everything from collectibles to contemptibles. Admission. ~ 1001 Rose Bowl Drive, Pasadena; 323-560-7469.

Another major Pasadena shopping district lies along **Colorado Boulevard**, the town's main artery and the route of the annual Rose Parade. **Vroman's Bookstore**, one of the area's oldest and finest bookstores, is among the revered shops along this boulevard. ~ 695 East Colorado Boulevard, Pasadena; 626-449-5320.

The pride of the Boulevard is Pasadena's **Paseo Colorado**, three blocks of open-air shopping with over 100 stores, restaurants, and businesses, as well as a 14-screen multiplex movie theater. Unlike Old Towne there is plenty of parking. ~ On Colorado Boulevard through to Green Street, between Los Robles and Marengo avenues; 626-795-8891.

Old Town Pasadena is a lively historic district that is the pride of the city. ~ Bordered by Holly and Green streets, Pasadena Avenue, and Arroyo Parkway.

Travelers will want to stop in at **Distant Lands**, one of the finest travel-related bookstores anywhere. In addition to travel literature, they also carry a complete selection of travel clothing, accessories, and luggage. ~ 56 South Raymond Avenue, Pasadena; 626-449-3220, 800-310-3220; www.distantlands.com, e-mail distantlands@earthlink.net.

Pasadena Antique Center & Annex, the city's largest gallery of shops, houses more than 130 antique dealers. Among them is **Djanet**, with a collection of antique glassware, and **Things of**

Interest, specializing in Mission-style furniture and accessories. ~ 480 South Fair Oaks Avenue, Pasadena; 626-449-7706.

The colorful exterior of **The Folk Tree** will inevitably draw you in to see the shop's amazing collection of folk art. Originating from Mexico and South America, the inventory includes a fascinating collection of dolls. Tours are available. ~ 217 South Fair Oaks Avenue, Pasadena; 626-795-8733; www.folktree.com.

For more international folk art, head three doors down to **The Folk Tree Collection**, where there's a large selection of folk art, jewelry, and clothing from all over the world, as well as changing art exhibits. ~ 199 South Fair Oaks Avenue, Pasadena; 626-793-4828; www.folktree.com.

Elsewhere in the San Gabriel Valley, there's **Santa Anita Fashion Park**, a colossal 150-store mall adjacent to Santa Anita Park. ~ Baldwin Avenue and West Huntington Drive, Arcadia.

NIGHTLIFE   Like almost everything else in the San Gabriel Valley, the entertainment scene centers around Pasadena.

The **Ice House** presents new and established comedians every night. Another section of the 1920s-era ice house, **The Ice House Annex**, features stand-up comedy. Closed Monday. Cover. ~ 24 North Mentor Avenue, Pasadena; 626-577-1894.

Barney's Ltd., an old-style saloon with village charm and friendly spirit, pours over 80 brands of beer from all over the world. ~ 93 West Colorado Boulevard, Pasadena; 626-577-2739.

Or consider the **Pasadena Playhouse**, a historic theater that has been the birthplace for numerous stars of stage and screen. A multitude of performances are produced in the 680-seat space. ~ 39 South El Molino Avenue, Pasadena; 626-356-7529; www.pasadenaplayhouse.org.

During the thoroughbred horse-racing season, beautiful Santa Anita Racetrack attracts huge crowds every day. At night the bawdy track crowd goes to sing along karaoke-style at the **100 to 1 Club**. ~ 100 West Huntington Drive, Arcadia; 626-445-3520.

PARKS   **FRANK G. BONELLI REGIONAL PARK** This 1799-acre facility combines tree-covered hills and theme-park attractions. For the outdoor-minded there are trails, stables, and a 250-acre lake with boating and fishing facilities; swimming is good at Swim Beach. Bicycles, boats, and horses can all be rented here. There are also picnic areas, restrooms, and a snack bar. The rest of the crowd beelines to **Raging Waters** (909-802-2200; www.ragingwaters.com, e-mail extreme@raging waters.com), an aquatic theme park with waterslides and simulated surfing waves. Open spring and summer. Visitors who can't decide between the natural and artificial head for the adjacent golf course and hot tubs. Day-use fee, $6 per car; free from

November through February except on weekends and holidays.
~ 120 Via Verde, San Dimas; 909-599-8411, fax 909-599-6020.

▲ Permitted at **East Shore RV Park,** located within the park.
There are 519 sites (with full hookups), $32 to $34 per night,
and 14 tent sites, $24 per night. ~ 909-599-8355, 800-809-3778.

ANGELES NATIONAL FOREST 🚶 🚲 🎿 🏠 ⛵ 🎣 🐎 🚴
🚤 Nature is rarely reducible to statistics, but numbers are
unavoidable in describing this 693,000-acre forest. There are four
rivers, eight lakes, a 10,000-foot peak, and 189 miles of fishing streams. The 36,000-acre San Gabriel Wilderness is contained within the National Forest.
Overall the forest attracts more than 30 million
visitors annually. Most are daytrippers intent on
sightseeing and picnicking, but campers and hikers,
enjoying 60 campgrounds and 556 miles of trails,
are also prevalent. Flora and fauna range from green-
winged teal to black bear to horned toads and rattlesnakes. This is also a prime ski area, with five winter
sports centers. Other facilities include picnic areas and
restrooms. Parking fee, $5 per day. ~ Route 2 is the main high-
way through the southern sector of the forest; the northern region is east of Route 5; 626-574-5200, fax 626-574-5233.

Stretching from San Ber-
nardino County across
the entire northern tier
of Los Angeles County,
the Angeles National
Forest separates the
Los Angeles Basin
from the desert.

▲ There are 60 campgrounds for tents and RVs (no hookups); $3 to $12 per night.

Though the beach isn't far away, Los Angeles
also contains several lakes that provide ample
opportunity for water sports.

Outdoor Adventures

If you'd like to waterski or windsurf, try **Frank G. Bonelli Park,**
but bring your own equipment. Vehicle fee. ~ 120 Via Verde, San
Dimas; 909-599-8411. Anglers can rent motorized fishing boats
at **Castaic Lake Recreation Area.** ~ 32132 Castaic Lake Drive,
Castaic; 661-775-6232.

WATER SPORTS

For those who are happier lolling about in a boat, there are
rowboat rentals at **Santa Fe Dam.** Vehicle fee. ~ 15501 East Arrow
Highway, Irwindale; 626-334-1065. Paddle boating is a big sport
at **MacArthur Park.** ~ 2230 West 6th Street, Los Angeles.

Though driving seems almost an addiction in the city, many Angelenos still manage to exercise. Filling your lungs with smoggy
air might not be the healthiest thing to do, but if you're interested in jogging anyway, join the troopers at **Elysian Park,** located
just north of downtown L.A. near the intersection of Routes 110
and 5. Visit **San Vicente Boulevard** in the Brentwood area or **Lacy
Park** at 1485 Virginia Road in San Marino. Another popular
area is the **arroyo** near the Rose Bowl in Pasadena, or **Griffith
Park** at 4730 Crystal Springs Drive in Los Angeles.

JOGGING

HANG GLIDING

What better way to let yourself go than by coasting or floating on high? The adventurous can try hang gliding at **Windsports Soaring Center,** which offers lessons and trips off the San Gabriel Mountains. ~ 12623 Gridley Street, Sylmar; 818-367-2430; www. windsports.com.

GOLF

In Los Angeles it's as easy to tee off at a golf course as it is to get teed off in a traffic jam. If you left your cart (or clubs) at home, you're in luck; most courses rent both.

One of the many challenging or interesting courses is the **Montebello Country Club,** a regulation 18-hole public course. They rent carts only. ~ 901 Via San Clemente, Montebello; 323-887-4565; www.themontebellocc.com. If you are in Pasadena, stop by the two 18-hole courses at the public **Brookside Golf Course.** Located right next to the Rose Bowl, this green features many lakes and trees. ~ 1133 North Rosemont Avenue; 626-796-0177. In Los Angeles, **Wilson and Harding Golf Courses** are both 18-hole, par-72 public greens. ~ Griffith Park; 323-664-2555; www.griffithparkgolfshop.com. **Westchester Golf Course** is a privately owned, public 15-hole course. You can also get in some driving practice. ~ 6900 West Manchester Boulevard; 310-670-5110; www.americangolf.com.

In the eastern end of the county part of the public, 18-hole **Marshall Canyon Golf Course** runs over a canyon. There's also a driving range. ~ 6100 North Stephens Ranch Road, La Verne; 909-593-8211; www.marshallcanyon.com. **Diamond Bar Golf Course** is another 18-hole, public green. ~ 22751 East Golden Springs Drive, Diamond Bar; 909-861-8282. The public 18-hole **San Dimas Canyon Golf Course,** designed by Dan Murray, is the premier facility in the Foothill area. ~ 2100 Terrebonne Avenue, San Dimas; 909-599-2313; www.americangolf.com. Duffers in Pomona head to the 18-hole **Mountain Meadows Golf Course,** a public course with three water holes, rolling hills, and tiered greens. ~ 1875 Fairplex Drive, Pomona; 909-623-3704; www. americangolf.com. Rosemead's **Whittier Narrows,** an Arnold Palmer–managed golf course, is also a good choice, with three public nine-hole, courses. ~ 8640 East Rush Street, Rosemead; 626-280-8225.

In the San Fernando Valley, **Knollwood Golf Course** is an 18-hole, public course with a driving range. ~ 12040 Balboa Boulevard, Granada Hills; 818-363-8161. Another option is the public **Sepulveda Golf Complex,** which features two 18-hole courses. ~ 16821 Burbank Boulevard, Encino; 818-986-4560.

TENNIS

Most public parks have at least one tennis court; the city's largest facility, **Griffith Park,** has many outdoor lighted courts. ~ 4730 Crystal Springs Drive, Los Angeles; 323-662-7772. Or try **Elysian**

Park, which has two unlighted courts. ~ Near the intersection of Route 5 and Route 110, Los Angeles.

Tennis clubs dot the county; one such club is the **Racquet Center**. The Pasadena location has nine lighted courts and seven racquetball courts. They also rent racquets and have lessons. ~ 920 Lohman Lane, South Pasadena, 323-258-4178. For further information about clubs and tournaments, contact the **Southern California Tennis Association**. ~ P.O. Box 240015, Los Angeles, CA 90024; 310-208-3838; www.usta.com/scta.

For more information on other local parks and their facilities, contact the nearest Los Angeles City and County Parks and Recreation Department office.

With its curving hills and flowering meadows, Griffith Park is a favorite spot among urban equestrians. Several places on the edge of the park provide facilities. **Sunset Ranch** offers trail rides on specific park trails, and one that takes you to a Mexican restaurant. Trips usually last from one to two hours. ~ 3400 North Beachwood Drive, Hollywood; 323-464-9612; www.sunsetranchhollywood.com.

RIDING STABLES

In Burbank consider **Circle K Stables** for smaller group rides. Trail rides can be as short as one hour or as long as five. ~ 914 South Mariposa Street; 818-843-9890. Another Burbank offering is **Griffith Park Horse Rentals**, which takes you on one- to two-hour rides into the hills of Griffith Park. Maximum group of 20. ~ 480 Riverside Drive; 818-840-8401.

> For a bike trip from the mountains to the sea, try the San Gabriel River Trail. It begins in Azusa and extends 24 miles to the Pacific near Long Beach.

Rent horses from **Bar S Stables** and lead yourself through the Glendale portion of the park. Guides can be arranged beforehand. You must be at least seven years old to ride. ~ 1850 Riverside Drive, Glendale; 818-242-8443.

Bikeways in Los Angeles are almost as plentiful as freeways. Unlike the freeways, few of them are normally congested. Many run parallel to parks, rivers, aqueducts, and lakes, offering a different view of this diverse area.

BIKING

Over 14 miles of bike routes wind through Griffith Park. Two notable excursions skirt many of the park attractions: **Crystal Springs Loop**, which follows Crystal Springs Drive and Zoo Drive along the park's eastern edge, passes the merry-go-round and Travel Town; **Mineral Wells Loop**, an arduous uphill climb, passes Harding Golf Course, then coasts downhill to Zoo Drive, taking in Travel Town and the zoo.

In the Mt. Washington area, the **Arroyo Seco Trail** includes a loop past Heritage Square, the Lummis House, and Casa de Adobe. The trail begins at the Montecito Heights Recreation Center on Homer Street and runs along an arroyo.

In the Whittier–El Monte area, bikers can choose a long jaunt along the 15-mile **Rio Hondo River Trail** or a leisurely go-round on the **Legg Lake Loop** in Whittier Narrows Recreation Area.

The flat, nine-mile **Sepulveda Basin Bikeway** circumnavigates the Sepulveda Dam Recreation Area in the heart of the San Fernando Valley.

The **Kenneth Newell Bikeway** begins on Arroyo Boulevard in Pasadena, then dips down to Arroyo Seco and the famed Rose Bowl. The bikeway follows a flood basin, climbs a steep hill into Linda Vista, and continues to Devil's Gate Dam and the world-renowned Jet Propulsion Laboratory.

For a look at the good life, check out the route from **San Gabriel Mission to the Huntington Library**, which winds from San Gabriel through the exclusive town of San Marino.

The most scenic bike path in the L.A. area is the **West Fork Trail** in the San Gabriel Mountains—6.7 miles of gentle, paved path that parallels the west fork of the San Gabriel River. Take Route 210 to Azusa, then Route 39 ten miles north to a parking lot a little past the Rincon Ranger Station.

HIKING   The idea of natural areas in Los Angeles seems to be a contradiction in terms. But the city is so vast—sprawling from the Pacific Ocean to the mountains—that even ambitious developers have been unable to pave it all. For backpackers and daytrippers alike, miles of hiking trails still lace the hills and canyons that lie just beyond the housing tracts and shopping malls. For more information and maps, call **Los Angeles County Riding and Hiking Trails.** ~ 626-575-5756, fax 626-652-0748. All distances listed for hiking trails are one way unless otherwise noted.

GRIFFITH PARK   Los Angeles' outback is found a few miles from the center of Downtown amid the forested hills of Griffith Park. With more than 55 miles of trails to explore, the park rests along the Hollywood Hills at the edge of the Santa Monica Mountains. For information and maps contact the local ranger station. ~ 323-913-7390, fax 213-485-8775.

Among the best hikes here is the **Mt. Hollywood Loop Trail** (6 miles). Beginning near the merry-go-round, the path follows a stream, passes deer and coyote habitats, then leads up out of the canyon onto the chaparral-covered slopes of Mt. Hollywood.

For a combination sightseeing-hiking venture take the **Mineral Wells Trail** (4.3 miles). The hike begins on a level bridle trail, then wends its way down toward the zoo, and back to Mineral Wells.

The **Pacific Electric Quarry–Bronson Cave Trail** (2.3 miles) snakes through Brush Canyon to an abandoned rock quarry and the Bronson Caves, an area ripe for exploring. If it seems like you've been here before, that's because this was the location for such TV shows as "Bonanza," "Mod Squad," and "Star Trek."

WHITTIER–EL MONTE AREA   Near Roland Heights, in Schabarum Regional County Park, the **Skyline Trail: Schabarum Park
to Hacienda Boulevard** (3 miles) traverses the Puente Hills. The
hike leads through wild mustard fields to an overlook with views
of the San Gabriel Valley.

Fourteen miles of trails abound in **Frank G. Bonelli Regional
Park** in San Dimas. To get an overview of the park, hike along
the southern hills above Puddingston Reservoir. Maps are available at the park headquarters.

SAN FERNANDO VALLEY   Leading up a 5074-foot peak, the
highest within the Los Angeles city limits, **Mount Lukens Stone
Canyon Trail** (3.3 miles) is a hearty uphill trek. On a clear day
the Pacific looms in the distance, beyond a jigsaw puzzle of housing tracts and rolling hills. The trailhead is located in Sunland off
Doske Road; be sure to bring water.

At the northern edge of the San Fernando Valley, **Placerita
Canyon to Sylmar Trail** (9 miles) offers conditioned hikers an opportunity to climb along a chaparral-covered hillside to an oak-
studded canyon. The hike begins in Placerita Canyon State and
County Park and goes along the Wilson Canyon Saddle. Another
challenging trek is the climb up **Manzanita Mountain** (1 mile),
with its picturesque views.

The old stage road that connected the San Fernando and San
Joaquin valleys is now the route of **Beale's Cut Trail** (.3 mile).
This short but steep hike cuts through the San Fernando Pass,
with its earthquake fault and twisted rock formations.

One of Los Angeles' hidden gems is **O'Melveny Park**, a 672-
acre preserve in the Santa Susana Mountains at the north end of
the San Fernando Valley. **O'Melveny Park Trail** (2.5 miles) begins   ◀ HIDDEN
in Bee Canyon and follows an old fire road past a stream, then
climbs through fields of wildflowers to a series of bluffs. After
the steep climb, you are rewarded with a panoramic view of Los
Angeles, the Santa Clarita Valley, and the San Gabriel Mountains.
The trailhead is near Sesnon Boulevard in Granada Hills.

AUTHOR FAVORITE

There are many ways to scale 5710-foot Mount Wilson. One particularly
pleasant route is the **Mount Wilson Trail** (7.5 miles), beginning from
Mira Monte Avenue in Sierra Madre. This path leads up Little Santa Anita
Canyon past oak and spruce trees to Orchard Camp, a way station
offering a perfect place for a picnic. From here the trail ascends through
dense chaparral to the ridge and Mount Wilson Road. This is also a
popular mountain-biking road.

In Chatsworth, **Devil's Canyon Trail** (1.5 miles) offers a peaceful walk along a streambed through stands of sycamore and oak trees. Look for the caves that have been etched into the sides of the canyon. Also in Chatsworth is a honeycomb of hiking trails winding around **Stoney Point,** located at the north end of Topanga Boulevard just before it meets Route 118. This huge rock outcropping draws some of the country's best rock climbers, so there's an aspect of theater here as well.

PASADENA AREA   The San Gabriel Mountains are crisscrossed with hiking trails ripe for exploring.

Several years ago the San Gabriel portion of the **Pacific Crest Trail,** which leads from Canada to Mexico, was completed. One part of that great system, the **Mill Creek Summit to Pacifico Mountain Trail** (4 miles) follows a route through spruce and oak forests to a view overlooking the Mojave Desert.

At the end of Chaney Trail Road in Altadena there's a lovely spot for a family hike through a tree-shrouded canyon. **Lower Millard Canyon Falls Trail** (.5 mile) leads to a 50-foot waterfall surrounded by huge boulders. If you're a little more adventurous, try **Upper Millard Canyon Trail** (2.5 miles).

An even more ambitious hike from the same trailhead is the **Mount Lowe Railway Trail** (3.5 miles). At the end you'll discover an abandoned rail line, the old "Railway to the Clouds," and the ruins of Ye Alpine tavern. It's a moderate trek offering spectacular views of Los Angeles.

In Altadena's Eaton Canyon, the strenuous **Altadena Crest Trail** (7 miles) explores the foothills of the San Gabriels. A side trip to **Eaton Falls** (.5 mile) follows the stream bed.

Big Santa Anita Canyon north of Sierra Madre is another popular area for hiking. **Sturtevant Falls Trail** (1.8 miles) leads upstream to a 50-foot waterfall. The trailhead is located in Chantry Flat. (Don't climb on the rocks at the waterfall; several people have been seriously hurt here.)

Not as well-known as popular Mount Wilson is a neighboring peak, 5994-foot **Mount Disappointment** (2.8 miles), which offers another opportunity to view Los Angeles from on high. You will walk through Douglas fir and Coulter pine forests and climb along chaparral-covered ridges. The trailhead is just beyond Red Box off the Mount Wilson Road.

It's all downhill to begin with when you hike **Devil's Canyon Trail** (5.5 miles). This trek through an alder-studded canyon, with a bubbling creek for company, goes from Upper Chilao Campground in the San Gabriel Wilderness.

The **Arroyo Seco Canyon Trail** (9.8 miles), beginning at Switzer's Picnic Area (off Route 2), is a challenging way to explore the serene canyons of the San Gabriels. The trail overlooks

Switzer Falls, joins the **Gabrieleño Trail** (3.5 miles), then descends to the tree-laden floor of the canyon. En route is Oakwilde Trail Camp, an ideal spot for an overnight visit. The trail continues to the mouth of the canyon, which overlooks the massive Jet Propulsion Laboratory.

Arriving in Los Angeles by car means entering a maze of freeways. For most Angelenos this is an every day occurrence; they know where they are going and are accustomed to spending a lot of time getting there. It's an intimate affair, a personal relationship between car and driver; they even refer to their freeways by name rather than number.

Transportation

CAR

For the visitor the experience can be very intimidating. The best way to determine a path through this labyrinth is by learning the major highways to and from town.

From the north and west, **Route 101**, the Ventura Freeway, extends from Ventura to Sherman Oaks, then turns southeast to become the Hollywood Freeway.

The Santa Monica Freeway, **Route 10**, cuts through the heart of Los Angeles. It begins in Santa Monica and then becomes the San Bernardino Freeway in downtown Los Angeles.

From Northern California, **Route 5**, the Golden State Freeway, runs south into the center of the city where it changes its name to the Santa Ana Freeway. **Route 405**, better known as the San Diego Freeway, cuts through the San Fernando Valley and the Westside, and then curves east towards Orange County.

Two airports bring visitors to the L.A. area: the very big, very busy Los Angeles International Airport and the less crowded

AIR

Los Angeles Freeway Names

NORTH–SOUTH FREEWAYS		EAST–WEST FREEWAYS	
(405) San Diego		(14) Antelope Valley	
(5) Golden State	north of Downtown	(118) San Fernando	
Santa Ana	south of Downtown	(101) Ventura	west of Hollywood
(170) Hollywood	in San Fernando Valley	(134) Ventura	
(101) Hollywood	Hollywood & Downtown	(210) Foothill	
(210) Foothill		(10) Santa Monica	west of Downtown
(2) Glendale		San Bernardino	east of Downtown
(110) Pasadena	north of Downtown	(60) Pomona	
Harbor	south of Downtown	(91) Redondo Beach	west of Route 710
(710) Long Beach		Artesia	Route 710 to Route 5
(605) San Gabriel		Riverside	east of Route 5
(57) Orange		(22) Garden Grove	

Burbank-Glendale-Pasadena Airport. Los Angeles International is convenient if you are headed for the downtown area or out to the coast. Traffic around this major hub is generally ferocious. Those planning to stay around Hollywood and Beverly Hills, in the San Fernando Valley, or out around Pasadena, are better advised to fly in to the Burbank-Glendale-Pasadena Airport.

Los Angeles International Airport, better known as LAX, is served by many domestic and foreign carriers. Currently (and this seems to change daily) the following airlines fly into LAX: Alaska Airlines, America West Airlines, American Airlines, Continental Airlines, Delta Air Lines, Hawaiian Airlines, Northwest Airlines, Southwest Airlines, and United Airlines.

International carriers are also numerous: Air Canada, Air France, Air New Zealand, All Nippon Airways, British Airways, Canadian Airlines International, China Airlines, Japan Airlines, KLM, Lufthansa German Airlines, Mexicana Airlines, Philippine Airlines, QUANTAS Airways, Singapore Airlines, and TACA International Airlines. ~ 310-646-5252; www.lawa.org/lax.

Flights to and from **Burbank-Glendale-Pasadena Airport** are currently provided by Alaska Airlines, America West Airlines, American Airlines, Skywest Airlines, Southwest Airlines, United Airlines, and United Shuttle. ~ 818-840-8847.

Taxis, limousines, and buses line up to transport passengers from LAX and Burbank. **SuperShuttle** travels between hotels, businesses, and residences to both Burbank and Los Angeles airports. ~ 818-556-6600.

BUS

Greyhound Bus Lines (800-231-2222) has service to the Los Angeles area from all around the country. The main L.A. terminal is at 1716 East 7th Street (213-629-8401). Other stations are found in Hollywood at 1715 North Cahuenga Boulevard (323-466-6381); Pasadena at 645 East Walnut Street (626-792-5116); Glendale at 400 West Cerritos Avenue (818-244-7295); and North Hollywood at 11239 Magnolia Boulevard (818-761-5119).

TRAIN

Amtrak will carry you into Los Angeles via the "Coast Starlight" from the North, the "San Diegan" from San Diego, the "Southwest Chief" from Chicago, and the "Sunset Limited" from New Orleans. The L.A. terminal, Union Station, is at 800 North Alameda Street. There are also stations in Pasadena at 150 South Los Robles Avenue and Glendale at 400 West Cerritos Avenue. ~ 800-872-7245.

CAR RENTALS

Having a car in Los Angeles is practically a must. Distances are great and public transportation leaves much to be desired. As you can imagine, it's not difficult to find a car rental agency. The challenge is to find the best deal. Be sure to request a mileage-free rental, or one with at least some free mileage. One thing is certain in the Los Angeles area, you'll be racking up mileage on the odometer.

If you arrive by air, consider renting a car at the airport. These cost a little more but eliminate the hassles of getting to the rental agency.

Looking for a car at Los Angeles International Airport will bring you to **Avis Rent A Car** (800-331-1212), **Budget Rent A Car** (800-527-0700), **Hertz Rent A Car** (800-654-3131), or **National Car Rental** (800-227-7368).

Agencies providing free airport pick-up service include **Enterprise Rent A Car** (800-736-8222) and **Thrifty Car Rental** (800-367-2277).

At the Burbank airport several companies rent autos: **Avis Rent A Car** (800-331-1212), **Enterprise Rent A Car** (800-736-8222), **Hertz Rent A Car** (800-654-3131), and **National Car Rental** (800-227-7368). **American Eagle Car and Truck Rental** (818-840-8816) offers free pick-up service from the airport.

Among the used car rental agencies in the Los Angeles area are **Rent A Wreck** (800-535-1391) and **G & R Rent A Car** (310-478-4208).

If there was ever a place to rent a limousine, Los Angeles is it. Dozens of companies specialize in "elegant service for elegant people." Check the Yellow Pages for listings.

PUBLIC TRANSIT

If you arrive in Los Angeles without a car, believe it or not you can still get around. **Los Angeles County Metropolitan Transportation Authority**, or MTA, has over 200 bus routes covering more than 2200 square miles. "Rapid" transit may be a misnomer, but buses do get you where you want to go. Seven customer service centers are located throughout Los Angeles; call for the nearest location. ~ 213-626-4455, 800-266-6883; www.mta.net.

The **Metro Red Line** runs between Downtown (from the Union Station rail passenger terminal) and the MacArthur Park area in seven minutes; it also extends along Wilshire Boulevard and into Hollywood and the San Fernando Valley. The **Metro Gold Line** runs from Union Station to Pasadena. The **Metro Blue Line** operates daily between Downtown and Long Beach. The **Metro Green Line** trains travel from Norwalk and Redondo Beach to Los Angeles International Airport.

When using the bus for an extended period of time, you can save money by purchasing an MTA Day, Weekly, Semi-Monthly, or Monthly Pass. The EZ Transit pass, good for a month, will get you on any Metro Bus or Metro Rail line. Passes are available at any ticket machine or Metro Customer Center.

For traveling around downtown Los Angeles or Westwood, the DASH shuttle service is available Monday through Saturday (except holidays). ~ 213-626-4455.

TAXIS

Several cab companies serve Los Angeles International Airport, including **United Independent Taxi** (323-934-6700) and **Yellow Cab** (213-627-7000).

From Burbank Airport, **Taxi Services** provides taxi service. ~ 818-843-8500, 818-558-3000.

THREE

Los Angeles Coast

L.A., according to a popular song, is a great big freeway. Actually, this sprawling metropolis by the sea is a great big beach. From Long Beach north to Malibu is a 74-mile stretch of sand that attracts visitors in the tens of millions every year. Life here reflects the culture of the beach, a freewheeling, hedonist philosophy that combines pleasure-seeking with healthfulness.

Perfectly fitted to this philosophy is the weather. The coastal climatic zone, called a maritime fringe, is characterized by cooler summers, warmer winters, and higher humidity than elsewhere in California. Sea breezes and salt air keep the beaches relatively free from smog. During summer months the thermometer hovers around 75° or 80° and water temperatures average 67°. Winter carries intermittent rain and brings the ocean down to a chilly 55°.

Add a broadly ranging coastal topography and Los Angeles has an urban escape valve less than an hour from downtown. The shoreline lies along the lip of the Los Angeles basin, a flat expanse interrupted by the sharp cliffs of the Palos Verdes Peninsula and the rocky heights of the Santa Monica Mountains. There are broad strands lapped by gentle waves and pocket beaches exploding with surf. Though most of the coast is built up, some sections remain raw and undeveloped.

Route 1, the Pacific Coast Highway, parallels the coast the entire length of Los Angeles County, tying its beach communities together. To the south lie Long Beach and San Pedro, industrial enclaves which form the port of Los Angeles, a world center for commerce and shipping. Embodying 35 miles of heavily developed waterfront, the port is a maze of inlets, islets, and channels protected by a six-mile breakwater. It is one of the world's largest manmade harbors; over $79 billion in cargo crosses its docks every year. Despite all this hubbub, the harbor supports over 125 fish species and over 90 types of birds, including several endangered species.

The great port dates to 1835 when a small landing was built on the shore. Following the Civil War an imaginative entrepreneur named Phineas Banning developed the area, brought in the railroad, and launched Los Angeles into the 20th century. Now Long Beach wears several hats. In addition to being a major port and manufacturing center, it is the site of a naval base and a revitalized tourist center.

Home to the retired ocean liner *Queen Mary* and the Aquarium of the Pacific, Long Beach also contains the neighborhood of Naples, a system of islands, canals, and footbridges reminiscent of Italy's gondola cities.

Once an amusement center complete with airship, carousel, and sword swallowers, the city became one big oil field during the 1920s. That's when wildcat wells struck rich deposits and the region was transformed into a two-square-mile maze of derricks. Even today the offshore "islands" hide hundreds of oil wells.

Commercial fishing, another vital industry in Long Beach and San Pedro, supports an international collection of sailors. Mariners from Portugal, Greece, and elsewhere work the waterfront and add to the ethnic ambience.

Just a few miles north, along the Palos Verdes Peninsula, blue collar gives way to white collar and the urban surrenders to the exotic. A region of exclusive neighborhoods and striking geologic contrasts, Palos Verdes possesses Los Angeles' prettiest seascapes. A series of 13 marine terraces, interrupted by sheer cliffs, descend to a rocky shoreline. For 15 miles the roadway rides high above the surf past tidepools, rocky points, a lighthouse, and secluded coves.

This wealthy suburban environment is replaced in turn by another type of culture, typified by blond-haired surfers. Santa Monica Bay, the predominant feature of the Los Angeles Coast, is a single broad crescent of sand extending 30 miles from Redondo Beach through Venice and Santa Monica to Point Dume. South Bay—comprising the towns of Redondo Beach, Hermosa Beach, and Manhattan Beach—is the surfing center of Southern California, where the sport was first imported from Hawaii. This strip of coast is also home to Los Angeles International Airport.

Like most of the coastal communities, South Bay didn't take off as a beach resort until the turn of the 20th century, after railroad lines were extended from the city center to the shore and several decades after downtown Los Angeles experienced its 1880s population boom.

It was well into the 20th century, 1962 to be exact, that neighboring Marina del Rey, the largest manmade small boat harbor in the world, was developed. Nearby Venice, on the other hand, was an early 1900s attempt to re-create its Italian namesake. Built around plazas and grand canals, Venice originally was a fashionable resort town with oceanfront hotels and an amusement park. Today studios and galleries have replaced canals and gondolas in this seaside artist colony. The place has become a center for thinkers at the cutting edge and street people who have stepped over it. Zany and unchartable, modern-day Venice is an open ward for artists, the place where bohemians go to the beach, where roller-skating is an art form and weightlifting a way of life.

The town of Santa Monica next door was originally developed as a beachside resort in 1875. Back in 1769 explorer Gaspar de Portolá had claimed the surrounding area for the Spanish crown. Over the years this royal domain has served as a major port, retirement community, and location for silent movies; today it is a bastion of brown-shingle houses, flower-covered trellises, and left-wing politics.

Bordering it to the north are the Santa Monica Mountains, a succession of rugged peaks that are part of the Transverse Range, the only mountains in California running east and west. Extending to the very edge of the sea, the Santa Monicas create Los Angeles' most varied terrain. White-sand beaches are framed by bald peaks, crystal waters and flourishing kelp beds attract abundant sea life and make for excellent fishing and skindiving, while the mountains provide a getaway for hikers and campers.

Lying along a narrow corridor between the Santa Monicas and the sea is Malibu, that quintessential symbol of California, a rich, glamorous community known for its movie stars and surfers. Once inhabited by Chumash Indians, whose skeletal remains are still occasionally uncovered, Malibu escaped Los Angeles' coastal development until 1928, when the aging widow who controlled the region like a personal fiefdom finally succumbed to the pressures of progress and profit. Within a few years it became a haven for Hollywood. Stars like Ronald Colman and John Gilbert found their paradise on the sands of Malibu. Like figures out of *The Great Gatsby*, they lived insouciant lives in movie-set houses.

By the 1960s artists and counterculturalists, seeking to flee a town that in turn had become too commercial and crowded, left Malibu for the outlying mountains. In Topanga Canyon they established freeform communities, undermined in

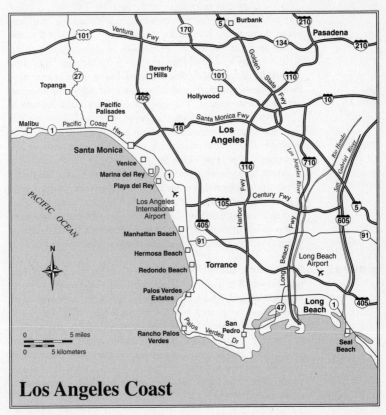

Los Angeles Coast

recent years by breathtaking real-estate prices, but still retaining vestiges of their days as a flower children's retreat.

The most romantic locale along the Los Angeles Coast lies 22 miles offshore. Santa Catalina, highlighted by Avalon, a resort town tucked between mountains and ocean, is a 21-mile-long island almost entirely undeveloped, given over to cactus and grazing buffalo. Through the centuries this solitary island has undergone many incarnations—habitat for Stone Age Indians; base for Russian fur hunters; center for pirates, smugglers, and gold prospectors; gathering place for the big bands of the 1930s; and strategic military base during World War II. Today it's a singular spot where visitors enjoy the amenities of Avalon and the seclusion of the island's outback. If Avalon, with its art-deco waterfront, provides a picture of Los Angeles circa 1933, the rest of the island is a window on Los Angeles in its natural state, wild and alluring, long before freighters embarked from Long Beach, surfers worked the South Bay, and movie moguls uncovered Malibu.

▼▼▼▼▼▼▼▼▼▼▼▼
Long Beach

Anchoring the southern end of Los Angeles County is Long Beach, one of California's largest cities (the fifth-largest, in fact). Back in the Roaring Twenties, after oil was discovered and the area experienced a tremendous building boom, Long Beach became known as "The Coney Island of the West." Boasting five and a half miles of beachfront and a grand amusement park, it was a favorite spot for daytripping Angelenos.

Several decades of decline followed, but in more recent years the metropolis launched a redevelopment plan dubbed the Queensway Bay Development. The star of this facelift is the Aquarium of the Pacific. Together with the *Queen Mary* and Shoreline Village, the aquarium rounded out an oceanfront triumvirate of family-oriented attractions, each of which is accessible to the others by a water taxi called the AquaBus.

Today Long Beach ranks together with neighboring San Pedro as one of the largest manmade harbors in the world and is a popular tourist destination. It's a revealing place, a kind of social studies lesson in modern American life. Travel Ocean Boulevard as it parallels the sea and you'll pass from quaint homes to downtown skyscrapers to fire-breathing smokestacks.

SIGHTS

For a dynamic example of what I mean, visit the enclave of **Naples** near the south end of town. Conceived early in the 20th century, modeled on Italy's fabled canal towns, it's a tiny community of three islands separated by canals and linked with walkways. Waterfront greenswards gaze out on Alamitos Bay and its fleet of sloops and motorboats. You can wander along bayside paths past comfortable homes, contemporary condos, and humble cottages. Fountains and miniature traffic circles, alleyways and boulevards, all form an incredible labyrinth along which you undoubtedly will become lost.

Adding to the sense of old Italia is the **Gondola Getaway,** a romantic hour-long cruise through the canals of Naples. For a hefty price (less, however, than a ticket to Italy), you can climb aboard a gondola, dine on hors d'oeuvres, and occasionally be serenaded with Italian music. Reservations of up to three weeks in advance are strongly suggested. ~ 5437 East Ocean Boulevard, Naples; 562-433-9595; www.gondola.net.

Housed in a converted skating rink, the **Museum of Latin American Art** is the only museum in the western United States to exclusively exhibit contemporary art from Latin America. The museum store also features the works of Latin American artists. For children there are hands-on art-making workshops on Sunday. Closed Monday. Admission. ~ 628 Alamitos Avenue; 562-437-1689, fax 562-437-7043; www.molaa.com, e-mail info@ molaa.com.

For a touch of early Spanish/Mexican culture, plan on visiting the region's old adobes. Built around 1800 with walls more than two feet thick, the adobe core of **Rancho Los Alamitos** is one of Southern California's oldest remaining houses. In its gardens, which cover more than three acres, are brick walkways and a variety of majestic trees. You can tour old barns (housing draft horses, sheep, and chickens), a blacksmith shop, and a feed shed. There's also a chuck wagon with a coffeepot still resting on the wood-burning stove. Closed Monday and Tuesday. ~ 6400 Bixby Hill Road (enter at guard gate at Palo Verde and Anaheim); 562-

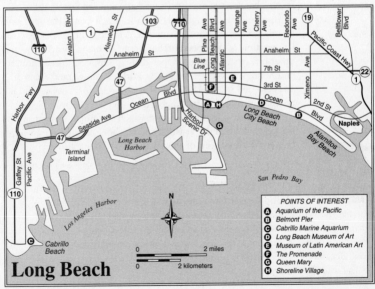

Long Beach

POINTS OF INTEREST

- Ⓐ Aquarium of the Pacific
- Ⓑ Belmont Pier
- Ⓒ Cabrillo Marine Aquarium
- Ⓓ Long Beach Museum of Art
- Ⓔ Museum of Latin American Art
- Ⓕ The Promenade
- Ⓖ Queen Mary
- Ⓗ Shoreline Village

0   2 miles

0   2 kilometers

431-3541, fax 562-430-9694; rancholosalamitos.com, e-mail info@rancholosalamitos.com.

Rancho Los Cerritos, a two-story Monterey Colonial home built in 1844, once served as headquarters for a 27,000-acre ranch. Now the adobe is filled with Victorian furniture and reflects the families and workers who lived and worked on the ranch in the 19th century. The site includes historic gardens, a California history research library and an orientation exhibit. Closed Monday and Tuesday. ~ 4600 Virginia Road; 562-570-1755, fax 562-570-1893; www.ranchoscerritos.org.

The Pacific Ocean may be Long Beach's biggest natural attraction, but many birds in the area prefer the **El Dorado Nature Center.** Part of the 450-acre El Dorado East Regional Park, this 103-acre wildlife sanctuary offers one- and two-mile hikes past two lakes and a stream. About 150 bird species as well as numerous land animals can be sighted. Though located in a heavily urbanized area, the facility encompasses several ecological zones. There's also a quarter-mile paved, handicapped-accessible nature trail. Closed Monday. Parking fee. ~ 7550 East Spring Street; 562-570-1745, fax 562-570-8530; www.ci.long-beach.ca.us/park/index.htm.

Another side of Long Beach is the steel-and-glass downtown area, where highrise hotels vie for dominance. The best way to tour this crowded commercial district is to stroll **The Promenade,** a six-block brick walkway leading from 3rd Street to the waterfront. There's a **tile mosaic** (Promenade and 3rd Street) at the near end portraying an idyllic day at the beach complete with sailboats, sunbathers, and lifeguards. Visit the **Long Beach Area Convention & Visitors Bureau,** home to maps, brochures, and other bits of information. Open daily in summer; closed Saturday and Sunday at other times. ~ 1 World Trade Center, Suite 300; 562-436-3645, 800-452-7829, fax 562-435-5653; www.visitlong beach.com, e-mail staff@longbeachcvb.org.

The latest addition to Long Beach's popular waterfront attractions is **The Pike at Rainbow Harbor.** Located on 18 acres beside the Aquarium of the Pacific, The Pike features a slew of

sights

AUTHOR FAVORITE

The **Long Beach Museum of Art** is a must. Dedicated to the past 300 years of design and decorative arts, this museum has ever-changing exhibits, bluff-top gardens, and an oceanview café. Closed Monday. Admission, except for the first Friday of every month. ~ 2300 East Ocean Boulevard; 562-439-2119, fax 562-439-3587; www.lbma.org, e-mail tours@lbma.org.

restaurants and places to play, including a pedestrian bridge over Shoreline Village Drive, a carousel, Ferris wheel and movie theater and video arcade.

Cross Ocean Boulevard and you'll arrive at a park shaded with palm trees and adjacent to **Shoreline Village**, a shopping center and marina disguised as a 19th-century fishing village. ~ 407 Shoreline Village Drive.

Another aspect of Long Beach rises in the form of oil derricks and industrial complexes just across the water. To view the freighters, tankers, and warships lining the city's piers, gaze out from the northern fringes of Shoreline Village.

Fittingly, the climax of a Long Beach tour comes at the very end, after you have experienced the three phases of urban existence. Just across the Los Angeles River, along Harbor Scenic Drive ("scenic" in this case meaning construction cranes and cargo containers), lies one of the strangest sights I've ever encountered. The first time I saw it, peering through the steel filigree of a suspension bridge, with harbor lights emblazoning the scene, I thought something had gone colossally wrong with the world. An old-style ocean liner, gleaming eerily in the false light, appeared to be parked on the ground. Next to it an overgrown geodesic dome, a kind of giant aluminum breast, was swelling up out of the earth.

Unwittingly I had happened upon Long Beach's top tourist attraction, the *Queen Mary*, once the world's largest ocean liner. Making her maiden voyage in 1936, the **Queen Mary** was the pride of Great Britain. Winston Churchill, the Duke and Duchess of Windsor, Greta Garbo, and Fred Astaire sailed on her, and during World War II, she was converted to military service.

Today she is the pride of Long Beach, a 1000-foot-long "city at sea" transformed into a floating museum and hotel that brilliantly re-create shipboard life. An elaborate walking tour carries you down into the engine room (a world of pumps and propellers), out along the decks, and up to each level of this multistage behemoth. There's a parking fee and admission to the ship (the admission fee is waived for hotel guests).

The *Queen Mary* is expertly refurbished and wonderfully laid out, an important addition to the Long Beach seafront and the anchor attraction for Queen Mary Seaport, which also includes the **Queen Mary Seawalk** shopping and dining area. Her neighbor is the world's largest clear-span geodesic dome. The dome once housed Howard Hughes' *Spruce Goose*, the largest plane ever built. Admission. ~ 1126 Queen's Highway; 562-435-3511, 800-437-2934, fax 562-437-4531; www.queenmary.com, e-mail attractions@queenmary.com.

The **Aquarium of the Pacific**, located at the waterfront Rainbow Harbor in downtown Long Beach, has three major permanent galleries designed to lead visitors on a "journey of discovery" through the waters of the Pacific Ocean. The journey begins in the temperate waters of Southern California and Baja, and includes tidepools and endangered sea turtles. The Bering Sea is the focus of the exhibit representing the icy waters of the northern Pacific, which are inhabited by sea otters, a giant octopus, and spider crabs. The coral reefs and lagoons of Palau in Micronesia are spotlighted in the Tropical Pacific Gallery, which also features the huge Tropical Reef exhibit, where microphone-equipped scuba divers swim along with schools of brilliant fish and sharks, answering questions for visitors. There's also an outdoor lagoon where visitors can touch sharks and a lorikeet forest where visitors can handfeed colorful birds. Admission. ~ 100 Aquarium Way; 562-590-3100, fax 562-590-3109; www.aquariumofpacific.org, e-mail info@lbaop.org.

> The *Queen Mary* carried so many troops across the Atlantic Ocean that Adolf Hitler offered $250,000 and the Iron Cross to the U-boat captain who sank her.

Long Beach's latest effort to draw tourists is the Soviet-built submarine **Scorpion**, which is docked alongside the *Queen Mary*. Visitors enter through the forward hatch of the 300-foot Foxtrot-class Russian sub, then squeeze their way along corridors for a look through the periscope and a self-guided tour of the torpedo room, crew quarters, and communications center. Admission. ~ 1126 Queen's Highway; 562-435-3511.

The **AquaBus**, a water taxi service, links the city's main waterfront attractions—the aquarium, Shoreline Village, the *Queen Mary*, Catalina Express, and the convention center—with daily service. ~ 800-429-4601.

Long Beach is also a departure point for the **Catalina Express** shuttle boats to Santa Catalina Island. Reservations recommended. ~ 310-519-1212, 800-897-7154; www.catalinaexpress.com.

Beyond all the shoreline hubbub, the venerable Pacific gray whales migrate along the "Whale Freeway" between late December and mid-April, and several enterprises in Long Beach offer whale-watching opportunities. The **Long Beach Area Convention & Visitors Bureau** can put you in touch with a whale-watching operator. ~ 800-452-7829; www.visitlongbeach.org, e-mail staff@longbeachcvb.org.

LODGING   The **Beach Plaza Hotel** has 40 units, some with ocean views, many offering kitchens and all with easy access to the beach. Each room is furnished in contemporary fashion. There's a pool and jacuzzi. ~ 2010 East Ocean Boulevard; 562-437-0771, 800-485-8758, fax 562-437-0900; www.beachplazahotel.net, e-mail yemaneh@verizon.com. MODERATE

Granted I'm a fool for gimmicks, but somehow the opportunity to stay aboard a historic ocean liner seems overwhelming.

Where else but at the **Hotel Queen Mary** can you recapture the magic of British gentility before World War II? What other hotel offers guests a "sunning deck"? Staying in the original state-rooms of this grand old ship, permanently docked on the Long Beach waterfront, you are surrounded by the art-deco designs for which the *Queen Mary* is famous. Some guest rooms are small (this *is* a ship!) and dimly illuminated through portholes, but the decor is classic. There are also restaurants, lounges, and shops on board. ~ 1126 Queen's Highway; 562-435-3511, 800-437-2934, fax 562-437-4531; www.queenmary.com, e-mail reservations@ queenmary.com. DELUXE.

DINING

One of the first small brewery/restaurants in the Long Beach area, the **Belmont Brewing Company** brews pale and amber ales, seasonal beers, and a dark, rich porter—Long Beach Crude— that closely resembles the real stuff pumped from nearby coastal oil derricks. Gourmet pizzas, fresh seafood, steaks, and pastas are served in the dining area, at the bar, and outside on the patio. I'd opt for the patio where you can enjoy watching the sun set over the water. Breakfast is served on the weekends. ~ 25 39th Place; 562-433-3891, fax 562-434-0604; www.belmontbrewing. com. MODERATE.

◀ HIDDEN

Southern cooking at the **Shenandoah Café** is becoming a tradition among savvy shore residents. The quilts and baskets decorating this understated establishment lend a country air to the place. Add waitresses in aprons dishing out hot apple fritters and it gets downright homey. Dinner and Sunday brunch are special events occasioned with "riverwalk steak" (filet in mustard caper sauce), prime rib, salmon on wild-rice pancake, gumbo, "granny's fried chicken," and Texas-style beef brisket. Try it! No breakfast or lunch Monday through Saturday. ~ 4722 East 2nd Street; 562-434-3469, fax 562-438-4299; www.shenandoahcafe.com, e-mail info@shenandoahcafe.com. MODERATE TO ULTRA-DELUXE.

◀ HIDDEN

The Porch Cafe, a gay-owned restaurant that serves great breakfasts and lunches, is a favorite with the town's large gay and lesbian population, as well as with straight folks who also appreciate the generous portions and reasonable prices. The breakfast special of eggs, French toast, bacon, and orange juice is available for under $6. No dinner. Closed Wednesday. ~ 2708 East 4th Street; 562-433-0118. BUDGET.

In downtown Long Beach the **King's Pine Avenue Fish House** is a prime spot for seafood. The private booths and dark wood trim lend an antique atmosphere to this open-kitchen establishment. The seafood platters are too numerous to recite (besides, the menu changes daily); suffice it to say that you can have them baked, broiled, sautéed, or grilled. For those not keen on seafood, there are also pasta, pizza, and chicken. ~ 100 West Broadway; 562-432-7463, fax 562-435-6143; www.kingsfishhouse. com. MODERATE TO DELUXE.

Back in the world of good eats and frugal budgets, **Acapulco Mexican Restaurant & Cantina** offers standard as well as innovative dishes. Tacos, burritos, and enchiladas are only the beginning; this comfortable eatery also serves several Mexican-style seafood dishes. ~ 6270 East Pacific Coast Highway; 562-596-3371, fax 562-431-0290. MODERATE.

The Reef on the Water is rambling, ramshackle, and wonderful. Built of rough-sawn cedar, it sits along the waterfront on a dizzying series of levels. The Continental American cuisine includes such contemporary choices as seafood collage and jumbo shrimp scampi. For the traditionalists, there are steaks, pasta, and swordfish. There's also Sunday brunch. ~ 880 Harbor Scenic Drive; 562-435-8013, fax 562-432-6823; www.specialtyrestau rants.com. MODERATE TO DELUXE.

What more elegant a setting in which to dine than aboard the *Queen Mary*. There you will find everything from snack kiosks to coffee shops to first-class dining rooms. The **Promenade Café** offers a reasonably priced menu of chicken, steak, and seafood dishes. They also have salads and sandwiches. The café is a lovely art-deco restaurant featuring period lamps and stunning views. Breakfast, lunch and dinner served. ~ 1126 Queen's Highway; 562-499-1595, fax 562-432-7674; www.queenmary.com. MODERATE TO DELUXE.

For a true taste of regal life aboard the old ship, cast anchor at **Sir Winston's**, the *Queen Mary*'s most elegant restaurant. The Continental and California cuisine in this dining emporium includes rack of lamb, veal medallion, muscovy duck, venison, châteaubriand, broiled swordfish, and Australian lobster. Sir Winston's is a wood-paneled dining room with copper-rimmed mirrors, white tablecloths, and upholstered armchairs. The walls are adorned with photos of the great prime minister and every window opens onto a full view of Long Beach. A semiformal dress code is enforced and jackets are requested. Reservations required. Dinner only. ~ 1126 Queen's Highway; 562-499-1657, fax 562-432-7674; www.queenmary.com, e-mail sirwinstons@ queenmary.com. ULTRA-DELUXE.

SHOPPING   The best street shopping in Long Beach is in Belmont Shore along **East 2nd Street**. This 15-block strip between Livingston Drive and Bayshore Avenue is a gentrified row. Either side is lined with art galleries, book shops, boutiques, jewelers, and import stores.

For **vintage-store and antiques** shoppers, Redondo Avenue, East Broadway, and East 4th Street in downtown Long Beach have nearly two dozen stores where you can find everything from Bauer pottery to antique furniture to Depression glass to beaded sweaters. Look for a copy of the Long Beach Antique and Vintage Shopping Guide to help you map out your itinerary.

Shoreline Village is one of those waterfront malls Southern California specializes in. With a marina on both sides, the buildings are New England–style shingle and clapboard structures designed to re-create an Atlantic Coast port town. ~ 407 Shoreline Village Drive; 562-435-2668; www.shorelinevillage.com.

There are more than half a dozen stores onboard the **Queen Mary**. There is a fee charged to board the ship. Concentrated in the Piccadilly Circus section of the old ship are several souvenir shops as well as stores specializing in artifacts and old-fashioned items. Perhaps the prettiest shopping arcade you'll ever enter, it is an art-deco masterpiece with etched glass, dentil molding, and brass appointments. ~ 1126 Queen's Highway; 562-435-3511; www.queenmary.com.

Adjacent to the *Queen Mary*, the **Queen Mary Seawalk** is a shopping plaza styled after a 19th-century British village and offering a variety of speciality and souvenir shops.

Panama Joe's Grill & Cantina cooks Thursday through Sunday night. The bands are R&B ensembles, rock groups, and assorted others, which create an eclectic blend of music. Your average Tiffany-lamp-and-hanging-plant nightspot, the place is lined with sports photos and proudly displays an old oak bar. ~ 5100 East 2nd Street; 562-434-7417; www.panamajoes.com.

NIGHTLIFE

E. J. Malloy's is a small sports bar with a comfortable pub-style interior including a long wood bar, brick walls, and plenty of televisions for watching a Lakers game with the locals. There's a fireplace, bar, and patio seating. The sports fans can get loud and rambunctious on game nights. ~ 3411 East Broadway; 562-433-3769, fax 562-987-3580.

Located right along the promenade in downtown Long Beach is **The Blue Café**. This tavern serves up live blues, swing, and alternative music seven nights a week and tasty dishes from the deli

AUTHOR FAVORITE

No matter how grand, regardless of how much money went into its design, despite the care taken to assure quality, any Long Beach nightspot is hard pressed to match the elegance of the **Observation Bar** aboard the *Queen Mary*. Once the first-class bar for this grand old ship, the room commands a 180° view across the bow and out to the Long Beach skyline. The walls are lined with fine woods, a mural decorates the bar, and art-deco appointments appear everywhere. The bar features live jazz as well as rock-and-roll on the weekends.

and grill. Hip hustlers hang out upstairs where there are plenty of billiard tables and a karaoke lounge on Friday nights. Closed Monday. Cover. ~ 210 Promenade North; 562-983-7111, fax 562-901-3057; www.thebluecafe.com.

If live music is not your thing, you can always adjourn aft to **Sir Winston's Piano Bar**, a cozy and elegant setting decorated with memorabilia of the WWII British leader. ~ 1126 Queen's Highway; 562-499-1657.

GAY SCENE   A long-time favorite is **Ripples**, which has a dance-club upstairs and a bar downstairs. There's also a pool table and patio. Live entertainment on Saturday and Sunday. Cover. ~ 5101 East Ocean Boulevard; 562-433-0357; www.clubripples.com. **Mineshaft** has pool tables, pinball machines, and live deejay music Tuesday, Friday, and Saturday. ~ 1720 East Broadway; 562-436-2433.

The Falcon is a gay bar complete with a CD player and dart boards. ~ 1435 East Broadway; 562-432-4146.

BEACHES & PARKS

ALAMITOS PENINSULA   The ocean side of this slender salient offers a pretty sand beach looking out on a tiny island. Paralleling the beach is an endless string of woodframe houses. The sand corridor extends all the way to the entrance of Alamitos Bay where a stone jetty provides recreation for anglers, occasional surfers, swimmers, and climbers with sturdy hiking shoes. Facilities include restrooms, lifeguards in summer, and volleyball courts; the paved bike path leading to Aquarium of the Pacific begins here. ~ Located along Ocean Boulevard between 54th Place and 72nd Place; park at the end of the road; 562-570-3100, 562-570-3109.

BAYSHORE BEACH   This hook-shaped strand curves along the eastern and southern shores of a narrow inlet. Protected from the ocean by a peninsula and breakwater, the beach faces the waterfront community of Naples; you can catch gondola rides through Naples' canals. Houses line the beach along most of its length. Protected from surf and tide, this is a safe, outstanding spot for swimming, and conditions are perfect for windsurfing. At the corner of Bayshore and Ocean there are basketball and handball courts as well as kayak and sailboat rentals. Restrooms are available at the beach; lifeguards in summer only. ~ Located along Bayshore Avenue and Ocean Boulevard; 562-570-3215, fax 562-570-3247.

LONG BEACH CITY BEACH   They don't call it Long Beach for nothing. This strand is broad and boundless, a silvery swath traveling much of the length of town. There are several islets parked offshore. Along the miles of beachfront you'll find numerous facilities and good size crowds. Bel-

mont Veterans Memorial Pier, a 1300-foot-long, hammerhead-shaped walkway, bisects the beach and offers fishing services. Fishing is good from the pier, where halibut and sea bass are common catches, and the beach is protected by the harbor breakwater, making for safe swimming. Along the beach you'll find restrooms, lifeguards, a snack bar, a playground, and volleyball courts. A paved bike path along Long Beach City Beach leads to the Aquarium of the Pacific. ~ Located along Ocean Boulevard between 1st and 72nd places. Belmont Pier is at Ocean Boulevard and 39th Place; 562-570-3100, 562-570-3109.

San Pedro

Overlooking the busy Port of Los Angeles and scored by shipping channels, San Pedro lies at the eastern end of the rocky Palos Verdes Peninsula. In 1542 Portuguese explorer Juan Cabrillo sailed into the bay and named it "Bay of Smokes," inspired by the hillside fires of the Gabrieleño Indians; San Pedro was given its current name by Spanish navigator Sebastian Vizcaino in 1602. The city began to develop its reputation as a major port in the mid-19th century, when the railroad came to town. Almost 100 years later, during World War II, Fort MacArthur was built on the bluff to protect the bustling harbor from invasion. Now the fort houses a small museum and a youth hostel. All manner of boats, from tankers to fishing vessels, cruise the bay in peace.

SIGHTS

The Los Angeles Harbor, a region of creosote and rust, is marked by 28 miles of busy waterfront. This landscape of oil tanks and cargo containers services thousands of ships every year.

◄ **HIDDEN**

Head over to the **22nd Street Landing** and watch sportfishing boats embark on high-sea adventures. Then wander the waterfront and survey this frontier of steel and oil. Here awkward, unattractive ships glide as gracefully as figure skaters and the machinery of civilization goes about the world's work with a clatter and boom. The most common shorebirds are cargo cranes. ~ At the foot of 22nd Street.

San Pedro is a departure point for the Catalina Express Shuttleboats to Santa Catalina Island. ~ 800-897-7154.

Ports O' Call Village, a shopping mall in the form of a 19th-century port town, is home to several outfits conducting harbor cruises. ~ The entrance is at the foot of 6th Street; 310-732-7696. The boats sail around the San Pedro waterfront and venture out for glimpses of the surrounding shoreline; for more information, call **Spirit Cruises**. ~ Ports O' Call Village; 310-548-8080; www.spiritdinnercruises.com.

Moored serenely between two bustling docks is the **S.S. Lane Victory**. This World War II cargo ship, a 455-foot-long National Historic Landmark, offers weekend cruises from mid-July to mid-

September as well as daily tours. Admission. ~ Berth 94; 310-519-9545, fax 310-519-0265; www.lanevictoryship.com.

For more of our history on the sea, stop by the **Los Angeles Maritime Museum**. This dockside showplace displays models of ships ranging from fully rigged brigs to 19th-century steam schooners to World War II battleships. Exhibits include a comprehensive display on the history of commercial (hard-hat) diving in Los Angeles Habor. Closed Monday. ~ Berth 84; 310-548-7618, fax 310-832-6537; www.lamaritimemuseum.org, e-mail museum@lamaritimemuseum.org.

HIDDEN ►

Another piece in the port's historic puzzle is placed several miles inland at the **Phineas Banning Residence Museum**. This imposing Greek Revival house, built in 1864, was home to the man who dreamed, dredged, and developed Los Angeles Harbor. Today Phineas Banning's Mansion, complete with a cupola from which he watched ships navigate his port, is furnished in period pieces and open for guided tours. Closed Monday and Friday. ~ 401 East M Street, Wilmington; 310-548-7777; www.banningmuseum.org.

By definition any shipping center is of strategic importance. Head up to **Fort MacArthur** and discover the gun batteries with which World War II generals planned to protect Los Angeles Harbor. From this cement-and-steel compound you can inspect the bunkers and a small military museum, then survey the coast. Once a site of gun turrets and grisly prospects, today it is a testimonial to the invasion that never came. ~ Angel's Gate Park, 3601 South Gaffey Street; 310-548-2631; www.ftmac.org, e-mail director@ftmac.org.

Extending along 6th Street between Mesa Street and Harbor Boulevard is the Sportswalk, featuring plaques dedicated to Olympic medalists as well as great collegiate and professional athletes.

Nearby, you can visit the **Bell of Friendship**, which the people of South Korea presented to the United States during its 1976 bicentennial. Housed in a multi-color pagoda and cast with floral and symbolic images, it rests on a hilltop looking out on Los Angeles Harbor and the region's sharply profiled coastline.

Down the hill at the **Cabrillo Marine Aquarium**, there is a modest collection of display cases with samples of shells, coral, and shorebirds. Several dozen aquariums exhibit local fish and marine plants, and there's a large outdoor touch tank. Closed Monday. ~ 3720 Stephen M. White Drive; 310-548-7562, fax 310-548-2649; www.cabrilloaq.org, e-mail info@cabrilloaq.org.

Nearby, 1200-foot **Cabrillo Fishing Pier** stretches into the Pacific from Cabrillo Beach, where on a clear day you can see Santa Catalina.

Of greater interest is **Point Fermin Park**, a 37-acre blufftop facility resting above spectacular tidepools and a marine preserve.

The tidepools are accessible from the Cabrillo Marine Aquarium, which sponsors exploratory tours, and via steep trails from the park. Also of note (though not open to the public) is the **Point Fermin Lighthouse**, a unique 19th-century clapboard house with a beacon set in a rooftop crow's nest. From the park plateau, like lighthouse keepers of old, you'll have open vistas of the cliff-fringed coastline and a perfect perch for sighting whales during their winter migration. ~ 805 Paseo del Mar; 310-548-7756; e-mail parkoffice@sanpedro.com.

Then drive along Paseo del Mar, through arcades of stately palm trees and along sharp sea cliffs, until it meets 25th Street. The sedimentary rocks throughout this region have been twisted and contorted into grotesque shapes by tremendous geologic pressures.

LODGING

Hostelling International—Los Angeles South Bay is located in the Army barracks of old Fort MacArthur. Set in Angel's Gate Park on a hilltop overlooking the ocean, it's a pretty site with easy access to beaches. Men and women are housed separately in dorms but couples can be accommodated. Kitchen facilities are provided. Reservations are highly recommended from June through August. ~ 3601 South Gaffey Street, Building 613; 310-831-8109, fax 310-831-4635; e-mail hisanpedro@aol.com. BUDGET.

San Pedro also has several chain hotels designed to serve the needs of departing or returning cruise ship passengers. Perhaps the most distinctive among them is the **Holiday Inn San Pedro**, which captures the flavor of a traditional European hotel. Behind the columned facade with its faux mansard roof are individually decorated Victorian-style rooms; some have kitchenettes. Two-room suites with harbor views and fireplaces are available. ~ 111 South Gaffey Street; 310-514-1414, 800-248-3188, fax 310-831-8262; www.holidayinnsanpedro.com. MODERATE TO DELUXE.

DINING

The vintage shopping mall at **Ports O' Call Village** is Los Angeles Harbor's prime tourist center. It's situated right on the San Pedro waterfront and houses numerous restaurants. Try to avoid the high-ticket dining rooms, as they are overpriced and serve mediocre food to out-of-town hordes. But there are a number of take-out stands and ethnic eateries, priced in the budget and moderate ranges, which provide an opportunity to dine inexpensively on the water. ~ The entrance is at the foot of 6th Street; 310-732-7696.

◄ HIDDEN

Of course local anglers rarely frequent Ports O' Call. The old salts are over at **Canetti's Seafood Grotto**. It ain't on the waterfront, but it is within casting distance of the fishing fleet. Which means it's the right spot for fresh fish platters at good prices. Dinner Friday and Saturday; breakfast and lunch all week. ~ 309 East 22nd Street; 310-831-4036. MODERATE.

Trade the Pacific for the Aegean and set anchor at **Papadakis Taverna.** The menu features moussaka, Greek-style cheese dishes, lamb baked in pastry, grilled contessa shrimp in tomato and feta and occasional specials like stuffed eggplant, fresh seafood, and regional delicacies. Dinner only. ~ 301 West 6th Street; 310-548-1186. MODERATE TO ULTRA-DELUXE.

SHOPPING

Los Angeles Harbor's answer to the theme shopping mall craze is **Ports O' Call Village,** a mock 19th-century fishing village. There are clapboard stores with shuttered windows, New England–style structures with gabled roofs, and storehouses of corrugated metal. Dozens of shops here are located right on the water, giving you a chance to view the harbor while browsing the stores. It's one of those hokey but inevitable places that I swear to avoid but always seem to end up visiting. ~ The entrance is at the foot of 6th Street; 310-732-7696, fax 310-547-5389.

NIGHTLIFE

Landlubbers can enjoy a quiet drink on the waterfront at **Ports O' Call Restaurant.** In addition to a spiffy oak bar, they have a dockside patio. ~ Ports O' Call Village; 310-833-3553.

BEACHES & PARKS

CABRILLO BEACH The edge of Los Angeles harbor is an unappealing locale for a beach, but here it is, a two-part strand, covered with heavy-grain sand and bisected by a fishing pier. One half faces the shipping facility; the other half looks out on the glorious Pacific and abuts on the Point Fermin Marine Life Refuge, a rocky corridor filled with outstanding tidepools and backdropped by dramatic cliffs. You'll also find restrooms, showers, picnic areas, lifeguards, an aquarium, a playground, and volleyball courts. Fires are permitted. Fishing can be done from the pier, and for surfing try the beachfront and near the jetty; this area is a windsurfing mecca. People do swim here, but I saw a lot of refuse from the nearby shipping harbor. After heavy rains, storm drainage increases the bacteria count; stick to the oceanside during these times. If you like tidepooling, beeline to Cabrillo—if not, there are hundreds of other beaches in the Golden State. Parking fee, $6.60. ~ 3720 Stephen M. White Drive; 310-372-2166, fax 310-372-6902.

ROYAL PALMS COUNTY BEACH Situated at the base of a sedimentary cliff, this boulder-strewn beach gains its name from a grove of elegant palm trees. This was an erstwhile hub of elegant activity in the 1920s; the Royal Palms country club and a Japanese-owned resort presided here until a violent storm destroyed them in 1939. Today the guests of honor are surfers and tidepoolers. While the location is quite extraordinary, I prefer another beach, Point Fermin Park's **Wilder Annex,** located to the east. This little gem also lacks sand, but is built on three tiers of a cliff.

The upper level is decorated with palm trees, the middle tier has a grassy plot studded with shady magnolias, and the bottom floor is a rocky beach with promising tidepools and camera-eye views of Point Fermin. Fishing is good at both parks, but swimming is not recommended. Surfing is popular at Royal Palms, where there are lifeguards, and off White Point, a peninsula separating the two parks. Snorkelers and divers take advantage of Diver's Cove, at the far east end of the parking lot. Facilities are limited to restrooms. Day-use fee, $6. ~ Both parks are located along Paseo del Mar in San Pedro. Royal Palms is near the intersection with Western Avenue and Wilder Annex is around the intersection with Meyler Street; 310-372-2166, fax 310-372-6902.

Palos Verdes Peninsula

Though Portuguese explorer Juan Cabrillo first described the area in 1542, the peninsula was home to the Gabrieleño Indians until 1827, when Don Dolores Sepulveda received 75,000 acres in an original land grant. By 1913, a consortium of New York investors owned most of the property, which it planned to divide into large estates. However, the first homes didn't start appearing here until the mid-20th century. Today it is an upscale resi-

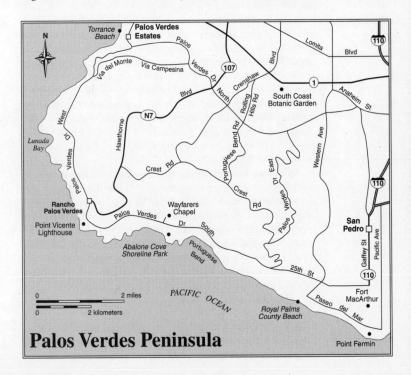

Palos Verdes Peninsula

dential neighborhood overlooking one of Southern California's loveliest stretches of coastline. Residents embrace an active lifestyle: Equestrian and hiking trails wind through lovely tree-shaded areas past pristine homes on large lots, and golfers try their luck on Los Angeles' only oceanfront golf course.

SIGHTS   The forces of nature seem to dominate as you proceed out along the Palos Verdes Peninsula from San Pedro. Follow 25th Street, then Palos Verdes Drive South and encounter a tumbling region where terraced hills fall away to sharp coastal bluffs.

As you turn **Portuguese Bend**, the geology of this tumultuous area becomes startlingly evident when the road begins undulating through landslide zones. The earthquake faults that underlie the Los Angeles basin periodically fold and collapse the ground here. To one side you'll see the old road, fractured and useless. Even the present highway, with more patches than your favorite dungarees, is in a state of constant repair.

Of course the terrible power of nature has not dissuaded people from building here. Along the ridgetops and curving hills below are colonies of stately homes. With its rocky headlands, tidepool beaches and sun-spangled views, the place is simply so magnificent no one can resist.

Most lordly of all these structures is the **Wayfarers Chapel**, a simple but extraordinary center designed by the son of Frank Lloyd Wright. Nestled neatly into the surrounding landscape, the sunlit chapel is built entirely of glass and commands broad views of the terrain and ocean. With its stone altar and easy repose the chapel was built to honor Emanuel Swedenborg, the 18th-century Swedish philosopher and mystic. A visitors center designed by Wrights's son, Eric Lloyd Wright, also graces the grounds. ~ 5755 Palos Verdes Drive South, Rancho Palos Verdes; 310-377-1650, fax 310-377-8589; www.wayfarerschapel.org, e-mail harveyt@wayfarerschapel.org.

The **Point Vicente Lighthouse** rises farther down the coast, casting an antique aura upon the area. While the beacon is not open to the public, the nearby **Point Vicente Interpretive Center** offers a small regional museum. This is a prime whale-watching spot in the winter when onlookers gather in the adjacent park to catch glimpses of migrating gray whales. (At press time, the center was closed for soil remediation work and construction; call ahead for reopening information.) Admission. ~ 31501 Palos Verdes Drive West, Rancho Palos Verdes; 310-377-5370, fax 310-544-5294; www.palosverdes.com/rpv.

For a vision of how truly beautiful this region is, turn off Palos Verdes Drive West in Palos Verdes Estates and follow Paseo

HIDDEN ▶   Lunado until it meets the sea at **Lunada Bay**. This half-moon inlet, backdropped by the jagged face of a rocky cliff, looks out upon an unending expanse of ocean. Steep paths lead down to a rocky shoreline rich in tidepools.

The road changes names to Paseo del Mar but continues past equally extraordinary coastline. There is a series of open fields and vista points along this shoreline preserve where you can gaze down from the blufftop to beaches and tidepools. Below, surfers ride the curl of frothing breaks and a few hardy hikers pick their way goat-like along precipitous slopes.

The setting is decidedly more demure at the **South Coast Botanic Garden**. This 87-acre garden is planted with exotic vegetation from Africa and New Zealand as well as species from other parts of the world. Admission. ~ 26300 South Crenshaw Boulevard, Palos Verdes; 310-544-6815, fax 310-544-6820; www.southcoastbotanicgarden.org.

Restaurants are a rare commodity along the Palos Verdes Peninsula. You'll find a cluster of them, however, in the Golden Cove Shopping Center. Granted, a mall is not the most appetizing spot to dine, but in this case who's complaining?

DINING

The Admiral Risty is one of those nautical cliché restaurants decorated along the outside with ropes and pilings and on the interior with brass fixtures. Know the type? Normally I wouldn't mention it, but the place has a full bar, a knockout view of the ocean, and happens to be the only member of its species in the entire area. My advice is to play it safe and order fresh fish (or never leave the bar). The menu is a surf-and-turf inventory of fish (prepared four ways), steak, chicken, and so on. Dinner and Sunday brunch. ~ 31250 Palos Verdes Drive West, Rancho Palos Verdes; 310-377-0050; www.admiral-risty.com, e-mail wayne@admiral-risty.com. DELUXE TO ULTRA-DELUXE.

> Malaga Cove is nick-named "RAT" beach because it's "right after Torrance."

For genuine elegance, make lunch or dinner reservations at **La Rive Gauche**, an attractively appointed French restaurant. With its upholstered chairs, brass wall sconces, and vintage travel posters, this cozy candlelit dining room is unique to the peninsula. The three-course dinner menu is a study in classic French cooking including veal chop with *foie gras* and truffles, duck à l'orange, and a selection of fresh seafood like Norway salmon and John Dory. A pianist adds to the romance. The lunch offerings, while more modest, follow a similar theme. In sum, gourmet cuisine, warm ambience, and a world-class wine list. No lunch on Monday. ~ 320 Tejon Place, Palos Verdes Estates; 310-378-0267, 888-646-8166, fax 310-373-5837. MODERATE TO ULTRA-DELUXE

ABALONE COVE SHORELINE PARK 🏃 🏄 🏊 ↵ The Palos Verdes Peninsula is so rugged and inaccessible that any beach by

BEACHES & PARKS

definition will be secluded. This gray-sand hideaway is no exception. It sits in a natural amphitheater guarded by sedimentary rock formations and looks out on Catalina Island. There are tidepools to ponder and a marine ecological reserve to explore, and the fishing and swimming are good. For surfing, try the east end of the cove. There are also picnic areas, restrooms, and lifeguards on weekends, holidays, and in summer. Parking fee, $5. ~ Off Palos Verdes Drive South in Rancho Palos Verdes. From the parking lot a path leads down to the beach; 310-377-1222.

TORRANCE BEACH 🚲 🏊 🎣 🏄 🌊 This beach is a lengthy stretch of bleach-blond sand guarded on one flank by the stately Palos Verdes Peninsula and on the other by an industrial complex and colony of smokestacks. Just your average middle-class beach; it's not one of my favorites, but it has the only white sand hereabouts. Also consider adjacent **Malaga Cove**, noted for tidepools, shells, and rock-hounding. Prettier than its pedestrian partner, Malaga Cove is framed by rocky bluffs. At Torrance there are restrooms, some concession stands, and lifeguards; around Malaga Cove you're on your own. Fishing for corbina is good at both beaches, and surfing is generally good (but better in winter) at Malaga Cove with steady, rolling waves ideal for beginners. For swimming I recommend Torrance, where lifeguards are on duty year-round. Parking fee, $5. ~ Paseo de la Playa in Torrance parallels the beach. To reach Malaga Cove, walk south from Torrance toward the cliffs; 310-372-2166, fax 310-372-6902.

▼▼▼▼▼▼▼▼▼▼▼▼
South Bay

The birthplace of California's beach culture lies in a string of towns on the southern skirt of Santa Monica Bay—Redondo Beach, Hermosa Beach, and Manhattan Beach. It all began here in the South Bay with George Freeth, "the man who can walk on water." It seems that while growing up in Hawaii, Freeth resurrected the ancient Polynesian sport of surfing and transplanted it to California. Equipped with a 200-pound, solid wood board, he introduced surfing to fascinated onlookers at a 1907 event in Redondo Beach.

It wasn't until the 1950s that the surfing wave crested. The surrounding towns became synonymous with the sport and a new culture was born, symbolized by blond-haired, blue-eyed surfers committed to sun, sand, and the personal freedom to ride the last wave. By the 1960s, a group of local kids called the Beach Boys were recording classic beach songs.

Sightseeing spots are rather scarce in these beach towns. As you can imagine, the interesting places are inevitably along the waterfront. Each town sports a municipal pier, with rows of knick-knack shops, cafés, and oceanview lounges, either along the pier or on the nearby waterfront.

In Redondo Beach, **Fisherman's Wharf** is home to surfcasters and hungry seagulls. Walk out past the shops, salt breeze in your face, and you can gaze along the waterfront to open ocean. Waves wash against the pilings. Beneath the wood plank walkway, sea birds dive for fish. These sights and sounds are repeated again and again on the countless piers that line the California coast.

In fact you'll find them recurring right up in Hermosa Beach at the **Municipal Pier**. Less grandiose than its neighbor, this 1320-foot concrete corridor is simply equipped with a snack bar and bait shop. From the end you'll have a sweeping view back along Hermosa Beach's low skyline. ~ Located at the foot of Pier Avenue, Hermosa Beach.

The **Manhattan Beach Pier**, which extends extends 900 feet from the beach, is the site of the **Roundhouse Marine Studies Lab and Aquarium**, a community marine science center full of local sea creatures. A mini-reef tank, shark tank, and touch tank make this a great place to take kids. ~ At the west end of Manhattan Beach Boulevard, Manhattan Beach; 310-379-8117, fax 310-937-9366; www.roundhousemb.com.

> The South Bay is the place for surfing, sunning, swimming, and soaking up the laid-back atmosphere.

The other sightseeing diversion in these parts is the stroll. The stroll, that is, along the beach. **Esplanade** in Redondo Beach is a wide boulevard paralleling the waterfront. Wander its length and take in the surfers, sunbathers, and swimmers who keep this resort town on the map. Or walk down to the waterline and let the cool Pacific bathe your feet.

In Hermosa Beach you can saunter along **The Strand**. This pedestrian thoroughfare borders a broad beach and passes an endless row of bungalows, cottages, and condominiums. It's a pleasant walk with shops and restaurants along the way.

The Strand continues along Manhattan Beach but lacks the commercial storefronts of Hermosa Beach. Wide and wonderful, the beach is lined by beautiful homes with plate-glass windows that reflect the blue hues of sea and sky. Together, these oceanfront walkways link the South Bay towns in a course that bicyclists can follow for miles.

Route 1 barrels through Los Angeles' beach towns and serves as the commercial strip for generic motels. As elsewhere, these facilities are characterized by clean, sterile rooms and comfortable, if unimaginative surroundings. Located within walking distance of the beach, the **Starlite Motel** offers 20 standard, motel-style units. ~ 716 South Pacific Coast Highway, Redondo Beach; 310-316-4314. BUDGET TO MODERATE.

The **Ramada Ltd.** features 40 rooms with refrigerators, microwaves, and TVs. Some of the rooms have jacuzzis. This establishment rests two blocks from the beach. Continental breakfast is included. ~ 435 South Pacific Coast Highway, Redondo Beach; 310-540-5998, fax 310-543-9828. BUDGET TO DELUXE.

The Portofino Hotel and Yacht Club is a big, brassy hotel set on King Harbor. The 163 units are decorated in contemporary fashion and look out either on the ocean or the adjoining marina. There is a decorous lobby as well as a waterside swimming pool and a restaurant; other facilities are nearby in the marina. ~ 260 Portofino Way, Redondo Beach; 310-379-8481, 800-468-4292, fax 310-372-7329; www.hotelportofino.com, e-mail reservations@theportofino.net. ULTRA-DELUXE.

The best bargain on lodging in South Bay is found at **Sea Sprite Motel & Apartments**. Located right on Hermosa Beach, this multibuilding complex offers oceanview rooms with kitchenettes at moderate to deluxe prices. The accommodations are tidy, well furnished, and fairly attractive. There is a swimming pool and sundeck overlooking the beach. The central shopping district is just two blocks away, making the location hard to match. You can also rent suites at deluxe prices or a two-bedroom beach cottage at an ultra-deluxe price. Be sure to ask for an oceanview room in one of the beachfront buildings. ~ 1016 The Strand, Hermosa Beach; 310-376-6933, fax 310-376-4107; www.seasprite motel.com, e-mail questions@seaspritemotel.com. MODERATE TO ULTRA-DELUXE.

At the **Hi View Motel**, you're only a step away from the beach, shopping malls, and restaurants. There are 21 standard rooms and 4 studio apartments (these are ultra-deluxe in price and rent by the week) for rent. ~ 100 South Sepulveda Boulevard, Manhattan Beach; 310-374-4608, fax 310-937-9542; e-mail reservations@hiviewmotel.com. BUDGET TO MODERATE.

The **Sea View Inn at the Beach** is a compound of five buildings a block up from the beach. Accommodations range from single and double rooms to suites to apartment-style units with kitchens. You'll find comfortable furniture, refrigerators, microwaves, and

SLEEP ON THE SHORE

One of the few Southern California beach hotels that is actually on the beach, the **Beach House at Hermosa** is a beautifully appointed, elegant three-story affair that offers 96 loft suites complete with fireplace, CD player, television, and continental breakfast. If you enjoy staying here, you might want to visit its sister facility up the coast in Half Moon Bay. ~ 1300 The Strand, Hermosa Beach; 310-374-3001, 888-895-4559, fax 310-372-2115; www.beach-house.com, e-mail tw@beach-house.com. DELUXE TO ULTRA-DELUXE.

air conditioning in every room; many have ocean views and balconies. In addition, it is close to the surf and lodging is rare in these parts. The inn offers complimentary bikes, boogie boards, towels and beach umbrellas and chairs. ~ 3400 Highland Avenue, Manhattan Beach; 310-545-1504, fax 310-545-4052; www.seaview-inn.com, e-mail info@seaview-inn.com. MODERATE TO ULTRA-DELUXE.

In downtown Redondo Beach, just a couple blocks from the water, are several small restaurants serving a diversity of cuisines. **DINING**

Petit Casino, a French bakery, serves quiche, soups, salads, and sandwiches (including the French standard, *croque monsieur*). ~ 1767 South Elena Avenue, Redondo Beach; 310-543-5585. BUDGET.

A family-run, longtime Redondo Beach favorite, **Captain Kidd's Fish Market and Restaurant** has live crabs and lobsters, fresh shrimp and clams, and at least 18 kinds of fresh fish. Pick what you want and they'll cook it to order, whether charbroiled, panfried, deep-fried, or simmered into a chowder, gumbo, jambalaya, or Italian-style cioppino stew. There's indoor and outdoor seating at the harbor's edge. ~ 209 North Harbor Drive, Redondo Beach; 310-372-7703, fax 310-379-1531; www.captainkidds.com, e-mail rmatey1@captainkidds.com. BUDGET TO MODERATE.

In addition to serving good Asian food, **Thai Thani** is an extremely attractive restaurant. Black trim and pastel shades set off the blond wood furniture and etched glass. There are fresh flowers all around plus a few well-placed wall prints. The lunch and dinner selections include dozens of pork, beef, vegetable, poultry, and seafood dishes. Unusual choices like spicy shrimp coconut soup, whole pompano smothered in pork, and whole baby hen make this a dining adventure. No lunch on the weekend. ~ 1109 South Pacific Coast Highway, Redondo Beach; 310-316-1580, fax 310-316-0812. BUDGET TO MODERATE.

A wider than usual selection of healthy dishes—not to mention the surfboard decor—sets the **GoodStuff Restaurant** at the entrance to Riviera Village apart from other restaurants in the area (there are also branches in Manhattan Beach and Hermosa Beach). The menu features a full range of meat, fish, and vegan entrées, salads, and sandwiches. There's even heart-healthy options for the not *quite* vegetarian such as ground turkey enchiladas. ~ 1617 Pacific Coast Highway, Redondo Beach; 310-316-0262, fax 310-316-3182; www.eatgoodstuff.com. BUDGET TO MODERATE.

The capital of "in" dining around the South Bay is **Chez Melange**. As the name suggests, and as current trends demand, the cuisine is eclectic, thanks to its on-site cooking school. You'll find a hip crowd ordering everything from caviar to sushi to Cajun meatloaf. ~ 1716 Pacific Coast Highway, Redondo Beach; 310-540-1222, fax 310-316-9283; www.chezmelange.com, e-mail melangeinc@aol.com. MODERATE TO ULTRA-DELUXE.

HIDDEN ▶   There is excellent thin-crust pizza at **Pedone's**. Popular with the beach crowd, it's a good spot for a quick meal in a convenient locale. ~ 1332 Hermosa Avenue, Hermosa Beach; 310-376-0949. BUDGET TO MODERATE.

No restaurants line the Strand in Manhattan Beach, so you'll have to make do with the pier's snack shop or hike up the hill into town, where you'll find **Mama D's Original Italian Kitchen** just around the corner. It has the feel of a genuine neighborhood eatery. There's usually a wait for supper, but the occasional tray of warm garlic bread, fresh from the oven, passed among the prospective diners reminds you why you're in line. Entrées include homemade ravioli, lasagna with *diablo* sauce, and *cioppino* with linguine. The thin New York–style pizza is a perennial favorite. ~ 1125-A Manhattan Avenue, Manhattan Beach; 310-546-1492. BUDGET TO MODERATE.

Café Pierre is an excellent choice for adventurous gourmets. Black chairs and cherry wood furnishings create a contemporary but warm atmosphere. You can feast on flamed filet mignon Roquefort, striped bass filet niçoise, and homemade pasta. Daily specials may include stuffed swordfish or venison. No lunch on Saturday and Sunday. ~ 317 Manhattan Beach Boulevard, Manhattan Beach; 310-545-5252, fax 310-546-6072; www.cafe pierre.com. MODERATE TO DELUXE.

SHOPPING   If they weren't famous Pacific beach communities, the South Bay enclaves of Redondo, Hermosa, and Manhattan beaches would seem like small-town America. Their central shopping districts are filled with pharmacies, supply shops, and shoe stores.

There are a few places of interest to folks from out of town. In Redondo Beach, scout out Catalina Avenue, particularly along its southern stretches. Shops in Hermosa Beach concentrate along Pier and Hermosa avenues, especially where they intersect. Likewise in Manhattan Beach, Manhattan Beach Boulevard is traversed by Highland and Manhattan avenues.

NIGHTLIFE   **The Lighthouse Café** spotlights blues, reggae, rock-and-roll, and funk bands; the different styles draw vastly different crowds. Cover on Friday and Saturday. ~ 30 Pier Avenue, Hermosa Beach; 310-372-6911; www.thelighthousecafe.net.

Locals bemoan the passing of Manhattan Beach's funky old La Paz Bar, a victim of urban gentrification that was recently turned into a parking lot. Since then, the surfer and beach-bum crowd HIDDEN ▶ from the La Paz has gravitated to the **Shellback Tavern** to carry on the endless beach party with tacos and burgers, loud music, cheap beer, and elbow-to-elbow tanned bodies. ~ 116 Manhattan Beach Boulevard, Manhattan Beach; 310-376-7857.

REDONDO BEACH 🚲 🏄 🏃 🏊 🚣 ⛵ Surfers know this strand and so should you. Together with neighboring Hermosa and Manhattan beaches, it symbolizes the Southern California beach scene. You'll find a long strip of white sand bordered by a hillside carpeted with ice plants. In addition to surfers, the area is populated by bicyclists and joggers, while anglers cast from the nearby piers. Not surprisingly, fishing is particularly good from nearby Fisherman's Wharf. The swimming at Redondo is good, and surfing is even better. Facilities include restrooms, lifeguards, and volleyball courts. ~ Along the Esplanade, Redondo Beach; 310-372-2166, fax 310-372-6902.

HERMOSA BEACH 🚲 🏄 🏃 ⛵ One of the great beaches of Southern California, this is a very, very wide (and very, very white) sand beach extending the entire length of Hermosa Beach. Two miles of pearly sand are only part of the attraction. There's also The Strand, a pedestrian lane that runs the length of the beach; Pier Avenue, an adjacent street lined with interesting shops; a quarter-mile fishing pier; and a local community known for its artistic creativity. Personally, if I were headed to the beach, I would head in this direction. The swimming is good and the surfing is very good around the pier and all along the beach. Lifeguards are on duty, and facilities include restrooms, volleyball courts, and a playground. Parking fee, $5. ~ At the foot of Pier Avenue, Hermosa Beach; 310-372-2166, fax 310-372-6902; www.watchwater.com.

MANHATTAN COUNTY BEACH 🚲 🏄 🏃 🏊 ⛵ Back in those halcyon days when their first songs were climbing the charts, the Beach Boys were regular fixtures at this silvery strand. They came to swim and check out the scene along The Strand, the walk-

---

AUTHOR FAVORITE

The Comedy & Magic Club features name acts nightly. Many of the comedians are television personalities with a regional, if not national, following. Jay Leno, for instance, frequently tests his new *Tonight Show* material on the club's Sunday-night crowd. The supper club atmosphere is upscale and appealing. There's a showroom that features star memorabilia. Reservations are required. Closed Monday. Cover. ~ 1018 Hermosa Avenue, Hermosa Beach; 310-372-1193, fax 310-379-2806; www.comedymagicclub.com.

way that extends the length of Manhattan Beach. What can you say, the gentlemen had good taste—the surfing here is some of the best in Southern California; the prime spot hereabouts is perhaps El Porto, located at the northern end of the beach. This sand corridor is wide as a desert, fronted by an aquamarine ocean and backed by the beautiful homes of the very lucky. If that's not enough, there's a fishing pier and an adjacent commercial area door-to-door with excellent restaurants. The swimming here is good, and the surfing is tops. Other facilities include restrooms, lifeguards, and volleyball courts. ~ At the foot of Manhattan Beach Boulevard, Manhattan Beach; 310-372-2166, fax 310-372-6902.

DOCKWEILER STATE BEACH 🚴 🛶 🚶 ⛱ 🛶 It's long, wide, and has fluffy white sand—what more could you ask? Rather, it's what less can you request. Dockweiler suffers a minor problem. It's right next to Los Angeles International Airport, one of the world's busiest terminals. Every minute planes are taking off, thundering, reverberating, right over the beach. To add insult to infamy, there is a sewage treatment plant nearby. Nevertheless, swimming and surfing are good, fires are permitted, and fishing is good from the jetties. You'll also find picnic areas and restrooms. Parking fee, $5 to $6.75. ~ At the foot of Imperial Highway, along Vista del Mar Boulevard, Playa del Rey; 310-322-4951, fax 310-726-0371.

▲ There is an RV park with 82 sites with full hookups and 35 without; $13 to $25 per night. Reservations are recommended and are accepted 7 to 90 days in advance.

▼▼▼▼▼▼▼▼▼▼▼▼
Venice

Venice, California, was the dream of one man, a tobacco magnate named Abbot Kinney. He envisioned a "Venice of America," a Renaissance town of gondoliers and single-lane bridges, connected by 16 miles of canals.

After convincing railroad barons and city fathers, Kinney dredged swampland along Santa Monica Bay, carved a network of canals, and founded this dream city in 1905. The place was an early-20th-century answer to Disneyland with gondola rides and amusement parks. The canals were lined with vaulted arches and rococo-style hotels.

Oil spelled the doom of Kinney's dream. Once black gold was discovered beneath the sands of Venice, the region became a landscape of drilling rigs and oil derricks. Spills polluted the canals and blackened the beaches. In 1929 the city of Los Angeles filled in most of the canals and during the subsequent decades Venice more resembled a tar pit than a cultural center.

But by the 1950s latter-day visionaries—artists and bohemians —rediscovered "Kinney's Folly" and transformed it into an avant-garde community. It became a magnet for Beats in the 1950s and hippies during the next decade. Musician Jim Morrison of The Doors lived here and Venice developed a reputation as a center for the cultural renaissance that Abbot Kinney once envisioned.

Today Venice seems to represent some sort of socially ideal community where there's room for everyone—aging hippies, retirees, world-class artists, and millionaire movie stars—to call Venice home. The reality, of course, is that gentrification of beachfront districts sent housing costs soaring. Still, the creative energy of Venice is hard to stifle. The town is filled with galleries and covered by murals, making it one of the region's most important art centers.

SIGHTS

The revolution might have sputtered elsewhere, but in Venice artists seized control. City Hall has become the **Beyond Baroque Literary Arts Center,** housing a library and bookstore devoted to small presses. Closed Sunday and Monday. ~ 681 Venice Boulevard; 310-822-3006; www.beyondbaroque.org.

Next door, the former **Venice Police Station** is home to SPARC, or the Social and Public Art Resource Center. Some of the jail cells of this imposing 1929 art deco–style building have been

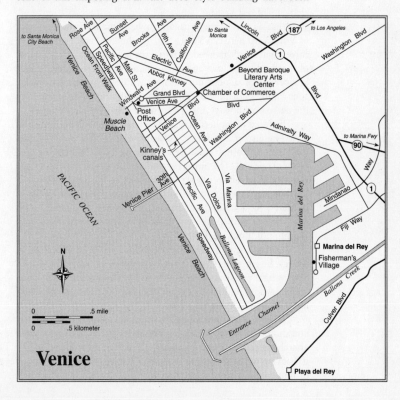

Venice

converted into an art gallery. The holding pen is intact and you'll walk through an iron door to view contemporary artwork by mostly local alternative, cutting-edge artists. The center also houses a gift shop and the UCLA/SPARC Cesar Chavez Digital Mural Lab. Closed Saturday and Sunday except by appointment. ~ 685 Venice Boulevard; 310-822-9560, fax 310-827-8717; www.sparcmurals.org, e-mail sparc@sparcmurals.org.

Both the Venice City Hall and Police Station are great places to learn about what's going on in the community. Also consider the **Venice Chamber of Commerce**. If you can find someone there (which is not always easy), you can obtain maps, brochures, and answers. ~ 583¾ North Venice Boulevard, Suite C; 310-396-7016, fax 310-314-7641.

The commercial center of Venice rests at the intersection of Windward Avenue and Main Street. Windward was the central boulevard of Kinney's dream city, and the Traffic Circle, marked today by a small sculpture, was to be an equally grand lagoon. Continue along Windward Avenue to the arcades, a series of Italian-style colonnades that represent one of the few surviving elements of old Venice.

What's left of **Kinney's canals** can be found a few blocks south of Windward between Venice and Washington boulevards. Here three small canals flanked by two larger ones comprise an enclave of charming bungalows and showy mini-mansion remodels. Strains of opera or jazz float out of open windows as resident ducks, squawking loudly, paddle along the canals and joggers run along the narrow walkways and over small arched wooden bridges.

The heart of modern-day Venice pulses along the **boardwalk**, a two-mile strip that follows Ocean Front Walk from Washington Street to Rose Avenue. **Venice Pier**, an 1100-foot fishing pier, anchors one end. The pier is renovated with excellent lighting and coin-operated telescopes for lovely views of the Strand. Between Washington Street and Windward Avenue, the promenade is bordered by a palisade of beachfront homes, two- and three-story houses with plate-glass facades. ~ Ocean Front Walk and Washington Boulevard.

Walking north, the real action begins around 18th Avenue, at **Muscle Beach,** where rope-armed heavies work out in the world-class weight pen, smacking punching bags and flexing their pecs, while gawking onlookers dream of oiling their bodies and walking with a muscle-bound strut.

The rest of the boardwalk is a grand open-air carnival that you should try to visit on the weekend. It is a world of artists and anarchists, derelicts and dreamers, a vision of what life would be if heaven were an insane asylum. Guitarists, jugglers, conga drummers, and clowns perform for the crowds. Kids on roller

Murals of Venice & Santa Monica

Nowhere is the spirit of Venice and Santa Monica more evident than in the murals adorning their walls. Both seaside cities house major art colonies, and numerous galleries and studios make them important centers for contemporary art.

Over the years, as more and more artists made their homes here, they began decorating the twin towns with their art. The product of this creative energy lives along street corners and alleyways, on storefronts and roadways. Crowded with contemporary and historic images, these murals express the inner life of the city.

Murals adorn nooks and crannies all over Venice. You'll find a cluster of them around Windward Avenue between Main Street and Ocean Front Walk. The interior of the **Post Office** is adorned with public art. There's a trompe l'oeil mural nearby on the old St. Marks Hotel that beautifully reflects the street along which you are gazing. Don't miss the woman in the upper floor window. ~ Windward Avenue and Main Street. On the other side of the building, facing the ocean, **Venice Reconstituted** depicts the unique culture of Venice Beach. ~ Windward Avenue and Speedway.

At last count Santa Monica boasted about two dozen outdoor murals. Route 1, or Lincoln Boulevard, is a corridor decorated with local artworks. **John Muir Woods** portrays a redwood forest. ~ Lincoln and Ocean Park boulevards. **Early Ocean Park and Venice Scenes** captures the seaside at the turn of the 20th century. ~ Located two blocks west of Lincoln Boulevard along Kensington Road in Joslyn Park.

Ocean Park Boulevard is another locus of creativity. At its intersection with the 4th Street underpass you'll encounter **Whale of a Mural**, illustrating whales and underwater life common to California waters, and **Unbridled**, depicting a herd of horses fleeing from the Santa Monica Pier carousel. One of the area's famous murals awaits you at Ocean Park Boulevard and Main street, where **Early Ocean Park** vividly re-creates scenes from the past.

For more information or a tour of these and other murals, contact the **Social and Public Art Resource Center**. ~ 685 Venice Boulevard; 310-822-9560; www.sparcmurals.org. The **Santa Monica Cultural Affairs Division** can also help. ~ 310-458-8350; www.arts.santamonica.org. Los Angeles has earned a reputation as the mural capital of the United States, making this tour a highpoint for admirers of public art.

skates and bicycles whiz past rickshaws and unicycles. Street hawkers and panhandlers work the unwary while singers with scratchy voices pass the hat. Vendors dispense everything from corn dogs to cotton candy, T-shirts to wind-up toys.

South of Venice and Washington Boulevard is **Marina del Rey**, the largest manmade small-boat harbor in the world. Over 6000 pleasure boats and yachts dock here. Private charters, dinner, dance and Sunday champagne brunch cruises are provided by **Hornblower Cruises & Events**. ~ 13755 Fiji Way; 310-301-9900, 800-668-4322; www.hornblower.com, e-mail md@hornblower.com.

The entire region was once a marsh inhabited by a variety of waterfowl. Personally, I think they should have left it to the birds. Marina del Rey is an ersatz community, a completely fabricated place where the main shopping area, **Fisherman's Village**, resembles a New England whaling town, and everything else attempts to portray something it's not. ~ 13755 Fiji Way; 310-823-5411.

With its endless condominiums, pretentious homes, and overpriced restaurants, Marina del Rey is an artificial limb appended to the coast of Los Angeles.

LODGING

HIDDEN ►

There's nothing quite like **The Venice Beach House**. That may well be because there are so few bed-and-breakfast inns in the Los Angeles area. But it's also that this is such a charming house, an elegant and spacious California craftsman–style home built in 1911 by Warren Wilson. The living room, with its beam ceiling, dark wood paneling, and brick fireplace, is a masterwork. Guests also enjoy a sunny alcove, patio, and garden. The stroll to the Venice boardwalk and beach is only one-half block. The nine guest rooms are beautifully appointed and furnished with antiques; each features patterned wallpaper and period artwork. I can't recommend the place highly enough. ~ 15 30th Avenue; 310-823-1966, fax 310-823-1842; www.venicebeachhouse.com, e-mail reservations@venicebeachhouse.com. DELUXE TO ULTRA-DELUXE.

PARKING POINTERS

Parking in Venice, especially on hot summer weekends, can be a pain, and an expensive one at that. Street parking close to the beach cannot be found after 10 or 11 in the morning; lots closest to the beach will charge between $9 and $12 per car. If you don't mind a bit of walking, try your luck in the public lots at Venice Boulevard and Pacific Avenue; a day of parking here should cost between $7 and $10. The best advice: come early and be patient.

Also consider the **Best Western Marina Pacific Hotel & Suites**. Located in the recreational center of Venice only 200 feet from the sand, this three-story, 88-unit hostelry has a small lobby and café downstairs. The guest rooms are spacious, nicely furnished, and well maintained; all have refrigerators, hairdryers, coffee-makers, and irons. Very large one-bedroom suites, complete with kitchen and fireplace, are also available. All rooms have small balconies. Amenities include a coin laundry. ~ 1697 Pacific Avenue; 310-452-1111, 800-421-8151, fax 310-452-5479; www.mp hotel.com, e-mail info@mphotel.com. DELUXE TO ULTRA-DELUXE.

For the international hostel-hopper, Venice Beach is a veritable heaven by the ocean. The **Venice Beach Cotel**, located right on the beach, offers both private and shared rooms. Passports are required at check-in. ~ 25 Windward Avenue; 310-399-7649, fax 310-399-1930; www.venicebeachcotel.com, e-mail reserva tions@venicebeachcotel.com. BUDGET.

Hostel California features ten units with shared baths: six dorm-style rooms hold six beds, four rooms are available for couples. Other amenities include kitchen and laundry facilities. Reservations are not taken for private rooms. ~ 2221 Lincoln Boulevard; 310-305-0250, fax 310-305-8590; www.hostelcalifornia.net, e-mail hoca90291@aol.com. BUDGET.

Situated a few blocks from a broad, pleasant beach, the **Inn at Playa del Rey** abuts the Ballona Wetlands, one of the last wet-lands habitats in Southern California. With 21 rooms and suites, many with fireplaces and whirlpool tubs, the gray-and-white clap-board inn looks more like a New England beach house than a California B&B. Bicycles are available for guests' use, and the out-door jacuzzi is a popular feature. In addition to a full breakfast, owner Susan Zolla provides afternoon wine and cheese. ~ 435 Culver Boulevard, Playa del Rey; 310-574-1920, fax 310-574-9920; www.innatplayadelrey.com, e-mail info@innatplayadel rey.com. DELUXE TO ULTRA-DELUXE.

DINING

The best place for finger food and junk food in all Southern California might well be the **boardwalk** in Venice. Along Ocean Front Walk are vendor stands galore serving pizza, frozen yogurt, hamburgers, falafel, submarine sandwiches, corn dogs, etc.

Regardless, there's really only one spot in Venice to consider for dining. It simply *is* Venice, an oceanfront café right on the boardwalk, **The Sidewalk Café**. Skaters whiz past, drummers beat rhythms in the distance, and the sun stands like a big orange wafer above the ocean. Food is really a second thought here, but eventually they're going to want you to spend some money. So, on to the menu . . . breakfast, lunch, and dinner are what you'd expect—omelettes, sandwiches, hamburgers, pizza, and pasta. There are also fresh fish dishes plus specialty salads, steak, spicy

◄ HIDDEN

chicken, and fried shrimp. Validated parking is a block away in the lot at Market and Speedway. ~ 1401 Ocean Front Walk at Horizon Avenue; 310-399-5547, fax 310-399-4512. MODERATE.

Take a walk down the boardwalk to **Venice Bistro**. This beachfront establishment is a casual dining room with a tile floor and brick walls. Cozy and comfortable, it features a menu that includes hamburgers, salads, pasta, and some Mexican dishes. There's a full bar. ~ 323 Ocean Front Walk; 310-392-7472. BUDGET TO MODERATE.

Or check out **Jody Maroni's Sausage Kingdom**, a beach stand with over a dozen types of sausage, all natural. There's sweet Italian, Yucatán chicken, Louisiana hotlinks, and, of course, Polish. All sausages are served with grilled onions and peppers on a poppy-seed roll. Breakfast served daily. Open until sunset; closed on rainy days. ~ 2011 Ocean Front Walk; 310-822-5639, fax 310-348-1510; www.jodymaroni.com, e-mail info@jodymaroni.com. BUDGET.

HIDDEN ▶ The landing ground for Venetians is a warehouse dining place called **The Rose Café**. There's a full-scale deli, bakery counter, and a restaurant offering indoor seating and outdoor patio service. The last serves lunch and dinner daily from a reasonably priced menu that may include entrées like linguine with smoked salmon, sautéed chicken, and a good selection of vegetarian dishes. A good spot for pasta and salad, The Rose Café, with its wall murals and paintings, is also a place to appreciate the vital culture of Venice. Call ahead for hours. ~ 220 Rose Avenue; 310-399-0711, fax 310-396-2660. BUDGET TO MODERATE.

In the mood for Asian cuisine? **Hama Restaurant** is a well-respected Japanese restaurant in the center of Venice. The place features an angular sushi bar, a long, narrow dining room, and a patio out back. The crowd is young and the place is decorated to reflect Venice's vibrant culture. There are paintings on display representing many of the area's artists. In addition to scrumptious sushi, Hama offers a complete selection of Japanese dishes including tempura, teriyaki, and sashimi. ~ 213 Windward Avenue; 310-396-8783, fax 310-392-9456. ULTRA-DELUXE.

"American comfort cooking"—barbecued pork ribs with ribbons of collard greens; roast chicken with a side of coffee-flavored barbecue sauce; fried calamari served with chipotle-pepper dipping sauce; calf's liver with pancetta; and iceberg lettuce with a creamy bleu-cheese dressing, for example—that's what **James' Beach** is all about. Frequented by the Venice arts-and-letters crowd, this art-filled restaurant (Billy Al Bengston designed the interior) offers daily dinner specials that are well conceived and reasonably priced. Dinner and weekend brunch; lunch Wednesday through Friday. ~ 60 North Venice Boulevard; 310-823-5396, fax 310-823-5397. MODERATE TO ULTRA-DELUXE.

Chef Joseph Manzare returns to L.A. (from Globe San Francisco) as chef/co-owner of **Globe Venice Beach**. When last in the Southland, he was head chef at Spago before it moved to Beverly Hills. The California cuisine menu features seafood, pasta, pizza, and mesquite-grilled T-bone. All is done with imagination and skill. No lunch on Saturday and Sunday. ~ 72 Market Street; 310-392-8720, fax 310-399-5953. MODERATE TO ULTRA-DELUXE.

To combine slumming with shopping, be sure to wander the **boardwalk** in Venice. Ocean Front Walk between Windward and Ozone avenues is lined with low-rent stalls selling beach hats, cheap jewelry, sunglasses, beach bags, and souvenirs. You'll also encounter **Small World Books**, a marvelous beachside shop crammed with fiction, mysteries (novels, that is), poetry, and other books. ~ 1407 Ocean Front Walk; 310-399-2360; www.smallworld books.com, e-mail info@smallworldbooks.com.

SHOPPING

> Venice, to quote Bob Dylan, represents "life and life only," but a rarefied form of life, slightly, beautifully askew.

L.A. Louver is one of Venice's many vital and original galleries. It represents David Hockney, R. B. Kitaj and other contemporary American and European artists. Closed Sunday and Monday. ~ 45 North Venice Boulevard; 310-822-4955, fax 310-821-7529; www.lalouver.com, e-mail info@lalouver.com.

There is also a covey of art galleries and antique shops along the 1200 to 1500 blocks of West Washington Boulevard. **Philip Garaway Native American Art** specializes in museum-quality antique American Indian art, 19th-century Navajo blankets, antique rugs, vintage kachina dolls, Western American Indian basketry, and Pueblo pottery dating from A.D. 700 to the 20th century. By appointment only. ~ Venice; 310-577-8555, fax 310-577-8557; e-mail philipgaraway@earthlink.net.

◄ HIDDEN

The **Beyond Baroque Literary Arts Center**, a clearinghouse for local talent, has a bookstore and sponsors poetry readings, dramatic revues, lectures, and concerts. It's located in the old Venice City Hall. Closed Sunday and Monday. ~ 681 Venice Boulevard; 310-822-3006; www.beyondbaroque.org.

The town's erstwhile jail, the **Social and Public Art Resource Center**, or SPARC, has a store offering Latin American and Southwestern folk art as well as a selection of art books, prints, and cards. ~ 685 Venice Boulevard; 310-822-9560; www.sparcmurals.org.

The **Townhouse**, set in a '20s-era speakeasy, has live music occasionally. Otherwise, stop by for a drink or a game of darts or pool. Occasional cover. ~ 52 Windward Avenue; 310-392-4040.

NIGHTLIFE

The **Venice Bistro** features a different style of live music every night—bluegrass, blues, rock, acoustic, folk—and there's never a cover charge. Call ahead for the schedule. ~ 323 Ocean Front Walk; 310-392-7472.

The Sidewalk Café is also a popular nightspot and gathering place, more for its central location than anything else. ~ 1401 Ocean Front Walk; 310-399-5547.

For an unusual way to spend the evening in the summer months, ask **Malibu Ocean Sports** about their moonlight kayak tours around Marina del Rey. The evening can include dinner at one of the marina's restaurants. ~ 310-456-6302; www.mali bukayaks.com.

BEACHES & PARKS

VENICE BEACH 🚴 🏊 🏄 🛶 This broad white-sand corridor runs the entire length of Venice and features Venice Pier. But the real attraction—and the reason you'll find the beach described in the "Dining," "Sights," and "Shopping" sections—is the boardwalk. A center of culture, street artistry, and excitement, the boardwalk parallels Venice Beach for two miles. As far as beach facilities, you'll find restrooms, showers, lifeguards, playgrounds, basketball courts, weightlifting facilities ($5 to use), a bike path, and handball and paddle ball courts. If you can tear yourself away from the action on the boardwalk, the swimming and surfing are good here, too. Closed on rainy days. ~ Ocean Front Walk in Venice parallels the beach; 310-399-2775, fax 310-577-1046.

▼▼▼▼▼▼▼▼▼▼

Santa Monica

Pass from Venice into Santa Monica and you'll trade the boardwalk for a promenade. It's possible to walk for miles along Santa Monica's fluffy beach, past pastel-colored condominiums and funky woodframe houses. Roller skaters and bicyclists galore crowd the byways and chess players congregate at the picnic tables.

A middle-class answer to mod Malibu, Santa Monica started as a seaside resort in the 1870s when visitors bumped over long, dusty roads by stagecoach from Los Angeles. After flirting with the film industry in the age of silent movies, Santa Monica reverted in the 1930s to a quiet beach town that nevertheless was notorious for the gambling ships moored offshore. It was during this period that detective writer Raymond Chandler immortalized the place as "Bay City" in his brilliant Philip Marlowe novels.

Today Santa Monica is *in*. Its clean air, pretty beaches, and attractive homes have made it one of the most popular places to live in Los Angeles. As real-estate prices skyrocketed, liberal politics ascended. Santa Monica is, in a manner of speaking, Southern California's answer to Berkeley.

SIGHTS

Highlight of the beach promenade (and perhaps all Santa Monica) is the **Santa Monica Pier**. No doubt about it, the place is a scene. Acrobats work out on the playground below, surfers catch waves offshore, and street musicians strum guitars. And I haven't even mentioned the official attractions. There's a late-19th-century carousel with hand-painted horses that was featured in that cinematic classic, *The Sting*. There are video parlors, pinball machines, skee ball, bumper cars, and a restaurant. ~ Located at the foot of Colorado Avenue.

At the Santa Monica Pier is **Pacific Park,** a family amusement park featuring 12 rides, 21 amusement games and an oceanfront food plaza. Reaching up to 55 feet in height, the Santa Monica West Coaster cruises around the park at 35 miles per hour and makes two 360-degree turns. The nine-story-high Ferris wheel offers a bird's-eye view of the beach and coastline. Other attrac-

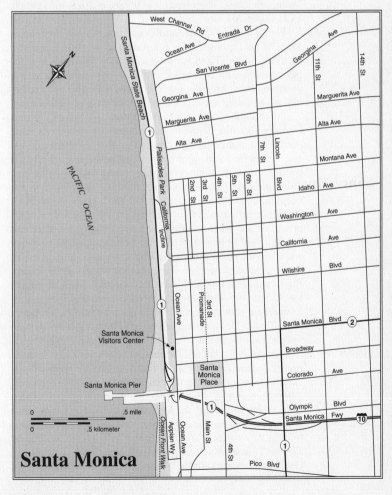

West Channel Rd

Entrada Dr

Ocean Ave

Santa Monica State Beach

San Vicente Blvd

Georgina Ave

11th St

14th St

Georgina Ave

Marguerita Ave

Marguerita Ave

Alta Ave

Palisades Park

1

Alta Ave

7th St

Lincoln

Montana Ave

PACIFIC OCEAN

2nd St

3rd St

4th St

5th St

6th St

Blvd

Idaho Ave

California Incline

Washington Ave

California Ave

Wilshire Blvd

Ocean Ave

3rd St Promenade

1

Santa Monica Blvd

2

Santa Monica
Visitors Center

Broadway

Santa
Monica
Place

Colorado Ave

Santa Monica Pier

0   .5 mile

0   .5 kilometer

Olympic Blvd

Santa Monica Fwy

10

Ocean Front Walk

Appian Wy

Ocean Ave

Main St

1

4th St

1

Santa Monica

Pico Blvd

tions include adult and kid bumper cars and a slew of kiddie rides. ~ 380 Santa Monica Pier; 310-260-8744, fax 310-260-8748; www.pacpark.com.

From here it's a jaunt up to the **Santa Monica Visitors Center** information kiosk. Here are maps, brochures, and helpful workers. ~ 1400 Ocean Avenue; 310-393-7593, 800-544-5319, fax 310-319-6273; www.santamonica.com, e-mail info@santamonica.com.

The booth is located in **Palisades Park**, a pretty, palm-lined greensward that extends north from Colorado Avenue more than a mile along the sandstone cliffs fronting Santa Monica beach. One of the park's stranger attractions here is the **Camera Obscura,** a periscope of sorts through which you can view the pier, beach, and surrounding streets. ~ In the Senior Recreation Center, 1450 Ocean Avenue.

For 25 cents, the **Tide Shuttle** takes you through the heart of Santa Monica's tourist zone, from Main Street to the Santa Monica Pier and the Third Street Promenade. It also stops at many beachfront hotels. Running every 15 minutes, the shuttle is a great way to visit the city's central attractions. Maps and schedules are available at the visitor center and most central hotels.

For a glimpse into Santa Monica's past, take in the **California Heritage Museum**. Heirlooms and antiques are housed in a grand American Colonial Revival home. The mansion dates to 1894 and is furnished entirely in period California pieces. There are photo archives, historic artifacts galore, and rotating exhibits of decorative and fine arts. Closed Monday and Tuesday. Admission. ~ 2612 Main Street; 310-392-8537, fax 310-396-0547.

Sympathetic as it is to liberal politics, Santa Monica is nonetheless an extremely wealthy town. In fact, it's a fusion of two very different neighbors, mixing the bohemian strains of Venice with the monied elements of Malibu. For a look at the latter influence, take a drive from Ocean Avenue out along **San Vicente Boulevard**. This fashionable avenue, with its arcade of magnolias, is lined on either side with lovely homes. But they pale by comparison with the estates you will see by turning left on **La Mesa Drive**. This quiet suburban street boasts a series of marvelous Spanish Colonial, Tudor, and contemporary-style houses.

HIDDEN ►   At first glance, the **Self Realization Fellowship Lake Shrine** in nearby Pacific Palisades is an odd amalgam of pretty things. Gathered along the shore of a placid pond are a Dutch windmill, a houseboat, and a shrine topped with something resembling a giant artichoke. In fact, the windmill is a chapel, the houseboat is a former stopping place of yogi and Self Realization Fellowship founder Paramahansa Yogananda, and the oversized artichoke is a golden lotus archway near which some of Indian leader Mahatma Gandhi's ashes are enshrined. A strange but potent collection of icons in an evocative setting, the Fellowship is a meditation garden open to people of any religion. Closed Monday. ~ 17190 Sunset Boulevard, Pacific Palisades; 310-454-4114, fax 310-459-7461; www. yogananda-srf.org.

Several miles inland at **Will Rogers State Historic Park**, on a hillside overlooking the Pacific, you can tour the ranch and home of America's greatest cowboy philosopher. Will Rogers, who started as a trick roper in traveling rodeos, hit the big time in Hollywood during the 1920s as a kind of cerebral comedian whose humorous wisdom plucked a chord in the American psyche.

From 1928 until his tragic death in 1935, the lariat laureate occupied this 31-room home with his family. The house is deceptively large but not grand; the woodframe design is basic and unassuming, true to Will Rogers' Oklahoma roots. Similarly the interior is decorated with Indian rugs and ranch tools. Western knickknacks adorn the tables and one room is dominated by a full-sized stuffed calf which Rogers utilized for roping practice. Well worth visiting, the "house that jokes built" is a simple expression of a vital personality. Admission. The house is undergoing a major restoration that is scheduled to be completed in late 2005. ~ 1501 Will Rogers State Park Road, Pacific Palisades; 310-454-8212, fax 310-459-2031.

LODGING

Ocean Avenue, which runs the length of Santa Monica, paralleling the ocean one block above the beach, boasts the most hotels and the best location in town. Among its varied facilities are several generic motels. These are all-American-type places furnished in veneer, carpeted wall-to-wall, and equipped with telephones and color televisions. If you book a room in one, ask for quiet accommodations since Ocean Avenue is a busy, noisy street.

A reasonably good bargain is the **Bayside Hotel**. Laid out in motel fashion, this two-story complex offers plusher carpets and

AUTHOR FAVORITE

Shutters on the Beach, perched directly on Santa Monica Beach, is cozy and sedate. The lobby has two large fireplaces and the 198 gray-and-white rooms are well appointed with dark walnut furniture. Most rooms have coastal views; all feature, yes, shutters, as well as marble baths with jacuzzis. The hotel has a lovely pool terrace, two restaurants, and an oceanview bar. ~ 1 Pico Boulevard; 310-458-0030, 800-334-9000; www.shuttersonthebeach.com, e-mail info@shuttersonthebeach.com. ULTRA-DELUXE.

plumper furniture than motels hereabouts. More important, it's just 50 yards from the beach across a palm-studded park. Some rooms have ocean views and fully equipped kitchens. ~ 2001 Ocean Avenue; 310-396-6000, 800-525-4447, fax 310-396-1000; www.baysidehotel.com, e-mail info@baysidehotel.com. MODERATE TO DELUXE.

Just off Ocean Avenue and a little quieter than most, the **Sea Shore Motel** has 19 guest rooms and one suite located two blocks from the beach and within walking distance of all Santa Monica sights. The rooms have terra-cotta tile floors, granite counter tops, and refrigerators. There's a sundeck and off-street parking. ~ 2637 Main Street; 310-392-2787, fax 310-392-5167; www.seashore motel.com, e-mail reservations@seashoremotel.com. MODERATE.

Of course the ultimate bargain is found at **Hostelling International—Santa Monica**. This four-story, dorm-like structure boasts 30,000 square feet, room for 228 beds. There are several common rooms, internet kiosks, a central courtyard, and a kitchen. In addition to facilities for independent travelers, the hostel has set aside nine private rooms for couples. ~ 1436 2nd Street; 310-393-9913, 800-909-4776, fax 310-393-1769; www. hiusa.org, e-mail reserve@hiusa.org. BUDGET TO MODERATE.

Despite its location on a busy street, **Channel Road Inn** conveys a cozy sense of home. Colonial Revival in style, built in 1910, this sprawling 14-room bed and breakfast offers guests a living room, library, and dining room as well as a jacuzzi and hillside garden. The guest rooms vary widely in decor—some traditional, others contemporary; some florid, others demure. ~ 219 West Channel Road; 310-459-1920, fax 310-454-9920; www. channelroadinn.com, e-mail info@channelroadinn.com. DELUXE TO ULTRA-DELUXE.

The **Viceroy Hotel** looks the part of a contemporary Southern California hotel. Located across the street from the beach, this sprawling 163-room facility boasts a pool, exercise room, and patio. There's a restaurant off the lobby as well as a lounge. ~ 1819 Ocean Avenue; 310-451-8711, 800-622-8711, fax 310-394-6657; www.viceroysantamonica.com. ULTRA-DELUXE.

Think of sunflowers backdropped by a deep blue Mediterranean sky. That's what the **Hotel Oceana Santa Monica** evokes. From its magnificent oceanfront setting to its lush courtyard planted with fragrant flowers, this exquisite hotel—reminiscent of the beauty of the Côte d'Azur—is a lesson in understated elegance. The lobby is decorated with a wrought-iron registration desk and floor-to-ceiling murals. Each guest suite comes with a fully equipped kitchen and is individually decorated in a French-impressionist style. The amenities include room service from Wolfgang Puck's Cafe, a fitness center, and a swimming pool. ~ 849 Ocean Avenue; 310-393-0486, 800-777-0758, fax 310-458-

1182; www.hoteloceana.com, e-mail beth@hoteloceana.com.
ULTRA-DELUXE.

The **Loews Santa Monica Beach Hotel**, a creamy yellow
structure contemporary Victorian," features a mock turn-of-the-
20th-century design. Its spectacular five-story glass atrium lobby
and most of the 340 rooms provide views of the famed Santa
Monica Pier. Rooms are furnished in rattan and wicker and offer
special amenities. Non-beachies love the oceanview indoor/out-
door pool. ~ 1700 Ocean Avenue; 310-458-6700, fax 310-458-
6761; www.loewshotels.com. ULTRA-DELUXE.

Hotel Shangri-La is private, stylish, and nothing short of beautiful. A 1939 art-deco building with a facade like the prow of a
steamship, the 55-room home-away-from-paparazzi is completely
up-to-date. The art moderne–era furniture has been laminated
and lacquered and each appointment is a perfect expression of the
period. Located on the palisades one block above Santa Monica
Beach, many rooms sport an ocean view and have a kitchen.
There's no pool or restaurant, but the hotel has a sundeck, serves
continental breakfast and afternoon tea, and is close to the beach,
shops, and pier. ~ 1301 Ocean Avenue; 310-394-2791, 800-345-
7829, fax 310-451-3351; www.shangrila-hotel.com. DELUXE TO
ULTRA-DELUXE.

DINING

Santa Monica is a restaurant town. Its long tradition of seafood
establishments has been expanded in recent years by a wave of
ethnic and California cuisine restaurants. While some of the most
fashionable and expensive dining rooms in L.A. are right here,
there are also many excellent, inexpensive cafés. Generally you'll
find everything from the sublime to the reasonable located within
several commercial clusters—near the beach along Ocean Avenue,
downtown on Wilshire and Santa Monica boulevards, and in the
chic, gentrified corridors of Main Street and Montana Avenue.

One of the best places in Southern California for stuffing
yourself with junk food while soaking up sun and having a whale
of a good time is the **Santa Monica Pier**. There are taco stands,
fish-and-chips shops, hot dog vendors, oyster bars, snack shops,
pizzerias, and all those good things guaranteed to leave you clutch-

GOURMET GHETTO

Every type of cuisine imaginable is found on the bottom level of **Santa
Monica Place**. This multitiered shopping mall has an entire floor of
take-out food stands. It's like the United Nations of dining, where
everything is affordably priced. ~ On Broadway between 2nd and
4th streets. BUDGET.

ing your stomach. The prices are low to modest and the food is amusement park quality. ~ At the foot of Colorado Avenue.

There's a sense of the Mediterranean at the sidewalk cafés lining Santa Monica's Ocean Avenue: palm trees along the boulevard, ocean views in the distance, and (usually) a warm breeze blowing. Any of these bistros will do (since it's atmosphere we're seeking), so try **Ivy at the Shore**. It features a full bar, serves espresso, and, if you want to get serious about it, has a full lunch and dinner menu with pizza, pasta, steaks, and Cajun dishes. ~ 1541 Ocean Avenue; 310-393-3113, fax 310-458-9259. ULTRA-DELUXE.

Considered a "botanical island," the Santa Monica Mountains support chaparral, coastal sage, and oak forests; mountain lions, golden eagles, and many of California's early animal species still survive here.

In business since the 1950s, **Chez Jays** is a Santa Monica institution. It's a sort of chic dive where aging surfers rub elbows with high-profile Hollywood stars. To say that the decor is unpretentious is an understatement, but the no-nonsense steaks are always tender and tasty and the seafood unfailingly fresh. Owner Jay Fiondella, a legend in his own right, still seats customers and just may regale you with tales of his colorful life if asked. The bar is always jam-packed with an eclectic array of locals. No lunch on Monday. ~ 1657 Ocean Avenue; 310-395-1741; www.chezjays.com. MODERATE.

A number of excellent eateries line Santa Monica's vaunted Third Street Promenade. This three-block-long walkway, filled with movie theaters and located in the downtown district, boasts some of the best coffeehouses and restaurants in the area.

Gotham Hall serves California cuisine, including free-range chicken marsala and seared ahi tuna. But the real show here is the decor—from the oblong mirrors and wavy-looking paint job in hues of aqua and pink on the walls to the purple pool tables and spotlights shining at odd angles from the beamed ceiling, this restaurant's look couldn't be more unique. Dinner only. ~ 1431 Third Street Promenade; 310-394-8865, fax 310-395-7040; www.gothamhall.com. MODERATE TO DELUXE.

If steak-and-kidney pie, bangers and mash, or shepherds' pie sound appetizing, head over to **Ye Olde King's Head**. You won't see a king's head on the wall of this British pub, but you will find British memorabilia alongside photographs of the celebrities who inhabit the pub. Like you, they are drawn here by the cozy ambience and the lively crowd. ~ 116 Santa Monica Boulevard; 310-451-1402, fax 310-393-6869; www.yeoldekingshead.com, e-mail ruth88@earthlink.net. MODERATE.

In the world of high chic, **Chinois on Main** stands taller than most. Owned by famous restaurateur Wolfgang Puck, the fashionable dining room is done in nouveau art deco–style with track lights, pastel colors, and a central skylight. The curved bar is hand-painted; contemporary artworks adorn the walls. Once you drink in the glamorous surroundings, move on to the menu, which includes Shanghai lobster with curry sauce, whole sizzling catfish, and grilled Szechuan beef. The appetizers and other entrées are equal in originality, a medley of French, Chinese, and California cuisine. This is an excellent restaurant with high standards of quality. No lunch Saturday through Tuesday. ~ 2709 Main Street; 310-392-9025, fax 310-396-5102; www.wolfgangpuck.com. DELUXE TO ULTRA-DELUXE.

◀ HIDDEN

The spot for breakfast in Santa Monica is **Rae's Restaurant**, a diner located on the edge of town several miles from the beach. With its formica counter and naugahyde booths, Rae's is a local institution, always packed. The breakfasts are hearty American-style feasts complete with biscuits and gravy. At lunch they serve the usual selection of sandwiches and side orders. Come dinner time they have fried shrimp, liver, fried chicken, steaks, and other platters at prices that seem like they haven't changed since the place opened in 1958. ~ 2901 Pico Boulevard; 310-828-7937. BUDGET.

The word's spread about **Louise's**. A friendly trattoria atmosphere, creative Italian fare, and reasonable prices account for its popularity. ~ 1008 Montana Avenue; 310-394-8888. MODERATE.

◀ HIDDEN

There's no denying that the tariff at quietly elegant **Melisse** is steep, but the exquisite service and food make it one of the Westside's finest eateries. A gracious and ever-present, but unhovering, waitstaff serves up perfectly cooked, French-inspired dishes such as wild king salmon with lima bean purée, lamb stew on vegetable risotto, and white corn raviolis with truffles. Dinner only. ~ 1104 Wilshire Boulevard; 310-395-0881, fax 310-395-3810; www. melisse.com, e-mail mail@melisse.com. ULTRA-DELUXE.

There are many who believe the dining experience at **Michael's** to be the finest in all Los Angeles. Set in a restored stucco structure and decorated with original artworks by David Hockney and Jasper Johns, it is certainly one of the region's prettiest dining rooms. The menu is French-American, with original entrées such as squab on duck liver, and scallops with papaya, shallots, and chevril. At lunch there is grilled salmon with a tomato-basil vinaigrette, Alaskan halibut with fava beans, chanterelle and citrus nage, and several elaborate salads. Haute cuisine is the order of the evening here. The artistry that has gone into the restaurant's cuisine and design have permanently established Michael's reputation. There is a cozy lounge and a garden terrace. No lunch Saturday. Closed Sunday. ~ 1147 3rd Street; 310-451-0843, fax 310-394-1830. ULTRA-DELUXE.

Montana Avenue is Santa Monica's version of designer heaven, making it an interesting, if inflationary, strip to shop. From 7th

SHOPPING

to 17th Street, chic shops and upscale establishments line either side of the thoroughfare.

Brenda Himmel, an elegant stationary and gift store, just oozes refinement and good taste. They sell buttery-leather journals, photo albums, engagement books, and sterling silver picture frames. ~ 1126 Montana Avenue; 310-395-2437.

For men's and women's fashion sportswear, try **Weathervane For Men**. ~ 1132 Montana Avenue; 310-395-0397.

Across the street, but no relation, is another **Weathervane**, this one featuring high-end designer casual clothing for women. Owner Jan Brilliot opened her shop in 1974, long before Montana Avenue had all the buzz. She journeys twice yearly to Paris and Italy looking for clothing that makes a statement. And her store certainly does with its architectural features and provocative art. You feel the thought and care that's gone into every detail. Closed Sunday. ~ 1209 Montana Avenue, Santa Monica; 310-393-5344.

Though they carry elegant traditional styles as well, **A. Mason** will offer you a look at worldwide cutting-edge fashion with their presentation of creations for women by emerging international talent. The emphasis in this special store is on originality. ~ 1511 Montana Avenue, Santa Monica; 310-394-7179.

Exuding class, with its wooden floors, thick carpets, and potpourri aroma, **Room with a View** sells all sorts of high-end household accessories. The linens are nothing but the best; sheets have lofty thread counts, and towels are luxuriously fluffy. Combined with to-die-for table settings and gleaming silver accent pieces, this is a place that makes credit card max-out a definite possibility. ~ 1600 Montana Avenue; 310-998-5858.

Browse **Main Street** and you'll realize that Montana Avenue is only a practice round. Block after block of this thoroughfare is filled with trendy fashion and stylish shops.

The shopper's parade stretches most of the length of Main Street, but the center of action resides around the 2700 block. **Galleria Di Maio** is an art-deco mall with several spiffy shops including **Suji**, which carries fun, romantic women's clothing. ~ 2525 Main Street; 310-396-7614.

FOR LOVERS OF LIBERAL LANGUAGE ...

There is one shop in particular that exemplifies Santa Monica's liberal politics. **Midnight Special Bookstore** specializes in politics and social sciences. Rather than current bestsellers, the window displays might feature books on Latin America, world hunger, Africa, or disarmament. ~ 1450 2nd Street; 310-393-2923; www.msbooks.com, e-mail books@ msbooks.com.

For designer labels at a fraction of their original cost, **The Address Boutique** is the place to go. The rich and famous from the nearby communities of Brentwood and Bel Air bring their hardly worn couturier clothes and accessories here to be resold. Why buy new when you can get a $1494 Vera Wang knit dress and jacket for $395 or a $2500 ivory satin Valentino gown for a mere $350? ~ 1116 Wilshire Boulevard; 310-394-1406; www.theaddressboutique.com.   ◄ *HIDDEN*

The last of Santa Monica's several shopping enclaves is in the center of town. Here you'll find **Santa Monica Place**, a mammoth triple-tiered complex with about 140 shops. This flashy atrium mall has everything from clothes to books to luggage to leather work, jewelry, toys, hats, and shoes. ~ On Broadway between 2nd and 4th streets; 310-394-1049; www.santamonicaplace.com.

Step out from this glittery gathering place and you'll immediately encounter the **Third Street Promenade**, a three-block walkway lined on either side with shops, upscale cafés, and movie theaters. ~ Located between Broadway and Wilshire Boulevard.

For the outward bound, **California Map & Travel Center** has it all—maps, directories, and guidebooks. Or, if you're planning a little armchair traveling at home, there are globes and travelogues. ~ 3312 Pico Boulevard; 310-396-6277; www.mapper.com.

The lively Third Street Promenade has several spots to enjoy a drink, but if you have your dancing shoes on, stop by **Gotham Hall**. Deejays spin hip-hop, dance, and house music in the Moroccan-style lounge Thursday through Saturday. Cover. ~ 1431 Third Street Promenade; 310-394-8865.   **NIGHTLIFE**

Ye Olde King's Head might be the most popular British pub this side of the Thames. From dart boards to dark wood walls, trophy heads to draft beer, it's a classic English watering hole. Known throughout the area, it draws crowds of local folks and expatriate Brits. ~ 116 Santa Monica Boulevard; 310-451-1402, fax 310-393-6869; www.yeoldekingshead.com, e-mail ruth88@earthlink.net.

McCabe's Guitar Shop is a folksy spot with live entertainment on weekends. The sounds are almost all acoustic and range from Scottish folk bands to jazz to blues to country. The concert hall is a room in back lined with guitars; performances run Friday through Sunday. Cover. ~ 3101 Pico Boulevard; 310-828-4497; www.mccabes.com.

For a raucous good time, try **O'Briens**. This bar is a loud, brash place that draws hearty crowds. There are live bands nightly, ranging from Irish rock to Texas blues. The decor is what you'd expect from an Irish pub, with old pictures and beer signs hanging from the walls. Cover on Friday and Saturday. ~ 2941 Main Street; 310-396-4725, fax 310-399-7514.

For blues, R&B, soul and jazz, try **Harvelle's**, which hosts local acts nightly. Cover. ~ 1432 4th Street; 310-395-1676; www. harvelles.com.

BEACHES & PARKS

SANTA MONICA CITY BEACH 🏊 🏄 ⛵ If the pop song is right and "L.A. is a great big freeway," then truly Santa Monica is a great big beach. Face it, the sand is very white, the water is very blue, the beach is very broad, and they all continue for miles. From Venice to Pacific Palisades, it's a sandbox gone wild. Skaters, strollers, and bicyclists pass along the promenade, sunbathers lie moribund in the sand, and volleyball players perform acrobatic shots. At the center of all this stands the Santa Monica Pier with its amusement park atmosphere. If it wasn't right next door to Venice this would be the hottest beach around. Lifeguards are on duty, and facilities include picnic areas, restrooms, and snack bars. Swimming and surfing are good, and anglers usually opt for the pier. Parking fee, $7. ~ Route 1, at the foot of Colorado Avenue; 310-458-8374.

WILL ROGERS STATE BEACH 🚲 🏄 🏊 Simple and home-spun he might have been, but Will Rogers was also a canny busi-nessman with a passion for real estate. He bought up three miles of beachfront property that eventually became his namesake park. It's a sandy strand with an expansive parking lot running the length of the beach. Route 1 parallels the parking area and beyond that rise the sharp cliffs that lend Pacific Palisades its name. The South Bay Bike Trail makes its northernmost appear-ance here. You'll find good swimming, and surfing is best in the area where Sunset Boulevard meets the ocean. Lifeguards are on duty. Facilities include restrooms, volleyball courts, and play-grounds. Day-use fees vary from $5 to $10, depending on crowds expected. ~ Located south along Route 1 from Sunset Boulevard in Pacific Palisades; 310-305-9545.

WILL ROGERS STATE HISTORIC PARK 🚶 🚲 🐎 The former ranch of humorist Will Rogers, this 186-acre spread sits in the hills of Pacific Palisades. The late cowboy's home is currently under-going restoration until late 2005 and is not open to visitors, al-though there are hiking trails leading around the property and out into adjacent Topanga Canyon State Park. Facilities include picnic areas, a museum (also undergoing restoration), and rest-rooms. Day-use fee, $5 per vehicle. ~ 1501 Will Rogers State Park Road, Pacific Palisades; 310-454-8212, fax 310-459-2031.

SANTA MONICA MOUNTAINS NATIONAL RECREATION AREA 🚶 🚲 🐎 One of the few mountain ranges in the United States to run transversely (from east to west), the Santa Monicas reach for 50 miles to form the northwestern boundary of the Los Angeles basin. This federal preserve, which covers part of the mountain

range, encompasses about 153,000 acres between Routes 1 and
101, much of which is laced with hiking trails (about 500 miles);
in addition to high country, it includes a coastal stretch from
Santa Monica to Point Mugu. ~ Several access roads lead into
the area; Mulholland Drive and Mulholland Highway follow the
crest of the Santa Monica Mountains for about 50 miles from
Hollywood to Malibu. The National Park Service visitor center
is located at 401 West Hillcrest Drive, Thousand Oaks; 805-370-
2301, fax 805-370-1850; www.nps.gov/samo.

▲ There is a group campground that accommodates 10 to 50
people; $2 per person, 10 person minimum. Reservations required.

Malibu

Malibu is a 27-mile-long ribbon lined on one side with
pearly beaches and on the other by the Santa Monica
Mountains. Famed as a movie star retreat and surfer's
heaven, it is one of America's mythic communities. It has been a
favored spot among Hollywood celebrities since the 1920s, when
a new highway opened the region and film stars like Clara Bow
and John Gilbert publicized the idyllic community. By the 1950s,
Malibu was rapidly developing and becoming nationally known
for its rolling surf and freewheeling lifestyle. The 1959 movie
Gidget cast Sandra Dee and James Darren as Malibu beach bums
and the seaside community was on its way to surfing immortality.

Today surfers by the dozens hang ten near the pier, just south
of where movie and television greats live behind locked gates in

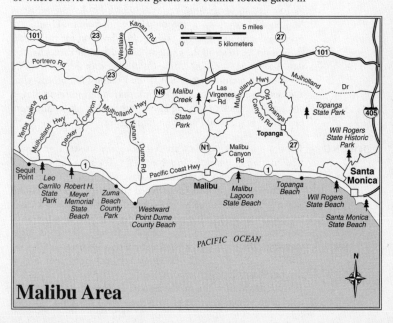

Malibu Area

lavish mansions on stretches of sand that are off-limits to normal folk. That lack of access may change, however, as there's a movement afoot to make these hitherto "private" beaches public.

SIGHTS   Today blond-mopped surfers still line the shore and celebrities continue to congregate in beachfront bungalows. Matter of fact, the most popular sightseeing in Malibu consists of ogling the homes of the very rich. **Malibu Road**, which parallels the waterfront, is a prime strip. To make it as difficult as possible for common riffraff to reach the beach, the homes are built townhouse-style with no space between them. It's possible to drive for miles along the water without seeing the beach, only the backs of baronial estates. Happily there are a few accessways to the beach, so it's possible to wander along the sand enjoying views of both the ocean and the picture-window palaces.

Among the Malibu beach accessways is one that local wags named after the "Doonesbury" character Zonker Harris.

What's amazing about these beachfront colonies is not the houses, but the fact that people insist on building them so close to the ocean that every few years several are demolished by high surf while others sink into the sand.

One of Malibu's loveliest houses is open to the public. The **Adamson House**, located at Malibu Lagoon State Beach is a stately Spanish Colonial Revival–style structure adorned with ceramic tiles. With its bare-beam ceilings and inlaid floors, the house is a study in early-20th-century elegance. The building is surrounded by landscaped grounds, which border the beach at Malibu and overlook a lagoon alive with waterfowl and are open to the public. Though there is an admission for the house, there is no fee to stroll the gardens. Closed Sunday through Tuesday. Admission. ~ 23200 Pacific Coast Highway; 310-456-8432.

Another seafront attraction is the **Malibu Pier**. Storm damage has closed the pier, and it's ironic that in this ultra-privileged community, a lack of funding has kept the necessary repairs from being made. ~ 23000 Pacific Coast Highway.

LODGING   There are several motels scattered along the coastal highway in Malibu, two of which I can recommend. **Topanga Ranch Motel** is a 30-unit complex that dates back to the 1920s. Here are cute little cottages painted white with red trim and clustered around a circular drive. Granted they're somewhat timeworn, but each is kept neat and trim with plain furnishings and little decoration. A few have kitchens. A good deal for a location right across the highway from the beach. ~ 18711 Pacific Coast Highway; 310-456-5486, fax 310-456-1447; www.topangaranchmotel.com, e-mail raycraig@earthlink.net. MODERATE.

At **Casa Malibu Inn on the Beach**, you'll be in a 21-room facility with two suites that actually overhangs the sand. Located smack in the center of Malibu, the building features a central courtyard with lawn furniture and ocean view, oceanfront red-brick patio plus a balcony dripping with flowering plants. The rooms are decorated in an attractive but casual fashion; some have private balconies, fireplaces, kitchens, and/or ocean or garden views. ~ 22752 Pacific Coast Highway; 310-456-2219, 800-831-0858, fax 310-456-5418; www.casamalibu.com, e-mail casamal ibu@earthlink.net. MODERATE TO ULTRA-DELUXE.

The **Malibu Beach Inn** is posh and each of its 47 guest rooms offers spectacular ocean views from private balconies. Minibars round out the amenities. Some rooms feature jacuzzis and fireplaces. The location on the beach, one block from the Malibu Pier, makes this an ideal getaway. ~ 22878 Pacific Coast Highway; 310-456-6444, 800-462-5428, fax 310-456-1499; www.malibubeachinn.com, e-mail reservations@malibubeachinn.com. ULTRA-DELUXE.

At the northern Zuma Beach end of Malibu, you'll find the 16-room **Malibu Country Inn** perched atop a hillside above Pacific Coast Highway. Draped in bougainvillea, this property also has four suites and a restaurant. Since the inn isn't directly on the beach, only some of the rooms have partial ocean views; but all have unobstructed mountain views, private decks, coffee makers, and a floral-wicker decor scheme. The suites include fireplace and spa tub. There's a small pool surrounded by a garden of roses and other flowers and herbs. Continental breakfast at the restaurant is included. ~ 6506 Westward Beach Road at Pacific Coast Highway; 310-457-9622, 800-386-6787, fax 310-457-1349; www.malibucountryinn.com, e-mail info@malibucountry inn.com. DELUXE TO ULTRA-DELUXE.

The **Reel Inn Restaurant** is my idea of heaven—a reasonably priced seafood restaurant. Located across the highway from the beach, it's an oilcloth restaurant with an outdoor patio and a flair for serving good, healthful food at low prices. Among the fresh fish lunches and dinners are salmon, snapper, lobster, and swordfish. ~ 18661 Pacific Coast Highway; 310-456-8221, fax 310-456-3568. BUDGET TO DELUXE.

DINING

For a possible celebrity sighting over your whole-wheat pancakes with strawberries and bananas, try **Coogie's Beach Cafe**. ~ Malibu Colony Plaza, 23700 Pacific Coast Highway; 310-317-1444, fax 310-317-1446. BUDGET TO MODERATE.

Cutting-edge Continental cuisine can be found at **Granita**, where chef Wolfgang Puck's culinary cohorts whip up original creations. Watch as they prepare grilled ahi tuna with wasabi puree, sesame asparagus and Chinese black bean sauce. Yow! The marble terrazo tile gives an underwater effect. Dinner only; brunch on weekends. Closed Monday. ~ Malibu Colony Plaza;

310-456-0488, fax 310-456-8317; www.wolfgangpuck.com, e-mail granita@wolfgangpuck.com. DELUXE TO ULTRA-DELUXE.

There's nothing fancy about **Malibu Fish & Seafood**. It's just a fish-and-chips stand across the highway from the beach with picnic tables under a covered patio outside, but the menu includes such tantalizing specialties as ahi tuna burgers and steamed lobster. The price is hard to beat when you add the ocean view. ~ 25653 Pacific Coast Highway; 310-456-3430, fax 310-456-8017. BUDGET TO DELUXE.

BeauRivage Mediterranean Restaurant, another gourmet gathering place, located across the highway from the ocean, boasts a cozy dining room and ocean-view terrace. With exposed-beam ceiling, brick trim, and copper pots along the wall, it has the feel of a French country inn. The dinner menu, however, is strictly Mediterranean. In addition to several pasta dishes, including gnocchi al pesto and linguine with clams, tomatoes, and garlic, there is New Zealand rack of lamb, Long Island duckling, Norwegian salmon, antelope, wild boar, and grilled Italian bass. Dinner and Sunday brunch served. ~ 26025 Pacific Coast Highway; 310-456-5733, fax 310-317-1589; www.beaurivagerestaurant.com, e-mail beaurivagemalibu@aol.com. MODERATE TO ULTRA-DELUXE.

The quintessential Malibu dining experience is **Geoffrey's**, a clifftop restaurant overlooking the ocean. The marble bar, white-washed stucco walls, stone pebble tiles, and flowering plants exude wealth and elegance. The entire hillside has been landscaped and beautifully terraced, creating a Mediterranean atmosphere. The menu, a variation on California cuisine, includes grilled filet mignon with a roasted shallot and Granny Smith cabernet reduction, and lobster bruschetta. The lunch and dinner menus are almost identical and on Saturday and Sunday they also serve brunch. The setting, cuisine, and high prices make Geoffrey's a

---

A SIDE ORDER OF ENLIGHTENMENT, PLEASE

Up in the Santa Monica Mountains, high above the clamor of Los Angeles, rests the **Inn of the Seventh Ray**. A throwback to the days when Topanga Canyon was a hippie enclave, this mellow dining spot serves organic "energized" foods to "raise your body's light vibrations." Entrées include buckwheat mushroom terrine and baked young leeks, asparagus and golden beet vichyssoise sauce. There is also a selection of fresh seafood, duckling, and lamb dishes. Open for lunch and dinner, the restaurant features dining indoors or outside on a pretty, tree-shaded patio, where coyotes can often be seen from your table. Far out. ~ 128 Old Topanga Canyon Road, Topanga; 310-455-1311, fax 310-455-0033; www.innoftheseventh ray.com. DELUXE TO ULTRA-DELUXE.

prime place for celebrity gazing. ~ 27400 Pacific Coast Highway; 310-457-1519, 800-927-4197, fax 310-457-7885; www.geof freysmalibu.com, e-mail gmalibu@earthlink.net. DELUXE TO ULTRA-DELUXE.

When you're out at the beaches around Point Dume or elsewhere in northern Malibu, there are two adjacent roadside restaurants worth checking out. **Coral Beach Cantina** is a simple Mexican restaurant with a small patio. The menu contains standard south-of-the-border fare. ~ 29350 Pacific Coast Highway; 310-457-5503. BUDGET TO MODERATE.

◄ *HIDDEN*

Over at **Zuma Sushi** they have a sushi bar and table service. In addition to the house specialty there are tempura and teriyaki dishes. Like its neighbor, this is a small, unassuming café. Dinner only. ~ 29350 Pacific Coast Highway; 310-457-4131. BUDGET TO MODERATE.

◄ *HIDDEN*

For a good meal near the beach there's **Neptune's Net Seafood**. Located across the highway from County Line Beach (at the Los Angeles–Ventura county border), it's a breezy café frequented by surfers. Fresh seafood, live lobster, sandwiches, burgers, and clam chowder, as well as oyster, shrimp, clam, and scallop baskets fill the bellies here. Ocean views at beach-bum prices. Closed one week before Christmas. ~ 42505 Route 1; 310-457-3095, fax 310-457-6314; www.neptunesnetseafood.com. BUDGET TO DELUXE.

◄ *HIDDEN*

Zuma Canyon Orchids offers elegant, exquisite prize-winning orchids that can be shipped anywhere in the world. If you call ahead for a reservation, they will even provide a tour of the greenhouses. Closed Sunday. ~ 5949 Bonsall Drive; 310-457-9771; www.zumacanyonorchids.com.

SHOPPING

Up in the secluded reaches of Topanga Canyon there are numerous artists and craftspeople who have traded the chaos of the city for the serenity of the Santa Monica Mountains. Craft shops come and go with frustrating regularity here, but it's worth a drive into the hills to see who is currently selling their wares.

For some easy listening, check out the scene at **BeauRivage Mediterranean Restaurant**. There's a piano player Monday through Thursday. A cozy bar and fireplace add charm to the scene. ~ 26025 Pacific Coast Highway; 310-456-5733; www.beaurivage restaurant.com.

NIGHTLIFE

Malibu is largely a bedroom community; it's not known for wild nightlife, unless it's a private party at one of the beachfront homes in the colony. For music, theater, dance, and art, Pepperdine University's **Smothers Theater** offers performances and exhibitions by visiting artists. ~ 24255 Pacific Coast Highway; 310-506-4522; www.pepperdine.edu/cfa.

Santa Monica Mountains

When you've had your fill of Malibu's sand and surf, take a detour from Route 1 up into the Santa Monica Mountains. This chaparral country filled with oak and sycamore forests offers sweeping views back along the coast. As long as you remember which direction the water is (south), it's hard to get lost no matter how crazily the roads wind and twist. But if you descend on the wrong side of the mountains—that is, the north side—into the vast suburban sprawl of the San Fernando Valley, it can be an all-day challenge to find your way back around the mountains to Los Angeles. You'll find a fair amount of solitude if you take this drive on a weekday; on weekends you can expect traffic and full parking lots.

TOPANGA CANYON   Topanga Canyon Boulevard (Route 27), perhaps the best known of these mountain roads, turns off Route 1 five miles west of Santa Monica, or eight miles east of the village of Malibu, near the temporarily closed J. Paul Getty Villa. It curves gradually up the rocky canyon to the rustic town of **Topanga**. Back in the '60s this was a fabled retreat for flower children. Even today vestiges of the hippy era remain in the form of health food stores, New Age shops, and organic restaurants. Many of the woodframe houses are handcrafted, and the community still vibrates to a slower rhythm than coastal Malibu and cosmopolitan Los Angeles. Turn right in town on Entrada Road to go for a walk in **Topanga State Park** (see below), the world's largest wilder-

BEACHES & PARKS

TOPANGA STATE PARK 🚶 🚴 🏇 Not much sand here, but you will find forests of oak and fields of rye. This 10,000-plus-acre hideaway nestles in the Santa Monica Mountains above Pacific Palisades. Along the 36 miles of hiking trails and fire roads are views of the ocean, San Gabriel Mountains, and San Fernando Valley. There are meadows and a stream to explore. The park climbs from 200 to 2100 feet in elevation, providing an introduction to one of Los Angeles' few remaining natural areas. Biking is restricted to the fire roads. Facilities include a hike-in camp and trails, picnic areas, and restrooms. Parking fee, $4. ~ From Route 1 in Malibu take Topanga Canyon Road up to Entrada Road. The park is at 20825 Entrada Road; 310-455-2465, fax 310-455-7085.

▲ There are eight hike-in sites, tents only; $2 per person per night.

TOPANGA BEACH 🏊 🚣 ⚓ This narrow sand corridor extends for over a mile. The adjacent highway breaks the quietude,

ness located entirely within the boundaries of a major city. The gentlest and prettiest trails for a short hike start at Trippet Ranch near the park entrance. There's a parking fee.

MULHOLLAND HIGHWAY   To reach the top of the world, retrace your route from Entrada a short distance back down Topanga Boulevard to where Old Topanga Canyon Road forks off to the northwest. Turn right, follow this road for about five miles to the intersection with Mulholland Highway, and turn left. With its panoramic views of the Los Angeles Basin and San Fernando Valley, Mulholland is justifiably famous. On weekend nights, Mulholland Drive (as it's known in town) is a rendezvous for lovers and a drag strip for daredevil drivers, but the rest of the time you'll find it a sinuous country road far from the madding mobs. If you have time and don't mind paying another parking fee, **Malibu Creek State Park** (see below), near the junction of Mulholland and Las Virgenes/Malibu Canyon Road, has a creek, a lake, lava rock formations, and miles of hiking trails.

KANAN DUME ROAD   Depending on how far you want to drive, any of the several roads that turn off Mulholland to the left will bring you out of the mountains at a nice beach; staying on Mulholland all the way to the end will, too. Our favorite is Kanan Dume Road, which comes out at **Westward Point Dume County Beach** (page 210). A great spot to while away the remainder of the afternoon, it's just 19 miles from Santa Monica on Route 1.

but the strand is still popular with surfers and those wanting to be close to Malibu services. The swimming is good; surfing and windsurfing are excellent around Topanga Creek. Lifeguards are on duty; facilities include restrooms, showers, picnic tables, and barbecues. Parking fee, $5. ~ Route 1, near Topanga Canyon Road in Malibu; 310-451-2906, fax 310-458-6445.

MALIBU CREEK STATE PARK 🚶 🚲 🐎 ⛵ 🎣 Once the location site for *M*A*S*H* and the original *Planet of the Apes*, this 7000-acre facility spreads through rugged, virgin country in the Santa Monica Mountains. Among its features are over 80 miles of hiking trails, four-acre Century Lake, and Malibu Creek, which is lined with willow and cottonwood. In spring the meadows explode with wildflowers; at other times of the year you'll encounter squirrels, rabbits, mule deer, coyotes, and bobcats. The bird life ranges from aquatic species such as ducks and great blue herons along the lake to hawks, woodpeckers, quail, and golden eagles. The lava hills, sloping grasslands, and twisted sedimentary rock formations make it an intriguing escape from the city. Facilities here include picnic areas, restrooms, and showers. Day-use fee, $5. ~ Located off Mulholland Highway at 1925 Las Virgenes Road, Calabasas; 818-880-0367, fax 818-706-3869.

▲ There are 60 sites for tents and trailers or RVs (no hookups); $15 per night. No wood fires. Reservations: 800-444-7275.

MALIBU LAGOON STATE BEACH 🏃 ☂ 🎣 ⛵ Not only is there a pretty beach here but an estuary and wetlands area as well. You can stroll the white sands past an unending succession of lavish beachfront homes, or study a different species entirely in the park's salt marsh. Here Malibu Creek feeds into the ocean, creating a rich tidal area busy with marine life and shorebirds. The surfing is world-renowned. This is also a very popular spot for swimming; lifeguards are on duty most of the year. Facilities include picnic areas and restrooms. Day-use fee, $5. ~ Pacific Coast Highway at Cross Creek Road in Malibu; 818-880-0350.

HIDDEN ► **WESTWARD POINT DUME COUNTY BEACH** 🏃 🚴 ☂ 🏄
🎣 🚣 This long narrow stretch is really a southerly continuation of Zuma Beach. Unlike its neighbor, it is conveniently located away from the highway and bordered by lofty sandstone cliffs. For white sand serenity this is a choice spot. Matter of fact, on the far side of Point Dume you'll encounter what was once a popular nude beach in **Pirate's Cove**. Swimming is good, but beware of dangerous currents. Surfing is good along Westward Beach and off Point Dume. Lifeguards are on duty and restrooms are available. Parking fee, $7. ~ The park entrance is located near the southern entrance to Zuma Beach County Park; take Westward Beach Road off of Route 1 about six miles west of Malibu. To reach the beach at Pirate's Cove, take the trail over the Point Dume Headlands; 310-457-2525, fax 310-457-1632.

ZUMA BEACH COUNTY PARK ☂ 🏄 🎣 🚴 🚣 ⛵ This long, broad beach is a study in the territorial instincts of the species. Los Angeles County's largest beach park, it is frequented in one area by Latinos; "Vals," young residents of the San Fernando Valley, have staked claim to another section, while families and students inhabit another stretch (Zuma 3 and 4). Not as pretty as other Malibu beaches, Zuma offers more space and better facilities, such as restrooms, lifeguards, playgrounds, volleyball courts, and proximity to restaurants and stores. Swimming and surfing are good; for information on surf conditions, call 310-457-9701. Parking fee, $7. ~ Route 1, approximately six miles west of Malibu; 310-457-2525, fax 310-457-1632.

ROBERT H. MEYER MEMORIAL STATE BEACHES 🏃 ☂ This unusual facility consists of three separate pocket beaches—**El Pescador**, **La Piedra**, and **El Matador**. Each is a pretty strand with sandy beach and eroded bluffs. Together they are among the nicest beaches in Malibu. My favorite is El Matador with its rock formations, sea stacks, and adjacent Malibu mansions. Use caution swimming at these beaches; there are unstationed lifeguards Memorial Day to Labor Day. Facilities include toilets. Access to the beaches is by stairs and short, steep trails. Parking for all beaches is $2. ~ Route 1, about 11 miles west of Malibu; 818-880-0350, fax 818-880-6165; e-mail info@csp-angeles.com.

LEO CARRILLO STATE PARK 🏃 🏄 ⛵ 🎣 🚣 Extending more than a mile, this white-sand corridor rests directly below Route 1. Named after Leo Carrillo, the TV actor who played sidekick Pancho in "The Cisco Kid," the beach offers tidepools and interesting rock formations. Nicer still is **Leo Carrillo North Beach**, a sandy swath located just beyond Sequit Point and backdropped by a sharp bluff. This entire area is a prime whale-watching site from February through April. At the south end of this 1600-acre park people have been known to bathe in the buff—but beware, if caught you will be cited. Facilities here include limited picnic areas, restrooms, showers, and lifeguards. Swimming and surfing are good; the best waves break around Sequit Point, and there's also excellent surfing a few miles north at **County Line Beach**. Day-use fee, $5. ~ On Route 1 about 14 miles west of Malibu. There's access to Leo Carrillo Beach North from the parking lot at 35000 Pacific Coast Highway; 818-880-0350; e-mail info@csp-angeles.com.

> Look for the natural tunnel under lifeguard tower #3 at Leo Carrillo State Park.

▲ There are 136 sites for tents and trailers or RVs (no hookups); $15 per night. Reservations: 800-444-7275.

Santa Catalina Island

There's something surprising about finding a little slice of the Mediterranean sitting in the middle of the sea just a short ferry ride from the urban sprawl of L.A. Along its 54 miles of shoreline, Santa Catalina Island offers sheer cliffs, pocket beaches, hidden coves, and some of the finest skin diving anywhere. To the interior, mountains rise sharply to over 2000 feet in elevation. Island fox, black antelope, and over 400 bison range the island while its waters teem with marlin, swordfish, and barracuda. Happily, this unique habitat is preserved for posterity and adventurous travelers by an arrangement under which 86 percent of the island lies undeveloped, protected by the Santa Catalina Conservancy. Avalon, the famous coastal resort enclave, is the only town on the island. The rest is given over to mountain wilderness and pristine shoreline.

As romantic as its setting is the history of the island. Originally part of the Baja coastline, it broke off from the mainland eons ago and drifted 100 miles to the northwest. Its earliest inhabitants arrived perhaps 4000 or 5000 years ago, leaving scattered evidence of their presence before being supplanted by the Gabrieleño Indians around 500 B.C. A society of sun worshippers, the Gabrieleños constructed a sacrificial temple, fished island waters, and traded ceramics and soapstone carvings with mainland tribes, crossing the channel in canoes.

Juan Rodríguez Cabrillo discovered Catalina in 1542, but the place proved of such little interest to the Spanish that other than Sebastian Vizcaíno's exploration in 1602 they virtually ignored it.

By the 19th century, Russian fur traders, attracted by the rich colonies of sea otters, succeeded in exterminating both the otters and the indigenous people. Cattle and sheep herders took over the Gabrieleños' land while pirates and smugglers, hiding in Catalina's secluded coves, menaced the coast. Later in the century Chinese laborers were secretly landed on the island before being illegally carried to the mainland.

Other visionaries, seeing in Catalina a major resort area, took control. After changing hands several times the island was purchased in 1919 by William Wrigley, Jr. The Wrigley family—better known for their ownership of a chewing gum company and the Chicago Cubs baseball team—developed Avalon for tourism and left the rest of the island to nature. Attracting big-name entertainers and providing an escape from urban Los Angeles, Avalon soon captured the fancy of movie stars and wealthy Californians. Today Avalon is the port of entry for the island.

SIGHTS   Set in a luxurious amphitheater of green mountains, **Avalon** is like a time warp of Southern California early in the 20th century. The architecture is a blend of Mediterranean and Victorian homes as well as vernacular structures designed by creative locals who captured both the beautiful and whimsical.

From the ferry dock you can wander **Crescent Avenue**, Avalon's oceanfront promenade. Stroll out along the **Avalon Pleasure Pier**, located at Crescent Avenue and Catalina Street, for a view of the entire town and its surrounding crescent of mountains. Located along this wood plank promenade are food stands, the harbormaster's office, and bait-and-tackle shops. The **Catalina Island Visitors Bureau and Chamber of Commerce** has an information center here that will help orient you to Avalon and the island. ~ #1 Green Pier; 310-510-1520, fax 310-510-7606; www.catalina. com, e-mail info@visitcatalina.org.

Among the pier kiosks is a ticket booth offering guided tours in a **semi-submersible vessel** out to a nearby cove filled with colorful fish and marine plant life. Known as Catalina's "undersea gardens," the area is crowded with rich kelp beds and is a favorite haunt of spotted and calico bass, golden adult Garibaldi, and

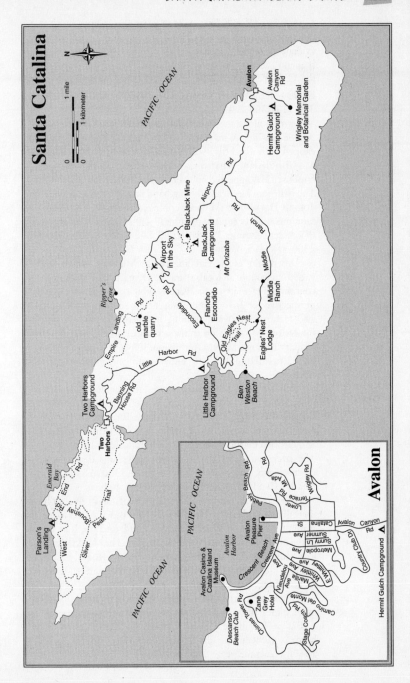

Santa Catalina

PACIFIC OCEAN

N

0 1 mile
0 1 kilometer

Avalon

Avalon Canyon Rd

Hermit Gulch Campground

Wrigley Memorial and Botanical Garden

Blackjack Mine

Airport Rd

Airport in the Sky

Blackjack Campground

Mt Orizaba

Ranch Rd

Middle

Middle Ranch

Ripper's Cove

Rd

old marble quarry

Empire Landing Rd

Escondido Rd

Rancho Escondido

Old Eagles Nest Trail

Eagles' Nest Lodge

Harbor Rd

Little

Banning House Rd

Two Harbors Campground

Little Harbor Campground

Ben Weston Beach

Emerald Bay

West End Rd

Parson's Landing

Silver Peak Trail

Bushsky Peak

Two Harbors

PACIFIC OCEAN

Avalon

PACIFIC OCEAN

Pebbly Beach Rd

Wrigley Rd

Lower Terrace Rd

Mt Ada

Catalina

St

Avalon Canyon Rd

Sunny Ln

Sumner Ave

Metropole Ave

Whitley Ave

Marilla Ave

Eucalidean Ave

Crescent Ave

Country Club Dr

Hermit Gulch Campground

Avalon Harbor

Avalon Pleasure Pier

Crescent Beach

Avalon Casino & Catalina Island Museum

Chimes Tower Rd

Zane Grey Hotel

Camino del Monte

Stage Coach Rd

Descanso Beach Club

PACIFIC OCEAN

leopard sharks. **Santa Catalina Island Company** has tours in the day and also at night when huge floodlights are used to attract sea life. In the summer they seek out the spectacular flying fish that seasonally inhabit these waters. They also offer coastal cruises and inland motor tours. Drop by their visitor information center. ~ 423 Crescent Avenue; 310-510-2000, 800-626-1496, fax 310-510-2300; www.scico.com.

Farther along the waterfront, dominating the skyline, sits the **Avalon Casino**. A massive circular building painted white and capped with a red tile roof, it was built in 1929 after a Spanish Moorish design. What can you say other than that the place is famous: it has appeared on countless postcards and travel posters. The ballroom has heard the big band sounds of Count Basie and Tommy Dorsey and the entire complex is a study in art deco with fabulous murals and tile paintings. ~ On Casino Way at the end of Crescent Avenue; 310-510-2000, 800-626-1496, fax 310-510-2300; www.scico.com.

Downstairs is the **Catalina Island Museum**, which holds a varied collection of local artifacts. Of particular interest is the contour relief map of the island, which provides an excellent perspective for anyone venturing into the interior. The museum also features an award-winning interactive exhibit chronicling the history of steamship transportation. Closed Thursday from January through March. Admission. ~ Avalon Casino; 310-510-2414, fax 310-510-2780; e-mail catalinaislmuseum@catalina isp.com.

Another point of particular interest, located one and a half miles inland in Avalon Canyon, is the **Wrigley Memorial and Botanical Garden**, a tribute to William Wrigley, Jr. The monument, an imposing 130-foot structure fashioned with glazed tiles and Georgia marble, features a spiral staircase in a solitary tower. The gardens, a showplace for native island plants, display an array of succulents and cactus. Admission. ~ 1400 Avalon Canyon Road; 310-510-2288; e-mail wmgarden@catalinas.net.

The most exhilarating sightseeing excursion in Avalon lies in the hills around town. Head out Pebbly Beach Road along the water, turn right on **Wrigley Terrace Road**, and you'll be on one of the many terraces that rise above Avalon. The old **Wrigley Mansion** (currently The Inn on Mt. Ada, Wrigley Road), an elegant estate with sweeping views, was once the (ho hum) summer residence of the Wrigley family.

Other scenic drives on the opposite side of town lie along Stage and Chimes Tower roads. Here you'll pass the **Zane Grey Hotel**, a 1926 pueblo adobe that was formerly the Western novel writer's home. ~ 199 Chimes Tower Road; 310-510-0966, fax 310-510-1340; www.zanegreypueblohotel.com.

Both routes snake into the hills past rocky outcroppings and patches of cactus. The slopes are steep and unrelenting. Below you blocks of houses run in rows out to a fringe of palm trees and undergrowth. Gaze around from this precarious perch and you'll see that Avalon rests in a green bowl surrounded by mountains.

> During Prohibition Catalina proved a favorite place among rumrunners and bootleggers.

One thing to remember about Catalina is that perhaps more than any other spot along the California coast, its tourism is seasonal. The season, of course, is summer, when mobs of people descend on the island. During the winter months everything slows down, storms wash through intermittently, and some facilities close. Spring and fall, when the crowds have subsided, the weather is good, and everything is still open, may be the best seasons of all.

Regardless of how you journey into Catalina's outback, there's only one way to get there, **Airport Road**. This paved thoroughfare climbs steadily from Avalon, offering views of the rugged coast and surrounding hills. Oak, pine, and eucalyptus dot the hillsides as the road follows a ridgetop with steep canyons falling away on either side. **Mt. Orizaba**, a flat-topped peak which represents the highest point on the island, rises in the distance.

A side road out to BlackJack Campground leads past **BlackJack Mine**, a silver mine closed since early in the century. Today little remains except tailing piles and a 520-foot shaft. Then the main road climbs to Catalina's **Airport in the Sky**, a small landing facility located at 1600-foot elevation.

From the airport you might want to follow a figure eight course in your route around the island, covering most of the island's roads and taking in as much of the landscape as possible (beyond the airport all the roads are dirt). Just follow Empire Landing Road, a curving, bumping track with side roads that lead down past an **old marble quarry** to **Ripper's Cove**. Characteristic of the many inlets dotting the island, the cove is framed by sharply rising hills. There's a boulder-and-sand beach here and a coastline bordered by interesting rock formations.

Two Harbors, at the intersection of the figure-eight's loops, is a half-mile wide isthmus connecting the two sections of Catalina Island. A small fishing pier, several tourist facilities, and a boat harbor make this modest enclave the only developed area outside Avalon.

From here **West End Road** curves and climbs, bends and descends along a rocky coast pocked with cactus and covered by scrub growth. There are Catalina cherry trees along the route and numerous coves at the bottom of steep cliffs. Not for the faint-hearted, West End Road is a narrow, bumpy course that winds high above the shore.

Anchored off **Emerald Bay** are several rock islets crowded with sea birds. From **Parson's Landing**, a small inlet with a brown-gray sand beach, dirt roads continue in a long loop out to the west end of the island, then back to Two Harbors.

Catalina possesses about 400 species of flora, some unique to the island, and is rich in wildlife. Anywhere along its slopes you are likely to spy quail, wild turkey, mountain goats, island fox, mule deer, and wild boar. Bison, placed on the island by a movie company filming a Western way back in the 1920s, graze seemingly everywhere. En route back toward Avalon, Little Harbor Road climbs into the mountains. From the hilltops around **Little Harbor** you can see a series of ridges that drop along sheer rockfaces to the frothing surf below.

> Gold fever swept Santa Catalina in 1863 as miners swept onto the island, but the rush never panned out.

Take a detour up to **Rancho Escondido**, a working ranch that boards champion Arabian horses. There's an arena here where trainers work these exquisite animals through their paces, and a "saddle and trophy room" filled with handcrafted riding gear as well as prizes from major horse shows.

Back at Little Harbor, Middle Ranch Road cuts through a mountain canyon past **Middle Ranch**, a small spread with livestock and oat fields. En route lies **Eagles' Nest Lodge**, a stagecoach stop dating to 1890. Numbered among the antique effects of this simple woodframe house are wagon wheels and a split-rail fence. Carry on to Airport Road then back to Avalon, completing this easy-eight route around an extraordinary island.

LODGING   One fact about lodging in Catalina everyone seems to agree upon is that it is overpriced. Particularly in the summer, when Avalon's population swells from about 3200 to over 10,000, hotels charge stiff rates for rooms. But what's a traveler to do? The island is both pretty and popular, so you have no recourse but to pay the piper.

It's also a fact that rates jump seasonally more than on the mainland. Summer is the most expensive period, winter the cheapest, with spring and fall somewhere in between. Weekend rates are also sometimes higher than weekday room tabs and usually require a two-night minimum stay.

The last fact of life for lodgers to remember is that since most of the island is a nature preserve, most hotels are located in Avalon.

Low-price lodgings are as rare as snow in Avalon. But at the **Hotel Atwater** you'll find accommodations to suit all budgets. The newer wing offers 26 country-style rooms in the deluxe-to-ultra-deluxe range. The older part of the hotel has wicker chairs and blond wood furniture. Besides, it has a friendly lobby with oak trim and tasteful blue furniture, plus dozens of rooms to choose from. Closed mid-November to April. ~ 125 Sumner Street; 310-

510-1788, 800-322-3434, fax 310-510-1673; www.scico.com.
MODERATE TO ULTRA-DELUXE.

One of Santa Catalina's most popular hotels is the **Pavilion Lodge**, a 73-room facility on Avalon's waterfront street. Designed around a central courtyard, it offers guests a lawn and patio for sunbathing. The rooms contain modern furniture, ceramic tile flooring, and Italian bedding. If you want to be at the heart of downtown in a comfortable if undistinguished establishment, this is the place. ~ 513 Crescent Avenue; 310-510-1788, fax 310-510-2073; www.scico.com. ULTRA-DELUXE.

Plainly put, the **Hotel Vista del Mar** is a gem. Each of the 15 spacious Mediterranean-style rooms is decorated in soft pastels and features a wet bar, fireplace, and full tiled bath. All surround an open-air atrium courtyard lobby, where guests enjoy ocean breezes and views from comfortable wicker rockers. One smaller room is priced deluxe, while courtyard rooms command ultra-deluxe rates. ~ 417 Crescent Avenue; 310-510-1452, 800-601-3836; www.hotel-vistadelmar.com, e-mail vista@catalinas.net. DELUXE TO ULTRA-DELUXE.

Farther along the same street is **Hotel Villa Portofino** with 35 rooms situated around a split-level brick patio. The accommodations are small but have been stylishly decorated with modern furniture, dressing tables, and wallpaper in pastel shades. There are tile baths with stall showers; a few have tubs. The oceanview suites have marble tubs. A small lobby downstairs has been finished with potted plants and marble. ~ 111 Crescent Avenue; 310-510-0555, 888-510-0555, fax 310-510-0839; www.hotelvilla portofino.com, e-mail vpstaff@catalinaisp.com. DELUXE TO ULTRA-DELUXE.

It's a big, bold, blue and white structure rising for five levels above the hillside. **Hotel Catalina** has been a fixture on the Avalon skyline since 1892. The 32-unit, completely non-smoking facility features a comfortable lobby complete with overhead fans, plus a sundeck and jacuzzi. The sleeping rooms are small but comfy with standard furnishings; many offer ocean views and all the rooms have ceiling fans, small refrigerators, and VCRs. There are also four trim little cottages that are warmly decorated. A bright, summer atmosphere pervades the place. ~ 129 Whittley Avenue; 310-510-0027, 800-540-0184, fax 310-510-1495; www.hotelcatalina.com, e-mail jarneson@catalinaisp.com. MODERATE TO DELUXE.

La Paloma Cottages, a rambling complex consisting of several buildings, features a string of eight contiguous cottages. These are cozy units with original decor and comfortable furnishings. There are also six larger family units (with kitchens) available in a nearby building. Set on a terraced street in a quiet part of town, La Paloma is attractively landscaped. There are no phones or daily maid service in the rooms. However, at **Las Flores**, an addition to the original hotel, you can get pricier rooms with maid service, phones, and a whirlpool bath to boot. ~ 326 Sunny Lane; 310-510-0737, 800-310-1505, fax 310-510-2424; www.catalina.com/lapaloma. html, e-mail lapaloma@catalinaisp.com. ULTRA-DELUXE.

Best Western Catalina Canyon Resort and Spa is a chic, modern 72-room complex complete with pool, jacuzzi, sauna, restaurant, and bar. This Mediterranean-style hotel sits on a hillside in Avalon Canyon. The grounds are nicely landscaped with banana plants and palm trees. Each guest room is furnished in an upscale beach style with wrought iron and granite, adorned with art prints, and decorated in a motif of natural colors. ~ 888 Country Club Drive; 310-510-0325, 800-253-9361, fax 310-510-0900; www.pacificahost.com ULTRA-DELUXE.

The romantic **Hotel St. Lauren** rises with a pink blush a block from the sand above Catalina's famed harbor. The Victorian-style hotel is a honeymoon paradise, with 42 spacious rooms and jacuzzi tubs in minisuites. ~ Metropole and Beacon streets; 310-510-2299, 800-645-2496, fax 310-510-1369; www.stlauren. com. DELUXE TO ULTRA-DELUXE.

Rare and incredible is the only way to describe **The Inn on Mt. Ada**. Nothing on the island, and few places along the California coast, compare. Perched on a hillside overlooking Avalon and its emerald shoreline, this stately hostelry resides in the old Wrigley mansion, a 7000-square-foot Georgian Colonial home built by the chewing gum baron in 1921. A masterwork of French doors and elegant columns, curved ceilings, and ornamental molding, the grande dame is beautifully appointed with antiques and plush furnishings. The entire ground floor—with rattan-furnished sitting room, oceanfront veranda, formal dining room, and spacious living room—is for the benefit of visitors. Wine and hors d'oeuvres

AUTHOR FAVORITE

Banning House Lodge, the only hotel on the island located outside Avalon, is an early-20th-century hunting lodge. Set in the isthmus that connects the two sections of Santa Catalina, it's a low-slung shingle building with a dining room and a mountain-lodge atmosphere. The living room boasts a brick fireplace. The rooms are trimly and individually decorated with throw rugs and wood furniture. The lodge provides an excellent opportunity to experience the island's outback. Continental breakfast is served in the lodge's breakfast room. ~ Two Harbors; 310-510-4228, fax 310-510-1303; www.scico.com. DELUXE TO ULTRA-DELUXE.

are served in the evening and there's a full breakfast and lunch served to guests and a limited number of visitors. The wonder of the place is that all this luxury is for just six guest rooms, two of which have semiprivate terraces, guaranteeing personal service and an atmosphere of intimacy. The private rooms are stylishly furnished in period pieces and adorned with a creative selection of artwork. The room fee includes a golf cart for transportation. Reserve at least two months in advance. Closed Christmas eve and Christmas day. ~ 398 Wrigley Road, P.O. Box 2560, Avalon, CA 90704; 310-510-2030, 800-608-7669, fax 310-510-2237; www.catalina.com/mtada. ULTRA-DELUXE.

DINING

As with Catalina hotels, there are a few points to remember when shopping for a restaurant. Prices are higher than on the mainland. With very few exceptions the dining spots are concentrated in Avalon; services around the rest of the island are minimal. Also, business is seasonal, so restaurants may vary their schedules, serving three meals daily during summer and weekends but only dinner during winter. The wisest course is to check beforehand.

Original Antonio's Deli is a hole-in-the-wall, but a hole-in-the-wall with panache. It's chockablock with junk—old pin-up pictures, record covers, dolls, and trophies. There's sawdust on the floor and a vague '50s theme to the place. The food—pizza, pasta, and hot sandwiches—is good, filling, and served daily at lunch and dinner. "Come on in," as the sign suggests, "and bask in the ambience of the decaying 1950s." ~ 114 Sumner Avenue; 310-510-0060; e-mail antonios@catalinaisp.com. BUDGET TO MODERATE.

The Beachcomber Café is a local gathering place located right on the beach. It's hard to match the views from the patio of this simple café. This is one place in Catalina that's open for breakfast, lunch, and dinner year-round. For lunch you can dine on vegetable platters, tacos, tostadas, salads, and sandwiches while gazing out at the pier and harbor. The dinner menu offers buffalo burgers, fried shrimp, teriyaki chicken, and steak. ~ 306-B Crescent Avenue; 310-510-1983, fax 310-510-1205. MODERATE TO DELUXE.

◄ HIDDEN

The other half of the vintage stucco-and-red-tile building housing the Busy Bee is the site of **Armstrong's Seafood Restaurant and Fish Market**. The interior is trimly finished in knotty pine and white tile with mounted gamefish on the walls. Since the establishment doubles as a fish market you can count on fresh seafood. The menu is the same at lunch and dinner with only the portions and prices changing. Mesquite-grilled dishes include mahimahi, scallops, swordfish, skewered shrimp, and steak. They also feature lobster, ahi, and orange roughy. You can dine indoors or on the patio right along the waterfront, making Armstrong's reasonable prices a bargain. ~ 306-A Crescent Avenue; 310-510-0113, fax 310-510-0266; www.armstrongseafood.com. MODERATE TO ULTRA-DELUXE.

Café Prego, a small Italian bistro complete with oilcloth tables and stucco arches, comes highly recommended. The specialties are seafood and pasta; you'll find a menu offering fresh swordfish, sea bass, halibut, and snapper, plus manicotti, rigatoni, lasagna, and fettuccine. There are also steak and veal dishes at this waterfront nook. It features good food and a cozy ambience. Dinner only. ~ 609 Crescent Avenue; 310-510-1218, fax 310-510-2997; e-mail pregocafe@catalinaisp.com. MODERATE TO ULTRA-DELUXE.

For a step upscale head down the street to **Ristorante Villa Portofino,** where you'll find pink stucco walls and candlelit tables set off by flowers. With art-deco curves and colorful art prints the place has a Mediterranean feel. The Continental cuisine includes several veal dishes, scampi, grilled filet mignon, lobster, and a selection of pasta dishes. This is the place for a romantic meal. Dinner only. Closed in January. ~ 101 Crescent Avenue; 310-510-2009; www.hotelvillaportofino.com. MODERATE TO ULTRA-DELUXE.

Buffalo Springs Station, situated up in the mountains at 1600 feet, is part of Catalina's Airport in the Sky complex. This facility serves egg dishes, hot cakes, buffalo burgers, and a variety of sandwiches. There's not much to the self-service restaurant itself, but it adjoins a lobby with stone fireplace and a tile patio that overlooks the surrounding mountains. Breakfast, lunch, and early dinner are served. ~ 310-510-2196, fax 310-510-2140. BUDGET.

HIDDEN ►   Catalina's remotest dining place is the **Harbor Reef Restaurant,** located way out in the Two Harbors area. This rambling establishment has a dining room done in nautical motif with fish nets and shell lamps. There's also an adjoining patio for enjoying the soft breezes that blow through this isthmus area. Fresh seafood and fresh fish are to be expected, of course, as are steak and pasta dishes. Reservations are recommended. ~ Two Harbors; 310-510-4235, fax 310-510-8690. MODERATE TO ULTRA-DELUXE.

Next to the Harbor Reef Restaurant there's an adjoining **snack bar** serving three meals daily; breakfast and lunch in winter months. It offers egg dishes, sandwiches, burgers, pizza, and burritos. ~ Two Harbors. BUDGET.

SHOPPING   The town of Avalon has a row of shops lining its main thoroughfare, Crescent Avenue, and other stores along the streets running up from the waterfront. Within this commercial checkerboard are also several mini-malls, one of which, **Metropole Market Place,** is a nicely designed complex. ~ Crescent and Whitney avenues.

Touring Catalina Sans Rental Car

When it comes time to venture further afield, you'll find that traveling around Santa Catalina Island is more complicated than it first seems. Preserving nature is probably what the island's caretakers had in mind when they made driving cars illegal on Catalina for non-residents. While golf carts are allowed in Avalon, visitors must navigate the remainder of the island's roads by two wheels, two feet, or a shuttle.

You can hike or bicycle to most places on the island, although permits are required outside Avalon. They can be obtained from the **Santa Catalina Island Conservancy**. ~ 125 Claressa Avenue; 310-510-2595; www.catalinaconservancy.org. Permits are also available at **The Airport in the Sky**. ~ 310-510-0143. You can also call **Two Harbors Visitors Services**. ~ P.O. Box 5086, Two Harbors, CA 90704; 310-510-0303.

Brown's Bikes rents bicycles, tandems, mountain bikes, and kids' bikes. Maps and helmets are included. ~ 107 Pebbly Beach Road; 310-510-0986. In Avalon proper, rent golf carts from outfits like **Island Rentals**. ~ 125 Pebbly Beach Road; 310-510-1456. You can also try **Catalina Auto Rental**, which rents golf carts as well as mountain bikes. Bike rentals include helmets. ~ 301 Crescent Avenue; 310-510-0111. There are also taxis in town.

Catalina Safari Bus provides a shuttle service to Two Harbors. ~ 310-510-2800, 800-785-8425. Santa Catalina Island Conservancy, the agency charged with overseeing the island, shuttles visitors to the airport and provides jeep tours.

Half the stores in town are souvenir or curio shops. I'd wait 'til you return to that shopping metropolis 26 miles across the sea.

NIGHTLIFE Like all other Catalina amenities, nightspots are concentrated in Avalon. The **Chi Chi Club** is the hottest danceclub on the island with live and deejay music (ranging from Top-40 and hip-hop to retro) and an enthusiastic crowd. Live comedy shows are offered on summer weekends. Cover on weekends. ~ 107 Sumner Avenue; 310-510-2828.

Also check the schedule for **Avalon Casino**. This fabulous vintage ballroom still hosts big bands and most of the island's major events. The Avalon also shows films at night in its restored golden-era motion picture theater. ~ Located at the end of Crescent Avenue; 310-510-2000.

BEACHES & PARKS If you are planning to camp on Catalina, there are a few things to know. First, there is a fee for camping and reservations are a must (reservation numbers are listed under the particular park).

In addition to designated beaches, camping is permitted in many of the island's coves. These are undeveloped sites with no facilities; most are readily accessible by boat. Patrolling rangers collect the fees here.

For information on hiking permits, camping, and transportation to campgrounds, contact the **Santa Catalina Island Conservancy** (125 Claressa Avenue, Avalon; 310-510-1421; www.catalina conservancy.org), **Two Harbors Enterprises** (P.O. Box 5086, Two Harbors; 310-510-4250), or the agent at **Two Harbors Campground** (310-510-2800) who seems to know just about everything relating to camping in the area.

CRESCENT BEACH 🚶 🚴 🏊 🦅 ⚓ 🛶 About as relaxing as Coney Island, this beach is at the center of the action. Avalon's main drag parallels the beach and a pier divides it into two separate strips of sand. Facing Avalon Harbor, the strand is flanked on one side with a ferry dock and along the other by the famous Avalon Casino. Full service facilities (including restrooms, showers, and beach rentals) are available on the street adjacent to the beach; lifeguards are also on duty. Fishing is good from the pier, and the harbor provides protection from the surf, making it an excellent swimming area. ~ Along Crescent Avenue in Avalon; 310-510-1520.

DESCANSO BEACH CLUB 🚶 🏊 🦅 ⚓ Somehow the appeal of this private enclave escapes me. A rock-strewn beach on the far side of the Avalon Casino, it seconds as a mooring facility for sailboats. Granted, there is a rolling lawn dotted with palm trees and the complex is nicely surrounded by hills. But with all the commotion at the snack bar and volleyball courts it's more like being on an amusement pier than a beach. Besides that, you have to pay to get onto the beach. Once there, you'll find good swimming, a restaurant, horseshoes, Ping-Pong tables, restrooms, a playground, and showers. ~ Located off Crescent Avenue past Casino Way; 310-510-1226.

HERMIT GULCH CAMPGROUND 🚶 🚲 This grassy field, dotted with palm and pine trees, is the only campground serving the Avalon area. Located up in Avalon Canyon inland from the beach, it provides a convenient and inexpensive way to visit Avalon and utilize its many services. There are pretty views of the surrounding hills and hiking trails are nearby. Facilities include picnic areas, restrooms, and showers. ~ Located on Avalon Canyon Road a mile from downtown Avalon; 310-510-8368, fax 310-510-2698; www.scico.com/camping.

▲ There are extensive camping facilities, ranging from tent cabins to basic camping to equipment rentals. There are 43 tent sites, $12 per person per night. Reservations are recommended in July and August.

BLACKJACK CAMPGROUND 🚶 🚲 Situated at 1600 feet elevation, this facility sits on a plateau below Mt. BlackJack, the island's second-highest peak. It's a lovely spot shaded by pine and eucalyptus trees and affording views across the rolling hills and out along the ocean. Among backcountry facilities this is about the least popular on the island. The campground has picnic areas, toilets, and showers. ~ Located south of The Airport in the Sky off Airport Road. Seasonal shuttle available from Avalon to BlackJack Trail Junction; 310-510-2800, fax 310-510-7254; www.scico.com/camping.

◄ *HIDDEN*

▲ There is a hike-in campground with 10 sites; $12 per person per night. Reservations are required.

BEN WESTON BEACH 🚶 🐟 🏊 🎣 A favorite among locals, this pewter-colored beach is surrounded by rocky hills. Located at the end of a long canyon road, it is serene and secluded. Avalon residents come here to flee the tourists, so you might consider making it your hideaway. This is a day-use beach only. Fishing and swimming are good, and it is one of the island's best spots for surfing. Facilities are limited to toilets. ~ Located about two miles south of Little Harbor off Middle Ranch Road.

LITTLE HARBOR CAMPGROUND 🐟 🏹 🏊 🎣 On the southwest shore of the island, this camp sits near a sandy beach between rocky headlands. It's studded with palm trees and occasionally filled with grazing bison, making it one of the island's prettiest facilities. In addition, Shark Harbor, a section of Little

> No one sails to Santa Catalina Island searching for bargains. Everything here has been shipped from the mainland and is that much more expensive as a result.

Harbor, is excellent for shell collecting and bodysurfing. Fishing, swimming, and skindiving are good here; facilities include picnic areas, toilets, and cold showers. ~ Located about seven miles east of Two Harbors along Little Harbor Road; 310-510-2800, fax 310-510-7254; www.scico.com/camping.

▲ The campground has a 150-person maximum (tents only); $12 per person per night.

TWO HARBORS CAMPGROUND 🏃 🚲 🚣 ⛵ 🏄 ⚓ Set along a series of terraces above a brown sand beach, this facility is adjacent to the services at Two Harbors. It's also a convenient base camp from which to hike out along the island's west end. Facilities include picnic areas, restrooms, and showers. The fishing and swimming are good, and the colorful waters here make skindiving especially rewarding. ~ Located next to Two Harbors in Little Fisherman's Cove; 310-510-2800, fax 310-510-7254; www.scico.com.

The Santa Catalina Island Conservancy runs Jeep eco-tours of the interior, where you may catch sight of foxes, bald eagles, and even American bison.

▲ The facilities here are extensive and include 45 tent sites and 13 tent cabins with added amenities, a 24-hour-a-day ranger, and more. Prices vary; call for information.

PARSON'S LANDING 🏃 🚲 🚣 ⛵ ⚓ The most remote of Catalina's campgrounds, this isolated facility sits along a small brown-gray sand beach with grass-covered hills in the background. Fishing, swimming, and skindiving are all good; facilities include picnic areas and toilets. The beach is ideal for shell combing, amethyst and beach glass. ~ Located seven miles west of Two Harbors along West End Road; 310-510-2800, fax 310-510-7254; www.scico.com.

▲ The campground holds a maximum of 45 people; there are 8 tent-only sites; $12 per person per night, plus $9 the first night.

Outdoor Adventures

SPORTS-FISHING

Fish the waters around Los Angeles and you can try your hand at landing a barracuda, calico bass, halibut, white sea bass, white croaker, or maybe even a relative of Jaws.

L.A. Harbor Sportfishing offers scheduled and chartered trips for yellowtail, bass, tuna, barracuda, and bonito. ~ 1150 Nagoya Way, Berth 79, San Pedro; 310-547-9916; www.laharborsportfishing.com. **Pierpoint Landing** has seven charter boats offering half-day to overnight fishing charters. ~ 200 Aquarium Way, Long Beach; 562-983-9300; www.pierpoint.net. **Redondo Sportfishing** offers half- and three-quarter-day trips in and around the Santa Monica Bay on three 65-foot boats. ~ 233 North Harbor Drive, Redondo Beach; 310-372-2111; www.redondosportfishing.com. For half- and three-quarter-day trips seeking yellowtail and white sea bass, contact **Marina del Rey Sportfishing**. ~ 13759 Fiji Way, Marina del Rey; 310-822-3625.

In Catalina you can contact the **Santa Catalina Island Visitors Bureau and Chamber of Commerce** for listings of private boat owners who outfit sportfishing expeditions. ~ 310-510-1520; www.catalina.com.

If you'd rather search for starfish than stars along L.A.'s coastline, you'll find an active diving scene.

DIVING

To explore Los Angeles' submerged depths, contact **Pacific Sporting Goods**, which provides lessons and equipment and organizes boat trips. ~ 11 39th Place, Long Beach; 562-434-1604. **Pacific Wilderness** is a PADI training center that sells and rents equipment. ~ 1719 South Pacific Avenue, San Pedro; 310-833-2422. Lessons at **Dive 'n Surf** are also PADI-certified; dive trips to Catalina and Santa Barbara are available. ~ 504 North Broadway, Redondo Beach; 310-372-8423; www.divensurf.com. For full-day trips around local islands call **Sea D Sea**. ~ 1911 South Catalina Avenue, Redondo Beach; 310-373-6355. **Blue Cheer Ocean Water Sports** runs trips from Ventura to Anacapa and Santa Cruz islands. ~ 1112 Wilshire Boulevard, Santa Monica; 310-828-1217; www.divers4hire.com. For NAUI certification classes and dive trips near the islands contact **Scuba Haus**. ~ 2501 Wilshire Boulevard, Santa Monica; 310-828-2916. **Malibu Divers** rents and sells gear and periodically runs full-day trips to Catalina. Private lessons are available. ~ 21231 Pacific Coast Highway, Malibu; 310-456-2396; www.malibudivers.com.

Without doubt Santa Catalina offers some of the finest scuba diving anywhere in the world. Perfectly positioned to attract fish from both the northern and southern Pacific, it teems with sea life. Large fish ascend from the deep waters surrounding the island while small colorful species inhabit rich kelp forests along the coast. There are caves and caverns to explore as well as the wrecks of rusting ships.

Several outfits rent skindiving and scuba equipment and sponsor dive trips, including **Catalina Divers Supply**. ~ 310-510-0330. **Island Charters, Inc.** offers similar services. ~ 310-510-2616. For guided or unguided full-day chartered trips try **Argo Diving Service**. ~ 310-510-2208.

During the annual migration (January through March) several outfits offer local whale-watching trips. **Pierpoint Landing** will take you out on the briny deep for a three-hour cruise. ~ 200 Aquarium Way, Long Beach; 562-495-6250. Out of Long Beach, **Harbor Breeze Corporation** takes two-and-a-half-hour trips along the coast. ~ Dock #2, 100 Aquarium Way, Long Beach; 310-831-0996; www.longbeachcruises.com. **Spirit Cruises** gives

WHALE WATCHING

you a guarantee with your trip. You see a whale or you get a gift certificate for a later trip. ~ Berth 77, San Pedro; 310-548-8080; www.spiritmarine.com. **L.A. Harbor Sportfishing** offers two-hour trips. ~ Berth 79, San Pedro; 310-547-9916; www.laharbor sportfishing.com.

SURFING & WIND-SURFING

"Surfing is the only life," so when in the Southland, sample a bit of Los Angeles' seminal subculture. Redondo, Hermosa, and Manhattan beaches have come to represent the L.A. scene. Other popular spots include Royal Palms State Beach and Torrance County Beach's Malaga Cove. If you're in Malibu, check out the waves at Topanga Beach, Malibu Surfrider Beach, and Leo Carrillo State Beach. Santa Catalina also has its share of waves: Ben Weston Beach for surfing and Shark Harbor for bodysurfing. Remember, it's more fun to hang ten than just hang out.

If you're visiting Los Angeles from winter to early spring, hop aboard a whale-watching vessel and keep your eyes peeled for plumes and tails.

Rent a surfboard, bodyboard, or wetsuit from **Manhattan Beach Bike and Skate Rentals**. Closed Tuesday in winter. ~ 1116 Manhattan Avenue, Manhattan Beach; 310-372-8500. **Jeffers** offers surfboards and boogieboards. ~ 39 14th Street, Hermosa Beach; 310-372-9492. You'll find surfboard, boogieboard, and wetsuit rentals in Malibu at **Zuma Jay Surfboards**. ~ 22775 Pacific Coast Highway, Malibu; 310-456-8044.

KAYAKING

For half-day ocean kayak tours along the Malibu coast, kayaking lessons, and kayak rentals, contact **Malibu Ocean Sports**. The tours last about two and a half hours and include some basic instruction. Tours are offered only on weekends between April and October. ~ 22935 Pacific Coast Highway; 310-456-6302, fax 310-456-6302; www.malibuoceansports.com.

On Catalina Island, **Descanso Beach Ocean Sports** offers rentals and several different guided expeditions in the waters around Catalina, among them a short 90-minute paddle to a cove near Avalon and a full-day excursion that includes hiking and picnicking. ~ Descanso Beach, Avalon; 310-510-1226, fax 310-510-3577; www.kayakcatalinaisland.com.

SKATING & SKATE-BOARDING

Los Angeles may well be the skating capital of California, and skateboarding, of course, is the closest thing to surfing without waves. Between the two of them, you can't get much more L.A., so find a way to put yourself on wheels.

To rent skates call **Manhattan Beach Bike and Skate Rentals**. ~ 1116 Manhattan Avenue, Manhattan Beach; 310-372-8500. **Rollerskates of America** has inline skates and gear. ~ 1312 Hermosa Avenue, Hermosa Beach; 310-372-8812. **Rentals on the**

Beach offers inline skates, bicycles, tandems, and other gear at three beach locations. ~ Near the parking lots at Washington Boulevard, Venice Boulevard, and Rose Avenue. **Spokes 'n Stuff** has two convenient locations and rents both inline skates and rollerskates. ~ At the parking lot on Admiralty Way at Jamaica Bay Inn Hotel, Marina del Rey, 310-306-3332; and near the Santa Monica Pier in Loews Santa Monica, 310-395-4748. Along the Santa Monica Pier, **Sea Mist Skate Rentals** has inline skates, rollerskates, mountain bikes, and everything else needed for a day on the South Bay Trail. ~ 1619 Ocean Front Walk, Santa Monica; 310-395-7076.

GOLF

Tee off in the gentle sea breeze—L.A.'s coastal climate is ideal for spending a day on the greens. Just don't swing too hard, because those golf balls don't float! Most courses have 18 holes and rent clubs and carts.

The beautiful **El Dorado Park Municipal Golf Course**, home of the Long Beach Open, has two putting greens and a driving range. ~ 2400 Studebaker Road, Long Beach; 562-430-5411. The 18-hole **Skylink Golf Course** is a duffer's delight with club and cart rentals, a driving range, night lighting, and a sports bar on the premises. ~ 4800 East Wardlow Road, Long Beach; 562-421-3388. The hilly **Recreation Park** offers both an 18-hole and a 9-hole course. ~ 5001 Deukmeijian Drive, Long Beach; 562-494-5000.

The coastal **Los Verdes Golf Course** is one of the finest public facilities in Southern California; along with spectacular views you'll find a driving range and two putting greens. ~ 7000 West Los Verdes Drive, Rancho Palos Verdes; 310-377-7370; www.americangolf.com.

If you can take a break from the action in Venice, head to the nine-hole **Penmar Golf Course**. ~ 1233 Rose Avenue, Venice; 310-396-6228.

Catalina Visitors Golf Club is a par-32 nine-hole course with plenty of sand traps. ~ 1 Country Club Drive, Avalon; 310-510-0530; www.scico.com.

TENNIS

A visit to the Los Angeles coast is reason enough to re-string your racquet and start enjoying the weather. These waterfront communities sport an abundance of hardtop courts, though there's usually a fee to play; call ahead to check.

There are 15 lighted courts available at **El Dorado Park**. ~ 2800 Studebaker Road, Long Beach; 562-425-0553. The **Billie Jean King Tennis Center** offers eight lighted courts. ~ 1040 Park Avenue, Long Beach; 562-438-8509. The **Alta Vista Tennis Courts** have eight lighted courts as well. Membership is required. ~ 715 Julia Avenue, Redondo Beach; 310-318-0670. Two lighted courts are available at **The Sport Center at King Harbor**. ~ 819 North Harbor Drive, Redondo Beach; 310-372-8868.

In Santa Monica, it's a good idea to call for reservations at public tennis courts during the summer. **Reed Park** has six lighted courts. ~ 1133 7th Street; 310-394-6011. **Memorial Park** offers four lighted courts. ~ Olympic Boulevard at 14th Street, Santa Monica; 310-394-6011. Also try one of the six courts at **Ocean View Park**. ~ Barnard Way south of Ocean Park Boulevard, Santa Monica; 310-394-6011.

BIKING   Though Los Angeles might seem like one giant freeway, there are scores of shoreline bike trails and routes for scenic excursions. Whether you're up for a leisurely and level beachfront loop, or a more strenuous trek through coastal cliffside communities, the weather and scenery make this area a beautiful place for a bike ride.

Foremost is the **South Bay Bike Trail**, with over 22 miles of coastal vistas. The trail, an easy ride and extremely popular, runs from RAT Beach in Torrance to Will Rogers State Beach in Pacific Palisades. The path intersects the Ballona Creek Bikeway in Marina Del Rey, which extends seven miles east and passes the Venice Boardwalk, as well as piers and marinas along the way.

Naples, a Venice-like neighborhood in Long Beach, provides a charming area for freeform bike rides. There are no designated paths but you can cycle with ease past beautiful homes, parks, and canals.

Of moderate difficulty is the **Palos Verdes Peninsula** coastline trail. Offering wonderful scenery, the 14-mile roundtrip ride goes from Malaga Cove Plaza in Palos Verdes Estates to the Wayfarers Chapel. (Part of the trail is a bike path, the rest follows city streets.)

The **Venice Boardwalk** is a casual, two-mile ride where a host of kooky characters and performers line the promenade, vying for your attention.

The **Santa Monica Loop** is an easy ride starting at San Vicente Boulevard and going up Ocean Avenue, past Palisades Park and the Santa Monica Pier. Most of the trail is on bike lanes and paths; five miles roundtrip.

In **Catalina**, free use of bikes is allowed only in Avalon. Elsewhere permits are required: they may be obtained from the **Santa Catalina Island Conservancy**. ~ 125 Claressa Avenue, Avalon; 310-510-2595; www.catalinaconservancy.org. Cross-channel carriers have special requirements for transporting bicycles and must be contacted in advance for complete details.

A strenuous but worthwhile excursion is a bike ride along **Mulholland Drive**. Not recommended during commuter hours, this route traverses the spine of the Santa Monica Mountains and offers fabulous views of the city and ocean.

For maps, brochures, and additional information on bike routes in Los Angeles contact the **Department of Transportation**. ~ 205 South Broadway, Suite 400; 213-485-9957.

Bike Rentals   To rent mountain bikes, cruisers, or tandems, try **Manhattan Beach Bike and Skate Rentals**. ~ 1116 Manhattan Avenue, Manhattan Beach; 310-372-8500. In Hermosa Beach, **Jeffers** rents beach cruisers. ~ 39 14th Street, Hermosa Beach; 310-372-9492. **Spokes 'n Stuff** offers mountain bikes, tandems, and cruisers. ~ Near the pier in Loews Santa Monica; 310-395-4748. Also in Santa Monica, **Sea Mist Skate Rentals** has mountain bikes and helmets. ~ 1619 Ocean Front Walk, Santa Monica; 310-395-7076. In Catalina try **Brown's Bikes**. ~ 107 Pebbly Beach Road, Avalon; 310-510-0986.

HIKING

The terrain of this region offers a wide array of pedestrian options, from beaches and tidepools to busy boardwalks to the trails of the rugged coast range. Depending on where you go for your hike, you may want your boots, spiffy street shoes, or Tevas. For a unique foray, try exploring a beached shipwreck or hiking in to the familiar-looking filming location of *M*A*S*H*. The only common denominators for hiking around here are the fine weather and sweeping vistas.

All distances listed for hiking trails are one way unless otherwise noted.

The Los Angeles portion of the **California Coastal Trail** begins on Naples Island in Long Beach. From here the trail is a varied journey across open bluffs, boat basins, rocky outcroppings accessible only at low tide, along beachwalks filled with rollerskaters, jugglers, and skate boarders, and up goat trails with stunning views of the Pacific Ocean.

PALOS VERDES PENINSULA   Set beneath wave-carved bluffs, the moderate **Palos Verdes Peninsula Trail** (5 miles) takes you along a rocky beachside past coves and teeming tidepools. The trail begins at Malaga Cove and ends at Point Vicente Lighthouse.

AUTHOR FAVORITE

For a nostalgic visit to the location of many movie and television shows, including *M*A*S*H* and *Love Is a Many Splendored Thing*, check out the **Craggs-Century Ranch Trail** (3.8 miles) in Malibu Creek State Park. The moderate trail travels along Malibu Creek to Rock Pool, the Gorge, and Century Lake. Continue over a rocky trail to view the *M*A*S*H* site.

If you're interested in exploring a shipwreck, head to Palos Verdes Estate Shoreline Preserve, near Malaga Cove, and hike the **Seashore–Shipwreck Trail** (2.25 miles). The moderate-to-difficult trail hugs the shoreline (and requires an ability to jump boulders), skirting tidepools and coves, until it arrives at what is left of an old Greek ship, the *Dominator*. Wear sturdy hiking shoes and bring water.

SANTA MONICA MOUNTAINS It's difficult to imagine, but Los Angeles does have undeveloped mountain wilderness areas prime for hiking. The Santa Monica Mountains offer chaparral-covered landscapes, grassy knolls, mountain streams, and dark canyons.

When visiting Will Rogers State Historic Park, take a moderate hike down **Inspiration Point Trail** (2-mile loop) for a view overlooking the Westside.

Topanga State Park has over 36 miles of trails. The **Musch Ranch Loop Trail** (5 mile loop) passes through five different types of plant communities. Or try the moderate **Santa Ynez Fire Road Trail** (7 miles), which guides you along the Palisades Highlands with views of the ocean and Santa Ynez Canyon. In spring wildflowers add to the already spectacular scenery.

Several trails trace the "backbone" of the Santa Monica Mountains. In fact, the **Backbone Trail** roughly follows the crest of these mountains, from Will Rogers State Historic Park to Point Mugu State Park—a 70-mile stretch. If you're not up for the long haul, you can pick up pieces of the trail at several points along the way, including the Circle X Ranch, Malibu Creek State Park, and Topanga State Park.

The moderate **Eagle Rock to Eagle Springs Loop Trail** (6 miles), for instance, begins in Topanga State Park and traverses oak and chaparral countryside on its way to Eagle Spring. Another section of the "Backbone Trail," **Malibu Creek State Park Loop** (15.5 miles roundtrip) begins near the crossroads of Piuma Road and Malibu Canyon Road. The difficult trail follows fire roads and offers choice views of the ocean and Channel Islands before it climbs up to Kanan-Dume Road. **Charmlee Park** is a little-visited wildflower paradise in the hills overlooking the ocean. A 1.75-mile trail offers great coastal views. Take Encinal Canyon Road four miles into the mountains from Pacific Coast Highway. **Solstice Canyon Park** is another hidden beauty with trails offering hikes of up to six miles. The moderate three-mile roundtrip to the Roberts Ranch House ruins follows a perennial stream and ends at the burned-out remains of a terraced dream house that retains a palm-shaded charm. Take Corral Canyon Road a quarter-mile north from Pacific Coast Highway.

HIDDEN ►

HIDDEN ►

An easy (though in spots difficult) climb up **Zuma Ridge Trail** (6 miles) brings you to the center of the Santa Monica Mountains

and affords otherworldly views of the Pacific. The trail begins off
Encinal Canyon Road, one and a half miles from Mulholland
Highway.

MALIBU   Zuma-Dume Trail (3 miles) in Malibu takes you on an
easy walk from Zuma Beach County Park, along Pirate's Cove
(which used to be a nude beach) to the Point Dume headlands
and Paradise Cove, a popular diving spot.

For a pleasant, easy hike along part of the Malibu coast dotted with coves and caves and providing terrific swimming, surfing, and skindiving, head out the **Leo Carrillo Trail** (1.5 miles),
located at Leo Carrillo State Beach. Or to hike up a gently sloping hill for a view of the coastline, take the easy, nearby **Yellow
Hill Trail** (2 miles).

SANTA CATALINA ISLAND   For a true adventure in hiking,
gather your gear and head for Santa Catalina. A network of spectacular trails crisscrosses this largely undeveloped island. Bring
plenty of water and beware of rattlesnakes and poison oak. You'll
also need a hiking permit, free from the Santa Catalina Island
Conservancy. ~ 125 Claressa Avenue, Avalon; 310-510-1421.

Empire Landing Road Trail (11.5 miles) begins at BlackJack
Junction and ends up at Two Harbors. The path passes a lot of
interesting terrain and provides glimpses of island wildlife, especially buffalo. (You can arrange with the ferry service to ride back
to the mainland from Two Harbors.)

Other routes to consider are **Sheep Chute Trail** (3.3 miles), a
moderate hike between Little Harbor and Empire Landing; and
Parson's Landing to Starlight Trail (4 miles), a strenuous trek between Silver Peak Trail and Parsons Landing.

Transportation

CAR

Route 1, which parallels the coast throughout Los Angeles County, undergoing several name changes during
its course, is the main coastal route. **Route 101** shadows the coast further inland, while **Route 405** provides access to
the Los Angeles basin from San Diego and **Route 10** arrives from
the east.

AIR

Two airports bring visitors to the Los Angeles coast area: the small
Long Beach Airport and the very big, very busy **Los Angeles International Airport** (LAX). (See Chapter Two for information pertaining to LAX.)

Presently, carriers into Long Beach are America West, Great
America Airways, SunJet International, and United Airlines.

The **Airport in the Sky**, set at 1600-foot elevation in the
mountains of Santa Catalina, may be the prettiest landing strip
anywhere. The small terminal building conveys a mountain lodge
atmosphere with a stone fireplace adorned by a trophy bison head.

~ 310-510-0143. **National Air,** also called **Catalina Vegas Airlines,** services the airport from the mainland. ~ 800-339-0359.

Another means of transportation to Catalina is **Island Express,** a helicopter service from Long Beach and San Pedro. They also offer around-the-island tours. ~ 310-510-2525; www.island express.com.

TRAIN

The closest **Amtrak** station is Union Station in downtown Los Angeles. (See Chapter Two for information.)

BOAT

Several companies provide regular transportation to Catalina by boat. The island is just 22 miles across the sea, but it's still necessary to make advance reservations. **Catalina Express** has service to Avalon and Two Harbors from the Catalina Terminal in San Pedro; service to Avalon leaves from Long Beach next to the *Queen Mary.* ~ 310-519-1212. **Catalina Passenger Service** makes daily trips to Catalina from Orange County. ~ 400 Main Street, Newport Beach; 949-673-5245.

BUS

Greyhound Bus Lines has service to the Los Angeles area from around the country. The Long Beach terminal is at 1498 Long Beach Boulevard (562-218-3011), and the Los Angeles terminal is at 1716 East 7th Street (213-629-8400).

CAR RENTALS

Avis Rent A Car (800-331-1212), **Budget Rent A Car** (800-527-0700), **Enterprise Rent A Car** (800-325-8007), **Hertz Rent A Car** (800-654-3131), and **National Car Rental** (800-227-7368) are located at, or within shuttle distance of, the Long Beach Airport.

To save even more money, try agencies that rent used cars. In the Long Beach area this includes **Robin Hood Rent A Car.** ~ 310-518-2292, 800-743-2992.

In Catalina, golf carts are the only vehicles permitted for sightseeing in Avalon. Check with **Catalina Auto and Bike Rental.** ~ 301 Crescent Avenue; 310-510-0111. **Island Rentals** is another option. ~ 125 Pebbly Beach Road; 310-510-1456. For further information on vehicle rentals on Catalina see the "Santa Catalina Island" section in this chapter.

PUBLIC TRANSIT

Long Beach Transit transports riders throughout the Long Beach area. Among the services is the Tour of the Art bus, which carries visitors between major points of interest. ~ 1963 East Anaheim, Long Beach; 562-591-2301; www.lbtransit.com.

MTA **Bus Line** serves all of Los Angeles County; disabled riders can call a hotline for information, 800-621-7828 (this number is functional only within the designated area). ~ 213-626-4455, 800-266-6883; www.mta.net.

In Santa Monica, call the **Big Blue Bus,** which hits such destinations as the LAX and downtown L.A. ~ Santa Monica Municipal Bus Lines, 612 Colorado Avenue; 310-451-5444; www.big bluebus.com.

In Catalina, **Catalina Safari Bus** provides daily buses from Avalon to Two Harbors and all campgrounds. This shuttle service also takes passengers from Avalon to the Airport in the Sky. ~ 310-510-2800, 800-785-8425.

Manhattan Beach Yellow Cab provides service in the South Bay. ~ 310-545-7520. In Santa Monica, call **Taxi Taxi.** ~ 310-828-2233. **Long Beach Yellow Cab** provides taxi service in Long Beach. ~ 562-435-6111. In Catalina you'll find the **Catalina Cab Company.** ~ 310-510-0025.

TAXIS

FOUR

Orange County

Places are known through their nicknames. More than official titles or proper names, sobriquets reveal the real identity of a region. "Orange Coast" can never describe the 42 miles of cobalt blue ocean and whitewashed sand from Seal Beach to San Clemente. That moniker derives from the days when Orange County was row on row with orchards of plump citrus. Today prestigious homes and marinas sprout from the shoreline. This is the "Gold Coast," habitat of beachboys, yachtsmen, and tennis buffs, the "American Riviera."

The theme that ties the territory together and gives rise to these nicknames is money. Money and the trappings that attend it—glamour, celebrity, elegance, power. Orange County is a sun-blessed realm of beautiful people, where politics is right-wing and real estate sells by the square foot.

Some half-dozen freeways crisscross the broad coastal plane where Spain's Gaspar de Portolá led the first overland expedition into present-day Orange County in 1769. Today, more than two million people live, work, and play where, during the mid-19th century, a few hundred Mexican ranchers tended herds of livestock on a handful of extensive land grants.

Ever since Walt Disney founded his fantasy empire here in the 1950s, Orange County has exploded with population and profits. In Disney's wake came the crowds, and as they arrived they developed housing projects and condominium complexes, mini-malls and business centers.

Along the coast progress also levied a tremendous toll but has left intact some of the natural beauty, the deep canyons and curving hills, soft sand beaches and sharp escarpments. The towns too have retained their separate styles, each projecting its own identifying image.

Seal Beach, Orange County's answer to small-town America, is a pretty community with a sense of serenity. To the south lies Huntington Beach, a place that claims the nickname "Surfing Capital of the World." The social capital of this beachside society is Newport Beach, a fashion-conscious center for celebrities, business mavens, and those to whom God granted little patience and a lot of money.

Corona del Mar is a model community with quiet streets and a placid waterfront. Laguna Beach is an artist colony so *in* that real estate prices have driven the artists *out*. Dana Point represents a marina development in search of a soul. San Juan Capistrano, a small town surrounding an old mission, is closer to its roots than any place in this futuristic area. San Clemente, which served as President Nixon's Western White House, is a trim, strait-laced residential community. Linking this string of beach towns together is Route 1, the Pacific Coast Highway, which runs south from Los Angeles to Capistrano Beach.

The geography throughout Orange County is varied and unpredictable. Around Newport Beach and Huntington Beach, rugged heights give way to low-lying terrain cut by rivers and opening into estuaries. These northerly towns, together with Dana Point, are manmade harbors carved from swamps and surrounded by landfill islands and peninsulas. Huntington Harbor, the first of its kind, consists of eight islands weighted down with luxury homes and bordered by a mazework of marinas. To the south, particularly around Laguna Beach, a series of uplifted marine terraces create bold headlands, coastal bluffs, and pocket coves.

Land here is so highly prized that it's not surprising the city fathers chose to create more by dredging it from river bottoms. The Gabrieleño and Juañero Indians who originally inhabited the area considered the ground sacred, while the Spanish who conquered them divided it into two immense land grants, the San Joaquin and Niguel ranchos.

Establishing themselves at the San Juan Capistrano mission in 1776, the Spanish padres held sway until the 19th century. By the 1830s American merchants from the East Coast were sending tall-masted trading ships up from Cape Horn. Richard Henry Dana, who sailed the shoreline, giving his name to Dana Point, described the area in *Two Years Before the Mast* as "the most romantic spot along the coast."

Orange County's first real spurt of growth came in the late 1850s when European immigrants, inspired by the agricultural successes of Franciscan missionaries, left the worked-out gold fields of the north to try their luck farming the fertile soil of the Santa Ana River Valley. German immigrants formed a successful winegrowing colony at Anaheim in 1857 and soon began planting the citrus trees that would eventually give the county its name.

By the 1860s, after California became a state, the Spanish ranchos were joined into the Irvine Ranch, a land parcel extending ten miles along the coast and 22 miles inland, and controlled with a steel fist by a single family.

They held in their sway all but Laguna Beach, which was settled in the 1870s by pioneers developing 160-acre government land grants. A freestyle community, Laguna developed into an artist colony filled with galleries and renowned for its cliff-rimmed beaches. Over the years artists and individualists—including the late LSD guru Timothy Leary and a retinue of hippies, who arrived during the 1960s— have been lured by the simple beauty of the place.

Laguna Beach has always relied on natural beauty, but Newport Beach has worked for its reputation. During the 1870s the harbor was built; channels were dredged, marshes filled, and stone jetties constructed as stern-wheelers began frequenting the "new port" between San Diego and Los Angeles. Newport Pier followed in 1888, allowing cattle hides and grain from Irvine Ranch to be loaded onto waiting ships.

While Laguna Beach developed as a resort community during the 1880s, it wasn't until 1904 that Newport Beach became a noted pleasure stop. That was the year the red trolley arrived and the town became the terminus for the Pacific Electric, Los Angeles' early streetcar line.

Within two years the population jumped sixfold and land values went into orbit. Balboa Pavilion was built in 1905 and soon became the center for Max Sennett–type bathing beauty contests. Years later it would be a dancehall and gambling casino, and finally a showroom for the Big Bands.

By the 1960s those brassy sounds had surrendered to the twanging strains of electric guitars as the Orange Coast earned its final nickname, "Surfer Heaven." Dick Dale, the "King of the Surf Guitar," hit the top of the charts with "Pipeline," setting off a wave that the Beach Boys and Jan and Dean rode to the crest. Down in Dana Point local boy Bruce Brown contributed to the coast culture in 1964 with a surf flick called *The Endless Summer*, which achieved cult status and earned for its director a reputation as "the Fellini of foam."

As the Orange Coast, particularly Huntington Beach, earned its surfing reputation in the 1960s, the entire county broke from the power of the Irvine Ranch. The suicide of a third-generation scion resulted in the land passing from a conservative family to an aggressive foundation. Within a few years it built Newport Center, the area's highrise district, and crowned it with the chic Fashion Island enclave. Orange County rapidly entered the modern age of multimillion-dollar development, adding a certain luster to its image (tarnished in the 1990s when risky investments forced the county temporarily into bankruptcy) and granting to its shoreline, for better or worse, an everlasting reputation as California's "Gold Coast."

Seal Beach

▼▼▼▼▼▼▼▼▼▼▼ Rare find indeed, this is a small town with a small-town beach tucked between Huntington Beach and Long Beach. In addition to a swath of fine-grain sand, there is a fishing pier from which you can engage in sportfishing. Oil derricks loom offshore and Long Beach rises in the misty distance. The beach, located along Ocean Avenue, features a pier and is popular with swimmers and surfers alike.

LODGING   It's only fitting that Seal Beach, Orange County's answer to a small town, houses the area's most appealing bed and breakfast. With its wrought-iron balcony, ornate fence, and garden ambi-

HIDDEN ►   ence, the **Seal Beach Inn and Gardens** has garnered a reputation for style and seclusion. Its 23 rooms are furnished in hardwood antiques and appointed with period wallhangings; some have balconies and fireplaces. Guests breakfast in a cozy "tea room," then adjourn to a cozy chair by the fireplace. The guest accommodations are named for flowers, many of which grow on the grounds. Indeed the landscaping, which includes early-20th-century lampposts, may be the most appealing feature of this fine old inn. ~ 212 5th Street; 562-493-2416, 800-443-3292, fax

562-799-0483; www.sealbeachinn.com, e-mail hideaway@seal-beachinn.com. DELUXE TO ULTRA-DELUXE.

DINING

You've probably discovered that Southern California is a land of extremes. One of the great examples of that is **Bonadonna's Shore House Cafe**. The decor, the atmosphere, and the menu all bring to mind the word "exaggeration." They describe their portions as "huge"—and that's *not* an exaggeration. Italian, Mexican,

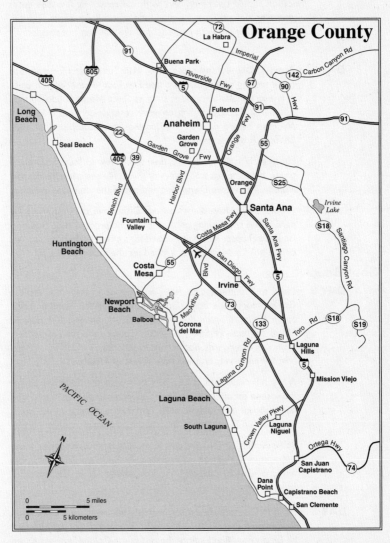

Text continued on page 240.

Disneyland and Beyond

You'll be hard-pressed to see all of Disneyland in a single day. To get the most out of your trip, plan a two-day visit. Ideally, a "Disneyland" vacation should last seven days, with the remaining five days spent sightseeing along the coast and visiting other theme parks. This itinerary is for families with grade school-age children, not toddlers.

DAY 1
- Arrive at **Disneyland**'s (page 276) Main Street early for maps and other touring essentials. Get a free Fast Pass to reserve your place in line at popular attractions such as *Space Mountain* (closed until summer 2005). Depending on your reservation time, ride *Space Mountain* before or after the *Indiana Jones Adventure* and *Jungle Cruise* in Adventureland.

- Lunch early at *Aladdin's Oasis*, then go to New Orleans Square and try to beat the lines at *Pirates of the Caribbean* and the *Haunted Mansion*. Then leave Disneyland and spend the afternoon relaxing.

- Around 5 p.m., have dinner outside Disneyland, then return to the park. Spend the evening on the rides in Fantasyland. Ride Frontierland's *Big Thunder Mountain Railroad* for a grand finale. If it's summer or the holiday season, stick around for the fireworks display.

DAY 2
- Head to Frontierland to make an afternoon reservation for the Golden Horseshoe Stage. Go directly to Tomorrowland and ride *Space Mountain* again, then ride *Star Tours, Autopia,* and *Honey, I Shrunk the Audience*. Stroll to Critter Country and see *Country Bear Playhouse*. Afterwards, hop aboard Frontierland's *Mark Twain Steamboat* for a leisurely cruise on the Rivers of America.

- While in Frontierland, catch a performance at the *Golden Horseshoe Stage*, then eat at the *Stage Door Café*. After lunch, ride the *Matterhorn Bobsleds* or re-ride favorite Fantasyland attractions. At 2 p.m. head to Main Street for the character flood from the current parade.

- Some evening options are: dine at the *Blue Bayou* overlooking those outrageous Caribbean pirates; visit *Tomorrowland Terrace* for live music; or dine by candlelight at Frontierland's *River Belle Terrace*.

DAY 3
- Head to Disneyland's smaller, less-stressful sister park, **California Adventure** (page 278). Go straight to *Soarin' Over California*, then hit *Grizzly River Run*. Explore the rest of the Golden State area, then grab an early lunch at the Pacific Wharf. Make your way to the

Hollywood Pictures Backlot and visit *Disney Animation*, *Jim Henson's MuppetVision 3D*, and *Who Wants to Be A Millionaire—Play It!* Finally, head over to Paradise Pier and ride *California Screamin'*. Spend the rest of the afternoon enjoying boardwalk-style games and rides. In the evening, wander through **Downtown Disney** (page 279).

DAY 4 • Get to **Knott's Berry Farm** (page 279) early and as soon as the gates open head for *Boomerang*, then *Montezooma's Revenge*. Do the rides in the Boardwalk section of the park, including *Windjammer*, then head to the *Log Peeler* and the rides in Fiesta Village, including *Jaguar*. Just before noon, head back toward the entrance and get in line at *Mrs. Knott's Chicken Dinner Restaurant*.

• Walk over to Ghost Town and, starting at the *Geode Shop*, move clockwise into the Wild Water Wilderness area to *Bigfoot Rapids*. Then check out *Mystery Lodge*. On a weekday, crowds will begin to thin in late afternoon, so head to any rides you haven't been on, then set off for the Boardwalk and ride *HammerHead*.

• In the evening, grab a tostada at *Herdez Cantina* and watch the *Incredible Waterworks Show* before you leave.

DAY 5 • Take a break from theme parks with a day on the beach. We recommend family-friendly **Bolsa Chica State Beach** (page 244).

• In the evening, take in the jousting matches at **Medieval Times** (page 290).

DAY 6 • Back in action, head up to **Universal Studios Hollywood** (page 76). Arrive 30 minutes before the park opens so you can be on the first tram, then take the *Back to the Future* ride. Order a snack from *Crepe de Paris* and stroll over to *Mel's Diner* to hear the Doo Wop singers. In the afternoon, work *Jurassic Park*, *E.T.*, and *Revenge of the Mummy* into your schedule. Finally, check the *TV Audience Ticket Booth* for shows that might be taping that evening or the next day.

DAY 7 • Spend the day at **SeaWorld San Diego** (page 338), which has enough shows and exhibits to fill the whole day.

• Alternatively, spend the morning at **San Diego Zoo's Wild Animal Park** (page 305). Have lunch in the park at **Thorn Tree Terrace**. On your way back to Anaheim, don't miss the amazing constructions at **LEGOLAND** (page 307).

Adapted from Hidden Disneyland & Beyond *(Ulysses Press). Consult this guide for ride ratings and additional information.*

Chinese, Texas chili, prime rib—they offer them all abundantly 24/7/365! ~ 941 East Pacific Coast Highway, Seal Beach; 562-430-0116. MODERATE.

Walt's Wharf restaurant specializes in creative seafood dishes but there's also Walt's oyster bar with a premium well, more than 40 imported beers, and more than 200 wines. Start off with appetizers such as the blackened ahi sashimi. Entrées vary with the catch of the day but may include oak-grilled mahimahi, sea bass with roasted macadamia nut sauce, or blackened Louisiana catfish with cilantro cream and fried polenta. ~ 201 Main Street; 562-598-4433, fax 562-598-8554; www.waltswharf.com, e-mail ww@waltswharf.com. MODERATE TO ULTRA-DELUXE.

For something different in a Mexican restaurant, try the **Yucatan Grill,** specializing in dishes from the Mexican Caribbean such as *cochinita pibil* (pork barbecued in banana leaves with a tangy sauce) and Mayan *dorado* (mahimahi with a pungent orange sauce). There are also offerings from other parts of the Caribbean, such as Jamaican jerk chicken and steak *cubano*. With seating both indoors and out, the atmosphere is supercasual. ~ 12147 Seal Beach Boulevard; 562-430-4422. MODERATE.

▼▼▼▼▼▼▼▼▼▼▼▼▼▼
Huntington Beach

In most of Orange County, a reference to "Duke" will conjure images of John Wayne, former resident and namesake of the airport here; in Huntington Beach, however, natives are more likely to assume you're talking about Duke Kahanamoku, the Hawaiian Olympic swimmer who brought the sport of surfing to the mainland in 1911. His bust stands at the foot of the Huntington Beach Pier, and his legacy continues through the international surfing competitions held here. At the surfing museum, located a few blocks from the beach, you can learn anything else you want to know about the history and culture of the sport.

There are, of course, many other ways to enjoy the beautiful coastline here: you can pedal the bike paths, dig for Pismo clams, hike in a wetlands preserve, and warm up at beach bonfires in the evening. But no matter what you do, you'll encounter surfing in some shape or form, even if it's only to admire a wave rider in the distance or watch a "woody," loaded with boards, driving through the streets. While the official story is that the discovery of offshore oil made Huntington Beach the largest city in Orange County, beach bums will argue that it was the discovery of how to ride the onshore breaks.

SIGHTS

As Route 1 buzzes south from Los Angeles it is bordered on one side by broad beaches and on the other by **Bolsa Chica Ecological Reserve.** An important wetlands area dotted with islands and overgrown in cord grass and pickleweed, this 300-acre preserve features a three-mile-long loop trail. Among the hundreds of animal species inhabiting or visiting the marsh are egrets, herons, and five endangered species. There are raucous seagulls as well as rare Belding's savannah sparrows and California least terns. There is an interpretive center (closed Monday) with scientific displays, educational material, and trail guides. ~ The accessways are across from the entrance to Bolsa Chica State Beach and at 3842 Warner Avenue; 714-846-1114, fax 714-846-4065; www. bolsachica.org, e-mail info@bolsachica.org.

Leave this natural world behind and you will enter the surf capital of California. In the mythology of surfing, Huntington Beach rides with Hawaii's Waimea Bay and the great breaks of Australia. Since the 1920s boys with boards have been as much a part of the seascape as blue skies and billowing clouds.

Synonymous with Huntington Beach is the **Huntington Beach Pier**. First built in 1904 for oil drilling purposes, it has been damaged by storms and extensively repaired four times. The pier's current incarnation, which opened in July 1992, is 1856 feet long, 38 feet above the water, and has a life expectancy of 100 years. But, as anyone who has lived by the ocean will agree, that century-long life span could be shortened dramatically by the next winter storm. ~ At the end of Main Street.

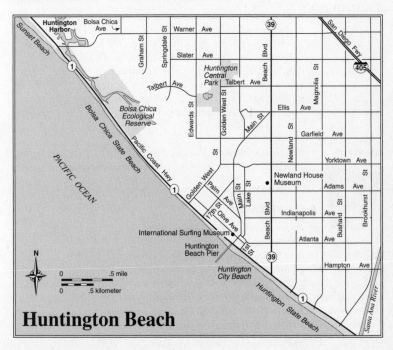

Huntington Beach

At the **Newland House Museum** visitors can see what life in 19th-century Huntington Beach was all about. Listed on the National Register of Historic Places and built in 1898, the grand dame is filled with furnishings and antiques from the town's early days. Closed Monday, Tuesday, and Friday, as well as on rainy days. ~ 19820 Beach Boulevard; 714-962-5777.

LODGING

The **Colonial Inn Youth Hostel** is a cavernous three-story house located four blocks from the beach. Capable of accommodating couples and families as well as individual travelers, its many rooms each contain two to eight beds. The house is in a residential neighborhood and has a kitchen, dining room, TV room, yard, and barbecue. Reservations recommended. ~ 421 8th Street; 714-536-3315, fax 714-536-9485; www.surfcityhostel.com, e-mail surf cityhostel@yahoo.com. BUDGET.

About four miles from the beach and 15 minutes from Disneyland, **The Comfort Suites** caters to leisure travelers and corporate clients. Stylish theme suites offer VCRs and include a continental breakfast. The large pink three-story building surrounded by palm trees is somewhat reminiscent of the Royal Hawaiian in Waikiki. A continental breakfast is included. ~ 16301 Beach Boulevard; 714-841-1812, 800-714-4040, fax 714-841-0241. MODERATE TO DELUXE.

The adventurous curiosity seeker might want to try staying at the **Edelweiss Inn**. Frankly, this 30-room hostelry has seen better days. In fact, it's very difficult to get the innkeeper to answer the phone. But it's located in the Bavarian Old World Village, a delightful replica of a Bavarian community built some 30 years ago by the same German builder who created the Alpine Village in Torrance. Shops and restaurants line the street. Bring your *liederhosen*: It's Oktoberfest year-round. ~ 7561 Center Avenue; 714-373-4999. BUDGET.

DINING

At **Louise's Trattoria** you can dine on fine Italian cuisine for reasonable prices. Try one of their fresh pasta dishes, such as rigatoni

AUTHOR FAVORITE

When Disneyland was young and I was a child, the Beach Boys' anthems gave me surfing daydreams, thwarted by the fact that I lived hundreds of miles from the nearest beach. So today I treasure the nostalgic **International Surfing Museum**. The showplace sits two blocks from the beach and features boards, boards, and more boards as well as an array of surfing paraphernalia. Hours vary; call for schedule. Admission. ~ 411 Olive Avenue, Huntington Beach; 714-960-3483, fax 714-960-1434; www.surfingmuseum.org, e-mail intsurfing@earthlink.net..

with grilled vegetables tossed in olive oil, or a California-style pizza with one of their inventive salads. Daily "chef's creations" guarantee you'll never tire of the menu. The restaurant is open and airy with modern decor, plenty of windows, and a patio overlooking the ocean. No lunch Monday through Thursday. ~ 300 Pacific Coast Highway; 714-960-0996, fax 714-960-7332. MODERATE TO ULTRA-DELUXE.

Harbor House Café is one of those hole-in-the-wall places ◄ HIDDEN packed with local folks. In this case it's "open 24 hours, 365 days a year" and has been around since 1939. Add knotty-pine walls covered with black-and-whites of your favorite movies stars and you've got a coastal classic. The menu, as you have surmised, includes burgers and sandwiches. Actually, it's pretty varied—in addition to croissant sandwiches there are Mexican dishes, seafood platters, chicken entrées, and omelettes. ~ 16341 Pacific Coast Highway; 562-592-5404. BUDGET TO MODERATE.

If you've ever been intimidated in a French restaurant, the **Moulin Rouge Bistro** is not that kind. Housed in a residential-style building with windows looking out on a shady green yard, this place has a family-oriented feel. The menu features a number of standard French selections, such as escargot florentine and the house specialty, châteaubriand *bouguetiere*, as well as a sampling of southeast Asian cuisine like the Vietnamese filet mignon *da-lat*, which is cubed beef tenderloin served on spring mix salad. No lunch. Closed Monday. ~ 10142 Adams Avenue; 714-593-3346, fax 714-593-3286. MODERATE.

Located at the Waterfront Hilton Beach Resort, **The West Coast** **NIGHTLIFE** **Club** is what one might call a gentlemen's club. Featuring seasonal live entertainment, a fireplace, floor-to-ceiling windows, and a patio for cigar lovers, it's a perfect spot for unwinding. Call ahead for hours. ~ 21100 Pacific Coast Highway; 714-960-7873; www.waterfrontbeachresort.hilton.com.

SURFSIDE BEACH 🐾 🛶 🎣 🚣 AND SUNSET BEACH **BEACHES**
🐾 🎣 🚣 These contiguous strands extend over three miles **& PARKS** along the ocean side of Huntington Harbor. Broad carpets of cushioning sand, they are lined with beach houses and lifeguard stands. Both are popular with local people. But Surfside, which fronts a private community and lacks facilities, is still a great beach to get away from the crowds. Sunset Beach has restrooms and lifeguards. Swimming and surfing are good at both beaches, although spectacular winter breaks near the jetty at the end of Surfside Beach make it the better choice during that season. For fishing, Sunset is the best bet. ~ Surfside runs north from Anderson Street, which provides the only public access to the beach; Sunset is off the Pacific Coast Highway, extending from Warner Avenue to Anderson Street in Sunset Beach.

BOLSA CHICA STATE BEACH 🏃 🚴 ⛵ 🏊 🚣 With three miles of fluffy sand, this is another in a series of broad, beautiful beaches. There are seasonal grunion runs and rich clam beds here; the beach is backdropped by the **Bolsa Chica Ecological Reserve**, an important wetlands area. Since the summer surf is gentler here than at Huntington Beach, Bolsa Chica is ideal for swimmers and families. You'll find picnic areas, restrooms, lifeguards, outdoor showers, snack bars, and beach rentals—and all these facilities do come with a cost. The fishing is good year-round at Bolsa Chica; swimming is better in the summer. For surfing, there are small summer waves and big winter breaks. Parking fee, $12. ~ Located along Pacific Coast Highway between Warner Avenue and Huntington Pier in Huntington Beach; 714-846-3460.

▲ There are 57 sites with water and electric hookups; $30 to $39 per night. Reservations required: 800-444-7275.

HUNTINGTON CITY BEACH 🚴 ⛵ 🏃 An urban continuation of the state beach to the south, this strand runs for several miles. This is one of the most famous surfing spots in the world. The Huntington Pier is the pride of the city. The surrounding waters are crowded with surfers in wet suits. A great place for water sports and people-watching. This surfer heaven gives way to an industrial inferno north of the pier where the oil derricks that plague offshore waters climb right up onto the beach, making it look more like the Texas coast than the blue Pacific. So stay south of the pier and make use of the fire pits, restrooms and outdoor showers, volleyball courts, and beach rentals. Swimming is good if you can find a time when the swells aren't too big, but the surf pumps year-round here (lifeguards are on duty year-round, too). Fishing tackle shops are nearby in Huntington Beach; if you're aiming to angle, try the pier. In October 2004, upgraded overnight camping will be available. Day-use fee, $7 to $9 and is subject to change. ~ Located along Pacific Coast Highway in Huntington Beach with numerous accesses; 714-536-5281, fax 714-374-1500.

> International surfing competitions are held throughout the summer months and in September at Huntington City Beach.

HUNTINGTON STATE BEACH 🏃 🚴 ⛵ 🏃 One of Southern California's broadest beaches, this strand extends for three miles. In addition to a desert of soft sand, it has those curling waves that surfer dreams (and movies) are made of. Pismo clams lie buried in the sand, a bike path parallels the water, and there is a five-acre preserve for endangered least terns. Before you decide to move here permanently, take heed: these natural wonders are sandwiched between industrial plants and offshore oil derricks. Nonetheless, your visit will be made more comfortable by the restrooms, fire rings, lifeguards, outdoor showers, dressing rooms, snack bars, volleyball, and beach rentals. The fishing is good here, and the surfing is excellent. Swimming is prime when the surf is low. Day-use fee, $5. ~ Located along Pacific Coast Highway in Huntington Beach; entrances are at Beach Boulevard, Newland Street, Magnolia Street, and Brookhurst Street; 714-536-1454, fax 714-536-0074.

▼▼▼▼▼▼▼▼▼▼▼
Newport Beach

Newport Beach is a mélange of manmade islands and a peninsula surrounding a harbor, and as a result, boating is the order of the day here. One of the largest pleasure harbors in the world, Newport Harbor is the starting point for the famous Tommy Bahama Ensenada Race, a 125-mile sailboat race to Baja held every April. There is also an annual Christmas Boat Parade, a nighttime procession of lighted boats.

In addition to recreational boats, fishing boats are a common sight; Newport Pier, the oldest in Southern California, is where the fishing boats return every morning to sell the day's catch. If you don't buy from them directly, you can still sample local seafood at the myriad waterfront area restaurants.

Although virtually the entire shoreline of the lower bay is developed, the upper bay, a narrow channel carved by a Pleistocene river, is a protected wetlands, and it offers perhaps the only escape from the constant flow of boat traffic and manmade vistas of the lower bay.

SIGHTS

For help finding your bearings around this labyrinth of waterways, contact the **Newport Harbor Area Chamber of Commerce**. Closed Saturday and Sunday. ~ 1470 Jamboree Road; 949-729-4400, fax 949-729-4417; www.newportbeach.com, e-mail info@newportbeach.com. The **Newport Beach Conference & Visitors Bureau** can also provide information. Closed Saturday and Sunday, except in the summer. ~ 3300 West Coast Highway; 949-719-6100, fax 949-719-6101, 800-942-6278; www.newportbeach-cvb.com, e-mail info@newportbeach-cvb.com.

While it cannot compete with Laguna Beach as an art center, the town does offer the **Orange County Museum of Art**. Specializing in contemporary art, this facility possesses perhaps the finest collection of post–World War II California art. Closed Monday. Admission. ~ 850 San Clemente Drive; 949-759-1122, 949-759-4848, fax 949-759-5623; www.ocma.net, e-mail ocma@pacbell.net.

Further evidence of Newport's creativity can be found at the **Lovell Beach House**. This private residence, set on the beach, is a modern masterpiece. Designed by Rudolf Schindler in 1926, it features a Bauhaus-like design with columns and cantilevers of poured concrete creating a series of striking geometric forms. ~ 13th Street and West Ocean Front.

One of Newport Beach's prettiest neighborhoods is **Balboa Island**, composed of two manmade islets in the middle of Newport Harbor. It can be reached by bridge along Marine Avenue or via a short ferry ride from Balboa Peninsula. Walk the pathways that circumnavigate both islands and you will pass clapboard cottages, Cape Cod homes, and modern block-design houses that seem made entirely of glass. While sailboats sit moored along the waterfront, streets that are little more than alleys lead into the center of the island.

Another dredged island, **Lido Isle**, sits just off Balboa Peninsula. Surrounded by Newport Harbor, lined with sprawling homes and pocket beaches, it is another of Newport Beach's wealthy residential enclaves.

Nearby **Lido Peninsula** seems like yet one more upscale neighborhood. But wait a minute, doesn't that house have a corrugated roofline? And the one next to it is made entirely of metal. Far from an ordinary suburban neighborhood, Lido Peninsula is a trailer park. In Newport Beach? Granted they call them "mobile homes" here, and many are hardly mobile with their brick foundations, flower boxes, and shrubs. But a trailer park it is, probably one of the fanciest in the country, with tin homes disguised by elaborate landscape designs, awnings, and wooden additions. Surreal to say the least.

The central piece in this jigsaw puzzle of manmade plots is **Balboa Peninsula**, a long, narrow finger of land bounded by Newport Harbor and the open ocean. High point of the peninsula is **Balboa Pavilion** located at the end of Main Street, a Victorian landmark that dates back to 1905, when it was a bathhouse for swimmers in ankle-length outfits. Marked by its well-known cupola, the bayfront building hosted the nation's first surfing tournament in 1932 and gave birth to its own dance sensation, the "Balboa." Today it's a mini-amusement park with carousel, Ferris wheel, photograph booths, skee ball, video games, and pinball machines.

Finding a parking space is one of the biggest challenges facing visitors to Balboa Peninsula. Be prepared to pump plenty of quarters into the metered spaces around Newport Pier, at the northern end of the peninsula, or pay $7 or more at an attendant lot near Balboa Pier, at the southern end.

Cruise ships to Catalina Island embark daily from the dock here and there are harbor cruises offered by **Catalina Passenger Service** aboard the *Pavilion Paddy*. The boat motors around the mazeway that is Newport Harbor. Fee. ~ 400 Main Street; 949-673-5245; www.catalinainfo.com, e-mail betsy@catalina info.com.

This is also home to the **Balboa Island Ferry**, a kind of floating landmark that has shuttled between Balboa Peninsula and Bal-

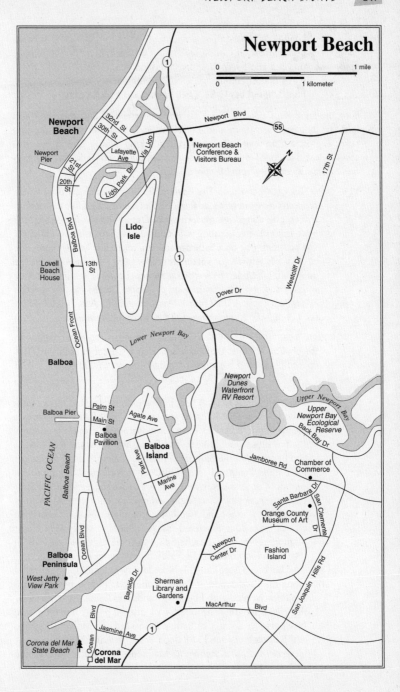

Newport Beach

0 _____ 1 mile
0 _____ 1 kilometer

Newport Beach

Newport Pier

Newport Blvd

55

32nd St
30th St
21st St
20th St
Lafayette Ave
Via Lido
Lido Park Dr

Newport Beach Conference & Visitors Bureau

N

17th St

Lido Isle

1

Balboa Blvd
13th St

Lovell Beach House

Ocean Front

Westcliff Dr

Dover Dr

Lower Newport Bay

Balboa

Newport Dunes Waterfront RV Resort

Upper Newport Bay

Upper Newport Bay Ecological Reserve

Back Bay Dr

PACIFIC OCEAN

Balboa Pier

Palm St
Main St
Balboa Pavilion

Agate Ave

Park Ave

Balboa Island

Marine Ave

Jamboree Rd

Chamber of Commerce

Santa Barbara Dr

San Clemente Dr

Orange County Museum of Art

Fashion Island

San Joaquin Hills Rd

Balboa Beach

Ocean Blvd

Bayside Dr

Newport Center Dr

Balboa Peninsula

West Jetty View Park

Sherman Library and Gardens

MacArthur Blvd

Ocean Blvd

Jasmine Ave

1

Corona del Mar State Beach

Corona del Mar

Adventures in Imagination

Sure, the Southern California Coast has sun, sand, and surf. But when your kids look like they need something a little different (you'll know it's time by the sunburnt expressions on their little faces), you're in luck: Orange County has that, too. No less than four kid-friendly museums dot the inland landscape, and each one is just a short drive from Newport Beach.

THE BOWERS KIDSEUM   The Bowers Kidseum gives a new twist to the children's museum genre, adding a dash of multicultural flair through activities, play things, and performances. Despite its diminutive size, the place ignites the imagination with dress-up, puppets, and scads of crafts and activities. Visit on a Saturday and you might just happen upon one of the family festivals (one Saturday each month). And there's always the interesting (albeit decidedly more grown-up) Bowers Museum next door with art and artifacts from around the world. Closed Monday through Friday. Admission. ~ 1802 North Main Street, Santa Ana; 714-480-1524, fax 714-480-0053; www.bowers.org, e-mail info@bowers.org.

DISCOVERY SCIENCE CENTER   Budding scientists can experiment with the physical world at the Discovery Science Center in Santa Ana. This science playground is gizmo and gadget heaven; 59,000 square feet of

boa Island since 1919. A simple, single-deck ferry that carries three cars (for about $1.50 each) and sports a pilot house the size of a phone booth, it crosses the narrow waterway every few minutes.

For those who'd like to paddle around Newport Bay, **kayaks** can be rented at the Balboa Fun Pavilion, next to the ferry launch on Balboa Peninsula (see "Outdoor Adventures"). A more romantic way to see Newport Bay is as a passenger aboard a gondola cruise, sipping champagne and nibbling chocolate. **Adventures at Sea** offers one- and two-hour gondola cruises, including an all-out three-course catered dinner cruise. ~ 3101 West Coast Highway, Newport Beach; 888-446-6365, fax 949-548-8856; www.gondola.com, e-mail travelguide@boatcharter.com.

The beach scene in this seaside city extends for nine miles along the Pacific side of Balboa Peninsula. Here a broad white-sand beach, lined with lifeguard stands and houses, reaches along the entire length. The centers of attention and amenities are **Newport Pier**, located at Balboa Boulevard and McFadden Place, and **Balboa Pier** found at Balboa Boulevard and Main Street. At Newport Pier, also known as McFadden's Pier, the skiffs of the

space with activities from a bed of nails (illustrating the principles of weight dispersion) to electronic finger painting. Admission. ~ 2500 North Main Street, Santa Ana; 714-542-2823, fax 714-542-2828; www. discoverycube.org.

CENTENNIAL HERITAGE MUSEUM   If newfangled science isn't your thing, go back in time at the Centennial Heritage Museum. The museum has household items and knickknacks from a bygone era: old-fashioned games, a Victrola, and even a washboard you can try. Outside the main structure, a 12-acre spread has a nature center and blacksmith shop. Closed Monday, Tuesday, and Saturday. Admission. ~ 3101 West Harvard Street, Santa Ana; 714-850-9452; www.centennialmuseum.org.

CHILDREN'S MUSEUM   For plain-old modern thrills, you can't beat the Children's Museum in La Habra. Housed in a renovated train depot, this cozy spot is kid heaven, where little ones can get in the driver's seat of an actual city bus (don't worry, it doesn't go anywhere!) or play operator on an old-time switchboard. There's lots (and lots and lots!) more. The highlight: a well-stocked stage (complete with lighting, props, and microphone) where pint-sized thespians can get ready for their close-ups. An extra perk for moms and dads: such imagination-fueled activities let beleaguered parents sit back and watch for a while. Admission. ~ 301 South Euclid Street, La Habra; 562-905-9693, fax 562-905-9698; www.lhcm.org.

Newport Dory Fishing Fleet are beached every day while local fishermen sell their catches. This flotilla of small wooden boats has been here so long it has achieved historic landmark status. At dawn the fishermen sail ten miles offshore, set trawl lines, and haul in the mackerel, flounder, rock fish, and halibut sold at the afternoon market.

To capture a sense of the beauty that still inheres in Newport Beach, take a walk out to **West Jetty View Park** at the tip of Balboa Peninsula. Here civilization meets the sea. To the left extend the rock jetties forming the mouth of Newport Harbor. Behind you are the plate-glass houses of the city. A wide beach, tufted with ice plants and occasional palm trees, forms another border. Before you, changing its hue with the phases of the sun and clouds, is the Pacific, a single sweep of water that makes those million-dollar homes seem fragile and tenuous. ~ Ocean Boulevard at Channel Road.

Not all the wealth of Newport Beach is measured in finances. The richness of the natural environment is evident as well when you venture through **Upper Newport Bay Ecological Reserve.**   ◄ *HIDDEN*

Whether you bike (see "Outdoor Adventures") or drive part way through the 752-acre reserve, you'll have the chance to glimpse what's left of an ancient landscape that was first carved out by glaciers some 300,000 years ago. Development has reduced the marshes to a fraction of what they used to be, but what's left is one of the last remaining coastal wetlands in California. The road passes limestone bluffs and sandstone hills. Reeds and cattails line the shore. Over 200 species of birds can be seen here; and six endangered species, including Belding's savannah sparrow, the brown pelican, and the light-footed clapper rail, live along the bay. Be sure to visit the interpretive center (949-923-6833). Closed Monday. Guided walking, electric pontoon boat, canoeing, and kayaking tours are available. ~ 600 Shellmaker; 949-640-6746, fax 949-923-2269; www.newportbay.org, e-mail info@newportbay.org.

Southern California's largest estuary, Upper Newport Bay is a vital stopping place for thousands of migrating birds on the Pacific Flyway.

Located at the far northwest end of Newport Bay, the unusual **Upper Newport Bay–Peter and Mary Muth Interpretive Center** isn't visible from the road. The rooftop is planted with native grasses that blend into the landscape, while the center itself is built underground. Hands-on interactive exhibits reveal the intricate workings of this complex ecosystem. Closed Monday. ~ 2301 University Drive; 949-923-2290, fax 949-642-3189; www.ocparks.com/unbic.

Back on Route 1, head south through **Corona del Mar** en route to Laguna Beach. A wealthy enclave with trim lawns and spacious homes, Corona del Mar offers a pretty coastal drive along residential Ocean Boulevard.

In Corona del Mar, drop by the **Sherman Library and Gardens**. Devoted to the culture and recent history of the "Pacific Southwest," this complex features a specialized library set in Early California–style buildings. Also inviting are the koi pond, botanical garden, and the tropical conservatory. Admission; free on Monday. ~ 2647 East Coast Highway, Corona del Mar; 949-673-2261, fax 949-675-5458; www.slgardens.org, e-mail info@slgardens.org.

LODGING   You'd have a hell of a time docking your boat at the **Little Inn by the Bay**. Actually it's on an island, but the island is a median strip dividing the two busiest streets on the Balboa Peninsula. Offering 17 standard motel rooms, the inn is a block from the beach and walking distance from many restaurants. ~ 2627 Newport Boulevard; 949-673-8800, 800-438-4466, fax 949-673-4943; www.littleinnbythebay.com, e-mail littlein@pacbell.net. DELUXE TO ULTRA-DELUXE.

A Spanish-style hotel with cream-colored walls and a tile-roofed tower, the **Balboa Inn** is ideally situated right next to the beach at Balboa Pier. Adding to the ambience is a swimming pool that looks out on the water. The 34 rooms, some of which have ocean views, are furnished in knotty pine, decorated with colorful prints, and supplied with jacuzzi tubs, brass fixtures, and fireplaces. ~ 105 Main Street; 949-675-3412, 877-225-2629, fax 949-673-4587; www.balboainn.com, e-mail info@balboainn.com. DELUXE TO ULTRA-DELUXE.

Portofino Beach Hotel, a 15-room B&B inn, rests on the beach in an early-20th-century building. Richly appointed with brass beds, armoires, and antique fixtures, the Portofino has a wine bar downstairs and two oceanfront parlors overlooking Newport Pier. Each room is decorated with antiques and equipped with a private bath; many have jacuzzis, skylights, fireplaces, and ocean views. There are also five two-bedroom apartments with kitchenettes. ~ 2306 West Ocean Front; 949-673-7030, 800-571-8749, fax 949-723-4370; www.portofinobeachhotel.com, e-mail info@portofinobeachhotel.com. DELUXE TO ULTRA-DELUXE.

On tiny Balboa Island you'll find the **Balboa Island Hotel**, a family-operated, three-bedroom, bed-and-breakfast affair. Set in a 1925 house, it's about one block from the water (of course, on Balboa Island everything is one block from the water). Each room of this B&B inn has been decorated in period and furnished with antiques. The place has a small, intimate, homey feel. Guests share bathrooms and there are two porches that serve as sitting rooms. ~ 127 Agate Avenue; 949-675-3613. MODERATE.

By way of full-facility destinations, Southern California–style, few places match the **Hyatt Regency Newport Beach**. Situated on a hillside above Upper Newport Bay, it sprawls across 26 acres and sports three swimming pools, three jacuzzis, a nine-hole pitch-and-putt course, and a tennis club. There are restaurants, a lounge, a lavishly decorated lobby, and a series of terraced patios. Guest rooms are modern in design, comfortably furnished, and tastefully appointed. An inviting combination of elegance and amenities. ~ 1107 Jamboree Road; 949-729-1234, 800-233-1234, fax 949-644-1552; www.hyattnewporter.com, e-mail info@hyattnewporter.com. DELUXE TO ULTRA-DELUXE.

DINING

Believed by many to be the finest dining in Newport Beach, **Pascal** provides a taste of Provence. The menu includes their popular rendition of sea bass, as well as rabbit, duck, and free-range chicken with a French accent. No dinner on Monday and no lunch on Saturday. Closed Sunday. ~ 1000 North Bristol Street; 949-752-0107, fax 949-261-9422; www.pascalnewportbeach. com. DELUXE TO ULTRA-DELUXE.

21 Ocean Front is a gourmet seafood dining place known for fine cuisine. Located on the beach overlooking Newport Pier, the interior is done (or rather, overdone) in a kind of shiny Victorian style with black trim and brass chandeliers. The secret is to close your eyes and surrender to the senses of taste and smell. At dinner the chef prepares carp and Hawaiian fish specials as well as abalone, Maine lobster, and *cioppino*. For those who miss the point there's rack of lamb, pork tenderloin, filet mignon, and Kobe beef (when available). Live entertainment and a wine cellar contribute to the extravagant atmosphere. Dinner only. ~ 2100 West Ocean Front; 949-673-2100, fax 949-673-2101; www. 21oceanfront.com, e-mail info@21oceanfront.com. DELUXE TO ULTRA-DELUXE.

Around **Balboa Pavilion** you'll find snack bars and amusement park food stands.

A place nearby that's worth recommending is **Newport Landing**, a double-decker affair where you can have an intimate supper downstairs in a wood-paneled dining room or a casual meal upstairs on a deck overlooking the harbor. The upper deck features live music on the weekend. Serving lunch, dinner, and weekend brunch, Newport Landing specializes in fresh fish selections (including *ono*, salmon, and halibut) but also serves lamb chops, hickory-smoked prime rib, and chicken with artichokes. ~ 503 East Edgewater Avenue; 949-675-2373, 877-526-3464, fax 949-675-0682; www.newport-landing.com, e-mail info@newport-landing.com. DELUXE TO ULTRA-DELUXE.

Who could imagine that at the end of Balboa Pier there would be a vintage 1940s-era diner complete with art-deco curves and red plastic booths. **Ruby's Diner** is a classic. Besides that it provides 270-degree views of the ocean. Of course the menu, whether breakfast, lunch, or dinner, contains little more than omelettes, hamburgers, sandwiches, chili, and salads. But who's hungry anyway with all that history and scenery to savor? ~ 1 Balboa Pier; 949-675-7829; www.rubys.com. BUDGET.

HIDDEN ▶   **Amelia's**, a family-run restaurant serving Italian dishes and seafood, is a local institution. At lunch you'll find them serving a multitude of pasta dishes, fresh fish entrées, sandwiches, and salads. Then in the evening the chef prepares calamari stuffed with crab, scallops, Icelandic cod, bouillabaisse, veal piccata, and another round of pasta platters. Dinner is served daily; lunch on Friday and Saturday. Sunday brunch. ~ 311 Marine Avenue; 949-673-6580, fax 949-673-5395. MODERATE TO DELUXE.

If you were hoping to spend a little less money, **Wilma's Patio** is just down the street. It's casual family dining at its best—open morning, noon, and night—with multicourse American, Chinese, and Mexican meals. ~ 203 Marine Avenue; 949-675-5542, fax 949-675-7243. BUDGET TO MODERATE.

With a bakery on the premises, you know that the pastries at **Haute Cakes** must be fresh. Enjoy the daily waffle special in a cozy, simple setting, or have a hot scrambler out in the courtyard. If you're in the mood for lunch, the grilled-eggplant-and-vegetable salad with a sandwich hits the spot. No dinner. ~ 1807 Westcliff Drive; 949-642-4114. BUDGET TO MODERATE.

If it's people watching you're after, **Baja Sharkeez** will deliver. This chain eatery specializes in Mexi-California food—gourmet burritos, mesquite-grilled platters, tacos, and fajitas. The atmosphere is nothing to write home about, but the service is friendly and it's a good place to go for an inexpensive meal before a day of sightseeing or hitting the beach. ~ 114 McFadden Place, Newport Beach; 949-673-0292; www.sharkeez.net. BUDGET.

Ironically enough, one of Newport Beach's top dining bargains lies at the heart of the region's priciest shopping malls. Encircling the lower level of **Fashion Island** is a collection of stands dispensing sushi, soup and sandwiches, Mexican food, pasta salads, hamburgers, and other light fare. ~ Fashion Island, 401 Newport Center Drive; 949-721-2000; www.shopfashionisland.com. BUDGET TO MODERATE.

A local favorite in Corona del Mar, the small town adjacent to Newport Beach, is **The Quiet Woman**, a small, dark, friendly place serving mesquite-grilled food. The lunch and dinner menus both feature steak and seafood. Live entertainment accompanies evening meals Wednesday through Saturday. No lunch on weekends. ~ 3224 East Coast Highway, Corona Del Mar; 949-640-7440; fax 949-640-5869; www.thequietwoman.com. DELUXE TO ULTRA-DELUXE.

◄ HIDDEN

SHOPPING

The streets radiating out from **Balboa Pavilion** (end of Main Street) are lined with beachwear stores, sundries shops, and souvenir stands. While there's little of value here, it is a good place to shop for knickknacks. The scene is much the same around **Newport Pier**, located at Balboa Avenue and McFadden Place.

AUTHOR FAVORITE

You won't miss **The Crab Cooker**. First, it's painted bright red; second, it's located at a busy intersection near Newport Pier; last, the place has been a local institution since the 1950s. Actually, you don't *want* to miss The Crab Cooker. This informal eatery, where lunch and dinner are served on paper plates, has fish, scallops, shrimp, crab, and oysters. There's a fish market attached to the restaurant, so freshness and quality are assured. ~ 2200 Newport Boulevard; 949-673-0100, fax 949-675-8445. MODERATE TO DELUXE.

For more specialized boutique shopping, cast anchor at **Lido Marina Village**. This well-heeled complex features a host of shops lining a brick courtyard and adjacent boardwalk. ~ 3400 Via Oporto; 949-675-8662, fax 949-673-8517.

Another Newport Beach shopping enclave lies along Marine Avenue on Balboa Island. This consumer strip is door-to-door with card shops, gift shops, and sundries stores. Without exaggerating, I would estimate that more than half the outlets here sell beachwear.

After all is said and done, but hopefully before the money is all spent, the center for Newport Beach shopping is **Fashion Island**. Situated at the heart of Newport Center, the town's highrise financial district, it is also the best place for beautiful-people watching. Every self-respecting department store is here. Neiman Marcus, Macy's, and Bloomingdale's are all represented. ~ 401 Newport Center Drive; 949-721-2000; www.shopfashionisland.com.

There's an outdoor plaza filled with fashion outlets and an atrium displaying one floor of designer dreams. If you don't believe Newport Beach is a match for Beverly Hills in flash and cash, take a tour of the parking lot. It's a showplace for Rolls Royces, Jaguars, and Mercedes, as well as more plebeian Volvos and Audis.

The **Entertainer** cruises around the bay on Friday and Saturday evenings and Sunday afternoons year-round. In addition to a delicious supper prepared fresh on board there is dancing on the upper deck to live music. The Sunday brunch cruise offers free flowing champagne. ~ 2431 West Pacific Coast Highway; 949-646-0155, 800-668-4322, fax 949-646-5924; www.horn blower.com, e-mail nb@hornblower.com.

For contemporary paintings, I particularly recommend **Southern California Art Projects and Exhibitions** (SCAPE), which displays the work of Ran Turner, R. Kenton Nelson, and other artists. Closed Monday. ~ 2859 East Coast Highway, Corona Del Mar; 949-723-3406, fax 949-723-3407; www.scapesite.com, e-mail info@scapesite.com.

NIGHTLIFE For a lively happy hour, televised sports, and pool games, check out **Cabo Cantina**, a watering hole near Balboa Pier. ~ 100 Main Street; 949-675-7760.

There's dancing, food, and drink specials Thursday through Saturday nights at **Baja Sharkeez**. Thursday night attracts a raucous college crowd fond of imbibing huge frozen drink concoctions. ~ 114 McFadden Place, Newport Beach; 949-673-0292; www.sharkeez.net.

BEACHES & PARKS **NEWPORT BEACH** Narrow at the northern end and widening to the south, this sandy strip extends for several miles along the base of the Balboa Peninsula. Newport Pier (also known as McFadden's Pier) and the surrounding facilities serve as the center of the strand. A wonderful beach, with entrances along its entire length, this is an important gathering place for the crowds that pour into town. There are restrooms, lifeguards, and beach rentals; at the foot of the pier you will find restaurants, groceries, and all amenities imaginable. The pier is also the place for fishing. Swimming and surfing are both good. If you want to ride the waves, try in the morning around Newport Pier and then in the afternoon at the 30th Street section of the beach. There are year-round breaks near the Santa Ana River mouth at the far north end of the beach. ~ The beach parallels Balboa Boulevard in Newport Beach. Newport Pier is between 20th and 21st streets; 949-644-3000.

BALBOA BEACH This broad sandy strip forms the ocean side of Balboa Peninsula and extends along its entire length. There are entrances to the beach from numerous side streets, but the center of the facility is around Balboa Pier, a concrete fishing pier. With a palm-shaded lawn and many nearby amenities, this beach, together with neighboring Newport Beach, is the most popular spot in town. Facilities include restrooms, showers, lifeguards, a playground, and beach rentals. Fishing is good from the pier. ~ The beach parallels Balboa Boulevard; Balboa Pier is at the end of Main Street; 949-644-3000.

WEST JETTY VIEW PARK Set at the very end of the Balboa Peninsula, this triangle of sand is perfectly placed. From the tip extends a rock jetty that borders Newport Harbor. You can climb the rocks and watch boats in the bay, or turn your back on these trifles and wander across the broad sand carpet that rolls down to the ocean. There are wonderful views of Newport Beach and the coast. If you're daring enough, you can challenge the waves at **The Wedge.** Known to bodysurfers around the world, the area between the jetty and beach is one of the finest and most dangerous shore breaks anywhere, the "Mount Everest of bodysurfing." If it's any comfort, there are lifeguards. Swimming is very dangerous; the shore break here is fierce. Bodysurfing is the main sport; surfing is permitted further down the beach and only in the winter. But take heed, these breaks are only for veteran bodysurfers. ~ At the end of Balboa and Ocean boulevards at the tip of the Balboa Peninsula; 949-644-3000.

> If the crowds at Corona del Mar State Beach are driving you crazy, you will find one possible escape valve: there are a pair of pocket beaches on the other side of the rocks next to the jetty.

NEWPORT DUNES WATERFRONT RV RESORT This resort has a broad, horseshoe-shaped beach about a half-mile in length. It curves around the lake-like waters of Upper Newport Bay, one mile inland from the ocean. Very popular with families and campers, it offers a wide range of possibilities, including playground activities, volleyball, a swimming pool, jacuzzi, and boat and watersport rentals. Lifeguards are on duty in the summer. Other facilities include restrooms, a café, groceries, picnic areas, and laundry. The park is very popular, so plan to come for the attractions, not peace and quiet. Parking fee, $8. ~ 1131 Back Bay Drive, Newport Beach; 949-729-3863, 800-765-7661, fax 949-729-1133; www.newportdunes.com, e-mail info@newportdunes.com.

▲ There are 405 sites for freestanding tents and RVs (all with hookups, some with cable TV and phone access); $23 to $38 per night.

CORONA DEL MAR STATE BEACH ⚓ 🛶 Located at the mouth of Newport Harbor, this park offers an opportunity to watch sailboats tacking in and out from the bay. Bounded on one side by a jetty, on the other by homes, with a huge parking lot behind, it is less than idyllic, yet it is also inevitably crowded. Throngs congregate because of its easy access, landscaped lawn, and excellent facilities, which include restrooms, picnic areas, lifeguards, showers, concession stands, and volleyball courts. The facilities area is slated to undergo construction in September 2004; its completion date is as of yet unknown. It's well protected for swimming and also popular for fishing—cast from the jetty bordering Newport Harbor. Skindiving is also good around the jetty. Parking fee, $6. ~ Located at Jasmine Avenue and Ocean Boulevard in Corona del Mar; 949-644-3000.

LITTLE CORONA DEL MAR STATE BEACH ⚓ 🎣 🛶 Another in the proud line of pocket beaches along the Orange Coast, this preserve features the **Corona del Mar Tidepool Reserve**. These are endangered and protected, and may be closed at times. The bluff to the north consists of sandstone that has been contorted into a myriad of magnificent lines. There's a marsh behind the beach thick with reeds and cattails. Unfortunately you won't be the first explorer to hit the sand; Little Corona is known to a big group of local people. The beach is also popular with swimmers, snorkelers, and skindivers; for anglers, try casting from the rocks. ~ There is an entrance to the beach at Poppy Avenue and Ocean Boulevard in Corona del Mar; 949-644-3000.

▼▼▼▼▼▼▼▼▼▼
Laguna Beach

Next stop on this cavalcade of coastal cities is Laguna Beach. Framed by the San Joaquin hills, the place is an intaglio of coves and bluffs, sand beaches and rock outcroppings. It conjures images of the Mediterranean with deep bays and greenery running to the sea's edge.

Little wonder that Laguna, with its wealthy residents and leisurely beachfront, has become synonymous with the chic but informal style of Southern California. Its long tradition as an artist colony adds to this sense of beauty and bounty, aesthetics and aggrandizement.

Laguna's traditional tranquility has weathered natural disasters quite well. Although hillside fires remain a threat, and winter storms sometimes leave debris on beaches, Laguna always recovers.

Part of Laguna Beach's artistic tradition is the **Festival of Arts and Pageant of the Masters**, staged every year during July and August. While the festival displays the work of approximately 150 local artists and craftspeople, the Pageant of the Masters is the high point, an event you *absolutely must not miss*. It presents a series of *tableaux vivants* in which local residents, dressed to resemble figures from famous paintings, remain motionless against a frieze that re-creates the painting. Elaborate make-up and lighting techniques flatten the figures and create a sense of two-dimensionality. If you attend, be sure to arrange lodging, transportation, and dining reservations ahead of time; check out the package deals offered by local hotels. Admission. ~ Irvine Bowl, 650 Laguna Canyon Road; 949-494-1145; 800-487-3378, fax 949-494-9387; www.lagunafestivalofarts.com.

During the 1960s freelance artists, excluded from the more formal Festival of the Arts, founded the **Sawdust Festival** across the street. Over the years this fair has become pretty established, but

SIGHTS

it still provides an opportunity from July to late August to wander along sawdust-covered paths past hundreds of arts and crafts displays accompanied by musicians and jugglers. Admission. ~ 935 Laguna Canyon Road; 949-494-3030, fax 949-494-7390; www.sawdust artfestival.org, e-mail info@sawdustartfestival.org.

Drive by the Bette Davis House, an English Tudor–style home where the silver screen diva lived in the early 1940s. ~ 1991 Ocean Way, Laguna Beach.

Laguna Beach's artistic heritage is evident in the many studios around town. The **Laguna Beach Visitors Bureau**, with its maps and brochures, can help direct you. They can also assist with hotel and restaurant reservations. Closed Sunday, except in July and August. ~ 252 Broadway; 949-497-9229, 800-877-1115, fax 949-376-0558; www.lagunabeachinfo.org, e-mail laguna@ lagunabeachinfo.com.

The **Laguna Art Museum** has a wonderfully chosen collection of historic and contemporary paintings and photographs, with an emphasis on the art of California. The oldest cultural institution in Orange County, it will help you find your way through the local art world. Closed Wednesday. Admission. ~ 307 Cliff Drive; 949-494-8971, fax 949-494-1530; www.lagunaartmuseum.org.

Beauty in Laguna is not only found on canvases. The coastline too is particularly pretty and well worth exploring (see the "Beaches & Parks" section below). One of the most enchanting areas is along **Heisler Park**, a winding promenade set on the cliffs above the ocean. Here you can relax on the lawn, sit beneath a palm tree, and gaze out on the horizon. There are broad vistas out along the coast and down to the wave-whitened shoreline. Paths from the park descend to a series of coves with tidepools and sandy beaches. The surrounding rocks, twisted by geologic pressure into curving designs, rise in a series of protective bluffs. ~ Located on Cliff Drive.

Cliff Drive streams along Heisler Park and then past a series of entranceways to sparkling coves and pocket beaches. At the north end of this shoreline street take a left onto Coast Highway, then another quick left onto Crescent Bay Drive, which leads to **Crescent Bay Point Park**. Seated high upon a coastal cliff, this landscaped facility offers magnificent views for miles along the Laguna shore.

When you're ready to leave the beach behind and head for the hills, take Park Avenue up from the center of Laguna Beach, turn right at the end onto Alta Laguna Boulevard, and right again to head back down on Temple Hills Drive and Thalia Street. This climbing course will carry you high into the **Laguna Hills** with spectacular vistas along the coastline and into the interior valleys.

HIDDEN ►

In town, in the Laguna-North section, you'll find a charming historical link with Laguna's past in this neighborhood of **1920s bungalows**. Built by year-round residents who worked or owned businesses in town to serve the seasonal visitors, the bungalows were humble interpretations of the Craftsman style popularized by Pasadena architects Charles and Henry Greene. The homeowners over the years individualized their dwellings by adding columns, changing roof styles, rebuilding entries, and making other modifications. Pick up a map at the Laguna Beach Visitors Bureau to follow a self-guided tour. ~ East of Coast Highway and north of Broadway.

South on Route 1, called the Pacific Coast Highway in these parts, you will pass through **Dana Point**. This ultramodern enclave, with its manmade port and 2500-boat marina, has a history dating back to the 1830s when Richard Henry Dana immortalized the place. Writing in *Two Years Before the Mast*, the Boston gentleman-turned-sailor described the surrounding countryside: "There was a grandeur in everything around."

Today much of the grandeur has been replaced with condominiums, leaving little for the sightseer. There is the **Ocean Institute** with a small sealife aquarium, a modern research vessel named the *R/V Sea Explorer*, and a 130-foot replica of Dana's brig, *The Pilgrim*. The institute also offers cruises, for a fee, on weekends and selected weekdays. The Institute is closed on most major holidays, the aquarium and ships are open only on weekends. ~ 24200 Dana Point Harbor Drive, Dana Point; 949-496-2274, fax 949-496-4296; www.ocean-institute.org.

LODGING

Boasting 70 guest rooms, a pool, spa, and sundeck overlooking the sea, the **Inn at Laguna Beach** offers great ocean views from its blufftop perch. Rooms are small, the construction uneven, and the furnishings modern at this coastside property. But continental breakfast and a local paper are brought to your room, gratis. ~ 211 North Coast Highway; 949-497-9722, 800-544-4479, fax 949-497-9972; www.innatlagunabeach.com, e-mail info@innat lagunabeach.com. DELUXE TO ULTRA-DELUXE.

The premier resting place in Laguna Beach is a sprawling 165-room establishment overhanging the sand. The **Surf & Sand Resort** is a blocky 1950s-era complex, an architectural mélange of five buildings and a shopping mall. The accent here is on the ocean: nearly every room has a sea view and private balcony, the pool sits just above the sand, and the beach is a short step away. A full-service hotel, the Surf & Sand has an oceanfront restaurant and lounge. Guest rooms are understated but attractive with raw-silk furnishings, unfinished woods, and sand-hued walls. ~ 1555 South Coast Highway; 949-497-4477, 800-524-8621, fax 949-494-2897; www.surfandsandresort.com, e-mail surfandsand resort@jcresorts.com. ULTRA-DELUXE.

Casa Laguna Inn, a hillside hacienda, has a dreamlike quality about it. The cottages and rooms are nestled in a garden setting complete with stone terraces and winding paths. Built in the 1930s, the Spanish-style complex features a courtyard, bell tower, and a heated swimming pool with an ocean view. The rooms are small, equipped with overhead fans, and furnished in antiques; many offer ocean views and have double-paned windows to block noise from the highway. Continental breakfast and afternoon tea are served in a restored landmark Mission house. ~ 2510 South Coast Highway; 949-494-2996, 800-233-0449, fax 949-494-5009; www.casalaguna.com, e-mail info@casalaguna.com. ULTRA-DELUXE.

It's not just the residential neighborhood that makes **The Carriage House** unique. The colonial architecture of the "New Orleans style" B&B inn also sets it apart. Within this historic landmark structure are six suites, each with a sitting room, a private bath, and separate bedroom; some have dining rooms and kitchenettes. All face a verdant brick courtyard filled with flowering plants and adorned with a tiered fountain—in case you get tired of the ocean views. Certainly the Carriage House is one of the prettiest and most peaceful inns along the entire Orange Coast. ~ 1322 Catalina Street; 949-494-8945, 888-335-8945, fax 949-494-6829; www.carriagehouse.com, e-mail crgehsebb@aol.com. DELUXE.

Accommodations with kitchen facilities are hard to come by in Laguna Beach. You'll find them in most of the units at **Capri Laguna**, a multilevel motel situated on the beach. This 48-unit resting place provides contemporary motel-style furnishings, plus a pool, sauna, and sundeck with barbecue facilities. Continental breakfast is included. ~ 1441 South Laguna Coast Highway; 949-494-6533, 800-225-4551, fax 949-497-6962; www.caprilaguna.com, e-mail caprilagun@aol.com. DELUXE TO ULTRA-DELUXE.

Holiday Inn Laguna Beach is fashioned in the luxurious style of the French Caribbean: the lobby is a breezy affair with provincial furnishings; the 54 guest rooms surround a lushly landscaped

AUTHOR FAVORITE

Even if you never stay there, you won't miss the **Hotel Laguna**. With its octagonal bell tower and Spanish motif, this huge whitewashed building dominates downtown Laguna Beach. The oldest hotel in Laguna, it sits in the center of town, adjacent to Main Beach. In addition to 65 guest rooms there is a restaurant, lounge, and lobby terrace. For a place on the water *and* at the center of the action, it cannot be matched. ~ 425 South Coast Highway; 949-494-1151, 800-524-2927, fax 949-497-2163; www.hotellaguna.com, e-mail hotellaguna@msn.com. DELUXE TO ULTRA-DELUXE.

courtyard complete with swimming pool and patio. For a touch of the tropics right here in Laguna Beach, you can't go astray at this hotel. ~ 696 South Coast Highway; 949-494-1001, 800-228-5691, fax 949-497-7107. ULTRA-DELUXE.

Tucked into a secluded canyon is **Aliso Creek Inn and Golf Resort**, an appealing 83-acre resort complete with swimming pools, jacuzzi, restaurant, lounge, and nine-hole golf course. Particularly attractive for families, every unit includes a sitting area, patio, and kitchen. Removed from the highway but within 400 yards of a beach, the resort is surrounded by steep hillsides that are populated by deer, rabbits and raccoon. Tying this easy rusticity together is a small creek that tumbles through the resort. ~ 31106 South Coast Highway; 949-499-2271, 800-223-3309, fax 949-499-4601; www.alisocreekinn.com, e-mail sales@aliso creekinn.com. ULTRA-DELUXE.

The **Ritz-Carlton Laguna Niguel**, set on a 150-foot-high cliff above the Pacific, is simply the finest resort hotel along the California coast. Built in the fashion of a Mediterranean villa, it dominates a broad sweep of coastline, a 393-room mansion replete with gourmet restaurants and dark wood lounges. An Old World interior of arched windows and Italian marble is decorated with one of the finest hotel collections of 18th- and 19th-century American and English art anywhere. The grounds are landscaped with willows, sycamores, and a spectrum of flowering plants. Tile courtyards lead to two swimming pools, a pair of jacuzzis, tennis courts, and a fitness and massage center. The rooms are equal in luxury to the rest of the resort. ~ 1 Ritz-Carlton Drive, Dana Point; 949-240-2000, 800-241-3333, fax 949-240-0829. ULTRA-DELUXE.

Most motels have a stream of traffic whizzing past outside, but the **Dana Marina Inn Motel**, situated on an island where the highway divides, manages to have traffic on both sides! The reason I'm mentioning it is not because I'm sadistic but because rooms in this 15-unit facility are inexpensive. The accommodations are roadside-motel style. ~ 34111 Pacific Coast Highway, Dana Point; 949-496-1300. MODERATE.

Four Sisters Inns, a bed-and-breakfast "chain" with several properties along the coast, has a 29-room property, **Blue Lantern Inn**, situated on an oceanside bluff in Dana Point. A contemporary building designed in classic Cape Cod–style, this bed and breakfast, offers lovely views. Each room features a fireplace and jacuzzi as well as a sitting area; most have decks overlooking the ocean. The tower rooms offer spectacular ocean views and telescopes for stargazing. The sitting rooms are spacious and comfortable and the inn provides a well-done, though self-conscious, re-creation of a classic era. Full breakfast and afternoon wine and hors d'oeuvres are served. Be sure to book rooms in advance.

~ 34343 Street of the Blue Lantern, Dana Point; 949-661-1304, 800-950-1236, fax 949-496-1483; www.foursisters.com, e-mail bluelanterninn@foursisters.com. DELUXE TO ULTRA-DELUXE.

DINING   Laguna Beach is never at a loss for oceanfront restaurants. But somehow the sea seems closer and more intimate at **Laguna Village Cafe,** probably because this informal eatery was once entirely outdoors, with tables placed at the very edge of the coastal bluff (now they've added indoor seating warmed by a fireplace). The menu is simple: egg dishes in the morning, and a single menu with salads, sandwiches, and smoothies during the rest of the day. There are also house specialties like calamari, abalone, scallops amandine, teriyaki chicken, skewered shrimp, and Chinese-style chicken dumplings. Closed at dusk. ~ 577 South Coast Highway; 949-494-6344, fax 949-494-1956; www.lagunavillagecafe.com. BUDGET TO MODERATE.

The **Penguin Malt Shop** is from another era entirely. The 1950s to be exact. A tiny café featuring counter jukeboxes and swivel stools, as well as penguin memorabilia brought in by customers, it's a time capsule with a kitchen. Breakfast and lunch are all-American affairs from ham and eggs to hamburgers to pork chops. It's cheap, so what have you got to lose? Step on in and order a chocolate malt with a side of fries. No dinner. ~ 981 South Coast Highway; 949-494-1353. BUDGET.

The **White House Tavern and Restaurant** seems nearly as permanent a Laguna Beach fixture as the ocean. Dating to early in the 20th century this simple wooden structure serves as bar, restaurant, and local landmark. The White House is lined with historic photos of Laguna Beach and works by local artists. You can drop by from early morning until late evening to partake of a menu that includes pasta, steak, chicken, and seafood dishes. ~ 340 South Coast Highway; 949-494-8088; www.lagunabeach whitehouse.com. MODERATE TO DELUXE.

Don't get sidetracked by the extensive martini menu at **230 Forest Avenue,** because what really shines here is the inventive food. The butternut squash soup or the Chinese chicken salad pave the way for the entrées: spicy lemon caper shrimp scampi, applejack brandy–smoked barbecued ribs, and Pacific Northwest cioppino, or the restaurant's signature hazelnut-crusted halibut. Then top the savory with sweet specialties such as bread pudding. ~ 230 Forest Avenue; 949-494-2545, fax 949-497-4789; www.230forestavenue.com. ULTRA-DELUXE.

Choose one place to symbolize the easy elegance of Laguna and it inevitably will be **Las Brisas**. Something about this whitewashed Spanish building with arched windows captures the natural-living-but-class-conscious style of the Southland. Its cliffside locale on the water is part of this ambience. Then there are the beautiful people who frequent the place. Plus there is a dual kitchen arrangement that permits formal dining in a white-tablecloth room or bistro dining on an outdoor patio. The menu consists of Continental-Mexican seafood dishes and other specialties from south of the border. Out on the patio there are sandwiches, salads, and appetizers. ~ 361 Cliff Drive; 949-497-5434, fax 949-497-9210; www.lasbrisaslagunabeach.com. MODERATE TO ULTRA-DELUXE.

For people watching and swimming pool–sized lattes, try **Zinc Café and Market**. Here you'll find sidewalk seating complete with the obligatory umbrellas. They serve vegetarian fare that attracts a casual-intellectual crowd. No dinner Monday through Wednesday. ~ 350 Ocean Avenue; 949-494-6302, fax 949-497-8294; www.zinccafe.com. BUDGET.

John Steinbeck wrote *Tortilla Flats* while living at 504 Park Avenue in Laguna Beach.

Five Feet Restaurant prepares a succulent interpretation of "modern Chinese cuisine" that carries you from catfish to lamb chinoise. Often on the ever-changing and always unique bill of fare are Hawaiian swordfish with garlic-parmesan crust and New York steak with shallot-hoisin sauce. Applying the principles of California cuisine to Chinese cooking and adding a few French flourishes, Five Feet has gained an impressive reputation. The decor is as avant-garde as the food. Dinner only. ~ 328 Glenneyre Street; 949-497-4955, fax 949-376-2003; www.fivefeetreastaurant.com. DELUXE TO ULTRA-DELUXE.

Dizz's Restaurant represents one of those singular dining spots that should not be overlooked. Funk is elevated to an art form in this woodframe house. The tiny dining room is decorated with art-deco pieces and 1930s-era tunes play throughout dinner. This studied informality ends at the kitchen, where talented chefs prepare international cuisine that includes veal piccata, Cornish game hen, chicken stuffed with cheese and shallots, pasta with prawns, and cioppino. Dinner only. Closed Monday. ~ 2794 South Coast Highway; 949-494-5250. DELUXE TO ULTRA-DELUXE.

The most remarkable aspect of the **Cottage Restaurant** is the cottage itself, an early-20th-century California bungalow. The place has been neatly decorated with turn-of-the-20th-century antiques, oil paintings, and stained glass. Meal time in this historic house is a traditional American affair. They serve eggs-and-bacon breakfasts starting at 7 a.m. Lunch consists of salads and sandwiches plus specials like top sirloin, fresh fish, and steamed vegetables. For dinner there is chicken fettuccine, top sirloin, broiled lamb, fresh shrimp, and swordfish as well as daily fresh fish specials. ~ 308 North Coast Highway; 949-494-3023, fax 949-497-5183; e-mail thecottagerestaurant@aol.com. MODERATE.

Ti Amo is a little jewel set on a coastal bluff. Situated in a former home, it offers intimate dining indoors or outside on the patio. The restaurant has Renaissance decor with Italian-style murals and heavy draperies. In addition to ocean views, it offers daily specials. On a typical evening you can expect such entrées as paella, fresh seafood, homemade pastas, and a variety of beef and poultry dishes. Desserts here—ranging from a light berry ice cream to a decadent chocolate cake—are not to be skipped. Dinner only. ~ 31727 South Coast Highway; 949-499-5350, fax 949-499-9760. MODERATE.

The **Harbor Grill**, located in Dana Point Harbor, lacks the view and polish of its splashy neighbors. But this understated restaurant serves excellent seafood dishes. The menu includes fresh swordfish and salmon with pesto sauce, but the real attraction is the list of daily specials. This might include sea bass with black-bean sauce, gumbo, and other fresh fish dishes. Lunch, dinner, and Sunday brunch are served in a light, bright dining room with contemporary artwork. Patio dining and a full bar are also options here. ~ 34499 Golden Lantern Street, Dana Point; 949-240-1416, fax 949-240-2013; www.harborgrill.com, e-mail grillman @home.com. MODERATE TO DELUXE.

If you'd prefer to dine alfresco overlooking the harbor, there's **Proud Mary's**, a little hole in the wall where you can order sandwiches, salads, hamburgers, and a few chicken and steak platters, then dine on picnic tables outside. Breakfast is served all day. No dinner. ~ 34689 Golden Lantern Street, Dana Point; 949-493-5853, fax 949-493-3911. BUDGET.

SHOPPING Laguna Beach claims to support more goldsmiths and jewelers than any place in the country. Add a few designer clothing shops plus antique stores and you have one very promising shopping spot. The center of this action lies along Route 1 (Coast Highway) between Bluebird Canyon Drive and Laguna Canyon Road.

Fine fashion is taken for granted at **Shebue**. This plush shop houses beautiful designer clothing for women. *Très chic* (and *très cher*). Closed Sunday. ~ 31678 South Coast Highway; 949-494-3148.

Since you're likely to be spending a good bit of time tooling around town wearing sandals, **Shelby's Laguna** will allow you to do so in style with its wide selection of beaded and sterling silver anklets and toe rings. Occasionally closed on Tuesday, call ahead. ~ 577 South Coast Highway; 949-494-7992; www.shelbys footjewels.com.

Tippecanoe's is a vintage clothing store with a collection of antique knickknacks. ~ 648 South Coast Highway; 949-494-1200.

For a huge selection of pre-1940s American Indian art, I particularly recommend **Len Wood's Indian Territory**. The gallery carries everything: Navajo rugs and blankets, Pueblo pottery,

Laguna Beach Art Galleries

Given its long tradition as an artist colony, it's little wonder that Laguna Beach is crowded with galleries and studios. The historic Gallery Row area, located along the 300 and 400 blocks of North Coast Highway around the Laguna Beach Art Museum, has more than 20 galleries. **Marion Meyer Contemporary Art** represents both emerging local artists and well-established international figures. Closed Wednesday. ~ 354 North Coast Highway; 949-497-5442. Impressionist local landscapes and seascapes at affordable prices are the stock in trade at **Studio 7 Gallery**. ~ 384-B North Coast Highway; 949-497-1080.

The downtown Village, along the quaint streets of Forest, Ocean, Coast Highway, Peppertree Lane, and Laguna Avenue, offers another assortment of galleries. The eclectic **Sherwood Gallery** has a reputation for its unconventional approach to art and its strong commitment to progressive artists. ~ 460 South Coast Highway; 949-497-2668; www.sherwoodgallery. com. At the three **Wyland Galleries** you'll find paintings from the world's leading environmental marine life artist. ~ 509 South Coast Highway, 218 Forest Avenue, and 2171 Laguna Canyon; 949-376-8000; www.wyland.com. The **Diane DeBilzan Gallery** features the colorful, contemporary work of William DeBilzan. ~ 224 Forest Avenue; 949-494-5757; www.dianedebilzangallery.com.

South Village, located along South Coast Highway between the 900 and 1800 blocks, is lined with a multitude of galleries. Foremost among them is the **Redfern Gallery**, specializing in museum-quality paintings of the California impressionist school (1890–1940s). ~ 1540 South Coast Highway; 949-497-3356; www.redferngallery.com. Early California impressionism is also the focus of **De Ru's Fine Arts**. Closed Monday and Tuesday. ~ 1590 South Coast Highway; 949-376-3785; www.derusfineart.com. **Blue-bird Gallery** carries both Early California and contemporary artists. Closed Monday and Tuesday. ~ 1540 South Coast Highway; 949-497-5377.

Russian impressionist paintings from the 1940s through the 1980s are exhibited at **J. Kamin Fine Art**, along with contemporary impressionism by artist Jacqueline Kamin. Closed Monday and Tuesday. ~ 1590 South Coast Highway; 949-494-5076; www.jkaminfineart.com. Another artist-owned gallery, the **Vladimir Sokolov Studio Gallery** presents works, including mixed media collages, by Mr. Sokolov. ~ 1540 South Coast Highway; 949-494-3633. The **Esther Wells Collection** features contemporary oil paintings, watercolors, and sculptures. ~ 1390 South Coast Highway; 949-494-2497; www.estherwellscollection.com.

Hopi kachinas, and Hopi, Navajo, and Zuni jewelry. Closed Sunday. ~ 305 North Coast Highway; 949-497-5747.

Laguna Beach's other shopping strip is Forest Avenue, a three-block promenade with specialty stores. **Laura Downing** is here, a clothing store specializing in upscale clothing and jewelry. ~ 241 Forest Avenue; 949-494-4300.

The Foxes Trot has an unpredictable inventory, a kind of cultural hodgepodge ranging from ethnic jewelry and clothing to African art. ~ 264 Forest Avenue; 949-497-3047.

NIGHTLIFE   **The White House Tavern and Restaurant** is a landmark 1917 building downtown. A wide-open dancefloor turns tradition upside down every night with live rock, reggae, Motown, blues, and funk. Cover. ~ 340 South Coast Highway; 949-494-8088, fax 949-494-0986.

One of Laguna Beach's hottest nightspots is also its most funky. **The Sandpiper** is a run-down club filled with dart boards, a pool table, and pinball machines. Often it is also filled with some of the finest sounds around. Rock, reggae, blues, and other music is live nightly, sometimes preformed by well-known groups. There's a deejay on Monday. Cover. ~ 1185 South Coast Highway; 949-494-4694.

Las Brisas, a sleek, clifftop restaurant overlooking the ocean, is a gathering place for the fast and fashionable. A wonderful place to enjoy a quiet cocktail, it features a tile bar as well as an open-air patio. Mariachis play one night each week in summer. ~ 361 Cliff Drive; 949-497-5434, fax 949-497-9210.

The ultimate evening destinations are located at the ultra-posh Ritz-Carlton Laguna Niguel. Here, along corridors of polished stone, is **The Club Grill and Bar**, a wood-paneled rendezvous decorated with 19th-century paintings of equestrian scenes. Also located in the Ritz-Carlton is **The Lounge**, an elegant two-tiered, glass-walled lounge with sweeping ocean views. The first offers a quartet nightly and the latter features a solo pianist. ~ 1 Ritz-Carlton Drive, Dana Point; 949-240-2000, 800-241-3333, fax 949-240-1061; www.ritzcarlton.com.

The **Wind and Sea Restaurant**, on the waterfront in Dana Point Harbor, features sparkling views and live musical entertainment nightly. ~ 34699 Golden Lantern Street, Dana Point; 949-496-6500, 800-241-3333, fax 949-496-2605; www.wind andsearestaurant.com..

GAY SCENE   Laguna Beach has always been a popular weekend getaway spot for gay men and lesbians living in Los Angeles, which is about a 90-minute drive north. Not only is the natural environment attractive—so is the town's socially progressive climate. Laguna Beach elected the nation's first openly gay mayor way back in 1983.

The **Coast Inn** itself has been a legendary gay resort for about 30 years. It's especially popular with young single gay men, attracted perhaps in part by the gay porn stars who have been known to stay there. Nightlife here centers around the **Boom Boom Room**. This beachy, three-tiered discotheque one-half block from the beach boasts a dancefloor, pinball machines, and two bars. The Wednesday-night drag show, The Dreamgirls Revue, is always popular. Cover Thursday, Friday, and Saturday. ~ 1401 South Coast Highway; 949-494-7588, fax 949-494-1735; www.boomroom.com, e-mail coastinn@boomboomroom.com.

There's a quieter gay scene at **Main Street**, which resembles "Cheers" with a predominantly male clientele. Monday- and Tuesday-night karaoke attract a large mixed crowd. ~ 1460 South Coast Highway; 949-494-0056.

CRYSTAL COVE STATE PARK This outstanding facility has a long, winding sand beach that is sometimes sectioned into a series of coves by high tides. The park stretches for over three miles along the coast and extends up into the hills. Grassy terraces grace the sea cliffs and the offshore area is designated an underwater preserve. Providing long walks along an undeveloped coastline and on upland trails in El Moro Canyon, it's the perfect park when you're seeking solitude. Facilities are limited to lifeguards (summer only) and restrooms. Onshore fishing is permitted (with a fishing license), and swimming is good. For surfing, try the breaks north of Reef Point in Scotchman's Cove, or head south to Abalone Point. Day-use fee, $5. ~ Located along the Coast Highway between Corona del Mar and Laguna Beach. There are entrances at Pelican Point, Los Trancos, Reef Point, and El Moro Canyon; 949-494-3539, fax 949-494-6911; www.crystalcovestatepark.com.

BEACHES & PARKS

Visit seals and sea lions at the Marine Mammal Rescue Center, open daily from 10 a.m. to 4 p.m. ~ 20612 Laguna Canyon Road; 949-494-3050; www.fslmmc.org

▲ Environmental camping is permitted at three campgrounds, a three- to four-mile hike inland from the parking lot; $10 per night. No open campfires allowed.

CRESCENT BAY This half-moon inlet is flanked by a curving cliff upon which the fortunate few have parked their palatial homes. Down on the beach, the sand is as soft and thick as the carpets in those houses. Offshore stands Seal Rock, with barking denizens whose cries echo off the surrounding cliffs. This, to say the least, is a pretty place. You can swim, skindive, sunbathe, explore the rocks and tidepools, or venture up to the vista point that overlooks this natural setting. The beach has restrooms, and lifeguards in summer. Fishing and swimming are good, and there's also very good bodysurfing and excellent skindiving. ~ Entrances to the beach are located near the intersection of Cliff Drive and Circle Way.

SHAW'S COVE, FISHERMAN'S COVE, AND DIVER'S COVE

These three miniature inlets sit adjacent to one another, creating one of Laguna Beach's most scenic and popular sections of shoreline. Each features a white sand beach backdropped by a sharp bluff. Rock formations at either end are covered in spuming surf and honeycombed with tidepool pockets (particularly at the south end of Shaw's Cove). Well-known to local residents, the beaches are sometimes crowded. There are lifeguards, but no facilities. Fishing is not permitted at Diver's Cove, and swimming, while generally good, can be hazardous at Fisherman's Cove because of rocks. Diver's Cove, in keeping with its name, is often awash with scuba divers, but skindiving is excellent along this entire shoreline. ~ All three coves rest along Cliff Drive. The walkway to Shaw's Cove is at the end of Fairview Street; the entrances to Fisherman's and Diver's are within 50 feet of each other in the 600 block of Cliff Drive.

> For a lighthouse keeper's view of the harbor and coast, visit the lookout points at the end of Old Golden Lantern or Blue Lantern streets in Dana Point.

HEISLER PARK, PICNIC BEACH, AND ROCK PILE BEACH

One of Laguna's prettiest stretches of shoreline lies along the clifftop in Heisler Park and below on the boulder-strewn sands of Picnic and Rock Pile beaches. The park provides a promenade with grassy areas and shade trees. You can scan the coastline from Laguna Beach south for miles, then meander down to the beach where sedimentary formations shatter the wave patterns and create marvelous tidepools. Picnic and Rock Pile form adjacent coves, both worthy of exploration. In addition to the tidepools, you'll find picnic areas, restrooms, lifeguards, and—get ready—shuffleboard. Fishing is excellent here and along most of the Laguna coast: perch, cod, bass, and halibut inhabit these waters. Swimming is permitted at Picnic Beach but not at Rock Pile Beach. For surfing, the south end of Rock Pile has some of the biggest waves in Laguna Beach. However, skindiving is also good at Picnic Beach, as the rocks offer great places to explore. ~ Heisler Park is located along Cliff Drive. Picnic Beach lies to the north at the end of Myrtle Street; Rock Pile Beach is at the end of Jasmine Street.

MAIN BEACH

You'll have to venture north to Muscle Beach in Venice to find a scene equal to this one. It's located at the very center of Laguna Beach, with shopping streets radiating in several directions. A sinuous boardwalk winds along the waterfront, past basketball players, sunbathers, volleyball aficionados, little kids on swings, and aging kids on roller skates. Here and there an adventuresome soul has even dipped a toe in the wa-wa-water. In the midst of this humanity on holiday stands the lifeguard tower, an imposing glass-encased structure that looks more like a conning tower and has become a Laguna Beach icon. There are also restrooms, showers, picnic areas, a playground, and a grassy area. Fishing is good, and swimming is very good, as the beach is well-guarded. And because the Laguna Beach Marine Life Refuge lies just offshore, this a popular place for diving and snorkeling. ~ Located at Coast Highway and Broadway.

STREET BEACHES Paralleling downtown Laguna for nearly a mile is a single slender strand known to locals by the streets that intersect it. Lined with luxury homes, it provides little privacy but affords easy access to the town's amenities. There are lifeguards, and everything you want, need, or couldn't care less about is within a couple blocks. Swimming is good, and excellent peaks are created by a submerged reef off Brooks Street, making it a prime surfing and bodysurfing locale. The surf is also usually up around Thalia Street. ~ Off Coast Highway there are beach entrances at the ends of Sleepy Hollow Lane, and Cleo, St. Ann's, Thalia, Anita, Oak, and Brooks streets.

ARCH COVE Stretching for more than a half mile, ◄ HIDDEN bordered by a palisade of luxury homes and resort hotels, this sandy swath is ideal for sunbathers. A sea arch and blowhole rise along the south end of the beach; the northern stretch is more populated and not as pretty. Lifeguards are on duty, and swimming, although not as protected as the pocket beaches, is still okay. For surfing, there are sizeable breaks around Agate Street. ~ Entrances to the beach are at the ends of Cress Street, Mountain Road, Bluebird Canyon Drive, Agate Street, and Pearl Street. As a result, you will hear sections of the strand referred to as "Agate Beach," "Pearl Beach," etc.

WOOD'S COVE An S-shaped strand backed by ◄ HIDDEN Laguna's ever-loving shore bluff, this is another in the town's string of hidden wonders. Three rock peninsulas give the area its topography, creating a pair of sandy pocket beaches. The sea works in, around, and over the rocks, creating a tumultuous presence in an otherwise placid scene. Swimming is well protected by rock outcroppings, and skindiving is good off the rocks; lifeguards are on duty. ~ Steps from Diamond Street and Ocean Way lead down to the water.

MOSS POINT This tiny gem is little more than 50 yards ◄ HIDDEN long, but for serenity and simple beauty it challenges the giant strands. Rocky points border both sides and sharp hills overlook the entire scene. The sea streams in through the mouth of a cove and debouches onto a fan-shaped beach. The cove is well protected for swimming, and there is a lifeguard; the surrounding rocks also provide interesting areas for skindiving. ~ Located at the end of Moss Street.

HIDDEN ► **VICTORIA BEACH** ⚓ 🏊 ⛵ Known primarily to locals, this quarter-mile sand corridor is flanked by homes and hills. The rocks on either side of the beach make for good exploring and provide excellent tidepooling opportunities. Amenities are few, but that's the price to pay for getting away from Laguna's crowds. At least there's a lifeguard, and even volleyball. Swimming is okay, but watch for the strong shore break and offshore rocks. Skindiving here is good. ~ From Coast Highway take Victoria Drive, then turn right on Dumond Street.

HIDDEN ► **ALISO CREEK BEACH PARK** 🚲 🏊 ⛵ 🎣 ⚓ Set in a wide cove and bounded by low coastal bluffs, this park is popular with local folks. The nearby highway buzzes past and the surrounding hills are adorned with houses. A sand scimitar with rocks guarding both ends, the beach is bisected by a fishing pier.

HIDDEN ► To escape the crowds head over to the park's **southern cove**, a pretty beach with fluffy sand, or check out the tidepools. Facilities include picnic areas, restrooms, showers, lifeguards, volleyball, and a snack bar. Fishing is good from the pier. When swimming, beware of strong shore breaks. Bodysurfing is a better bet than board surfing at Aliso. ~ Along the Coast Highway in South Laguna; there's a public accessway to the southern cove along the 31300 block of Coast Highway.

HIDDEN ► **SOUTH LAGUNA COVES** 🏊 ⛵ 🎣 Hidden by the hillsides that flank South Laguna's waterfront are a series of pocket beaches. Each is a crescent of white sand bounded by sharp cliffs of conglomerate rock. These in turn are crowned with plate-glass homes. Two particularly pretty inlets can be reached via accessways called **1000 Steps** and **West Street**. Both beaches have seasonal lifeguards and restrooms. Swimming is good, and the bodysurfing is excellent in both coves. Parking fee. ~ Both accessways are on Coast Highway in South Laguna—1000 Steps is at 9th Avenue; West Street is (surprise!) at West Street.

SALT CREEK BEACH PARK 🚲 🏊 ⛵ 🎣 ⚓ This marvelous locale consists of two half-mile sections of beach divided by a lofty point on which the Ritz-Carlton Laguna Niguel Hotel stands. Each beach is a broad strip of white sand, backdropped by bluffs and looking out on Santa Catalina Island. The hotel above dominates the region like a palatial fortress on the Mediterranean. Though both beaches are part of Salt Creek, the strand to the south is also known as **Dana Strand**. It's possible to walk from one beach to the other. Both beaches have restrooms and seasonal lifeguards; at Salt Creek (north) there is also a snack bar. The swimming is good at either beach, but for fishing you're better off at Dana Strand. It's also a good spot if you're hoping to hang ten. Salt Creek has two well-known breaks, "The Gravels," just north of the outcropping separating the two beaches, and at "The Point" itself. Parking fee. ~ Dana Strand is reached via a long stairway at the end of Selva Road. The staircase to Salt Creek is on Ritz-Carlton Drive. Both lie off Coast Highway in Laguna Niguel; 949-923-2280, fax 949-661-2641.

DOHENY STATE BEACH This park wrote the book on oceanside facilities. In addition to a broad swath of sandy beach there is a five-acre lawn complete with private picnic areas, beach rentals, restrooms with changing areas, lifeguards, horse-shoe pits, volleyball courts, and food concessions. The grassy area offers plenty of shade trees. Surfers work the north end of the beach, leaving plenty of room for swimmers to the south. Dana Point Harbor, with complete marina facilities, borders the beach. For fishing, try the jetty in Dana Point Harbor. Swimming is not particularly good here, as the ocean bottom is rocky, but surfing is comfortable for beginners, particularly on a south swell. Day-use fee, $5. ~ Located off Dana Point Harbor Drive in Dana Point; 949-496-6171, fax 949-496-9469; www.dohenystatebeach.org.

▲ There are 121 tent/RV sites (no hookups), including 32 beach sites, $21 to $31 per night. Reservations: 800-444-7275.

San Juan Capistrano

When you're ready to flee Southern California's ultramodern coastline, Camino Capistrano is the perfect escape valve. Perhaps you've heard the 1939 tune "When the Swallows Return to Capistrano." The lyrics, just to refresh your memory, describe the return of flocks of swallows every March 19. And return they still do, though in ever-decreasing numbers and not always on March 19. When you're ready to follow the swallows, head up Camino Capistrano to the mission and get out your telephoto lens—swal-lows are small and fast. They remain in the area until October, when winter's approach prompts them to depart for Argentina,

AUTHOR FAVORITE

sights The **Capistrano Depot** is a vital part of the town's history. Today it houses a restaurant and a saloon, but the beautifully preserved 1894 depot is still operating as a train station. Built of brick in a series of Spanish-style arches, the old structure also features railroad memora-bilia. An antique Pullman, a brightly colored freight car, and other vin-tage cars line the tracks. ~ 26701 Verdugo Street; 949-487-2322, fax 949-493-4243; www.capistranodepot.com.

where, blissfully, they are welcomed by no similar ditties. While you're here, take time to explore the beautiful mission and local architectural gems.

SIGHTS

Seventh in the state's chain of 21 missions, the **Mission San Juan Capistrano** was founded in 1776 by Father Junípero Serra. Considered "the jewel of the missions," it is a hauntingly beautiful site, placid and magical.

There are ponds and gardens here, ten acres of standing adobe buildings, and the ruins of the original 1797 stone church, which was destroyed by an earthquake in 1812. The museum displays American Indian crafts, early ecclesiastical artifacts, and Spanish weaponry, while an Indian cemetery memorializes the enslaved people who built this magnificent structure. There is a living-history program on the second Saturday of every month, with costumed "characters" playing the role of Father Serra and others, and craftspeople showing how old-time crafts were made. On select Saturday nights during the summer, you can hear live music under the stars. In addition, a variety of festivals, folk-art exhibits, and cultural programs (including an interactive Achajamen Indian presentation) are held throughout the year; call for details.

The chapel at San Juan Capistrano—the oldest continually used building in California—is the only remaining church used by Father Serra.

The highlight of the mission is the chapel, a 1777 structure decorated with Indian designs and a baroque altar. Admission. ~ 31522 Camino Capistrano and Ortega Highway; 949-234-1300, fax 949-240-8091; www.missionsjc.com.

In the surrounding blocks are a dozen or so 19th-century structures. The **O'Neill Museum** is housed in a tiny 1870s Victorian and furnished with Victorian decor. Closed Monday and Saturday. ~ 31831 Los Rios Street; 949-493-8444, fax 949-493-0061; www.sjchistoricalsociety.com.

Jolting you back to contemporary times are two buildings near the Capistrano Depot, both constructed in the 1980s. The **New Church of Mission San Juan Capistrano**, a towering edifice next to the town's historic chapel, is a replica of the original structure. Spanish Renaissance in design, the new church even re-creates the brilliantly painted interior of the old mission. ~ 31522 Camino Capistrano.

Across the street is the **San Juan Capistrano Regional Library**, an oddly eclectic building. Drawing heavily from the Moorish-style Alhambra in Spain, the architect, Michael Graves, also incorporated ideas from ancient Egypt and classical Greece. Closed Friday. ~ 31495 El Camino Real; 949-493-1752, fax 949-240-7680; www.ocpl.org.

One of San Juan Capistrano's many historic points, a 19th-century building, **El Adobe de Capistrano** has been converted into a restaurant. The interior is a warren of white-washed rooms, supported by *vigas* and displaying the flourishes of Spanish California. Stop by for a drink next to the old jail (today a wine cellar) or tour the building. (Counterpoint to all this dusty history is a display of Nixon memorabilia.) If you decide to dine, the menu includes lunch, dinner, and Sunday brunch. Naturally the cuisine is Mexican, but also includes a number of American steak and seafood entrées. ~ 31891 Camino Capistrano; 949-493-1163, fax 949-493-4565; www.welcometoeladobedecapistrano.com. MODERATE TO DELUXE.

Who can match the combination of intimacy and French and Belgian cuisine at **L'Hirondelle**? It's quite small, and conveys a French-country atmosphere. The restaurant offers a varied menu beginning with escargots, crab-stuffed mushrooms, and crab crêpes. Entrées include roast duck, rabbit in wine sauce, rack of lamb, bouillabaisse, sautéed sweetbreads, and fresh fish specials. No lunch on Tuesday; brunch only on Sunday. Closed Monday. ~ 31631 Camino Capistrano; 949-661-0425, fax 949-661-3405; www.sjc.net/dining/l'hirondelle. MODERATE TO ULTRA-DELUXE.

Situated in a beautifully restored train depot, **Sarducci's Capistrano Depot** offers creative American cuisine at reasonable prices. Picture windows overlooking the depot add flourish, and guests can dine on lovely oak tables. Be sure to try the blackened ahi tuna with mustard-soy sauce. Lovers of veggies should definitely not miss the chef's eggplant parmesan and asparagus and sun-dried tomato pasta. ~ 26701 Verdugo Street; 949-487-2322, fax 949-493-4243; www.capistranodepot.com. MODERATE TO ULTRA-DELUXE.

The mission town of San Juan Capistrano has many shops clustered along its main thoroughfare, Camino Capistrano. Not surprisingly, the most common establishment in this centuries-old town is the antique store. In line with contemporary times, there are also pocket malls featuring boutiques, jewelers, and other outlets.

Particularly noteworthy is **The Old Barn**, a warehouse-size store filled to the rafters with antiques. ~ 31792 Camino Capistrano; 949-493-9144.

Swallows Inn is a hellbent Western bar with ranch tools tacked to the walls. Wednesday through Sunday nights, you can kick up your heels to live country-and-western, except when the music takes on a rock-and-roll, jazz, or blues feel. ~ 31786 Camino Capistrano; 949-493-3188; www.swallowsinn.com.

BEACHES & PARKS

CAPISTRANO BEACH PARK 🚲 🏊 🚤 🏄 This is a big rectangular sandbox facing the open ocean. Like many beaches in the area it offers ample facilities and is often quite crowded. Bounded by sedimentary cliffs and offering views of Dana Point Harbor, the beach is landscaped with palm and deciduous trees. The park is particularly popular with families and surfers, who all take advantage of the picnic areas, bonfire pits, restrooms, showers, lifeguards, volleyball and basketball courts, and rollerblade rentals. Swimming is good here, but it's the surfing that's the big draw. "Killer Capo" breaks are about 400 yards offshore along the northern fringes of the beach (near Doheny State Park), and "Dody's Reef" breaks are about one-half mile to the south, but are not predictable. Parking fee. ~ Located along Coast Highway in Capistrano Beach.

▼▼▼▼▼▼▼▼▼▼▼

San Clemente

If any place is the capital of Republican politics, it is San Clemente, a seaside town that sets the standard for Southern California's notorious conservatism because of one man. Richard Milhous Nixon, President of the United States from 1969 until his ignominious resignation during the Watergate scandal in 1974, established the Western White House on a 25-acre site overlooking the ocean.

SIGHTS

La Casa Pacífica, a magnificent Spanish-style home, was famous not only during Nixon's presidency, but afterwards when he retreated to San Clemente to lick his wounds. There are stories of Nixon, ever the brooding, socially awkward man, pacing the beach in a business suit and leather shoes.

San Clemente boasts an average temperature of 70 degrees and 342 days of sunshine per year.

The Nixon house is located off Avenida del Presidente in a private enclave called Cypress Shore. You can see it, a grand white stucco home with red tile roof, on the cliffs above San Clemente State Beach. Just walk south from the beach entrance about one-half mile toward a point of land obscured by palms; the house is set back in the trees.

Another point of interest (quite literally) is **San Clemente Municipal Pier**, a popular fishing spot and centerpiece of the city beach. There are food concessions, bait and tackle shops, and local crowds galore. ~ Foot of Avenida del Mar.

For more information on the area, call the **San Clemente Chamber of Commerce**. ~ 1100 North El Camino Real; 949-492-1131, fax 949-492-3764; www.scchamber.com.

LODGING

Algodon Motel is a standard 18-unit facility several blocks from the beach. Some units have kitchens. Not much to write home about, but it is clean and affordable. ~ 135 Avenida Algodon; 949-492-3382. BUDGET.

For families and extended stays, a stint at the **Seahorse Resort** is a sure bet. Located right on the beach, accommodations vary from studios to one- and two-bedroom suites. All boast modern conveniences as well as uncluttered views of the ocean and pier, full kitchens, and private patios and balconies. Complimentary beach chairs, umbrellas, and boogie boards are avaialble. ~ 602 Avenida Victoria; 949-492-1720, fax 949-498-8857; www.sea horsesanclemente.com. ULTRA-DELUXE.

DINING

Center of the casual dining scene in San Clemente is along the beach at the foot of the municipal pier (end of Avenida del Mar). Several takeout stands and cafés are here. The **Fisherman's Restaurant and Bar**, a knotty-pine-and-plate-glass establishment, sits right on the pier, affording views all along the beach. With a waterfront patio it's a good spot for seafood dishes at lunch or dinner. There is also breakfast on Saturday, and Sunday brunch. ~ 611 Avenida Victoria; 949-498-6390, fax 949-498-8681. MODERATE TO DELUXE.

SHOPPING

Though it sounds forbidding, **The Mole Hole Unique Gift Gallery** is a colorful and inviting shop specializing in limited-edition collectibles from around the world. Wee Forest Folk, hand-painted Limoges boxes, Franz porcelain, and bronze from "The Frogman" are part of the unusual selection. You'll also find art glass and sculpture from internationally known artists. ~ Ocean View Plaza, 638 Camino de los Mares, Suite G140; 949-443-1670, 800-863-5395, fax 949-443-1681; www.themolehole.net, e-mail moleweb@themolehole.net.

BEACHES & PARKS

SAN CLEMENTE CITY BEACH 🏖 🎣 Running nearly the length of town, this silver strand is the pride of San Clemente. Landlubbers congregate near the municipal pier, anglers work its waters, and surfers blanket the beachfront. There are railroad tracks and coastal bluffs paralleling the entire beach. Eden this ain't: San Clemente is heavily developed, but the beach is a pleasant place to spend a day. There are restaurants and other amenities at the municipal pier including picnic areas, restrooms, lifeguards, and a playground. The **Ole Hanson Beach Club** (105 Avenida Pico; 949-361-8207; admission) at the north end of the beach is a public pool with dressing rooms. Fishing is best from the pier, and surfing is good alongside of the pier. The beach is also good for swimming. ~ The pier is located at the foot of Avenida del Mar in San Clemente.

SAN CLEMENTE STATE BEACH 🏃 🏖 🎣 Walk down the deeply eroded cliffs guarding this coastline, and you'll discover a long narrow strip of sand that curves north from San Diego County up to San Clemente City Beach. There are camping areas and picnic plots on top of the bluff. Down below a railroad track parallels the beach and surfers paddle offshore. You can stroll north toward downtown San Clemente or south to President Nixon's old home. Beach facilities include lifeguards, picnic areas, and restrooms. Surf fishing is best in spring, and surfers will find year-round breaks at the south end of the beach. Swimmers should beware of rip currents. Day-use fee, $12. ~ Located off Avenida Calafia in San Clemente; 949-492-3156.

▲ There are 160 tent/RV sites (71 with hookups); $36 for tents, $48 for hookups.

Inland Orange County

Moving away from the Pacific Ocean, Orange County sprawls eastward towards and beyond the Santa Ana River, an ever-expanding region marked by constant sunshine and conservative politics. Like much of inland Orange County, Anaheim appears as a vast and bewildering plane of urbanization, an uninspiring amalgam of housing tracts and shopping centers.

Within this densely populated and frenetic city lies the virtual epicenter of visitor appeal—Disneyland. And just a short drive north of Anaheim is California's second-largest theme park, Knott's Berry Farm. Disneyland and Knott's Berry Farm are by no means the only things going on in Orange County: You'll also discover prehistoric fossil beds, unusual edifices, and winding roads that lead into the distant mountains.

SIGHTS   **DISNEYLAND** Almost everyone, no matter how reclusive, regardless of age, race, or creed, inevitably visits **Disneyland**. Cynics—who snicker at its fantasy formula, orderliness, ultra-cleanliness, cornball humor, and conservative overtones—nevertheless often seem to be swept away by the pure joy of Uncle Walt's fertile imagination.

When Walt Disney cleared away orange groves to open his dream park back in 1955, he provided 18 attractions and promised that Disneyland would never stop growing. Today the entire resort complex includes upscale hotels, a second theme park called **Disney's California Adventure**, and **Downtown Disney**, a massive dining, shopping, and entertainment district. While absolutely nothing about it is "hidden," Disneyland can provide one of life's great escapes.

If at all possible, plan your Disneyland visit to avoid the peak summer months. Huge crowds mean long waiting lines. In any case, it's a good idea to arrive as the park opens and to go directly down Main Street (the park's entry corridor) to be among the first wave of visitors fanning out into the park's many theme lands.

The Magic Kingdom is divided into eight areas. *Main Street* portrays an all-American town at the turn of the 20th century.

Adventureland, a region of jungle rivers filled with hippos and crocodiles, is home to "Indiana Jones™ Adventure," one of Disneyland's most thrilling and popular rides.

With cactus, adobe buildings, and Western-style trading posts, *Frontierland's* main draw is "Big Thunder Mountain Railroad," which simulates a runaway mine train.

Iron-trellised balconies, winding streets, and sidewalk cafés make *New Orleans Square* one of the prettiest themed areas. Here

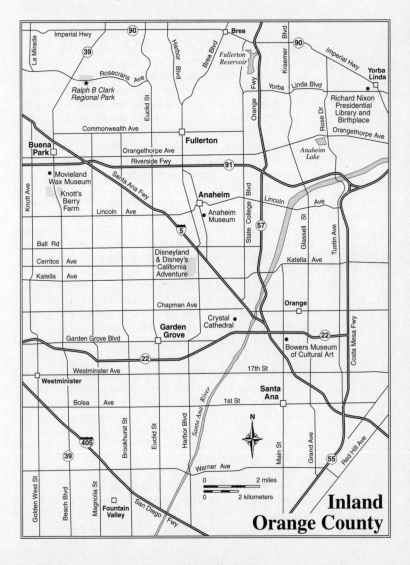

Inland Orange County

are two perennial favorites: "Pirates of the Caribbean" and "The Haunted Mansion."

In *Critter Country* you can listen to a jamboree performed by mechanical bears or venture down the harrowing "Splash Mountain" log ride.

At the center of *Mickey's Toontown* is "Mickey's House," where toddlers can visit with Mr. Mouse himself and view his personal possessions.

Sleeping Beauty's castle, Pinocchio's village, and the white-knuckle "Matterhorn Bobsleds" are only some of the highlights of *Fantasyland*.

Still dedicated to the future and its limitless prospects, *Tomorrowland* has been rebuilt with 3-D films and imaginative surroundings to portray technological wonders. "Star Tours" and "Space Mountain" (Space Mountain is closed for renovations until 2005), Tomorrowland's most sensational rides, should be early on your agenda. Also, don't miss "Honey, I Shrunk The Audience."

The list of things to see and do in Disneyland is staggering: take a jungle cruise, ride a Mississippi paddlewheeler, watch parades and live entertainment, eat at a mind-boggling array of restaurants, shop for just about anything, and have your picture taken with Mickey Mouse.

During off-peak periods, most adults can tour the park in a day. If you take children or visit during peak periods when lines are long, plan on a couple of days (see "Beyond the Theme Parks" on page 281). In addition to one-day general admission tickets, Disneyland now employs "Park Hopper" tickets, which include admission to both parks and unlimited use of rides and attractions. Two- and three-day passes are discounted but a family of four can figure on spending at least $250 a day, including meals, snacks, and souvenirs. Even at that, not many will argue the value of a day or two at the "Happiest Place on Earth." ~ 1313 South Harbor Boulevard, Anaheim; 714-781-4000, fax 714-781-1575; www.disney.com.

DISNEY'S CALIFORNIA ADVENTURE Immediately adjacent to Disneyland, this long-awaited park opened in 2001 and celebrates the California lifestyle with rides, entertainment, and exhibits. While you'll find plenty of thrills here, you'll also encounter a certain level of education, Disney-style, on California's history, environment, and diverse cultures. The park is divided into four major sections:

Sunshine Plaza is the welcome area and portal for the rest of the park. Here, a glistening sun sculpture sits high above a continuous wave fountain. More of a meeting place than anything else, this area is also prime viewing grounds for the park's parades, including the ever-popular "Electrical Parade."

Paradise Pier is a California beachfront - themed area with rides and attractions that would have been found on the old piers of Long Beach or Venice Beach from the 1930s to the '60s. There's "California Screamin'," an old-fashioned wooden coaster with new-fashioned tricks, "King Triton's Carousel," featuring sea creatures instead of horses, and a whole line of low-tech carnival-style boardwalk games.

Get the scoop on showtimes and wait times at popular attractions, and ride closures at the Information Board, located in front of the walkway to Paradise Pier in Disney's California Adventure.

The *Hollywood Pictures Backlot* pays tribute to L.A.'s favorite industry, recreating cafés, shops, and theaters in grand movieland style. "Jim Henson's Muppet Vision 3D" features Kermit, Miss Piggy, and the rest of the gang in a special-effects extravaganza. In the Disney Animation Pavilion, you'll find a very interesting interactive exhibit delineating the animation process—you can even draw your own cartoon. Don't miss "Who Wants To Be A Millionaire—Play It," where you can match wits with other park guests.

Appropriately enough, the *Golden State* area celebrates the beauty and culture of California with six distinct districts that represent California's diversity. Probably the most memorable attraction here is "Soarin' Over California," a free-flight simulation sweeping you over the wonders of the state. The wizards at Disney Imagineering have augmented this trip with the fragrances of California. Yes, you will actually smell the blooms as you soar over the orange groves of central California and the fresh scent of pine from Yosemite National Park!

Most of the attractions here are best appreciated by kids over eight, but there are several areas (the Redwood Creek Challenge Trail, for example) that the little ones love. ~ 1313 South Harbor Boulevard, Anaheim; 714-781-4000, fax 714-781-1575; www. disney.com.

DOWNTOWN DISNEY There is no admission charge for this separate shopping, dining, and entertainment area. Here, sandwiched between the two parks, you'll find mainly souvenir shops alongside some fine upscale restaurants where, unlike the eateries in Disneyland, alcohol is served. One kid-friendly spot is the *Rainforest Cafe*, which makes you feel like you're dining in the Amazon. A popular restaurant and nightclub is the *House of Blues*, which features nationally touring bands and singers nightly. If you're visiting on a Sunday, make a point of catching the Gospel Brunch at the House of Blues. A truly inspired idea—and the Delta-inspired food is good. ~ 1313 South Harbor Boulevard, Anaheim; 714-781-4000, fax 714-781-1575; www.disney.com.

KNOTT'S BERRY FARM California's second biggest theme park, Knott's Berry Farm, lies just five miles away in Buena Park. While some have alluded to it as a country cousin to Disneyland, this 160-acre theme park is both larger and some 15 years older than its sophisticated neighbor. "The Farm," as it is known locally, actually began life back in 1920 when Walter and Cornelia Knott planted a ten-acre berry and rhubarb patch and opened a roadside stand. Eventually the stand evolved into a "Chicken Dinner Restaurant" to which Walter Knott added a mock California Gold Rush town, complete with narrow-gauge railroad.

The original restaurant still serves up Mrs. Knott's chicken dinners—at the rate of 1.5 million a year—and Walter's *Old West Ghost Town*, though rickety with age, looks much as it did in the beginning. To be sure, the park has grown right along with Disneyland, in a sort of symbiotic surge, meeting the demands of increasing attendance. Be sure to experience the "Ghost Rider," the longest and most popular wooden roller coaster in the Western United States.

Knott's *Wild Water Wilderness* resembles a 1900s California river wilderness park highlighted by "Mystery Lodge," an exploration of the traditions of the American Indians who lived on the Pacific Northwest Coast, and "Bigfoot Rapids," a wet and wild ride down California's longest manmade whitewater river.

The Boardwalk, a colorfully themed area, was designed to celebrate the vigor and vitality of Southern California's fabled beach culture. Check out the thrill rides "HammerHead," "Supreme Scream," "Boomerang," and "Kingdom of the Dinosaurs." Don't miss "Perilous Plunge," billed as the world's tallest, steepest, and wettest water ride with a 45-foot, 180-degree splash at the bottom.

A south-of-the-border entertainment center, *Fiesta Village* is complete with California mission replicas, open markets, strolling mariachis, and two wild rides: "Montezooma's Revenge" and "Jaguar."

Geared toward young kids, *Camp Snoopy* is the official home of Charles Schultz's beloved "Peanuts" pals—Snoopy, Linus, Lucy, and Charlie Brown. Life-size versions of the popular cartoon characters roam the six-acre area hugging guests and posing for pictures. Modeled after the Sierra Nevada mountains, Camp Snoopy features a lake, waterfalls, petting zoo, animal show, and kiddie and family rides.

Indian Trails is the park's fifth theme area, a two-acre plot exhibiting the culture, entertainment, and crafts of American Indians. Admission. ~ 8039 Beach Boulevard, Buena Park; 714-220-5200, fax 714-220-5047; www.knotts.com.

Consult *Hidden Disneyland & Beyond* (Ulysses Press) for further information on Southern California's theme parks.

BEYOND THE THEME PARKS Theme parks aren't the only visitor attractions in the inland reaches of Orange County. Their

Queen of
the Canyonlands

Hidden deep in Santiago Canyon, the **Modjeska House** was formerly the retreat of Madame Helena Modjeska, who is remembered as the greatest Polish actress in history. A talented tragedienne, Madame Modjeska left Europe and moved to California with her venturesome husband, Count Karol Chlapowski. While the count tried unsuccessfully to develop a vineyard, Madame Modjeska began acting in the United States, achieving stardom in such roles as Mary Queen of Scots, Cleopatra, and Lady Macbeth. Although she never lost her Polish accent, she starred in 12 Shakespeare plays. (To read more on Madame Helena Modjeska, pick up a copy of her autobiography, *Memories and Impressions*.)

The forest of live oak trees on the banks of Santiago Creek conjured visions of "fantastic stage scenery," prompting Modjeska to name her retreat Arden, after the magical forest in Shakespeare's *As You Like It*. Modjeska and her husband the Count commissioned New York architect Stanford White to design a pastoral palace for them here, a white-frame ranch house they lived in until they retired to Newport Beach. The house later served as a country club and a private home until the county bought the site and turned it into a museum. Today, the north peak of nearby Saddleback Mountain is named Modjeska Peak in her honor.

The home is open to the public for docent-led tours four days a month. All visits to this National Historic Landmark must be arranged in advance. Fee. ~ 949-855-2028.

very existence, in fact, has spawned the growth of other travel destinations. The **Movieland Wax Museum**, with its collection of more than 300 wax figures of movie and television stars, has grown up right in the shadow of Knott's Berry Farm. Movie buffs and stargazers will either love or loathe this wax mausoleum, which presents stars frozen in realistic scenes from their most famous movies or television roles. Admission. ~ 7711 Beach Boulevard, Buena Park; 714-522-1154, fax 714-739-9668; www.movie landwaxmuseum.com.

Ripley's Believe It or Not! Museum, one of the many Ripley "Odditoriums" around the country, is just across the street. Filled with the usual strange artifacts and curiosities (the bearded lady, the six-legged cow), this particular Ripley's also features objects donated by people from all over the world. Adding to the local theme is the Earthquake Tunnel, which deliberately puts you on shaky ground. Admission. ~ 7850 Beach Boulevard, Buena Park; 714-522-7045, fax 714-739-9668; www.ripleysbuenapark.com.

Located on a prehistoric fossil field that may be as extensive as the famed La Brea Tar Pits, **Ralph B. Clark Regional Park** offers an interpretive center with fossil displays and a working paleontology lab. With large shady picnic areas, hiking and biking trails, and extensive playgrounds, this is an inviting spot to spend a low-key afternoon. Closed Monday. ~ 8800 Rosecrans Avenue, Buena Park; 714-973-3170, fax 714-670-8074; www.ocparks. com.

Museums catering to broader interests include the **Anaheim Museum**, with permanent exhibits depicting the city's meteoric growth from a 19th-century farm society. Two galleries showcase works by nationally known artists, and a lower-level children's center offers activities to busy the little ones. Closed Sunday through Tuesday. ~ 241 South Anaheim Boulevard, Anaheim; 714-778-3301, fax 714-778-6740.

AUTHOR FAVORITE

sights One of urban Orange County's most unusual edifices is the **Crystal Cathedral**, a spectacular glass cathedral that rises in the shape of a star to a height of 124 feet. The pipe organ, amplified by banks of speakers that would be the envy of any rock concert promoter, is one of the largest in the world. Through the cathedral's 10,661 panes of glass you can see both the steel tubing that forms the structure's skeleton and the cars that assemble every Sunday to attend "drive-in services" in the parking lot. ~ 12141 Lewis Street, Garden Grove; 714-971-4000, fax 714-971-4315; www.crystalcathedral.org.

Also try the excellent **Bowers Museum of Cultural Art,** where cultural art exhibits include pre-Columbian collections as well as displays from the Pacific Rim and Africa. Closed Monday. Admission. ~ 2002 North Main Street, Santa Ana; 714-567-3600, fax 714-567-3633; www.bowers.org, e-mail rweinberg@bowers.org.

For an expanded sense of Orange County's cultural life, head down Costa Mesa way to Two Town Center, located on Bristol Street across from the South Coast Plaza Shopping Center. Here Japanese-American sculptor Isamu Noguchi has created **California Scenario,** a sculpture garden surrounded by office towers. An abstract expression of the Golden State, this stone-and-steel creation reflects the many faces of California.

The state's majestic redwoods are represented along Forest Walk, a curving path lined with granite. At the Energy Fountain, a stainless steel cone, resembling the nose of a rocket, symbolizes the space-age vitality of the state. The Desert Land section features an array of plants and cacti, including the native tricereus, golden barrel cactus, and agave. The featured piece, Noguchi's tribute to the lima bean farmers who once worked this region, is a collection of bronze-colored granite boulders, precisely cut and fit together to resemble a mound of the noble beans. ~ Costa Mesa; 714-384-5500, fax 714-384-5515.

Covering 60 acres and containing 990 rooms, 3 restaurants and lounges, 2 shops, and almost as many gimmicks as the Magic Kingdom itself, **Disneyland Hotel** is a self-contained world. Situated anywhere else it would rank as a full-blown destination. You can swim, sun on a sandy "beach," watch a light show, shop, dine, drink—or even sleep here. And if that isn't enough, step out front to the monorail station and three minutes later you are at the real thing! ~ 1150 West Magic Way, Anaheim; 714-778-6600, fax 714-956-6597; www.disney.com. ULTRA-DELUXE.

LODGING

The **Disney's Paradise Pier Hotel** is situated on four and a half acres of beautifully landscaped grounds. The 502 guest rooms are elegantly understated with colorful decor and modern furnishings. Two swimming pools, a spa, a boutique, and two restaurants are among the amenities. Located next door to the Disney monorail station, the hotel also provides its guests with special perks such as an early admission to Disneyland's Main Street area. ~ 1717 Disneyland Drive, Anaheim; 714-999-0990, fax 714-776-5763; www.disney.com. ULTRA-DELUXE.

Located inside Disney's California Adventure, the **Grand Californian Hotel** is a classy, Craftsman-style retreat. At 751 rooms, it's not exactly intimate, but the lodge-like atmosphere, quiet courtyards, and carefully landscaped grounds are reminiscent of a stately turn-of-the-20th-century inn. You'll find an up-

Orange County's Outback

To explore the last vestiges of Orange County's open country, plan to spend a day wandering the ridges and valleys of the Santa Ana Mountains along the county's southeastern fringes. It's your final chance to catch a glimpse of Orange County as it looked back in 1769 when the Spanish first probed the region's rugged, chaparral-covered mountains. But at the rate new housing tracts are pushing into the region, you'd better hurry!

LIVE OAK CANYON   Heading south on Route 5, exit onto El Toro Road (Route S18) and head northeast toward those lovely mountains. Continue for about seven miles to Live Oak Canyon Road, turn right, and you'll slip beneath a canopy of live oaks. This leafy tunnel into Orange County's distant past is also the way to **O'Neill Regional Park** (page 291), a 3100-acre preserve that makes a perfect spot for a picnic lunch. Returning to El Toro Road, which becomes Santiago Canyon Road, the route curves up what locals call Modjeska Grade, leaving in its wake a spate of subdivision projects that spoil the view for solace seekers.

MADAME MODJESKA   Turn right on Modjeska Valley Road, another winding lane, then left at the junction of Modjeska Canyon and Foothill roads (there's a large tree forming an island between the two streets). As you enter the rustic town of Modjeska, watch for the fire station on your left; across from it lies a small bridge leading to Hill Road. Once over the bridge, the first gate on the left belongs to one of Orange County's

scale restaurant featuring (what else?) California cuisine, two lounges, a casual café, three pools, and a fitness center. A special feature is Pinocchio's Workshop, a child activity center, where kids can eat and play from 5 p.m. 'til midnight while mom and dad sneak out for a night on the town. ~ 1600 South Disneyland Drive, Anaheim; 714-635-2300, fax 714-300-7301; www.disney. com. ULTRA-DELUXE.

The **Anaheim Marriott**, located two blocks from Disneyland, offers an outstanding luxury-hotel experience. Two towers, 19 and 17 stories in height, are centered on 15 acres of flower-filled grounds. The lobby reflects a soft, contemporary feel with a sunken sitting area. Framed by a tropical palm court, the area has the atmosphere of a sunlit atrium. The hotel has a connecting indoor/outdoor pool, an outdoor pool, two whirlpools plus saunas, and a Nautilus-equipped fitness center. Its 1033 rooms are medium-sized with small balconies, some with Disneyland

most important historic treasures, the **Modjeska House**. In fact, the house is one of two National Historic Landmarks in Orange County (the other is the Richard Nixon Library and Birthplace in Yorba Linda). This hillside mansion was built for Madame Helena Modjeska, reputed to be Poland's greatest actress. For more information on Madame Modjeska and the home, see "Queen of the Canyonlands" on page 281.

TUCKER WILDLIFE SANCTUARY   A mile farther along Modjeska Canyon Road lies Tucker Wildlife Sanctuary, a 12-acre refuge that's home to more than 170 species of birds and animals, which can be viewed along a series of short loop trails. Tucker is best known for its hummingbirds; all seven varieties known to exist in California can be seen here. An island of conservation in a sea of development, the preserve is also home to hawks and woodpeckers. Guided tours are available during the week only (fee). Closed Monday. ~ 714-649-2760.

IRVINE LAKE   Back on Santiago Canyon Road, continue northwest to Irvine Lake, a 731-acre private lake. Stocked and maintained with the serious angler in mind, these waters have produced a state record 59-pound catfish as well as trophy-sized triploid rainbow "super trout" in the 20-pound range. Bass up to nearly 15 pounds have been caught, and there are bluegill and white sturgeon as well. Closed Tuesday in summer. Admission. ~ 714-649-9111; www.irvinelake.net. To wrap up this backcountry adventure, continue for four miles on Santiago Canyon Road to Chapman Avenue, turn left and go three miles to the Newport Freeway (Route 55), then proceed south to Route 5 or 405. Either will carry you back to the civilization from which you temporarily escaped.

views. ~ 700 West Convention Way, Anaheim; 714-750-8000, 800-228-9290, fax 714-750-9100; www.marriott.com/laxah, e-mail anaheim@marriott.com. ULTRA-DELUXE.

Nearby, you can't miss the cavernous, 1572-room **Anaheim Hilton**, a glass-enclosed monolith. The airy atrium lobby, set off by brass railings and green tones, holds five restaurants, two lounges, and assorted shops, along with a pond and fountain. The modern guest rooms are individually decorated. ~ 777 Convention Way, Anaheim; 714-750-4321, 800-222-9923, fax 714-740-4737. ULTRA-DELUXE.

One of the nicest of the hundreds of hotels and motels encircling the perimeter of Disneyland is **Best Western Park Place Inn**. Crisp, contemporary styling sets it apart from many of its neighbors. All of the 199 accommodations are fresh and colorful. There's a pool, sauna, and jacuzzi. You can walk to Disneyland, which is right across the street from the inn. ~ 1544 South Harbor Boulevard, Anaheim; 714-776-4800, 800-854-8175, fax 714-758-1396; www.stovallshotels.com. DELUXE.

Best Western Raffles Inn & Suites offers a compromise between the huge highrise hotels and roadside motels in central Orange County. Just three stories high and sensibly sized (108 rooms), it actually conveys a bit of the "inn" feeling. It looks like one, too, with its tree-shrouded manor house facade. Rooms feature contemporary furnishings and all contain kitchenettes. ~ 2040 South Harbor Boulevard, Anaheim; 714-750-6100, 800-654-0196, fax 714-740-0639; www.bestwesternrafflesinn.com, e-mail reservations@dknhotels.com. DELUXE.

Their motto, "Comfort without Extravagance," is pretty much the truth at the **Welcome Inn**. Located two minutes from Knott's and ten from Disneyland, this well-run family business offers clean, simple, no-frills accommodations. ~ 2912 West Lincoln Avenue, Anaheim; 714-527-2455. BUDGET.

A bit off the mainstream but still only a few blocks from Knott's Berry Farm is **Fullerton "A" Inn**. This 43-room motel may be the best low-cost lodging in close proximity to Knott's. Rooms are clean, air-conditioned, and nicely furnished in a contemporary mode. There is also a pool on the premises. ~ 2601 West Orangethorpe Avenue, Fullerton; 714-773-4900. BUDGET.

Colony Inn is a rambling 90-room complex across the street from Knott's. It's clean, well maintained, and has a pool. ~ 7800 Crescent Avenue, Buena Park; 714-527-2201, 800-982-6566, fax 714-826-3826; www.colonyinnbuenapark.com, e-mail info@colonyinnbuenapark.com. BUDGET.

For visitors planning to bike Santiago Canyon Road, explore O'Neill Regional Park, or fish the Santa Ana River lakes, the nicest motel is **Sky Palm International Lodge**. It has 27 clean and spacious guest rooms, plus a pool with cabaña. ~ 210 North

AUTHOR FAVORITE

Orange County's most original dining adventure is at **The Hobbit**. Here you'll be ushered into a gracious old 1930s hacienda for a magical evening of food and wine. Dinner begins with a tour of the wine cellar, where guests select their favorite wines. For two or three hours you are tempted with a parade of hot and cold hors d'oeuvres, soup, salad, fowl, beef, and fish courses, followed by sorbet and dessert. During "intermission" you can visit the chef in his immaculate kitchen or stroll in the art gallery and gardens. The menu is prix-fixe; reserve weeks in advance. Dinner only. Closed Monday. ~ 2932 East Chapman Avenue, Orange; 714-997-1972, fax 714-997-3181; www.hobbitrestaurant.com. ULTRA-DELUXE.

Tustin Avenue, Orange; 714-639-6602, 800-833-4477, fax 714-639-5581. MODERATE.

Restaurants of every description surround Disneyland, most offering moderately priced but mediocre food. An exception, one of the area's best values for atmosphere and satisfying dining, is **Mr. Stox**, which boasts a versatile menu of steaks, rack of lamb, veal, pasta, and mesquite-grilled fresh seafood. Special touches include savory herbs and spices grown in a garden out back, plus homemade breads and desserts and an award-winning wine cellar. No lunch on weekends. ~ 1105 East Katella Avenue, Anaheim; 714-634-2994, fax 714-634-0561; www.mrstox.com, e-mail mr stox@mrstox.com. DELUXE TO ULTRA-DELUXE.

A full sushi bar in Disneyland? That's exactly what **Yamabuki** has to offer, as well as tempura and teriyaki. Laid out in a Japanese-style fashion, the dining area includes a traditional *tatami* room where guests are invited to take off their shoes, sit on cushion-covered straw mats, and indulge in the culinary delights of authentic Japanese cuisine. No lunch on weekends. ~ Disney's Paradise Pier Hotel, 1717 Disneyland Drive, Anaheim; 714-239-5683, fax 714-776-5763; www.disneyland.com. DELUXE TO ULTRA-DELUXE.

A top restaurant in these parts can be found at the Anaheim Marriott Hotel. **JW's Steakhouse** offers hearty fare such as steak and prime rib, as well as chicken and seafood dishes. The candle-lit ambience, attentive service, and contemporary flourishes add to the experience. Reservations recommended. Hotel occupancy dictates restaurant's availability so call ahead. ~ 700 West Convention Way, Anaheim; 714-703-3187, fax 714-750-9100; www.marriott.com. DELUXE TO ULTRA-DELUXE.

Somewhat distant from metropolitan Orange County is **La Vie En Rose**. Portraying a Norman farmhouse, complete with eight-sided steeple, it's an intimate dining room with French-country appointments. The theme of rural Normandy is carried to completion by waitresses who stream forth with hearty and authentic provincial dishes like *escalope de veau à la Normande* (sautéed veal scallopine with apple brandy cream sauce) and *carré d'agneau aux herbes fraîches* (rack of lamb with fresh herbs). Be sure to make reservations for this prix-fixe dinner. No lunch Saturday. Closed Sunday. ~ 240 South State College Boulevard, Brea; 714-529-8333, fax 714-529-2751; www.lavnrose.com, e-mail lavn rose@earthlink.com. ULTRA-DELUXE.

Antonello Ristorante, Orange County's best-decorated and top-rated Italian eatery, is a re-creation of an actual Italian street setting. Window flower boxes give the place a genuine Old Country feel. When it comes to cuisine, the nouvelle treatments of traditional Northern Italian dishes are outstanding. Pasta, breads, and desserts are made fresh daily and are quite good, but try something you won't find in run-of-the-mill Italian restaurants, like scampi *al anice* or raviolini stuffed with braised veal. Highly recommended. No lunch on Saturday. Closed Sunday. ~ 1611 Sunflower Avenue, Santa Ana; 714-751-7153, fax 714-751-8650; www.antonello.com, e-mail info@antonello.com. MODERATE TO ULTRA-DELUXE.

For a multicourse feast, Moroccan-style, reserve a tent at **Marrakesh**. Decorated in the fashion of North Africa with tile floor and cloth drapes, this well-known dining room conveys a sense of Morocco. There are belly dancers Wednesday through Sunday and any night of the week you can experience *harira* (an aromatic soup), *tajine fassi* (chicken with marinated lemon rinds), couscous, and a host of rabbit, lamb, quail, duck, and chicken dishes. Dinner only. ~ 1976 Newport Boulevard, Costa Mesa; 949-645-8384, fax 949-645-8387; www.marrakesh restaurant.com. DELUXE.

To savvy diners, **Chanteclair** spells "enchantment." Entering the château along a brick walkway flanked by Italian terra-cotta planters, you'll encounter a dining room furnished with antiques. Magnificent to the eye as well as the palate, Chanteclair is one of Orange County's best (and most expensive) dining spots. The menu changes seasonally but may include filet mignon with truffle sauce, châteaubriand, and potato-crusted Chilean sea bass with vanilla-bean butter lead the list of favorite dishes. Dressy attire is suggested. No lunch Saturday. Closed Sunday. ~ 18912 MacArthur Boulevard, Irvine; 949-752-8001, fax 949-955-1394; www.chanteclairrestaurant.com. DELUXE TO ULTRA-DELUXE.

At **Chinatown Restaurant and Bar**, the list of entrées includes 20 original house specialties such as gunpowder scallops. Exciting and varied, Chinatown should not be overlooked. ~ 4139 Campus Drive, Irvine; 949-856-2211, fax 949-856-2404. BUDGET TO MODERATE.

Upscale, contemporary **Prego** packs 'em in both for tasty, authentic Italian food and a breathtaking interior scheme. Arched ceilings and a sizzling open-fire rotisserie greet the eye. Hardwood floors are accented by marbletop tables and beige wood chairs with brown leather cushions. Aromas of saffron, oregano, and steaming pasta will quickly turn your attention to eating, however, and that's a real pleasure at Prego. The big surprise is Prego's pizza, superb pies baked in a huge woodburning oven. *Buon appetito!* No lunch on weekends. ~ 18420 Von Karman Avenue, Irvine; 949-553-1333, fax 949-553-1868; www.pregoirvine.com. MODERATE TO ULTRA-DELUXE.

Chef/owner Tatsuya Osako has been serving up sushi and other Japanese delights at the **Tachibana Restaurant** since 1975, when he could smell the orange blossoms out the back door. Now, tucked away in a corner of the rambling Saddleback Valley

Plaza with not an orange tree in sight, he still serves a splendid *oyako donburi*. ~ 23684 El Toro Road, Suite E, Lake Forest; 949-837-4361. MODERATE.

Trabuco Oaks Steak House is popularly known as "the home of the two-pound cowboy steak." Don't be put off by its run-down facade or funky-rustic decor; nobody in Orange County turns out a bigger, tastier steak or better french fries (they're hand-cut daily). The dog-eared menu lists ribs, chicken, fish, and spaghetti as well, but you should stick to steak here. Leave your tie at home (they cut 'em and tack 'em to the walls), but be sure to bring a business card to add to the thousands plastered around the place. Dinner only. ~ 20782 Trabuco Oaks Drive, Trabuco Canyon; 949-586-0722, fax 949-858-1506; www.trabucooaks steakhouse.com. MODERATE TO ULTRA-DELUXE.

SHOPPING

Inland Orange County is a maze of suburban shopping centers large and small. Which is all right if you're really intent on buying but rather unappealing when you simply want to browse. For those charming little boutiques and artisan shops, stick to the beach area.

Hobby City looks like a miniature Knott's Berry Farm, an-chored by a "perfect half-scale replica" of the White House. It also features an intriguing array of 24 specialized shops, each de-voted entirely to the hobbyist and collector. Among them are stamp, coin, gem, antiques, and doll dealers. ~ 1238 South Beach Boulevard, Anaheim; 714-527-2323, fax 714-236-9762.

In spite of its discount-store facade, the **Crystal Factory** is a treasure trove of crystal and glassware. It's possible to spend from two bucks to two grand on everything from stemware to hand-blown crystal lamps. While browsing you can watch craftspeople engrave crystal items. ~ 8010 Beach Boulevard, Buena Park; 714-952-4135, fax 714-952-4921; www.crystalfactory.com.

Fill a 16,000-square-foot building with 145 separate cubicles and you've got the **Old Chicago Antique Market**. Independent vendors sell wares ranging from fine old furniture to '50s mem-orabilia. ~ 18319 Euclid Street, Fountain Valley; 714-434-6487, fax 714-557-0990.

ANTIQUE ALERT

Serious antique shoppers always head over to Orange where there's a gaggle of great shops. Considered the "antique capital of Southern California," **Orange Circle Antique Mall** is the biggest and one of the best. Housed in a refurbished 1909 brick building are some 120 independently oper-ated booths, each offering something different. Estate jewelry, col-lectibles, mahogany armoires . . . you name it. ~ 118 South Glassell Street, Orange; 714-538-8160, fax 714-997-1410.

Biggest and best of the Orange County malls is **South Coast Plaza**. Some say this is the most distinguished retail address on the West Coast, loaded with sleek signature shops, showcase stores, and a host of specialty boutiques. ~ 3333 South Bristol Street, Costa Mesa; 714-241-1700, 800-782-8888; www.south coastplaza.com.

NIGHTLIFE   The place to cut a rug in Anaheim is **The Boogie**, a vast 20,000-square-foot hall where a deejay spins Top-40 and hip-hop Thursday through Saturday. Dress code: "Dress to impress". Cover. ~ 1721 South Manchester Avenue, Anaheim; 714-956-1410; www.theboogie.net.

The spot to watch the game (or play one) is **Brian's Beer & Billiards**, where the TVs and the pool tables compete with spicy barbecue for your attention. ~ 1944 North Placentia Avenue, Fullerton; 714-993-1401.

You'll find live house-band music, rustic surroundings, and a rowdy party atmosphere at the **Rockin' Taco Cantina**, located in the oldest building in downtown Fullerton. In the spotlight are three piano players who take turns on two baby grand pianos to perform "dueling pianos" renditions of audience requests. Closed Monday. ~ 111 Harbor Boulevard, Fullerton; 714-525-8226.

On Wednesday, you can two-step to live country music at **Crazy Horse Steak House & Saloon**, Orange County's most popular and long-lived nightspot. On Thursday, Friday, and Saturday you'll encounter disco and '80s dance music. Cover. ~ 71 Fortune Drive, Irvine; 949-585-9000; www.crazyhorse2000.com.

THEATER   **Grove Shakespeare at the Gem Theater** presents a Shakespeare festival from mid-April through November, in which professional actors including some Hollywood celebrities appear in the Bard's plays. Three plays are performed in rotation in the outdoor amphitheater, with three others on the indoor stage. ~ 12852 Main Street, Garden Grove; 714-741-9555; www.gtc.org.

AUTHOR FAVORITE

It seems hokey at first: dining with your fingers in an imitation 11th-century castle while knights ride into battle. Actually, **Medieval Times** is a brilliant concept, a re-creation of a medieval tournament, complete with games of skill and jousting matches. It can get pretty wild when the knights—highly trained horsemen and stuntmen—perform dangerous jousting and sword-fighting routines. ~ 7662 Beach Boulevard, Buena Park; 714-521-4740; www.medievaltimes.com.

Orange County Performing Arts Center is one of Southern California's great cultural assets, a 3000-seat theater that regularly features the New York City Ballet and Joffrey Ballet, plus a host of visiting dance, opera, and musical companies. The more-intimate 250-seat Founders Hall features cabaret and jazz acts. ~ 600 Town Center Drive, Costa Mesa; 714-556-2787; www.ocpac.org.

Offering the best in classic and new plays, **South Coast Repertory Theatre** has established itself as a major theatrical presence in California and nationwide. ~ 655 Town Center Drive, Costa Mesa; 714-708-5500 or 714-708-5555 (for tickets); www.scr.org.

CANYON RV PARK AND CAMPGROUND 🚶 🚲 🛶 Unique among Orange County parks, this one's only for camping. Situated in the heart of Santa Ana Canyon, it covers 66 acres, a fraction of which has been developed for campgrounds. The balance is a natural streamside wilderness that includes a nature trail flanked by cottonwood, oak, and willow trees. There are restrooms, showers, a seasonal pool, and nature and bike trails. ~ 24001 Santa Ana Canyon Road, Anaheim; 714-637-0210, fax 714-637-9317; www.canyonrvpark.com.

▲ There are tent sites when space allows and 137 RV sites; $35 with hookups.

IRVINE REGIONAL PARK 🚶 🚲 🐎 This 477-acre park offers more than ten miles of biking, hiking, and equestrian trails. There's a lagoon, petting zoo, train rides, and pony stables with rides for the kids. You'll find picnic areas, playground, nature center, bike and aquacycle rentals, restrooms, and a snack bar. Parking fee, $2 on weekdays, $4 on weekends. ~ 1 Irvine Park Road, Orange; 714-973-6835.

O'NEILL REGIONAL PARK 🚶 🚲 🐎 Originally part of an 1841 Mexican land grant, this 3300-acre county park straddles Trabuco and Live Oak canyons in a delightfully undeveloped region of the Santa Ana Mountains. Topography varies from oak-lined canyon bottomlands and grassy meadows to chaparral-covered hillsides. There's a surprising variety of wildlife that can be spotted while hiking on the nature trails: opossum, raccoon, rabbit, and coyote are frequently seen, as are hawk, quail, dove, and roadrunner. Far more elusive, but ever present in the park, is the mountain lion. Amenities include picnic areas, restrooms, and showers. Parking fee, $2 on weekdays, $4 on weekends. ~ 30892 Trabuco Canyon Road, 18 miles east of Route 405 via El Toro Road exit; 949-923-2260, fax 949-858-9156.

▲ There are 85 tent/RV sites (no hookups); $12 per night.

RONALD W. CASPERS WILDERNESS PARK 🚶 🚲 🐎 A gem of a park, this is Orange County's largest preserve, covering 8000 acres of rugged mountain and canyonland bordering Cleveland National Forest. Within this vast domain are more than 40 miles of marked trails for hiking, biking, and horseback riding. There are picnic areas, restrooms, showers, a nature center, and a playground. Day-use fee, $2 weekdays, $4 weekends. ~ 33401 Ortega Highway (Route 74), San Juan Capistrano; 949-923-2210, fax 949-728-0346.

▲ There are 55 tent/RV sites and an equestrian camp with 28 sites; $12 per night.

▼▼▼▼▼▼▼▼▼▼▼▼▼

Outdoor Adventures

Whether you want to snatch a tuna or watch a spouting whale, the Orange County coast offers plenty of possibilities.

SPORT-FISHING & WHALE WATCHING

Davey's Locker offers half- and full-day sportfishing charters for yellowtail, bass, and barracuda. ~ 400 Main Street, Balboa; 949-673-1434; www.daveyslocker.com. For trips to Catalina and Clemente islands for bass, dorado, and tuna, contact **Dana Wharf Sportfishing**. ~ 34675 Golden Lantern Street, Dana Point; 949-496-5794; www.danawharfsportfishing.com. Dana Wharf Sportfishing and Davey's Locker also sponsor two-hour whale-watching cruises during migratory season (December to late March).

Inland you can fish at **Irvine Lake**, possibly landing a bluegill, "super trout," bass, or white sturgeon. Closed Tuesday in summer. ~ 4621 Santiago Canyon Road; 714-649-9111; www.irvine lake.net.

DIVING

The coastal waters abound in interesting kelp beds rich with sea life; several companies are available to help you through the kelp.

For monthly diving lessons and rentals on Catalina, contact **Aquatic Center**. ~ 4537 West Coast Highway, Newport Beach; 949-650-5440; www.aquaticcenter.net. **Laguna Sea Sports** rents equipment and provides lessons. ~ 925 North Coast Highway, Laguna Beach; 949-494-6965; www.scuba-superstore.com.

SURFING

Orange County is surfer heaven, so when you're in the area, don't miss out on Orange County's wild waves.

Practically all the beaches here are surfable; these are just a few spots to get you started. Early risers head to Newport Pier at Newport Beach. If you're in town during the winter, try the jetty at the end of Surfside Beach. World-renowned Huntington City Beach hosts international surfing competitions in the summer. The south end of San Clemente State Beach offers great breaks any time of the year. Large waves can be found at Salt Creek Beach Park and the south end of Rock Pile Beach; Capistrano Beach Park is known for its "Killer Capo" breaks. Beginners choose to learn at Doheny State Beach. For surf reports call 949-492-1011.

If bodysurfing is your thing, the Wedge at West Jetty View Park is the place to do it.

For surfboards, boogieboards, wetsuit rentals, sales, and repairs, contact **Huntington Surf and Sport**. ~ 300 Pacific Coast Highway, Huntington Beach; 714-841-4000; www.huntington surfandsport.com. **Hobie Sports** also rents boards and wetsuits. ~ 24825 Del Prado, Dana Point; 949-496-2366. **Stewart's Surf Boards** sells and rents surfboards, boogieboards, and wetsuits. Inquire about lessons—many of the employees offer private instruction. ~ 2102 South El Camino Real, San Clemente; 949-492-1085.

KAYAKING & BOATING

With elaborate marina complexes at Huntington Beach, Newport Beach, and Dana Point, this is a spectacular area for boating. If you yearn to make some waves, call one of the outfits listed below.

Fishing skiffs are available for rent at **Davey's Locker**. ~ 400 Main Street, Balboa; 949-673-1434; www.daveyslocker.com. In Newport Beach, try **Marina Sailing** for lessons or six-passenger charters. ~ 300 Pacific Coast Highway, Suite F, Newport Beach; 949-548-8900; www.marinasailing.com. Electric boats, motorboats, sailboats, kayaks, and offshore runabouts can be rented at **Balboa Boat Rentals**. ~ 510 East Edgewater, Balboa; 949-673-7200; www.boats4rent.com. **Embarcadero Marina**, located at the public launch ramp, rents sailboats, fishing skiffs, and an electric duffy. ~ 34512 Embarcadero Place, Dana Point; 949-496-6177; www.danaharbor.com.

GOLF

The climate and terrain of Orange County make for excellent golfing. Take a break from Southern California freeways, and do some driving on the greens instead.

Tee up in Newport at the 18-hole executive **Newport Beach Golf Course**, but expect to carry your own clubs: this course has no electric carts. ~ 3100 Irvine Avenue, Newport Beach; 949-

---

ROAD RUNNING

If you'd rather shake up the cellulite than the water, you can do it on Orange County's miles of beaches and running trails. Mecca for Orange County runners is the **Santa Ana Riverbed Trail**, a smooth asphalt ribbon stretching 20.6 miles from Anaheim to Huntington Beach State Park. There are par courses and excellent running trails at both **Laguna Niguel Regional Park** (La Paz and Aliso Creek Road) and **Mile Square Regional Park** (16801 Euclid Avenue in Fountain Valley). In Mission Viejo there's a beautiful two-and-a-half-mile trail around **Lake Mission Viejo**. And then there are the miles and miles of beaches for which Orange County is renowned.

852-8681. The enchanting nine-hole **Aliso Creek Golf Course** is set in the middle of a steep canyon with a creek winding through it. ~ 31106 Coast Highway, Laguna Beach; 949-499-1919; www.alisocreekinn.com. The coastal course at **The Golf Links at Monarch Beach** is designed by Robert Trent Jones, Jr., and has a beautiful view of the water. ~ 22 Monarch Beach Resort North, Dana Point; 949-240-8247; www.monarchbeachgolf.com. If you're looking for a dry course with ocean views, visit the **San Clemente Municipal Golf Course**. ~ 150 East Avenida Magdalena, San Clemente; 949-361-8384. Situated in a narrow canyon, the public, par-72 **Shorecliffs Golf Course** has a driving range and putting green. The greens are small and the course is fast and in good condition. Carts are mandatory. ~ 501 Avenida Vaquero, San Clemente; 949-492-1177.

Richard Nixon used to play the greens at Shorecliffs Golf Course in San Clemente.

The inland sections of Orange County also feature numerous golf links. Among them is **Dad Miller Golf Course**. ~ 430 North Gilbert Street, Anaheim; 714-765-3481. Visit the **Anaheim Hills Golf Course**, which features a double-decker driving range. ~ 6501 Nohl Ranch Road, Anaheim; 714-998-3041. A natural creek running along 14 of the 18 holes at **Fullerton Golf Course** ensures lots of water hazards. ~ 2700 North Harbor Boulevard, Fullerton; 714-871-7411. For a flat, wide-open, 36-hole walking course, visit **Mile Square Golf Course**. ~ 10401 Warner Avenue, Fountain Valley; 714-968-4556; www.milesquaregolfcourse.com.

TENNIS   Even though public courts are hard to find in this area, who says Orange County is elitist? There are still many private clubs, and given the wonderful climate and the way you'll fit in wearing those white shorts and tennis sweaters, it's probably worth the club fee after all.

In Newport Beach, you can try one of the eight lighted, plexi-paved courts at **Hotel Tennis Club**. A pro is available for lessons. Fee. ~ Marriott Hotel, 900 Newport Center Drive, Newport Beach; 949-729-3566. Laguna Beach's **Moulton Meadows Park** has two courts. ~ Del Mar and Balboa avenues, Laguna Beach; 949-497-0716. **Laguna Niguel Regional Park** features four lighted tennis courts. ~ 28241 La Paz Road, Laguna Niguel; 949-923-2240. There are eight lighted courts at **Dana Hills Tennis Center**. Fee. ~ 24911 Calle de Tenis, Dana Point; 949-240-2104.

Strangely enough, San Clemente is the one Orange County town that does seem to have an abundance of public courts. **Bonito Canyon Park** offers two lighted courts. ~ 1304 Calle Valle, San Clemente; 949-361-8264. There are four lighted courts at **San Luis Rey Park**. ~ 109 Avenida San Luis Rey, San Clemente; 949-361-8264. **San Gorgonio Park** has one unlit court. ~ 2916 Via San

Gorgonio, San Clemente; 949-361-8264. **Verde Park** also has two courts for day-use only. ~ 301 Calle Escuela; 949-361-8264.

The **Anaheim Tennis Center** offers 12 lighted courts. Fee. ~ 975 South State College Boulevard, Anaheim; 714-991-9090. In Buena Park, **Ralph B. Clark Regional Park** has four lighted courts. ~ 8800 Rosecrans Avenue, Buena Park; 714-973-3170.

BIKING

Wind and wheels are a perfect blend with Southern California's weather, and you can avoid adding to the smog and sitting in traffic by tooling around on a bike rather than in a car. Whether you like road riding or mountain biking, you'll find a suitable place to cycle in Orange County. **Route 1**, the Pacific Coast Highway, offers cyclists an opportunity to explore the Orange County coastline. The problem, of course, is the traffic. Along **Bolsa Chica State Beach**, however, a special pathway runs the length of the beach. Another way to avoid traffic is to mountain-bike; **Moro Canyon** in Crystal Cove State Park is a favorite off-road riding area.

Call the **Newport Beach Department of Public Works** and ask for a copy of the "Bikeways" map; it shows all the trails in Newport Beach. ~ City Hall, 3300 Newport Boulevard; 949-644-3311; www.city.newport-beach.ca.us.

Other interesting areas to explore are **Balboa Island** and the **Balboa Peninsula** in Newport Beach. Both offer quiet residential streets and are connected by a ferry that permits bicycles. A popular inland ride is along **Santiago Canyon Road**; leaving from Orange the route skirts Irvine Lake and Cleveland National Forest.

Bike Rentals   **Sandpiper Bicycle Repair** is a full-service shop renting hybrids, tandems, and inline skates. Closed Monday. ~ 231 Seal Beach Boulevard, Seal Beach; 562-594-6130. **Rainbow Bicycle Company** rents, repairs, and sells mountain bikes. ~ 485 North Coast Highway, Laguna Beach; 949-494-5806; www.teamrain.com.

HIKING

All distances listed for hiking trails are one way unless otherwise noted.

COASTAL ORANGE COUNTY   Though heavily developed, the Orange Coast still provides several outstanding trails. All are located near the beaches and offer views of private homes and open ocean.

The California Coastal Trail extends over 40 miles from the San Gabriel River in Seal Beach to San Mateo Point in San Clemente. Much of the route follows sandy beachfront and sedimentary bluffs. There are lagoons and tidepools, fishing piers, and marinas en route.

At the **Bolsa Chica Ecological Reserve Trail** (1.5 miles) you can say hello to birds traveling along the Pacific Flyway. A migratory rest stop, this lagoon features a loop trail that runs atop a levee past fields of cord grass and pickleweed.

Huntington Beach Paved Bike and Hike Trail (8.5 miles) parallels the Pacific from Bolsa Chica Lagoon to Beach Boulevard in Huntington Beach. Along the way it takes in Huntington Pier, a haven for surfers, and passes an army of unspeakably ugly oil derricks.

Newport Trail (2.5 miles) traces the ocean side of Balboa Peninsula from Newport Pier south to Balboa Pier, then proceeds to the peninsula's end at Jetty View Park. Private homes run the length of this pretty beach walk.

Back Bay Trail (3.5 miles) follows Back Bay Drive in Newport Beach along the shores of Upper Newport Bay. This fragile wetland, an important stop on the Pacific Flyway, is an ideal bird-watching area.

Crystal Cove Trail (2.5 miles) provides a pleasant seaside stroll. Starting from Pelican Point at the western boundary of Crystal Cove State Park, the paved path leads to the beach. The trail continues another mile to a cluster of cottages at Crystal Cove, then follows an undeveloped beach to Abalone Point, a 200-foot high promontory.

Aliso Creek Canyon Hiking Trail (1 mile) begins near the fishing pier at Aliso Beach County Park in South Laguna, leads north through a natural arch, and passes the ruins of an old boat landing.

INLAND ORANGE COUNTY Rising along the entire length of Orange County's eastern perimeter, the Santa Ana Mountains offer several challenging and surprisingly uncrowded trails inside the **Cleveland National Forest** (909-736-1811).

Holy Jim Trail (5 miles) is a good Santa Ana sampler, with a creek, waterfall, oak woodland, and chaparral-covered slopes. It leads to Bear Springs, where hikers can take a three-mile optional

AUTHOR FAVORITE

Skirting the Upper Newport Bay Ecological Reserve are about ten miles of bikeway, with some hills, but nothing too strenuous. You can park for about $8 at Newport Dunes (an RV resort) or try for one of the spots in the small Big Canyon lot in the reserve. Back Bay Drive, a multi-use paved roadway, has a double-wide bike route; it links up with a dedicated bike route around the northern perimeter of the reserve. Eventually, along the western flank, the bike route gives way to a bike lane on city-streets to complete the loop around the reserve. ~ Back Bay Drive at Jamboree Road.

climb on **Main Divide Truck Trail** to the crest of 5687-foot Santiago Peak. The trail begins on Holy Jim Road, six miles from O'Neill Regional Park.

Bear Canyon Trail (3.5 miles) is a broad, well-graded, and rather pleasant hike climbing through brush and meadow country to refreshing Pigeon Springs. Arrive at the spring early in the morning and you'll likely see deer, coyote, or even bobcat drinking from the cool waters. From Pigeon Springs there's an optional five-mile hike to Sitton Peak via **Verdugo and Sitton Peak Trail**. The trail is on Route 74, 20 miles east of Route 5.

Nearby **Chiquito Basin Trail** (9 miles) switchbacks past a sparkling waterfall and over oak-studded slopes to shady Lion Canyon. Don't be confused: the trailhead (just east of Bear Canyon trailhead) is signed San Juan Loop Trail, but Chiquito Basin Trail branches off a mile up.

Should you be city-bound during your visit to Orange County you can still get out and stretch the legs, thanks to the **Santa Ana Riverbed Trail** (28 miles). True to the name, it follows the Santa Ana River on a smooth asphalt surface from Imperial Highway in Anaheim south to Route 1 at Huntington Beach State Park. A great way to hike to the beach, it's also popular with joggers and bikers.

Transportation

Several major highways crisscross Orange County. **Route 1,** known in this area as the **Pacific Coast Highway**, ends its long journey down the California Coast in Capistrano Beach. A few miles farther inland, **Route 405** runs from Long Beach to Irvine, with feeder roads leading to the main coastal towns.

CAR

AIR

John Wayne International Airport, located in Santa Ana, is the main terminal in these parts. Major carriers presently serving it include Alaska Airlines, Aloha Airlines, America West, American Airlines, Continental Airlines, Delta Air Lines, Frontier Airlines, Northwest Airlines, Southwest Airlines, and United Airlines. ~ 18601 Airport Way, Santa Ana; 949-252-5200; www.ocair.com.

BUS

Greyhound Bus Lines (800-231-2222; www.greyhound.com) serves Orange County, stopping in Anaheim, Santa Ana, Irvine, and San Clemente. Most stops are flag stops. Finally, there's the San Clemente station. ~ 2421 South El Camino Real; 949-366-2646.

TRAIN

Amtrak's "San Diegan" travels between Los Angeles and San Diego, with Orange County stops at Fullerton, Anaheim Stadium, Santa Ana, San Juan Capistrano, and San Clemente. ~ 800-872-7245; www.amtrak.com.

CAR RENTALS Arriving at John Wayne International Airport, you'll find the following car rental agencies: **Alamo Rent A Car** (800-327-9633), **Avis Rent A Car** (800-230-4898), **Budget Rent A Car** (800-221-1203), **Hertz Rent A Car** (800-654-3131), and **National Car Rental** (800-227-7368). For less expensive (and less convenient) service, try **Enterprise Rent A Car** (800-736-8222).

PUBLIC TRANSIT **Orange County Transportation Authority,** or RIDE from southern Orange County, has bus service throughout Orange County, including most inland areas. Along the coast it stops at beach fronts including Seal Beach, Huntington Beach, Newport Beach, Corona del Mar, Laguna Beach, San Juan Capistrano, and San Clemente. ~ 714-636-7433; www.octa.net.

In addition, **Los Angeles County Metropolitan Transit Authority** (MTA) serves some areas of Orange County including Fullerton, Disneyland, and Knott's Berry Farm. ~ 213-626-4455; www.mta.net.

FIVE

San Diego

San Diego County's 4261 square miles occupy a Connecticut-sized chunk of real estate that forms the southwestern corner of the continental United States. Geographically, it is as varied a parcel of landscape as any in the world. Surely this spot is one of the few places on the planet where, in a matter of hours, you can journey from bluff-lined beaches up and over craggy mountain peaks and down again to sun-scorched desert sands.

Moving east from the Pacific to the county's interior, travelers discover lush valleys and irrigated hillsides. Planted with citrus orchards, vineyards, and rows of vegetables, this curving countryside eventually gives way to the Palomar and Laguna mountains—cool, pine-crested ranges that rise over 6500 feet.

But it is the coast—some 76 sparkling miles stretching from San Mateo Point near San Clemente to the Mexican border—that always has held the fascination of residents and visitors alike.

When Portuguese explorer Juan Rodríguez Cabrillo laid eyes on these shores in 1542, he discovered a prospering settlement of Kumeyaay Indians. For hundreds of years, these native peoples had been living in quiet contentment on lands overlooking the Pacific; they had harvested the rich estuaries and ventured only occasionally into the scrubby hills and canyons for firewood and game.

Sixty years passed before the next visitor, Spanish explorer Sebastian Vizcaíno, came seeking a hideout for royal galleons beset by pirates. It was Vizcaíno who named the bay for San Diego de Alcala.

In 1769, the Spanish came to stay. The doughty Franciscan missionary Junípero Serra marched north from Mexico with a company of other priests and soldiers and built Mission San Diego de Alcala. It was the first of a chain of 21 missions and the earliest site in California to be settled by Europeans. Father Serra's mission, relocated a few miles inland in 1774, now sits incongruously amid the shopping centers and housing developments of Mission Valley.

California's earliest civilian settlement evolved in the 1820s on a dusty mesa beneath the hilltop presidio that protected the original mission. Pueblo San Diego quickly developed into a thriving trade and cattle ranching center after the ruling Spanish colonial regime was overthrown and replaced by the Republic of Mexico.

By the end of the century, new residents, spurred partly by land speculators, had taken root and developed the harbor and downtown business district. After the rails finally reached San Diego in 1885, the city flourished. Grand Victorian buildings lined 5th Avenue all the way from the harbor to Broadway and 1400 barren acres were set aside uptown for a city park.

After its turn-of-the-20th-century spurt of activity, the city languished until World War II, when the U.S. Navy invaded the town en masse to establish the 11th Naval District headquarters and one of the world's largest Navy bases. San Diego's reputation as "Navytown USA" persisted well after the war-weary sailors went home. Despite the closure of the San Diego Naval Training Center, some 103,000 Navy and Marine personnel are still based in San Diego and at Camp Pendleton to the north. With 101,000 family members, 26,000 civilian Navy employees, and 59,000 Navy retirees, the military presence remains a major influence, but this is changing as high-tech industries locate in San Diego, bringing "new economy" diversity and a spirit of renewal.

The military has not been the only force to foster San Diego's growth. In the early 1960s, construction began on an important university that was to spawn a completely new industry. Many peg the emergence of the "new" San Diego to the opening of the University of California's La Jolla campus. Not only did the influx of 15,000 students help revive a floundering economy, it tended to liberalize an otherwise insular and conservative city.

Truth is, San Diego is no longer the sleepy, semitransparent little resort city it once was. Nowhere is the fact more evident than in the downtown district, where a building boom brought new offices, condominiums, and hotels.

But for all the city's manmade appeal, it is nature's handiwork and an ideal Mediterranean climate that most delights San Diego visitors. With bays and beaches bathed in sunshine 75 percent of the time, less than ten inches of rainfall per year and average temperatures that mirror a proverbial day in June, San Diego offers the casual outdoor lifestyle that fulfills vacation dreams. There's a beach for every taste, ranging from broad sweeps of white sand to slender scimitars beneath eroded sandstone bluffs.

Situated a smug 120 miles south of Los Angeles on Route 5, San Diego is not so much a city as a collection of communities hiding in canyons and gathered on small shoulders of land that shrug down to the sea. As a result, it hardly seems big enough (a bit over 1.25 million) to rank as America's seventh largest city. Total county population is 2.8 million, and nine of ten residents live within 30 miles of the coast.

The city of San Diego is divided into several geographic sections. To the south lies Coronado, nestled on a peninsula jutting into San Diego Bay and connected to the mainland by a narrow sandbar known as the Silver Strand.

Although they are within the boundaries of the city of San Diego, the seaside communities of Ocean Beach, Mission Beach, Pacific Beach, and La Jolla have developed their own identities, moods, and styles.

"OB," as the first of these is known, along with Mission and Pacific beaches, exults in the sunny, sporty Southern California lifestyle fostered by nearby Mission Bay Park. These neighboring communities are fronted by broad beaches and an almost continuous boardwalk that is jammed with joggers, skaters, and cyclists. The beaches are saturated in the summer by local sun-seekers, but they have much to offer visitors.

Like a beautiful but slightly spoiled child, La Jolla is an enclave of wealth and stubborn independence that calls itself "The Village" and insists on having its own post office, although it's actually just another part of the extended San Diego family. Mediterranean-style mansions and small cottages shrouded by jasmine and hibiscus share million-dollar views of beaches, coves, and wild, eroded sea cliffs. Swank shops and galleries, trendy restaurants and classy little hotels combine in a Riviera-like setting that rivals even Carmel for chicness.

North County is a string of beach towns stretching from Oceanside south to Del Mar, where outdoor enthusiasts can find their fill of white-sand beaches, world-class golf courses, and state parks. Shops and restaurants dot Route 101, the coastal highway that threads through the towns of Oceanside, Carlsbad, Leucadia, Encinitas, Cardiff-by-the-Sea, and Del Mar. A varied area, these towns

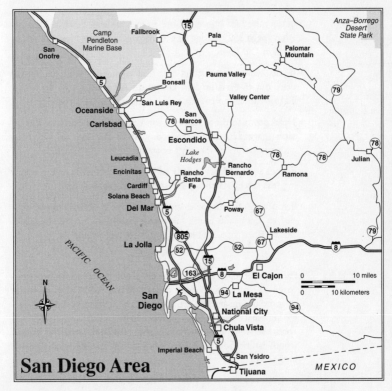

San Diego Area

Text continued on page 304.

Three-day Weekend

History, Culture, and Wildlife

This tour will introduce you to the many facets of San Diego in a brief visit. Conspicuously absent here is **SeaWorld San Diego** (page 338), an all-day theme park that's a must-see if you have kids. Another all-day adventure for those who have extra time is a visit to **Tijuana** (page 380).

DAY 1
- Start your day in **Old Town** (page 348) with a tour on the Old Town Trolley, then stroll through the lively **Bazaar del Mundo** marketplace.

- Visit the **Junipero Serra Museum** (page 350) for an account of San Diego's birth.

- In the mood for Mexican food? Enjoy a leisurely lunch at **Casa de Pico** (page 352) or one of the many other good Mexican restaurants in Old Town.

- If you wish, round out the historical segment of your tour with a drive out to **Mission San Diego de Alcala** (page 350), the first California mission church, now surrounded by suburban sprawl.

- Head down to the waterfront for a **San Diego Harbor Excursion** (page 370) to see the commercial shipping and U.S. Navy activity that drives the city's economy.

- Enjoy a seafood feast at **Star of the Sea** (page 371) or the adjoining, less pricey **Anthony's Fish Grotto** (page 372).

- If you're still bursting with energy after this busy day, why not drive out to Coronado island for cocktails at the classy **Babcock & Story Bar** (page 376) in the Hotel del Coronado?

DAY 2
- Pack a picnic lunch and plan your day around a visit to **Balboa Park** (page 357), where you can choose among world-class museums devoted to fine art, folk art, photography, astronomy, natural history, aerospace technology, anthropology, sports, and model railroads. Between museums, take plenty of time to stroll this magnificently landscaped 1400-acre park with its Spanish colonial revival architecture.

- Dine in Downtown San Diego's Gaslamp Quarter at **Ida Bailey's Restaurant** (page 368), an elegant Victorian-style restaurant named for the madam who used to run a house of ill-repute there. Later, stick around the Quarter and hop your way among the many nightclubs of San Diego's premier entertainment zone.

DAY 3
- Drive up north to the **San Diego Zoo's Wild Animal Park** (page 305) to spend the morning watching the free-roaming wildlife from the monorail and walkways.

- Returning from the animal park, stop for lunch in Del Mar at **The Fish Market** (page 315).

- Follow the coast highway down to La Jolla. Round out your wildlife-watching day with a stop at the **Birch Aquarium at Scripps** (page 330).

- Head up to the top of the bluffs in **Torrey Pines State Reserve and Beach** (page 331) for a great sunset view.

- Return to La Jolla for dinner at one of the village's many great restaurants, such as **George's at the Cove** (page 333).

boast residents from every walk of life—from the ultra-wealthy (as found in La Costa and Del Mar), to the Southern Californian artisans (as found in Leucadia), to the short-haired Marines of Oceanside.

It is safe to say that the San Diego area is not as eccentric and sophisticated as San Francisco, nor as glamorous and fast-paced as Los Angeles. But those who still perceive it as a laid-back mecca for beach bums—or as a lunch stop en route to Mexico—are in for a huge surprise.

▼▼▼▼▼▼▼▼▼▼▼▼▼
North San Diego County

Stretching along the coast above San Diego is a string of towns with a host of personalities and populations. Residents here range from the county's wealthiest folks in Rancho Santa Fe to Marine privates at Oceanside's Camp Pendleton to yogis in retreat at Encinitas. This part of the county really shines, however, in its many sparkling beaches.

The best way to see North County's fine beaches is to cruise along Old Route 101, which preceded Route 5 as the north–south coastal route. It changes names in each beach town along the way, but once you're on it you won't be easily sidetracked.

SIGHTS
Your first sightseeing opportunity in San Diego County is at **San Onofre State Beach**, about 16 miles north of Oceanside. Unique in that it's actually two beaches, North and South, this certainly is one of the county's most scenic beach parks. Its eroded sandstone bluffs hide a variety of secluded sandy coves and pocket beaches. But all this beauty is broken by an eerie and ungainly structure rising from the shoreline. Dividing the park's twin beaches is a mammoth facility, potent and ominous, the **San Onofre nuclear power plant**. Admission. ~ 949-492-0802, fax 949-492-8412.

Old Route 101 leads next into **Oceanside**, gateway to Camp Pendleton Marine Base. San Diego County's third-largest city is busy renovating its beachfront and image. The refurbished fishing pier is a lengthy one, stretching almost 2000 feet into the Pacific.

If you'd like to learn more about California's "cultural" side, stop by the **California Surf Museum**, which features exhibits on the history of the sport and its early pioneers. On display is the very first surfing trophy, named after Tom Blake, one of the first waterproof cameras that was used to capture up-close footage, an exhibit that chronicles the history of surfboard shaping, and wooden boards from the pre-'60s era. A museum shop offers vintage books and videos. Closed Tuesday and Wednesday. ~ 223 North Coast Highway, Oceanside; 760-721-6876; www.surfmuseum.org, e-mail csm@surfmuseum.org.

From Oceanside, Mission Avenue, which merges with Route 76, will carry you to **Mission San Luis Rey**. Known as the "King of the Missions" (and named originally after a king of France), this beautifully restored complex was originally constructed in 1798 and represents the largest California mission. Today you can visit the museum chapel and cemetery while walking these historic grounds. Admission. ~ 4050 Mission Avenue, Oceanside; 760-757-3651, fax 760-757-4613; www.sanluisrey.org.

Continue east on Route 76 to **Guajome County Park**, a 557-acre playground that offers a variety of natural, historical, and recreational opportunities. The park is centered around 1850s-era **Rancho Guajome Adobe**, considered one of the region's best examples of early Spanish architecture. Just a few miles away is a 25-acre fishing lake. Hiking and horseback riding trails thread the property, and there are picnic areas, restrooms, a playground, and a campground. Parking fee. ~ Guajome Lake Road, south off of Route 76, Oceanside; 858-565-3600; www.sdparks.org.

Heading inland on Route 78 will bring you to **Escondido**. One of the fastest growing places in California, it is also home to 40 percent of the state's 59,000 acres of avocados. Planted in neat rows, they climb the hillsides north and east of town.

There's no finer wildlife sanctuary in the country than the remarkable **San Diego Zoo's Wild Animal Park**. This 1800-acre spread, skillfully landscaped to resemble Asian and African habi-

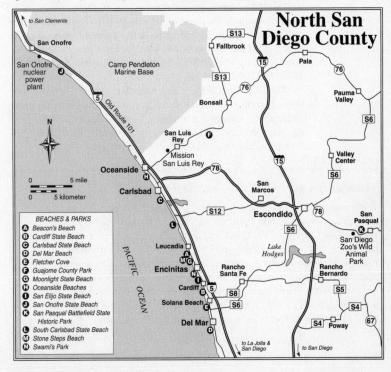

North San Diego County

0   5 mile
0   5 kilometer

BEACHES & PARKS
A Beacon's Beach
B Cardiff State Beach
C Carlsbad State Beach
D Del Mar Beach
E Fletcher Cove
F Guajome County Park
G Moonlight State Beach
H Oceanside Beaches
I San Elijo State Beach
J San Onofre State Beach
K San Pasqual Battlefield State Historic Park
L South Carlsbad State Beach
M Stone Steps Beach
N Swami's Park

tats, houses over 3500 animals. Among them are several endangered species not found in zoos elsewhere. Many of the animals roam free while you view them from a monorail. After visiting the fearsome lions and gorillas, you can follow that line of children to the "Petting Kraal," where the kids can fluff up a variety of exotic deer. Admission. ~ 15500 San Pasqual Valley Road, Escondido; 619-234-6541; www.wildanimalpark.org.

Two miles east of the animal park is **San Pasqual Battlefield State Historic Park**, where an interpretive center tells the story of a strange and little-known battle. It seems that during the Mexican War in 1846 about 100 U.S. Dragoons, including the famous scout Kit Carson, suffered an embarrassing defeat at the hands of the California Mexicans. Today a small monument here marks the battle site. Closed Monday through Friday. ~ 15808 San Pasqual Valley Road, Escondido; 760-737-2201.

On a more modern note, **Welk Resort**, an elaborate resort complex, contains a museum in its theater lobby that features the famous "one-ana-two" entertainer's (Lawrence, that is) memorabilia. High camp at its most bizarre. Closed during theater performances; call ahead. ~ 8860 Lawrence Welk Drive, Escondido; 760-749-3000; www.welkresort.com.

In addition to avocado and citrus groves, Escondido boasts a number of vineyards. You can chat with the folks at **Ferrara Winery** and stroll around the vineyards. A small family enterprise, the winery has been producing vintages for three generations. Wine tasting is free. ~ 1120 West 15th Avenue, Escondido; 760-745-7632, fax 760-743-2675.

The **Deer Park Winery and Auto Museum** offers tastings of wines from its Napa and Escondido vineyards and displays a fine collection of vintage automobiles. Closed Tuesday and Wednesday. Admission. ~ 29013 Champagne Boulevard, Escondido; 760-749-1666, fax 760-751-1666; www.deerparkwinery.com.

TURF AND SURF

While seasonal, **Del Mar Race Track** and companion **Fairgrounds** are the main attractions in Del Mar. The track was financed in the 1930s by such stars as Bing Crosby and Pat O'Brien to bring thoroughbred racing to the fairgrounds. It was no coincidence that this town, "where the turf meets the surf," became a second home for these and many other top Hollywood stars. Track season is from the end of July to mid-September. The rest of the year you can bet on races televised via satellite. Admission. ~ Route 5 and Via de la Valle, Del Mar; race track 858-755-1141, fairgrounds 858-755-1161; www.delmarracing.com, e-mail marys@dmtc.com.

Orfila Vineyards and Winery, a producer of chardonnay, merlot, viognier, and syrah, is open daily for tastings and tours. ~ 13455 San Pasqual Road, about six miles southeast of Escondido; 760-738-6500, 800-868-9463, fax 760-745-3773; www.orfila.com.

Also southeast of Escondido, **Bernardo Winery** is the oldest operating winery in the county. You can take a self-guided tour any day and taste wine for free. ~ 13330 Paseo del Verano Norte, San Diego; 858-487-1866, fax 858-673-5376; www.bernardo winery.com.

Back on coastal Route 5 and farther south of Oceanside is **Carlsbad,** a friendly, sunny beachfront town that has been entirely redeveloped, complete with cobblestone streets and quaint shops. Originally the place established its reputation around the similarity of its mineral waters to the springs of the original Karlsbad in the Czech Republic. But don't waste your time looking for the fountain of youth, the spring has long since dried up. Go to the beach instead.

Added to Southern California's theme park lineup is LEGO-LAND, patterned after the park in Denmark where Legos are made. Designed with kids ages two to twelve in mind, attractions include cruises, rides (such as roller coasters), and walkways that take visitors past huge, elaborate constructions made from the colorful plastic snap-together bricks, including models of the Golden Gate Bridge, the New York skyline, the Taj Mahal, 18-foot giraffes, a larger-than-life Albert Einstein, a buffalo herd, and much more. Even grown-ups are likely to be amazed. Closed Tuesday and Wednesday except in summer. Admission. ~ LEGO-LAND Drive, Carlsbad; 760-918-5346, fax 760-918-5375; www. legoland.com.

Another opportunity for hands-on fun awaits at the **Children's Discovery Museum of North County.** Here, kids can explore the science of light and color, fish, and spend time in a bubble. Closed Monday. Admission. ~ 2787 State Street, Carlsbad; 760-720-0737, fax 760-720-0336; www.museumforchildren.org, e-mail vaavoom@aol.com.

Encinitas is popularly known as the "Flower Capital of the World" and the hillsides east of the beach are a riot of colors. A quick call to the friendly folks at the local **Chamber of Commerce and Visitors Center** will net you information concerning the area. ~ 138 Encinitas Boulevard, Encinitas; 760-753-6041, fax 760-753-6270; www.encinitaschamber.com, e-mail info@ encinitaschamber.com.

A self-guided walking tour at **Quail Botanical Gardens** treats visitors to 30 acres of colorful plants and flowers, including the area's natural chaparral, and gardens that display rainforest vegetation, orchids and bamboo. A lookout tower provides a 360-degree view of the grounds. Admission. ~ 230 Quail Gardens

Drive at Encinitas Boulevard, Encinitas; 760-436-3036; www.qbgardens.com.

Yogis, as well as those of us still residing on terra firma, might want to make a stop at Paramahansa Yogananda's **Self Realization Fellowship Retreat**. The gold-domed towers of this monastic retreat were built by an Indian religious sect in the 1920s and are still used as a retreat. Although the gardens inside the compound are beautifully maintained and open to the public daily, Yogananda's house is only open on Sunday. The views, overlooking the famous "Swami's" surfing beach, are spectacular. Closed Monday. ~ 215 K Street, Encinitas; 760-753-2888, fax 760-753-8156; www.yogananda-srf.org.

Although **Del Mar** is inundated every summer by "beautiful people" who flock here for the horse racing, the town itself has retained a casual, small-town identity. Its trim, Tudor-style village center and luxurious oceanfront homes reflect the town's subtle efforts to "keep up with the Joneses" next door (i.e., La Jolla).

On the east side of Route 5, about five miles inland on either Via de la Valle or Lomas Santa Fe Drive, is **Rancho Santa Fe**. If La Jolla is a jewel, then this stylish enclave is the crown itself. Residing in hillside mansions and horse ranches parceled out from an old Spanish land grant are some of America's wealthiest folks. Rancho Santa Fe is like Beverly Hills gone country. The area became popular as a retreat for rich industrialists and movie stars in the 1920s when Douglas Fairbanks and Mary Pickford built their sprawling **Fairbanks Ranch**. To make a looping tour of this affluent community, drive in on Via de la Valle, then return to Route 5 via Linea del Cielo and Lomas Santa Fe Drive.

LODGING   Many of San Diego's best beaches lie to the north, between Oceanside and Del Mar. Sadly, most of the good hotels do not. But don't worry, among those listed below all but a handful are either oceanfront or oceanview properties.

The Mediterranean-style **Southern California Beach Club** is a 43-suite, time-share facility situated on the beach near Oceanside Pier. Each suite is graciously appointed with quality furnishings in contemporary hues of peach, heather, and blue. Kitchens are standard; other extras include a mini-gym, a rooftop jacuzzi, and laundry facilities. ~ 121 South Pacific Highway, Oceanside; 760-722-6666, fax 760-722-8950. DELUXE TO ULTRA-DELUXE.

San Luis Rey Downs is a casual little resort nestled northeast of Oceanside, along the San Luis Rey River. There are only 26 rooms, neat, clean, and basic, in a two-story woodframe lodge overlooking the golf course. But this inviting hideaway also offers a restaurant, lounge, pool, jacuzzi, and nearby tennis courts. ~ 31474 Golf Club Drive, Bonsall; 760-758-3762, 800-783-6967,

fax 760-758-1597; www.slrd.com, e-mail reservations@slrd.com.
MODERATE TO ULTRA-DELUXE.

Palm Tree Lodge is clearly the nicest of the reasonably priced
motels in Escondido. Family-owned and -operated, it is sparkling
clean and well maintained. Some of the 38 rooms have kitchens
and fireplaces. You'll also find a restaurant, pool, and sundeck on
the premises. Pets are welcome. ~ 425 West Mission Avenue, Escondido; 760-745-7613, 800-745-1062, fax 760-745-3377; www.
palmtreelodge.com, e-mail joy@palmtreelodge.com. MODERATE.

Carlsbad offers several nice oceanview facilities, including
Tamarack Beach Resort, a Mediterranean contemporary-style
hotel. Finished in peach and aqua hues, the Tamarack rents standard rooms as well as one- and two-bedroom suites. Most are
smashingly decorated in upbeat tones and textures and incorporate such touches as potted plants and photographic prints. Suites,
though ultra-deluxe-priced, may be the best value on the North
Coast. They have kitchens and private balconies. Guests can make
use of the oceanview restaurant, clubhouse, fitness center, jacuzzis,
video library, and activities program as well as enjoying the adjacent beach. Complimentary continental breakfast is included.
~ 3200 Carlsbad Boulevard, Carlsbad; 760-729-3500, 800-334-
2199, fax 760-434-5942; www.tamarackresort.com, e-mail tam
arack@pacbell.net. ULTRA-DELUXE.

Advertised as "a very special bed and breakfast," the **Pelican
Cove Inn** is a lovely Cape Cod–style house with eight guest rooms.
Each features a fireplace and is well-furnished with antique pieces,
including feather beds; some rooms have spa tubs. Visitors share
a sundeck and patio with gazebo. The inn is located just two
blocks from the beach. ~ 320 Walnut Avenue, Carlsbad; 760-434-

AUTHOR FAVORITE

Affordability and quiet are the order of the day at **Ocean Palms Beach
Resort**. This tidy, 57-room mom-and-pop complex is so near the sea you can
hear it, but a row of expensive beach houses blocks the view from all but
one beachfront building. Some sections of the rambling ocean manor date
back to 1939, and "new" additions have a tropical feel to them, so the general decor could best be described as "beach bungalow." An oldie but
goodie in this case, however. The place is clean and lovingly maintained
and features a landscaped patio and pool area, complete with two
jacuzzis and sauna. All rooms have fully equipped kitchens. ~ 2950
Ocean Street, Carlsbad; 760-729-2493, 888-802-3224, fax 760-729-
0579; www.opalms.com, e-mail info@ocean-palms.net. MODERATE
TO ULTRA-DELUXE.

5995, 888-735-2683, fax 760-434-7649; www.pelican-cove.com, e-mail pelicancoveinn@pelican-cove.com. MODERATE TO ULTRA-DELUXE.

The **Best Western Beach Terrace Inn** is a 49-unit establishment with stucco facade and the feel of a motel. There's a pool and jacuzzi, plus a single feature that differentiates the Beach Terrace from most other places hereabouts—it is located right on the beach. A broad swath of white sand borders the property, making the price for a room with kitchen a worthwhile investment. ~ 2775 Ocean Street, Carlsbad; 760-729-5951, 800-433-5415, fax 760-729-1078; www.beachterraceinn.com. DELUXE TO ULTRA-DELUXE.

Sporting a fresh look, the fabled **La Costa Resort & Spa** can justly claim to be one of the world's great "total" resorts. This luxurious 400-acre complex boasts 474 guest rooms, two 18-hole championship golf courses, 21 tennis courts (hard, clay, *and* grass), 10 shops, 2 restaurants, and one of the country's largest and most respected spa and fitness centers. Simply put, the place is awesome. With rooms *starting* well up in the ethereal range, La Costa's appeal to the well-monied few is apparent. ~ 2100 Costa del Mar Road, Carlsbad; 760-438-9111, 800-854-5000, fax 760-438-3758; www.lacosta.com, e-mail info@lacosta.com. ULTRA-DELUXE.

Located on a lofty knoll above the Pacific, **Best Western Encinitas Inn and Suites** is built on three levels and looks like a condominium. With a pool and jacuzzi, it has many of the same features. The 90 rooms include private balconies overlooking the ocean. Deluxe continental breakfast is served at the poolside cabaña. ~ 85 Encinitas Boulevard, Encinitas; 760-942-7455, 866-362-8648, fax 760-632-9481; www.bwencinitas.com. DELUXE.

HIDDEN ►

The best reasonably priced lodging near the beach in Encinitas is **Moonlight Beach Motel**. This three-story, 24-unit family-run motel is tucked away in a residential neighborhood overlooking Moonlight Beach State Park. Guest rooms are modern as well as clean, and contain everything you'll need, including full kitchens. Most of the accommodations command ocean views. ~ 233 2nd Street, Encinitas; 760-753-0623, 800-323-1259, fax 760-944-9827. MODERATE.

Every room is individually decorated at **Cardiff-by-the-Sea Lodge** with themes such as Old World, Southwest, and Mediterranean, and many rooms have ocean views, fireplaces and in-room whirlpools. It's a bed and breakfast, but not of the converted-home variety; everyone has a private entrance and bath. Breakfast is served buffet-style in a center courtyard, but you can take it to your room or up to the rooftop garden and savor a panoramic view of the Pacific. ~ 142 Chesterfield Avenue, Cardiff; 760-944-

6474, fax 760-944-6841; www.cardifflodge.com, e-mail innkeeper @cardifflodge.com. DELUXE TO ULTRA-DELUXE.

It's all in the name when it comes to locating **Del Mar Motel on the Beach,** the only motel between Carlsbad and La Jolla on the beach. All 48 rooms in this plain stucco building are steps from the sand. That's undoubtedly where you'll spend your time because there is little about the rooms to enchant you. They are basic in design, equipped with refrigerators, color TVs, and air conditioning. Because the hotel is at a right angle to the beach, only two rooms have full views of the water. ~ 1702 Coast Boulevard, Del Mar; 858-755-1534, 800-223-8449, fax 858-259-5403; www. delmarmotelonthebeach.com, e-mail thedelmarmotel@cs.com. DELUXE TO ULTRA-DELUXE.

A two-story Spanish Mediterranean inn conveniently situated a few blocks from downtown Del Mar, **Les Artistes** honors several of the world's favorite artists: Diego Rivera, Georgia O'Keeffe, Erté, Claude Monet, and Paul Gauguin. The owner, who is an architect from Thailand, designed each room in the style and spirit of the artist. Other architectural delights include a pond filled with water lilies and koi, and a classic Spanish-style courtyard with a fountain. ~ 944 Camino del Mar, Del Mar; 858-755-4646; www.les artistesinn.com. MODERATE TO ULTRA-DELUXE.

Built on the site of a once-famous Del Mar Beach getaway, **L'Auberge Del Mar Resort and Spa** replicates the old hotel's nostalgic past of the '20s, '30s, and '40s. The original Tudor/Craftsman inn's rich lobby is dominated by a replica of the huge original brick fireplace. Along with 120 guest rooms and suites, the inn features a restaurant with patio dining, bar, full-service European spa, tennis courts, leisure and lap pools, shops, a park amphitheater, and partial ocean views. Each room has its own patio. ~ 1540 Camino del Mar, Del Mar; 858-259-1515, 800-553-1336, fax 858-755-4940; www.lauberge delmar.com, e-mail laubergereservations@destinationhotels.com. ULTRA-DELUXE.

L'Auberge Del Mar was frequented by Hollywood greats such as Bing Crosby, Jimmy Durante, and Rudolph Valentino.

For an elegant country inn consider **The Inn at Rancho Santa Fe.** Widely known among the world's genteel, it's a country inn comprised of Early California–style *casitas* on a 20-acre site. Situated five miles inland from Solana Beach, the inn offers individually decorated guest rooms as well as one-, two-, and three-bedroom cottages. Many rooms and all cottages feature private sun terraces, fireplaces, and kitchenettes. Displayed in the homespun lobby is a priceless collection of antique hand-carved model ships. There are tennis courts, a swimming pool, a jacuzzi, an exercise room, croquet, and a restaurant. ~ 5951 Linea del Cielo, Rancho Santa Fe; 858-756-1131, 800-843-4661, fax 858-759-

1604; www.theinnatrsf.com, e-mail reservations@theinnatrsf.com. ULTRA-DELUXE.

One of the county's leading resorts is **Rancho Bernardo Inn**. World-class golf and tennis aside, this handsome hacienda-style complex is a gracious country retreat. The 287 rooms here are decorated with original artwork and potted palms. There are two pools, seven jacuzzis, a fitness center, and a spa. ~ 17550 Bernardo Oaks Drive, Rancho Bernardo; 858-675-8500, 800-542-6096, fax 858-675-8437; www.jcresorts.com, e-mail ranchobernardoinn@ jcresorts.com. ULTRA-DELUXE.

DINING

The **Harbor House Café** is a great place for breakfast. Decorated with brightly colored murals, this eatery serves up innovative omelettes, buckwheat pancakes, and delicious home fries. For lunch, try the mushroom burger with sautéed onions, mushrooms, and jack cheese. Patio dining is also available. No dinner. ~ 714 North Coast Highway, Oceanside; 760-722-2254. BUDGET.

HIDDEN ►

For a downright homey café, try **Robin's Nest**, a country-style establishment with good eats and a gregarious chef. The menu features omelettes, soups, and burgers. With a decor of soft blues and artwork by local artists, this place is quite popular with locals and has an outdoor patio that faces the harbor. Breakfast and lunch served daily; served from May through September. ~ 280-A Harbor Drive South, Oceanside; 760-722-7837, fax 949-492-2665; www.robinsnestcafe.com. MODERATE.

Legends California Bistro at La Costa Resort & Spa bills its food as "Consciousness-in-cooking". This translates to incorporating Ayurveda guidelines from the Chopra Center. Breakfast offerings may include a power smoothie, apple walnut crêpes, or a tofu scramble. Lunch is a variety of health-conscious bites such as ahi tuna tartar, crisp salads, sandwiches, ansd veggie stirfries. Dinner is a more upscale affair with seafood, lamb, and steak dishes. Sunday champagne and jazz brunch is served. ~ 2100 Costa del Mar Road, Carlsbad; 760-438-9111, 800-854-5000; www.lacosta.com, e-mail info@lacosta.com. DELUXE.

Neimans, an eye-catching Victorian landmark, houses both a dining room and café/bar. My favorite for lunch or dinner is the café, where LeRoy Neiman lithographs hang on the walls and the menu includes trendy dishes such as coconut shrimp, chicken kabob, and citrus-macadamia salmon. They also serve burgers, pasta, and salads. The Sunday brunch in the sprawling early 1900s dining room is a definite "must," featuring a tremendous buffet assortment of breakfast and lunch items. ~ 300 Carlsbad Village Drive, Carlsbad; 760-729-4131, fax 760-729-6131; www.neimans. com, e-mail neimans1@hotmail.com. MODERATE TO DELUXE.

For light, inexpensive fare there's the **Daily News Café**. Breakfast features eggs, pancakes, French toast, and their "world famous" sticky buns, while the heartier lunch fare includes an array of soups, salads, sandwiches, and burgers. Breakfast and lunch only. ~ 3001-A Carlsbad Boulevard, Carlsbad; 760-729-1023. BUDGET.

Pasta lovers should be sure to try the *penne* or *fusilli* in vodka-tomato sauce at **When In Rome**. The art-filled Roman decor provides the proper atmosphere, and the Italian owners certainly know their trade. All the breads and pastas are made fresh daily. Entrées include a variety of veal and seafood items. Dinner only. ~ 1108 South Coast Highway, Encinitas; 760-944-1771, fax 760-944-3849; www.wheninrome.signonsandiego. com. MODERATE TO ULTRA-DELUXE.

Most visitors to Encinitas never lay eyes on the **Potato Shack**   ◄ HIDDEN **Café**, hidden away on a side street. But locals start packing its pine-paneled walls at dawn to tackle North County's best and biggest breakfast for the buck. There are three-egg omelettes and manhole-size pancakes, but best of all are the home-style taters and the old-fashioned biscuits and gravy. Lunch is also served, but the Potato Shack is really a breakfast institution, and as such serves breakfast until 2 p.m. ('til 2:30 p.m. on weekends). No dinner. ~ 120 West I Street, Encinitas; phone/fax 760-436-1282. BUDGET.

Another popular feeding spot is **Sakura Bana Sushi Bar**. The sushi here is heavenly, especially the *sakura* roll, crafted by Japanese masters from shrimp, crab, scallop, smelt egg, and avocado. The bar serves only sushi and sashimi, but table service will bring you such treats as teriyaki, tempura, and shrimp *shumai*. No lunch Saturday or Sunday; closed Monday. ~ 1031 South Coast Highway, Encinitas; 760-942-6414. MODERATE.

Encinitas' contribution to the Thai food craze is an intimate café called **Siamese Basil**, set along the town's main drag. At lunch and dinner this white-washed eatery serves up about six

AUTHOR FAVORITE

Whatever you do during your North County visit, don't pass up the chance to dine at **El Bizcocho**. Tucked away in the upscale Rancho Bernardo Inn, an Early California–style resort, this award-winning restaurant rates among greater San Diego's best. The traditional French haute cuisine menu includes a nice balance of beef, veal, fish, and fowl dishes. Try the roast duckling for two or indulge in the creamy lobster bisque. Dinner only. Closed Sunday. ~ 17550 Bernardo Oaks Drive, Rancho Bernardo; 858-675-8550, fax 858-675-8443; www.jcresorts.com. ULTRA-DELUXE.

dozen dishes. You can start with the spicy shrimp soup and satay, then graduate to an entrée menu that includes noodle, curry, seafood, and vegetable selections. House specialties include roast duck with soy bean and ginger sauce, honey-marinated spare ribs, and barbecued chicken. ~ 527 South Coast Highway, Encinitas; 760-753-3940. BUDGET TO MODERATE.

Best of the beachfront dining spots in Cardiff is **Charlie's by the Sea**, where the surf rolls right up to the glass. Here you can choose from an innovative selection of fresh seafood items or an all-American menu of grilled chicken, steak, and prime rib. Charlie's has a smartly decorated contemporary setting with a full bar, but still creates an easy, informal atmosphere. Sunday brunch. ~ 2526 South Coast Highway, Cardiff; 760-942-1300, fax 760-942-1228; www.charliesbythesea.com, e-mail charliesbythesea@sbcglobal.net. MODERATE TO DELUXE.

HIDDEN ►

Mention the words "Mexican food" in Solana Beach and the reply is sure to be **Fidel's**. This favored spot has as many rooms and patios as a rambling hacienda. Given the good food and cheap prices, all of them are inevitably crowded. Fidel's serves the best *tostada suprema* anywhere and the burritos, enchiladas, and *chimichangas* are always good. ~ 607 Valley Avenue, Solana Beach; 858-755-5292, fax 858-755-2392. MODERATE.

Il Fornaio, an Italian restaurant/bakery, boasts magnificent ocean views, outside dining terraces, elegant Italian marble floors and bar, trompe l'oeil murals, and an enormous exhibition kitchen. The place is packed with eager patrons ready to sample the pastas, pizzas, rotisserie, meats, and *dolci* (desserts). There's also Sunday brunch. ~ 1555 Camino del Mar, Del Mar Plaza, Del Mar; 858-755-8876, fax 858-755-8906; www.ilfornaio.com. MODERATE TO DELUXE.

Since life is lived outdoors in Southern California, **Pacifica Del Mar**, part of a local restaurant mini-chain, features a terrace overlooking the ocean as well as a white-tablecloth dining room.

CRÈME DE LA CRÈME

Mille Fleurs tops everyone's list as San Diego's best French restaurant. The à la carte menu, which changes daily, provides exquisite appetizers, soup, and such entrées as rack of lamb with black-olive crust, grilled Alaskan halibut with saffron sauce, and loin of antelope. A sophisticated interior features fireside dining, Portuguese tiles, and stunning trompe l'oeil paintings. There is also a Spanish courtyard for dining as well as a piano bar. No lunch on the weekend. ~ 6009 Paseo Delicias, Rancho Santa Fe; 858-756-3085; www.millefleurs.com, e-mail milfleurs@aol.com. ULTRA-DELUXE.

The Pacific Rim accent here is on seafood, as in barbecued sugar-spiced salmon, Chinese five-spice ahi salad, and miso-marinated sea bass. ~ 1555 Camino del Mar, Del Mar Plaza, Del Mar; 858-792-0476, fax 858-792-0848; www.pacificadelmar.com, e-mail kipp@pacificadelmar.com. DELUXE TO ULTRA-DELUXE.

The place is mobbed all summer long, but **The Fish Market** remains one of my favorite Del Mar restaurants. I like the noise, nautical atmosphere, oyster bar, on-the-run service, and the dozen or so fresh fish items. Among the best dishes are the sea bass, yellowtail, orange roughy, and salmon, either sautéed or mesquite charbroiled. ~ 640 Via de la Valle, Del Mar; 858-755-2277, fax 858-755-3912; www.thefishmarket.com. MODERATE TO ULTRA-DELUXE.

Scalini, housed in a classy contemporary-style building with arched windows overlooking a polo field, is strictly star-quality northern Italian fare. The place has been decorated in a mix of modern and antique furnishings and wrapped in all the latest Southern California colors. But the brightest star of all is the menu. The mesquite-broiled veal chops and osso buco are exceptional. There are many good homemade pasta dishes including lobster fettuccine, linguine, and tortellini. Dinner only. ~ 3790 Via de la Valle, Del Mar; 858-259-9944, fax 858-259-2270; www.scalini sandiego.com. DELUXE TO ULTRA-DELUXE.

Delicias, a comfortable and spacious restaurant with an adjoining bar, is decorated in a mixture of antiques and wicker, accented by woven tapestries and flowers. The chefs in the open-view kitchen whip up contemporary California cuisine. Delicious food, personable service. No lunch. ~ 6106 Paseo Delicias, Rancho Santa Fe; 858-756-8000, fax 858-759-1739. MODERATE TO ULTRA-DELUXE.

SHOPPING

Jewelry is a high art form at **The Collector Fine Jewelry,** where every piece is crafted by hand. The owners go right to the source for the best gems—Colombia for emeralds, Burma for rubies, and Africa for diamonds. Closed Sunday. ~ 912 South Live Oak Park Road, Fallbrook; 760-728-9121, 800-854-1598; www.col lectorfinejewelry.com.

Mega-malls are popping up all around San Diego these days, but few match Escondido's **Westfield Shoppingtown North County.** This 87-acre complex has a half-dozen major department stores and a host of independent shops. ~ 272 East Via Rancho Parkway and Route 15, Escondido; 760-489-2332; www.westfield.com.

Carlsbad has blossomed with a variety of trendy shops. You will see many beach-and-surf-type shops, as well as a variety of gift shops. Swing by the **Village Faire Shopping Centre,** a New England–style specialty mall that has Sunday afternoon concerts in July and August. ~ 300 Carlsbad Village Drive, Carlsbad; www.villagefaire.com.

If little else, Solana Beach harbors an enclave of good antique stores. One of the best is the **Antique Warehouse**, with its collection of 101 small shops. Closed Tuesday. ~ 212 South Cedros Avenue, Solana Beach; 858-755-5156; www.antique-warehouse.com.

A seacoast village atmosphere prevails along Del Mar's half-mile-long strip of shops. Tudor-style **Stratford Square**, the focal point, houses a number of shops in what is the area's first commercial building. **Earth Song Bookstore** offers traditional books as well as an eclectic selection of titles focusing on health, spirituality, and psychology. ~ 1440 Camino del Mar, Del Mar; 858-755-4254.

Carolyn's is a consignment shop with designer fashions from the closets of the community's best-dressed women. Closed Sunday. ~ 1310 Camino Del Mar, Del Mar; 858-481-4133.

The stylized **Del Mar Plaza** is a welcome addition. Home to over 20 retail shops, this tri-level mall sells everything from fashion accessories to upscale home furnishings and has a host of eateries. ~ 1555 Camino del Mar, Del Mar; 858-792-1555; www.delmarplaza.com.

Flower Hill Mall, a rustic mall, has the usual fashion and specialty shops. But the real draw here is **Bookworks** (858-755-3735; www.book-works.com) and an adjoining coffeehouse called **Pannikin Coffee and Tea** (858-481-8007). Together they're perfect for a relaxed bit of book browsing and a spot of tea. ~ 2670 Via de la Valle, Del Mar; 858-481-7131.

Detouring, as every sophisticated shopper must, to Rancho Santa Fe, you'll find an assortment of chic shops and galleries along Paseo Delicias. One of my favorites is **Marilyn Mulloy Estate & Fine Jewelers**, with its collection of old and new pieces. Closed Sunday. ~ 6024 Paseo Delicias, Rancho Santa Fe; 858-756-4010. There are lots of millionaires per acre here, but bargains can still be found: **Country Friends** is a charity-operated repository of antique furniture, silver, glass, and china priced well below local antique shops. Closed Sunday. ~ 6030 El Tordo, Rancho Santa Fe; 858-756-1192.

NIGHTLIFE   **Aquaterra**, a classy and contemporary watering hole at Pala Mesa Resort, attracts mainly golfers fresh from a round on the links. ~ 2001 South Route 395, Fallbrook; 760-728-5881.

For a harbor view and daily entertainment, cast an eye toward **Monterey Bay Canners**. ~ 1325 Harbor Drive North, Oceanside; 760-722-3474.

HIDDEN ►   **First Street Bar** is a neighborhood bar with three pool tables. It is consistently on the best neighborhood bar list, voted on by locals. ~ 656 South Coast Highway, Encinitas; 760-944-0233.

Solana Beach's low-profile daytime image shifts gears in the evening when the-little-town-that-could spotlights one of North County's hottest clubs. The **Belly Up Tavern** is a converted quonset hut that now houses a concert club and often draws big-name rock, reggae, jazz, and blues stars. Cover. ~ 143 South Cedros Avenue, Solana Beach; 858-481-9022, 858-481-8140 (box office); www.bellyup.com.

Tucked away in the Flower Hill Mall, **Pannikin Coffee and Tea** brings a true taste of culture in the form of live jazz, classical guitarists, and poetry readings on Friday nights. ~ 2670 Via de la Valle, Del Mar; 858-481-8007.

SAN ONOFRE STATE BEACH 🏃🚴🏊🏄🛶🚣⛵ San Diego County's northernmost beach is about 16 miles north of Oceanside, uneasily sandwiched between Camp Pendleton and the San Onofre nuclear power plant. It's well worth a visit if you're not put off by the nearby presence of atomic energy. San Onofre has a number of sections separated by the power plant and connected via a public walkway along the seawall. On the north side of the power plant, off Cristianitos Road, is San Mateo Campground, with developed sites. Eroded bluffs rumple down to the beach creating a variety of sandy coves and pockets. South of Bluffs and not far from famous Trestles Beach is Surf Beach, a favorite with surfers and kayakers. The southern side of the plant is Bluffs Campground, a superb campground with trailer spaces and primitive tent sites, the only primitive campsite anywhere on San Diego County beaches. Gentle surf, which picks up considerably to the north, makes this a good swimming and bodysurfing spot. You'll find restrooms, lifeguards, and trails. Parking fee, $12. ~ From Route 5, take Basilone Road exit and follow the signs to the beach; 949-492-0802, fax 949-492-8412.

BEACHES & PARKS

> It is more than a rumor that some discreet nude sunbathing takes place at the end of beach path #6 at San Onofre.

▲ There are 221 tent/RV sites (no hookups) at Bluffs Campground (949-492-4872), $21 per night; and 157 tent and RV sites (hookups and showers) at San Mateo Campground, $21 to $30 per night. Reservations: 800-444-7275.

OCEANSIDE BEACHES 🚴🏊🏄🛶🚣🚤⛵ Over three miles of clean, rock-free beaches front North County's largest city, stretching from Buena Vista Lagoon in the south to Oceanside Harbor in the north. Along the entire length the water can get rough in the summer and fall, and it's important to be wary of riptides here. Lots of Marines from nearby Camp Pendleton favor this beach. The nicest section of all is around Oceanside Pier, a 1900-foot-long fishing pier. Nearby, palm trees line a grassy promenade dotted with picnickers; the sand is as clean as a whistle. Added to the attractions is **Buena Vista Lagoon**, a bird sanctuary and na-

◄ HIDDEN

ture reserve. Facilities include picnic areas, restrooms, lifeguards, basketball courts, and volleyball courts. There are kayak rentals at the harbor; the only boat ramp for miles around is located here. Restaurants are at the end of the pier and harbor. Try fishing from the pier, rocks, or beach. Swimming is good and surfing is reliable year-round. Day-use fee, up to $5. ~ Located along The Strand in Oceanside; 760-435-4018, fax 760-435-4022; www.ci.oceanside.ca.us.

▲ Limited to a few RV sites in a parking lot with no hookups; $15 per night.

CARLSBAD STATE BEACH 🏊 🛶 🏃 ⚓ ♪ Conditions here are about the same as at South Carlsbad (see below), a sand and rock beach bordered by bluffs. Rock and surf fishing are quite good at this beach and even better at the adjoining Encinas Fishing Area (at the San Diego Gas and Electric power plant), where Agua Hedionda Lagoon opens to the sea. The beach extends another mile or so to the mouth of the Buena Vista Lagoon. Facilities include restrooms and lifeguards. The beach offers swimming, surfing, and skindiving. ~ The park entrance is at Tamarack Avenue, west of Carlsbad Boulevard, Carlsbad; 760-438-3675, fax 760-438-2762.

SOUTH CARLSBAD STATE BEACH 🏊 🛶 🏃 ⚓ ♪ This is a big, bustling beachfront rimmed by bluffs. The pebbles strewn everywhere put towel space at a premium, but the water is gentle and super for swimming. The beach has restrooms, lifeguards, showers, groceries, and beach rentals. Swimming, fishing, surfing, and skindiving are popular activities. ~ Located west of Carlsbad Boulevard south of Palomar Airport Road, Carlsbad; 760-438-3143, fax 760-438-2762.

▲ There are 196 blufftop tent/RV sites (no hookups), $21 to $31 per night. Reservations: 800-444-7275.

BEACON'S BEACH 🏊 🛶 🏃 ⚓ ♪ A broad sand corridor backdropped by coastal bluffs, this beach has appeal, though it's certainly not North County's finest. The strand is widest at the north end, but the breakers are bigger at the south end, a favorite with local surfers. Swimming, surfing, and skindiving are good. ~ There is a trail off the parking lot at Leucadia Boulevard and Neptune Avenue, Encinitas; 760-633-2740, fax 760-633-2626; www.ci.encinitas.ca.us.

HIDDEN ▶

STONE STEPS BEACH 🏊 🏃 ♪ Locals come here to hide away from the tourists. It is indeed stony and narrow to boot, but secluded and hard to find. Much like Moonlight to the south, its surf conditions are good for several types of water sports. There are no facilities; a lifeguard is stationed here in summer. ~ The staircase to the beach is located at South El Portal Street, off Neptune Avenue, Leucadia.

MOONLIGHT STATE BEACH 🏄 🐋 🎣 🏃 🏕 🚣 A very popular beach, Moonlight boasts a big sandy cove flanked by sandstone bluffs. Surf is relatively tame at the center, entertaining swimmers and bodysurfers. Volleyball courts, a playground and fire circles are added attractions. Surfers like the wave action to the south, particularly at the foot of D Street. There are picnic areas, firepits, restrooms, showers, lifeguards, a snack bar, equipment (surfboards, boogieboards, beach gear) rentals, and places to fish. ~ 400 B Street, Encinitas; 760-633-2740, fax 760-633-2626; www.ci.encinitas.ca.us.

SWAMI'S PARK 🏄 🐋 🎣 🏃 🏕 North County's most famous surfing beach derives its name from an Indian guru who founded the Self Realization Fellowship Temple here in the 1920s. The gold-domed compound is located on the cliff-top just to the north of the park. A small, grassy picnic area gives way to stairs leading to a narrow, rocky beach favored almost exclusively by surfers, though divers and anglers like the spot as well. The reef point break here makes for spectacular waves. The stretch between this beach and D Street is a marine refuge, so don't get any ideas about taking an invertebrate home with you. Facilities include restrooms, picnic areas, lifeguards, and a funky outdoor shower. ~ 1298 South Route 101 about one mile south of Encinitas Boulevard, Encinitas; 760-633-2740, fax 760-633-2626; www.ci.encinitas.ca.us.

SAN ELIJO STATE BEACH 🏃 🏄 🐋 🎣 🏕 🚣 Although the beach is wide and sandy, low tide reveals a mantle of rocks just offshore and there are reefs, too, making this another of North County's most popular surf fishing and skindiving spots. Lifeguards are stationed here during summer. There is a campground atop the bluff overlooking the beach. Most amenities are located at the campground and include restrooms, showers, beach rentals, and groceries. Day-use fee, $4. ~ Off South Route 101 north of Chesterfield Drive, Cardiff; 760-753-5091; e-mail sanelijo@ixpres.com.

Surfers brave big breakers at "Turtles" and "Pipes" reefs at the north end of San Elijo State Beach.

▲ There are 171 tent/RV sites (some hookups), $21 to $39 per night. Reservations: 800-444-7275.

CARDIFF STATE BEACH 🚲 🏄 🏃 🏕 This strand begins where the cliffs of Solana Beach end and where the town's most intriguing feature, a network of tidepools, begins. Popular with surfers because of the interesting pitches off its reef break, this wide, sandy beach is part of a two-mile swath of state beaches. At the beach there are restrooms, cold showers, and lifeguards (summer only). Fishing, swimming, and surfing are popular activities here. Day-use fee, $6. ~ Off South Route 101 directly west of San Elijo Lagoon, Cardiff; 760-753-5091.

FLETCHER COVE 🏄 🛶 🧗 🚣 ⚓ Lined by cliffs and carpeted with sand, this is a popular spot for water sports. There's a natural break in the cliffs where the beach widens and the surf eases up to allow comfortable swimming. Surfers gather to the north and south of Plaza Street where the beach is narrow and the surf much bigger. It's also a prime area for grunion runs. Facilities include restrooms, outdoor showers, lifeguards, and basketball courts. ~ Located at the end of Plaza Street, Solana Beach; 858-755-1560, fax 858-793-7734; e-mail msafety@cosb.org.

DEL MAR BEACH 🏄 🛶 🧗 🚣 ⚓ Though rather narrow from Torrey Pines to about 15th Street, the beach widens further north. The part around 15th Street is action central, with teens playing sand volleyball and frisbee while the elders read magazines beneath their umbrellas. Surfers congregate at the foot of 13th Street. Quintessential North County! There are picnic tables, a snack bar, restrooms, showers, and lifeguards. Fishing is good, and there are regular grunion runs. There is typical beach surf with smooth peaks, year-round. ~ Easiest beach access is at street ends from 15th to 29th streets off Coast Boulevard, one block below South Route 101, Del Mar; 858-755-1556, fax 858-259-3264; www.delmar.ca.us, e-mail msafety@cosb.org.

Inland San Diego County

Touring Inland San Diego County's rugged backcountry means wandering through a landscape filled with rambling hills, flowering meadows, and rocky peaks. There are old missions and gold mines en route, as well as farms and ranches. More than anything else, exploring this region consists of driving over miles of silent country road.

SIGHTS **Mission San Antonio de Pala** has been conducting mass since it was built in 1816. The original chapel and bell tower have been faithfully restored, and the long, low walls of the church interior are still decorated with primitive Indian frescoes. Located on the Pala Indian Reservation, it is the only mission primarily serving American Indians. Closed Monday and Tuesday. Admission. ~ Pala Mission Road, Pala; 760-742-3317, fax 760-742-3040.

From Pala, you can drive east along Route 76 to Pauma Valley, and then pick up scenic Route S6 south, which will carry you from the pine-rimmed high country of Cleveland National Forest to a verdant region of citrus groves. Route S6 south eventually brings you to the avocado-growing town of Escondido.

If you continue east on Route 76, you will reach a spiraling road that leads to that great silver dome in the sky, **Palomar Observatory**. With a clear shot heavenward from its 6100-foot-high perch, one of the world's largest reflecting telescopes scans the night

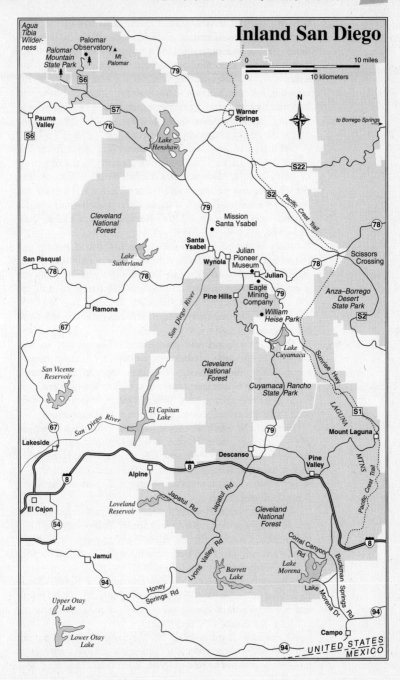

Inland San Diego

Agua Tibia Wilderness

Palomar Observatory

Palomar Mountain State Park

Mt Palomar

S6

S7

Pauma Valley

76

S6

Lake Henshaw

Warner Springs

to Borrego Springs

S22

S2

Pacific Crest Trail

Cleveland National Forest

79

Mission Santa Ysabel

78

Santa Ysabel

Lake Sutherland

Wynola

Julian Pioneer Museum

Julian

Scissors Crossing

San Pasqual

78

78

Pine Hills

Eagle Mining Company

79

Anza–Borrego Desert State Park

S2

Ramona

San Diego River

William Heise Park

67

Lake Cuyamaca

San Vicente Reservoir

Cleveland National Forest

Cuyamaca Rancho State Park

Sunrise Hwy

El Capitan Lake

79

S1

LAGUNA

Mount Laguna

67

San Diego River

Lakeside

Descanso

Pine Valley

MTNS

Pacific Crest Trail

8

Alpine

8

El Cajon

Japatul Rd

Japatul Rd

54

Loveland Reservoir

Cleveland National Forest

Corral Canyon Rd

8

Jamul

Lyons Valley Rd

Barrett Lake

Lake Morena

Buckman Springs Rd

94

Honey Springs Rd

Lake Morena Dr

94

Upper Otay Lake

Lower Otay Lake

Campo

94

UNITED STATES

MEXICO

0   10 miles

0   10 kilometers

N

skies for celestial secrets. Staffed by scientists and astronomers from the California Institute of Technology, this is an active research facility and, only reluctantly, a tourist attraction. You can glimpse the 200-inch Hale Telescope from the visitor's gallery, view a movie on how research is conducted, and look at photos in the museum, but there's little else to see or do. Unless of course you have the time and the legs to hike around the mountain (see the "Hiking" section at the end of this chapter). ~ On Mount Palomar at the end of Route S6 off Country Road 76; 760-742-2119.

Southwest of Mount Palomar, Route 76 ends at Route 79, which then courses south through backcountry to the tiny town of Santa Ysabel. **Mission Santa Ysabel**, where a 20th-century church stands on the site of an 1818 branch chapel, lacks the appeal of its sister missions. It does, however, feature Indian burial grounds and a museum. ~ 23013 Route 79, Santa Ysabel; 760-765-0810, fax 760-765-3494.

Most of the pilgrims in these parts are bound not for the chapel but for **Dudley's Bakery**, where dozens of kinds of bread, including a delicious jalapeño loaf, come steaming from the oven. Closed Monday and Tuesday. ~ 30218 Route 78 at Route 79, Santa Ysabel; 760-765-0488, 800-225-3348, fax 760-765-1565; www.dudleysbakery.com, e-mail dudleysbakery@dudleys bakery.com.

HIDDEN ►   Down the road in **Julian**, deemed a state historic site, you will come upon the belle of Southern California mountain mining towns. During the 1890s, the local mines employed 2000 miners, who hauled up $15 million in gold ore. Today the region produces red apples rather than gold nuggets and Julian, with its dusty aura of the Old West, has become a major tourist attraction.

Some of the falsefront stores located along **Main Street** are 19th-century originals. Have a look, for instance, at the 1897 **Julian Hotel**, and don't miss the **Julian Drug Store**, an old-style soda fountain serving sparkling sarsaparilla and conjuring images of boys in buckskin and girls in bonnets. The white clapboard **Town Hall** still stands.

Over at the **Julian Pioneer Museum**, the townsfolk have turned an old blacksmith's shop into a charming hodgepodge of local collectibles. Closed Monday from April through November; open weekends only from December through March. Admission. ~ 2811 Washington Street, Julian; 760-765-0227.

Although the tunnels of the **Washington Mine** (the first hardrock mine in Julian) have long since collapsed, the Julian Historical Society displays mining memorabilia depicting the mining era. ~ At the end of C Street, Julian.

Operations closed in 1942, but the **Eagle Mining Company** still offer tours of the tunnels of the Eagle and High Peak mines, and an opportunity to pan for gold. What seems certain to be a "tourist trap" is actually an interesting and educational experience. Open daily, weather-permitting. Admission. ~ At the end of C Street, Julian; 760-765-0036.

But remember, these days apples are actually the main business in Julian and dozens of orchards drape the hillsides below town. The countryside all around is quilted with pear and peach orchards as well, and there are Appaloosa ranches and roadside stands selling fruits and jams.

Route 79 points south from Julian along the ridge of the Laguna Mountains to the charred remains of **Cuyamaca Rancho State Park**. Isolated Indian country that was turned into a Spanish rancho in the 19th century, this former alpine sanctuary suffered a huge fire in October 2003 and is closed until further notice. For further information, call 760-767-5311; www.cuyamaca.statepark.org.

Near Lake Cuyamaca, Route S1 (Sunrise Highway), leads southeast to **Mount Laguna,** a region rich in recreational areas and desert views. You can continue your backcountry adventure by following the highway (which becomes Buckman Springs Road) south toward the Mexican border. This is rough, arid, scrub country, but you'll find an oasis at **Lake Morena**, where an oak-shaded park borders a fishing lake. Farther south lies the high desert outpost of **Campo**, with its sun-baked streets and 19th-century ruins. From here you can head south across the border or west toward the seaside metropolis of San Diego.

LODGING

Overnighting in the Mount Palomar area is limited to camping, except for the **Lazy H Ranch**. When the proprietor said the place "dates back to the '40s," I wondered which '40s—it has the look and feel of an early California homestead. The 11 rooms include amenities you'd expect from a budget-priced establishment—and no TVs or phones. But here you can adjourn to the Spanish-style patio, stroll through a garden with lemon trees, or take a dip in the pool. ~ 18767 Route 76, Pauma Valley; 760-742-3669, fax 760-742-3305. BUDGET.

AUTHOR FAVORITE

The 23-room **Julian Lodge**, designed after a 19th-century hotel, is a wood-frame structure that nicely recaptures the original. The rooms are small but well decorated with country Victorian furnishings. The breakfast parlor, where an expanded continental breakfast is served, is also quite homey, with oak tables and an inviting fireplace. ~ 2720 C Street, Julian; 760-765-1420, 800-542-1420, fax 760-765-2752; www.julianlodge.com. MODERATE TO DELUXE.

HIDDEN ▶   One of Southern California's oldest hostelries, the 1897 **Julian Hotel Bed and Breakfast** is a Victorian charmer. The place is often full, particularly on weekends, so reserve in advance. Two charming cottages and 18 rooms are done in period fashion with plenty of brass, lace, porcelain, and mahogany; all feature private baths. In addition to a historic building, guests share a lovely sitting room. ~ Main and B streets, Julian; 760-765-0201, 800-734-5854, fax 760-765-0327; www.julianhotel.com, e-mail b&b@julianhotel.com. MODERATE TO ULTRA-DELUXE.

Located on three acres in the heart of Julian's historic district, **Orchard Hill Country Inn** is a winsome getaway. The two-story lodge houses ten guest rooms done in American country decor, while four California Craftsman–style bungalows feature 12 suites complete with fireplaces, whirlpool tubs, and wrap-around porches. Stroll through the gardens of native plants and fruit trees or head for the hammock for a little cat nap. A full breakfast and afternoon hors d'oeuvres are included in the tab. ~ 2502 Washington Street, Julian; 760-765-1700, 800-716-7242, fax 760-765-0290; www.orchardhill.com, e-mail information@orchardhill.com. ULTRA-DELUXE.

HIDDEN ▶   **Shadow Mountain Ranch Bed and Breakfast**, a large, attractive country house near Julian, provides the area's most unique lodging in its "enchanted cottage," complete with pot-bellied stove; the "gnome home," with a stone waterfall shower; and "grandma's attic cottage," containing all of granny's antiques. For the adventurous, they even have a tiny treehouse with built-in toilet. There are more conventional rooms and cottages available as well. Full breakfast is included in the price. Reservations strongly recommended. Two-night minimum stay required on weekends. ~ 2771 Frisius Road, Pine Hills; phone/fax 760-765-0323; e-mail jcketch@julianweb.com. MODERATE TO DELUXE.

Also consider **Pine Hills Lodge**, a wonderfully rustic complex with a lodge and cabins that date back to 1912. Surrounded by pines and cedars, this cozy retreat features six European-style rooms (with shared bath) in the lodge. The ten cozy deluxe-priced cabins are woodframe structures complete with clawfoot tubs. Located at 4500 feet elevation, Pine Hills is a mini-resort featuring a restaurant, bar, and dinner theater. ~ 2960 La Posada Way, Pine Hills; 760-765-1100, fax 760-765-1121; www.pinehillslodge.com, e-mail info@pinehillslodge.com. MODERATE TO DELUXE.

The **Ramona Valley Inn** is a 39-room roadside motel, clean and comfortable, located 22 miles west of Julian. There's a pool; some rooms have kitchenettes. ~ 416 Main Street, Ramona; 760-789-6433, 800-648-4618, fax 760-789-2889. MODERATE.

Magnolia Travelodge is the nicest of a gaggle of affordable motels lining Route 8. You won't confuse its Spanish stucco styling with the Alhambra, but you will find the 48 attractively furnished rooms quite comfortable; all are equipped with microwaves and refrigerators. ~ 471 North Magnolia Avenue, El Cajon; 619-447-3999, 800-578-7878, fax 619-447-8403. MODERATE.

It's not listed or advertised anywhere, but if you need clean, cozy, low-cost lodgings, check out the **St. Francis Motel**. This trim 37-room court offers small, simply decorated rooms, some with kitchens. There is a pool. ~ 1368 East Main Street, El Cajon; 619-444-8147, fax 619-444-7290. BUDGET TO MODERATE.

El Rey is a favorite among smart locals and savvy travelers. The tasty Mexican-American fare includes huge servings of enchiladas, tostadas, tacos, and quesadillas. On the gringo side of the menu, there's steak, chicken, and seafood dishes. The rustic interior is paneled with pine. Closed Monday. ~ 16220 Route 76, Pauma Valley; 760-742-3343. BUDGET TO MODERATE.

DINING

◄ HIDDEN

The **Lazy H Ranch** serves up steaks, prime rib, chicken, and fish dishes in a family-style dining room set in the leafy environs of a four-acre orchard. Closed Monday. ~ Route 76, Pauma Valley; 760-742-3669. MODERATE TO DELUXE.

Hikers will appreciate **Palomar Mountain General Store**, whose adjacent vegetarian café serves hearty soups, salads, sandwiches, and hot entrées at lunch and dinner. The store is open daily; the café is closed Tuesday and Wednesday from Labor Day to Memorial Day. ~ Routes S6 and S7, Palomar Mountain; store 760-742-3496, café 760-742-4233, fax 760-742-2220. BUDGET.

The **Julian Grill**, situated in a 1920-vintage house, is cozy and folksy, especially around the living room fireplace. The menu emphasizes such hearty fare as steaks, prime rib, seafood, scampi, and chicken breast. They also feature sophisticated chef's specials like chicken Jerusalem. There's patio dining and a full bar. Champagne brunch is served on Sunday. No dinner on Monday. ~ 2224 Main Street, Julian; 760-765-0173; www.juliangrill.com. MODERATE TO DELUXE.

At **Romano's Dodge House** you will feel like a family guest. This intimate Italian restaurant, with its homespun ambience,

◄ HIDDEN

JUST LIKE MOM USED TO MAKE...

At least a dozen places in Julian prepare the local specialty, apple pie. But buyer beware: all pies are not created equal: some are definitely better than others. The pies at the **Julian Pie Company**, for instance, always have flaky crusts and just the right mix of apples, cinnamon, and sugar. ~ 2225 Main Street, Julian; 760-765-2449; www.julianpie.com, e-mail julianpiecompany@aol.com. BUDGET.

dishes out delicious chicken cacciatore, lasagna, and authentic homemade sausage. With its reasonable prices, Romano's is hard to beat. Closed Tuesday. ~ 2718 B Street, Julian; 760-765-1003, fax 760-765-3435; www.romanosjulian.com, e-mail panda@the grid.net. MODERATE.

HIDDEN ►

For buffalo burgers and local gossip, the townsfolk all head over to **Buffalo Bill's**. This friendly café, with its all-American cuisine and Early American decor serves up a standard-fare breakfast and lunch menu. No dinner. ~ 2603 B Street, Julian; 760-765-1560. BUDGET.

Las Delicias is a Mexican-Italian-American hybrid that serves comfort food along the lines of burritos, chicken-fried steak plates and hearty pastas. Breakfast, lunch and dinner. ~ 401 West Main Street, El Cajon; 619-442-7768, fax 619-442-7769. BUDGET TO MODERATE.

SHOPPING

Even if you're not in the market for nuts, dried fruit, or candy, a visit to **Bates Nut Farm** is mandatory. Name the nut and they have it—walnuts, cashews, pistachios, pecans, almonds, and peanuts—attractively displayed with an equally amazing variety of dried and glazed fruits, jellies, honey, and candy. ~ 15954 Woods Valley Road, Valley Center; 760-749-3333; www.batesnutfarm.biz.

Main Street in Julian is lined with dozens of antique, gift, clothing, and curio shops. Among the more intriguing ones are the **Antique Boutique**, with an especially nice selection of furniture and collectibles. ~ 2626 Main Street, Julian; 760-765-0541. **Julian's Toy Chest** features unusual educational toys and children's books. ~ 2116 Main Street, Julian; 760-765-2262. Located in the same building, **Quinn Knives** is where you can buy anything from a sword to a Swiss Army knife. ~ 2116 Main Street, Julian; 760-765-2230. Nearby is the **Old Julian Book House**, specializing in used and out-of-print antiquarian volumes. Call for hours. ~ 2230 Main Street, Julian; 760-765-1989. **Harvest Ranch Market** is an epicure's delight. Deli items, farm-fresh produce, international gourmet foods, picnic supplies, and rack after rack of fine wines are available at this pleasant country store. ~ 759 Jamacha Road, El Cajon; 619-442-0355.

NIGHTLIFE

Built in 1926 as a training camp for Jack Dempsey, **Pine Hills Lodge & Dinner Theatre** uses the champ's old ring as a dinner theater stage. And it looks as though they've scored a knockout. Nationwide, professional companies perform year-round. Admission. ~ 2960 La Posada Way, Pine Hills; 760-765-1100; www.pinehillslodge.com.

East County Performing Arts Center is the cultural flagship of the region, offering everything from chamber music to popular music. The cultural calendar here includes orchestras, dance companies, and pop concerts. ~ 210 East Main Street, El Cajon; 619-440-2277; www.ecpac.com.

The **Lamplighter Community Theatre** presents a year-round series of stage plays by a local theater group. ~ 8053 University Avenue, La Mesa; 619-464-4598; www.lamplighterstheater.org.

PALOMAR MOUNTAIN STATE PARK 🚶🚴⛵ Thick forests of pine, fir, and cedar combine with rambling mountain meadows to create a Sierra Nevada–like atmosphere. The average elevation here on the side of Mount Palomar is 5500 feet, so the evenings are cool and heavy snow is common in the winter. Doane Pond is stocked with trout. Biking is allowed on paved roads. Facilities include picnic areas, barbecues, restrooms, and showers. Day-use fee, $6. ~ Route S7 on top of Mount Palomar; 760-742-3462.

PARKS

CLEVELAND NATIONAL FOREST 🚶🚴🐎🎿 A major mountain preserve, this sprawling retreat is divided into three districts, two of which encompass more than 400,000 acres in San Diego County. Northernmost is the Palomar District, covering 189,000 acres around the famous observatory and stretching south beyond Lake Henshaw. Its main feature is the rugged Agua Tibia Wilderness Area, with several excellent trails. Horseback riding is permitted on trails designated for equestrian use. Farther south, the 216,000-acre Descanso District adjoins Cuyamaca Rancho State Park. Here the Laguna Mountain Recreation Area offers camping, picnicking, and hiking. There are picnic areas and restrooms. Day-use fee, $5. ~ Access to the Palomar District is via Routes 79, S6, and S7; the Descanso District and the Laguna Mountain Recreation Area are located on Route S1 (Sunrise Highway) a few miles north of Route 8; 619-445-6235, fax 619-445-1753; www.r5.fs.fed.us/cleveland.

> William Heise Park is one of the few county parks where the snowfall is sufficient for winter recreation.

▲ There are five campgrounds in the Palomar District, three of which accommodate RVs (no hookups); $12 to $15 per night. There are six campgrounds in the Descanso District, all of which accommodate both tents and RVs (no hookups); $10 to $14 a night. Reservations: 877-444-6777.

WILLIAM HEISE PARK 🚶🐎 Beautifully situated in a forest of pines and oaks, this preserve rests at 4200-foot elevation near the Laguna Mountains and Julian. The park is largely undeveloped and provides more than 1000 acres of hiking and riding trails (although only 200 trails are open for use after the 2003 wildfires). Picnic areas, restrooms, a playground, and showers are available. Parking fee, $2. ~ From Route 79 (one mile west of Julian) go south on Pine Hills Road for two miles, then east on Frisius Road for two more miles; 858-565-3600, fax 858-495-5840; www.co.san-diego.ca.us/parks.

◄ HIDDEN

▲ There are 100 tent/RV sites (no hookups), $14 to $16 per night; and 4 cabins equipped with heat and electricity, $35 per night.

ANZA-BORREGO DESERT STATE PARK Comprising more than 600,000 acres, Anza-Borrego is the largest state park in California and encompasses rugged mountains as well as desert terrain. Lucky visitors may also get a glimpse of the area's most famous inhabitant, the desert bighorn sheep. For more details on Anza-Borrego, see Chapter Seven.

LAKE MORENA PARK 🏃 🐎 🎣 🚃 🚤 🎿 As its name suggests, the highlight of this hideaway is a 1000-acre lake renowned for its bass, crappie, bluegill, and catfish. Located near the Mexican border, the park covers a total of 3250 acres, which range from flat terrain to low hills covered with oak and scrub. There are picnic areas, restrooms, and showers. Fishing facilities and boat rentals are available. Parking fee, $2. ~ Off Route 8 (Buckman Springs Road) in the southeast corner of San Diego County; 858-565-3600, fax 858-495-5840; www.scparks.org.

▲ There are 80 tent/RV sites; 50 have hookups; $12 to $16 per night. Ten wilderness cabins are also available; $25 per night.

LOS PEÑASQUITOS CANYON PRESERVE 🏃 🐎 This 3000-acre parcel, a canyonland wilderness several miles from the coast, features narrow rock gorges, mesa plateaus, and streamside woodlands. There are hiking trails as well as historic adobe houses to explore. Restrooms are available. Parking fee, $2. ~ Located off Black Mountain Road near Mira Mesa.

La Jolla

▼▼▼▼▼▼▼▼▼▼

A certain fascination centers around the origins of the name La Jolla. It means "jewel" in Spanish, but according to Indian legend it means "hole" or "caves." Both are fairly apt interpretations: this Mediterranean-style enclave perched on a bluff above the Pacific is indeed a jewel; and its dramatic coves and cliffs are pocked with sea caves. Choose your favorite interpretation but for goodness sake don't pronounce the name phonetically—it's "La Hoya."

La Jolla is a community within the city of San Diego, though it considers itself something more on the order of a principality—like Monaco. Locals call it "The Village" and boast that it's an ideal walking town, which is another way of saying La Jolla is a frustrating place to drive around. Narrow, curvy 1930s-era streets are jammed with traffic and hard to follow. A parking place in The Village is truly a jewel within the jewel.

The beauty of its seven miles of cliff-lined sea coast is La Jolla's *raison d'être*. Spectacular homes, posh hotels, chic boutiques, and gourmet restaurants crowd shoulder to shoulder for a better view of the ocean. Each of the area's many beaches has its own particular character and flock of local devotees. Though most beaches are narrow, rocky, and not really suitable for swimming or sunbathing, they are the best in the county for surfing and skindiving.

To get the lay of the land, wind your way up **Mount Soledad** (east on Nautilus Street from La Jolla Boulevard), where the view extends across the city skyline and out over the ocean. That large white cross at the summit is a memorial to the war dead and the setting for sunrise services every Easter Sunday.

Ah, but exploring The Village is the reason you're here, so head back down Nautilus Street, go right on La Jolla Boulevard, and continue until it leads into **Prospect Street**. This is La Jolla's hottest thoroughfare and the intersection with **Girard Avenue**, the town's traditional "main street," is the town epicenter. Here, in the heart of La Jolla, you are surrounded by the elite and elegant.

Although Girard Avenue features as wide a selection of shops as anyplace in San Diego, Prospect Street is much more interesting and stylish. By all means, walk Prospect's curving mile from the cottage shops and galleries on the north to the **Museum of Contemporary Art San Diego** on the south. The museum, by the way, is a piece of art in itself, one of many striking contemporary structures in La Jolla, originally designed by noted architect Irving Gill. The museum's highly regarded collection focuses on

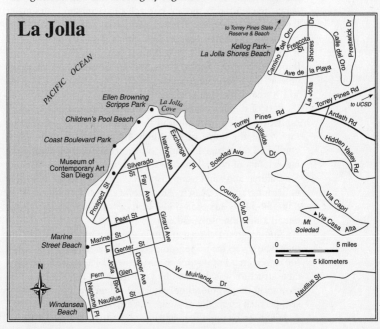

La Jolla

Minimalist, California, Pop, and other avant-garde developments in painting, sculpture, and photography. Closed Wednesday. Admission. ~ 700 Prospect Street; 858-454-3541, fax 858-454-6985; www.mcasd.org, e-mail info@mcasd.org.

The Museum of Contemporary Art San Diego's modern lines belie the fact that it was designed as a private villa back in 1915.

During this stroll along Prospect Street, also visit the lovely La Valencia Hotel, a very pink, very prominent resting place nicknamed "La V." This pink lady is a La Jolla landmark and a local institution, serving as both village pub and town meeting hall. You can feel the charm and sense the rich tradition of the place the moment you enter. While "La V" has always been a haven for the gods and goddesses of Hollywood, the Gregory Peck and Olivia de Haviland gang of old has been replaced by a client roster of current stars like Will Smith and Jada Pinkett. ~ 1132 Prospect Street; 858-454-0771, 800-451-0772, fax 858-456-3921; www.lavalencia.com, e-mail info@lavalencia.com.

Another center of interest lies at the northern end of La Jolla. The best beaches are here, stretching from the ritzy La Jolla Shores to the scientific sands at Scripps Beach.

Driving along North Torrey Pines Road you will undoubtedly cross the **University of California–San Diego** (858-534-2230) campus, a sprawling 1200 acres set on a mesa above the Pacific Ocean. Home to over 22,000 undergraduate and graduate students, the university boasts natural chaparral canyons, green lawns, and eucalyptus groves, contrasted with urban student plazas and buildings. Spread throughout this expansive campus is the **Stuart Collection of sculpture**, featuring permanent outdoor sculptures by leading contemporary artists. Maps are available at the information kiosk. ~ 858-534-2117, fax 858-534-9713; stuartcollection.ucsd.edu.

Part of the university is the **Scripps Institution of Oceanography**, the oldest institution in the nation devoted to oceanography and the home of the **Birch Aquarium at Scripps**. Here you'll find 60 marine life tanks, a manmade tidepool, breathtaking exhibits of coastal underwater habitats, interactive displays for children and adults, and displays illustrating recent advances in oceanographic research. Admission. ~ 2300 Expedition Way; 858-534-3474, fax 858-534-7114; www.aquarium.ucsd.edu, e-mail aquariuminfo@ucsd.edu.

Another research center, the **Salk Institute**, created by the man whose vaccine helped vanquish polio, is renowned not only for its research but its architecture as well. The surrealistic concrete structure was designed by Louis Kahn in 1960 to be an environment that would stimulate original thinking. It is a stunning site, perched on the lip of a high canyon overlooking the Pacific. A daily tour, by appointment only, is conducted in the morning.

~ 10010 North Torrey Pines Road, just north of the University of California–San Diego campus; tour information, 858-453-4100 ext. 1200, fax 858-625-2404; www.salk.edu.

Next to the institute is the **Torrey Pines Glider Port**, where you can watch hang-gliding and paragliding masters soar over the waves from atop a 360-foot cliff. ~ 2800 Torrey Pines Scenic Drive; 858-452-9858, 877-359-8326, fax 858-452-9983; www.flytorrey.com, e-mail aircal@ix.netcom.com.

Trails leading down to the notorious **Black's Beach** begin here. Black's is San Diego's unofficial, illegal, ever-loving nude beach. And a beautiful strip of natural landscape it is.

◄ *HIDDEN*

Bordering Black's on the north is **Torrey Pines State Reserve and Beach**, whose 1750-acre preserve was established to protect one of the world's rarest pine trees, the Torrey Pine. The tree itself is a gnarled and twisted specimen. Centuries ago these pines covered the southern coast of California; today they are indigenous only to Santa Rosa Island, off the coast of Santa Barbara, and to the reserve. A network of trails through this blufftop reserve makes hiking sheer pleasure. Among the rewards are the views, extending along the cliffs and ocean, and the chance to walk quietly among La Jolla's rare treasures. ~ Located west of North Torrey Pines Road, two miles north of Genesee Avenue.

Like a Monopoly master, La Jolla possesses the lion's share of "Park Place" accommodations in the San Diego area. Understandably, there are no budget hotels in this fashionable village by the sea.

LODGING

Sands of La Jolla is a small, 39-room motel on a busy thoroughfare just a quick drive away from the bustle of Girard Avenue and Prospect Street. Rooms (kitchenettes are available) are not exactly designer showcases, but they are tastefully appointed and neatly maintained. Amenities include a heated pool and mini-fridges. ~ 5417 La Jolla Boulevard; 858-459-3336, 800-643-0530, fax 858-454-0922; www.sandsoflajolla.com, e-mail sandsoflajolla@aol.com. MODERATE.

Small, European-style hotels have always been popular in La Jolla, and the granddaddy of them all is the **The Grande Colonial**. Established in 1913, the 75-room establishment features rooms lavishly decorated with historically inspired furnishings. Oceanfront rooms provide matchless views. There's a restaurant on site. ~ 910 Prospect Street; 858-454-2181, 800-826-1278, fax 858-454-5679; www.thegrandecolonial.com, e-mail info@thegrande colonial.com. ULTRA-DELUXE.

More than just a hotel, **La Valencia** is a La Jolla institution and one of the loveliest hotels in San Diego. Resplendent in pink stucco and Spanish tile, it is perched on a breezy promontory overlooking the coves and sea cliffs of La Jolla. From the moment guests enter via a trellis-covered tile loggia into a lobby that could pass for King Juan Carlos' living room, they are enveloped in elegance. The 106 private accommodations reflect the European feel—that is, they tend to run on the small side and are furnished in reproduction antiques. Ah, but out back there's a beautiful garden terrace opening onto the sea and tumbling down to a free-form swimming pool edged with lawn. Facilities include a gym, sauna, whirlpool, and three distinctive restaurants. ~ 1132 Prospect Street; 858-454-0771, 800-451-0772, fax 858-456-3921; www.lavalencia.com, e-mail info@lavalencia.com. ULTRA-DELUXE.

Also smack dab in the Village is the **Empress Hotel**, a five-story L-shaped building set on a quiet street just a stone's throw from both the beach and the bustle of Prospect Street. A contemporary establishment blending Victorian and European boutique styles, its 73 spacious rooms and suites offer amenities such as mini-fridges, bathrobes, coffeemakers, and high-speed internet; two "Green" suites have filtered air and water. If you're looking to splash out, you probably can't get any fancier than one of the two jacuzzi suites outfitted with a baby grand piano and ocean views. There are also fitness facilities, a sauna, a spa, and a restaurant. Enjoy complimentary continental breakfast on the flower-lined patio. ~ 7766 Fay Avenue; 858-454-3001, 888-369-9900, fax 858-454-6387; www.empress-hotel.com, e-mail reservations 411@empress-hotel.com. ULTRA-DELUXE.

Tucked away on the north fringe of the village is **Andrea Villa Inn**, a classy looking 49-unit motel that packs more amenities than some resorts. There is a pool, a jacuzzi, and continental breakfast service. The rooms are spacious and professionally decorated with quality furniture. Be forewarned however, that some guests have complained that the inn was not as clean as they would have liked. ~ 2402 Torrey Pines Road; 858-459-3311, 800-411-2141, fax 858-459-1320; www.andreavilla.com, e-mail info@andreavilla.com. DELUXE.

Just as the village boasts San Diego's finest selection of small hotels, it can also claim a well-known bed and breakfast. **The Bed and Breakfast Inn at La Jolla**, listed as a historical site, was designed as a private home in 1913 by the architect Irving Gill. The John Phillip Sousa family resided here in 1921. Faithfully restored by its present owners as a 15-room inn, it stands today as Gill's finest example of Cubist-style architecture. Ideally situated a block and a half from the ocean, this inn is the essence of La Jolla. Each guest room features an individual decorative theme carried out in period furnishings. Some have fireplaces and ocean views. All have private baths. Bicycles are available for guests' use. ~ 7753 Draper Avenue; 858-456-2066, 800-582-2466, fax 858-456-1510; www.innlajolla.com, e-mail bed+breakfast@innlajolla.com. ULTRA-DELUXE.

La Jolla's only true beachfront hotel is **Sea Lodge on La Jolla Shores Beach**. Designed and landscaped to resemble an old California hacienda, this 128-room retreat overlooks the Pacific on a mile-long beach. With its stuccoed arches, terra-cotta roofs, ceramic tilework, fountains, and flowers, Sea Lodge offers a relaxing south-of-the-border setting. Guest rooms are large; most feature balconies, some have kitchens, and all have access to the usual amenities: fitness room, sauna, jacuzzi, pool, and tennis courts. ~ 8110 Camino del Oro; 858-459-8271, 800-237-5211, fax 858-456-9346; www.sealodge.com. ULTRA-DELUXE.

> A great stop for picnic supplies is the La Jolla Farmers Market, held Sunday at the La Jolla Elementary School. ~ Center and Girard streets.

Just north of UCSD, the **Hilton La Jolla Torrey Pines**, adorned with marble and polished wood, is an outstanding white-glove establishment. Here, art deco visits the 21st century in a series of terraces that lead past plush dining rooms, multi-tiered fountains, a luxurious swimming pool, and a fitness center. Avid golfers will appreciate its location—the 18th fairway of the Torrey Pines Golf Course, and the site of the 2008 U.S. Open. ~ 10950 North Torrey Pines Road; 858-558-1500, 800-762-6160, fax 858-450-4584; www.lajollatorreypines.hilton.com, e-mail santp-reservations@hilton.com. ULTRA-DELUXE.

DINING

Just as it is blessed with many fine hotels, La Jolla is a restaurant paradise. **George's at the Cove** based its climb to success on its knockout view of the water, a casual, contemporary environment, fine service, and a trendsetting regional menu. Daily menus incorporate the freshest seafood, beef, lamb, poultry, and pasta available. Downstairs in the fine-dining room are selections such as sesame-crusted tuna with eggplant-miso purée, and roasted lamb loin and braised lamb shoulder with spicy Medjool date cous cous. The food presentation alone is a work of art. ~ 1250 Prospect Place; 858-454-4244, fax 858-454-5458; www.georgesatthecove.com. MODERATE TO ULTRA-DELUXE.

◄ HIDDEN

For no-frills sushi and *bento* boxes, head for **Yummy Maki Yummy Box**, located in a nondescript strip mall. The seafood is fresh, and the service is courteous and attentive. No lunch. Closed Sunday. ~ 3211 Holiday Court #101; 858-587-9848. BUDGET.

Jose's Court Room, a noisy, down-to-earth Mexican pub, is the best place in town for quick, casual snacks. They offer all the typical taco, tostada, and enchilada plates plus tasty sautéed shrimp and chicken *ranchero* dinners. There's also a Mexican-style weekend breakfast. ~ 1037 Prospect Street; 858-454-7655. BUDGET TO MODERATE.

Illuminated only by the flickering of candles and the incandescent glow of fish tanks, the **Manhattan** at the Empress Hotel features cozy booths, boisterous patrons, and a singing maître d', successfully replicating a New York City family-style Italian restaurant. Popular dishes include cannelloni, veal marsala, and chicken piccata; in addition there are wonderful caesar salads and tiramisu. No lunch Sunday or Monday. ~ Empress Hotel, 7766 Fay Avenue; 858-459-0700, fax 858-454-4741. MODERATE TO ULTRA-DELUXE.

Set in an early-1900s bungalow surrounded by a white picket fence, **The Cottage** serves up breakfast and lunch fare melding California, Southwest, and Mediterranean flavors: French toast, Mediterranean omelette, vegetable frittata, fish tacos, penne pesto, and Napa Valley beef stew. Dinner brings Santa Fe shrimp brochettes, meatloaf, Cajun jambalaya pasta, and steak. A shady patio table is ideal when the sun's out (which is often). No dinner from October through May. ~ 7702 Fay Avenue; 858-454-8409, fax 858-454-0284; www.cottagelajolla.com. BUDGET TO MODERATE.

HIDDEN ▶

If, during your shopping foray down Girard Avenue, you come across a line of locals snaking out of a small, unassuming eatery, you've no doubt reached **Girard Gourmet**. You may have to wait to partake of the deli goods (salads, quiches, sandwiches, pastries), but it's worth it. Take it to go, or dine out on the sidewalk or inside in an alpine-like setting. ~ 7837 Girard Avenue; 858-454-3321, fax 858-454-2325; www.funcookies.com, e-mail info@funcookies.com. BUDGET.

SHOPPING

Once a secluded seaside village, La Jolla has emerged as a world-famous resort community that offers style and substance. The shopping focuses on Girard Avenue (from Torrey Pines Road to Prospect Street) and along Prospect Street. Both are lined with designer boutiques, specialty shops, and art galleries.

For two levels of hip and stylish designer duds and shoes, stop by **Let's Go**. ~ 7863 Girard Avenue; 858-459-2337; www.houseofstyle.com.

In La Jolla's numerous galleries, traditional art blends with contemporary paintings, and rare Oriental antiques complement

AUTHOR FAVORITE

Housed as it is in a landmark 1903 cottage covered with wisteria, **John Cole's Book Shop** provides a refuge from these slick, chic La Jolla boutiques. Its nooks and crannies are lined with books ranging from best sellers to rare editions. Closed Sunday and Monday. ~ 780 Prospect Street; 858-454-4766.

20th-century bronze sculpture. The **Tasende Gallery** has a large display area and patio garden that pack in contemporary art by big names like Henry Moore and Roberto Matta. The gallery showcases sculpture, paintings, and drawings as well. Closed Sunday and Monday. ~ 820 Prospect Street; 858-454-3691.

The dark red **Whaling Bar** attracts lots of La Jolla's big fish. A fine place to relax and nibble gourmet hors d'oeuvres. ~ La Valencia Hotel, 1132 Prospect Street; 858-454-0771.

NIGHTLIFE

Among the most romantic restaurants in town, **Top O' The Cove** features an equally romantic bar with live entertainment on Saturday. ~ 1216 Prospect Street; 858-454-7779.

A panoramic view of the ocean makes **French Gourmet at the Larias** the perfect place to enjoy live music Tuesday through Saturday. ~ Hotel La Jolla, 7955 La Jolla Shores Drive; 858-459-0541.

The **Comedy Store** features comedians exclusively, many with national reputations. Closed Monday and Tuesday. Cover. ~ 916 Pearl Street; 858-454-9176; www.thecomedystore.com.

D. G. Wills Books is a tiny literary haven featuring lectures and poetry readings, as well as an occasional jazz night. ~ 7461 Girard Avenue; 858-456-1800.

◄ *HIDDEN*

The **La Jolla Music Society** hosts year-round performances by such notables as Anne Sophie Von Otter, the Mark Morris Dance Group, and the Royal Philharmonic Orchestra. ~ 858-459-3728; www.ljms.org.

The prestigious **La Jolla Playhouse**, located on the University of California's San Diego campus, produces innovative dramas and musicals and spotlights famous actors during the summer and fall. ~ 858-550-1010; www.lajollaplayhouse.com.

TORREY PINES STATE RESERVE AND BEACH 🏃 ⚓ 🏊 🛶 A long, wide, sandy stretch adjacent to Los Peñasquitos Lagoon and Torrey Pines State Reserve, this beach is highly visible from the highway and therefore heavily used. It is popular for sunning, swimming, surf fishing, and volleyball. Nearby trails lead through the reserves with their lagoons, rare trees, and abundant birdlife. Keep in mind that food is prohibited in the reserve but allowed on the beach. The beach is patrolled year-round, but lifeguards are on duty only in summer. Restrooms are available. Day-use fee, $4 per vehicle. ~ Located just south of Carmel Valley Road, Del Mar; 858-755-2063, fax 858-509-0981; www.torreypine. org, e-mail torreypines@ixpres.com.

BEACHES & PARKS

BLACK'S BEACH 🏄 🚾 🛶 One of the world's most famous nude beaches, on hot summer days it attracts bathers by the thou-

◄ *HIDDEN*

sands, many in the buff. The sand is lovely and soft and the 300-foot cliffs rising up behind make for a spectacular setting. Hang-gliders and paragliders soar from the glider port above to add even more enchantment. Swimming is dangerous; beware of the currents and exercise caution as the beach is infrequently patrolled. Surfing is excellent; one of the most awesome beach breaks in California. Lifeguards are here in summer. ~ From Route 5 in La Jolla follow Genesee Avenue west; turn left on North Torrey Pines Road, then right at Torrey Pines Scenic Drive. There's a parking lot at the Torrey Pines Glider Port, but trails to the beach from here are very steep and often dangerous. If you're in doubt just park at the Torrey Pines State Reserve lot one mile north and walk back along the shore to Black's during low tide.

SCRIPPS BEACH 🏃 ⛵ With coastal bluffs above, narrow sand beach below, and rich tidepools offshore, this is a great strand for beachcombers. Two **underwater reserves** as well as museum displays at the Scripps Institution of Oceanography are among the attractions. There are museum facilities at Scripps Institution. ~ Scripps Institution is located at the 8600 block of La Jolla Shores Drive in La Jolla. You can park at Kellogg Park–La Jolla Shores Beach and walk north to Scripps.

KELLOGG PARK–LA JOLLA SHORES BEACH 🏊 🏊 The sand is wide and the swimming is easy at La Jolla Shores; so, naturally, the beach is covered with bodies whenever the sun appears. Just to the east is Kellogg Park, an ideal place for a picnic, swimming, and surfing. There are restrooms, a playground, and lifeguards. ~ Off Camino del Oro and Costa Boulevard.

The spectacular natural beauty of La Jolla Cove makes it one of the most photographed beaches of Southern California.

ELLEN BROWNING SCRIPPS PARK AND LA JOLLA COVE 🏊 ⛵ This grassy park sits on a bluff overlooking the cove and is the scenic focal point of La Jolla. The naturally formed cove is almost always free of breakers, has a small but sandy beach, and is a popular spot for swimmers and divers. It's also the site of the **La Jolla Ecological Reserve**, an underwater park and diving reserve. There are picnic areas, restrooms, shuffleboard, and lifeguards. ~ 1100 Coast Boulevard at Girard Avenue.

CHILDREN'S POOL BEACH 🏊 🏄 At the north end of Coast Boulevard Beach (see below) a concrete breakwater loops around a small lagoon. Harbor seals like to sun themselves on the rock promontories here. Despite its name, the beach's strong rip currents and seasonal rip tides can make swimming hazardous, so check with lifeguards. There are lifeguards and restrooms. Fishing is good from the surf. ~ Located off of Coast Boulevard in La Jolla.

COAST BOULEVARD PARK After about a half-mile of wide sandy beach, the bluffs and tiny pocket beaches that characterize Windansea (see below) reappear at what locals call "Coast Beach." The pounding waves make watersports unsafe, but savvy locals find the smooth sandstone boulders and sandy coves perfect for reading, sunbathing, and picnicking. ~ Paths lead to the beach at several points along Coast Boulevard.

MARINE STREET BEACH Separated from Windansea to the south by towering sandstone bluffs, this is a much wider and more sandy strand, favored by sunbathers, swimmers, skindivers, and frisbee-tossing youths. The rock-free shoreline is ideal for walking or jogging. The beach is good for board and bodysurfing; watch for rip currents and high surf. ~ Turn west off La Jolla Boulevard on Marine Street.

WINDANSEA BEACH This is surely one of the most picturesque beaches in the country. It has been portrayed in the movies and was immortalized in Tom Wolfe's 1968 nonfiction classic, *The Pumphouse Gang*, about the surfers who still hang around the old pumphouse (part of the city's sewer system), zealously protecting their famous surf from outsiders. Windansea is rated by experts as one of the best surfing locales on the West Coast. In the evenings, crowds line the Neptune Place sidewalk, which runs along the top of the cliffs, to watch the sunset. North of the pumphouse are several sandy nooks sandwiched between sandstone outcroppings. Romantic spot! There are lifeguards in the summer. ~ At the end of Nautilus Street.

HERMOSA TERRACE PARK This beach is said to be "seasonally sandy," which is another way of saying it's rocky at times. Best chance for sand is in the summer when this is a pretty good sunning beach. The surfing is good. There are no facilities. ~ Off Winamar Avenue; a paved path leads to the beach.

BIRD ROCK Named for a large sandstone boulder about 50 yards off the coast, this beach is rocky and thus favored by divers. The surf rarely breaks here, but when it does this spot is primo for surfing; exercise caution. Fishing is also good. Facilities are nonexistent. ~ At the end of Bird Rock Avenue.

SOUTH BIRD ROCK Tidepools are the attractions along this rocky, cliff-lined beach. Surfing is best in summer. ~ From Midway or Forward streets in La Jolla follow paths down to the beach.

TOURMALINE SURFING PARK A year-round reef break and consistently big waves make La Jolla one of the best surfing areas on the West Coast. Tourmaline is popular with surfers. Skindiving is permitted, as is swimming. You'll find picnic areas and restrooms. ~ At the end of Tourmaline Street.

▼▼▼▼▼▼▼▼▼▼▼▼
Mission Bay Park Area

Dredged from a shallow, mosquito-infested tidal bay, 4600-acre Mission Bay Park is the largest municipal aquatic park in the world. For San Diego's athletic set it is Mecca, a recreational paradise dotted with islands and lagoons and ringed by 27 miles of sandy beaches.

Here, visitors join with residents to enjoy swimming, sailing, windsurfing, waterskiing, fishing, jogging, cycling, golf, and tennis. Or perhaps a relaxing day of kite flying and sunbathing.

SIGHTS

More than just a playground, Mission Bay Park features a shopping complex, resort hotels, restaurants, and the popular marine park, **SeaWorld San Diego**. This 189-acre park-within-a-park is one of the world's largest oceanarium. Admission. ~ SeaWorld Drive; 619-226-3901, fax 619-226-3996; www.seaworld.com.

Among the attractions are killer whales; one of the largest penguin colonies north of Antarctica; a "Forbidden Reef" inhabited by bat rays and over 100 moray eels; and "Rocky Point Preserve," an exhibit boasting a wave pool, pettable dolphins, and a colony of California sea otters. "Manatee Rescue," only one of three U.S. manatee exhibits outside of Florida, is a venture designed to relieve the Florida SeaWorld of its overflowing supply of rehabilitating manatees. The exhibit provides over 800 feet of underwater viewing. The park also includes "Journey to Atlantis," a wet and wild ride that takes thrill seekers on a tour of Poseidon's island nation; a Sky Tower that lifts visitors nearly 300 feet above Mission Bay; a helicopter simulator dubbed the "Wild Arctic" that takes visitors to an Arctic research station to explore two capsized sailing ships from a century-old wreck and see native Arctic mammals; and "Shipwreck Rapids," a wet and winding ride in a raft-like innertube.

One of the best bargains at SeaWorld is the guided tour of the park (fee). It's expert guides take the guests on adventures that may include the Shark Laboratory, the animal care area, and killer whale facility. I prefer simply to watch the penguins waddling about on a simulated iceberg and zipping around after fish in their glass-contained ocean, or to peer in at the fearsome makos at "Shark Encounter." The park's magnificent marine creatures are all the entertainment I need.

Down along the oceanfront, **Mission Beach** is strung out along a narrow jetty of sand protecting Mission Bay from the sea. Mission Boulevard threads its way through this eclectic, wall-to-wall mix of shingled beach shanties, condominiums, and luxury homes.

The historic 1925 "Giant Dipper" has come back to life after years of neglect at **Belmont Park**. One of only two West Coast seaside coasters, this beauty is not all the park has to offer. There's

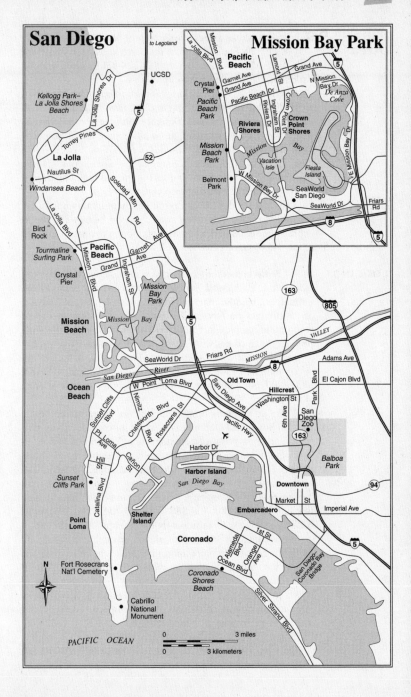

San Diego

to Legoland

UCSD

Kellogg Park–
La Jolla Shores
Beach

La Jolla Shores Dr

5

Torrey Pines Rd

La Jolla

Nautilus St

Windansea Beach

52

Soledad Mtn Rd

Bird
Rock

La Jolla Blvd

Tourmaline
Surfing Park

**Pacific
Beach**

Garnet Ave

Grand   Ave

Crystal
Pier

Mission Blvd

Ingraham St

**Mission
Beach**

Mission   Bay

Mission
Bay
Park

5

SeaWorld Dr

San Diego River

Friars Rd

MISSION   VALLEY

163

805

8

Adams Ave

**Ocean
Beach**

W Point Loma Blvd

Nimitz   Blvd

Chatsworth   Blvd

Rosecrans   St

Old Town

San Diego Ave

Hillcrest

Washington   St

El Cajon Blvd

Park Blvd

6th Ave

**San
Diego
Zoo**

163

Pacific   Hwy

Sunset Cliffs Blvd

Pt Loma Ave

Canon St

Hill St

Harbor Dr

Harbor Island

Harbor Island

San   Diego   Bay

**Balboa
Park**

Downtown

Market   St

94

*Sunset
Cliffs Park*

Catalina Blvd

**Shelter
Island**

Embarcadero

Imperial Ave

**Point
Loma**

Coronado

Alameda Blvd

Orange   Ave

Ocean Blvd

1st St

San Diego–Coronado Bay Bridge

5

N

Fort Rosecrans
Nat'l Cemetery

*Coronado
Shores
Beach*

Silver Strand Blvd

Cabrillo
National
Monument

PACIFIC   OCEAN

0   3 miles

0   3 kilometers

Mission Bay Park

La Jolla Blvd

Mission Blvd

**Pacific
Beach**

Garnet Ave

Crystal
Pier

Grand Ave

*Pacific
Beach
Park*

Pacific Beach Dr

Lamont St

Ingraham St

Grand Ave

N Mission
Bay Dr

5

*De Anza
Cove*

**Riviera
Shores**

Riviera Dr

Crown Point Dr

**Crown
Point
Shores**

Mission

*Mission
Beach
Park*

W Mission Bay Dr

*Vacation
Isle*

Bay

*Fiesta
Island*

E Mission Bay Dr

**Belmont
Park**

**SeaWorld
San Diego**

SeaWorld Dr

Friars
Rd

8

5

also a carousel, a video arcade, a large indoor swimming pool, and a host of shops and eateries along the beach and boardwalk. ~ 3146 Mission Boulevard or on the beach at Mission Boulevard and West Mission Bay Drive; 858-228-9283; www.belmont park.com, e-mail info@belmontpark.com.

Pacific Beach, which picks up at the northern edge of the bay, is the liveliest of the city beaches, an area packed with high school and college students. Designer shorts, a garish Hawaiian shirt, strapped-on sunglasses, and a skateboard are all you need to fit in perfectly along the frenetic boardwalk at "PB." If you're missing any or all of these accoutrements, Garnet Avenue is the city's core, lined with skate and surf shops and funky boutiques, as well as colorful bars and taco eateries.

Stop and see the 1920s **Crystal Pier** with its tiny hotel built out over the waves. Or take a stroll along the boardwalk, checking out the sunbathers, skaters, joggers, and cyclists. ~ Located at the end of Garnet Avenue.

LODGING   Pacific Beach boasts the San Diego County lodging with the most character of all. **Crystal Pier Hotel** is a throwback to the 1930s. Fittingly so, because that's when this quaint-looking assemblage of 29 cottages on Crystal Pier was built. This blue-and-white woodframe complex, perched over the waves, features tiny little cottages. Each comes with a kitchen and patio-over-the-sea, not to mention your own parking place on the pier. A unique discovery indeed. ~ 4500 Ocean Boulevard, Pacific Beach; 858-483-6983, 800-748-5894, fax 858-483-6811; www.crystalpier.com. ULTRA-DELUXE.

There aren't many beachfront facilities along Pacific Beach, Mission Beach, and Ocean Beach, except for condominiums. One particularly pretty four-unit condominium, **Ventanas al Mar**, overlooks the ocean in Mission Beach. Its contemporary two- and three-bedroom units feature fireplaces, jacuzzis, kitchens, and washer-dryers. They sleep as many as eight people. In the summer, these rent by week only. ~ 3631 Ocean Front Walk, Mission Beach; 858-488-1580, 800-869-7858, fax 858-488-1584; www. billluther.com, e-mail vacation@billluther.com. ULTRA-DELUXE.

A real bargain is **Banana Bungalow**, a privately run hostel right on Pacific Beach. The accommodations are of the co-ed bunk-bed variety for the backpacking set who don't mind sharing rooms with strangers. You must be a traveler with an out-of-state license or passport. A complimentary breakfast is served every morning. Accommodations are on a first-come, first-served basis. ~ 707 Reed Avenue, Pacific Beach; 858-273-3060, 800-546-7835, fax 858-273-1440; www.bananabungalow.com. BUDGET.

Only one Mission Bay resort stands out as unique—the **San Diego Paradise Point Resort & Spa**. Over 40 acres of lush gardens, lagoons, and white-sand beach surround the bungalows of this 462-room resort. Except for some fancy suites, room decor is basic and pleasant, with quality furnishings. But guests don't spend much time in their rooms anyway. At Paradise Point there's more than a mile of beach, catamaran and bike rentals, a spa, a fitness center, five tennis courts, five pools, a basketball court, sand volleyball, two restaurants, and an 18-hole putting course. A self-contained island paradise. ~ 1404 West Vacation Road, Mission Beach; 858-274-4630, 800-344-2626, fax 858-581-5929; www.paradisepoint.com, e-mail reservations@paradis epoint.com. ULTRA-DELUXE.

Critic's choice for the area's best omelettes is **Broken Yolk Café**. Choose from nearly 30 of these eggy creations or invent your own. If you can eat it all within an hour, the ironman/woman special—including a dozen eggs, mushrooms, onions, cheese, etc.—costs only $1.98. Faint or fail and you pay much more. They make soups, sandwiches, and salads, too. Outdoor patio seating is available. Breakfast and lunch only. ~ 1851 Garnet Avenue, Pacific Beach; 858-270-0045, fax 858-270-4745; www.brokenyolkcafe. com. BUDGET.

DINING

The most creative restaurant in Pacific Beach is **Château Orleans**, one of the city's finest Cajun-Creole restaurants. Tasty appetizers fresh from the bayous include Louisiana crabcakes and Southern-fried 'gator bites. Yes, indeed, they eat alligators down in Cajun country, and you should be brave enough to find out why. Mardi Gras gumbo chocked with crawfish, Uncle Bubba's prime rib steak, chicken sauce piquant, and colorful jambalaya are typical menu choices. Everything is authentic except the decor, which thankfully shuns board floors and bare bulbs in favor of carpets, original New Orleans artwork, and patio seating in a New Orleans–style garden. Live jazz and blues Thursday through Saturday. Dinner only. Closed Sunday. ~ 926 Turquoise Street, Pacific Beach; 858-488-6744, fax 858-488-6745; www.chateauorleans.com. MODERATE TO DELUXE.

The Château Orleans features live jazz and blues Thursday through Saturday.

The Mission Cafe is a casual neighborhood restaurant where folks are likely to chat with whoever is dining next to them. The ambience is funky, the furniture eclectic, and the walls are enlivened with local art. Blending Asian and Latin influences, the cuisine emphasizes food that is healthy, tasty, and original. There are breakfast standards with a twist—the French toast is served with berries and blueberry purée. If you're in the mood for something more Mexican, order the *plata verde con huevos* (slightly sweet tamales with eggs, roasted chile verde and cheese). For lunchtime there are such creations as ginger-sesame chicken roll-up or Baja shrimp wrap. You can also choose from several soups, salads, and sandwiches. No dinner. ~ 3795 Mission Boulevard, Mission Beach; 858-488-9060. BUDGET.

SHOPPING Commercial enterprises in the beach communities cater primarily to sun worshipers. Beachie boutiques and rental shops are everywhere. A shopping center on the beach, **Belmont Park** has a host of shops and restaurants. ~ 3146 Mission Boulevard, Mission Bay Park.

The Promenade Mall at Pacific Beach, a modern, Mediterranean-style shopping complex, houses a dozen or so smartly decorated specialty shops and restaurants. A farmer's market is held here on Saturday. ~ Located on Mission Boulevard between Pacific Beach Drive and Reed Street, Pacific Beach; 858-490-9097.

Garnet Avenue is the place in "PB" to hook up with laidback street styles, skintight clubwear, one-of-a-kind outfits, and tattoos. **Anatomic Rag** carries vintage wear that'll tickle the fancy of modern-day hep cats and kittens. ~ 1336 Garnet Avenue, Pacific Beach; 858-274-3597.

NIGHTLIFE **Blind Melons,** beside the Crystal Pier, is best described as a Chicago beach bar featuring punk rock on Tuesday, a national blues act twice a month, and local acts the other nights of the week. Cover. ~ 710 Garnet Avenue, Pacific Beach; 858-483-7844; www. home.fan.rr.com/melonsx.

The **Cannibal Bar** features a variety of live music Wednesday through Sunday. Bands may play blues, ska, rock, or even jazz. Closed Monday and Tuesday. Cover. ~ Catamaran Hotel, 3999 Mission Boulevard, Pacific Beach; 858-488-1081; www.catama ranresort.com.

The Pennant is a Mission Beach landmark where local beachies congregate en masse on the deck to get rowdy and watch the sunset. The entertainment here is the clientele. ~ 2893 Mission Boulevard, Mission Beach; 858-488-1671.

BEACHES & PARKS **PACIFIC BEACH PARK** 🚲 🏊 🎣 ⚓ At its south end, "PB" is a major gathering place, its boardwalk crowded with teens and assorted rowdies, but a few blocks north, just before Crystal Pier, the boardwalk becomes a quieter concrete promenade that follows scenic, sloping cliffs. The beach widens here and the crowd becomes more family oriented. The surf is moderate and fine for swimming and bodysurfing. Pier and surf fishing are great for corbina and surf perch. South of the pier Ocean Boulevard becomes a pedestrian-only mall with a bike path, benches, and picnic tables. Amenities include restrooms, lifeguards, and restaurants. ~ Located near Grand Avenue and Pacific Beach Drive.

MISSION BAY PARK 🛶 🦆 🎣 🚣 🏊 🚤 🛥 One of the nation's largest and most diverse city-owned aquatic parks, Mission Bay has something to suit just about everyone's recreational interest. Key areas and facilities are as follows: **Dana Landing** and **Quivira Basin** make up the southwest portion of this 4600-acre park. Most boating activities begin here, where port headquarters and a large marina are located. Adjacent is **Bonita Cove**, used for swimming, picnicking and volleyball. There is a softball field at **Mariner's Point**. Mission Boulevard shops, restaurants, and recreational equipment rentals are within easy walking distance. **Ventura Cove** houses a large hotel complex but its sandy beach is open to the public. Calm waters make it a popular swimming spot for small children.

> Mission Bay Park was a vast tidal marsh until 1944, when the city converted the land into an aquatic park.

Vacation Isle and **Ski Beach** are easily reached via the bridge on Ingraham Street, which bisects the island. The west side contains public swimming areas, boat rentals, and a model yacht basin. Ski Beach is on the east side and is the favorite spot in the bay for waterskiing. **Fiesta Island** is situated on the southeast side of the park. It's ringed with soft sand swimming beaches and laced with jogging, cycling, and skating paths. A favorite spot for fishing from the quieter coves and for kite flying. On the south side of Fiesta Island sits **South Shores**, a large boat launching area.

Over on the **East Shore**, you'll find landscaped picnic areas, a physical fitness course, playgrounds, a sandy beach for swimming, and the park information center. **De Anza Cove**, at the extreme northeast corner of the park, has a sandy beach for swimming plus a large private campground. **Crown Point Shores** provides a sandy beach, picnic area, nature study area, physical fitness course, and a waterski landing.

Sail Bay and **Riviera Shores** make up the northwest portion of Mission Bay and back up against the apartments and condominiums of Pacific Beach. Sail Bay's beaches aren't the best in the park and are usually submerged during high tides. Riviera Shores has a better beach with waterski areas.

Santa Clara and **El Carmel Points** jut out into the westernmost side of Mission Bay. They are perfect for water sports: swimming, snorkeling, surfing, waterskiing, windsurfing, and boating. Santa Clara Point is of interest to the visitor with its recreation center, tennis courts, and softball field. A sandy beach fronts San Juan Cove between the two points.

Just about every facility imaginable can be found somewhere in the park. There are also catamaran and windsurfer rentals, playgrounds and parks, frisbee and golf, and restaurants and groceries. ~ Located along Mission Boulevard between West

Mission Bay Drive and East Mission Bay Drive; 619-221-8900, fax 619-581-9984.

▲ The finest and largest of San Diego's commercial campgrounds is **Campland On The Bay** (2211 Pacific Beach Drive; 800-422-9386; www.campland.com), featuring 600 hookup sites for RVs, vans, tents, and boats; $30 to $155 per night.

MISSION BEACH PARK 🚲 🏊 🎣 The wide, sandy beach at the southern end is a favorite haunt of high schoolers and college students. The hot spot is at the foot of Capistrano Court. A paved boardwalk runs along the beach and is busy with bicyclists, joggers, and roller skaters. Farther north, up around the old Belmont Park roller coaster, the beach grows narrower and the surf rougher. The crowd tends to get that way, too, with heavy-metal teens, sailors, and bikers hanging out along the sea wall, ogling and sometimes harassing the bikini set. This is the closest San Diego comes to Los Angeles' colorful but funky Venice Beach. Facilities include restrooms, lifeguards, and a boardwalk lined with restaurants and beach rentals. Surfing is popular along the jetty. ~ Located along Mission Boulevard north of West Mission Bay Drive.

▼▼▼▼▼▼▼▼▼▼▼▼▼
Point Loma Area

The Point Loma peninsula forms a high promontory that shelters San Diego Bay from the Pacific. It also provided Juan Rodríguez Cabrillo an excellent place from which to contemplate his 16th-century discovery of California. For those of us today interested in contemplating life—or just zoning out on a view—Point Loma peninsula presents the perfect opportunity.

SIGHTS

Heading south from Mission Beach, the first thing you'll encounter on your way to Cabrillo National Monument is **Ocean Beach**, whose reputation as a haven for hippie hold-outs is not entirely undeserved. One of San Diego County's most dramatic coastlines then unfolds as you follow Sunset Cliffs Boulevard south.

After making a left on Hill Street, take a right on Catalina Boulevard. You'll enter the monument through the U.S. Navy's Fort Rosecrans, home to a variety of sophisticated military facilities and the haunting **Fort Rosecrans National Cemetery**. Here, thousands of trim, white markers march down a grassy hillside in mute testimony to San Diego's fallen troops and deep military roots.

Naturally, **Cabrillo National Monument** features a statue of the navigator facing his landing site at Ballast Point. The sculpture itself, a gift from Cabrillo's native Portugal, isn't very impressive but the view is outstanding. With the bay and city spread below, you can often see all the way from Mexico to the La Jolla mesa. The visitors center includes a small museum. The nearby **Old Point Loma Lighthouse** guided shipping from 1855 to 1891.

Admission. ~ 1800 Cabrillo Memorial Drive, Point Loma; 619-557-5450, fax 619-557-5469; www.nps.gov/cabr.

On the ocean side of the peninsula is **Whale Watch Lookout Point,** where, during winter months, you can observe the southward migration of California gray whales. Close by is a superb network of tidepools.

LODGING

Ensconced in a plain vanilla, two-story former church building, the **Hostelling International—San Diego Point Loma** is filled up with 61 economy-minded guests almost every night during the summer. Comfortable bunk beds are grouped in 13 rooms housing from two to eight persons in youth-hostel fashion. Family rooms and private rooms are also available, and there is a common kitchen and dining area. The courtyard has Ping-Pong and other recreational activities. ~ 3790 Udall Street, Point Loma; 619-223-4778, fax 619-223-1883; www.sandiegohostels.org, e-mail pointloma@sandiegohostels.org. BUDGET.

A rare beachfront find in residential Point Loma is the **Inn at Sunset Cliffs**. This trim, white, two-story, 25-room apartment hotel sits right on the seaside cliffs. Rooms are neat and clean but very basic. You can practice your swing on a miniature putting green, or lounge by the pool. There are also bachelor and studio apartments (with kitchenettes). ~ 1370 Sunset Cliffs Boulevard, Point Loma; 619-222-7901, 866-786-2543, fax 619-222-4201; www.innatsunsetcliffs.com, e-mail info@innatsunsetcliffs.com. DELUXE TO ULTRA-DELUXE.

Manmade Shelter and Harbor Islands jut out into San Diego Bay, providing space for several large resorts. For a relaxing, offbeat alternative to these mammoth hotels try **Humphrey's Half Moon Inn**. Surrounded by subtropical plants, this nautical 182-room complex overlooks the yacht harbor and gives the feeling of staying on an island. The rooms are tastefully decorated with a Polynesian theme. There is a pool, spa, putting green, a concert venue, and restaurant. ~ 2303 Shelter Island Drive, Point Loma; 619-224-3411, 800-542-7400, fax 619-224-3478; www.halfmooninn.com, e-mail res@halfmooninn.com. DELUXE TO ULTRA-DELUXE.

HAM IT UP

Aside from being a popular restaurant and lounge, **Tom Ham's Lighthouse** is a real lighthouse and the official Coast Guard–sanctioned beacon of Harbor Island. This scrimshaw-filled nautical lounge is a piano bar Wednesday through Friday. ~ 2150 Harbor Island Drive; 619-291-9110; www.tomhamslighthouse.com.

DINING   A marine view and whirling ceiling fans at **Humphrey's by the Bay** suggest Casablanca. California coastal cuisine is the fare, which means lots of fresh seafood. Breakfast, lunch, and dinner are served. ~ Adjacent to the Half Moon Inn, 2241 Shelter Island Drive, Point Loma; 619-224-3577, fax 619-224-9438; www. humphreysbythebay.com. DELUXE TO ULTRA-DELUXE.

The air at **South Beach Bar & Grille** is decidedly salty, with fishing trophies, a long wooden bar overlooking the pier, and a fun-loving sun-bronzed crowd. It's the perfect environment in which to enjoy grilled fish tacos (mahi, shark, wahoo), steamed clams and mussels, seafood burritos and other mouth-watering choices—washed down with a selection from the dozen beers on tap. ~ 5059 Newport Avenue, Ocean Beach; 619-226-4577. BUDGET.

SHOPPING   **Newport Avenue** in Ocean Beach is the area's best bet for shopping. The blocks closest to the beach are lined with stores exuding a bohemian air: eclectic clothing and jewelry, black-light posters, smoking paraphernalia. Farther down is arguably San Diego County's largest antique district.

In addition, the 4900 block of Newport Avenue hosts a **farmer's market** every Wednesday afternoon.

NIGHTLIFE   Alternative rock and pop bands, mainly local, perform Wednesday through Saturday to a young crowd at **Dream Street**. Cover. ~ 2228 Bacon Street, Ocean Beach; 619-222-8131; www.dream streetlive.com.

A mellower mood can be had nightly at nearby **Winston's**, where live blues, rock, and reggae are the preferred sounds. Cover. ~ 1921 Bacon Street, Ocean Beach; 619-222-6822.

Even musicians head outdoors during San Diego summers. **Humphrey's by the Bay** hosts the city's most ambitious series of jazz, comedy, funk, and mellow rock shows, which include an impressive lineup of name artists in a beautiful oceanview concert venue. ~ 2241 Shelter Island Drive, Point Loma; 619-224-3577.

BEACHES   **OCEAN BEACH** 🏊 🏄 🐕 Where you toss down your towel
& PARKS   at "OB" will probably depend as much on your age as your interests. Surfers, sailors, and what's left of the hippie crowd hang out around the pier; farther north, where the surf is milder and the beach wider, families and retired folks can be found sunbathing and strolling. At the far north end is San Diego's first and only dog beach, complete with a doggie drinking fountain. There are picnic areas, restrooms, and restaurants. Fishing is good from the surf or the fishing pier. Swimming and surfing is very popular here. ~ Take Ocean Beach Freeway (Route 8) west until it

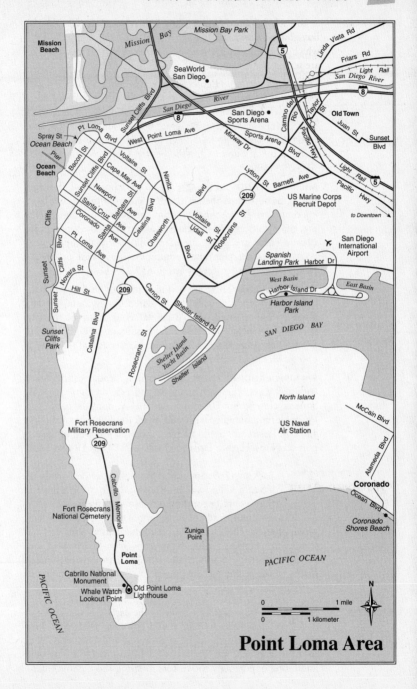

Point Loma Area

ends; turn left onto Sunset Cliffs Boulevard, then right on Voltaire Street; 619-235-1100.

SUNSET CLIFFS PARK 🏃 🚶 🛶 🏄 🎣 The jagged cliffs and sandstone bluffs along Point Loma peninsula give this park a spectacular setting. High-cresting waves make it popular with expert surfers, who favor the rocky beach at the foot of Ladera Avenue. Tidepools evidence the rich marine life that attracts many divers. Winding staircases (at Bermuda and Santa Cruz avenues) and steep trails lead down to some nice pocket beaches. ~ Located off of Sunset Cliffs Boulevard south of Ocean Beach; 619-235-1100.

SHELTER ISLAND 🚶 🚤 🛥 🎣 Like Harbor Island, its neighbor to the northeast, Shelter Island functions primarily as a boating center, but there's a beach facing the bay for swimming, fishing, and picnicking. A landscaped walkway runs the length of the island. There are picnic areas, a children's playground, restrooms, a fishing pier, and restaurants. ~ Located on Shelter Island Drive near Rosecrans Street; 619-235-1100.

HARBOR ISLAND There are no sandy beaches on this manmade island, but there is a walkway bordered by lawn and benches along its entire length. You'll get fabulous views of the city. Facilities here include restrooms and restaurants. ~ Located south of San Diego International Airport on Harbor Island Drive; 619-686-6200, fax 619-686-6400.

SPANISH LANDING PARK 🚶 This is a slender sandy beach with walkways, a grassy picnic area, and a children's playground. Situated close to San Diego International Airport, the park overlooks Harbor Island Marina and offers lovely views of the bay and city. Restrooms are available. ~ Located just west of the airport on North Harbor Drive; 619-686-6200, fax 619-686-6400.

▼▼▼▼▼▼▼▼▼▼▼▼
Old Town Area

Back in 1769, Spanish explorer Gaspar de Portolá selected a hilltop site overlooking the bay for a mission that would begin the European settlement of California. A town soon spread out at the foot of the hill, complete with plaza, church, school, and the tile-roofed adobe casas of California's first families. Through the years, Spanish, Mexican, and American settlements thrived until an 1872 fire destroyed much of the town, prompting developers to relocate the commercial district nearer the bay.

SIGHTS
Some of the buildings and relics of the early era survived and have been brought back to life at **Old Town San Diego State Historic Park**. Lined with adobe restorations and brightened with colorful shops, the six blocks of Old Town provide a lively and interesting opportunity for visitors to stroll, shop, and sightsee.

~ Park headquarters, 4002 Wallace Street; 619-220-5422, fax 619-220-5421.

The state historic park sponsors a free walking tour at 11 a.m. and 2 p.m. daily, or you can easily do it on your own by picking up a copy of the *Old San Diego Gazette*. The paper, which comes out once a month and includes a map of the area, is free at local stores. You can also hop aboard the **Old Town Trolley** for a delightful two-hour narrated tour of Old Town and a variety of other highlights in San Diego and Coronado. It makes eight stops, and you're allowed to get on and off all day long. Fee. ~ 4010 Twiggs Street; 619-298-8687, 800-868-7482, fax 619-298-3404; www.historictours.com.

As it has for over a century, everything focuses on **Old Town Plaza**. Before 1872 this was the social and recreational center of the town: political meetings, barbecues, dances, shootouts, and bullfights all happened here. ~ San Diego Avenue and Mason Street.

Casa de Estudillo is the finest of the original adobe buildings. It was a mansion in its time, built in 1827 for the commander of the Mexican Presidio. ~ Located at the Mason Street corner of the plaza.

Casa de Bandini was built in 1829 as a one-story adobe but gained a second level when it became the Cosmopolitan Hotel in the late 1860s. **Seeley Stables** next door is a replica of the barns and stables of Albert Seeley, who operated the stage line. Nowadays it houses a collection of horse-drawn vehicles and Western

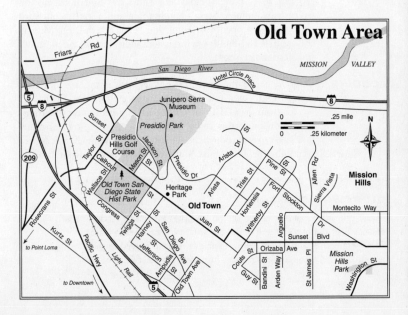

memorabilia, and has a video presentation. ~ At Mason and Calhoun streets.

The **San Diego Union** building was Old Town's first frame building and the place where the *San Diego Union* was first printed in 1868. It has been restored as a 19th-century printing office. ~ Located at San Diego Avenue.

Shoppers seem to gravitate in large numbers toward the north side of the plaza to browse the unusual shops comprising **Bazaar del Mundo**. Built in circular fashion around a tropical courtyard, this complex also houses several restaurants.

The original mission and Spanish Presidio once stood high on a hill behind Old Town. This site of California's birthplace now houses **Junipero Serra Museum**, a handsome Spanish Colonial structure containing an excellent collection of American Indian and Spanish artifacts from the state's pioneer days and relics from the Royal Presidio dig sites. Open Friday through Sunday. Admission. ~ Presidio Drive; 619-297-3258, fax 619-297-3281; www.sandiegohistory.org.

Within five years after Father Serra dedicated the first of California's 21 missions, the site had become much too small for the growing numbers it served. So **Mission San Diego de Alcala** was moved from Presidio Hill six miles east into Mission Valley. Surrounded now by shopping centers and suburban homes, the "Mother of Missions" retains its simple but striking white adobe facade topped by a graceful *campanario*. There's a library (open 10 a.m. to 12 p.m., Tuesday and Thursday) containing mission records in Junípero Serra's handwriting and a lovely courtyard with gnarled pepper trees. Admission. ~ 10818 San Diego Mission Road; 619-281-8449; www.missionsandiego.com, e-mail info@missionsandiego.com.

LODGING A good bet in the lower price categories is the appropriately named **Old Town Inn**. Strolling distance from Old Town, and across from the Old Town Trolley and Transit Center (the transportation hub), this spiffy little 84-room family-owned motel has two types of rooms: the economy units and the handicapped-accessible deluxe rooms, some of which have full kitchens. A

OLD TOWN VICTORIANA

About one and a half blocks east of Old Town lies **Heritage Park**, an area dedicated to the preservation of the city's Victorian past. Seven historic 1880s-era houses and an old Jewish temple have been moved to the hillside site and beautifully restored. ~ Juan and Harney streets.

guest laundry is available, as is a heated outdoor pool, and a complimentary deluxe breakfast buffet every morning. ~ 4444 Pacific Highway; 619-260-8024, 800-643-3025, fax 619-296-0524; www.oldtown-inn.com. MODERATE.

For the romantic, **Heritage Park Inn**, a storybook 1889 Queen Anne mansion with a striking turret, is an enchanting bed and breakfast. Set on a grassy hillside, it provides a tranquil escape. Choose from 12 distinctive chambers (all with private baths), each furnished with museum-quality antiques. Most feature ornate brass or four-poster canopy beds and old-fashioned quilts; three have jacuzzi tubs. ~ 2470 Heritage Park Row; 619-299-6832, 800-995-2470, fax 619-299-9465; www.heritageparkinn.com, e-mail innkeeper@heritageparkinn.com. DELUXE TO ULTRA-DELUXE.

For a choice of motels with a variety of prices, try looking for accommodations along **Hotel Circle**, on the north side of Presidio Park. The road loops under a portion of Route 8. Most properties around the circle are large chain hotels designed for vacation travelers, with resort facilities including large pools, tennis courts, and spas or fitness centers; many share the use of the 27-hole Riverwalk Golf Club. Rates are generally lower than at downtown hotels.

Among them is the 417-room **Red Lion Hanalei Hotel**, whose tall palm trees, courtyard, and tiki-style bar aim for a Polynesian ambience. ~ 2270 Hotel Circle North; 619-297-1101, 800-733-5466, fax 619-297-6049; www.redlion.com, e-mail sales@hanalei hotel.com. DELUXE.

The **Handlery Hotel Resort** is a lowrise 217-room complex adjacent to the golf course, with an outdoor pool, jacuzzi, and poolside gym. ~ 950 Hotel Circle North; 619-298-0511, 800-676-6567, fax 619-298-9793; www.handlery.com, e-mail sales@handlery.com. DELUXE.

The **Town and Country Hotel** is geared toward travelers who mix business with pleasure, featuring its own convention center as well as four swimming pools and an adjacent shopping mall. ~ 500 Hotel Circle North; 619-291-7131, 800-772-8527, fax 619-291-3584; www.towncountry.com. ULTRA-DELUXE.

Hawthorn Suites San Diego has 50 one-bedroom and two-bedroom, two-bath suites ideal for traveling families, as well as an outdoor barbecue area. ~ 1335 Hotel Circle South; 619-299-3501, 800-527-1133, fax 619-294-7882; www.hawthornsuites sandiego.com. MODERATE TO DELUXE.

The 280 rooms at **Days Inn–Hotel Circle**, which holds the distinction of being the largest Days Inn in California, feature Nintendo for kids, as well as ironing boards and irons; some rooms have kitchenettes. ~ 543 Hotel Circle South; 619-297-8800, 800-227-4743, fax 619-298-6029; www.daysinnhc.com. MODERATE.

DINING

Mexican food and atmosphere abound in Old Town, especially in the Bazaar del Mundo. Here five restaurants lure a steady stream of diners into festive, flowered courtyards. **Casa de Pico** is a great place to sit and munch cheese nachos and sip margaritas. Mexican entrées are served outside or in one of the hacienda-style dining rooms. ~ 2754 Calhoun Street; 619-296-3267, fax 619-296-3113; www.casadepico.com. BUDGET TO MODERATE.

Next door, in a magnificent 1829 hacienda, **Casa de Bandini**, you will find the cuisine a bit more refined. Seafood is good here, especially the crab enchiladas, and the health-conscious will like the low-fat menu. Mariachis often play at both restaurants. ~ Mason and Calhoun streets; 619-297-8211, fax 619-297-2557; www.casadebandini.com. MODERATE.

Like Balboa Park nearby, the four-building Balboa Park Inn was built in 1915 for the Panama–California Exposition.

Two Old Town charmers provide satisfying diversions from a Mexican diet. **Berta's** specializes in Latin American cuisine. *Vatapa* (coconut sauce over mahi-mahi, scallops, and shrimp) and *cansado* (a plate of pinto beans, rice, salsa, plantain, and green salad) are wonderfully prepared. Closed Monday. ~ 3928 Twigg Street; phone/fax 619-295-2343. MODERATE.

Fresh, innovative seafood is the calling card at **Café Pacifica**, where a billion points of light sparkle from the wood-beamed ceiling and candles create a warm, intimate setting. California cuisine meets Pacific Rim panache, with preparations such as ginger-stuffed seared halibut and swordfish with soy-peanut glaze. Seating is also available at the bar and, in warm weather, the patio with removable roof. Dinner only. ~ 2414 San Diego Avenue; 619-291-6666, fax 619-291-0122; www.cafepacifica.com, e-mail info@cafepacifica.com. MODERATE TO ULTRA-DELUXE.

HIDDEN ►

Less than a mile from Old Town lies a pair of excellent ethnic take-out shops that few visitors ever find. **El Indio** opened in 1940 as a family-operated *tortillería*, then added an informal restaurant serving quesadillas, enchiladas, tostadas, burritos, tacos, and taquitos. Quality homemade Mexican food at Taco Bell prices; you can sit indoors, out on the patio, or order to go. Open for breakfast, lunch, and dinner. ~ 3695 India Street; 619-299-0333; www.el-indio.com. BUDGET.

Another one-of-a-kind fast-food operation with an equally fervent following, **Saffron Chicken** turns out zesty Thai-grilled chicken on a special rotisserie. The aroma is positively exquisite and so is the chicken served with jasmine rice, Cambodian salad, and the five tangy sauces. Eat on an adjacent patio or take a picnic to the beach. Also, next door is **Saffron Noodles**, owned by the same restaurateurs. ~ 3731-B India Street; 619-574-0177. BUDGET TO MODERATE.

Historic Old Town is blessed with several exciting bazaars and **SHOPPING**
shopping squares. By far the grandest is the **Bazaar del Mundo**,
Old Town's version of the famous marketplaces of Spain and
Mexico. Adobe casitas house a variety of international shops.
Here **Fabrics and Finery** (619-296-3161) unfurls cloth, buttons,
and craft accessories from around the world, and **Ariana** (619-
296-4989) features clothing and wearable art. ~ Calhoun Street
between Twiggs and Juan streets.

From Friday through Sunday, **Kobey's Swap Meet** converts the
parking lot of the San Diego Sports Arena into a giant flea market
where over 1000 sellers hawk new and used wares. Admission. ~
Sports Arena Boulevard; 619-226-0650.

The prevailing culture in Old Town is Mexican, as in mariachis **NIGHTLIFE**
and margaritas. The **Old Town Mexican Café y Cantina**, a festive, friendly establishment, has a patio bar. ~ 2489 San Diego
Avenue; 619-297-4330.

O'Hungry's, a nearby restaurant, features an acoustic guitar-
ist every night but Monday. ~ 2547 San Diego Avenue; 619-
298-0133.

Located near the airport in Middletown, an area just north
of Downtown, **The Casbah** has hosted the likes of Nirvana and
Smashing Pumpkins, among others, before they made it big.
Rock, punk, rockabilly, and pop bands rock out nightly at this
San Diego institution for live alternative music. Cover. ~ 2501
Kettner Boulevard; 619-232-4355; www.casbahmusic.com.

For country-and-western dancing, try **In Cahoots**, which has
free dance lessons every night but Wednesday. There are also occasional live acts. Cover Wednesday through Saturday. Closed
Monday. ~ 5373 Mission Center Road; 619-291-8635, fax 619-
291-1723; www.incahoots.com.

Hillcrest & San Diego Gay Scene

Ironically, it's thanks to the strong presence
of the U.S. Navy that San Diego has such a
significant gay scene. After World War II,
thousands of newly discharged men and
women who had discovered their sexual identities during their
military service opted to remain in places like San Diego and San
Francisco instead of returning home. The long-time military
presence contributed to the fairly conservative personality of San
Diego's gay community, but a more liberalizing effect began to
take place in the 1960s with the arrival of the University of
California in La Jolla. Today, San Diego's gay and lesbian community is more out than it's ever been, and the center of attention is the section of town just to the northwest of Balboa Park
called Hillcrest.

The '50s architecture and neon give the area a campy feel (a neon sign, which works intermittently, hangs across University Avenue at 5th Avenue and signals entrance into Hillcrest). Bookstores, trendy boutiques, and coffeeshops line University Avenue, 5th Avenue, and Robinson Street—all within easy walking distance of one another. And because Hillcrest boasts some of the best movie houses and restaurants in San Diego, you'll see everyone there: gay yuppies, leather-clad lesbians, stylish hipsters, and Ozzie and Harriet lookalikes.

LODGING

Since many of its guests hail from outside the U.S., the **Hillcrest Inn Hotel** considers itself an international hotel. Right in the hub of Hillcrest activity, the 45 modestly furnished rooms, outfitted with microwaves and refrigerators, provide guests with a comfortable stay. Fatigued wayfarers will appreciate the sun patio and spa after long days of sightseeing. ~ 3754 5th Avenue; 619-293-7078, 800-258-2280, fax 619-293-3861; www.hillcrest inn.net, e-mail hillcrestinn@juno.com. BUDGET TO MODERATE.

The **Balboa Park Inn** is a popular caravansary with gays and straights alike. Its 26 rooms are decorated in different themes; you can choose to luxuriate in *Gone With the Wind's* "Tara Suite," get sentimental in 1930s Paris, or go wild in Greystoke. Some suites boast jacuzzi tubs, kitchens, and faux fireplaces, and *everyone* can request a continental breakfast served in bed. A courtyard and sun terrace round out the facilities of this winsome getaway. Reservations recommended. ~ 3402 Park Boulevard; 619-298-0823, 800-938-8181, fax 619-294-8070; www.balboaparkinn.com, e-mail info@balboaparkinn.com. MODERATE TO ULTRA-DELUXE.

DINING

Judging by the name itself, you'd think **Hamburger Mary's** was a typical burger joint. It peddles burgers, yes, but with washboards, surfboards, and murals decorating the walls, it definitely ain't typical. Besides hamburgers, you'll find steak and halibut dinners, vegetarian plates, and salads, which can be eaten outdoors on the patio. Afterward, you'll want to join the festivities at Kickers, the gay country-western bar in the same building. Sunday brunch is also served. ~ 308 University Avenue; 619-491-0400, fax 619-491-0160; www.hamburgermarys.com, e-mail mary@hamburgermarys.com. BUDGET TO MODERATE.

HIDDEN ►

Bread lovers will think they have landed in paradise when they enter **Bread & Cie**. The aroma of fig, jalapeño, cheese, and rosemary breads lingers in this amazing bakery, which also serves sandwiches, pastries, and cappuccinos. Be prepared to wait at lunchtime. ~ 350 University Avenue; 619-683-9322, fax 619-683-9299; e-mail kaufworld@earthlink.net. BUDGET.

Attracting attention has never been a problem for the **Corvette Diner**. Although it's usually crammed full of families and high school kids, the decor is not to be missed. Cool 1950s music, a soda fountain (complete with resident jerks), rock-and-roll memorabilia, dancing waitresses, and a classy Corvette have proven a magnetic formula for this Hillcrest haven. The place is jammed for lunch and dinner. Simple "blue-plate" diner fare includes meatloaf, chicken-fried steak, and hefty burgers named for 1950s notables like Dion, Eddie, and Kookie. ~ 3946 5th Avenue; phone/fax 619-542-1001; www.cohnrestaurants.com/corvette. html. MODERATE.

Around the corner and up the block is another diner complete with black-and-white tile, neon, shiny chrome and naugahyde booths. **City Delicatessen & Bakery**, however, whips up Jewish deli treats such as matzo ball soup, lox and bagels, and beef brisket. You'll also find burgers, steaks, salads, and sandwiches; breakfast is served all day. A popular late-night spot. ~ 535 University Avenue; 619-295-2747, fax 619-295-2129. BUDGET TO MODERATE.

Located in the heart of Hillcrest, **California Cuisine** offers sumptuous dishes for your discriminating palate. Beef tenderloin and New Zealand lamb loin are among the many items on their ever-changing menu, as are pasta, salads, and vegetarian fare. You also get a taste of promising local artists whose original work adorns the walls. No lunch Saturday and Sunday. Closed Monday. ~ 1027 University Avenue; 619-543-0790, fax 619-543-0106; www.californiacuisine.cc, e-mail info@californiacuisine.cc. MODERATE TO DELUXE.

SHOPPING

Obelisk carries gay, lesbian, and bisexual reading material, as well as gift items to tickle your fancy—jewelry, shirts, and cards —to name a few. ~ 1029 University Avenue; 619-297-4171.

Unlike other antique stores in the area, **Circa a.d.** offers anything but American antiques. It proudly displays a vast assortment of Asian, European, and African art, jewelry, textiles, and pottery, specializing in goods from around the Pacific Rim. It even carries bonsai trees. ~ 3867 4th Avenue; 619-293-3328; www. circaad.com, e-mail info@circaad.com.

AUTHOR FAVORITE

Searching high and low for that Betty Page calendar? How about some sweater-girl paper dolls? **Babette Schwartz**, the local drag queen, has a store that carries an array of novelty items and retro toys, including Wonder Woman lunchboxes and Barbie dolls. ~ 421 University Avenue; 619-220-7048; www.babette.com.

Appeasing vinyl junkies and casual listeners alike, **Off the Record** is jam-packed with new, used, and out-of-print CDs, LPs, and singles (both vinyl and plastic). You'll also find T-shirts, posters, books, magazines, and other music-related paraphernalia. ~ 3849 5th Avenue; 619-298-4755.

NIGHTLIFE   The **Brass Rail**, which opened in 1958, is one of San Diego's oldest gay bars. The bartenders' famed congeniality keeps the primarily male clientele coming back year after year for more— more drinks and more dancing (which is in full swing every weekend). Saturday is Latino night. Cover on weekends. ~ 3796 5th Avenue; phone/fax 619-298-2233.

A few doors down from the Brass Rail and next to the Hillcrest Inn Hotel is **David's Coffee House**. Designed to look like a living room with a couch and antique furniture, this popular coffeehouse is a home away from home for travelers and locals alike; pets are also welcome. Aside from knocking back espresso and admiring the passing scenery, you can engage your neighbor with a board game or surf the web. David's Coffee House donates a portion of its proceeds to local AIDS organizations. ~ 3766 5th Avenue; 619-296-4173.

Also in this same stretch of 5th Avenue, **The Loft** is a gay bar offering jukebox music and pool playing. ~ 3610 5th Avenue; 619-296-6407.

The short trek to University Avenue brings you to Hamburger Mary's restaurant, home of **Kickers**. This C&W bar keeps gay, lesbian, and straight folks kickin' with free line dancing and two-step lessons Thursday through Saturday. On Sunday, disco is the soundtrack for the tea dance. Cover for tea dance. ~ 308 University Avenue; 619-491-0400; www.hamburgermarys.com.

The real action on University Avenue is over at the Rainbow Block. First there's **Flicks**, a video bar that flashes visual stimuli on its six big screens while playing dance and progressive music. Depending on the evening, you might catch some live music, or you could pop in for a Monday night round of the dating game. Occasional cover. ~ 1017 University Avenue; 619-297-2056; www.sdflicks.com.

At the far end of the block, **Rich's** heats up Friday through Sunday with high-energy dancing until 2 a.m. The deejay-mixed music sets the beat: groove, techno, house, and tribal rhythms. Music isn't the only stimulation; your eyes will be dazzled by the specially created visual effects. Each night has a different theme. On Friday nights Rich's go-go boys "work it." Saturdays boast varied themes and are about good music (a deejay host) and dancing. To finish off the weekend, there is The Tea on Sunday with the doors opening at 9 p.m. Cover. ~ 1051 University Avenue; 619-295-2195; www.richs-sandiego.com.

Beyond the Rainbow Block you can take a pleasant stroll along the north side of Balboa Park to **The Flame**. Touted as "San Diego's hottest women's nightclub," this postmodern apocalypse features a dancefloor, pool tables, and darts. Although men are always welcome here, Tuesday is officially "Boys' Night." Dancing runs seven nights a week with deejays spinning everything from Top 40 to Gothic trance. No cover Tuesday through Thursday. ~ 3780 Park Boulevard; 619-295-4163; www.theflame-sd.com.

A young, hip mixed crowd patronizes **Six Degrees** on any given night along with weekday happy hour and Sunday barbecue. Customers enjoy karaoke on Wednesday and Sunday. Entertainment is split between live bands and deejays playing Top-40 and hip-hop. Occasional cover. ~ 3175 India Street; 619-296-6789.

Other gay bars around town include **Bourbon Street**, a French Quarter–style bar that features an outdoor patio and nightly entertainment. Live music Thursday through Sunday. ~ 4612 Park Boulevard; 619-291-0173; www.bourbonstreetsd.com. The action at the **Chee Chee Club**, a local cruise bar and the oldest gay establishment in San Diego, revolves around shooting pool and playing pinball. Occasional performers present shows for the mostly male crowd. ~ 929 Broadway; 619-234-4404. **Shooterz**, a popular sports bar, boasts two large-screen TVs, five pool tables, pinball, and video games. **The Odyssey Club**, located inside, is a mixed danceclub. Occasional cover. ~ 3815 30th Street; 619-574-0744; www.shooterzbar.com.

Balboa Park and the San Diego Zoo

It's unclear as to whether it was intelligent foresight or unbridled optimism that prompted the establishment of Balboa Park. Certain that a fine neighborhood would flourish around it, city fathers in 1868 set aside 1400 acres of rattlesnake-infested hillside above "New Town" as a public park. The park's eventual development, and most of its lovely Spanish Baroque buildings, came as the result of two world's fairs—The Panama–California Exposition of 1915–16 and the California–Pacific International Exposition of 1935–36.

Today Balboa Park ranks among the largest and finest of America's city parks. Wide avenues and walkways curve through luxurious subtropical foliage leading to nine major museums, three art galleries, four theaters, picnic groves, the world's largest zoo, a golf course, and countless other recreation facilities. Its verdant grounds teem with cyclists, joggers, skaters, picnickers, weekend artists, and museum mavens.

Balboa Park's museums charge an admission fee but every Tuesday select museums can be visited free.

The main entrance is from 6th Avenue onto Laurel Street, which becomes El Prado as you cross Cabrillo Bridge. Begin your visit at the **Balboa Park Visitors Center**, located on the northeast corner of Plaza de Panama. They provide plenty of free pamphlets and maps on the park. ~ House of Hospitality, 1549 El Prado; 619-239-0512; www.balboapark.org.

From here you can stroll about, taking in Balboa Park's main attractions. To the right, as you head east on the pedestrian-only section of El Prado, is the **Casa de Balboa**. This building houses several worthwhile museums, including the **San Diego Model Railroad Museum** (619-696-0199, fax 619-696-0239; www.sdmodel railroadm.com, e-mail sdmodrailm@abac.com), which features the largest permanent model railroad layouts in North America. Children under 15 enter free. Closed Monday. Here, too, is the **San Diego Historical Society's** extensive collection of documents and photographs spanning the urban history of San Diego. Closed Monday and Tuesday. The **Museum of Photographic Arts** (619-238-7559, fax 619-238-8777; www.mopa.org, e-mail info@mopa.org) has exhibits of internationally known photographers. Admission except on the second Tuesday of the month.

Continuing east to the fountain, you'll see the **Reuben H. Fleet Science Center** on your right. Among the park's finest attractions, it features one of the largest planetariums and the world's first IMAX dome theater. The galleries offer various hands-on exhibits and displays dealing with modern phenomena. Admission. ~ 619-238-1233, fax 619-685-5771; www.rhfleet.org.

Across the courtyard is the **San Diego Natural History Museum** with displays devoted mostly to the natural heritage of Southern and Baja California. Traveling exhibitions and giant-screen films cover more global topics. Admission. ~ 619-232-3821, fax 619-232-0248; www.sdnhm.org, e-mail lenstad@sdnhm.org

Going back along El Prado, take a moment to admire your reflection in the Lily Pond. With the old, latticed **Botanical Building** in the background, the scene is a favorite among photographers. The fern collection inside is equally striking.

Next is the **Timken Museum of Art**, considered to have one of the West Coast's finest collections of European and Early American paintings. The displays include works by Rembrandt and Copley, as well as an amazing collection of Russian icons. Closed Monday and the month of September. ~ 619-239-5548, fax 619-531-9640; www.timkenmuseum.org, e-mail info@timken museum.org.

Right next door on the plaza is the **San Diego Museum of Art**, with an entrance facade patterned after the University of Salamanca in Spain. The museum treasures include a permanent collection of Italian Renaissance, Dutch, and Spanish Baroque paintings and sculpture, a display of Asian art, a gallery of impressionist paintings, contemporary art, and an American collection, as well as touring exhibitions. Closed Monday. Admission. ~ 619-232-7931, fax 619-232-9367; www.sdmart.com, e-mail info@sdmart.org.

Across El Prado from the Museum of Art is the **Mingei International Museum**. The Mingei (which means "art of the people" and is pronounced *min-gay*), has a superb collection of world folk art, craft, and design from countries around the world. Closed Monday. Admission. ~ 1439 El Prado; 619-239-0003, fax 619-239-0605; www.mingei.org, e-mail mingei@mingei.org.

◄ *HIDDEN*

The grandest of all Balboa Park structures, built as the centerpiece for the 1915 Panama–California Exposition, is the 200-foot Spanish Renaissance **California Tower**. The **San Diego Museum of Man**, at the base of the tower, is a must for anthropology buffs and those interested in Egyptian mummies and American Indian cultures. Admission. ~ 619-239-2001, fax 619-239-2749; www.museumofman.org.

On display at the San Diego Aerospace Museum is Black Bird, the world's fastest plane.

Another museum not to be missed is the **San Diego Aerospace Museum**, several blocks south of the plaza. It contains over 65 aircraft including a replica of Charles Lindbergh's famous *Spirit of St. Louis*, the original of which was built in San Diego. Admission. ~ 619-234-8291; www.aerospacemuseum.org, e-mail info@aerospacemuseum.org.

En route you'll pass the **Spreckels Organ Pavilion**. Those 4416 pipes make it the world's largest outdoor instrument of its kind.

Sports fans will want to take in the **Hall of Champions Sports Museum** in the historic Federal Building. It houses the Breitbard Hall of Fame and exhibits that feature world-class San Diego athletes from more than 40 sports. The museum also has an interactive sports center. Admission. ~ 2131 Pan-American Plaza; 619-234-2544, fax 619-234-4543; www.sandiegosports.org.

You'll want to attend a play at the **Old Globe** to absorb the full greatness of this Tony Award–winning stage, but for starters you can stroll around the 581-seat theater, famed for its Shakespearean presentations. Located in a grove on the north side of California Tower, the **Old Globe** is part of the trio of theaters that includes the **Cassius Carter Centre Stage** and the outdoor **Lowell Davies Festival Theatre**. Admission. ~ 619-239-2255; www.oldglobe.org, e-mail tickets@theoldglobe.org.

SAN DIEGO ZOO   North of the Balboa Park museum and theater complex is San Diego Zoo, which needs no introduction. It quite simply is the world's top-rated zoo. The numbers alone are mind-boggling: 4000 animals, representing 800 species, spread out over 100 acres. Most of these wild animals live in surroundings as natural as man can make them. Rather than cages there are glass enclosures where orangutans roam free on grassy islands and multihued birds fly through tropical rainforests. All around is a manmade jungle forest overgrown with countless species of rare and exotic plants.

Of particular merit is "Polar Bear Plunge." Here you can watch the polar bears as they gracefully swim underwater in their deep saltwater bay. At "Ituri Forest," Funani and Koboko delight all with their infamous underwater hippo ballet. The zoo's state-of-the-art primate exhibit, the "Gorilla Tropics," is a two-and-a-half-acre African rainforest that is home to eight lowland gorillas and hundreds of jungle birds. Within this area is "Pygmy Chimps at Bonobo Road," home to frolicsome troupes of pygmy chimps and Angolan colobus monkeys. At the nearby "Sun Bear Forest," an equatorial rainforest, you'll encounter sun bears and lion-tailed macaques. One of the first pandas to be born and survive in captivity can be seen at the "Panda Research Station."

> For a bird's-eye view of the entire San Diego Zoo, you can take the "Skyfari" aerial tramway.

At the **Children's Zoo**, where there are just as many adults as kids, you can watch a large variety of bugs crawling around, and there's a petting zoo. Don't miss the pygmy marmosets. They are the world's smallest monkeys, weighing in at only four ounces when full grown. Admission. ~ Located off Park Boulevard; 619-234-3153, fax 619-231-0249; www.sandiegozoo.org.

LODGING   My vote for the prettiest and most hospitable of San Diego's bed and breakfasts goes to the **Keating House Bed and Breakfast**. This historically designated 1888 Victorian home in a sunny hillside residential neighborhood between Balboa Park and downtown offers nine comfy-cozy rooms—seven in the main house and two in the cottage out back. The cottage rooms feature private baths. With its gabled roof, hexagonal window turret, and conical peak, this beautifully restored Queen Anne is every bit as nice inside. A garden completes the homey scene. ~ 2331 2nd Avenue; 619-239-8585, 800-995-8644, fax 619-239-5774; www.keating house.com, e-mail inn@keatinghouse.com. MODERATE TO DELUXE.

Another attractive bed and breakfast in the Balboa Park area is **Carole's B&B Inn**, built in 1904 and situated on a quiet residential street. The main house has eight antique-furnished guest rooms (some with shared bath), while an annex across the street contains two garden studio apartments with private baths and kitchenettes, a one-bedroom cottage, and a two-bedroom apartment. In addition to a sitting room with player piano and a conference room, the inn has a swimming pool. ~ 3227 Grim Avenue; 619-280-5258, 800-975-5521; www.carolesbnb.com. MODERATE TO ULTRA-DELUXE.

The best value for your dollar among reasonably priced hotels in the area is the 67-room **Comfort Inn**. They feature wood furniture, designer color schemes, and high-grade carpeting. The inn has a pool-sized jacuzzi and serves a continental breakfast. Conveniently located near Balboa Park just a few blocks from the city center. ~ 719 Ash Street; 619-232-2525, 800-404-6835, fax 619-687-3024; www.comfortinnsandiego.com. MODERATE TO DELUXE.

Dmitri's Guesthouse offers five rooms (two with shared bath) close to Horton Plaza. Each suite comes with a ceiling fan and a refrigerator (one includes a full kitchen). Feel free to shed your clothing on the sundeck and immerse yourself in the hot tub or swimming pool. Situated in a century-old house, Dmitri's serves a continental breakfast poolside every morning. Reservations recommended. ~ 931 21st Street; 619-238-5547; www.dmitris.com, e-mail dmitrisbb@aol.com. MODERATE TO DELUXE.

DINING

Located in Balboa Park's House of Hospitality is the **Prado Restaurant**, surrounded by lovely Spanish terraces and burbling fountains. Pasta, seafood, poultry, and meat dishes here blend Latin and Italian flavors. For lunch, you may find fancy panini sandwiches, pasta, and fish tacos, while dinner choices might include wild-mushroom risotto, grilled jumbo prawns in a spiced coconut broth, and honey chipotle–marinated ribeye steak; the dessert menu is equally mouth-watering. Patio seating and a pitcher of sangria is a must during the warm months. No dinner on Monday. ~ 1549 El Prado; 619-557-9441, fax 619-557-9170; www.pradobalboa.com. MODERATE TO ULTRA-DELUXE.

When you're visiting the San Diego Zoo, consider **Albert's Restaurant**. Named for the gorilla who once occupied the area, this sit-down eatery offers a variety of salads, sandwiches, fresh pastas, and fish and meat entrées. No dinner except in summer (late June through Labor Day). ~ 2920 Zoo Drive, the San Diego Zoo; 619-685-3200, fax 619-685-3204; www.sandiegozoo.org. MODERATE TO DELUXE.

A couple of San Diego's better restaurant finds lie "uptown" just east of Route 5. **Fifth and Hawthorn** is a neighborhood sensation, but not many tourists find their way to this chic little dining room. The owners present an array of tasty dishes, specializing in fresh seafood ranging from sea bass with ginger. Usually available is filet mignon with green peppercorn and cabernet sauce. No lunch on weekends. ~ 515 Hawthorn Street at 5th Avenue; 619-544-0940, fax 619-544-0941. MODERATE TO DELUXE.

As its name suggests, **Liaison** is an intimate bistro with beautiful French doors, a wood-burning fireplace, and a patio with a waterfall. Add candlelight and superb French cuisine, and you're talking about the perfect place for a rendezvous. The five- or six-course, prix-fixe dinner varies and may include lamb curry served with rice, medallions of filet mignon with béarnaise sauce, and salmon served in a crayfish butter sauce. Or select dishes à la carte. For a romantic dinner, this place comes highly praised. Reservations are recommended. Dinner only. Closed Sunday and Monday. ~ 2202 4th Avenue; 619-234-5540; www.liaisonsan diego.com. MODERATE TO DELUXE.

SHOPPING A haven for art lovers is **Spanish Village Art Center**. Over 35 studios are staffed by artists displaying their work and giving daily demonstrations. For sale are original paintings, sculpture, handblown glass and fine jewelry. ~ 1770 Village Place, near the San Diego Zoo entrance; 619-233-9050, fax 619-239-9226; www. spanishvillageart.com.

NIGHTLIFE **The Globe Theatres** presents classic and contemporary plays, including Shakespeare with innovative twists, in three Balboa Park theaters. ~ Balboa Park; 619-239-2255; www.theoldglobe.org.

Bertrand at Mr. A's is the critics' choice for "best drinking with a view." The atmosphere at this elegant restaurant is one of monied luxury, and gentlemen are expected (but not required) to wear jackets. ~ 2550 5th Avenue, 12th floor; 619-239-1377.

▼▼▼▼▼▼▼▼▼▼▼▼▼▼

Downtown San Diego

At one time downtown San Diego was a collection of porn shops, tattoo parlors, and strip-tease bars. Billions of dollars invested in a stunning array of new buildings and in the restoration of many old ones have changed all that. Within the compact city center there's Horton Plaza, an exciting example of avant-garde urban architecture, and the adjacent Gaslamp Quarter, which reveals how San Diego looked at the peak of its Victorian-era boom in the 1880s.

SIGHTS **Horton Plaza** is totally unlike any other shopping center or urban redevelopment project. It has transcended its genre in whimsical, rambling paths, bridges, towers, piazzas, sculptures, fountains, and live greenery. Fourteen different styles, ranging from Renaissance to postmodern, are employed in its design. Mimes, minstrels, and fortune tellers meander about the six-block complex performing for patrons. The success of this structure sparked downtown's renewal by revamping local businesses and attracting more tourists.

Horton Plaza was inspired by European shopping streets and districts such as the Plaka of Athens, the Ramblas of Barcelona, and Portobello Road in London. ~ The Plaza is bounded by Broadway and G Street and 1st and 4th avenues.

The **Gaslamp Quarter** is one of America's largest national historic districts, covering a 16-block strip along 4th, 5th, and 6th avenues from Broadway to the waterfront. Architecturally, the Quarter reveals some of the finest Victorian-style commercial buildings constructed in San Diego during the 50 years between the Civil War and World War I. This area, along 5th Avenue, became San Diego's first main street. The city's core began on the bay where Alonzo Horton first built a wharf in 1869.

It was this same area that later fell into disrepute as the heart of the business district moved north beyond Broadway. By the 1890s, prostitution and gambling were rampant. Offices above street level were converted into bordellos and opium dens. The area south of Market Street became known as the "Stingaree," an unflattering reference coined by the many who were stung by card sharks, con men, and of course, con ladies.

Rescued by the city and a dedicated group of preservationists, the area not only survived but played a major role in the massive redevelopment of downtown San Diego. The city added wide brick sidewalks, period street lamps, trees, and benches. In all, more than 100 grand old Victorian buildings were restored to their original splendor. See "Walking Tour" in this chapter for more details.

Make a point to visit the **Villa Montezuma–Jesse Shepard House**, situated a few blocks east of the Gaslamp Quarter. This ornate, Queen Anne–style Victorian mansion, magnificently restored, was constructed by a wealthy group of San Diegans in

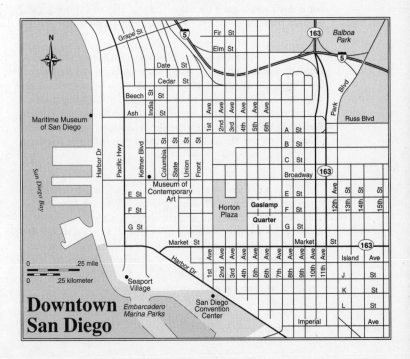

The Gaslamp Quarter

History buffs and lovers of antique buildings should don their walking shoes for a tour of the Gaslamp Quarter, accompanied by a map available at the William Heath Davis House Museum. The 16-block district contains over 90 historic buildings, most of which now house galleries, shops, restaurants, and upscale hotels. Here are a few of the highlights.

WILLIAM HEATH DAVIS HOUSE   Start your tour at the William Heath Davis House, the oldest surviving wooden structure in the downtown area, this 1850 "saltbox" prefabricated family home was framed on the East Coast and shipped around Cape Horn to San Diego. It is now filled with museum exhibits recounting the house's history. Call for museum hours. ~ 410 Island Avenue; 619-233-4692, fax 619-233-4148; www.gaslampquarter.org, e-mail tracey@gaslampquarter.org.

ROYAL PIE BAKERY   Just down the street from the William Heath Davis House is what was once the Royal Pie Bakery. Almost unbelievably, a bakery was on this site from 1871 until 1996. Around the turn of the 20th century, the bakery found itself in the middle of a red-light district, but it didn't stop turning out cakes and pies even though a notorious bordello operated on the second floor. It's now a restaurant. ~ 554 4th Street.

FIFTH AVENUE   Go back down Island Avenue to 5th Avenue and turn left. Not only was this block part of the Stingaree, but it was the heart of San Diego's Chinatown. The **Nanking Café** (now Royal Thai) was the only restaurant on the street when it was built in 1912; today there are 95 restaurants in the district. ~ 467 5th Avenue. The nearby **Timken Building**, notable for its fancy arched brick facade, was erected in 1894. ~ 5th Avenue and Market Street. Across the street is the **Backesto**

1887 as a gift to a visiting musician. Culture-hungry civic leaders actually "imported" world-famous troubadour Jesse Shepard to live in the opulent dwelling as something of a court musician to the city's upper crust. Shepard stayed only two years but decorated his villa to the hilt with dozens of stained-glass windows and elaborate hand-carved wood trim and decorations. Open Friday through Sunday. Admission. ~ 1925 K Street; 619-239-2211, fax 619-232-6297; www.sandiegohistory.org, e-mail ad missions@sandiegohistory.org.

Providing contrast to all this preserved history is the **Museum of Contemporary Art**'s downtown space, adjacent to the American

Building, a beautifully restored late-19th-century structure. The tall, Romanesque Revival **Keating Building** was one of the most prestigious office buildings in San Diego during the 1890s, complete with such modern conveniences as steam heat and a wire-cage elevator. ~ 5th Avenue and F Street. Next door is the **Ingersoll Tutton Building**. When this 90-foot-long structure was built in 1894 for $20,000 it was the most expensive building on the block! ~ 832 5th Avenue.

COMMERCE ROW   Most of the block on the other side of 5th Avenue, from F up to E streets, represents the most architecturally significant row in the Gaslamp Quarter. From south to north, there's the **Marston Building** on the corner of F Street. Built in 1881, it was downtown San Diego's leading department store. Next is the 1887 **Hubbell Building**, originally a dry goods establishment. The **Nesmith-Greeley Building** next door is another example of the then-fashionable Romanesque Revival style with its ornamental brick coursing. Featuring twin towers and intricate Baroque Revival architecture, the 1888 **Louis Bank of Commerce** is probably the most beautiful building in the quarter. It originally housed a ground-floor oyster bar that was a favorite haunt of Wyatt Earp. The famous Western lawman-turned-real-estate speculator resided in San Diego from 1886 to 1893 and operated three Gaslamp Quarter drinking establishments. Be sure to go to the fourth floor to see the beautiful skylight.

CHINESE BENEVOLENT SOCIETY   As you return south through the Gaslamp District, take a short detour west (right) along G Street, then south (left) on 3rd Avenue, to see the Chinese Benevolent Society, established in 1920, when police had shut down the bordellos and the Gaslamp District had become completely Chinese. Today, Chinese holidays are still celebrated in the street in front of the Benevolent Society. ~ 428 3rd Avenue. Continue south to Island Avenue and turn east (left) to return to your starting point.

Plaza Trolley Transfer Station. Two floors and four galleries showcase an internationally renowned collection and temporary exhibits featuring cutting-edge contemporary art. Educational tours and a well-stocked bookstore complement the exhibits. Closed Wednesday. ~ 1001 Kettner Boulevard at Broadway; 619-234-1001, fax 619-232-4875; www.mcasd.org.

LODGING

Among the few decent downtown budget overnight spots, **Hotel Churchill** is about the cleanest and most livable. Billed as "small, quaint, and unique," this venerable seven-story, 92-room hotel is mostly quaint. Built in 1915, it was somewhat tastelessly remodeled to "depict an authentic medieval English castle." To really save money during a downtown stay, ask for one of the rooms with a shared bathroom. ~ 827 C Street; 619-234-5186, fax 619-231-9012. BUDGET.

Treat yourself to a nice dinner with the money you save staying at **Hostelling International—San Diego Downtown**, centrally located in the Gaslamp Quarter. Featuring a blue-and-yellow trompe l'oeil mural on the outside, this Mediterranean-style hostelry has 25 sex-segregated dorm facilities and 17 private rooms, as well as a fully equipped kitchen and common area. Unlike other hostels, there is no curfew. Reservations recommended. ~ 521 Market Street, 619-525-1531, 800-909-4776, fax 619-338-0129; www.sandiegohostels.org, e-mail downtown@sandiegohostels.org. BUDGET.

The redlight district was called the Stingaree, after the dangerous sting rays in San Diego Bay—in either place, you were bound to get badly stung.

Chain hotels are normally not included in these listings, but because of the lack of good, low-cost lodgings downtown, I'm compelled to tell you about **Super 8 Bayview**. This 98-room property offers pleasant, affordable rooms downtown. Queen-sized beds complement a bright, functional, and contemporary environment; you'll also find a pool and jacuzzi here. ~ 1835 Columbia Street; 619-544-0164, 800-537-9902, fax 619-237-9940. MODERATE.

A recommended midtown hotel is the **Best Western Bayside Inn**. Small enough (122 rooms) to offer some degree of personalized service, this modern highrise promises nearly all the niceties you would pay extra for at more prestigious downtown hotels, including a harbor view. Furnishings and amenities are virtually on a par with those found in the typical Hilton or Sheraton. There is a pool and spa, plus a restaurant and cocktail lounge. ~ 555 West Ash Street; 619-233-7500, 800-341-1818, fax 619-239-8060; www.baysideinn.com, e-mail tichotels@sandiego.com. MODERATE.

Located in the heart of the Gaslamp Quarter, the **Bristol Hotel** is an elegant boutique hotel that leaves a lasting impression. Ultra-modern in decor, its clean, minimalist lines are boldly accented with vivid splashes of color. The 102 rooms offer one king-sized or two queen beds, and art lovers will revel in the hotel's art collection, which includes works by Peter Max, Andy Warhol, Roy Lichtenstein, and other Pop art greats. ~ 1055 1st Avenue; 619-232-6141, 800-662-4477, fax 619-232-1948; www.thebristolsandiego.com. DELUXE TO ULTRA-DELUXE.

No downtown hotel has a more colorful past than the **Horton Grand Hotel**. This 132-room Victorian gem is actually two old hotels that were disassembled piece by piece and resurrected a few blocks away. The two were lavishly reconstructed and linked by an atrium-lobby and courtyard. The 1880s theme is faithfully executed in the hotel's antique-furnished rooms, each of which has a fireplace. Such amenities as a concierge and afternoon tea (served Saturday) combine with friendly service and perfect location to make it one of the city's best hotel values. ~ 311 Island Avenue; 619-544-1886, 800-542-1886, fax 619-239-3823; www.hortongrand.com, e-mail horton@connectnet.com. DELUXE TO ULTRA-DELUXE.

Built in 1910 in honor of the 18th president by his son Ulysses S. Grant, Jr., the **U.S. Grant Hotel** reigned as downtown San Diego's premier hotel for decades. The U.S. Grant is a showcase boasting 285 rooms, a restaurant, and a lounge. It is quite possibly the most elegant and certainly the most beautifully restored historic building in the city. There's a marble-floored lobby with cathedral-height ceilings and enormous crystal chandeliers. Rooms are richly furnished with mahogany poster beds, Queen Anne–style armoires, and wing-back chairs. ~ 326 Broadway; 619-232-3121, 800-996-3426, fax 619-232-3626; www. usgrant.net. ULTRA-DELUXE.

Visitors to Horton Plaza are bombarded with dining opportunities. But for those who can resist the temptation to chow down on pizza, french fries, and enchiladas at nearby fast-food shops, there is a special culinary reward. On the plaza's top level sits **Panda Inn**. Here the plush, contemporary design alludes only subtly to Asia with a scattering of classic artwork. But the menu is all-Chinese. Three dishes stand out: crispy beef, lemon scallops, and chicken with garlic sauce. Lunch and dinner menus together present more than 100 dishes. Dine on the glassed-in veranda for a great view of the harbor. Brunch on Sunday. ~ 506 Horton Plaza; 619-233-7800, fax 619-233-5632; www.pandainn.com. BUDGET TO DELUXE.

DINING

There are no shortages of restaurants in the Gaslamp either, with the majority offering sidewalk tables from which to watch the passing parade of horse-drawn carriages, bike taxis and pedestrians.

Fans of the late Jim Croce ("Bad, Bad Leroy Brown," "Time in a Bottle") will surely enjoy a visit to **Croce's Restaurants and Bars**. Located in the heart of the Gaslamp Quarter and managed enthusiastically by Jim's widow, Ingrid Croce, the restaurants feature an eclectic mix of dishes served in a friendly setting. Daily dinner specials vary and are best described as contemporary American ranging from salads to pasta, beef, chicken, and fresh fish dishes. No breakfast or lunch on weekdays. ~ 802 5th Avenue; 619-233-4355, fax 619-232-9836; www.croces.com, e-mail ingrid@croces.com. MODERATE TO DELUXE.

Just down the block, **Dakota Grill & Spirits** occupies two floors of San Diego's first skycraper (1914). Black-clad, bolo-tied waitstaff bustle around with wood-fired pizza, hearty rotisserie meats, and grilled seafood whipped up by cooks in the open kitchen. Among the offerings: grilled pork prime rib with apricot mustard glaze, chicken breast with honey-mustard sauce, and seafood fettuccini in cream sauce. There's piano music Wednesday through Saturday. ~ 901 5th Avenue; 619-234-5554; www. cohnrestaurants.com, e-mail info@cohnrestaurants.com. MODERATE TO DELUXE.

History, atmosphere, and great cooking combine to make dining at **Ida Bailey's Restaurant** a memorable experience. Located in the Horton Grand Hotel, Ida's was once a brothel, operated back in the 1890s by a madam of the same name. Things are tamer now, but the rich Victorian furnishings serve as a reminder of San Diego's opulent past. The chef serves a varied menu highlighted by old-fashioned American fare, including Victorian pot roast, rack of lamb, and tenderloin. Breakfast, lunch, and dinner are served. ~ 311 Island Avenue; 619-544-1886, fax 619-239-3823; www.hortongrand.com, e-mail horton@connectnet.com. MODERATE TO DELUXE.

Nearby, a suit of armor marks the entrance to **Sevilla**. Inside, clouds float across the ceiling, red-tiled roofs and striped awnings extend from walls with shuttered windows, and gaslamps dot the dining room, evoking the festive atmosphere of a Spanish plaza. Diners combine plates of *tapas* (*bocadillos*, marinated lamb, *empanadas*) over glasses of sangria, or indulge in full-sized traditional meals such as *zarzuela* (a savory seafood stew) and paella. Save room for the equally marvelous desserts. Dinner only. ~ 555 4th Avenue; 619-233-5979; www.cafesevilla.com. MODERATE TO DELUXE.

SHOPPING The **Westfield Shoppingtown Horton Plaza** is anchored by three department stores and a flood of specialty and one-of-a-kind shops complete the picture. Along the tiled boulevard are shops and vendors peddling their wares. ~ Between Broadway and G Street, 1st and 4th avenues; 619-239-8180; www.westfield.com.

On the second level, the **San Diego City Store** (619-238-2489) sells retired street signs, keychains and the like. There are men's apparel shops, shoe stores, jewelry shops, and women's haute couture boutiques, dozens of stores in all.

The **Gaslamp Quarter**, along 5th Avenue, is a charming 16-square-block assemblage of shops, galleries, and sidewalk cafés in the downtown center. Faithfully replicated in the quarter are Victorian-era street lamps, red-brick sidewalks, and window displays thematic of turn-of-the-20th-century San Diego.

A favorite spot for antique lovers is **The Cracker Factory**, which offers three floors of antiques and collectibles in the restored 1913 Bishop Cracker Factory. Legend speaks of resident ghost named "Crunch" who shuffles through mounds of broken crackers here searching for a small brass cookie cutter. ~ 448 West Market Street; 619-233-1669.

Other intriguing Gaslamp Quarter shops include **Le Travel Store**, which sells innovative and hard-to-find travel gear, packs and luggage, guidebooks, maps, and travel accessories—there's even a travel agency inside the store. ~ 745 4th Avenue; 619-544-0005; www.letravelstore.com. **Palace Loan & Jewelry** offers top-of-the-line pre-owned merchandise at bargain prices in a building that once housed a saloon and gambling parlor owned by Wyatt Earp. Closed Sunday. ~ 951 4th Avenue; 619-234-3175.

You can watch Cuban exiles roll *panatelas, toropedos, presidentes,* and *robustos* from Cuban-seed tobacco grown in other parts of the Caribbean at the **Cuban Cigar Factory**. ~ 551 5th Avenue; 619-238-2429; www.cubancigarfactory.com.

NIGHTLIFE

The sun is certainly the main attraction in San Diego, but the city also features a rich and varied nightlife, offering the night owl everything from traditional folk music to high-energy discos. There are piano bars, singles bars, and a growing number of jazz clubs.

Call the **San Diego Performing Arts League** for its monthly arts calendar and information about inexpensive events. ~ 619-238-0700; www.sandiegoperforms.com. KIFM Radio (98.1 FM) hosts **Jazz Hotline**, a 24-hour information line that provides the latest in jazz happenings. ~ 619-543-1401.

THE BEST BARS   In the Gaslamp Quarter, **5th Quarter** has live entertainment nightly, usually featuring house bands. Occasional cover. ~ 600 5th Avenue; 619-236-1616; www.5quarter.com.

4th & B features national musical acts and well-known comedians. ~ 345 B Street; 619-231-4343; www.4thandb.com

It's a non-stop party at the **Bitter End**, a three-level bar and nightclub that has something to offer everyone. Top-40 music complete with videos is blasted on the first level, high-energy dance music can be found on the second, and a more mellow crowd kicks back to jazz on the top level. Cover. ~ 770 4th Avenue; 619-338-9300; www.bitterend.com.

Lawman Wyatt Earp once ran three gambling halls in the Gaslamp Quarter.

Fans of the immortal Jim Croce will love **Croce's Jazz Bar** (619-233-4355), built as a memorial to the late singer-songwriter by his wife, Ingrid. Family mementos line the walls in tribute to a talented recording artist. Live entertainment nightly. Just next door, **Croce's Top Hat Bar** (619-233-6945) is a snazzy New Orleans–style club featuring live R&B. Closed Sunday through Thursday. Cover. ~ 802–820 5th Avenue; www.croces.com.

Karl Strauss Restaurant and Brewery Downtown may well have the best beer in town—San Diego's original microbrew. ~ 1157 Columbia Street; 619-234-2739; www.karlstraus.com.

Plaza Bar, at the distinctive Westgate Hotel, is a graceful period French lounge where prominent locals and visitors enjoy classy piano entertainment nightly. ~ 1055 2nd Avenue; 619-238-1818, www.westgatehotel.com.

THEATER In addition to performances of the San Diego Opera, the **San Diego Civic Theatre** presents a variety of entertainment ranging from pop artists to plays to dance performances. ~ 1100 3rd Avenue; 619-570-1100; www.sandiegotheatres.org.

The **San Diego Repertory Theatre** performs dramas, comedies, and musicals. ~ At the Lyceum Horton Plaza; 619-544-1000; www.sandiegorep.com.

OPERA AND DANCE With performances at the San Diego Civic Theatre, the **San Diego Opera** presents such international stars as Patricia Racette, Ferruccio Furlanetto, and Anja Henteros. The season runs from January through May. ~ 1100 3rd Avenue; 619-232-7636, fax 619-231-6915; www.sdopera.com.

California Ballet Company and School presents a diverse repertoire of contemporary and traditional ballets at area theaters. ~ 4819 Ronson Court; 858-560-5676; www.californiaballet.org.

If you're a culture vulture with a limited pocketbook, try Times Arts Tix, a 24-hour recording listing half-priced theater, music, and dance tickets. ~ 619-497-5000.

San Diego Harbor

San Diego's beautiful harbor is a notable exception to the rule that big-city waterfronts lack appeal. Here, the city embraces its bay and presents its finest profile along the water.

SIGHTS The best way to see it all is on a harbor tour. A variety of vessels dock near Harbor Drive at the foot of Broadway. **San Diego Harbor Excursion** provides leisurely trips around the 22-square-mile harbor, which is colorfully backdropped by commercial and naval vessels as well as the dramatic cityscape. Ferry service to Coronado Island from downtown is also operated by Harbor Excursion. Fee. ~ 1050 North Harbor Drive; 619-234-4111, fax 619-522-6150; www.sdhe.com. My favorite sunset harbor cruises are aboard the 150-foot yacht *Spirit of San Diego*. Admission. ~ 1050 North Harbor Drive; 619-234-8687; 800-442-7847; www.sdhe.com, e-mail george@sdhe.com.

All along the cityside of the harbor from the Coast Guard Station opposite Lindbergh Field to Seaport Village is a lovely landscaped boardwalk called the **Embarcadero**. It offers parks where you can stroll and play, a floating maritime museum, and a thriving assortment of waterfront diversions.

The **Maritime Museum of San Diego** is composed of four vintage ships and one visiting ship on loan from Fox Studios until 2005; most familiar is the 1863 *Star of India*, the world's oldest iron-hulled merchant ship still afloat. Visitors go aboard for a hint of what life was like on the high seas more than a century ago. You can also visit the 1898 ferry *Berkeley*, which helped in the evacuation of San Francisco during the 1906 earthquake, and the 1904 steam yacht *Medea*. Admission. ~ 1492 North Harbor Drive; 619-234-9153, fax 619-234-8345; www.sdmaritime.com, e-mail info@sdmaritime.com.

Nautical buffs or anyone concerned about American naval power will be interested in the **U.S. Navy** presence in San Diego harbor. As headquarters of the Commander Naval Base, San Diego hosts one of the world's largest fleets of fighting ships—from aircraft carriers to nuclear submarines. Naval docks and yards are off-limits but you'll see the sprawling facilities and plenty of those distinctive gray-hulled ships during a harbor cruise. Naval vessels moored at the Broadway Pier hold open house on weekends.

The Marine Center presents colorful **military reviews** most Fridays. Marching ceremonies begin at exactly 10 a.m. at the Marine Corps Recruiting Depot (619-524-1772). ~ The center may be reached from downtown by going north on Pacific Highway to Barnett Avenue, then follow the signs.

Near the south end of the Embarcadero sits the popular shopping and entertainment complex known as **Seaport Village**. Designed to replicate an Early California seaport, it comprises 14 acres of bayfront parks and promenades, shops, restaurants, and galleries. You'll also find a carousel, free weekend concerts, and magicians and musicians entertaining the masses. ~ Kettner Boulevard and West Harbor Drive; 619-235-4013, fax 619-696-0025; www.seaportvillage.com, e-mail info@seaportvillage.com.

On the south side, overlooking the water, is the 45-foot-high **Mukilteo Lighthouse**, official symbol of the village, a recreation of a famous lighthouse located in Washington state. Nearby is the **Broadway Flying Horses Carousel**, a hand-carved, turn-of-the-20th-century model that originally whirled around on Coney Island.

Nearby, the **San Diego Convention Center** looks like an erector set gone mad. An uncontained congeries of flying buttresses, giant tents, and curved glass, it is fashioned in the form of a ship, seemingly poised to set sail across San Diego Harbor. This architectural exclamation mark is certainly worth a drive-by or a quick tour. ~ 111 West Harbor Drive; 619-525-5000, fax 619-525-5005; www.sdcc.org.

You'd be remiss to visit San Diego without enjoying a fresh seafood feast at a spot overlooking the harbor. Why not go first class at **Star of the Sea**? This place wears more awards than a Navy admiral. Dramatically set over the water and elegantly dec-

DINING

orated, Star of the Sea presents a remarkable seasonal seafood menu. Live jazz on Thursday. Reservations are recommended. Dinner only. ~ 1360 North Harbor Drive; 619-232-7408, fax 619-232-1877; www.starofthesea. com, e-mail starmail@afgcorp.com. ULTRA-DELUXE.

Seaport Village hosts a variety of open-air entertainments, from blues, jazz, and salsa bands to wandering magicians and mimes.

If your budget can't handle the "Star," check out the place next door—**Anthony's Fish Grotto**, whose menu includes fresh catch-of-the-day, seafood kabobs and lobster *thermidor*. ~ 1360 North Harbor Drive; 619-232-5103, fax 619-232-1877; www.gofishanthonys.com. BUDGET TO DELUXE.

SHOPPING   **Seaport Village** was designed to capture the look and feel of an Early California waterfront setting. Its 57 shops dot a 14-acre village and include the usual mix of boutiques, galleries, clothing stores, and gift shops. ~ Kettner Boulevard and West Harbor Drive; 619-235-4013; www.seaportvillage.com, e-mail info@sea portvillage.com.

NIGHTLIFE   There's a wonderful view of San Diego Bay from the Seaport Village restaurant **Edgewater Grill**, where a tropical setting creates a lovely relaxed atmosphere. ~ 861 West Harbor Drive; 619-232-7581.

BEACHES & PARKS   **EMBARCADERO MARINA PARKS** ♨ The center city's only real waterfront park is a breezy promenade situated on the bay and divided into two sections. The northern part has a nicely landscaped lawn and garden, picnic tables, and benches. The southern half features a fishing pier, basketball courts, and an athletic course. Restrooms are available. ~ Enter at the southern end at Harbor Drive and 8th Street; at the northern end, from Seaport Village shopping center; 619-686-6225, fax 619-686-6200; www. portofsandiego.org.

Coronado

An isolated and exclusive community in San Diego Bay, Coronado is almost an island, connected to the mainland only by the graceful San Diego–Coronado Bay Bridge and by a long, narrow sandspit called the Silver Strand. Long a playground of the rich and famous, the city's hotels reflect this ritzy heritage.

SIGHTS   Once known as the "Nickel Snatcher," the Coronado Ferry for years crossed the waters of San Diego Harbor between the Embarcadero and Coronado. All for five cents each way. That's history, of course, but the 1940-vintage, double-deck *Silvergate* still plies the waters. The **San Diego Bay Ferry** leaves from the Bay Café on North Harbor Drive at the foot of Broadway on the hour and docks 15 minutes later at the Ferry Landing Marketplace on the Coronado side. ~ San Diego Harbor Excursion; 619-234-4111, fax 619-522-6150; www.sdhe.com.

The town's main attraction is the **Hotel del Coronado**, a red-roofed, Victorian-style, wooden wonder, and National Historic Landmark. Explore the old palace and its manicured grounds, discovering the intricate corridors and cavernous public rooms. It was Elisha Babcock's dream, when he purchased 4100 acres of barren, wind-blown peninsula in 1888, to build a hotel that would be the "talk of the Western world." Realizing Babcock's dream from the beginning, it attracted presidents, dignitaries, and movie stars. You might even recognize it from the movie *Some Like It Hot*. ~ 1500 Orange Avenue; 619-435-6611, fax 619-522-8262; www.hoteldel.com, e-mail delinquiries@hoteldel.com.

Although shadowed by its noted neighbor, the **Glorietta Bay Inn** is a worthy landmark in its own right. It was built in 1908 as the private mansion of sugar scion John D. Spreckels. From here you can cruise the quiet neighborhood streets that radiate off Orange Avenue between the bay and the ocean, enjoying the town's handsome blend of cottages and historic homes. ~ 1630 Glorietta Boulevard; 619-435-3101, 800-283-9383, fax 619-435-6182; www.gloriettabayinn.com, e-mail info@gloriettabay inn.com.

El Cordova Hotel is in the heart of Coronado. Originally built as a private mansion in 1902, El Cordova's moderate size (40 rooms) and lovely Spanish-hacienda architecture make it a relaxing getaway spot. A pool and patio restaurant are added niceties. ~ 1351 Orange Avenue; 619-435-4131, 800-229-2032, fax 619-435-0632; www.elcordovahotel.com. DELUXE TO ULTRA-DELUXE.

LODGING

Nothing can detract from the glamour of the **Hotel del Coronado**. With its turrets, cupolas, and gingerbread facade, it is one of the great hotels of California. The last in a proud line of extravagant seaside resorts, the Hotel del Coronado has long been the relaxing place of Hollywood stars and ten United States presidents. Remember, however, this celebrated Victorian landmark is a major tourist attraction, so in addition to guests, who usually fill its 688 rooms to capacity, a large number of visitors crowd the lobby, grounds, and shops every day. Be aware, too, that many rooms are in two structures adjacent to the original building and though more comfortable are not the real thing. "Hotel Del" has two pools, a long stretch of beach, nine eating areas, three tennis courts, a fitness center, a spa, and a gallery of shops. Reservations recommended. ~ 1500 Orange Avenue; 619-522-8000, 800-435-6611, fax 619-522-8262; www.hoteldel.com, e-mail delinquiries@hoteldel.com. ULTRA-DELUXE.

Across the street rises the **Glorietta Bay Inn**, the 1908 Edwardian mansion of sugar king John D. Spreckels which has been transformed into an elegant 100-room hotel. Rooms and suites in the mansion reflect the grandeur of Spreckels' time; more typical accommodations are available in the contemporary inn buildings that surround the mansion. Continental breakfast, ladies and gentlemen, is served on the mansion terrace. ~ 1630 Glorietta Boulevard; 619-435-3101, 800-283-9383, fax 619-435-6182; www.gloriettabayinn.com, e-mail info@gloriettabayinn.com. DELUXE TO ULTRA-DELUXE.

A farmer's market is held at Ferry Landing Marketplace on Tuesday afternoons.

The **Coronado Victorian House** is quite possibly the only hotel anywhere to offer dance, exercise, and gourmet cooking classes with a night's stay. Located in an 1894 historic building near the beach and downtown Coronado, the decor of this seven-room bed and breakfast includes Persian rugs, stained-glass windows, and private baths with clawfoot tubs; rooms are named after artists and dancers. Those guests not interested in the extracurricular activities are invited to relax and enjoy such healthy and home-cooked specialties as baklava, stuffed grape leaves, and homemade yogurt. Two-night minimum. ~ 1000 8th Street; 619-435-2200, 888-299-2822; www.coronadovictorian.com. ULTRA-DELUXE.

DINING

Visitors crossing over to Coronado invariably tour the famous Hotel del Coronado, and many are lured into the **Crown-Coronet Room**. Its grand Victorian architecture and enormous domed ceiling (the chandeliers were designed by *Wizard of Oz* author L. Frank Baum) set a tone of elegance and style unmatched anywhere on the Pacific Coast. The place is so magnificent the food seems unimportant. Most critics, in fact, assert that dinner (served every night except Monday; reservations recommended) in the hotel's **Prince of Wales Room** is better, but the Sunday brunch at the Crown Room will never disappoint. Reservations recommended for Sunday brunch. ~ 1500 Orange Avenue; 619-435-6611, fax 619-522-8262; www.hoteldel.com. ULTRA-DELUXE.

Locals looking to avoid the crowds at "Hotel Del" usually head for **Chez Loma**. Set in a charming 1889 Victorian house, it serves a lovely Continental/French dinner—excellent *canard rôti* (traditional roast duck with cherry, green peppercorn, and burnt orange sauce). Dine inside or out. Dinner only. ~ 1132 Loma Avenue; 619-435-0661, fax 619-435-3770; www.chezloma.com, e-mail chef@chezloma.com. DELUXE TO ULTRA-DELUXE.

Peohe's, located at the Ferry Landing Marketplace, is primarily praised for its panoramic views of San Diego Bay and for its tropical decor. The dining room features green palms and rushing cascades of water flowing into ponds of live fish. The dinner menu is mostly fresh fish plus lobster, shrimp, and a daily featured "catch." There are also prime rib, chicken, and lamb. Sunday brunch is another option. ~ 1201 1st Street; 619-437-4474; www.peohes.com. DELUXE TO ULTRA-DELUXE.

SHOPPING

Coronado's fancy Orange Avenue in the village center harbors an assortment of unusual shops in the **El Cordova Hotel**. ~ 1351 Orange Avenue; 619-435-4131; www.elcordovahotel.com.

The **Ferry Landing Marketplace** is a modern shopping area complete with boutiques, specialty shops, galleries, and eateries. ~ 1201 1st Street; 619-435-8895.

The **Hotel del Coronado** is a city within a city and home to many intriguing specialty shops, such as **Babcock & Story Emporium**, which has a selection of bath and body products, kitchenware, and gardening accessories. ~ 1500 Orange Avenue; 619-435-6611; www.delshop.com.

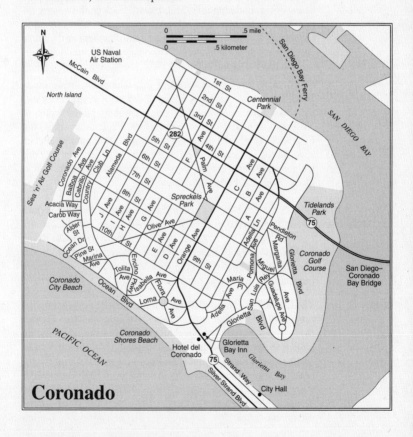

Coronado

NIGHTLIFE If you're out Coronado way, stop for a cocktail in the Hotel del Coronado's **Babcock & Story Bar**. Live entertainment Wednesday through Sunday night. ~ 1500 Orange Avenue; 619-435-6611; www.hoteldel.com.

Check out the boisterous Irish scene at **McP's**, a full swinging bar and grill with shamrock-plastered walls and a bartender with the gift of gab. McP's is a Navy SEAL hangout, so as one glib bartender noted, it's the most likely place in town to pet a seal. Entertainment includes live rock and jazz bands on a nightly basis. ~ 1107 Orange Avenue; 619-435-5280; www.mcpspub.com.

The historic Spreckels Building in Coronado is a vintage-1917 opera house that has been restored to a 347-seat venue called the **Lamb's Players Theatre**. ~ 1142 Orange Avenue; 619-437-0600; www.lambsplayers.org.

BEACHES & PARKS

CORONADO SHORES BEACH 🏊 🏄 🚣 It's the widest beach in the county but hardly atmospheric, backed up as it is by a row of towering condominiums. Still, crowds flock to this roomy expanse of clean, soft sand where gentle waves make for good swimming and surfing. The younger crowd gathers at the north end, just south of the Hotel del Coronado. There are lifeguards. ~ Located off Ocean Boulevard.

CORONADO CITY BEACH 🏊 🏄 🚣 That same wide sandy beach prevails to the north. Here the city has a large, grassy picnic area known as **Sunset Park** where frisbees and the aroma of fried chicken fill the air. Facilities include firepits, restrooms, and lifeguards. The beach offers good fishing and swimming. Surfing is restricted to the north end during the busy summer months; it's generally safe, but be wary of unpredictable breaks. ~ On Ocean Boulevard north of Avenue G.

▼▼▼▼▼▼▼▼▼▼▼▼▼▼▼▼
South San Diego County

Linking downtown with the Mexican border city of Tijuana, 20 miles south, a string of seaside cities straddle Route 5. While thriving as manufacturing, commercial, and residential communities, Imperial Beach, Chula Vista, and National City are beginning to develop as tourist industries.

SIGHTS The **Chula Vista Nature Center** is located in the Sweetwater National Wildlife Refuge on San Diego Bay and, through interactive exhibits especially appealing to children, offers a close-up look at the history and geology of Southern California wetlands. There is a shark and ray tank, birds of prey exhibits, and a composting garden. Closed Monday. Admission. ~ 1000 Gunpowder Point Drive, Chula Vista; 619-409-5900, fax 619-409-5910; www.chulavistanaturecenter.org, e-mail barbara@chulavistanaturecenter.org.

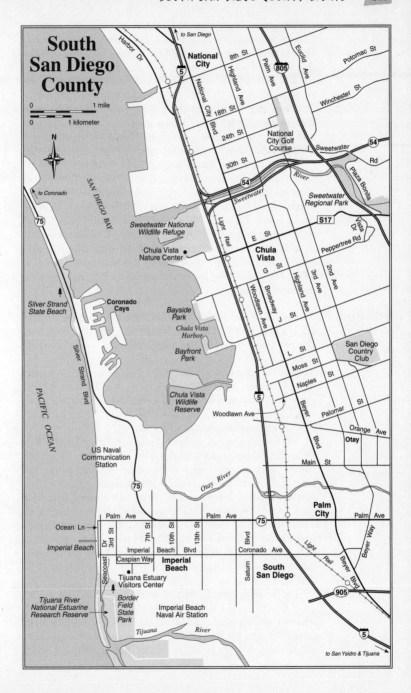

South San Diego County

0 _____ 1 mile
0 _____ 1 kilometer

N

Harbor Dr

to San Diego

National City

8th St

Highland Ave

Palm Ave

805

Euclid Ave

Potomac St

5

National City Blvd

18th St

Winchester St

24th St

National City Golf Course

Sweetwater

54

30th St

Rd

54

River

Plaza Bonita

Sweetwater

Sweetwater Regional Park

to Coronado

SAN DIEGO BAY

75

Light Rail

E St

S17

Vista Dr

Sweetwater National Wildlife Refuge

Chula Vista

Peppertree Rd

Chula Vista Nature Center

G St

Highland Ave

3rd Ave

2nd Ave

Silver Strand State Beach

Coronado Cays

Broadway

Woodlawn Ave

J St

Bayside Park

J St

Chula Vista Harbor

L St

San Diego Country Club

Silver Strand Blvd

Bayfront Park

Moss St

Naples St

PACIFIC OCEAN

Chula Vista Wildlife Reserve

5

St

Beyer

Palomar St

Woodlawn Ave

Orange Ave

Otay

US Naval Communication Station

Blvd

Main St

75

Otay River

Palm City

Palm Ave

Palm Ave

Palm Ave

75

Ocean Ln

3rd St

7th St

10th St

13th St

Blvd

Light Rail

Beyer Way

Imperial Beach

Imperial Beach Blvd

Coronado Ave

Beyer Blvd

Seacoast Dr

Caspian Way

Imperial Beach

Saturn

South San Diego

Tijuana Estuary Visitors Center

Border Field State Park

Imperial Beach Naval Air Station

905

Tijuana River National Estuarine Research Reserve

Tijuana   *River*

5

to San Ysidro & Tijuana

Visitors to Chula Vista also have an opportunity to glimpse Olympic athletes in training at the **U.S. Olympic Training Center**. Guided tours are conducted from the visitors center hourly, Monday through Saturday, from 10 a.m. to 3 p.m., and on Sunday, from 11 a.m. to 3 p.m. ~ 2800 Olympic Parkway, Chula Vista; 619-656-1500, fax 619-482-6200; www.usolympicteam.com.

Along this southern coastline is the **Tijuana River National Estuarine Research Reserve**, which comprises the county's largest and most pristine estuarine sanctuary (Tijuana Slough National Wildlife Refuge) and a three-mile stretch of sandy beach (Border Field State Park). For nature lovers, this haven of salt marsh and sand dunes is a must-see diversion: more than 370 species of birds are found there. The visitors center features exhibits and a library. Trails lead to the beach and wildlife refuge at this fascinating wetland (see the "Beaches & Parks" and "Hiking" sections in this chapter for more information). ~ Visitors center: 301 Caspian Way, Imperial Beach; see "South San Diego County Beaches & Parks" for directions to the state park; 619-575-3613, fax 619-575-6913; www.tijuanaestuary.com, e-mail trn err@ixpress.com.

LODGING
Among all those identical motels grouped around the freeway exits in Chula Vista, **The Traveler Inn & Suites** is perhaps your best bet. Conveniently located just a block from the highway, this family-owned 85-unit motel is early Holiday Inn throughout, but its rates hark back to 1960s. Not that you would really expect them, but extras include two pools, a spa, laundry facilities, and cable TV. Continental breakfast is served. ~ 235 Woodlawn Avenue, Chula Vista; 619-427-9170, 800-748-6998, fax 619-427-5247; thetravelerinn.com. MODERATE.

Situated on a main commercial street just a few blocks from the trolley station and the freeway, the **Chula Vista Travel Inn** has 77 clean and tidy rooms and suites overlooking a pool and hot tub. The palm trees and stucco-and-tile exterior exude a Mediterranean air; accommodations are standard motel style with phone, cable TV, and coffee makers, and some rooms have spas. There are laundry facilities and an adjacent greasy-spoon diner. Continental breakfast is included. ~ 394 Broadway, Chula Vista; 619-420-6600, 800-447-0416, phone/fax 619-420-5556; www.travelinnsandiego.com, e-mail travelinn7@aol.com. BUDGET TO DELUXE.

The **Seacoast Inn of Imperial Beach** is the only hostelry located directly on the sands of Imperial Beach. Decked out with a heated outdoor pool and hot tub, this 38-room complex looks good inside and out. Beachside units are especially nice and have full kitchens. It helps to make summer reservations well in advance. ~ 800 Seacoast Drive, Imperial Beach; 619-424-5183, 800-732-2627, fax 619-424-3090; www.theseacoastinn.com. DELUXE.

There's no shortage of fast-food joints along Broadway. **Roberto's Taco Shop** has been serving up cheap and tasty Mexican fare since the early 1980s. Rolled tacos, burritos bursting with juicy shredded beef, savory chicken fajitas—it's hard to go wrong here. Open 24 hours. ~ 444 Broadway, Chula Vista; 619-425-0444. BUDGET.

DINING

Each July Imperial Beach hosts the annual U.S. Open Sandcastle Competition, attracting huge crowds.

La Bella Pizza Garden is like an annex to Chula Vista's town hall, and owner Kitty Raso is known as the "Mayor of Third Avenue." But the food will interest you far more than the latest political gossip. Besides pizza, there's great lasagna, rigatoni, and ravioli. La Bella features tender veal dishes, too, from a menu that amazingly rarely strays beyond budget prices. Best Italian food for the money in San Diego, and it's open from 7 a.m. to 1 a.m. every day. ~ 373 3rd Avenue, Chula Vista; 619-426-8820, fax 619-426-1302; www.labellapizza.com. BUDGET.

The pastel-colored, open-air **Chula Vista Center** is anchored by Macy's, Mervyn's, and Sears, and comprises over 60 chain stores as well as unique boutiques. Kids love the carousel. ~ 555 Broadway, Chula Vista; 619-427-6700; www.chulavista.com.

SHOPPING

For something more unique, you might peruse the eclectic offerings on 3rd Avenue between E and G streets. This historic strip harbors shops laden with antiques, religious curios and books, and kitschy knickknacks.

If you're looking for nighttime entertainment in these areas, you'll probably want to consider a trip downtown or to Tijuana (see the "South of the Border" feature in this chapter). Otherwise, be content with scattered restaurant bars and local pubs.

NIGHTLIFE

SILVER STRAND STATE BEACH ⟋ This one-mile strip of fluffy white sand fronts a narrow isthmus separating the Pacific Ocean and San Diego Bay. It was named for tiny silver sea shells found in abundance along the shore. The water here is shallow and fairly calm on the ocean side, making it a good swimming beach. Things are even calmer and the water much warmer on the bay shore. Silver Strand State Beach is also popular for shell hunting. Facilities include picnic areas, restrooms, lifeguards (summer only), showers, and food concessions (summer only). Parking fee, $6. ~ Located on Route 75 and Coronado Cays Boulevard between Imperial Beach and Coronado; 619-435-5184.

BEACHES & PARKS

Text continued on page 382.

South of the Border

Tijuana, a favorite day-trip destination for San Diego visitors, has been amazingly transformed in recent years from a bawdy bordertown to a modern, bustling city of more than two million people. Gone, or very well hidden, are the borderline attractions that once lured sailors and marines. In their place is a colorful center of tourism suitable for the entire family.

A major revitalization effort brought highrise buildings, broad boulevards, huge shopping centers, and classy shops and restaurants. But don't get the idea Tijuana has become completely Americanized. It still retains much of its traditional Mexican flavor and offers visitors an exciting outing and some surprising cultural experiences.

Perhaps the most impressive attraction, ideal for learning about Mexico, is the **Centro Cultural Tijuana**. Here the striking 85-foot-high Omnimax Space Theater is a silvery sphere held up by a stylized hand that symbolizes the earth housing a world of culture. Inside, the giant 180° screen shows various films pertaining to Mexico. The complex, designed by Pedro Ramírez Váquez, architect of Mexico City's famous Anthropological Museum, houses five exhibit halls, a restaurant, a bookstore, and a multilevel cultural and historical museum. Admission. ~ Paseo de los Héroes at Calle Mina; 52-66-46-87-96-00; www.cecut.gob.mx.

No doubt a major reason to visit "TJ" is to shop. The central shopping district is downtown, along Avenida Revolución, where arcades, stalls, and hawkers line the boulevard promoting the usual selection of tourist trinkets, piñatas, colorful flowers, serapes, pottery, and lace. There are numerous shops featuring quality merchandise such as leather goods, designer clothes, perfumes, artwork, and jewelry at incredible savings. **La Villa del Tobaco** has a broad selection of cuban cigars and smoking accessories. ~ 2015 3rd Street; 52-66-85-85-58. **Tolan-Arte de México** offers authentic Mexican folk art and fashions. ~ Avenida Revolución between Calles 7 and 8; 52-66-46-88-36-37.

American currency is accepted everywhere but small bills are recommended since getting change can sometimes be a problem. U.S. residents receive a duty and federal tax exemption on the first $400 in personal goods purchased in Mexico. One liter of alcoholic beverage is allowed for those 21 years and older.

Spectator sports are a popular pastime for Tijuana visitors, including greyhound racing at **Hipódromo Caliente Race Track**. ~ Boulevard Agua Caliente, 52-66-46-33-73-47 in Tijuana; 619-231-1919 from San Diego. Or catch a colorful bullfight at **Toreo de Tijuana**. ~ Boulevard Agua Caliente. Or try **Plaza Monumental**. ~ Located six miles west via Highway 1D. Call **Five Star Tours** for tickets and information. ~ Located in the Amtrak Santa Fe station, 1050 Kettner Boulevard, San Diego; 619-232-5049.

Call the **Baja Visitors Information** for information about all events. You can also visit their office in Mission Valley and pick up helpful literature. Closed Sunday. ~ 6855 Friars Road #26, San Diego; 619-298-4105. The **Tijuana Chamber of Commerce Tourism Information** will provide visitors with information on the city's shops and restaurants. ~ 9365 Avenida de los Heroes; 52-66-46-84-05-37.

Tijuana has some exceptional restaurants. **La Costa** serves succulent seafood in a quiet, comfortable atmosphere. ~ Calle 7a between Avenida Revolución and Avenida Constitución; 52-66-46-85-84-94. MODERATE TO DELUXE.

Should you decide to stay longer than a day, enjoy Tijuana's stylish hotel, **The Grand Hotel Tijuana**. This 422-room luxury complex boasts dramatic city views from its 28-story glass towers and offers three restaurants, two bars, a gallery of shops, tennis courts, swimming pool, and a health club. ~ Boulevard Agua Caliente No. 4558; 800-026-6007 in Tijuana; 800-472-6385 in San Diego; www.grand hoteltijuana.com, e-mail ghotelt2@telnor.net. DELUXE TO ULTRA-DELUXE.

Just a little farther south of Tijuana along the coast, the small towns of Rosarito Beach and Ensenada provide a less commercial glimpse of Mexico. A modern highway makes the trip easy and comfortable.

If you venture down south, remember to bring your valid passport or identification for return to the U.S. and a copy of *Hidden Baja* (Ulysses Press). If you do not want to drive across the border, you can take a trolley to the border, walk on a pedestrian overpass across the International border, and then take a taxi into town for about $7 per person.

▲ There are 137 sites for self-contained RVs and trailers (no hookups); $24 per night.

IMPERIAL BEACH 🏖 🏊 🚻 🛏 A wide, sandy beach, popular at the south end with surfers; boogie-boarders and swimmers ply the waters between the two jetties farther north, just past the renovated fishing pier. The crowd is mostly young with many military personnel. There are restrooms and lifeguards. There is also a deli nearby. Surfing is very popular on both sides of the pier and rock jetties. ~ Take Palm Avenue exit west off Route 5 all the way to the water; 619-686-6200, fax 619-686-6200.

BORDER FIELD STATE PARK 🚶 🚲 🐎 True to its name, this oceanfront park within the Tijuana River National Estuarine Research Reserve actually borders on Mexico. It features a three-mile-long stretch of sandy beach, backed by dunes and salt marshes studded with daisies and chaparral. Equestrian and hiking trails crisscross this unsullied wetlands area which adjoins a federal wildlife refuge at the mouth of the Tijuana River. Sounds idyllic except for the constant racket from Border Patrol helicopters and the ever-present threat of untreated sewage drifting north from Mexico. Picnic areas and restrooms are available, and a visitors center houses exhibits and a library. Fishing and swimming are not recommended because of pollution. ~ Take the Dairy Mart Road exit off Route 5 and go west. The name changes to Monument Road about a mile before reaching the park entrance. The visitors center is at 301 Caspian Way, Imperial Beach; 619-575-3613, fax 619-575-6913; www. tijuanaestuary.com, e-mail trnerr@ixpress.net.

Outdoor Adventures

SPORT-FISHING

The lure of sportfishing attracts thousands of enthusiasts to San Diego every year. Yellowtail, sea bass, bonito, and barracuda are the local favorites, with marlin and tuna the prime objectives for multiday charters. Most outfitters provide bait and rent tackle.

For deep-sea and local sportfishing, contact **Helgren's Sportfishing**; five-day excursions lead down into Mexico. ~ 315 Harbor Drive South, Oceanside; 760-722-2133; www.helgrenssportfishing.com. **Seaforth Sportfishing** uses 36- to 85-foot boats for their runs. Longer trips in summer head out to Mexican waters for albacore. ~ 1717 Quivira Road, Mission Bay; 619-224-3383; www.seaforth.com. **Islandia Sportfishing** offers trips for albacore, mackerel, and skipjack. ~ 1551 West Mission Bay Drive, Mission Bay; 619-222-1164; www.islandiasportfishing.com. **H & M Landing** arranges half-day jaunts to local kelp beds or 18-day expeditions past the tip of Baja for giant yellowfin tuna. ~ 2803 Emerson Street, Point Loma; 619-222-1144; www.hmlanding.com. Call **Fish 'N Cruise** for custom-designed charters. ~

1551 Shelter Island Drive, San Diego; 619-224-2464; www.san diegoyachts.com. **Point Loma Sportfishing** operates a fleet of ten boats. Their daytrip goes down to Mexico for tuna. ~ 1403 Scott Street, Point Loma; 619-223-1627; www.pointlomasportfish ing.com. Also in Point Loma is **Fisherman's Landing**, which takes groups of 6 to 35 on fishing excursions. The 23-day charter winds up in Cabo San Lucas. ~ 2838 Garrison Street, Point Loma; 619-222-0391; www.fishermanslanding.com.

Spearfishing is very popular off La Jolla beaches, especially south of La Jolla Cove. Contact **San Diego Divers Supply** for supplies, tours, and information. ~ 4004 Sports Arena Boulevard, San Diego; 619-224-3439. Note: Spearfishing is not allowed in protected reserves from La Jolla Cove north.

WHALE WATCHING

The stately progress of our fellow mammalians in migration is a wonderful sight to behold. To get an even closer look at these mammoth cetaceans, book a charter with one of the many whale-watching companies; most outfitters guarantee marine sightings. The season generally runs from late December through late February (mid-January is the best time).

Helgren's Sportfishing sets sail from mid-December to mid-April—that's when you'll see California gray whales. ~ 315 Harbor Drive South, Oceanside; 760-722-2133; www. helgrensportfishing.com. **Islandia Sportfishing** serves the Mission Bay area, accommodating up to 150 guests. ~ 1551 West Mission Bay Drive, Mission Bay; 619-222-1164; www.islandiasportfishing. com. In Point Loma, **H & M Landing** takes you out on 65- to 85-foot boats in search of whales. ~ 2803 Emerson Street, Point Loma; 619-222-1144; www.hmland ing.com. **Point Loma Sportfishing** offers three-hour trips through local waters. ~ 1403 Scott Street, Point Loma; 619-223-1627; www.pointlomasportfishing.com. **San Diego Harbor Excursion** provides three-hour whale-watching tours during winter. ~ 1050 North Harbor Drive; 619-234-4111, 800-442-7847; www.sdhe.com.

A free whale-watching station at Cabrillo National Monument on Point Loma features a glassed-in observatory.

DIVING

San Diego offers countless spots for diving. The rocky La Jolla coves boast the clearest water on the California coast. Bird Rock, La Jolla Underwater Park, and the underwater Scripps Canyon are ideal havens for divers. In Point Loma try the colorful tidepools at Cabrillo Underwater Reserve; at "No Surf Beach" (located on Sunset Cliff Boulevard) pools and reefs are for experienced divers only.

For diving rentals, sales, instruction, and tips, contact **Underwater Schools of America**. ~ 225 Brooks Street, Oceanside; 760-722-7826; www.usascuba.com. **San Diego Shark Diving Ex-**

peditions offers one-day trips off the coast of San Diego to dive within the safety of a shark cage and observe (or photograph) free-swimming blue, white, and mako sharks. For the less adventurous, there are two-tank trips to kelp beds or Wreck Alley and three-tank trips to the Coronado Islands. Reservations are a must. ~ 6747 Friar's Road #112, San Diego; 619-299-8560; www.sdsharkdiving.com. **Ocean Enterprises** teaches a variety of diving classes. They also rent and sell gear. ~ 7710 Balboa Avenue, San Diego; 858-565-6054; www.oceanenterprises.com. You can also arrange dives with **San Diego Divers Supply**. They provide instruction, sell gear, and do repairs. ~ 4004 Sports Arena Boulevard, San Diego, 619-224-3439. In Pacific Beach, the **Diving Locker** offers open-water certification. They also rent and sell gear. ~ 1020 Grand Avenue, Pacific Beach; 858-272-1120; www.divinglocker.com.

SURFING & WIND-SURFING

The surf's up in the San Diego area. Pacific, Mission, and Ocean beaches, Tourmaline Surfing Park, and Windansea, La Jolla Shores, Swami, and Moonlight beaches are well-known hangouts for surfers. Sailboarding is concentrated within Mission Bay. Oceanside is home to annual world-class boogie-board and surfing competitions.

For surfboard, bodyboard, wetsuit, and snorkel rentals and sales, try **Mitch's**. ~ 631 Pearl Street, La Jolla; 858-459-5933. **Surfride** rents and sells surfboards, boogieboards, bodyboards, fins, and wetsuits. ~ 1909 South Coast Highway, Oceanside; 760-433-4020; www.surfride.com. **Hansen Surfboards** rents recreational gear such as snorkel equipment, surfboards, and bodyboards, as well as wetsuits. ~ 1105 South Coast Highway, Encinitas; 760-753-6595; www.hansensurf.com. **C. P. Water Sports** has windsurfing rentals and lessons. ~ 1775 East Mission Bay Drive, Mission Bay; 619-275-8945. Surfboards, boogieboards, and sailboards are available at **Mission Bay Sportscenter**. They have wetsuits and surfing instruction as well. ~ 1010 Santa

UP, UP AND AWAY

Hot-air ballooning is a romantic pursuit that has soared in popularity in the Del Mar area. A number of companies provide spectacular dawn and sunset flights, most concluding with a traditional champagne toast. Contact **A Skysurfer Balloon Company** for daily sunset flights over the coastal valley area. The 45-minute to an hour affair includes on-board champagne and soft drinks, and concludes with a first-flight certificate. ~ 2658 Del Mar Heights Road, Del Mar; 858-481-6800, 800-660-6809; www.sandiegohotairballoons.com.

Clara Place, Mission Bay; 858-488-1004; www.missionbaysport center.com.

Fabulous weather allows plenty of opportunities to sail under the Coronado Bridge, skirt the gorgeous downtown skyline, and even get a taste of open ocean in this Southern California sailing mecca.

BOATING & SAILING

Several sailing companies operate out of Harbor Island West in San Diego, including **Harbor Sailboats**. They offer instruction as well as sailboat rentals. ~ 2040 Harbor Island Drive, Suite 104, San Diego; 619-291-9568; www.harborsailboats.com. For sailboat rentals and party yacht charters, try **San Diego Yacht Charters**. ~ 1880 Harbor Island Drive, San Diego; 619-297-4555; www.sdyc.com.

Motorboat, sailboat, and kayak rentals can be found at **C. P. Water Sports**. ~ 1775 East Mission Bay Drive, Mission Bay; 619-275-8945. Powerboat, sailboat, catamaran, and kayak rentals are also available from **Mission Bay Sportscenter**. In addition, they can teach you how to sail and waterski. ~ 1010 Santa Clara Place, Mission Bay; 858-488-1004; www.missionbaysportscenter. com. **Seaforth Mission Bay Boat Rental** rents motorboats, sailboats, paddleboats, canoes, and kayaks. Sailing lessons are available. ~ 1641 Quivira Road, Mission Bay; 619-223-1681; www.sea forthboatrental.com. The **Coronado Boat Rentals** has motorboats and sailboats. ~ 1715 Strand Way, Coronado; 619-437-1514.

Charter a yacht through **Hornblower Dining Yachts**. ~ 1066 North Harbor Drive, San Diego; 619-234-8687; www.horn blower.com.

Torrey Pines Glider Port is an expert-rated hang-gliding and paragliding site, located atop a towering sandstone bluff overlooking Black's Beach. Lesson packages and half-hour tandem flights are available. If you're not yet an expert, there is a great vantage point to watch from. ~ 2800 Torrey Pines Scenic Drive, La Jolla; 858-452-9858; www.flytorrey.com, e-mail info@flytorrey.com.

HANG GLIDING

You don't have to look far for a green to practice your swing. Most courses in San Diego rent clubs and carts so you're in luck if you didn't plan ahead.

GOLF

NORTH SAN DIEGO COUNTY   The 18-hole **Emerald Isle Golf Course** is a public executive green. ~ 660 South El Camino Real, Oceanside; 760-721-4700; www.emeraldislegolf.net. Tee off at **Oceanside Golf Course**, a public, 18-hole course. At the 13th hole, take a minute to admire the view of rolling hills, and majestic mountains. ~ 825 Douglas Drive, Oceanside; 760-433-1360. You'll have to caddy your clubs by pull cart at the executive, public **Rancho Carlsbad Golf Course**, a par-56, 18-hole green. ~ 5200 El Camino Real, Carlsbad; 760-438-1772. The par-58

Lake San Marcos Executive Course is open to the public. ~ 1556 Camino del Arroyo, San Marcos; 760-744-9092. Tee off at the Welk Resort Village Golf Courses, which has two public, 18-hole courses: the executive Fountain and the smaller Oaks Par 3. Both are dotted with lakes and ponds. ~ 8860 Lawrence Welk Drive, Escondido; 760-749-3000. The public, 18-hole championship Rancho Bernardo Inn Golf Course includes a cart with the greens fee. ~ 17550 Bernardo Oaks Drive, Rancho Bernardo; 858-487-0700.

INLAND SAN DIEGO COUNTY For the Inland San Diego County area, consider the public, 18-hole Fallbrook Golf Club, which rents only carts. ~ 2757 Gird Road, Fallbrook; 760-728-8334. The 18-hole San Luis Rey Downs Golf Resort & Country Club is a public facility. ~ 31474 Golf Club Drive, Bonsall; 760-758-9699, 800-783-6967; www.slrd.com. In El Cajon, the semiprivate Singing Hills Golf Courses features three 18-hole courses: two championship and one par 3. The 12th hole on the Willow Glen championship course is over a fountain. There's also a driving range. ~ 3007 Dehesa Road, El Cajon; 619-442-3425; www.singinghills.com.

San Diego has been the backdrop for a number of Hollywood films including, *Charlie's Angels: Full Throttle, Bruce Almighty, Traffic* and *The Scorpion King.*

LA JOLLA Beautiful Torrey Pines Municipal Golf Course is famous for its two 18-hole, par-72 championship courses. ~ 11480 North Torrey Pines Road, La Jolla; 619-570-1234.

MISSION BAY PARK AREA Mission Bay Golf Resort is a public, 18-hole course. It's San Diego's only night-lighted course. ~ 2702 North Mission Bay Drive, Mission Bay; 858-581-7880.

BALBOA PARK A duffer's delight, the 18-hole Balboa Park Municipal Golf Course is a par-72 championship course. It also features a nine-hole executive course. ~ Golf Course Drive, Balboa Park; 619-570-1234.

CORONADO The Coronado Municipal Golf Course, an 18-hole green, runs along Glorietta Bay. ~ 2000 Visalia Row, Coronado; 619-435-3121.

TENNIS NORTH SAN DIEGO COUNTY North County suffers from a lack of public tennis courts; however, Del Mar has free courts located off 22nd Street between Camino del Mar and Jimmy Durante Boulevard. Kit Carson Park in Escondido has ten courts available, four of which are lighted. ~ 3333 Bear Valley Parkway, Escondido; 760-839-4691.

INLAND SAN DIEGO COUNTY Pala Mesa Resort is equipped with four lighted courts and an instructor available for lessons. ~ 2001 Old Route 395, Fallbrook; 760-723-5571, 800-722-

4700; www.palamesa.com. In Bonsall, try the six outdoor, lighted courts at **San Luis Rey Downs Tennis Club**. Fee. ~ 31474 Golf Club Drive, Bonsall; 760-758-1318, 800-783-6967; www.slrd. com. The **Parkway Sports Center** in El Cajon has four lighted courts. Instruction is available. Fee. ~ 1055 Ballantyne Street, El Cajon; 619-442-9623.

SAN DIEGO   San Diego has many private and public hardtop courts. The **Barnes Tennis Center** has 25 outdoor courts, 19 of which are lighted. ~ 4490 West Point Loma Boulevard, San Diego; 619-221-9000; www.barnestenniscenter.com. You'll find two unlighted courts at the **Cabrillo Recreation Center**. ~ 3051 Canon Street, Point Loma; 619-531-1534. If you're in Ocean Beach, try the 12 courts at **Peninsula Tennis Club**, which are outdoor and lighted. Fee. ~ 2525 Bacon Street, Ocean Beach; 619-226-3407. Some of the nine outdoor courts at the **La Jolla Recreation Center** are lighted. Fee. ~ 7632 Draper Avenue, La Jolla; 858-454-4434.

CORONADO   The **Coronado Tennis Center** has eight outdoor courts, three of which are lighted. ~ 1501 Glorietta Boulevard; 619-435-1616.

RIDING STABLES

San Diego's backcountry boasts hundreds of miles of riding trails. Cleveland National Forest, Palomar Mountain Park, William Heise Park, and Cuyamaca Rancho State Park all feature fine mountain riding. **Julian Stables** offers hour-long trail rides throughout a 30-acre ranch. Riders are rewarded with views of the Volcan Mountain Preserve and the peaks of Cuyamaca Rancho State Park. Reservations are required. ~ P.O. Box 881, Julian, CA 92036; 760-765-1598; www.julianactive.com, e-mail info@julianactive.com. For treks through the Anza–Borrego Desert, **Smokehouse Horse Rental & Equine Encounters** leads guided tours from October to May. Lessons and pony rides are offered daily. Reservations are required. ~ 302 Palm Canyon Drive, Borrego Springs; 760-767-5850; www.smoketree.micron pc.web.com, e-mail sthorpe@uia.net.

BIKING

North County's **Old Route 101** provides almost 40 miles of scintillating cycling along the coast from Oceanside to La Jolla. Traffic is heavy but bikes are almost as numerous as autos along this stretch. Bike lanes are designated along most of the route.

Cycling has skyrocketed in popularity throughout San Diego County, especially in coastal areas. The **Mission Bay Bike Path** (18 miles) starts at the San Diego Convention Center, winds along the harbor, crosses Mission Bay, and heads up the coast to La Jolla. **Balboa Park** and **Mission Bay Park** both have excellent bike routes (see the "Balboa Park and the San Diego Zoo" and

"Mission Bay Park Area" sections of this chapter). Check with Regional Transit about their special "biker" passes.

Inland, **Julian** makes a good base for bicycling the hilly country roads such as the nine-mile loop to Wynola.

Bike Rentals and Tours   To rent a bicycle (mountain, road, or kid's) in downtown San Diego, contact **Pennyfarthings Bicycle Store.** ~ 630 C Street; 619-233-7696. **Holland's Bicycles** sells, rents, and repairs cruisers, mountain bikes, and tandems. Rentals come with helmets and locks. ~ 977 Orange Avenue at 10th Street, Coronado; 619-435-3153; www.hollandsbicycles.com.

HIKING   Most of the San Diego County coastline is developed for either residential or commercial purposes, limiting the hiking possibilities. There are some protected areas set aside to preserve remnants of the county's unique coastal chaparral communities and tidelands. These reserves offer short hiking trails. Inland San Diego County, particularly in the Palomar and Laguna mountains, also provides backpacking opportunities. A trail map packet is available from the San Diego County Department of Public Works. ~ 858-694-3215.

Serious hikers might consider taking on the San Diego section of the **California Coastal Trail.** It follows the shoreline from the Mexican border to San Onofre State Beach.

All distances listed for hiking trails are one way unless otherwise noted.

NORTH SAN DIEGO COUNTY   Three Lagoons Trail (5 miles) originates on the beach in Leucadia and heads north along the sand past three saltwater lagoons, ending in Carlsbad. The best place to begin is at the beach parking lot at Grandview Street in Leucadia.

INLAND SAN DIEGO COUNTY   Rising along San Diego County's northern border, the Palomar Mountain Range provides a number of demanding trails. Well-protected and maintained within Cleveland National Forest, they offer hikers a prime wilderness experience. ~ 858-673-6180, 760-788-9250.

Observatory Trail (1 mile) is one of the area's easiest treks and rewards the hiker with a view of that famous silver hemisphere, the Palomar Observatory.

AUTHOR FAVORITE

The one-mile **La Jolla Coastal Walk**, a dirt path atop La Jolla Bluffs, affords some of the most spectacular views anywhere on the San Diego County coastline. It begins on Coast Boulevard just up the hill from La Jolla Cove and continues past a sea cave accessible from the trail.

The Agua Tibia Wilderness Area in the northwest corner of Cleveland National Forest is the setting for rugged **Dripping Springs Trail** (6.8 miles). Ascending the side of Agua Tibia Mountain, the trail leads through precipitous canyons to vista points with views of the Pacific, more than 40 miles away.

Scott's Cabin Trail (1 mile) wends through varied terrain in Palomar Mountain State Park. This moderate trail passes the remains of a homesteader's cabin, descends into a fir forest, and climbs to a lookout tower.

The challenging **Stonewall Peak Trail** (2 miles) zigzags to the summit of 5730-foot Stonewall Peak, with views of an 1870-era mine site along the way. Nearby, the moderate **Azalea Glen Trail** (4 mile loop) passes through open meadows as well as forests of oak and pine. **Paso Nature Trail** (.8 mile) is an easy, self-guided loop designed to introduce visitors to the local flora.

LA JOLLA Without a doubt, the 1750-acre **Torrey Pines State Park and Reserve** offers the county's best hiking. It was named for the world's rarest pine tree *(Pinus torreyana)* which the reserve was established to protect. An estimated 6000 of the gnarled and twisted trees cling to rugged cliffs and ravines, some growing as tall as 60 feet.

Several major trails offer hikers a variety of challenges and natural attractions. Most are easily walked loops through groves of pines, such as **Guy Fleming Trail** (.6-mile loop), which scans the coast at South and North overlooks, and **Parry Grove Trail** (.5-mile loop), which passes stands of manzanita, yucca, and other shrubs. There are more strenuous treks such as the **Razor Point Trail** (.6 mile), which follows the Canyon of the Swifts, then links up with the **Beach Trail** (.8 mile); and the south fork of **Broken Hill Trail** (1.3 miles), which zigzags to the coast past chamiso and scrub oak (the north fork is 1.2 miles).

Del Mar Beach Trail (3 miles) leads from the Del Mar Amtrak Station along the beach past flatrock tidepools and up to the bluffs of Torrey Pines State Reserve.

POINT LOMA AREA **Cabrillo National Monument** offers the moderate **Bayside Trail** (1 mile). It begins at the Old Point Loma Lighthouse, beautifully restored to its original 1855 condition, and meanders through the heart of a scenic coastal chaparral community. A wide variety of native plants including prickly pear cactus, yucca, buckwheat, and Indian paintbrush grow along the path. In addition to stunning views of San Diego, there are remnants of the coastal defense system built here during World Wars I and II. ~ 619-557-5450; www.nps.gov/cabr.

SOUTH SAN DIEGO COUNTY Four miles of hiking trails crisscross the dunes and marshes of the largely undeveloped **Tijuana River National Estuarine Research Reserve**, which forms the coastal border between the United States and Mexico. Trails lead through dunes anchored by salt grass, pickleweed, and sand verbena. The marshy areas, especially those in the wildlife refuge around the Tijuana River estuary, provide feeding and nesting grounds for several hundred species of native and migratory birds, including hawks, pelicans, plovers, terns, and ducks.

Border Field to Tijuana River Trail (1.5 miles) is a level beach walk past sand dunes and the Tijuana River Estuary.

Transportation

Even though it is located in California's extreme southwest corner, San Diego is the hub of an elaborate highway network. The city is easily reached from north or south via **Route 5**; **Route 8** serves drivers from the east; and **Route 15** is the major inland freeway for travelers arriving from the mountain west. **Route 76** runs inland from Oceanside to the Palomar Mountains, then becomes **Route 79**, which leads to Julian. From Carlsbad, **Route 78** connects the coast with inland communities like Escondido.

CAR

AIR

San Diego International Airport (Lindbergh Field) lies just three miles northwest of downtown San Diego and is easily accessible from either Route 5 or Route 8. The airport is served by most major airlines, including Alaska Airlines, America West Airlines, American Airlines, Continental Airlines, Delta Airlines, Frontier Airlines, JetBlue Airways, Northwest Airlines, Southwest Airlines, United Airlines, and USAir.

Taxis, limousines, and buses provide service from the airport. **San Diego Transit System** bus #992 carries passengers to downtown. ~ 619-233-3004. Or try the **Southwest Shuttle**, which travels to major points in the city as well as to Orange County and Los Angeles. ~ 619-231-1123.

BUS

Greyhound Bus Lines (800-231-222; www.greyhound.com) services San Diego from around the country. The terminal is downtown at 120 West Broadway and 1st Avenue; 619-239-3266. Greyhound also carries passengers inland from San Diego to Escondido at 700 West Valley Parkway, 760-745-6522; and El Cajon at 250 South Marshall Avenue, 619-444-2591. There's also an Oceanside station at 205 South Tremont Street; 760-722-1587.

TRAIN

Chugging to a stop at historic Santa Fe Depot, at 1050 Kettner Boulevard and Broadway downtown, is a nice and convenient way to arrive in San Diego. **Amtrak** offers several coast-hugging roundtrips daily between Los Angeles and San Diego, with stops at Oceanside and Solano Beach. ~ 800-872-7245; www.amtrak.com.

CAR RENTALS

Much like the rest of Southern California, San Diego is spread out over a wide area and is best seen by car. Car rental companies abound. Most major rental agencies have franchises at the airport. These include **Avis Rent A Car** (800-831-2847), **Dollar Rent A Car** (800-800-4000), **Hertz Rent A Car** (800-654-3131), and **National Car Rental** (800-227-7368).

For better rates (but less convenient service) try agencies located near the airport that provide pick-up service: **Thrifty Car Rental** (800-367-2277), **Rent A Wreck** (800-535-1391), and **Budget Car & Truck Rental** (800-527-0700).

North County Transit District, or NCTD, covers the general area from Camp Pendleton to Del Mar along the coast. NCTD operates numerous North County bus routes that service the communities of Oceanside, Carlsbad, Encinitas, Leucadia, Cardiff, Solana Beach, Del Mar, and Rancho Santa Fe. ~ 619-233-3004, 800-266-6883 (San Diego County only).

PUBLIC TRANSIT

Several modern and efficient public transportation systems operate throughout San Diego. Information and schedules are available for all systems by calling **Regional Transit**. ~ 619-233-3004, 800-266-6883 (San Diego County only).

The Regional Transit bus system is the city's largest public transportation network, with lines linking all major points. All Regional Transit stops are marked with a blue rectangle.

The city's newest and most venturesome mode of public transportation is the **San Diego Trolley**. The light rail system's line operates daily. Understandably, the line running between Mission San Diego and the Mexican border is known as the "Tijuana Trolley," or the Blue Line. It also serves Old Town and the south bay cities of National City, Chula Vista, and Imperial Beach. The Orange Line travels between Santee and downtown, including Seaport Village and the Gaslamp Quarter. ~ 619-233-3004.

National City Transit serves National City. ~ 619-233-3004. **Chula Vista Transit** serves Bonita and the city of Chula Vista. ~ 619-233-3004. ATC/Vancom runs from downtown San Diego to National City and Chula Vista and on to the San Ysidro international Otay Mesa borders. In addition, ATC/Vancom runs from Coronado along the Silver Strand to Imperial Beach. ~ 800-858-0291.

For Inland San Diego, NCTD provides bus service from Escondido to Ramona. **Northeast Rural Bus System** takes passengers from El Cajon to Julian, Santa Ysabel, and Cuyamaca Rancho. ~ 760-767-4287.

In North County (Del Mar to Carlsbad), you can call **Yellow Cab** (760-753-6044) or **Oceanside Yellow Cab** (760-722-4217).

TAXIS

San Diego is not a taxi town in the usual big-city sense, but there's a cab if you need it—just a telephone call away. Leading companies include **Silver Cab** (619-280-5555), **Yellow Cab** (619-

234-6161), **Orange Cab** (619-291-3333), and **USA Cab** (619-231-1144).

WALKING TOURS

Several San Diego organizations and tour operators offer organized walks: **Gaslamp Quarter Historical Foundation** conducts two-hour, docent-led walking tours of the restored downtown historic district on Saturday at 11 a.m. Fee. ~ 410 Island Avenue; 619-233-4692.

Walking tours of **Old Town State Historic Park** are offered weekdays at 11 a.m. and weekends at 11 a.m. and 2 p.m. through park headquarters. ~ 4002 Wallace Street; 619-220-5422.

Join **Coronado Touring** for a leisurely one-and-a-half-hour guided stroll through quaint Coronado. Tours leave from the Glorietta Bay Inn (1630 Glorietta Boulevard) at 11 a.m. on Tuesday, Thursday, and Saturday. Fee. ~ 619-435-5993.

SIX

Central Coast

To call any one section of the California Coast the most alluring is to embark upon uncertain waters. Surely the Central Coast, that 200-mile swath from Ventura to San Simeon, is a region of rare beauty. Stretching across Ventura, Santa Barbara, and San Luis Obispo counties, it embraces many of the West's finest beaches.

Five of California's 21 missions—in Ventura, Santa Barbara, Lompoc, San Luis Obispo, and farther inland in Solvang—lie along this stretch. Chosen by the Spanish in the 1780s for their fertile pastures, natural harbors, and placid surroundings, they are a historic testimonial to the varied richness of the landscape.

The towns that grew up around these missions, evocative of old Spanish traditions, are emblems of California's singular culture. Santa Barbara, perhaps the state's prettiest town, is a warren of whitewashed buildings and red tile roofs, backdropped by rocky peaks and bounded by a five-mile palm-fringed beach.

Ventura and San Luis Obispo represent two of California's most underrated towns. In addition to a wealthy heritage, Ventura has beautiful beaches and San Luis Obispo is set amid velvet hills and rich agricultural areas. Both are less expensive than elsewhere and offer many of the same features without the pretensions.

Offshore are the Channel Islands, a 25-million-year-old chain and vital wildlife preserve. Sandblasted by fierce storms, pristine in their magnificence, they are a china shop of endangered species and unique life forms. While the nearby reefs are headstones for the many ships that have crashed here, the surrounding waters are crowded with sea life.

Together with the rest of the coast, the islands were discovered by Juan Rodríguez Cabrillo in 1542. The noted explorer found them inhabited by Chumash Indians, a collection of tribes occupying the coast from Malibu to Morro Bay. Hunters and gatherers, the Chumash were master mariners who built woodplank canoes called *tomols*, capable of carrying ten people across treacherous waters to the Channel Islands. They in turn were preceded by the Oak Grove Tribes, which inhabited the region from 7000 to 3000 B.C.

Once Gaspar de Portolá opened the coast to Spanish colonialists with his 1769 explorations, few Indians from any California tribes survived. Forced into servitude and religious conversion by the padres, the Chumash revolted at Santa Barbara Mission and Mission de la Purísima Concepción in 1824. They held Purísima for a month before troops from Monterey overwhelmed them. By 1910 the Westerners who had come to save them had so decimated the Indians that their 30,000 population dwindled to 1250.

By the mid-1800s these lately arrived white men set out in pursuit of any sea mammal whose pelt would fetch a price. The Central Coast was a prime whale-hunting ground. Harpooners by the hundreds speared leviathans, seals, and sea lions, hunting them practically to extinction. Earlier in the century American merchants, immortalized in Richard Henry Dana's *Two Years Before the Mast*, had combed the coast trading for cattle hides.

The land that bore witness to this colonial carnage endured. Today the Central Coast and its offshore islands abound in sea lions, harbor seals, Northern fur seals, and elephant seals. Whales inhabit the deeper waters and gamefish are plentiful. The only threats remaining are those from developers and the oil industry, whose offshore drilling resulted in the disastrous 1969 Santa Barbara spill.

The Central Coast traveler finds a Mediterranean climate, dry and hot in the summer, tempered by morning fog and winds off the ocean, then cool and rainy during winter months. Two highways, Routes 1 and 101, lead through this salubrious environment. The former hugs the coast much of the way, traveling inland to Lompoc and San Luis Obispo, and the latter, at times joining with Route 1 to form a single roadway, eventually diverges into the interior valleys.

Almost as much as the ocean, mountains play a vital part in the life of the coast. Along the southern stretches are the Santa Monica Mountains, which give way farther north to the Santa Ynez Mountains. Below them, stretching along the coastal plain, are the towns of Oxnard, Ventura, Santa Barbara, and Goleta.

Both mountain systems are part of the unique Transverse Range, which, unlike most North American mountains, travels from east to west rather than north and south. They are California's Great Divide, a point of demarcation between the chic, polished regions near Santa Barbara and the rough, wild territory around San Luis Obispo.

Arriving at the ocean around Point Conception, the Transverse Range separates the curving pocket beaches of the south and the endless sand dunes to the north. Here the continent takes a sharp right turn as the beaches, facing south in Santa Barbara, wheel about to look west across the Pacific.

Amid this geologic turmoil lies Lompoc, the top flower seed–producing area in the world, a region of agricultural beauty and color beyond belief, home to 40 percent of the United States' flower crop. To the north are the Nipomo Sand Dunes, extending 18 miles from Point Sal to Pismo Beach, one of the nation's largest dune systems. A habitat for the endangered California brown pelican and the California least tern, these are tremendous piles of sand, towering to 450 feet, held in place against the sea wind by a lacework of ice plant, grasses, verbena, and silver lupine. They are also the site of an Egyptian city, complete with walls 110 feet high and a grand boulevard lined with sphinxes and pharaohs. Today, like other glorious cities of yesteryear, it lies buried beneath the sand.

In San Luis Obispo oceanfront gives way to ranch land as the landscape reveals a Western visage. Unlike Spanish-style Santa Barbara to the south and Monterey to the north, San Luis Obispo has defined its own culture, a blend of hardriding ranch hand and easygoing college student. Its roots nonetheless are similar, deriving from the Spanish, who founded their mission here in 1772, and the 19th-century Americans who built the town's gracious Victorian homes.

Rich too in natural history, the region between San Luis Obispo and Morro Bay is dominated by nine mountain peaks, each an extinct volcano dating back 20 million years. Last in the line is Morro Rock, an imposing monolith that's surrounded by a fertile wetlands that represents one of the country's ten most vital bird habitats.

Farther north civilization gives way to coastal quietude. There are untracked beaches and wind-honed sea cliffs, a prelude to Big Sur farther up the coast. Among the few signs of the modern world are the artist colony of Cambria and that big house on the hill, Hearst Castle, California's own eighth wonder of the world. Symbol of boundless artistry and unbridled egotism, it is also one of the Central Coast's many wonders.

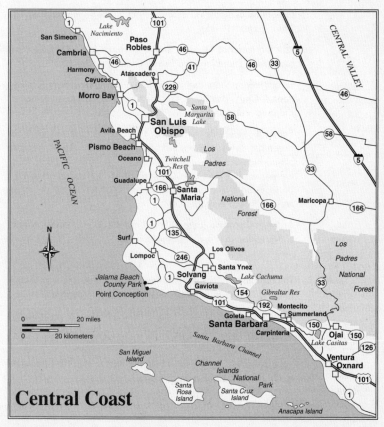

Central Coast

Text continued on page 398.

The Central Coast

This excursion takes you up the coast, avoiding the freeway wherever possible, for a visit to Hearst Castle, the area's biggest "must-see" attraction. The only trick is to book your reservations for the Hearst Castle tour(s) well in advance—in most cases, *months* ahead. The return trip takes you on a journey through California's wild Sierra Madre.

DAY 1
- Head north from the Los Angeles area on Route 101, leaving early enough to arrive in Santa Barbara by around 10 a.m.

- Explore Santa Barbara's historic district on the self-guided **Red Tile Tour** (pages 414–15).

- Visit the restored **Mission Santa Barbara** (page 412), the most beautiful of Padre Junipero Serra's California missions.

- Before leaving Santa Barbara, stop by **Brophy Brothers Restaurant & Clam Bar** (page 423) for a fresh seafood lunch and enjoy the spectacular harbor views from their patio.

- Follow legendary Route 1 north as it changes back and forth between fast divided highway and pastoral two-lane road, all the while playing hide-and-seek with the ocean. If you have extra time along the way, explore **San Luis Obispo**'s pretty downtown (page 438), or stop for a hike or a swim at one of the beaches and parks around **Morro Bay** (page 440).

- Arrive in **Cambria** (page 451) and check into your choice of bed-and-breakfast inns for a two-night stay.

DAY 2
- The high point of the day is a visit to the opulent **Hearst Castle** (page 452). Take Tour 1 and one of the other three tours.

- Spend the remainder of the day in blissful relaxation, exploring the art galleries of cute little Cambria or enjoying Moonstone Beach and San Simeon Creek in **San Simeon State Park** (page 456).

- Have dinner in town and return to your B&B or check out the music at **Camozzi's Saloon** (page 456).

DAY 3 • After breakfast, take Route 1 south for 52 miles to the little town of Guadalupe, and turn east (left) on Route 166.

• Drive through Santa Maria and up into the Sierra Madre, a distance of 74 miles to the junction with Route 33. Turn south (right) and continue for another 57 miles. Allow at least half a day for this drive. There are no notable sightseeing highlights along the way, just the solitude and dramatic mountain landscapes of **Los Padres National Forest** (page 451) rising from the sea to over 9000 feet elevation.

Unlikely as it may seem, Route 101 will take you back to central Los Angeles in under an hour—depending on traffic conditions.

Ventura–Oxnard Area

Situated 60 miles northwest of Los Angeles and 30 miles to the southeast of Santa Barbara, the 18th-century mission town of Ventura has generally been overlooked by travelers. History has not been so remiss. Long known to the Chumash Indians, who inhabited a nearby village named Shisholop, the place was revealed to Europeans in 1542 by the Portuguese explorer Juan Rodríguez Cabrillo. Father Junípero Serra founded a mission here in 1782 and the region soon became renowned for its fruit orchards. Oxnard is known chiefly as an agricultural community, contributing a large share of the area's produce.

SIGHTS

Today Ventura preserves its heritage in a number of historic sites. Stop by the **Ventura Visitors & Convention Bureau** for brochures and maps. ~ 89 South California Street, Suite C, Ventura; 805-648-2075, 800-333-2989; www.ventura-usa.com, e-mail tourism@ventura-usa.com.

Downtown Ventura is compact and walkable, and the highlight of a stroll through Ventura is **San Buenaventura Mission**, a whitewash and red-tile church flanked by a flowering garden. The dark, deep chapel is lined with Stations of the Cross paintings and features a Romanesque altar adorned with statues and pilasters. My favorite spot is the adjacent garden with its tile fountain and stately Norfolk pines. Entrance to the mission is actually through a small gift shop a few steps to the east. Admission. ~ 211 East Main Street, Ventura; 805-643-4318; www.sanbuenaventura mission.org, e-mail mission@sanbuenaventuramission.org.

Then cross Main Street to the **Ventura County Museum of History & Art,** which traces the region's secular history with displays of Chumash Indian artifacts and a farm implement collection. The art gallery features revolving exhibits of local painters and photographers. There's a collection of 32,000 photos depicting Ventura County from its origin to the present. One gallery features a permanent display of George Stuart's historical figures. The artist is exacting in his detail, right down to eyelashes and fingernails, when crafting a Martin Luther King, Jr., or Abraham Lincoln. A public library and archive houses maps, manuscripts, and photographs pertaining to Ventura County. Closed Monday. Admission. ~ 100 East Main Street, Ventura; 805-653-0323, fax 805-653-5267; www.vcmha.org.

Just west of the mission, the **Albinger Archaeological Museum** sits at the site of an archaeological dig that dates back 3500 years, representing five different native cultures. The small museum displays arrowheads, shell beads, crucifixes, and pottery uncovered here. At the dig site itself you'll see the foundation of an 18th-century mission church, an ancient earth oven, and a remnant of the Spanish padres' elaborate aqueduct system. Closed Monday and Tuesday. ~ 113 East Main Street, Ventura; 805-648-5823, fax 805-653-5267.

About four blocks west of the mission sits the **Ortega Adobe Historic Residence**, a small, squat home built in 1857 that eventually gave birth to Ortega Chile. With its woodplank furniture and bare interior it provides a strong example of how hard and rudimentary life was in that early era. Closed Monday and Tuesday. ~ 215 West Main Street, Ventura; 805-658-4726, fax 805-648-1030.

Backtrack to San Buenaventura Mission and wander down **Figueroa Plaza**, a broad promenade decorated with tile fountains and flowerbeds. This is the site of the town's old Chinatown section, long since passed into myth and memory. Be sure to contemplate the colorful mural depicting the history and contributions of Ventura's Chinese population.

Figueroa Street continues to the waterfront, where a **promenade** parallels the beach. This is a prime area for water sports, and countless surfers, with their blond hair and black wetsuits, will be waiting offshore, poised for the perfect wave. Along the far end of the esplanade, at the **Ventura Pier**, you'll encounter one more Southern California species, the surf fisherman.

If it's not too hazy, the outline of Anacapa, one of the **Channel Islands**, should be visible from the pier and other high spots in

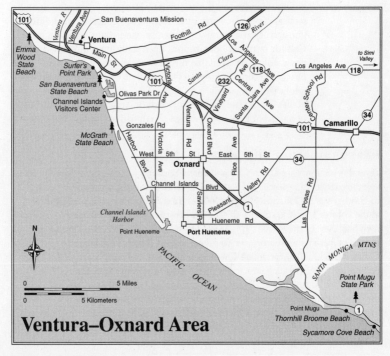

Ventura–Oxnard Area

Ventura. Day trips to Anacapa, which lies about 14 miles offshore, can be arranged through **Island Packers**. Tours are limited in December and January; call ahead. ~ 1691 Spinnaker Drive, Ventura Harbor; 805-642-1393; www.islandpackers.com. For an orientation to the special habitat of the Channel Islands, visit the **Channel Islands Visitors Center** at Ventura Harbor. ~ 1901 Spinnaker Drive, Ventura Harbor; 805-658-5730. (For more information about the islands and excursions to visit them, see "The Channel Islands" in this chapter.)

Another local wonder is the **Ventura County Courthouse**, a sprawling neoclassical-style structure. Now serving as the town's city hall, the place is a mélange of Doric columns, bronze fixtures, and Roman flourishes. But forget the marble entranceway and grand staircase—what makes it memorable is the row of friars' heads adorning the facade. Where else but in Southern California would a dozen baroque priests stare out at you from the hall of justice? ~ 501 Poli Street, Ventura.

The **Olivas Adobe** is a spacious hacienda surrounded by flowering gardens. This two-story gem, with balconies running the full length of the upper floor, is a study in the Monterey-style architecture of 19th-century California. The rooms are furnished in period pieces and there is a museum adjacent to the house, providing a window on the world of California's prosperous Spanish settlers. Special events such as summer concerts, a Halloween ghost story tour, and a Christmas candlelight tour are staged. Call for information. Grounds open daily, museum closed weekdays. Tours are available on the weekends. ~ 4200 Olivas Park Drive, Ventura; 805-644-4346, fax 805-648-1030; e-mail olivas adobe@yahoo.com.

It's mostly the agricultural fields of strawberries and the bustle of suburbia that you'll notice as you drive through the Oxnard

HARBOR-HOPPING DINE AROUND

Several restaurants are at the Channel Islands Harbor, and one of the most enjoyable dining experiences in Southern California is to harbor-hop from one to another via the **Harbor Hopper Water Taxi**. Start out with a cocktail at the Lobster Trap (Casa Sirena Hotel, 3605 Peninsula Road; 805-985-6311), then hop over to the Whale's Tail (3950 Bluefin Circle; 805-985-2511) for a starter of freshly shucked oysters. Continue to Port Royal (3900 Bluefin Circle; 805-382-7678) for grilled Chilean sea bass. It costs about $5 per person per hop; operating hours vary by season and weather. And don't wait too late to get started. Oxnard is an early-to-bed sort of place— most restaurants will be closed by 10 p.m. The hotel concierge can help you make arrangements. ~ 805-985-4677, fax 805-382-3305.

area. But the city also has a seven-mile stretch of shoreline and the **Channel Islands Harbor**, a busy commercial port providing a departure point for trips to the Channel Islands. The **Harbor Hopper Water Taxi** is a fun way to see the waterfront homes, as well as a convenient mode of transport for a culinary tour of the harbor (see "Harbor-Hopping Dine Around" next page). Closed Monday, except holidays. ~ 805-985-4677, fax 805-382-3305.

Several of Ventura County's late-19th-century homes were relocated to an area called **Heritage Square** in downtown Oxnard. Most of the houses are given over to small professional offices, but there are historic exhibits and a community theater as well. Tours are available on Saturday or by appointment. ~ 715 South A Street, Oxnard; 805-483-7960; e-mail heritagesquare@aol.com.

East of Ventura and Oxnard in the suburban town of Simi Valley lies the **Ronald Reagan Presidential Library**. Here you'll find a visual history of Reagan's 1980s-era presidency in the form of film clips, videos, artifacts, and photos. There's a piece of the Berlin Wall, a re-creation of the White House cabinet room, a replica of the Oval Office, and, re-creating Reagan's earlier years, memorabilia from his boyhood and Hollywood career. Admission. ~ 40 Presidential Drive, Simi Valley; 805-577-4000, 800-410-8354, fax 805-577-4074; www.reagan.utexas.edu.

For something spacious, plush, and formal consider the **Bella Maggiore Inn**. Set in downtown Ventura, this 25-room hostelry follows the tradition of a provincial Italian inn. There are European appointments and antique chandeliers in the lobby and a Roman-style fountain in the courtyard. The accommodations I saw were painted in soft hues and decorated with pastel prints. The furniture was a mixture of cane, washed pine, and antiques. ~ 67 South California Street, Ventura; 805-652-0277, 800-523-8479, fax 805-648-5670; www.bellamaggioreinn.com, e-mail bminn@pacbell.net. MODERATE TO DELUXE.

LODGING

◄ HIDDEN

Up the hill, overlooking Ventura and the ocean, sits **The Brakey House Bed & Breakfast**. This 1890 house illustrates the inn's turn-of-the-20th-century theme. Each of the five guest rooms is individually decorated in both antiques and reproductions, such as mission-style beds; some rooms have jacuzzi tubs. A full gourmet breakfast is served. ~ 411 Poli Street, Ventura; 805-643-3600, fax 805-653-7329; www.brakeyhouse.com, e-mail innkeeper@brakeyhouse.com. MODERATE TO ULTRA-DELUXE.

Get into the nautical theme of the area by staying aboard a 35-foot Chinese junk that's securely docked in Ventura Harbor. **Boatel Bunk and Breakfast** offers accommodations for two on restored wooden boats. Breakfast is included, but you'll have to go

◄ HIDDEN

Text continued on page 404.

The Channel
Islands

Gaze out from the Ventura or Santa Barbara shoreline and you will spy a fleet of islands moored offshore. At times fringed with mist, on other occasions standing a hand's reach away in the crystal air, they are the Channel Islands, a group of eight volcanic islands.

Situated in the Santa Barbara Channel 11 to 60 miles from the coast, they are a place apart, a wild and storm-blown region of sharp cliffs, rocky coves, and curving grasslands. Five of the islands—Anacapa, Santa Cruz, Santa Rosa, San Miguel, and Santa Barbara—comprise Channel Islands National Park while the surrounding waters are a marine sanctuary.

Nicknamed "North America's Galápagos," the chain teems with every imaginable form of life. Sea lions and harbor seals frequent the caves, blowholes, and offshore pillars. Brown pelicans and black oystercatchers roost on the sea arches and sandy beaches. There are tidepools crowded with brilliant purple hydrocorals and white-plumed sea anemones. Like the Galápagos, this isolated archipelago has given rise to many unique life forms, including over 40 endemic plant species and the island fox, which grows only to the size of a house cat.

The northern islands were created about 30 million years ago by volcanic activity. Archaeological discoveries indicate that they could be among the oldest sites of human habitation in the Americas. When explorer Juan Cabrillo revealed them to Europe in 1542 they were populated with thousands of Chumash Indians.

Today, long since the Chumash were removed and the islands given over to hunters, ranchers, and settlers, the Channel Islands are largely uninhabited. All five, however, are open to hikers and campers. At the mainland-based **Channel Islands National Park Visitors Center** there are contemporary museum displays, an observation deck, an indoor tidepool, and an excellent 23-minute movie to familiarize you with the park. Also on display is a skeleton of a pygmy mammoth found on Santa Rosa Island in 1994. ~ 1901 Spinnaker Drive, Ventura; 805-658-5730, fax 805-658-5799; www.nps.gov/chis.

Nearby at **Island Packers** you can arrange transportation to the islands. This outfit schedules regular daytrips by boat to Anacapa, Santa

Barbara, Santa Cruz, Santa Rosa, and San Miguel islands. ~ 1691
Spinnaker Drive, Ventura; 805-642-1393; www.islandpackers.com.
Channel Islands Aviation will fly you to Santa Rosa Island for a day of
fishing or hiking or overnight camping. Flights leave at 9 a.m. and return
around 3:30 p.m. ~ 805-987-1301; www.flycia.com.

Island Packers leads seasonal tours of **Santa Cruz**, the largest and most
diverse of the islands. Here you will find an island just 24 miles long that
supports 600 species of plants, 130 types of land birds, and several
unique plant species. There are Indian middens, earthquake faults, and
two mountain ranges to explore. To the center lies a pastoral valley
while the shoreline is a rugged region of cliffs, tidepools, and offshore
rocks. Note: Camping is not allowed on Nature Conservancy property
but *is* permitted on the eastern part on national park land. Call ahead to
make reservations. ~ 1691 Spinnaker Drive, Ventura; 805-642-1393;
www.islandpackers.com.

Anacapa Island, the island closest to shore, is a series of three islets
parked 11 miles southwest of Oxnard. There is a nature trail here. Like
the other islands, it is a prime whale-watching spot and is surrounded by
the giant kelp forests that make the Channel Islands one of the nation's
richest marine environments.

The varied landscape of **Santa Rosa Island** includes grasslands,
volcanic formations, and marshes. You may spot harbor and elephant
seals as you stroll the island's beaches. Nature and history draw visitors
to **San Miguel**, where you can hike to the caliche forest or visit a
monument to Juan Cabrillo, the first European to discover California.
Santa Barbara Island is a good spot for birdwatching. Hikers can
traverse the five and a half miles of trails here.

Outdoor aficionados will be glad to hear that camping is allowed in the
national park. However, you must obtain a permit by calling 800-365-
2267. All campgrounds have picnic tables and pit toilets, but generally,
water must be carried in—and trash must be carried out. Fires are not
permitted.

Whether you are a sailor, swimmer, daytripper, hiker, archaeologist,
birdwatcher, camper, tidepooler, scuba diver, seal lover, or simply an
interested observer, you'll find this amazing island chain a place of
singular beauty and serenity.

topside for the shower. ~ 1567 Spinnaker Drive, Slip D-8, Ventura Harbor; 805-598-2628; www.bunkinajunk.com. DELUXE.

Besides being an all-suite property, the **Embassy Suites Mandalay Beach Resort** is the only full-service hotel on the beach in this area. As you might expect, the oceanfront suites are almost always sold out on weekends, so plan ahead and reserve early. A full, complimentary breakfast is included in the price. ~ 2101 Mandalay Beach Road, Oxnard; 805-984-2500, 800-362-2779, fax 805-984-8339; www.embassymandalay.com, e-mail info@ embassymandalay.com. ULTRA-DELUXE.

DINING

Landmark No. 78 is exactly what its name states: a beautifully restored 1912 Victorian residence listed on the historic register. Today it's home to fine dining, featuring pasta, steak, and seafood dishes. There is much to recommend it. For one thing, it's not on the main drag, and, for another, the house claims to have its own ghost, Rosa, whose story is a sad one. ~ 211 East Santa Clara Street, Ventura; 805-643-3264 or 805-643-6267, fax 805-643-3267; www.landmark78.com. MODERATE.

HIDDEN ►

The brick-walled, flower-filled **Nona's Courtyard Café** provides a cool and charming indoor spot for lunch or dinner. Salads and sandwiches are tasty and generous, as are the pastas, risottos, chicken, and other entrées. No dinner Monday and Tuesday. ~ Bella Maggiore Inn, 67 South California Street, Ventura; 805-641-2783. MODERATE.

Try **Eric Ericsson's Fish Company**, a small snuggery done in casual California style with indoor/outdoor seating. At lunch they could be serving fish chowder, seafood pasta, poached shrimp, or fresh fish tacos. Then for dinner they might charbroil mahimahi, salmon, swordfish, or sea bass, depending on the season. They also have a walk-up snack shack where you can grab a smoothie, burger, or breakfast sandwich for your stroll along the beach. ~ 668 Harbor Boulevard, Ventura; 805-643-4783, fax 805-643-2904. MODERATE TO ULTRA-DELUXE.

NIGHTLIFE

Bombay Bar & Grill, known for a 200-foot bar, offers live entertainment nightly with a musical medley that varies from rock to funk, ska, and jazz. The room in back hosts live deejays on select weekends. Cover on weekends. ~ 143 South California Street, Ventura; 805-643-4404; www.bombaybarandgrill.com.

If a little high-energy entertainment is what you're looking for, try **Nicholby's**. Upstairs above the antique store, they dish out a mix of live music and deejay-spun tunes. It's a young scene, funky and hip. Cover. ~ 410 East Main Street, Ventura; 805-653-2320; www.nicholbys.com.

There is an improvisational comedy crew working out of the **Livery Theatre**, which, until a few years ago, was actually a working stable with some ramshackle attached buildings. Now it's a stylish complex of offices, shops, and the theater, which hosts a variety of events on weekends—from live music to comedy improv to interactive theater performances. ~ 34 North Palm Street, Ventura; 805-643-5701; www.liverytheatre.org.

POINT MUGU STATE PARK 🚶 🚴 🏇 🚙 🏊 ⚓ This outstanding facility extends along four miles of beachfront and reaches back six miles into the Santa Monica Mountains. Much of the landscape is characterized by hilly, chaparral-cloaked terrain. Vegetation is plentiful, and the campgrounds are very open. The beaches—which include **Sycamore Cove Beach, Thornhill Broome,** and **Point Mugu Beach**—are wide and sandy, with rocky outcroppings and a spectacular sand dune. To the interior, the park rises to 1266-foot Mugu Peak and to Tri-Peaks, 3010 feet in elevation. There are two large canyons as well as wide, forested valleys. More than 70 miles of hiking trails lace this diverse park. Facilities include picnic areas, restrooms, and lifeguards. Swimming and bodysurfing are popular but watch for rip currents. There is good surf a few miles south of the park at **County Line Beach.** ~ Route 1, ten miles south of Oxnard. Information center at Sycamore Cove; 818-880-0350, fax 818-880-6165.

BEACHES & PARKS

The lush riverbanks of the Santa Clara River in McGrath State Beach make for some of the best birdwatching in the state.

▲ There are three separate park campgrounds. At Sycamore Canyon there are 45 tent/RV sites (no hookups); $20 per night. Thornhill Broome Beach has 63 primitive tent/RV sites (no hookups) right on the beach; $15 per night. And La Jolla Valley has 12 sites (hike-in only) that cost $2 per person per night. Reservations are recommended for Sycamore Canyon and Thornhill Broome Beach campgrounds; call 800-444-7275.

MCGRATH STATE BEACH 🚴 🚙 🏊 ⚓ This long, narrow park extends for two miles along the water. The beach is broad and bounded by dunes. A lake and wildlife area attract over 200 bird species. The Santa Clara River, on the northern boundary, is home to bobcats, squirrels, possums, weasels, and other wildlife. Together the lake and preserve make it a great spot for camping or daytripping at the beach. There are restrooms, showers, and lifeguards. Swimming and surfing is recommended for strong swimmers only; watch for rip currents. Day-use fee, $4. ~ 2211 Harbor Boulevard, Oxnard; 805-654-4744 or 805-648-4127.

▲ There are 174 tent/RV sites (no hookups); $21 per night. Reservations strongly recommended: 800-444-7275.

SAN BUENAVENTURA STATE BEACH 🚴 🚙 🏊 ⚓ In the world of urban parks this 114-acre facility ranks high. The broad sandy beach, bordered by dunes, extends for two miles to the

Ventura pier. Since the pier is a short stroll from the city center, the beach provides a perfect escape hatch after you have toured the town. Facilities include picnic areas, restrooms, outdoor showers, food vendors, and lifeguards. The breakwaters here provide excellent swimming. Surfing is popular at **Surfer's Point Park**, foot of Figueroa Street; and at **Peninsula Beach**, at the north end of Spinnaker Drive. Fishing from the 1700-foot pier is good, and anglers may catch bass, shark, surf perch, corbina, and halibut. The nearby rock jetties are a haven for crabs and mussels. Day-use fee, $4. ~ Located along Harbor Boulevard southeast of the Ventura Pier in Ventura; 805-648-4807 or 805-648-4127.

EMMA WOOD STATE BEACH 🏃 🚵 🏊 ⛵ 🛶 Sandwiched between the ocean and the Union Pacific railroad tracks, this slender park measures only 109 acres. Because of tide fluctuations, the beach can become extremely rocky, making it undesirable for swimmers and sunbathers. There is a marsh at one end inhabited by songbirds and small mammals. Considering the fabulous beaches hereabouts, I rank this one pretty low. Restrooms are available. Cabezon, perch, bass, and corbina are caught here. Day-use fee, $4. ~ Located on the northwest boundary of Ventura just off Route 101; 805-648-4807 or 805-648-4127.

▲ There's camping nearby along the small, rocky beaches north of Emma Wood State Beach at three different campgrounds. **Emma Wood–North Beach** has 90 first-come, first-serve tent/RV sites (no hookups); $15 per night; for information, call 805-648-4807 or 805-648-4127. **Faria County Park** is a bit smaller with 42 tent/RV sites (no hookups); $20 per night. **Hobson County Park** is smaller still with 31 tent/RV sites (no hookups); $20 per night.

▼▼▼▼▼▼▼▼▼▼
Ojai Area

To Chumash Indians the word *ojai* signified the nest. And to the generations of mystics, health aficionados, artists, and admirers who have settled here, the place is indeed a secluded abode. Geographically it resembles its Chumash namesake, nestling in a moon-shaped valley girded by the Topa and Sulphur Mountains.

A town of 7900 souls, Ojai is an artist colony crowded with galleries and studios. The site is also a haven for the health conscious, with spas and hot springs. To the metaphysically minded it is a center for several esoteric sects.

Ever since the 1870s, when author Charles Nordhoff publicized the place as a tourist spot, it has been popular with all sorts of visitors. The cultural life of the town focuses around a series of annual music festivals that runs from May to October and range in style from classical to country-and-western to blues. For sport there is nearby Lake Casitas, Los Padres National Forest, 4500-foot mountains, and a 400-mile network of hiking trails.

Inland just 14 miles from Ventura, Ojai is a valley so extraordinary it was used as the setting for Shangri-La in the movie *Lost Horizon* (1937). Sun-bronzed mountains rise in all directions, fields of wildflowers run to the verge of forested slopes, and everywhere there is tranquility, making it clear why the region is a magnet for mystics.

SIGHTS

Set on top of a hill overlooking Ojai Valley is the **Krotona Institute of Theosophy**. This 118-acre forested estate is a center for "students of Theosophy and the ancient wisdom." A spiritual-philosophical movement that developed late in the 19th century, Theosophy combines science with religion and draws from the classic philosopher Pythagoras. Visitors can tour the library, shop in the bookstore, and enjoy the grounds, which are beautifully landscaped. Closed Monday. ~ 2 Krotona Hill, Ojai; 805-646-2653, fax 805-646-7679; www.theosophical.org, e-mail krotona @doc.k.net.

Another sect, the **Krishnamurti Foundation**, has an equally secluded library in the hills on the other side of town. Closed Monday and Tuesday. ~ 1130 McAndrew Road, Ojai; 805-646-4948.

At nearby **Meditation Mount**, where the grounds and meditation rooms are open daily, there are special community meditative sessions to celebrate the full moon. ~ 10340 Reeves Road, Ojai; 805-646-5508, fax 805-646-3303; www.meditation.com, e-mail meditation@meditation.com.

Before venturing to these ethereal heights, stop off at the **Ojai Valley Chamber of Commerce and Visitor's Bureau**, which has maps and brochures of the area. Closed Tuesday. ~ 150 West Ojai Avenue, Ojai; 805-646-8126, fax 805-646-9762; www.ojai chamber.org, e-mail info@ojaichamber.org.

AUTHOR FAVORITE

An excellent Ojai sightseeing jaunt follows Route 150 west as it snakes down from the hills. The valleys are covered with scrub growth and small farms and the heights support lofty forests. The road skirts **Lake Casitas**, whose 60-mile shoreline is a labyrinth of coves and inlets. This is a lovely spot for biking, bird-watching, or fishing. Ten miles from Ojai the road joins Route 192, which leads to Santa Barbara. This meandering country road, in the hills above Carpinteria, traverses pretty pastureland. All around lies a quiltwork of orchards, fields, and tilled plots. Shade trees overhang the road and horses graze in the distance.

The 1917 Mission Revival **Post Office** is also downtown. ~ 201 East Ojai Avenue, Ojai. While you are there, visit the Spanish-style **City Hall**. You'll find a secluded garden there. ~ 401 South Ventura Street, Ojai; 805-646-5581, fax 805-646-1980.

To capture the spirit of Ojai, hike, bicycle, or drive the back roads and mountain lanes. **Grand Avenue loop** will carry you past orange orchards and horse ranches to the foot of the mountains. It leads along thick stone walls built by Chinese laborers during the 19th century. ~ Take Ojai Avenue, Route 150, east from town; turn left on Reeves Road, left again on McAndrew Road, left on Thatcher Road, and left on Carne Road. This returns to Route 150, completing the ten-mile loop.

East End drive follows Route 150 west past palm trees and farmhouses. Three miles from town, on a promontory with a stone bench inscribed "The Ojai Valley," is the overlook from which actor Ronald Colman gazed down on Shangri-La in *Lost Horizon*. With deep green orchards below and sharp gold mountains above, it truly evokes that fictional utopia.

The highway winds high into the sun-scorched mountains past forests of pine and oak. Paralleling the Sespe River, Route 33 bisects rocky defiles and skirts 7500-foot Reyes Peak. For 60 miles the road tracks through the mountains until it meets Route 166, where the alternatives are heading east to the Central Valley or west toward the coastline.

LODGING The premier mountain resort hereabouts is **Ojai Valley Inn & Spa**, a 220-acre retreat with tennis courts, a few swimming pools, and 18-hole golf course. Set in a pastoral valley with spectacular mountain vistas, the complex has been refurbished and modernized. Rooms are quite spacious, imaginatively decorated, and share the resort's oh-so-incredible views. There is an ample lobby for lounging, plus such amenities as a tennis center, putting green, hiking trails, horseback riding, and restaurants. ~ 905 Country Club Road, Ojai; 805-646-5511, 800-422-6524, fax 805-646-7969; www.ojairesort.com, e-mail info@ojairesort.com. ULTRA-DELUXE.

For less lavish accommodations consider **Rose Garden Inn**. It's a 17-unit affair with large, attractive rooms, paneled entirely in knotty cedar and carpeted wall-to-wall. Some rooms have fireplaces and all have refrigerators and microwaves. Guests can use the pool, whirlpool, and sauna. A full complimentary breakfast is included in the rate. ~ 615 West Ojai Avenue, Ojai; 805-646-1434, 800-799-1881, fax 805-640-8455; www.rosegardeninn.com, e-mail info@rosegardeninn.com. MODERATE TO DELUXE.

Because of its surrounding mountains Ojai is extremely popular with the health conscious. One of the region's leading spas, **The Oaks at Ojai**, caters to this interest. It provides a full menu of physical activity including aerobic exercise, weight training, yoga classes, body conditioning, and massage. Guests take all their meals—low-calorie vegetarian, fish, or poultry plates—at the spa. The accommodations include comfortable, spacious rooms in the lodge and in outdoor multiunit cottages. Included in the tab are three meals, fitness classes, and use of the pool, saunas, jacuzzi, and other health facilities. ~ 122 East Ojai Avenue, Ojai; 805-646-5573, 800-753-6257, fax 805-640-1504; www.oaksspa.com, e-mail info@oaksspa.com. DELUXE.

DINING

Everyone's favorite Ojai restaurant is the **Ranch House**. Little wonder since this dining terrace rests in a tranquil garden surrounded by ferns, bamboo, and rose bushes. A flowering hedge shelters one side while a statue of Buddha gazes out from the other. Nearby, a graceful footbridge curves across a koi pond. Dinner includes venison tenderloin, grilled diver scallops, freshwater striped bass, and veal in cream sauce. Desserts come from the restaurant's bakery, as do the three varieties of bread served with each meal. Dinner and Sunday brunch only. Closed Monday. ~ South Lomita Avenue, Ojai; 805-646-2360; www.theranchhouse. com. DELUXE TO ULTRA-DELUXE.

For fine French-Belgian dining **L'Auberge**, a venerable old house replete with brick fireplace and chandeliers, sets the tone. You can also dine on the terrace, choosing from a menu that includes scampi, frogs' legs, poached sole, tournedos, pepper steak, sweetbreads, and duckling in orange sauce. Lunch is on weekends only and features almost a dozen different crêpes. ~ 314 El Paseo Road, Ojai; 805-646-2288; www.laubergeojai.com. MODERATE TO DELUXE.

Even if you're not staying at the Ojai Valley Inn, make a point of having lunch at the inn's **Oak Cafe & Terrace**. Set under a trellised patio next to the golf course, with ancient oak trees towering above and the mountains looming in the background, it's the perfect setting for a grilled-chicken salad, a sandwich of grilled local vegetables, or one of the pasta dishes. ~ Ojai Valley Inn & Spa, 905 Country Club Road, Ojai; 805-646-5511; www.ojaire sort.com, e-mail info@ojairesort.com. MODERATE TO DELUXE.

THE PINK MOMENT

If you're visiting Ojai from late October to February, be sure to be outside as sunset approaches to catch what's known as the **Pink Moment**. The rays of the setting sun turn the Topa Topa Mountains a rosy pink. It's a spectacular sight, especially if you can share it with someone special.

SHOPPING   The center of the shopping scene in the mountain resort town of Ojai is **Arcade Plaza**, a promenade between Ojai Avenue and Matilija Street that extends from Montgomery Street to Signal Street. Within this tile-roofed warren and along surrounding blocks are crafts stores and galleries. Many are operated by the community of artisans that has grown over the years in Ojai.

An even more extensive collection of pottery is on display at the **Human Arts Gallery**. There are also paintings, handblown glass pieces, and handwrought jewelry items. ~ 310 East Ojai Avenue, Ojai; 805-646-1525.

For women's fashions consider **Priscilla**, specializing in casual chic clothing for professional women. Closed Tuesday and Wednesday. ~ 320 East Ojai Avenue, Ojai; 805-646-9782. For stylish fashions, visit the **Barbara Bowman** shops, owned by the well-known designer. ~ 125 and 133 East Ojai Avenue, Ojai; 805-646-2970.

Primavera Gallery showcases a fine collection of glass, including a series of handpainted chandeliers by Ulla Darni. ~ 214 East Ojai Avenue, Ojai; 805-646-7133; www.primaveraart.com.

For museum-quality traditional pottery, head east from town to **The Pottery**. Otto Heino has been working in porcelain and stoneware for decades. After browsing the showroom visitors can wander the landscaped grounds viewing the carp pond, cactus garden, and peacocks. Closed Monday. ~ 971 McAndrew Road, Ojai; 805-646-3393.

NIGHTLIFE   There's live rock, jazz, or blues at the **Ojai Brew Pub** on Friday and Saturday nights. Wednesday night is open-mic night, so there's no telling what entertainment to expect. ~ 423 East Ojai Avenue #101, Ojai; 805-646-8837; www.ojaibrewpub.com.

World Famous Deer Lodge Tavern & Restaurant, a jukebox-and-pool-table bar, has dancing to rhythm-and-blues and rock bands every Friday and Saturday. Occasional cover. ~ 2261 Route 33, Ojai; 805-646-4256.

AUTHOR FAVORITE

Farther outside town, in a hilltop estate flanked by gardens, is the **Beatrice Wood Studio**, a place that you absolutely must visit. Beatrice Wood, whose autobiography is titled *I Shock Myself*, is a regional institution. Tremendously talented, she was a potter for six decades. Her work shows incredible range. Pieces are wrought as figurines of people and animals: vases feature forms in bas-relief; pitchers are shaped as people, their arms pouring spouts; couples are cast in bed or standing forlornly. Open by appointment Tuesday through Friday, and without appointment on Saturday afternoon. ~ 8560 Ojai-Santa Paula Road, Ojai; 805-646-3381; www.beatricewood.com, e-mail info@beatricewood.com.

Or check out the weekend poetry readings or musical performances that may be taking place during the summer at **Local Hero Bookstore** downtown. ~ 254 East Ojai Avenue, Ojai; 805-646-3165.

◄ *HIDDEN*

LAKE CASITAS RECREATION AREA 🏃 🚴 🚤 ⛵ 🚣 ⬦

PARKS

This is a 6200-acre park surrounded by forested slopes and featuring a many-fingered lake. No swimming is permitted since Casitas is a reservoir, but fishing and boating are encouraged. Outlying mountains and the proximity of Ojai make it a particularly popular locale. Facilities include picnic areas, restrooms, showers, a snack bar, a bait-and-tackle shop, and a grocery store. For bike rentals and boat rentals, call 805-649-2043. Bass, trout, and channel catfish are caught in these waters. Day-use fee, $6.50 per vehicle. ~ 11311 Santa Ana Road about ten miles east of Ventura; 805-649-2233, fax 805-649-4661.

▲ There are 400 sites in total, 156 with hookups. Camping costs $22 to $44 with hookups, $16 to $18 without.

From Ventura, Route 101 speeds north and west to Santa Barbara. For a slow-paced tour of the shoreline, take the Old Pacific Coast Highway

▼▼▼▼▼▼▼▼▼▼▼▼▼▼
Santa Barbara Area

instead. Paralleling the freeway and the Southern Pacific Railroad tracks, it rests on a narrow shelf between sharply rising hills and the ocean. The road glides for miles along sandy beaches and rocky shoreline, passing the woodframe communities of Solimar Beach and Seacliff Beach.

Past this last enclave the old road ends as you join Route 101 once more. With the Santa Ynez Mountains looming on one side and the Pacific extending along the other, you'll pass the resort town of Carpinteria. The temperature might be 80° with a blazing sun overhead and a soft breeze off the ocean. Certainly the furthest thing from your mind is the North Pole, but there it is, just past Carpinteria—the turnoff for Santa Claus Lane.

Tucked between a curving bay and the Santa Ynez Mountains lies one of the prettiest places in all California. It's little wonder that the Spanish who settled **Santa Barbara**, establishing a presidio in 1782 and a mission several years later, called it *la tierra adorada*, the beloved land.

SIGHTS

Discovered by a Portuguese navigator in 1542, it was an important center of Spanish culture until the Americans seized California in the 19th century. The town these Anglo interlopers built was an early-20th-century community. But a monstrous earthquake leveled the downtown area in 1925 and created a *tabula rasa* for architects and city planners.

Faced with rebuilding Santa Barbara, they returned the place to its historic roots, combining Spanish and Mission architecture to create a Mediterranean metropolis. The result is modern-day Santa Barbara with its adobe walls, red tile roofs, rounded archways, and palm-lined boulevards.

Mission Santa Barbara is the only California mission that has been continuously used by Franciscan fathers throughout its 200-year history.

Sightseeing Santa Barbara is as simple as it is rewarding. First, stop at the **Santa Barbara Visitors Center**. The myriad materials here include more pamphlets, books, and booklets than you ever want to see. The most important piece is a map entitled "Santa Barbara" that outlines a "Red Tile Tour" for walkers as well as a lengthier "Scenic Drive." Together they form two concentric circles along the perimeters of which lie nearly all the city's points of interest. ~ 1 Garden Street, Santa Barbara; 805-965-3021 or 805-568-1811, fax 805-966-5954; www.sbchamber.org.

SCENIC DRIVE The Scenic Drive around Santa Barbara, a 21-mile circular tour, incorporates several of the sites covered along the Red Tile Tour. To avoid repetition, begin at the **Santa Barbara Museum of Art** with its collection of American and European paintings and photography, Asian art, and classical sculpture. Closed Monday. Admission. ~ 1130 State Street; 805-963-4364, fax 805-966-6840; www.sbmuseart.org.

Then head up to **Mission Santa Barbara**, which sits on a knoll overlooking the city. Founded in 1786 and restored in 1820, this twin-towered beauty, known as the "Queen of the Missions," follows a design from an ancient Roman architecture book. The interior courtyard is a colonnaded affair with a central fountain and graceful flower garden. The chapel itself is quite impressive with a row of wrought-iron chandeliers leading to a multicolored altar. There are also museum displays representing the original Indian population and early-19th-century mission artifacts. Also visit the Mission Cemetery, a placid and pretty spot where frontier families and about 4000 Chumash Indians are buried in the shade of a Moreton Bay fig tree. Admission. ~ 2201 Laguna Street; 805-682-4713, fax 805-682-6067; www.sbmission.org.

Farther uphill at the **Santa Barbara Museum of Natural History** are successive rooms devoted to marine, plant, vertebrate, and insect life. Excellent for kids, it also features an extensive collection of artifacts from the local Chumash tribe. You'll recognize the museum by the 72-foot skeleton of a blue whale out front. There is also a lizard lounge and a planetarium with a space lab. Admission. ~ 2559 Puesta del Sol Road; 805-682-4711, fax 805-569-3170; www.sbnature.org, e-mail info@sbnature2.org.

Nearby Mission Canyon Road continues into the hills for close-up views of the rocky Santa Ynez Mountains and a tour of

Santa Barbara Botanic Garden. Trails here wind past eight different habitats, including a desert section carpeted with cactus and a meadow filled with wildflowers. In the spring, near the top of the garden, beyond the ancient Indian step, where the forest edges down from the mountains, is a stand of cool, lofty redwood trees. Be sure to visit the traditional Japanese teahouse and tea garden exhibit. Guided tours daily. Admission. ~ 1212 Mission Canyon Road; 805-682-4726, fax 805-563-0352; www. sbbg.org, e-mail info@sbbg.org. ◄ HIDDEN

Backtrack to Alameda Padre Serra and cruise this elite roadway past million-dollar homes with million-dollar views. From this thoroughfare a series of side roads leads through the exclusive bedroom community of **Montecito.** Here a variety of architectural styles combine to create a luxurious neighborhood.

Montecito is where the real money is in the Santa Barbara area. A drive through this community, which flanks Santa Barbara on the south, will give you only a glimpse of the well-tended natural beauty of the place because homes for the most part are secluded behind walls and lavish landscaping. One former resident, Madame Ganna Walska, turned her hillside estate into what is now one of the most famous private gardens in the country: **Lotusland.** By the time she arrived in Santa Barbara in 1941, Madame, a Polish-born opera singer, was on her sixth husband.

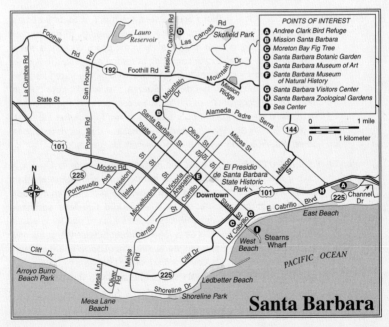

Santa Barbara

Text continued on page 416.

Santa Barbara's Red Tile Tour

For a lesson in Santa Barbara's colorful history, embark on the 14-block Red Tile Tour, which introduces visitors to many of the town's landmarks.

SANTA BARBARA COUNTY COURTHOUSE   The Red Tile loop begins at the Santa Barbara County Courthouse, the city's grandest building. This U-shaped Spanish–Moorish "palace" covers almost three sides of a city block. The interior is a masterwork of beamed ceilings, arched corridors, and palacio tile floors. On the second floor of this 1929 courthouse are murals depicting California history. The highlight of every visit is the sweeping view of Santa Barbara at the top of the clock tower. From the Santa Ynez Mountains down to the ocean, all that meets the eye are palm trees and red tile roofs. No tours on Sunday. ~ 1100 block of Anacapa Street; 805-962-6464, fax 805-967-4104.

HILL–CARRILLO ADOBE   Two blocks down, the Hill–Carrillo Adobe is an 1826-vintage home built by a Massachusetts settler for his Spanish bride. The house is closed to the public but can be viewed from the street. ~ 11 East Carrillo Street.

ANTIQUE BUILDINGS   Along State Street, the heart of Santa Barbara's shopping district, many stores occupy antique buildings. **El Paseo** represented one of the most original malls in the entire country. It was a labyrinthine shopping arcade consisting of several complexes. Today, it is composed mostly of offices. ~ 814 State Street. Incorporated into the architectural motif is **Casa de la Guerra**, a splendid house built in 1818 for the commander of the Santa Barbara presidio and described by Richard Henry Dana in his classic book *Two Years Before the Mast*. Closed Monday through Wednesday. Admission. ~ 15 East de la Guerra Street; 805-965-0093; www.sbthp.org, e-mail info@sbthp.org.

PLAZA DE LA GUERRA   Across the street rests Plaza de la Guerra, a palm-fringed park where the first city hall stood in 1875. Nearby, another series of historic structures has been converted into a warren of shops and offices. In the center of the mall is **Presidio Gardens**, a tranquil park with a carp pond and elephant-shaped fountains that spray water through their trunks. ~ On de la Guerra Street between Anacapa and Garden streets. The **Santiago de la Guerra Adobe** and the **Lugo Adobe**, set in a charming courtyard, are other 19th-century homes that have been converted to private use. ~ 114 East de la Guerra Street.

SANTA BARBARA HISTORICAL MUSEUM   The Santa Barbara Historical Museum certainly looks its part. Set in an adobe building with tile roof and wrought-iron window bars, the facility sits behind heavy wooden doors. Within are fine art displays and a series depicting the Spanish, Mexican, and early American periods of Santa Barbara's history. There is a pleasant courtyard in back with a fountain and shade trees, a perfect place for a sightseer's siesta. Closed Monday. ~ 136 East de la Guerra Street; 805-966-1601, fax 805-966-1603; www.santabarbaramuseum.com.

CASA DE COVARRUBIAS   A right turn on Garden Street carries you to Casa de Covarrubias. Most places in town are a little too neatly refurbished to provide a dusty sense of history. But this L-shaped house, and the adjacent **Historic Fremont Adobe**, are sufficiently wind-blasted to evoke the early 19th century. The former structure, dating to 1817, is said to be the site of the last Mexican assembly in 1846; the latter became headquarters for Colonel John C. Fremont after Americans captured the town later that year. ~ 715 Garden Street. Turn back along Garden Street and pass the **Rochin Adobe**. This 1856 adobe, now covered with clapboard siding, is a private home. ~ 820 Garden Street.

EL PRESIDIO DE SANTA BARBARA STATE HISTORIC PARK   It's a few steps over to El Presidio de Santa Barbara State Historic Park, which occupies both sides of the street and incorporates some of the city's earliest buildings. Founded in 1782, the Presidio was one of four military fortresses built by the Spanish in California. Protecting settlers and missionaries from Indians, it also served as a seat of government and center of Western culture. Today only two original buildings survive. **El Cuartel**, the guards' house, served as the soldiers' quarters. The **Cañedo Adobe**, also built as a military residence, is now the offices of the Santa Barbara Trust for Historic Preservation. Most interesting of all is the **Santa Barbara Presidio Chapel**, which re-creates an early Spanish church in its full array of colors. Compared to the plain exterior, the interior is a shock to the eye. Everything is done in red and yellow ochre and dark blue. The altar is painted to simulate a great cathedral. Drapes and columns, difficult to obtain during Spanish days, have been drawn onto the walls. Even the altar railing is painted to imitate colored marble. Admission. ~ 123 East Cañon Perdido Street; 805-966-9719; www.sbthp.org, e-mail info@sbthp.org.

LOBERO THEATRE   The last stop on this walking tour will carry you a step closer to the present. The Lobero Theatre was constructed in 1924. It is a three-tiered design that ascends to a 70-foot-high stage house. The original Lobero dates back to 1873, Santa Barbara's first theater. The Lobero presents a variety of performing arts. Call Monday through Saturday for tickets. ~ 33 East Cañon Perdido Street; 805-963-0761, fax 805-963-8752; www.lobero.com.

He persuaded her to buy a Montecito estate in order to establish a spiritual center for Tibetan scholar-monks. When that idea, along with the marriage, failed, Madame turned to horticulture. The result was a magnificent private garden that visitors may tour on a reservations-only basis. The gardens are closed Sunday through Tuesday and mid-November to mid-February. Admission. ~ 805-969-9990, fax 805-969-4423; www.lotusland.org, e-mail info@lotusland.org.

After exploring the town's shady groves and manicured lawns, you can pick up **Channel Drive**, a spectacular street that skirts beaches and bluffs as it loops back toward Santa Barbara. From this curving roadway you'll spy oddly shaped structures offshore. Looking like a line of battleships ready to attack Santa Barbara, they are in fact **oil derricks**. Despite protests from environmentalists and a disastrous 1969 oil spill, these coastal waters have been the site of drilling operations for decades. Those hazy humps farther out past the wells are the Channel Islands.

The **Andree Clark Bird Refuge** is a placid lagoon filled with geese and other freshwater fowl. There are three tree-tufted islands in the center and a trail around the park. ~ 1400 East Cabrillo Boulevard.

Upstaging all this is the adjacent **Santa Barbara Zoological Gardens** with its miniature train ride and population of monkeys, lions, elephants, giraffes, and exotic birds. Admission. ~ 500 Niños Drive; 805-962-6310; www.sbzoo.org, e-mail zooinfo @sbzoo.org.

Cabrillo Boulevard hugs the shore as it tracks past **East Beach**, Santa Barbara's longest, prettiest strand. With its rows of palm trees, grassy acres, and sunbathing crowds, it's an enchanting spot.

Every Sunday morning, the greenbelt at East Beach next to Stearns Wharf turns into an **outdoor art show**. Dozens of local and regional artists exhibit their artwork, photography, jewelry, and crafts. Quality varies, of course, but the setting is unbeatable. ~ Cabrillo Boulevard at State Street.

For a taste of sea air and salt spray, walk out along **Stearns Wharf**. From the end of this wooden pier you can gaze back at Santa Barbara, realizing how aptly author Richard Henry Dana described the place: "The town is finely situated, with a bay in front, and an amphitheater of hills behind." Favored by local anglers, the wharf is also noted for the **Sea Center**, a working marine laboratory where visitors can engage in the work of scientist who study, monitor, and determine how best to protect the ocean. Admission. ~ At the foot of State Street, 211 Stearns Wharf; 805-682-4711, fax 805-569-3170.

If you tire of walking, remember that Stearns Wharf is the departure point for the **Santa Barbara Old Town Trolley**, an old-fashioned vehicle that carries visitors along the waterfront, through the downtown area, and out to the mission. Fee. ~ 805-965-0353, fax 805-965-1075; www.sbtrolley.com.

The **Moreton Bay Fig Tree** is a century-old giant with branches ◄ *HIDDEN* that spread 160 feet. This magnificent specimen stands as the largest tree of its kind in the United States. ~ Chapala and Montecito streets.

Back along the waterfront, Cabrillo Boulevard continues to the **Yacht Harbor**, where 1200 pleasure boats, some worth more than homes, lie moored. The walkway leads past yawls, ketches, sloops, and fishing boats to a breakwater. From here you can survey the fleet and take in the surrounding mountains and ocean. ~ West Cabrillo Boulevard and Castillo Street.

To continue this seafront excursion, follow Shoreline, Cliff, and Marina drives as they parallel the Pacific, past headlands and beaches, en route to **Hope Ranch**. Santa Barbara is flanked by two posh communities: Montecito in the east and this elite enclave to the west. It's a world of country clubs and cocktail parties, where money and nature meet to create forested estates.

NORTH OF SANTA BARBARA   Route 101 streams northwest past a series of suburban communities, including Goleta and Isla Vista, where the **University of California–Santa Barbara** is located. Stop by the visitors center to pick up a campus map and brochures for one of the state's most beautiful universities, or

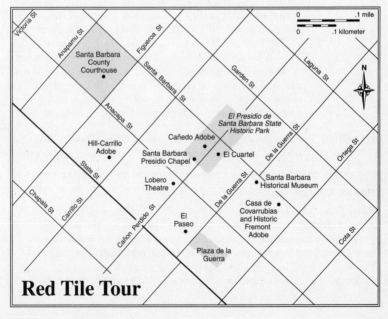

join a guided tour. Closed weekends. ~ 805-893-2487, fax 805-893-8610; www.admit.ucsb.edu.

Cutting a swath between mountains and ocean, the road passes a series of attractive beach parks, then turns inland toward the mountains and interior valleys.

About 35 miles from Santa Barbara Routes 101 and 1 diverge. For a rural drive past white barns and meandering creeks, follow **Route 1**. En route to Lompoc it passes farmlands, pastures, and rolling hills. About five miles south of Lompoc, you

HIDDEN ▶

can follow **Jalama Road**, a country lane that cuts through sharp canyons and graceful valleys on a winding 15-mile course to the ocean, ending at a beach park.

This journey becomes a pilgrimage when Route 1 approaches **La Purísima Mission**. The best restored of all 21 California missions, this historic site has an eerie way of projecting you back to Spanish days. There's the mayordomo's abode with the table set and a pan on the stove, or the mission store, its barrels overflowing with corn and beans. The entire mission complex, from the church to the tallow vats where the fat from slaughtered cattle was rendered into soap, was re-created in the 1930s by the Civilian Conservation Corps. Founded nearby in 1787, the mission was re-established at this site in 1813. Today you can tour the living quarters of priests, soldiers, and Indians, the workshops where weaving, leathermaking, and carpentry were practiced, and the mission's original water system. You can also see animals such as burros and goats in their period mission setting. Living-history events occur here periodically; call ahead for details. Admission. ~ 2295 Purisima Road, Lompoc; 805-733-3713, fax 805-733-2497; www.lapurisimamission.org, e-mail lapurmis@sbcco.org.

In spring and summer, the hills around **Lompoc** dazzle with thousands of acres of cultivated flowers. The countryside is a rainbow of color throughout the season. Then, in fall, fields of poppies, nasturtiums, and larkspurs bloom.

LODGING

Two centralized reservation agencies provide an idea of the full range of accommodations available in the Santa Barbara area.

MERRY KITSCH-MAS

Santa Claus Lane? It's a block-long stretch of trinket shops and toy stores with a single theme. It's one of those places that's so tacky you feel like you've missed something if you pass it by. If nothing else, you can mail an early Christmas card. Just drop it in the mailbox at **The Candy Kitchen** and it will be postmarked (ready for this?) "Santa Claus, California." ~ 3821 Santa Claus Lane, Carpinteria; 805-684-8425.

One is **Coastal Escapes Accommodations.** ~ 5320 Carpinteria Avenue, Carpinteria; 800-292-2222; www.coastalescapes.com. **Santa Barbara Hotspots** can also give information on prices and availability. ~ 36 State Street, Santa Barbara; 805-564-1637, 800-793-7666; www.hotspotsusa.com. Since room rates in Santa Barbara fluctuate by season and day of the week, it's advisable to check.

South of Santa Barbara in Carpinteria, the **Eugenia Motel** has ten rooms (four with kitchens). Each is small, carpeted, and clean. The furniture is comfortable though nicked. The baths have stall showers. ~ 5277 Carpinteria Avenue, Carpinteria; 805-684-4416. BUDGET TO MODERATE.

Because of its excellent beach, many families spend their entire vacation in Carpinteria, so most facilities rent by the week or month. Among the less expensive spots is **La Casa del Sol Motel.** This multi-unit complex has 23 units, including some suites with jacuzzis. The one I saw was paneled in knotty pine and trimly furnished. Small pool and laundry facilities are found on-site. No reservations accepted ~ 5585 Carpinteria Avenue, Carpinteria; 805-684-4307; www.casadelsolmotel.com. MODERATE.

For modest-priced accommodations within a block or two of the beach, check out **Cabrillo Boulevard.** This artery skirts the shoreline for several miles. Establishments lining the boulevard are usually a little higher in price. But along the side streets leading from Cabrillo are numerous generic motels. From these you can generally expect rooms that are small but tidy and clean. The wall-to-wall carpeting is industrial grade, the furniture consists of naugahyde chairs and formica tables, and the artworks make you appreciate minimalism. There's usually a swimming pool and surrounding terrace, plus a wall of ice machines and soda dispensers.

There are two such places located a block from Santa Barbara's best all-around beach. **Pacific Crest Motel** has 25 units renting at affordable prices. ~ 433 Corona del Mar Drive, Santa Barbara; 805-966-3103. MODERATE TO ULTRA-DELUXE. Next door, that generic facility, **Motel 6,** has 51 guest rooms. ~ 443 Corona del Mar Drive, Santa Barbara; 805-564-1392, 800-466-8356. MODERATE.

Over in the West Beach area, **Beach House Inn & Apartments** has 12 quiet units located two blocks from the beach and harbor. Rooms here are larger than usual, most have fully equipped kitchens, but there's no pool. Small pets are allowed. ~ 320 West Yanonali Street, Santa Barbara; 805-966-1126, fax 805-969-6058; www.thebeachhouseinn.com, e-mail beachhouseinn@hotmail.com. DELUXE.

Montecito Del Mar Hotel, a block farther away, has 23 units, including doubles and suites with kitchens and fireplaces. Ask for a room with a kitchen. There's no pool but there are three outdoor jacuzzis. Continental breakfast is served. ~ 316 West Montecito Street, Santa Barbara; 805-962-2006, 888-464-1690, fax 805-962-1016; www.montecitodelmar.com, e-mail e-mail@ montecitodelmar.com. MODERATE TO DELUXE.

For chic surroundings there is **The Villa Rosa Inn**. Built during the 1930s in Spanish palazzo fashion, it was originally an apartment house. Today it is an 18-room inn with raw wood furnishings and private baths. There's a pool and spa in the courtyard. Guests co-mingle over continental breakfast and afternoon wine and cheese, then settle into plump armchairs around a tile fireplace with port and sherry in the evening. The spacious rooms, some with fireplaces, are pleasantly understated and located half a block from the beach. ~ 15 Chapala Street, Santa Barbara; 805-966-0851, fax 805-962-7159; www.villarosainnsb.com, e-mail info@villarosainnsb.com. DELUXE TO ULTRA-DELUXE.

The Eagle Inn is an attractive Mediterranean-style apartment house converted into a 29-room hotel. Just two blocks from the beach, most of the rooms have king beds with jacuzzi tubs. ~ 232 Natoma Avenue, Santa Barbara; 805-965-3586, 800-767-0030, fax 805-966-1218; www.theeagleinn.com, e-mail info@theeagle inn.com. ULTRA-DELUXE.

Small and intimate as bed and breakfasts tend to be, the **Simpson House Inn** is even more so. Close to downtown, it resides along a quiet tree-lined block secluded in an acre of English gardens complete with fountains and intimate sitting areas. The century-old Victorian inn features 15 guest rooms, restored-barn suites, and garden cottages—all decorated with antiques and fine art. Some feature private decks or patios, fireplaces, and jacuzzis. A gourmet breakfast is served on the veranda or to private patios or rooms; beverages are served in the afternoon, and hors d'oeuvres and wine are provided in the evening. Bikes and croquet complete the package. ~ 121 East Arrellaga Street, Santa Barbara; 805-963-7067, 800-676-1280, fax 805-564-4811; www.simpsonhouseinn.com. ULTRA-DELUXE.

The **Old Yacht Club Inn** is two inns in one. The main facility is a 1912 California Craftsman–style house with five rooms. There is a cozy parlor downstairs where wine and cheese are served in the evening. Next door, in a 1927 vintage stucco, there are seven guest rooms with private baths. Some have been decorated by different families and feature personal photographs and other heirlooms, other rooms feature elegant European decor. The inn is just one block from East Beach, serves a full gourmet breakfast and provides bikes, beach chairs, and towels to guests. Occasionally, owner Nancy Donaldson offers an elegantly prepared five-course gourmet Saturday dinner to guests. The inn books far in advance on these nights, but it's well worth the wait. ~ 431 Corona del Mar Drive, Santa Barbara; 805-962-1277,

800-676-1676, fax 805-962-3989; www.oldyachtclubinn.com, e-mail info@oldyachtclubinn.com. DELUXE TO ULTRA-DELUXE.

The Glenborough Inn is laid out in similar fashion. The main house is a 1906 California Craftsman design with extensive wood detailing and period furniture. A suite in the main house is decorated in turn-of-the-20th-century nouveau style with a fireplace, private entrance, garden, and jacuzzi tub. The second house is an 1880s-era cottage with rooms and suites that have fireplaces and private baths. The theme in both abodes is romance. The rooms are beautifully fashioned with embroidered curtains, inlaid French furniture, some canopied beds, crocheted coverlets, and needlepoint pieces; several have jacuzzi tubs. Guests enjoy a gourmet breakfast brought to their door, and nightly tea and cookies; they also share a cozy living room that has a tile fireplace. ~ 1327 Bath Street, Santa Barbara; 805-966-0589, 800-962-0589; www.glenboroughinn.com, e-mail santabarbara@glenboroughinn.com. DELUXE TO ULTRA-DELUXE.

Down the road at the **Bath Street Inn** you'll encounter a Queen Anne Victorian constructed in 1890. Enter along a garden walkway into a warm living room with a marble-trimmed fireplace. The patio in back is set in another garden. Some of the guest rooms on the second floor feature the hardwood floors and patterned wallpaper that are the hallmarks of California bed and breakfasts. The third floor has a cozy sloped roof and a television lounge for guests. Rooms include private baths, televisions, breakfast, and evening refreshments. ~ 1720 Bath Street, Santa Barbara; 805-682-9680, 800-341-2284, fax 805-569-1281; www.bathstreetinn.com, e-mail bathstin@slicom.com. DELUXE TO ULTRA-DELUXE.

AUTHOR FAVORITE

Upham Hotel is "the oldest cosmopolitan hotel in continuous operation in Southern California." Established in 1871, it shares a sense of history with the country inns, but enjoys the lobby and restaurant amenities of a hotel. Victorian in style, the two-story clapboard is marked by sweeping verandas and a cupola; the accommodations here are nicely appointed with hardwood and period furnishings. Around the landscaped grounds are garden cottages, some with private patios and fireplaces, and a carriage house with five Victorian-style rooms. Continental breakfast, afternoon wine and cheese, and cookies at bedtime are included. ~ 1404 de la Vina Street, Santa Barbara; 805-962-0058, 800-727-0876, fax 805-963-2825; www.uphamhotel.com, e-mail upham.hotel@verizon.net. ULTRA-DELUXE.

Santa Barbara's two finest hotels dominate the town's two geographic locales, the ocean and the mountains. **Four Seasons Biltmore Hotel** is a grand old Spanish-style hotel set on 20 acres beside the beach. It's the kind of place where guests play croquet or practice putting on manicured lawns, then meander over to the hotel's Coral Casino Beach and Cabaña Club. There are several dining rooms as well as tennis courts, swimming pools, and a complete spa. The refurbished rooms are quite large and have an airy feel, with light wood furnishings and full marble baths. Many are located in multiplex cottages and are spotted around the magnificent grounds that have made this one of California's most famous hotels since it opened back in 1927. ~ 1260 Channel Drive, Santa Barbara; 805-969-2261, 800-332-3442, fax 805-565-8323; www.fourseasons.com. ULTRA-DELUXE.

El Encanto Hotel & Garden Villas sits back in the Santa Barbara hills and is a favorite hideaway among Hollywood stars. The hotel's 84 rooms are set in cottages and villas that dot this ten-acre retreat. The grounds are beautifully landscaped and feature a lily pond, tennis court, and swimming pool. The views are simply spectacular. Rooms are very spacious with attached sitting rooms, plus extra features like room service, refrigerator, and terrycloth bathrobes. Some have private patios. The decor is French country with a lot of brass and etched-glass fixtures. ~ 1900 Lasuen Road, Santa Barbara; 805-687-5000, 800-346-7039, fax 805-687-3903; www.elencantohotel.com. ULTRA-DELUXE.

John and Jackie Kennedy spent part of their honeymoon at San Ysidro Ranch.

In the Santa Ynez foothills above Montecito sits another retreat where the rich and powerful mix with the merely talented. **San Ysidro Ranch** sprawls across 500 acres, most of which is wilderness traversed by hiking trails. There are tennis courts, a pool, a bocce ball court, and complete fitness facilities. The grounds vie with the Santa Barbara Botanic Garden in the variety of plant life: there are meadows, mountain forests, and an orange grove. The Stonehouse Restaurant serves gourmet dishes and the complex also features sitting rooms and lounges. Privacy is the password: all these features are shared by guests occupying just 38 units. The accommodations are dotted around the property in cottages and small multiplexes. Pets are welcome; 24-hour room service is available. Rooms vary in decor, but even the simplest are trimly appointed and spacious with hardwood furnishings, wood-burning fireplaces, king-size beds, and a mountain, ocean, or garden view. Many have hot tubs. ~ 900 San Ysidro Lane, Montecito; 805-969-5046, 800-368-6788, fax 805-565-1995; www.sanysidro ranch.com. ULTRA-DELUXE.

About 20 miles north of Santa Barbara, there is a private campground, **El Capitan Canyon**, about one-half mile inland from El Capitan State Beach. This is not a spot to pitch your own tent, however; instead, you choose from a variety of cabins and tent cabins. This sprawling 100-acre complex features picnic areas, restrooms, showers, a store, a pool, a playground, game areas, and an outdoor theater that has live music on Saturday ~ 11560 Calle Real, Goleta; 805-685-3887, 866-352-2729, fax 805-968-6772; www.elcapitancanyon.com, e-mail info@elcapitancanyon.com. MODERATE TO ULTRA-DELUXE.

At **The Palms** you cook your own steak or halibut dinner, or have them prepare a shrimp, scallop, crab, lobster, or chicken meal. A family-style restaurant with oak chairs and pseudo-Tiffany lamps, it hosts a salad bar and adjoining lounge. Dinner only. ~ 701 Linden Avenue, Carpinteria; 805-684-3811, fax 805-684-2149. BUDGET TO DELUXE.

DINING

A step upscale at **Clementine's Steak House** they feature filet mignon, fresh fish dishes, vegetarian casserole, steak teriyaki, and Danish-style liver. It's dinner only here, but the meal—which includes soup, salad, vegetable, starch dish, homemade bread, and pie—could hold you well into the next day. The interior has a beamed ceiling and patterned wallpaper. Lean back in a captain's chair and enjoy some home-style cooking. Closed Monday. ~ 4631 Carpinteria Avenue, Carpinteria; phone/fax 805-684-5119. MODERATE TO DELUXE.

For a scent of Santa Barbara salt air with your lunch or dinner, **Brophy Brothers Restaurant & Clam Bar** is the spot. Located out on the Breakwater, overlooking the marina, mountains, and open sea, it features a small dining room and patio. If you love seafood, it's heaven; if not, then fate has cast you in the wrong direction. The clam bar serves all manner of clam and oyster concoctions, and the restaurant is so committed to fresh fish they print a new menu daily to tell you what the boats brought in. When I was there the daily fare included fresh snapper, shark, scampi, salmon, sea bass, halibut, and mahimahi. ~ 119 Harbor Way, Santa Barbara; 805-966-4418; e-mail brophybrothers@prodigy. net. BUDGET TO DELUXE.

One of the more romantic restaurants in Santa Barbara is the **Wine Cask**, where you can dine outside in a lovely courtyard or indoors under the colorful hand-painted ceiling mural that dates from the 1920s. Among the innovative entrées are seared peppercorn-crusted ahi and herb-crusted Colorado lamb loin, as well as chicken, beef, and pastas. Appetizers are equally creative and tempting. Don't forget to check out the wine list with more than 3500 vintages. No lunch on weekends. ~ 813 Anacapa Street, Santa Barbara; 805-966-9463; www.winecask.com, e-mail winecask@winecask.com. ULTRA-DELUXE.

Best of Santa Barbara's low-priced restaurants is **La Tolteca**, not to be confused with La Tolteca Restaurant on Milpas Street. This self-order café serves delicious Mexican food. Everything is fresh, making it *the* place for tacos, tostadas, burritos, tamales, and enchiladas. Menu items are served à la carte, so you can mix and match to get exactly what you want. You can sit at one of the few tables inside or out near the sidewalk. Breakfast, lunch, and dinner. ~ 616 East Haley Street, Santa Barbara; 805-963-0847, fax 805-963-3057. BUDGET.

Another south-of-the-border favorite is **La Super Rica**. The menu includes *alambre de pechuga* (marinated chicken strips fried with peppers and onions on a warm tortilla), and chile rellenos. The homemade salsa is recommended. ~ 622 North Milpas Street, Santa Barbara; 805-963-4940. BUDGET.

HIDDEN ►

Santa Barbara natives have been eating at **Joe's Café** since 1928. Crowds line the coal-black bar, pile into the booths, and fill the tables. They come for a meat-and-potatoes lunch and dinner menu that stars prime rib. This is where you go for pork chops, steak, and French dip. The walls are loaded with mementos and faded photographs; softball trophies and deer antlers decorate the place; and the noise level is the same as the Indy 500. Paradise for slummers. ~ 536 State Street, Santa Barbara; 805-966-4638. BUDGET TO DELUXE.

Downey's, a small, understated dining room, numbers among Santa Barbara's premier restaurants. The dozen tables here are set amid sage-colored walls lined with local artwork. The food is renowned: specializing in California cuisine, Downey's has a menu that changes daily. A typical evening's entrées are salmon with forest mushrooms, lamb loin with grilled eggplant and chiles, sea bass with artichokes, duck with fresh papaya chutney, and

AUTHOR FAVORITE

The graphics on the wall tell a story about the cuisine at **The Palace Grill**. Portrayed are jazz musicians, catfish, redfish, and scenes from New Orleans. The message is Cajun, Creole, and Italian, and this lively, informal bistro is very good at delivering it. This restaurant prepares softshelled crab, blackened filet mignon, crawfish *étouffée*, jambalaya, pastas, and grilled steak. For dessert, Honey, we have Key lime pie and bread pudding soufflé. ~ 8 East Cota Street, Santa Barbara; 805-963-5000, fax 805-962-3200; www.palacecafe.com. MODERATE TO DELUXE.

swordfish cooked over a mesquite grill. There is a good wine list featuring California vintages. Very highly recommended. Dinner only. Closed Monday. ~ 1305 State Street, Santa Barbara; 805-966-5006, fax 805-966-5000; www.downeyssb.com. ULTRA-DELUXE.

Hanging out in coffeehouses is my favorite avocation. There's no better spot in Santa Barbara than **Sojourner Coffeehouse**. Not only do they serve espresso and cappuccino, but lunch, dinner, and weekend brunch as well. Everyone seems to know everyone else in this easygoing café. They come to kibitz and enjoy the tostadas, rice-and-vegetable plates, and gourmet salads. The accent is vegetarian so expect daily specials like polenta cake royale, sweet tomato linguini, or garden Indian dhal. ~ 134 East Cañon Perdido, Santa Barbara; 805-965-7922; www.sojournercafe.com, e-mail sojo@sojournercafe.com. BUDGET TO MODERATE.

For truly prodigious breakfasts, locals know that nondescript **Esau's** is *the* place. Pancakes, omelettes, scrambles and homemade hash are nicely prepared and served in generous portions. If there's a queue (usually the case on weekends), look for a stool at the counter. ~ 403 State Street, Santa Barbara; 805-965-4416. BUDGET.

◄ HIDDEN

Cafe del Sol is the rarest of creatures, an upscale "Santa Barbara–style" eatery, where you'll find a tortilla deli/bar. Here you can sample tapas, Mexican appetizers, and margaritas. A large bank of windows allows dining room guests a view of the Andree Clark Bird Refuge while they dine on a menu varying from lamb shanks and fish to pasta and enchiladas. ~ 30 Los Patos Way, Santa Barbara; 805-969-0448, fax 805-969-5347. MODERATE.

On the beach at Arroyo Burro Beach Park is the **Brown Pelican**. It's a decent restaurant with great ocean views—what more need be said? Sandwiches, salads, hamburgers, and several fresh seafood and pasta dinners are served. Breakfast is available daily until 11 a.m. or later. Trimly appointed and fitted with a wall of plate glass, it looks out upon a sandy beach and tawny bluffs. ~ 2981½ Cliff Drive, Santa Barbara; 805-687-4550, fax 805-569-0188; e-mail thepelican@aol.com. MODERATE TO ULTRA-DELUXE.

Dining at **El Encanto** is pleasurable not only for the fine California and French cuisine but for the sweeping vistas as well. The restaurant resides in a hillside resort overlooking Santa Barbara. There's a luxurious dining room as well as a terrace for dining outdoors. Dinner is a gourmet experience. Changing weekly according to harvest and catch, the menu could include sautéed sea bass with a tarragon crust, roast tenderloin of beef with garlic mashed potatoes, or angelhair pasta with roasted garlic and organic red and yellow tomatoes. The appetizers and desserts are equally outrageous, as are the breakfast and lunch courses. Jackets are required for men at dinner. There's brunch on Sunday. ~ 1900

Lasuen Road, Santa Barbara; 805-687-5000, fax 805-687-3903; www.elencantohotel.com. DELUXE TO ULTRA-DELUXE.

The **Stonehouse Restaurant**, located at the legendary San Ysidro Ranch, serves breakfast, lunch, dinner, and Sunday brunch in the style of new California cuisine, with an international flavor. You can begin with fresh oysters or lobster, then indulge in the spring rolls with a ginger glaze for dipping, skillet-roasted rack of lamb, salmon garlic brulée, or charred yellowfin tuna with a mango garnish. Top off the meal with something scrumptious from the ever-changing dessert selection. ~ 900 San Ysidro Lane, Montecito; 805-969-5046, 800-368-6788, fax 805-565-1995; www.sanysidroranch.com. ULTRA-DELUXE.

SHOPPING   Since Santa Barbara's shops are clustered together, you can easily uncover the town's hottest items and best bargains by concentrating on a few key areas. The prime shopping center lies along State Street, particularly between the 600 and 1300 blocks.

Paseo Nuevo is, literally, a new *paseo*—a mall, really, with department stores, chain shops, and a few homegrown merchants lining a tastefully designed Spanish-style pedestrian promenade. ~ 651 Paseo Nuevo, Santa Barbara; 805-963-2202, fax 805-564-4239; www.sbmall.com.

Located on upper State Street, **La Cumbre Plaza** is a large, open-air shopping complex that features over 60 restaurants and retail stores. Don't miss the farmer's market held every Wednesday from 11 a.m. to 1 p.m. ~ 120 South Hope Street; 805-687-6458.

La Arcada Court is another spiffy mall done in Spanish style. The shops, along the upper lengths of State Street, are more chic and contemporary than they are elsewhere. **Santa Barbara Baggage Company** (805-966-2888) sells luggage, handbags, wallets, business bags, and gifts. Closed Sunday. ~ 1114 State Street, Santa Barbara.

Near the corner of State and Cota streets is the center for vintage clothing. **Yellowstone Clothing** features Hawaiian shirts, used Levi's, and other old-time favorites. ~ 527 State Street, Santa Barbara; 805-963-9609.

NIGHTLIFE   **The Palms** features local rock-and-roll bands Friday and Saturday nights. There's a small dancefloor here for footloose revelers. ~ 701 Linden Avenue, Carpinteria; 805-684-3811.

The State Street strip in downtown Santa Barbara offers several party places. **Zelo** has dancing to a variety of deejay music including hip-hop, disco, funk, and salsa. Live bands perform outside on weekends. Cover. ~ 630 State Street, Santa Barbara; 805-966-5792.

Up at **Acapulco Restaurant,** in La Arcada Court, you can sip a margarita next to an antique wooden bar or out on the patio. ~ 1114 State Street, Santa Barbara; 805-963-3469.

If for no other reason than the view, **Harbor Restaurant** is a prime place for the evening. A plate-glass establishment, it sits out on a pier with the city skyline on one side and open ocean on the other. The bar upstairs, **Longboards,** features sports television and surf videos. ~ 210 Stearns Wharf, Santa Barbara; 805-963-3311.

For sunset views, nothing quite compares to **El Encanto Lounge & Garden Villas.** Located in the posh El Encanto Hotel high in the Santa Barbara hills, it features a split-level terrace overlooking the city and ocean. ~ 1900 Lasuen Road, Santa Barbara; 805-687-5000, 800-346-7039; www.elencantohotel.com.

You can also consider the **Lobero Theatre,** which presents dance, drama, concerts, and lectures. ~ 33 East Cañon Perdido Street, Santa Barbara; 805-963-0761; www.lobero.com.

La Sala is the elegant lobby lounge at the Four Seasons Biltmore where live music and dancing—the kind in which couples actually hold each other in their arms—have become very popular on Friday and Saturday nights. The music varies nightly. ~ 1260 Channel Drive, Santa Barbara; 805-969-2261, 800-332-3442, fax 805-565-8323.

Or head into the mountains about 27 miles outside Santa Barbara and catch a show at the **Circle Bar B Dinner Theatre.** This well-known facility offers a menu of comedies and musicals. Open weekends only from April through October. ~ 1800 Refugio Road, 27 miles north of Santa Barbara; 805-967-1962; www.circlebarbtheatre.com.

RINCON BEACH COUNTY PARK 🏊 🧍 🛶 Wildly popular with nudists and surfers, this is a pretty white-sand beach backed by bluffs. At the bottom of the wooden stairway leading down to the beach, take a right along the strand and head over to the seawall. There will often be a bevy of nude sunbathers snuggled here between the hillside and the ocean in an area known as **Bates**

BEACHES & PARKS

SMALL CRAFT WARNING

For over 20 years Santa Barbara County artists and craftspeople have turned out for the **Arts & Crafts Show.** Every Sunday and holiday from 10 a.m. until dusk they line East Cabrillo Boulevard. The original artwork for sale includes paintings, graphics, sculptures, and drawings. Among the crafts are macrame, stained glass, woodwork, textiles, weaving, and jewelry. If you are in town on a Sunday make it a point to stop by.

Beach, or **Backside Rincon**. Be warned: Nude sunbathing is illegal. Occasionally the sheriff *will* crack down on nudists. Surfers, on the other hand, turn left and paddle out to Rincon Point, one of the most popular surfing spots along the entire California coast. There are picnic areas and restrooms. ~ Located three miles southeast of Carpinteria; from Route 101 take the Bates Road exit.

CARPINTERIA STATE BEACH This ribbon-shaped park extends for nearly a mile along the coast. Bordered to the east by dunes and along the west by a bluff, the beach has an offshore shelf that shelters it from the surf. As a result, Carpinteria provides exceptionally good swimming and is nicknamed "the world's safest beach." Wildlife here consists of small mammals and reptiles as well as seals and many seabirds. Don't bring your pets; dogs are not allowed on the beach. It's a good spot for tidepooling; there is also a lagoon here. The Santa Ynez Mountains rise in the background. Facilities include picnic areas, restrooms, dressing rooms, showers, and lifeguards (during summer only). Swimming is excellent, and skindiving is good along the breakwater reef, a habitat for abalone and lobsters. Surfing is very good in the "tar pits" area near the east end of the park. If you are into fishing, cabezon, corbina, and barred perch are caught here. Day-use fee, $8. ~ Located at the end of Palm Avenue in Carpinteria; 805-684-2811.

▲ There are 261 tent/RV sites, about half with hookups, from $21 to $39 per night. Reservations: 800-444-7275.

SUMMERLAND BEACH Part of this narrow strip of white sand used to be a popular nude beach. It's backed by low-lying hills, which afford privacy from the nearby freeway and railroad tracks. The favored skinny-dipping spot is on the east end between two protective rock piles. Gay men sometimes congregate farther down the beach at Loon Point, but families are rapidly taking over. Nudists beware: law enforcement at the beach has been stepped up in response to public demand. There are no facilities here, but nearby **Lookout Park** (805-969-1720) has picnic areas, restrooms, and a playground. Swimming is popular, and there is good bodysurfing here. ~ Located in Summerland six miles east of Santa Barbara. Take the Summerland exit off Route 101 and get on Wallace Avenue, the frontage road between the freeway and ocean. Follow it east for three-tenths of a mile to Finney Road and the beach.

EAST BEACH Everyone's favorite Santa Barbara beach, this broad beauty stretches more than a mile from Montecito to Stearns Wharf. In addition to a fluffy sand corridor there are grassy areas, palm trees, and a wealth of service facilities. Beyond the wharf the strand continues as **West Beach**. The area known as "Butterfly Beach" at the far east end is frequented by nude sunbathers. Facilities include restrooms, showers, lifeguards, a playground, a weight room, and volleyball courts. Fishing and swimming are recommended. **Cabrillo Pavilion Bathhouse** (1118 East Cabrillo Boulevard, Santa Barbara; 805-897-2680) provides lockers, showers, and a weight room for a small daily fee. There's a restaurant next door. Other facilities are at Stearns Wharf. ~ In Santa Barbara along East Cabrillo Boulevard between the Andree Clark Bird Refuge and Stearns Wharf. Butterfly Beach can be reached by following East Cabrillo Boulevard east past the Cabrillo Pavilion Bathhouse until the road turns inland. From this juncture continue along the beach on foot. Although sunbathers use the beach as a clothing-optional area, this spot, just beyond the Clark Mansion, is sometimes patrolled by the sheriff to discourage nudity; 805-564-5418.

LEDBETTER BEACH 🚲 ≈ 🎣 👤 ♨ A crescent of white sand, this beach rests along a shallow cove. While it's quite pretty here, with a headland bordering one end of the strand, it simply doesn't compare to nearby East Beach. There are picnic areas, restrooms, lifeguards (summer only), and a restaurant. Surfing is good, particularly for beginners, west of the breakwater. ~ Located along the 800 block of Shoreline Drive in Santa Barbara; 805-564-5418.

SHORELINE PARK ≈ The attraction here is not the park but the beach that lies below it. The park rests at the edge of a high bluff; at the bottom, secluded from view, is a narrow, curving length of white sand. It's a great spot to escape the Santa Barbara crowds while enjoying a pretty beach. Stairs from the park lead down to the shore, though the beach is inaccessible at high tide. Topside in the park are picnic areas, restrooms, and a playground.

◆◆

THE WRITING ON THE WALL

Rare and intricate cave paintings by Chumash Indians decorate the sandstone walls at **Chumash Painted Cave State Historic Park**. Strange animal and human figures, as well as various abstract shapes, appear in vivid red, white, and black colors. The oldest paintings here are thought to be 1000 years old, but some of them are quite recent. The Chumash still consider their art sacred—these paintings are one of the only examples on view to the public. ~ On Painted Caves Road, three miles south of San Marcos Pass. Take Route 154 out of Santa Barbara and turn right on Painted Caves Road. The cave is on the left, up a narrow, steep road. Warning: Trailers and RVs should not attempt this road.

~ Located in Santa Barbara along Shoreline Drive; 805-564-5418.

HIDDEN ►   **MESA LANE BEACH** 🏊 This is the spot Santa Barbarans head when they want to escape the crowds at the better-known beaches. It's a meandering ribbon of sand backed by steep bluffs. You can walk long distances along this secluded beach during low tide, but be careful not to get stranded when the tide comes in. There are no facilities so be sure to pack a snack. ~ There's a stairway to the beach at the end of Mesa Lane, off Cliff Drive in Santa Barbara.

ARROYO BURRO BEACH PARK 🐎 🏊 ⚓ 🎣 🚤 This 13-acre facility is a little gem on summer days. The sandy beach and surrounding hills are packed with locals, who often refer to it as "Henry's Park." If you can arrive at an uncrowded time you'll find beautiful scenery along this lengthy strand. There are picnic areas, restrooms, lifeguards (during the summer), a restaurant, a bar, and a snack bar. Swimming and fishing is good and surfing is excellent west of the breakwater. You can also see wildlife in the adjacent Douglas Preserve. ~ 2981 Cliff Drive, Santa Barbara; 805-568-2461.

HIDDEN ►   **MORE MESA** 🏊 According to nude-beach aficionado Dave Patrick, this is the region's favorite bare-buns rendezvous. Thousands of sunbathers gather at this remote site on a single afternoon. "On a hot day," Patrick reports, "the beach almost takes on a carnival atmosphere, with jugglers, surfers, world-class frisbee experts, musicians, dancers, joggers, and volleyball champs." A scene that should not be missed. No facilities. ~ Located between Hope Ranch and Goleta, three miles from Route 101. Take the Turnpike Road exit from Route 101; follow it south to Hollister Avenue, then go left; from Hollister turn right on Puente Drive, right again on Vieja Drive, then left on Mockingbird Lane. At the end of Mockingbird Lane a path leads about three-quarters of a mile to the beach.

On the inland side of Gaviota State Park a hiking trail leads up to Gaviota Hot Springs and into Los Padres National Forest.

EL CAPITAN STATE BEACH 🚶 🏊 🎣 ⚓ 🚤 Another one of Southern California's sparkling beaches, El Capitan stretches along three miles of oceanfront. The park is 168 acres and features a nature trail, tidepools, and wonderful opportunities for hiking along the beach. El Capitan Creek, fringed by oak and sycamore trees, traverses the area. Seals and sea lions often romp offshore and in winter gray whales cruise by. Swimming is good; surfing is good off El Capitan Point. This beach is also a good place to catch grunion. Facilities include picnic areas, restrooms, showers, a store, and seasonal lifeguards. Day-use fee, $5. ~ Located in Goleta off Route 101 about 20 miles north of Santa Barbara; 805-968-1033.

▲ There are 140 tent/RV sites (no hookups) in the park near the beach; $21 per night. Reservations: 800-444-7275.

REFUGIO STATE BEACH 🚶 🚲 ⛵ 🎣 ⛲ ♿ 🅿️ This is a 39-acre park with over a mile of ocean frontage. You can bask on a sandy beach, lie under palm trees on the greensward, and hike or bicycle along the two-and-a-half-mile path that connects this park with El Capitan. There are also interesting tidepools. Facilities include picnic areas, restrooms, showers, seasonal lifeguard, and a store. Fishing, swimming, and surfing are good. Day-use fee, $5. ~ Located on Refugio Road, off Route 101 about 23 miles north of Santa Barbara; 805-968-1033.

▲ There are 82 tent/RV sites (no hookups); $21 per night. Reservations: 800-444-7275.

SAN ONOFRE BEACH 🚶 ⛵ This nude beach is a rare find indeed. Frequented by few people, it is a pretty white-sand beach that winds along rocky headlands. There's not much here except beautiful views, shore plant life, and savvy sunbathers. Wander for miles past cliffs and coves. ~ Located off Route 101 about 30 miles north of Santa Barbara and two miles south of Gaviota. Driving north on Route 101 make a U-turn on Vista del Mar Road; drive south on Route 101 for seven-tenths of a mile to a dirt parking area. Cross the railroad tracks; a path next to the railroad light signal leads to the beach.

GAVIOTA STATE PARK 🚶 ⛵ 🎣 ⛲ ♿ 🚤 🅿️ This mammoth 2776-acre facility stretches along both sides of Route 101. The beach rests in a sandy cove guarded on either side by dramatic sedimentary rock formations. A railroad trestle traverses the beach and a fishing pier extends offshore. Facilities include picnic areas, restrooms, showers, and lifeguards. Day-use fee, $5. ~ The beach is located off Route 101 about 30 miles northwest of Santa Barbara; 805-968-1033.

▲ There are 40 tent/RV sites (no hookups); $14 per night. The vegetation is sparse from the forest fires a few years ago, and there is no drinking water, so bring your own. Sites are first-come, first-served.

JALAMA BEACH COUNTY PARK 🎣 ♿ 🅿️ This remote park sits at the far end of a 14-mile-long country road. Nevertheless, in summer there are likely to be many campers here. They come because the broad sandy beach is fringed by coastal bluffs and undulating hills. Jalama Creek cuts through the park, creating a wetland frequented by the endangered California brown pelican. Point Conception lies a few miles to the south, and the area all around is undeveloped and quite pretty (though Vandenberg Air Force Base is situated north of the beach). This is a good area for beachcombing as well as rock-hounding for chert, agate, travertine, and fossils. Facilities include picnic areas, restrooms, hot showers, a store, a snack bar, and a playground. Swimming is not recommended because of dangerous rip currents. There are no lifeguards stationed here. Surfing is good at Tarantula Point about one-half mile south of the park. You can surf-fish for perch or fish from the rocky points for cabezon and rock fish. Day-use fee, $6. ~ From Lompoc take Route 1 south for five miles; turn onto Jalama Beach Road and follow it 15 miles to the end; 805-736-3504, fax 805-735-8020.

▲ There are 110 tent/RV sites (28 with electrical hookups); $18 to $25 per night.

Santa Ynez Valley

The mountain road from Santa Barbara, Route 154, curves up into the Santa Ynez Mountains past forests of evergreen and oak. All along the roadside are rocky promontories with broad views back toward the city and out over the ocean. Along the way, you can visit the charming Danish town of Solvang. Oenophiles will enjoy exploring the burgeoning wineries in the Santa Ynez Valley.

SIGHTS

Turn off onto Stagecoach Road, head downhill a mile and rein in at **Cold Spring Tavern**, smack dab between Santa Barbara and Santa Ynez Valley. Back in the 1880s this squat wood structure served as a rest stop for stagecoaches coming through San Marcos Pass. Next door is a split-log cabin with stone fireplace. ~ 5995 Stagecoach Road, off Route 154, Santa Barbara; 805-967-0066, fax 805-964-5995; www.coldspringtavern.com.

The Santa Ynez Valley is horse country. Stud farms and working ranches dot the countryside and thoroughbreds graze in the meadows.

Beyond the mountain pass, amid striated hills and rolling ranch country, lies **Cachuma Lake**. Fed by creeks from Los Padres National Forest, this eight-mile-long lake is a jewel to the eye. Boating and fishing facilities lie nearby, and hiking trails lead into the nearby wilderness. Day-use fee, $6. ~ 805-686-5054; www.cachuma.com.

Thirty miles from Santa Barbara the mountains open onto the Santa Ynez Valley. Here a string of sleepy towns creates a Western-style counterpoint to California's chic coastline. **Santa Ynez** is a falsefront town. Downtown **Ballard** is one block long; the town was settled in 1880 and features the **Ballard School**, a little red schoolhouse that was constructed a few years later. ~ 2425 School Street, Ballard.

Nearby **Los Olivos** is complete with a white steeple church that dates back to 1897. It is also home to **Mattei's Tavern**. This former stagecoach inn, constructed in 1886, is a fine old wood-frame building with a trellised porch. ~ Route 154, Los Olivos; 805-688-4820.

The valley's other town, the most famous of all, does not resemble any of the others. It doesn't really resemble anything in California. **Solvang** is a town that looks like it was designed by Walt Disney. The place is a Danish village complete with cobblestone walks, gaslights, and stained-glass windows. Steep-pitched roofs with high dormers create an Old World atmosphere here. Stores and homes reveal the tall, narrow architecture of Scandinavia, and windmills dominate the view. What saves the place from being a theme park is that Solvang actually is a Danish town. Emigrants from Denmark established a village and school here in 1911.

Bethania Lutheran Church illustrates Danish provincial architecture. The model of a fully rigged ship hanging from the ceiling is traditional to Scandinavian churches. ~ At Atterdag Road and Laurel Avenue, Solvang.

To further confuse things, the centerpiece of Solvang in no way fits the architecture of the town. **Mission Santa Inés** does, however, meet the building style of the rest of California. Founded in 1804, the mission church follows the long, narrow rectangular shape traditional in Spanish California. The altar is painted brilliant colors and the colonnaded courtyard is ablaze with flowers. A small museum displays 18th-century bibles and song books, and one chapel contains a 17th-century statue of polychromed wood. ~ On Mission Drive, Solvang.

To escape the bustle of Solvang, take a ride out Alisal Road. After six miles this rustic road arrives at **Nojoqui Falls**. There's ◄ *HIDDEN* a picnic park here and a short hiking trail up to hillside cascades.

The Santa Inez Valley is a prime winegrowing region with several dozen wineries scattered around the valley. The **Buttonwood Winery** is a small winery that bottles sauvignon blanc, semillon, marsanne, merlot, cabernet sauvignon, and franc and syrah. This family business turns out well-regarded wine under the Kalyra label. ~ 1500 Alamo Pintado Road, Solvang; 805-688-3032.

For a long country ride, travel out Zaca Station and Foxen Canyon roads in Los Olivos. A string of wineries begins with the most elegant. **Firestone Vineyard** is set in stone-trimmed buildings and features a courtyard and picnic areas. The largest winery in the valley, it offers several estate-grown varietal wines. Tasting fee. ~ 5000 Zaca Station Road, Los Olivos; 805-688-3940; www.firestonewine.com, e-mail info@firestonewine.com.

Zaca Mesa Winery sits about nine miles from Route 101. Set in a modern woodframe building with an attractive tasting room, it's a beautiful winery with vineyards lining Foxen Canyon Road. Other wineries lie farther along the road and throughout the Santa Ynez Valley. ~ 6905 Foxen Canyon Road, Los Olivos; 805-

688-3310, 800-350-7972; www.zacamesa.com, e-mail zmail@ zacamesa.com.

LODGING Up in the Santa Ynez Valley, tucked between the Santa Ynez and San Rafael mountains, lies **Alisal Guest Ranch**. A 10,000-acre working cattle ranch, Alisal represents one of the original Spanish land grants. Part of the ranch is an exclusive resort featuring 73 units, two 18-hole golf courses, swimming pool, spa, tennis courts, and dining room. Guests ride horseback through the property and fish and sail on a mile-long lake. Square dances, hay rides, and summer barbecue dinners add to the entertainment. Breakfast and dinner are included. ~ 1054 Alisal Road, Solvang; 805-688-6411, 800-425-4725, fax 805-688-2510; www.alisal.com, e-mail sales@alisal.com. ULTRA-DELUXE.

> For visitors, wandering around Solvang means catching a ride on a horse-drawn Danish streetcar, then popping into a Danish bakery for hot pretzels or *aebleskiver*, a tasty Danish pastry.

Inexpensive lodging in the Santa Ynez Valley usually means finding a place in Solvang. This Danish town has numerous motels, many of which line Route 246. Be sure to reserve in advance; they fill up fast, particularly in summer and on weekends.

One I recommend is **Solvang Gardens Lodge**. Designed in old Danish style, one room is decorated in floral themes, and many have the warm, knotty-pine walls of a cozy mountain lodge. Several rooms feature kitchens, kitchenettes, and fireplaces. On the grounds are lovely English gardens, lily pond, waterfalls, and fountains to take in. ~ 293 Alisal Road, Solvang; 805-688-4404; www.solvangardens.com, e-mail info@solvangardens.com. BUDGET TO MODERATE.

DINING A vestige of the Old West, **Cold Spring Tavern** is a former stage-coach stop dating back to the 19th century. The floors tilt, the bar is wood plank, and the walls are stained with a century of use; a cow head with antlers decorates the stone fireplace. Dinner in this roughhewn time capsule features marinated rabbit, steak, pork back ribs, and fresh seafood. The evening special might be elk or buffalo, but that is a rare occasion. At lunch you can order a venison steak sandwich, *chile verde*, or a buffalo burger. Make a point of stopping by. Dinner reservations are recommended. Breakfast is served on weekends. ~ 5995 Stagecoach Road, off Route 154, Santa Barbara; 805-967-0066, fax 805-964-5995; www.cold springtavern.com. DELUXE TO ULTRA-DELUXE.

There's yet another stagecoach-stop-turned-restaurant in the Santa Ynez Valley. **Mattei's Tavern** is a mammoth old building that served as an inn back in the 1880s. Today you can dine in a rustically decorated room or out on the patio. Dinner features steaks, prime rib, pasta, and fresh seafood dishes. For a sense of history and a good meal, it's a safe bet. Reservations are recommended. Dinner only. ~ 2350 Railway Avenue, Los Olivos; 805-688-4820. DELUXE.

This Danish town is also famous for its bakeries. **Solvang Bakery** has excellent Danish pastries and other Scandinavian treats. ~ 460 Alisal Road, Solvang; 805-688-4939. BUDGET.

Barbecued artichokes are a tasty way to start your meal at the **Hitching Post II**, which is well-known for its steaks and barbecue. This popular eatery also serves ostrich—if you haven't tried it, what better place to start? Dinner only. ~ 406 East Route 246, Buellton; 805-688-0676, 805-686-1946. DELUXE TO ULTRA-DELUXE.

SHOPPING

The Danish town of Solvang is a choice spot to shop for imported products from Northern Europe. Walk the brick-paved streets and you'll encounter everything from cuckoo clocks to lace curtains. Many of the shops line **Copenhagen Drive**.

There are Danish handknit sweaters, music boxes, tiles, and pewter items. The toy stores are designed to resemble dollhouses and shops throughout town feature the tile roofs and high gables of Scandinavian stores.

With the feel of a small European village, it's no wonder that Solvang's shopping choices would include antiques. The **Solvang Antique Center** houses 65 different dealers in the Old Mill Shops building. Lovely old things abound every which way you turn. Peruse thousands of baubles, fine furniture, paintings, clocks, timepieces, and museum-quality heirloom pieces. ~ 486 1st Street, Solvang; 805-688-6222, fax 805-686-4044; www.solvang antiques.com, e-mail info@solvangantiques.com.

In the nearby town of **Los Olivos** several art galleries and antique shops will help round out your shopping spree.

NIGHTLIFE

Carousing at **Cold Spring Tavern**, a log cabin set high in the mountains outside Santa Barbara, is like being in an old Western movie. Every Friday night and Saturday and Sunday afternoons you can pull up a stool and listen to the rock, country-and-western, and rhythm-and-blues bands that ride through. ~ 5995 Stagecoach Road, off Route 154, Santa Barbara; 805-967-0066; www.coldspringtavern.com.

And don't forget the **Solvang Theaterfest**, one of the West's oldest repertory groups. Performing during summer months in an open-air theater, they present musicals and dramas. Box office is closed Monday and Tuesday. ~ 420 2nd Street, Solvang; 805-922-8313, fax 805-922-3074; www.pcpa.org, e-mail pcpa@pcpa.org.

AJ Spurs hosts live music every Friday and Saturday night. This is an elegant Western saloon with log walls, a stone fireplace, and frontier artifacts. ~ 350 East Route 246, Buellton; 805-686-1655; www.ajspurs.com.

PARKS **CACHUMA LAKE COUNTY PARK** 🚶 🚲 🛶 🚤 🎣 ⛵ Surrounded by the 4000-foot Santa Ynez Mountains and 6000-foot San Rafael Mountains, this is one of the prettiest lakes along the entire Central Coast. Oak forests and fields of tall grass border much of the shoreline. A great place for families and people exploring the backcountry above Santa Barbara. The many amenities include picnic areas, restrooms, a swimming pool, a snack bar, a store, a nature center (805-688-4515), a boat launch and rentals (805-688-4040), lake cruises (805-686-5050, 805-686-5055 on weekends), seasonal bike rentals, a par course, a game field, and hiking trails. Swimming is not permitted in lake, but there is a pool (open summer only). The lake has trout, perch, bass, bluegill, crappie, and catfish. Day-use fee, $6 per vehicle. ~ Located on Route 154 north of Santa Barbara; 805-688-4658; www.cachuma.com.

▲ There are 350 tent sites ($18 per night), 35 partial hookups ($25 per night), and 150 full hookups ($25 per night). Sites are first-come, first-served.

▼▼▼▼▼▼▼▼▼▼▼▼▼▼▼
San Luis Obispo Area
Craggy volcanic peaks and rolling hills dramatically punctuate this stretch of coastline lying about halfway between Los Angeles and San Francisco. The towns of San Luis Obispo, Morro Bay, and Pismo Beach are popular stopovers on the long scenic drive between northern and southern California. The county's growing wine industry also draws visitors to tasting rooms and winery tours. San Luis Obispo (don't say "San Louie"—pronounce the "s") is the region's commercial center, as well as the site of California Polytechnic State University (Cal Poly). Home of an old Spanish mission, pretty San Luis has enough small-city sophistication and cultural offerings to impress even big-city cosmopolites, while Pismo Beach and Morro Bay retain their earthier California beach town character.

SIGHTS **PISMO BEACH** An unattractive congeries of mobile homes and beach rental stands, Pismo Beach and its immediate neighbor Oceano are nondescript towns that have a single saving grace—the dunes of Oceano, several miles south of town. Wave after wave after wave of these ever-changing hills of sand parallel the beach, like a crystalline continuation of the ocean.

Otherwise, Pismo Beach, with its population of 8500 people, is a tacky tourist enclave known for an annual clam festival and for the migrating monarch butterflies that land just south of the town pier every year from late November to March. Traveling north, you reach Pismo Beach after Route 1 completes its lengthy inland course through Lompoc and Guadalupe, then rejoins Route 101 and returns to the coast.

Those vaunted sand piles comprise the most extensive coastal dunes in California. From Pismo Beach the sand hills run six miles south where they meet the 450-foot-high **Guadalupe dunes** (see "Beaches & Parks" section), forming a unique habitat for wildflowers and shorebirds.

Back in the 1930s and 1940s a group of bohemians, the "Dunites," occupied this wild terrain. Comprised of nudists, artists, and mystics, the movement believed that the dunes were a center of cosmic energy. Today the area is filled with beachcombers, sunbathers, and off-highway vehicles.

At the **Oceano Dunes State Vehicular Recreation Area** (see "Beaches & Parks" section below), you may drive your car onto the beach and operate off-highway and all-terrain vehicles in a specified area of the park.

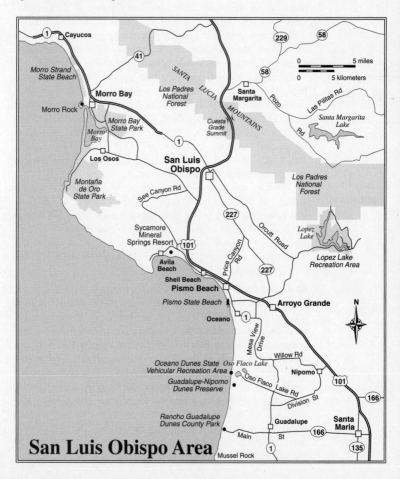

San Luis Obispo Area

Aside from exploring the dunes and studying the monarchs, Pismo Beach has a large jazz festival in February and October, as well as tidepools teeming with sea life just west of the pier. Stop by the **Pismo Beach Visitor Information Center** for brochures and maps of the San Luis Bay region. ~ 581 Dolliver Street, Pismo Beach; 805-773-4382, 800-443-7778, fax 805-773-6772; www.classiccalifornia.com.

An ironic twist of fate that has led to the decline of adjacent **Avila Beach** may turn out to be the town's salvation. In 1989, it was discovered that an oil pipeline leak was contaminating the ground underneath the tiny beachside enclave. As a result, property values plunged, and the town took on an increasingly run-down look. Recently, it was decided that the town's commercial core—a two-block stretch overlooking a white-sand beach and three fishing piers—would be torn down to remove tons of contaminated soil below. Much of the cleanup was completed in 2001; a new pier and a grassy community park are the result. Rebuilding the business district continues, with refurbished shops and restaurants slowly bringing the town back to life.

There are hot springs in the hills around Avila Beach. **Sycamore Mineral Springs Resort** has tapped these local waters and created a lovely spa with hotel units, a gift shop, and a swimming pool. The real attractions here, however, are the redwood hot tubs. Very private, they are dotted about on a hillside and shaded by oak and sycamore. Admission. ~ 1215 Avila Beach Drive, Avila Beach; 805-595-7302, 800-234-5831, fax 805-595-4007; www.sycamoresprings.com, e-mail info@smsr.com.

HIDDEN ►

From Pismo Beach, you can buzz into San Luis Obispo on Route 101 or take a quiet country drive into town via **See Canyon Road**. The latter begins in Avila Beach and corkscrews up into the hills past apple orchards and horse farms. Along its 13-mile length, half unpaved, you'll encounter mountain meadows and ridgetop vistas. During the fall harvest season you can pick apples at farms along the way.

SAN LUIS OBISPO San Luis Obispo, a pretty jewel of a town, lies 12 miles from the ocean in the center of an expansive agricultural region. Backdropped by the Santa Lucia Mountains, the town focuses around an old Spanish mission. Cowboys from outlying ranches and students from the campuses of Cal Poly and Cuesta College add to the cultural mix, creating a vital atmosphere that has energized San Luis Obispo's rapid growth.

Parking on weekends and during the summer can be a nightmare, but don't let that deter you. The town is completely walkable, so once you've found a spot in one of the numerous small public lots, two parking garages, or on the street (bring quarters), leave the car there and set out on foot. Your first stop should be the **San Luis Obispo Chamber of Commerce**. Here you can pick up brochures about the area's attractions, including a map for a self-guided walking tour. ~ 1039 Chorro Street, San Luis Obispo; 805-781-2777, fax 805-786-2769; www.visitslo.com, e-mail slo chamber@slochamber.org.

A self-guided tour of this historic town logically begins at **Mission San Luis Obispo de Tolosa**. Dating to 1772, the old Spanish outpost has been nicely reconstructed, though the complex is not as extensive as La Purísima Mission in Lompoc. There's a museum re-creating the American Indian, Spanish, and Mexican eras as well as a pretty church and a gift shop. Mission Plaza, fronting the chapel, is a well-landscaped park. ~ Chorro and Monterey streets, San Luis Obispo; 805-543-6850, fax 805-781-8214; www.missionsanluisobispo.org.

The **San Luis Obispo Art Center** exhibits works by the area's artists. Closed Monday from Labor Day to Memorial Day. ~ 1010 Broad Street at Monterey Street, San Luis Obispo; 805-543-8562.

St. Stephen's Episcopal Church is a narrow, lofty, and strikingly attractive chapel. Built in 1867, it was one of California's first Episcopal churches. ~ Nipomo and Pismo streets, San Luis Obispo.

The **Dallidet Adobe**, constructed by a French vintner in 1853, is another local architectural landmark. ~ On Toro Street between Pismo and Pacific streets, San Luis Obispo. A block away and about a century later Frank Lloyd Wright designed the **Kun-**

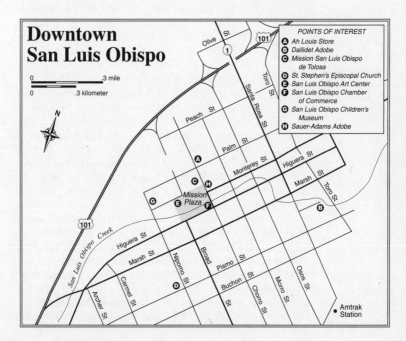

Downtown San Luis Obispo

0 _____ .3 mile
0 _____ .3 kilometer

N

POINTS OF INTEREST
Ⓐ Ah Louis Store
Ⓑ Dallidet Adobe
Ⓒ Mission San Luis Obispo de Tolosa
Ⓓ St. Stephen's Episcopal Church
Ⓔ San Luis Obispo Art Center
Ⓕ San Luis Obispo Chamber of Commerce
Ⓖ San Luis Obispo Children's Museum
Ⓗ Sauer-Adams Adobe

Olive St
Toro St
Santa Rosa St
Peach St
Palm St
Monterey St
Higuera St
Marsh St
Mission Plaza
Higuera St
Marsh St
Nipomo St
Broad St
Pismo St
Buchon St
Carmel St
Archer St
Chorro St
Morro St
Osos St
San Luis Obispo Creek
Amtrak Station

dert **Medical Building**. ~ Pacific and Santa Rosa streets, San Luis Obispo.

The **Ah Louis Store** symbolizes the Chinese presence here. A sturdy brick building with wrought-iron shutters and balcony, it dates to 1874 and once served the 2000 Chinese coolies who worked on nearby railroad tunnels. ~ 800 Palm Street, San Luis Obispo.

Around the corner, the **Sauer-Adams Adobe**, covered in clapboard, is an 1860s-era house with a second-story balcony. By the turn of the century, Victorian-style homes had become the vogue. Many of San Luis Obispo's finest Victorians are located in the blocks adjacent to where Broad Street intersects with Pismo and Buchon streets. ~ 964 Chorro Street, San Luis Obispo.

Those with young ones in tow can stop by the **San Luis Obispo Children's Museum**. In this imaginative environment kids can race to a fire engine, vote in a voting booth, learn the principles of photography, and discover a Chumash Indian cave. Closed Monday. Admission. ~ 1010 Nipomo Street, San Luis Obispo; 805-544-5437; www.slokids.org, e-mail slokids@slonet.org.

MORRO BAY   As Route 1 angles north and west from San Luis Obispo toward the ocean, separating again from Route 101, you will encounter a procession of nine volcanic peaks. Last in this geologic parade is a 576-foot plug dome called **Morro Rock**. The pride of Morro Bay, it stands like a little Gibraltar, connected to the mainland by a sand isthmus. You can drive out and inspect the brute. Years ago, before conservationists and common sense prevailed, the site was a rock quarry. Today it's a nesting area for peregrine falcons.

Young children might enjoy playing on the whale's tail or just watching the boats in the Morro Bay marina at Tidelands Children's Park, at the south end of Embarcadero.

Morro Bay is one of those places with obscure natural treasures that are often overlooked at first glance. That's because Morro Bay is largely a working fishing town, not a pretty recreational harbor with a gleaming fleet of expensive, handsome vessels, like Newport Harbor in Orange County. Morro Bay comes with a gritty legacy, first as a busy 19th-century port for the region's cattle and dairy industry, then as a naval training base during World War II. In the 1950s, a power plant was built on the site, providing a tax base that led to the town's incorporation. The real working waterfront of Morro Bay lies to the north of Harbor Street, in the shadow of the three giant smokestacks of the power plant. A walk along the touristy waterfront stretch called the Embarcadero, which is south of Harbor Street, reveals a predictable mix of tacky tourist shops and so-called galleries, along with plenty of restaurants offering fish and chips and "harbor views." The **Morro Bay Chamber of Commerce** offers plenty of brochures and information about the area. Closed Sunday. ~ 880 Main Street, Morro Bay; 805-772-4467, 800-231-0592, fax 805-772-6038; www.morrobay.org.

But the real pleasures of Morro Bay lie hidden behind its ugly manmade features.

The best place to learn something of the local natural environment is at the small **Morro Bay State Park Museum of Natural History**. It's located at White Point, a rocky outcropping (Indian mortar holes are still visible) in Morro Bay State Park, with fine views of the surrounding estuary, which is a protected habitat for 250 migratory and resident bird species and one of the largest salt marshes in California. From this height there are also views of the sandspit, Morro Bay, and Morro Rock. "Rocky," the museum's mascot, helps out with the museum's educational displays of local history and wildlife. Lots of hands-on interactive exhibits make it enjoyable for restless children. And a docent is always on hand to answer questions. Admission. ~ Morro Bay State Park Road (from Morro Bay, follow Main Street into the state park), Morro Bay; 805-772-2694, fax 805-772-7129; www.mbspmuseum.org.

The Morro Bay Estuary is one of the largest unspoiled coastal marshes in California. This unique environment, where salty sea meets fresh water, is a stopover for hundreds of migratory birds, including blue heron, who nest and rear their young at the **Morro Bay Heron Rookery**. When this eucalyptus grove was threatened some years ago with development, the people of California purchased it to retain it as a permanent nesting site. It is now the only remaining large rookery of great blue heron on the California coast between San Francisco and Mexico. Nesting begins in January, when the birds choose mates and build nests. Eggs are laid in February and hatch in late March. The nestlings are fed by both parents until they're able to fly away a few months later, sometime in late June or early July. ~ Morro Bay State Park Road, just south of Park View Drive, Morro Bay.

◄ HIDDEN

The Los Osos/Morro Bay chapter of the Small Wilderness Area Preservation offers monthly walks through **El Morro Elfin Forest**, an ecological preserve of pygmy oaks and other unusual flora. ~ Santa Ysabel Avenue at 15th Street, Los Osos; 805-528-4540.

◄ HIDDEN

At the mouth of Morro Bay, Morro Rock competes for attention, sadly, with the three concrete smokestacks of the power plant across the harbor, something that seems even to embarrass the locals. But turn your back on the travesty as they do, and gaze across the bay instead to the **sandspit** that holds back the Pacific and extends in a narrow sliver for four miles and teems with bird and other wildlife.

For a bit of underwater exploration, take a dive, so to speak, in a semi-submersible vessel with **Sub-Sea Tours** for a look at Morro Bay's giant kelp forest and the marine life that inhabits it.

◄ HIDDEN

Otters are occasionally spotted on the tours. ~ Marina Square, 699 Embarcadero; 805-772-9463; www.subseatours.com. For something more formal, **Tigers Folly Too** sponsors harbor cruises in an old-fashioned paddlewheeler. Closed Monday to Friday in the winter. ~ 1205 Embarcadero, at the Harbor Hut Restaurant, Morro Bay; 805-772-2257.

LODGING   Lodging in the Pismo Beach–Shell Beach area generally means finding a motel. None of these seaside towns has expanded more than a few blocks from the waterfront, so wherever you book a room will be walking distance from the beach.

Adam's Pirate Cove Inn is a 20-unit hostelry (14 with kitchenettes). The furniture and decoration is standard motel, though a volleyball court and horseshoe pit distinguishes this place from its peers. ~ 1000 Dolliver Street, Pismo Beach; 805-773-2065, fax 805-773-0425. MODERATE.

If it's panoramic Pacific Coast views you are after, try the **Best Western Shore Cliff Lodge**. Perched on the cliffs just off Route 101, the hotel offers spacious, although conventional, rooms with private balconies, microwaves, and refrigerators. There is a restaurant, lounge, pool, spa, sauna, and tennis courts. Guest rooms aren't cheap, but what a view! ~ 2555 Price Street, Pismo Beach; 805-773-4671, 800-441-8885, fax 805-773-2341; www.shore cliff.com. MODERATE TO ULTRA-DELUXE.

The small, seven-room **Beachcomber Inn** is neat and clean and just a block from the beach. Quaintly furnished with wicker furniture and floral prints, rooms also come equipped with microwaves and coffee makers. None of the rooms, however, have a full-on ocean view. Two-night minimum on the weekend. ~ 541 Cypress Street, Pismo Beach; 805-773-5505, fax 805-773-0880; www.pismobeach.com/beachcomberinn, e-mail bcomberinn@ aol.com. DELUXE TO ULTRA-DELUXE.

San Luis Obispo also offers several distinctive accommodations, including the **Petit Soleil**, a classic motel that's been transformed into a B&B with a French flavor. Here the 15 non-smoking rooms are simple but comfortable with queen-size beds. The view is of the surrounding hills, and a night's stay includes a trip to the inn's bounteous breakfast buffet, and afternoon hors d'oeuvres and wine. ~ 1473 Monterey Street, San Luis Obispo; 805-549-0321, 800-676-1588, fax 805-549-0383; www.petitsoleil slo.com, e-mail john&diane@petitsoleilslo.com. MODERATE TO ULTRA-DELUXE.

Sycamore Mineral Springs Resort reposes on a hillside one mile inland from Avila Beach. Situated in a stand of oak and sycamore trees are 74 rooms and suites. Each has a private patio spa; there are also redwood hot tubs scattered about in the surrounding forest and a swimming pool. The rooms are decorated in contemporary style. An on-site yoga institute and restaurant round out the amenities. ~ 1215 Avila Beach Drive, San Luis Obispo; 805-595-7302, 800-234-5831; www.sycamoresprings. com, e-mail info@smsr.com. DELUXE TO ULTRA-DELUXE.

Heritage Inn Bed & Breakfast is a San Luis Obispo anomaly. There aren't many country inns in town and this one is not even representative of the species. It sits in a neighborhood surrounded by motels and a nearby freeway, though it is in walking distance of historic downtown. What's more, the house was moved— lock, stock, and bay windows—to this odd location. Once inside, you'll be quite pleased. There's a warm, comfortable sitting parlor and seven guest rooms, all furnished with antiques, reflecting the house's 1902 birthdate; some accommodations include window seats and terraces that look out to a lovely creekside garden.

> For your pick of typical motels in San Luis Obispo, head for the stretch of Monterey Street north of California Boulevard known as Motel Row.

Three rooms have private baths; the other four share two baths, and four rooms have fireplaces. There's a cat in residence—allergics beware. Full breakfast is included. ~ 978 Olive Street, San Luis Obispo; 805-544-7440, fax 805-544-2819; www.heritage innslo.com. MODERATE TO DELUXE.

The **Garden Street Inn**, located in the beautiful downtown district, is a beautifully restored 1887 Victorian that has 13 rooms and suites. Each is individually decorated in such themes as "Walden," "Amadeus," and "Emerald Isle." Some accommodations honor local history; others are filled with family mementoes. A full breakfast is served in the bay-windowed morning room and the innkeeper's reception in the afternoon features hors d'oeuvres and local wines. ~ 1212 Garden Street, San Luis Obispo; 805-545-9802, 800-488-2045, fax 805-545-9403; www.garden streetinn.com, e-mail innkeeper@gardenstreetinn.com. DELUXE TO ULTRA-DELUXE.

The **Apple Farm Inn** represents another example of a classic country inn set in a neighborhood of drive-in motels. The carefully landscaped property, including a stream that runs by the old Victorian-style buildings, takes you away from the hubbub of Monterey Street and into Old America complete with apple pies fresh from the Inn's bakery and a working, water-powered mill. ~ 2015 Monterey Street, San Luis Obispo; 805-544-2040, 800-374-3705, fax 805-544-2452; www.applefarm.com, e-mail info@ applefarm.com. ULTRA-DELUXE. The adjoining **Trellis Court** has all the advantages of the Apple Farm Inn but its 34 smaller rooms are more affordably priced. While no two rooms are the same in either accommodation, they all have working gas fireplaces. MODERATE.

The most outlandish place in town is a roadside confection called the **Madonna Inn**. Architecturally it's a cross between a castle and a gingerbread house, culturally it's somewhere between light opera and heavy metal. The lampposts are painted pink, and the gift shop contains the biggest, gaudiest chandeliers you've ever seen. Personally, I wouldn't be caught dead staying in the place, but I would never miss an opportunity to visit. If you prove more daring than I, there are 109 rooms on the 2000-acre ranch, each decorated in a different flamboyant style ranging from an African Safari to something out of the Flintstones. Rooms offer a wide variety of amenities including waterfall showers and seven-foot bathtubs. There is a café, a formal dining room with live music, and a fabulous bakery. ~ 100 Madonna Road, San Luis Obispo; 805-543-3000, 800-543-9666, fax 805-543-1800; www.madonna inn.com. DELUXE TO ULTRA-DELUXE.

There are countless motels to choose from in Morro Bay, ranging across the entire spectrum in price and amenities. For information on availability contact the **Morro Bay Chamber of Commerce**. Closed Sunday. ~ 880 Main Street, Morro Bay; 805-772-4467, 800-231-0592, fax 805-772-6038; www.morrobay.org.

Located next to Tidelands Park at the quieter southern portion of Embarcadero is the 32-room **Embarcadero Inn**. All rooms, which are spacious, very clean, and comfortable, face the bay; several come with gas fireplaces and balconies. Other amenities include VCRs, refrigerators, and coffee makers, as well as a continental breakfast each morning. One room is disabled-friendly. ~ 456 Embarcadero, Morro Bay; 805-772-2700, 800-292-7625, fax 805-772-1060; www.embarcaderoinn.com. MODERATE TO ULTRA-DELUXE.

HIDDEN ▶   A flower-filled garden surrounds the **Marina Street Bed and Breakfast**, a yellow New England–style home with bay windows located two blocks from the bay and Morro Rock. Operated by Vern and Claudia Foster, retired teachers from Colorado, the inn has four separately themed rooms: the Bordeaux Room, with a tiger oak sleigh bed and bay view; the green-and-apricot-hued Garden Room, with a willow four-poster canopy bed and bay view; the nautically themed Dockside Room; and the romantic Battenberg Room, with delicate touches of lace throughout. The morning's full gourmet breakfast is served in the dining room and might include an apple-pecan panache or a spicy sausage casserole. ~ 305 Marina Street, Morro Bay; 805-772-4016, 888-683-9389, fax 805-772-0667; www.marinastreetinn.com, e-mail vfoster1 05@aol.com. DELUXE.

Fashionable but casual, **The Inn at Morro Bay** is a waterfront complex with the amenities of a small resort: a restaurant, a lounge, a swimming pool, and an adjacent golf course. It sits on ten acres overlooking Morro Bay and contains 98 guest rooms. Many rooms have feather beds, fireplaces, hot tubs, shuttered windows, and oak armoires. ~ 60 State Park Road, Morro Bay; 805-772-5651,

800-321-9566, fax 805-772-4779; www.innatmorrobay.com, e-mail resv@innatmorrobay.com. DELUXE TO ULTRA-DELUXE.

Fish-and-chip joints are everywhere on the Central Coast, but **DINING** Pismo Fish & Chips is special—mainly because it's good, but also because it's a local institution. The fish is fresh, the portions gen- **◄ HIDDEN** erous, and the service friendly. Closed Monday. ~ 505 Cypress Street, Pismo Beach; 805-773-2853. BUDGET TO DELUXE.

If you missed the swinging doors in the saloon you'll get the idea from the moose head trophies and branding irons. "Taste the Great American West" is the motto for **F. McLintocks Saloon & Dining House**. Every evening, when the oak pit barbecue really gets going, there are a dozen kinds of steak, ribs, and seafood. If popularity means anything, this place is tops. It's always mobbed. So dust off the Stetson and prepare to chow down. Dinner only. ~ 750 Mattie Road, Shell Beach; 805-773-1892, 800-866-6372, fax 805-773-5183; www.mclintocks.com, e-mail fmc@mclin tocks.com. DELUXE TO ULTRA-DELUXE.

Sick of seafood by now? Tired of saloons serving cowboy-sized steaks? Happily, San Luis Obispo has several ethnic restaurants. Two are located in The Creamery, a turn-of-the-20th-century dairy plant that has been transformed into a shopping mall. **Tsurugi Japanese Restaurant** features a sushi bar and dining area deco-rated with oriental screens and wallhangings. At lunch and din-ner there are shrimp tempura, chicken teriyaki, *nigiri*, and other Asian specialties. The atmosphere is placid and the food quite good. No lunch on Sunday. ~ 570 Higuera Street, San Luis Obispo; phone/fax 805-543-8942. MODERATE.

At **Tortilla Flats** they've fashioned an attractive restaurant from the brick walls, bare ducts, and exposed rafters of the old creamery. It's lunch, dinner, and Sunday brunch at this Mexican eatery that is particularly popular with the college crowd. The bar serves pitchers of margaritas. ~ 1051 Nipomo Street, San Luis Obispo; 805-544-7575; www.tortillaflats.com, e-mail goodfood@ tortillaflats.com. BUDGET TO MODERATE.

FARMERS' FEAST

If you're in San Luis Obispo on a Thursday evening, be sure to stop by the **Farmers Market**. Farmers from the surrounding area turn out to sell fresh fruits and vegetables. They barbecue ribs, cook sweet corn and fresh fish, then serve them on paper plates to the throngs that turn out weekly. Puppeteers and street dancers perform as the celebration as-sumes a carnival atmosphere. ~ At Higuera Street between Osos and Nipomo streets, San Luis Obispo.

Italy enters the picture with **Cafe Roma,** a delightful restaurant decorated in country Tuscan style. Copper pots as well as portraits from the old country decorate the walls. Lunch and dinner include Italian sausage, veal marsala, steak *fiorentina*, and several daily specials. Run by an Italian family, it serves excellent food; highly recommended. No lunch on weekends. Closed Sunday. ~ 1020 Railroad Avenue, San Luis Obispo; 805-541-6800, fax 805-786-2522; www.caferomaslo.com, e-mail marco@caferomaslo.com. MODERATE TO DELUXE.

HIDDEN ►

For a low-priced meal in a white-tablecloth restaurant with views of the surrounding hills, beat a path to the California Polytechnic campus. **Vista Grande Restaurant** serves Cal Poly students as well as the public in a comfortable plate-glass dining room. Open for lunch and Sunday brunch, it features salad, pasta, fish, and vegetarian dishes. No lunch on Saturday, and dinner only during performances at the arts center across the street. Hours vary in summer, so call ahead. ~ On the Cal Poly campus, off Grand Avenue, San Luis Obispo; 805-756-1204, fax 805-756-6457. MODERATE.

The **Corner View Restaurant & Bar** is a friendly neighborhood bar with better-than-average fare—entrées range from warm spinach salad, to stroganoff to fish and chips. No breakfast on weekdays. ~ 1141 Chorro Street, San Luis Obispo; 805-546-8444. MODERATE.

You needn't cast far in Morro Bay to find a seafood restaurant. Sometimes they seem as ubiquitous as fishing boats. One of the most venerable is **Dorn's Original Breakers Café.** It's a bright, airy place with a postcard view of the waterfront from indoor and patio tables. While they serve all three meals, in the evening you better want seafood because there are about two dozen fish dishes and only a couple of steak, chicken, pasta, and veal platters. For breakfast try their out-of-this-world blueberry pancakes with a healthy dollop of whipped cream. ~ 801 Market Street, Morro Bay; 805-772-4415, fax 805-772-4695. MODERATE TO DELUXE.

DOWN WHERE THE LIGHTS ARE BRIGHT

San Luis Obispo's quaint downtown is home to a lively bar scene where college students and cowboys mix it up. From intimate coffeehouses and restaurants with live music to bars featuring 25-cent beers, you're likely to find something entertaining—walk around Monterey, Higuera, and Marsh streets and the paths that connect them, until you find what you want. Or just head over to the 700 block of Higuera Street, where a triangle of bars offers something for everyone.

The **Galley Restaurant** is a bit of a surprise, as much for the unexpectedly well-prepared food—fresh fish, of course, is featured extensively on the menu—as for the friendly, but unobtrusive, and well-trained staff and the quiet classical or jazz background music. It sits on a dock over the water. Reservations are recommended. ~ 899 Embarcadero, Morro Bay; 805-772-2806. DELUXE TO ULTRA-DELUXE.

The picturesque setting—a grove of eucalyptus trees beside a small marina in Morro Bay State Park—is enough to recommend the small, rustic **Bayside Café**, where you can sit outside on the heated deck and take in the scenery. Locals come here for fresh fish, of course, and California/Mexican-inspired dishes like lime and garlic chicken, chicken pasta Vera Cruz, and chile verde. Desserts, like *tres leches* cake, are all homemade. No credit cards. No dinner Monday through Wednesday. ~ Morro Bay State Park Road (from Morro Bay, follow Main Street into the park), Morro Bay; 805-772-1465. MODERATE.

◄ HIDDEN

Fine California cuisine is the order of the day at **The Inn at Morro Bay**. Situated in a waterfront resort, the dining room looks out over Morro Bay. In addition to great views and commodious surroundings, it features an enticing list of local items with Pacific flavors. All three meals are served, but the highlight is dinner. The menu might include home-smoked salmon in bouillabaisse, filet mignon, or an assortment of fresh pastas. There's a Sunday champagne brunch. ~ 60 State Park Road, Morro Bay; 805-772-5651, 800-321-9566, fax 805-772-4779; www.innatmorrobay.com. MODERATE TO DELUXE.

SHOPPING

In the old Spanish town of San Luis Obispo, the best stores are located along the blocks surrounding Mission Plaza. Stroll the two blocks along Monterey Street between Osos and Chorro streets, then browse the five-block stretch on Higuera Street from Osos Street to Nipomo Street. These two arteries and the side streets between form the heart of downtown.

The Creamery is an old dairy plant converted into an ingenious shopping center with several small artists' galleries, restaurants, and shops. ~ 570 Higuera Street, San Luis Obispo.

In Morro Bay, the waterfront Embarcadero offers the ubiquitous souvenir/T-shirt emporiums that predominate in such touristy enclaves.

Up the hill, along Morro Bay Boulevard and Main Street, there are several antique and vintage stores that for collectors might offer an enjoyable afternoon of browsing. The Chamber of Commerce puts out a brochure and map pinpointing these shops.

NIGHTLIFE

The **Frog and Peach Pub** is your standard sports bar. More than 70 beers and a TV in every corner make it the perfect place to watch the game. The interior is dark and calm, while the back patio gets a bit more rowdy. When they host live rock or blues music (which is most nights), there is usually a cover. ~ 728 Higuera Street, San Luis Obispo; 805-595-3764.

Across the street at **Mother's Tavern** the mood is a little more mellow. With live rock, blues, or disco every night, this bar serves an upscale, older clientele out for a good time. There's often a line at the door and the generous dancefloor fills quickly, but it is usually possible to grab an intimate table upstairs. Occasional cover. ~ 725 Higuera Street, San Luis Obispo; 805-541-8733.

The mood is definitely not mellow at **The Library Lounge** next door. Despite its name's quiet, studious connotations, this is the seen-and-be-seen scene for local college students. In fact, every Cal Poly mother should be a little suspicious when her student starts spending inordinate amounts of time at "the library." The deejay music is loud, the dancefloor is packed, and nightly drink specials keep the crowd going. Occasional cover. ~ 723 Higuera Street, San Luis Obispo; 805-542-0199.

There's live entertainment every night in the conservatory at **The Inn at Morro Bay**. Appointed with bentwood furniture and pastel paneling, it's a beautiful bar. The most striking feature of all is the view, which extends out across the water to Morro Rock; an ideal location for watching the sunset. ~ 60 State Park Road, Morro Bay; 805-772-5651; www.innatmorrobay.com.

The **Performing Arts Center of San Luis Obispo County** is located on the Cal Poly campus. Seating 1298, it gives the region a year-round professional performance venue. ~ 805-756-2787 or 888-233-2787 for schedule and tickets; wwwpacslo.org.

GAY SCENE There's no particular neighborhood in San Luis that's become the preferred turf for gay men and lesbians or that has a concentration of gay-oriented business. In fact, although there are a fair number of gays and lesbians living in the SLO area, their profile is generally conservative, quiet, and "pretty closeted," as one gay business owner put it.

But the area is not without committed resources: the **Gay and Lesbian Alliance of the Central Coast** (GALA) operates a community center and provides a meeting place for various groups. ~ 11573 Los Osos Valley Road, San Luis Obispo; 805-541-4252; www.ccgala.org.

HIDDEN ► The gay-friendly atmosphere at **Linnaea's Café**, a "hipster hangout" downtown, attracts the city's young gays and lesbians, as well as artists and other creative types. It's usually open until midnight, late for this neck of the woods. ~ 1110 Garden Street, San Luis Obispo; 805-541-5888; www.linnaeas.com.

The **Big Sky Café** is another popular and gay-friendly spot and can be recommended for its American-style cooking. ~ 1121 Broad Street, San Luis Obispo; 805-545-5401; www.bigskycafe.com.

RANCHO GUADALUPE DUNES COUNTY PARK 🚶‍♂️🚴🏊‍♂️⛵
The Sahara Desert has nothing on this place. The sand dunes
throughout the area are spectacular; they provide a habitat for
California brown pelicans, Western least terns, and other endangered birds and plants. The Santa Maria River, which empties
here, forms a pretty wetland area. Fishing is very popular here.
Primitive restrooms are on site. Be sure to visit
the **Dunes Center** (closed Monday) for exhibits
on mammals, dune formation, birds, reptiles, orientation videos and maps, and visitor information.
~ From Route 1 in Guadalupe, follow Main Street
(Route 166) west for three miles to the beach. Wind-
blown sand sometimes closes the road, so call beforehand; 805-343-2455 (Dunes Center), fax 805-343-0442;
www.dunescenter.org, e-mail info@dunescenter.org.

**BEACHES
& PARKS**

The 450-foot Mussel
Rock in Rancho
Guadalupe Dunes
County Park is the
highest dune on the
West Coast.

OCEANO DUNES STATE VEHICULAR RECREATION AREA This
is the only spot in California where standard and four-wheel-drive
vehicles may still be driven right on the beach. A 1500-acre section of dunes is open year-round to four-wheelers and all-terrain
vehicles. OHVs can be driven only in designated areas and must
be registered and display flags. Day-use fee, $4 per vehicle. ~ Off
Route 1, south of downtown Pismo Beach. Enter on Pier Avenue
or Grand Avenue; 805-473-7223 (recorded) or 805-473-7220;
www.ohv.parks.ca.gov.

▲ There are primitive campsites, with only chemical toilets;
$6 per vehicle. Reservations are recommended: 800-444-7275.
To access the campsite, you must drive across two miles of sand
and cross a creek, which can be treacherous during high tide.

PISMO STATE BEACH 🚶‍♂️🐟🏊‍♂️🚣⛵ This spectacular
beach runs for six miles from Pismo Beach south to the Santa
Maria River. Along its oceanfront are some of the finest sand dunes
in California, fluffy hills inhabited by shorebirds and tenacious
plants. A freshwater lagoon abuts the campgrounds. Also home
to the pismo clam, it's a wonderful place to hike and explore. Surfing is popular here, but exercise caution in the water—rip tides
occur here occasionally. Lifeguards on duty in the summer. There
are picnic areas here, and restrooms with hot showers at both
campgrounds. Fishing for cod and red snapper is good from the
Pismo Pier (at the end of Hinds Avenue, Pismo Beach). You can
also dig for pismo clams along the beach (check for local restrictions). ~ The park parallels Route 1 in Pismo Beach; 805-489-
1869, fax 805-489-6004.

▲ There are tent/RV sites (limited hookups); $13 to $25 per
night. Call 800-444-7275 for reservations. There is also camping
at **Oceano Memorial County Park** (near Mendel Drive and Pier
Avenue, Oceano; 805-781-5930) at 24 tent/RV sites (full hookups); $29 per night. Sites are first-come, first-served.

HIDDEN ▶ **PIRATE'S COVE OR MALLAGH LANDING** 🏊 This crescent-shaped nude beach is a beauty. Protected by 100-foot cliffs, it curves for a half mile along a placid cove. At one end is a rocky headland pockmarked by caves. Restaurants and groceries are in Avila Beach. Swimming and skindiving are very good because the beach is in a sheltered area. ~ Located ten miles south of San Luis Obispo in Avila Beach. From Route 101 take Avila Beach Drive west for two miles, turn left on Cave Landing Road (the road travels immediately uphill), and go six-tenths of a mile to a dirt parking lot; crude stairs lead down to the beach.

MONTAÑA DE ORO STATE PARK 🚶🚴🐎🏊🎣🛶 This 13,000-acre facility is one of the finest parks along the entire Central Coast. It stretches more than seven miles along the shore, past a sandspit, tidepools, and sharp cliffs. There are remote coves for viewing seals, sea otters, and migrating whales and for sunbathing on hidden beaches. Monarch butterflies roost in the eucalyptus-filled canyons and a hiking trail leads to Valencia Peak, with views scanning almost 100 miles of coastline. Wildlife is abundant along 50 miles of hiking trails. Chaparral, Bishop pine, and coast live oak cover the hills; in spring wildflowers riot, giving the park its name, "Mountain of Gold." You can go fishing, but swimming is not recommended because of the lack of lifeguards, occasional rip tides, and chilly water. Surfing is good around Hazard Canyon. There are picnic areas and primitive restrooms. ~ Located on Pecho Valley Road about ten miles south of Morro Bay; 805-528-0513, fax 805-528-6857.

▲ There are 50 tent/RV sites (no hookups); $15 per night. Reservations strongly recommended for this busy campground from mid-May through Labor Day: 800-444-7275.

MORRO BAY STATE PARK 🚶🚴🎣🛶🛶 Located amid one of the biggest marshlands along the California coast, this 2435-acre domain is like an outdoor museum. The tidal basin attracts over 250 species of sea, land, and shore birds. Great blue herons roost in the eucalyptus trees. There's a marina where you can rent canoes or kayaks to explore the salt marsh and nearby sandspit, and a natural-history museum with environmental displays. The campground is closed for renovations and is slated to reopen in 2005. Day-use fee, $3. ~ On State Park Road in Morro Bay; 805-772-7434, fax 805-772-5760.

MORRO STRAND STATE BEACH 🏊🎣🛶🛶 Another of the Central Coast's long, skinny parks, this sandy beach stretches almost two miles along Morro Bay. Private homes border one side, but in the other direction there are great views of Morro Rock. It's a good place for beachcombing, fishing, and surfing. This beach is subject to rip currents and there are no lifeguards on duty. There are restrooms and cold showers. ~ Located parallel to Route 1 north of Morro Bay; park entrance is along Yerba Buena Street; 805-772-2560, fax 805-772-5760.

▲ There are 85 tent/RV sites; $20 per night. Reservations recommended Memorial Day through Labor Day: 800-444-7275.

LOS PADRES NATIONAL FOREST 🚶 🚴 🐎 🛶 The southern section of this mammoth forest parallels the coast from Ventura to Carmel. Rising from sea level to almost 9000 feet, it contains the Sierra Madre, San Rafael, Santa Ynez, Santa Lucia, and La Panza mountains. Characterized by sharp slopes and a dry climate, most of the region is covered with chaparral and oak. But there are coast redwoods, piñon pines, and an amazing diversity of other plant life. Animals you might see include golden eagles, quail, owls, woodpeckers, wild pig, mule deer, and black bear. The northern and southern sectors of the national forest contain over 1500 miles of hiking trails, almost 500 miles of streams, and a cross-country ski trail on Mt. Pinos. For information and permits contact forest headquarters at 6755 Hollister Avenue, Suite 150, Goleta, CA 93117. Day-use permit is $5; call ahead for purchase instructions. ~ Route 33 cuts through the heart of Los Padres. Route 101 provides numerous access points; 805-968-6640, fax 805-961-5729.

The endangered California condor, which with its nine-foot wingspan is the largest land bird in North America, has recently been reintroduced to Los Padres National Forest.

▲ There are 83 tent/RV sites (no hookups) and 250 trail camps; prices vary from free to $18 per night.

Cambria and San Simeon Area

Cambria itself is a seaside town that was originally settled in the 1860s and later expanded into a major seaport and whaling center. As the railroad replaced coastal shipping, Cambria declined, only to be resurrected during the past few decades as an artist colony and tourist center.

SIGHTS

If your approach to Cambria is along Route 1 from the south, you'll first pass the privately owned village of **Harmony**, which was a dairy cooperative in the early part of the century. Since the 1970s, however, it's been an artisans' colony of sorts, with the old dairy buildings converted to gift shops and glassmaking and pottery studios. In recent years, Harmony has been purchased by a new owner and the restaurant has been mostly closed, and the creative energy seems less vibrant than in the past. The post office is still in operation, however, and on a hill overlooking the town, you'll find **Harmony Cellars**, a winery offering daily tastings. ~ Harmony Valley Road and Route 1; phone/fax 800-432-9239 (winetasting information); www.harmonycellars.net.

A few miles north of Harmony is the turnoff for **Cambria**. The town is divided into two separate sections: the East Village and West Village. Galleries, gift shops, and antique stores abound in both villages, so it really doesn't matter where you start exploring the town. The **Chamber of Commerce** is located in the West Village. ~ 767 Main Street, Cambria; 805-927-3624; www.cambria chamber.org, e-mail info@cambriachamber.org.

Start wandering around and you'll find that it's a pretty place, with ridgetop homes, sandy beaches, and rocky coves. But like many of California's small creative communities, Cambria has begun peering too long in the mirror. The architecture along Main Street has assumed a cutesy mock-Tudor look and the place is taking on an air of unreality.

Still, there are many fine artists and several exceptional galleries here. It's a choice place to shop and seek out gourmet food. While you're at it, head up to **Nit Wit Ridge**. That hodgepodge house on the left, the one decorated with every type of bric-a-brac, was the home of Art Beal, a.k.a. Captain Nit Wit, who died in 1992. He worked on this folk-art estate, listed in the National Register of Historic Landmarks, from 1928 until his death. ~ Hillcrest Drive just above Cornwall Street.

Then take a ride along **Moonstone Beach Drive**, a lovely oceanfront corridor with vista points and tidepools. It's a marvelous place for beachcombers and daydreamers.

Funny thing about travel, you often end up visiting places in spite of themselves. You realize that as soon as you get back home friends are going to ask if you saw this or that, so your itinerary becomes a combination of the locales you've always longed to experience and the places everyone else says you "must see."

The world-renowned **Hearst Castle** is one of the latter. Built by newspaper magnate William Randolph Hearst and designed by architect Julia Morgan, the Hearst San Simeon State Historical Monument includes a main house that sports 37 bedrooms, three guesthouses, and part of the old Hearst ranch, which once stretched 40 miles along the coast.

The entire complex took 27 years to build. In the 1930s and 1940s, when Hearst resided here and film stars like Charlie Chaplin, Mary Pickford, Clark Gable, and Cary Grant frequented the place, the grounds contained the largest private zoo in the world.

An insatiable art collector, Hearst stuffed every building with priceless works. Casa Grande, the main house, is fronted by two cathedral towers and filled with Renaissance and Gothic art. To see it is overwhelming. There is no place for the eye to rest. The main sitting room is covered everywhere with tapestries, bas-relief works, 16th-century paintings, Roman columns, and a carved wood ceiling. The walls are fashioned from 500-year-old choir pews, the French fireplace dates back 400 years; there are hand-carved tables and silver candelabra (I am still describing the same room), overstuffed furniture, and antique statuary. It is the most lavish mismatch in history.

Hearst Castle crosses the line from visual art to visual assault. The parts are exquisite, the whole a travesty. And yet, as I said, you must see the place. It's so huge that four different two-hour tours are scheduled daily to various parts of the property.

A fifth tour of "The Ranch," as Hearst called the castle, is conducted at night, on most Fridays and Saturdays only from March through May and September through December. It begins at sunset and takes in the gardens that are illuminated by 100 historic light fixtures. Docents dressed in 1930s fashions appear as Hearst's domestic staff and celebrated guests.

In the visitors center, which is located just off Route 1, there's a National Geographic Theater that shows the film *Hearst Castle—Building the Dream* on a huge five-story-tall movie screen. Admission. ~ 805-927-6811; www.hearstcastle.org.

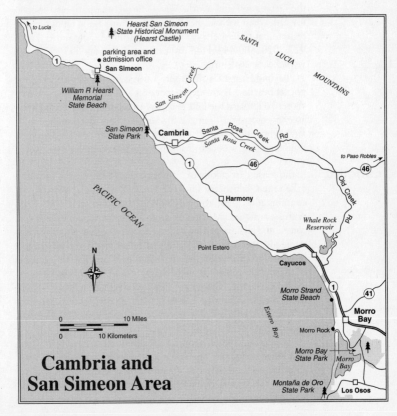

Cambria and San Simeon Area

All tours of the castle, which is on the hilltop above, depart from the center. The five-mile bus ride up takes several minutes; a tour guide will greet you upon your arrival at the top. The tours involve considerable walking and include many stairs.

> Ninety species of wild animals—including lions, tigers, yaks, and camels—roamed about Hearst Castle.

Since over one million people a year visit, the guided tours are often booked solid. I recommend that you reserve as much as two months in advance and plan on taking Tour 1, which covers the ground floor of Casa Grande, a guesthouse, the pools, and the gardens. Call 800-444-4445 for reservations.

Ultimately you'll find that in spite of the pomp and grandiosity, there is a magic about the place. In the early morning, when tour shuttles begin climbing from sea level to the 1600-foot-elevation residence, fog feathers through the surrounding valleys, obscuring everything but the spiked peaks of the Santa Lucia Mountains and the lofty towers of the castle. The entire complex, overbearing as it is, evokes a simpler, more glamorous era, before the Depression and World War II turned the nation's thoughts inward, when without blinking a man could build an outlandish testimonial to himself. Admission. ~ Route 1, San Simeon; 805-927-2020, 800-444-4445 (tour reservations), fax 805-927-2041; www.hearstcastle.org.

Beyond Hearst Castle, Route 1 winds north past tidepools and pocket beaches. There are pretty coves and surf-washed rocks offshore. To leeward the hills give way to mountains as the highway ascends toward the dramatic Big Sur coastline. Two hundred miles farther north sits the city that Hearst made the center of his publishing empire, an oceanfront metropolis called San Francisco.

LODGING   In the coastal art colony of Cambria is an 1873 bed and breakfast called the **Olallieberry Inn**. The Greek Revival clapboard house contains nine guest rooms, done in Victorian style with 19th-century antiques. Most rooms have fireplaces, some have balconies, and all have private baths. The rose-colored carpet and curtains, together with the carefully selected linens, add an element of luxury to this well-appointed establishment. The sitting room is attractively furnished with oak wood. A full breakfast is included in the rate. Closed the first two weeks of January. ~ 2476 Main Street, Cambria; 805-927-3222, 888-927-3222, fax 805-927-0202; www.olallieberry.com, e-mail olallieinn@olallieberry.com. MODERATE TO ULTRA-DELUXE.

If you would prefer a more rustic atmosphere, head up to **Cambria Pines Lodge**. Set one and a half miles from the beach, amid 25 acres of Monterey pines, are rambling split-rail lodges with additional cabins dotted about the property. The main building offers a spacious lobby with stone fireplace plus a restaurant and lounge with nightly entertainment; other amenities include a swimming pool, sauna, jacuzzi, and a day spa. For a more luxurious stay, hotel-style suites are available. All prices include breakfast. ~ 2905 Burton Drive, Cambria; 805-927-4200, 800-445-6868, fax 805-927-4016; www.cambriapineslodge.com, e-mail info@cambriapineslodge.com. DELUXE TO ULTRA-DELUXE.

North of Hearst Castle, where Route 1 becomes an isolated coastal road with few signs of civilization, are two hostelries. **Piedras Blancas Motel** has 14 standard motel-type rooms. Most of the units have ocean views. ~ Route 1, seven miles north of Hearst Castle; 805-927-4202, fax 805-927-5725. MODERATE TO ULTRA-DELUXE.

Farther along, on a ridge poised between the highway and ocean, sits the more appealing **Ragged Point Inn**. This 30-unit facility has attractive rooms furnished with contemporary hardwood furniture. Some of the rooms have gas fireplaces and jacuzzi tubs. Another compelling reason to stay is the beautiful ocean view from this clifftop abode. Despite the inn's proximity to the road, it's peaceful and quiet here; a variety of wildlife wanders and flutters through the grounds and sea sounds fill the air. A steep trail leads down to a rock-and-sand beach, while other trails take you away from the ocean to see the Santa Lucia Mountains. ~ Route 1, 15 miles north of Hearst Castle; 805-927-4502, fax 805-927-8862; www.raggedpointinn.net, e-mail info@raggedpointinn.net. DELUXE TO ULTRA-DELUXE.

DINING

In a small town like this, when a restaurant has managed to stay in business since 1986, you know they're doing something right. **Mustache Pete's** stirs up fine Italian cooking six days a week. Along with gourmet pizza they offer cooking-related souvenirs. Closed Sunday. ~ 4090 Burton Drive, Cambria; 805-927-8589, fax 805-927-0976; www.mustachepetes.com. MODERATE.

Ethnic and vegetarian food lovers will fare well at **Robin's**. Set in a 1930s Mexican-style house, it serves homemade lunches and dinners. Selections range from burritos to tandoori prawns to stir-fried tofu. It's an eclectic blend with the accent on European and Asian cuisine. Patio seating is available. ~ 4095 Burton Drive, Cambria; 805-927-5007, fax 805-927-1320; www.robins restaurant.com. MODERATE.

SHOPPING

Located a few miles south of Hearst Castle, the seaside enclave of Cambria has developed into an artist colony and become an important arts-and-crafts center, with numerous galleries and specialty shops. Several antique shops are also here; like the crafts stores, they cluster along Main Street and Burton Drive.

Among the foremost galleries in here is **Seekers Collection & Gallery**. It's a glass menagerie inhabited by contemporary, one-of-a-kind vases, goblets, and sculptures. ~ 4090 Burton Drive, Cambria; 805-927-4352, 800-841-5250; www.seekersglass.com.

The Soldier Gallery is a journey back to childhood. Part toy store and part aviation gallery, it serves as headquarters for thousands of hand-painted toy soldiers from around the world. Some of these are deployed in battle formation, re-enacting a clash from the Civil War. This unique shop has been featured in the *Wall Street Journal*. ~ 789 Main Street, Cambria; 805-927-3804; www.soldiergallery.com.

NIGHTLIFE **Camozzi's Saloon** is a century-old bar with longhorns over the bar, wagon wheels on the wall, and a floor that leans worse than a midnight drunk. The place is famous. Besides that, it has a rock band on Saturday. ~ 2262 Main Street, Cambria; 805-927-8941.

BEACHES & PARKS **SAN SIMEON STATE PARK** 🚶 🚲 🏊 〰️ ⚓ This wide sand corridor reaches for about two miles from San Simeon Creek to Santa Rosa Creek. It's a wonderful place to wander, and the streams, with their abundant wildlife, add to the enjoyment. Unfortunately, Route 1 divides the beach from the camping area and disturbs the quietude. Other parts of the park are very peaceful, especially the **Moonstone Beach** section in Cambria, known for its moonstone agates and otters. There are picnic areas, restrooms, and showers. ~ Route 1, Cambria; 805-927-2020, fax 805-927-2041.

▲ There are two campgrounds in the park with a total of 204 campsites. The larger San Simeon Creek has tent/RV spots (no hookups); $20 per night. At Washburn there are 70 tent/RV sites (no hookups); $15 per night. Reservations: 800-444-7275.

WILLIAM R. HEARST MEMORIAL STATE BEACH 🚶 🚲 🏊 〰️ ⚓ Located directly below Hearst Castle, this is a placid crescent-shaped beach. The facility measures only two acres, including a grassy area on a rise above the beach; there is a 1000-foot-long fishing pier. Scenic San Simeon Point curves out from the shoreline, creating a pretty cove and protecting the beach from surf. Swimming and fishing are very good. Facilities include picnic areas and restrooms. ~ On Route 1 opposite Hearst Castle; 805-927-2020, fax 805-927-2041; www.hearstcastle.com.

▼▼▼▼▼▼▼▼▼▼▼▼▼

Outdoor Adventures

SPORTS-FISHING Interested in hooking calico bass or yellowtail? Then book a half-day or overnight charter to the Channel Islands, a few of the more popular trips at **Channel Island Sportfishing**. There's also a 24-hour full tackle shop here that rents equipment, too. ~ 4151 South Victoria Avenue, Oxnard; 805-985-8511; www.sportfishingreport.com. **Sea Landing** offers half-, three-quarter-, and full-day cruises.

Look to catch calico bass, red snapper, barracuda, and an occasional tuna. ~ 301 West Cabrillo Boulevard, Santa Barbara; 805-963-3564. **Patriot Sportfishing** specializes in deep-sea and rock fishing and targets salmon and albacore seasonally. ~ Pier 3, Avila Beach; 805-595-7200; www.patriotsportfishing.com. **Virge's Sportfishing** books three-quarter-day charters for rock cod (in the fall) and overnight charters for albacore (from July to December). They also offer multiday trips from November to June. ~ 1215 Embarcadero, Morro Bay; 805-772-1222; www.virges.com.

If you're in the mood for a whale-watching excursion, take your pick from numerous companies. You can also opt for either of two whale-watching seasons. From January through May, you'll see California gray whales on their northern migration. The second season, from June to September, brings blue and humpback whales to the Channel Islands.

WHALE WATCHING

Contact **Channel Island Sportfishing** for tours from January through March. ~ 4151 South Victoria Avenue, Oxnard; 805-985-8511; www.sportfishingreport.com. For excursions in both seasons, call **Captain Don's**. From February through May, Captain Don's sails along the Santa Barbara coast on a 90-foot boat looking for gray whales around the Channel Islands. You're bound to see a sea lion, otter, or dolphin on the harbor cruise. ~ Stearns Wharf, Santa Barbara; 805-969-5217; www.captdon.com. **Sea Landing** will take you whale watching from December through October on the 75-foot *Condor Express*. ~ 301 West Cabrillo Boulevard, Santa Barbara; 805-963-3564; www.condorcruises.com. **Patriot Sportfishing** operates whale-watching tours from the end of December through April. The three-hour trips go in search of the California gray whale. ~ Pier 3, Avila Beach; 805-595-7200; www.patriotsportfishing.com. **Virge's Sportfishing** offers day trips to see gray whales from the end of December through April. ~ 1215 Embarcadero, Morro Bay; 805-772-1222; www.virges.com.

GO FISH

The waters off the Central Coast and the Channel Islands provide excellent fishing. In the summer, you can fish the surface for barracuda, calico bass, and yellowtail, or the shallow waters for ling cod. Due to the relatively shallow water in the Central Coast area, winter bottom fishing is some of the best in the world. Common catches are rock cod, cabazon, red snapper, and blue bass. Most charter companies in the area sell bait and rent tackle.

KAYAKING   Sea kayaking is excellent along the Central Coast and out to the Channel Islands. Many outfits offer tours, rentals, and lessons.

You can rent a kayak or arrange instructional paddling trips to the sea caves of Santa Cruz Island with **Aquasports**. ~ 111 Verona Avenue, Goleta; 805-968-7231, 800-773-2309; www.island kayaking.com. **Adventours Outdoor Excursions, Inc.** can arrange trips combining kayaking with other outdoor activities such as camping, hiking, biking, and backpacking. ~ P.O. Box 215, Santa Barbara, CA 93102; 805-898-9569; www.adventours.com. **Good Clean Fun** offers rentals, instructional guided tours north along the coast, and lessons. ~ 136 Ocean Front, Cayucos; 805-995-1993; www.gcfsurf.com. **Kayak Horizons** provides you the means to hobnob with seals and local birds. ~ 551 Embarcadero, Morro Bay; 805-772-1119; www.kayakhorizons.com. Paddle around the bay in a rented canoe or sit-on-top kayak from **Subsea Tours & Kayaks**. ~ Marina Square, 699 Embarcadero; 805-772-3349.

DIVING   For those more interested in watching fish, several companies charter dive boats and also offer scuba diving rentals and lessons. The waters around the Channel Islands provide some of the world's best diving spots.

Ventura Dive and Sport, a five-star PADI facility, has one-, two-, or three-day diving excursions to the northern Channel Islands, where you will see a wide array of sea life, including harbor seals and bat rays. ~ 1559 Spinnaker Drive #108, Ventura; 805-650-6500; www.venturadive.com. In Santa Barbara, call **Anacapa Dive Center** for scuba instruction, rentals, and trips to the Channel Islands. ~ 22 Anacapa Street, Santa Barbara; 805-963-8917; www.anacapadivecenter.com. Dive charters to local waters and the Channel Islands are arranged by **Sea Landing**. They offer one-day open-water trips as well as two-, three-, and five-day charters. ~ 301 West Cabrillo Boulevard, Santa Barbara; 805-963-3564; www.truth aquatics.com.

In the Santa Barbara area, surfers head to Rincon, Ledbetter, Santa Claus Lane, and La Conchita.

SURFING   There's good surfing all along the Central Coast. Catch a wave with surfboard rentals from the following enterprises.

The **Santa Barbara Adventure Company** will not only teach you how to surf, they will take you kayaking along the coast and over to the Channel Islands, or guide you on a mountain biking adventure. They rent all the gear and have professional guides for every activity. ~ P.O. Box 208, Santa Barbara, CA 93102; 805-452-1942, 888-596-6687; www.sbadventureco.com.

In Cayucos **Good Clean Fun** rents and sells wetsuits, surfboards, and boogieboards. ~ 136 Ocean Front, Cayucos; 805-

995-1993; www.gcfsurf.com. **Wavelengths Surf Shop** offers wet-suits and surfboards to surfers ready to take on the waves. For a good location, try The Rock right down the street from the shop. ~ 998 Embarcadero, Morro Bay; 805-772-3904.

The Central Coast and the Channel Islands are prime areas for boating. You can rent your own boat or go on one of the various cruises and charters offered.

BOATING & SAILING

To sail the Pacific, visit the Channel Islands, watch whales, or take a romantic sunset champagne cruise, contact **Santa Barbara Sailing Center** for boat rentals and charters. They also offer a variety of lessons. ~ The Breakwater, Santa Barbara; 805-962-2826, 800-350-9090; www.sbsail.com. **Sea Landing** offers cruises and charters. Sunset dinner trips are a specialty. ~ 301 West Cabrillo Boulevard, Santa Barbara; 805-963-3564. In the summer **Captain Don's** has sunset and dinner cruises as well as sightseeing tours. ~ Stearns Wharf, Santa Barbara; 805-969-5217; www.captdons.com. **Pacific Sailing** provides sailboat charters and instruction. ~ 1583 Spinnaker Drive, Dock D-9, Ventura Harbor; 805-658-6508; www.pacsail.com.

Golf enthusiasts will enjoy the weather as well as the courses along the Central Coast. Courses have 18 holes unless otherwise stated.

GOLF

VENTURA–OXNARD AREA   The **River Ridge Golf Club** is a links-style course with an island green on the 14th hole. ~ 2401 West Vineyard Avenue, Oxnard; 805-983-4653; www.riverridge-golf-club.com. A flat course, **Olivas Park** comes complete with driving range and putting green. ~ 3750 Olivas Park Drive, Ventura; 805-642-4303.

SANTA BARBARA AREA   **Santa Barbara Golf Club**'s course is dotted with oaks, pines, and sycamores. ~ Las Positas Road and McCaw Avenue, Santa Barbara; 805-687-7087. The executive nine-hole **Twin Lakes Golf Course** meanders around two lakes. ~ 6034 Hollister Avenue, Goleta; 805-964-1414. Two miles north of Twin Lakes is **Sandpiper Golf Course**, a championship course right on the ocean. ~ 7925 Hollister Avenue, Goleta; 805-968-1541; www.sandpipergolf.com. A creek winds through the nine-hole **Ocean Meadows Golf Course**, which is a relatively flat playing field. ~ 6925 Whittier Drive, Goleta; 805-968-6814; www.oceanmeadowsgolf.com.

SAN LUIS OBISPO AREA   A creek runs through the par-3, nine-hole **Pismo State Beach Golf Course**. ~ 25 Grand Avenue, Grover City; 805-481-5215. The nine-hole **Laguna Lake Golf Course** is a hilly green surrounded by mountains. They also have a putting green and chipping area. ~ 11175 Los Osos Valley Road, San Luis Obispo; 805-781-7309. **Avila Beach Resort Golf Course** is dotted with trees and water hazards. The driving range over-looks the beach. ~ Anabay Drive, Avila Beach; 805-595-4000; www.avilabeachresort.com. Lined with lofty pine trees, part of **Morro Bay Golf Course** overlooks the ocean. ~ 201 State Park Road, Morro Bay; 805-782-8060. **Sea Pines Golf Course** offers a nine-hole green whose gently rolling hills are speckled with mature pines. ~ 1945 Solano, Los Osos; 805-528-1788; www.seap inesgolfresort.com.

TENNIS

Tennis, anyone? This area offers a number of opportunities for tennis fiends. **Moranda Park Tennis Complex** has eight lighted courts situated in a beautiful park setting. Equipment rentals available. ~ 200 Moranda Parkway, Port Hueneme; 805-986-3587. **Santa Barbara Municipal Courts** features four facilities with a total of 32 courts; 14 are lighted. Bring your own equipment. Fee. ~ 1414 Park Place; 805-564-5517. **Cuesta College** has eight courts that open to the public on the weekend. ~ Route 1, San Luis Obispo; 805-546-3207. **Sinsheimer Park** has six courts. ~ 900 Southwood Drive, San Luis Obispo; 805-781-7300. Additional courts are located at **French Park**, off Poinsettia Street. For night games, try the lighted courts at the high school, on the corner of San Luis Drive and California Street. There are four more courts at **Shell Beach and Florin roads**.

RIDING STABLES

Circle Bar B Stables takes riders on a one-and-a-half-hour trip through a canyon, past waterfalls, and then up to a vista point overlooking the Channel Islands. A half-day lunch ride is also available. Reservations are required. ~ 1800 Refugio Road, Goleta; 805-968-3901; www.circlebarb.com. To ride right on the beach, you can go on one of **Pacific Dunes Ranch Riding Stables** guided tours or rent a horse from them to explore the area on your own in the off-season. Closed Wednesday, Thursday, and rainy days. ~ 1205 Silverspur Place, Oceano; 805-489-8100. The **Ojai Valley Inn** has its own stable, but nonguests may ride as well. Reservations required. Make arrangements with the concierge. ~ 905 Country Club Road, Ojai; 805-646-5511, 800-422-6524.

BIKING

Biking the Central Coast can be a rewarding experience. The coastal route, however, presents problems in populated areas during rush hour.

The town of **Ventura** offers an interesting bicycle tour through the historical section of town with a visit to the county historical museum and mission. Another bike tour of note, off of Harbor Boulevard, leads to the Channel Islands National Park Visitors Center. The **Ventura River Trail** (6 miles) is an asphalt trail featuring locally designed sculptures and links to coastal, mountain, and downtown trails. A bike map of Ventura County is available at the **Ventura Visitors Bureau.** ~ 89 South California Street #C, Ventura; 805-648-2075; www.goventura.org.

Santa Barbara is chock full of beautiful bike paths and trails. Two notable beach excursions are the **Atascadero Recreation Trail,** which starts at the corner of Encore Drive and Modoc Road and ends over seven miles later at Goleta Beach, and **Cabrillo bikeway,** which takes you from Andree Clark Bird Refuge to Leadbetter Beach. Also, the **University of California–Santa Barbara** has many bike paths through the campus grounds and into Isla Vista.

> The Goleta Valley bike-way travels from Santa Barbara to Goleta along Cathedral Oaks Road.

Up the coast, a stunning, three-mile bike path links **El Capitan** and **Refugio** state beaches.

Exploring the shores of Morro Bay is popular with cyclists. For the hardy biker a ride up **Black Mountain** leads to sweeping views of the Pacific Ocean.

Bike Rentals and Tours   **Adventours Outdoor Excursions, Inc.** offers bike tours to the Santa Ynez Mountains, the Santa Ynez Valley wine country, and the Santa Barbara coast. ~ P.O. Box 215, Santa Barbara, CA 93102; 805-898-9569; www.adventours.com. In the summer **Beach Rentals** rents tandems, three-wheelers, mountain bikes, and inline skates. ~ Embassy Suites Mandalay Beach Resort Inn, 2101 Mandalay Beach Road, Oxnard, 805-984-2500; and 22 State Street, Santa Barbara, 805-966-2282.

HIKING

With its endless beaches and mountain backdrop, the Central Coast is wide open for exploration. Shoreline paths and moun-tain trails crisscross the entire region. All distances listed for hik-ing trails are one way unless otherwise noted.

First among equals in this hiker's dreamland is the **California Coastal Trail,** the 1200-mile route that runs the entire length of the state. Here it begins at Point Mugu and travels along state beaches from Ventura County to Santa Barbara. In Santa Bar-bara the trail turns inland toward the Santa Ynez Mountains and Los Padres National Forest. It returns to the coast at Point Sal, then parallels sand dunes, passes the hot springs at Avila Beach, and continues up the coast to San Simeon.

VENTURA–OXNARD AREA   Bounded by the Santa Monica and Santa Ynez mountains and bordered by 43 miles of shoreline, Ventura County offers a variety of hiking opportunities. (Note, however, that some trails were damaged in recent Southern California fires.) For more information on local hiking trails and guided trail walks in the area, contact the City of Ventura Community Services Department at 805-658-4733.

Ocean's Edge Trail (.6 mile) is a lovely shore hike from the Emma Wood State Beach to Seaside Wilderness Park; popular with birders.

River's Edge Trail (.3 mile) is a great hike for exploring the riparian woodlands along the Ventura River.

OJAI AREA   For information on trails in the region, call the Ojai Chamber of Commerce and Visitors Center at 805-646-8126; www.ojaichamber.org.

Nine miles east of Ojai, **Santa Paula Canyon Trail** (3 miles) provides an easy hike to Santa Paula Creek. The path leads to waterfalls and a camp situated in a lovely area.

In Matilija Canyon the **Middle Matilija Trail** (8.4 miles) offers a moderately difficult backpacking hike in a stunning oak-filled area.

Near Ojai, the **Murietta Trail** (1.5 miles) is a good place to bring the kids for an easy trek.

SANTA BARBARA AREA   What distinguishes Santa Barbara from most of California's coastal communities is the magnificent Santa Ynez mountain range, which forms a backdrop to the city and provides excellent hiking terrain.

A red steel gate marks the beginning of **Romero Canyon Trail** (7 miles) on Bella Vista Road in Santa Barbara. After joining a fire road at the 2350-foot elevation, the trail follows a stream shaded by oak, sycamore, and bay trees. From here you can keep climbing or return via the right fork, a fire road that offers an easier but longer return trip.

San Ysidro Trail (1.2 miles) begins at Park Lane and Mountain Drive in Santa Barbara, follows a stream dotted with pools and waterfalls, then climbs to the top of Camino Cielo ridge. For a different loop back, it's only a short walk to Cold Springs Trail.

Also located in the Santa Ynez Mountains is **Rattlesnake Canyon Trail** (1.75 miles). Beginning near Skofield Park, the trail follows Mission Creek, along which an aqueduct was built in the early 19th century. Portions of the waterway can still be seen. This pleasant trail offers shaded pools and meadows.

Cold Springs Trail, East Fork (4.5 miles) heads east from Mountain Drive in Santa Barbara. The trail takes you through a canyon covered with alder and along a creek punctuated by pools

AUTHOR FAVORITE

The three-mile **Gaviota Hot Springs and Peak Trail** begins in Gaviota State Park, with a delicious first stop at the mineral pools at Gaviota Hot Springs (about a half mile from the trailhead). After a leisurely dip you can continue on a somewhat strenuous route into Los Padres National Forest, climbing to Gaviota Peak for a marvelous view of ranch land and the Pacific.

and waterfalls. It continues up into Hot Springs Canyon and crosses the flank of Montecito Peak.

Cold Springs Trail, West Fork (5 miles) leads off the better known East Fork. It climbs and descends along the left side of a lushly vegetated canyon before arriving at an open valley.

Tunnel Trail (2.9 miles) is named for the turn-of-the-20th-century tunnel through the mountains that brought fresh water to Santa Barbara. The trail begins at the end of Tunnel Road in Santa Barbara and passes through various sandstone formations and crosses a creek before arriving at Mission Falls.

San Antonio Creek Trail (1.7 miles), an easy hike along a creek bed, starts from the far end of Tucker's Grove County Park in Goleta. In the morning or late afternoon you'll often catch glimpses of deer foraging in the woods.

Thirty-five miles of coastline stretches from Stearns Wharf in Santa Barbara to Gaviota State Beach. There are hiking opportunities galore along the entire span.

Summerland Trail (1-mile loop), starting at Lookout Park in Summerland, takes you along Summerland Beach, past tiny coves, then along Montecito's coastline to the beach fronting the Biltmore Hotel.

Goleta Beach Trail (2 miles) begins at Goleta Beach County Park in Goleta and curves past tidepools and sand dunes en route to Goleta Point. Beyond the dunes is Devereux Slough, a reserve populated by egrets, herons, plovers, and sandpipers. The hike also passes the Ellwood Oil Field where a Japanese submarine fired shots at the mainland United States during World War II.

SAN LUIS OBISPO AREA   The San Luis Obispo area, rich in wildlife, offers hikers everything from seaside strolls to mountain treks. Many of the trails in this area are in the Los Padres National Forest (for information, call 805-925-9538).

Guadalupe-Nipomo Dunes Preserve (2.5 miles) is especially rewarding for dune lovers. This wetland area is a habitat for many endangered birds. The boardwalk trail passes a freshwater lake, a willow community, and many dunes, ending at Pismo Beach. At Oso Flaco Lake there's an entrance kiosk with trail and hiking information. ~ 805-343-2455; www.dunescenter.org.

The **Point Sal Trail** (6 miles) offers an excellent opportunity to hike in a forgotten spot along the coast. (But beware, it's not for inexperienced hikers or those afraid of heights.) Alternating between cliffs and seashore, the trail takes you past tidepools, pelicans, cormorants, and basking seals. An excellent whale-watching area, the trail ends near the mouth of the Santa Maria River.

The golden mustard plants and poppies along the way give **Montaña de Oro Bluffs Trail** (2 miles) its name ("Mountain of Gold"). This coastal trail takes you past Spooner's Cove (a mooring place for bootleggers during Prohibition). You'll pass clear tidepools, sea caves, basking seals, otters, and ocean bluffs.

For an interesting hike along the sandspit that separates Morro Bay from Estero Bay, try the **Morro Bay Sandspit Trail** (5 miles). The trail passes sand dunes and ancient Chumash shell mounds. Stay on the ocean side of the sandspit to avoid the muck.

Several trails in the vicinity of **Lopez Lake Recreational Area** offer opportunities to see the region's flora and fauna. Deer, raccoon, fox, and wood-rats predominate, along with a variety of birds species (not to mention rattlesnakes and poison oak). ~ 805-788-2381; www.slocountyparks.com.

At the entrance to the park, **Turkey Ridge Trail** (.8 mile) is a strenuous climb through oak and chaparral and offers splendid views of the lake and the Santa Lucia Mountains.

Two Waters Trail (1.3 miles) connects the Lopez and Wittenberg arms of Lopez Lake. It is a moderate hike that offers marvelous views. The trailheads are at Encinal or Miller's Cove.

Blackberry Spring Trail (.8 mile) commences at upper Squirrel campground and passes many plant species used by the Chumash Indians. This is a moderate hike with a 260-foot climb that connects with High Ridge Trail.

Little Falls Creek Trail (2.75 miles) begins along Lopez Canyon Road (High Mountain Road) and ascends 1350 feet up the canyon past a spectacular waterfall. Views of the Santa Lucia wilderness await you at the top of the mountain.

▼ ▼ ▼ ▼ ▼ ▼ ▼ ▼ ▼ ▼ ▼
Transportation

CAR

As it proceeds north from the Los Angeles area, coastal highway **Route 1** weaves in and out from **Route 101**. The two highways join in Oxnard and continue as a single roadway until a point 30 miles north of Santa Barbara. Here they diverge, Route 1 heading toward the coast while Route 101 takes an inland route. The highways merge again near Pismo Beach and continue north to San Luis Obispo. Here Route 1 leaves Route 101 and begins its long, beautiful course up the coast past Morro Bay and San Simeon.

AIR

Santa Barbara and San Luis Obispo have small airports serving the Central Coast. Airlines that stop at the **Santa Barbara Municipal Airport** include America West Express, American Eagle, Delta Connection, Horizon Air, and United Express. ~ 805-967-7111; www.flysba.com.

The **Santa Barbara Airbus** can be scheduled to meet arrivals at the airport; it otherwise goes to Carpinteria, Goleta, and downtown Santa Barbara, as well as Los Angeles International Airport. ~ 805-964-7759, 800-423-1618; www.sbairbus.com. There are also a number of taxi companies available. For the disabled, call **Easy Lift Transportation**. ~ 805-681-1181.

San Luis Obispo Municipal Airport is serviced by Sky West, United Express, American Eagle Airlines, and America West Express. ~ 805-781-5205.

Ground transportation from San Luis Obispo Municipal Airport is provided by Big City Cab. ~ 805-543-1234. Or try Yellow Cab of Five Cities. ~ 805-489-1155.

Greyhound Bus Lines (800-231-2222; www.greyhound.com) has **BUS** continual service along the Central Coast from both Los Angeles and San Francisco. The Ventura bus terminal is located at 291 East Thompson Boulevard (805-653-0164). Santa Barbara has one at 34 West Carrillo Street (805-965-7551). The terminal in San Luis Obispo is at 150 South Street (805-543-2121).

For those who want spectacular views of the coastline, try Am- **TRAIN** trak's "Coast Starlight." This train hugs the shoreline, providing rare views of the Central Coast's cliffs, headlands, and untracked beaches. Amtrak stops in Oxnard, Santa Barbara, and San Luis Obispo on its way north to Oakland and Seattle. ~ 800-872-7245; www.amtrak.com.

The larger towns in the Central Coast have car rental agencies; **CAR** check the Yellow Pages to find the best bargains. **RENTALS**

To pick up a car in the Oxnard–Ventura area, try Avis Rent A Car (800-331-1212), Budget Rent A Car (800-527-0700), or Hertz Rent A Car (800-654-3131).

At the airport in Santa Barbara try Avis Rent A Car (800-331-1212), Budget Rent A Car (800-527-0700), Hertz Rent A Car (800-654-3131), or National Car Rental (800-227-7368). Agencies located outside the airport with free pick-up include Enterprise Rent A Car (800-325-8007).

In San Luis Obispo, car-rental agencies at the airport include Avis Rent A Car (800-331-1212), Hertz Rent A Car (800-654-3131), and Thrifty Car Rental (800-367-2277). Among those with free pickup service, try Enterprise Rent A Car (800-325-8007).

Public transportation in the Central Coast is fairly limited. In the **PUBLIC** Ventura area you'll find South Coast Area Transit, or SCAT, which **TRANSIT** serves Oxnard, Port Hueneme, Ojai, and Ventura. ~ 805-487-4222; www.scat.org.

In the Santa Barbara area, the Santa Barbara Metropolitan Transit stops in Summerland, Carpinteria, Santa Barbara, Goleta, and Isla Vista. ~ Carrillo and Chapala streets; 805-683-3702; www.sbmtd.gov.

The San Luis Obispo area has San Luis Obispo Transit, or SLO, which operates on weekdays during daylight hours and even less frequently on weekends. ~ 805-541-2877; www.slocity.org.

SEVEN

Low Desert

East of metropolitan Los Angeles lies a land of brilliant greens and dusty browns, scorched flats and snow-thatched mountains. The Colorado Desert, the hottest, driest desert in the country, covers a broad swath of California's southeastern quarter. Here winter, with daily highs in the 70s and 80s, attracts sun worshippers, while summer brings withering heat waves.

It's a place where visitors can swim and ski in the same day. Little wonder that its entertainment capital, Palm Springs, has become a celebrity playground. Ever since 1930, when silent film stars Ralph Bellamy and Charlie Farrell began buying up desert land at $30 an acre, Hollywood has been vacationing in Palm Springs. The racquet club that Bellamy and Farrell initiated soon attracted Humphrey Bogart, Ginger Rogers, and Clark Gable. Latter-day luminaries like Bob Hope, Frank Sinatra, and Kirk Douglas continued to strengthen the spot's celebrity cachet.

Only 400 feet above sea level, the town nestles beneath mountains two miles high. Today Palm Springs is the golf capital of the world, sponsoring over 100 tournaments every year. In addition to dozens of golf courses, the region boasts hundreds of tennis courts and a swimming pool for every five residents. Together with satellite towns like Rancho Mirage and Palm Desert, it has become an opulent enclave in which billboards are prohibited, buildings are limited to heights of 30 feet, and manicured lawns are more common than cactus plants.

It was the Agua Caliente Indians who inhabited the area originally and discovered the desert's hot mineral baths. These American Indians hunted and gathered in the surrounding mountains and attributed magical healing powers to the natural springs. Eventually the United States government divided the entire territory into alternating squares of real estate, giving the odd-numbered sections to the Southern Pacific Railroad and deeding the rest to the Agua Calientes.

Today much of this valuable Indian property is leased to tourist resorts. Located just 100 miles from Los Angeles, the desert has become a major travel destination. Visitors arrive not only to soak in the sun and spas of Palm Springs, but also to tour the palm groves of Indio. The date-growing center of the country, this bland agricultural town is a date palm oasis, with gardens reaching from road's edge to the fringe of the mountains. Little Indio's day in the sun arrives every February when it hosts the Riverside County Fair & National Date Festival, a gala celebration complete with ostrich and camel races, Arabian Nights pageantry, and booths displaying over 100 varieties of dates.

Farther south lies the Salton Sea, California's largest lake, a briny trough that sits astride the notorious San Andreas Fault. Nearby Anza–Borrego Desert State Park stretches across parts of three counties and encompasses a half-million acres of gem-like springs, rock promontories, and sandstone chasms. Created about 150 million years ago by an earthquake fault system, the region includes the Jacumba Mountains, a granite jumble filled with eerie rock formations. Named for Juan Bautista de Anza, the Spanish explorer who trekked through this region in 1774, and *borrego*, the desert sheep that inhabit its hillsides, Anza–Borrego was a vital route for 1850s-era stagecoaches and mail wagons.

Joshua Tree National Park, the area's other major park, lies astride the Low and High deserts, rising from the scorching Colorado Desert to the cooler climes and higher elevations of the Mojave. Noted for its cactus gardens and stands of Joshua trees, this vast preserve was formerly home to the Chemehuevi Indians. Miners entered the territory following the Civil War, striking gold in 1873. Within a few years, cattle ranchers also arrived, creating vast ranges and driving the Indians from the land.

Rising between Los Angeles and Palm Springs, creating a gateway to the Low Desert is the Inland Empire. Bounded to the north by the San Bernardino Mountains, which rise over 11,000 feet and embrace the popular resort areas of Lake Arrowhead and Big Bear Lake, it is bordered on the east by the San Jacinto Mountains.

A Spanish explorer named Pedro Fage uncovered the Inland Empire during a 1772 expedition and in the 1830s missionaries began colonizing the region. By the next decade powerful Spanish families had transformed the territory into sprawling cattle and horse ranches.

Then in 1851 a party of Mormons settled here, staying for only six years but leaving an indelible legacy. They planted wheat, harvested lumber, and founded the city of San Bernardino.

Located at the foot of Cajon Pass along a vital route between Los Angeles and the East Coast, the area expanded in importance. The railroad arrived in 1875; and during the same decade Luther and Eliza Tibbetts planted three orange saplings shipped across the country from Washington, D.C., giving birth to the Inland Empire's vaunted citrus industry.

Together with Riverside and Redlands, San Bernardino sprouted with orange and lemon trees. Growth slackened during the first half of the 20th century, but began to accelerate once again in the 1950s. Today the Inland Empire, with its trim orchards, burgeoning cities, and mountain lakes, is one of the Golden State's fastest growing regions, a fitting entranceway to the increasingly popular Low Desert.

▼▼▼▼▼▼▼▼▼▼▼▼▼▼▼▼▼

San Bernardino Mountains

One of the highest ranges in California, the San Bernardinos rise to over 11,000 feet elevation. Together with the San Gabriels to the west, they provide a pine-rimmed barrier between the Los Angeles Basin and Mojave Desert. A popular winter and water sports area, the mountains are encompassed within San Bernardino National Forest and offer a string of alpine lakes and lofty peaks.

During the 1860s prospectors combed the area in search of gold. After their luck petered out, loggers and cattle ranchers took over the territory. Later in the century, as dams created the mountain lakes, herds of tourists began roaming the landscape.

Today a single highway, Route 18, nicknamed "Rim of the World Drive," courses through the entire region. Beginning in Crestline, north of San Bernardino, it winds east to Big Bear Lake, offering postcard vistas of the San Bernardino region.

SIGHTS   Before departing on this mountaintop cruise, follow Route 138 from Crestline out to **Silverwood Lake**, the least developed of this region's mountain pools. Here a state recreation area provides opportunities to fish, boat, swim, and explore the secluded fringes of the lake (see the "Beaches & Parks" section in this chapter). Admission. ~ 760-389-2303.

The prettiest and most precious of the alpine gems is **Lake Arrowhead**, a socially exclusive enclave encircled by private homes. Popular with Hollywood notables and Los Angeles business executives, the lake has public facilities along the south shore. The closest most people come to the remaining shoreline is aboard the **Arrowhead Queen**, a 65-passenger paddlewheeler that tours the lake. Fee. ~ Lake Arrowhead Village; 909-336-6992, fax 909-866-1084.

Larger, friendlier, and less formal than Lake Arrowhead, **Big Bear Lake** stretches for seven miles at a 7000-foot altitude. Lined with resort facilities, it is generally less expensive and less private than its counterpart to the west. Created in the 1880s by a single arch dam, Big Bear is a popular ski area in winter. During summer months it offers a full array of aquatic amenities.

To tour the lake, you can climb aboard the **Big Bear Queen**. While on board, the most unusual place you'll pass will be that stark white dome on the north shore. Called the **Big Bear Solar Observatory**, the telescope is a research station for scientists from the New Jersey Institute of Technology. No boat tours are available from November to April. Fee. ~ Big Bear Marina, Big Bear Lake; 909-866-3218, fax 909-866-3846; www.bigbearmarina.com.

HIDDEN ▶   Miners nicknamed part of this territory "Starvation Flats," but a few of them struck it rich in **Holcomb Valley**. During the 1860s this conifer-studded region boasted a boom town that ri-

Text continued on page 472.

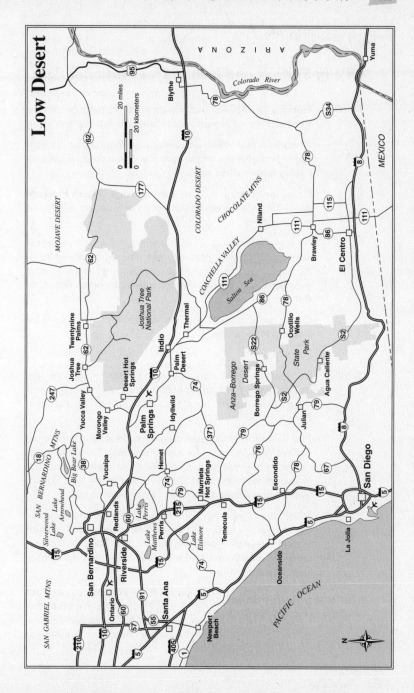

Low Desert

Palm Springs and Joshua Tree National Park

DAY 1 • From the Los Angeles area, hop on Route 10 and drive to Palm Springs. It's about 100 miles and normally takes less than two hours.

• Check into your choice accommodation from among the wide range of Palm Springs lodging options and head down to **Louise's Pantry** (page 493) for lunch.

• Escape the midday heat in the **Palm Springs Desert Museum** (page 485), an air-conditioned showplace of desert art, culture, and natural history.

• You may wish to round out your afternoon indulging in one of the three big Palm Springs pastimes—golf, shopping, or sunbathing by the pool. Or you could opt to continue learning about the desert environment with a visit to the incomparable **Moorten Botanical Garden** (page 486).

• Change out of your shorts or swimsuit and into evening attire for dinner at **Melvyn's** (page 493).

DAY 2 • Rising early to beat the desert heat on this wonderfully scenic day trip, take Route 62 north out of Palm Springs to Twentynine Palms and the Oasis Visitors Center entrance to **Joshua Tree National Park** (page 500).

• Tour the park in all its desert diversity, beginning with a drive out to **Keys View** (page 501) for a lovely panorama. Then drive southeast along the main park road, making the transition from the Mojave Desert to the Colorado Desert and ending up at Cottonwood Visitors Center, the southern gateway to the park.

• Take Route 10 west for 25 miles, exiting at Indio and continuing west on Route 111 to the rich-and-famous community of **Palm Desert** (page 488). From there, head south on Route 74, the spectacular 50-mile **Palms to Pines Tour** (page 489) through the Santa Rosa Mountains.

• If you're returning to Palm Springs for any reason, you can reach Route 10 by taking the right fork at Mountain Center and following Route 243 as it descends through San Bernardino National Forest. Or, to head back to L.A., simply take the left fork and stay on Route 74. With a short jog north on Route 215, Route 74 continues west, treating you to another burst of breathtaking scenery as it winds over the Elsinore Mountains and through Cleveland National Forest before bringing you back to Route 5 at San Juan Capistrano, about 30 miles south of the city.

valed Los Angeles in size. Today rough dirt roads lead to the last vestiges of those golden days. From Fawnskin on the north shore of Big Bear Lake, you can pick up Poligue Canyon Road and other well-marked roads, which bump for five miles past Wilber's Grave, the log remains of Two-Gun Bill's Saloon, Hangman's Tree, and an old log cabin.

A favored destination for children is **Moonridge Animal Park**. Featuring animals indigenous to the San Bernardino Mountains, the zoo contains bobcats, mountain lions, timber wolves, and grizzly and black bears that have been injured or abandoned. Admission. ~ On Moonridge Road, two miles south of Route 18, Big Bear Lake; 909-866-0183, fax 909-584-7177; www.moon ridgezoo.org, e-mail moonridgap@aol.com.

LODGING

For reasonably priced accommodations, head uphill about a mile from the lake. **Arrowhead Tree Top Lodge**, an attractive wood-frame motel with a pool, has 20 units available. Paneled in knotty pine, they are carpeted wall to wall and equipped with veneer furniture. There are also suites with kitchens. A pool rounds out the amenities. ~ 27992 Rainbow Drive, Lake Arrowhead; 909-337-2311, 800-358-8733, fax 909-337-1403; www.arrow headtreetop.com, e-mail mtnroom@aol.com. MODERATE TO ULTRA-DELUXE.

For a location right on Big Bear Lake, you need look no farther than **Shore Acres Lodge**. Here 11 woodframe cabins rest in the shade of a pine grove. Each is a full-facility unit with living room, bedroom, and kitchen; several feature two bedrooms and can easily sleep a family. The interiors are bland but quite trim and contemporary. Located away from the main road, Shore Acres is a quiet, private enclave with a pool (summer only), jacuzzi, dock, and swings. ~ 40090 Lakeview Drive, Big Bear Lake;

AUTHOR FAVORITE

Saddleback Inn beautifully plays the role of mountain lodge. The vintage 1920 structure, complete with steep-pitched roof, gables, and stone chimney, holds 34 comfortable units. The architecture is a mix of formal and country styles and the location is just across from the village and the lake. A restaurant and lounge round out the amenities in the main building, but the true attraction is the cluster of cottages dotting the property. Similar to the lodge rooms, they feature washed pine furniture, Laura Ashley designs, fireplaces, and tile baths with jacuzzi tubs. ~ 300 State Route 173, Lake Arrowhead; 909-336-3571, 800-858-3334, fax 909-336-6111; www.saddlebackinn.com, e-mail mtnrooms@aol.com. DELUXE.

909-866-8200, 800-524-6600, fax 909-866-1580; www.bigbear vacations.com, e-mail shoreacres@bigbear.net. ULTRA-DELUXE.

Located "on the quiet side of the lake," the **Quail Cove Lakeside Lodge** features six pine-paneled, rustic cabins with full kitchens, wood-burning fireplaces, and private baths. The whole property borders a bay on one side and a creek on the other, where kids swim all summer long. There's boat access, and the fishing is prime. Other amenities include porches and barbecues. Pets are welcome. ~ 39111 North Shore Drive, Fawnskin; 909-866-5957, 800-595-2683; www.quailcove.com, e-mail quailcove@ bigbear.com. MODERATE TO ULTRA-DELUXE.

For a true bed-and-breakfast experience, stay at **Windy Point Inn**. Situated lake-, forest-, and mountainfront, this quaint establishment offers five rooms with private baths. Each room is filled with light thanks to picture windows and skylights. The decor is contemporary and amenities feature down comforters, wet bars, fridges, wood-burning fireplaces, whirlpool tubs, and private decks. There's a spacious sitting room with a fireplace where you can spend a cold winter's day chatting with other visitors. A full country breakfast is served every morning, as are afternoon hors d'oeuvres. ~ 39015 North Shore Drive, Fawnskin; 909-866-2746, fax 909-866-1593; www.windypointinn.com. DELUXE TO ULTRA-DELUXE.

At the **Cedar Glen Inn**, there's a simple, wood-paneled café, where they serve breakfast until 2 p.m. at inexpensive prices. There is a sandwich lunch menu and they serve dinner, too, but the bargain here is eggs, eggs, eggs. No dinner on Tuesday. ~ 28942 Hook Creek Road, Cedar Glen; 909-337-8999. BUDGET TO MODERATE.

DINING

◀ *HIDDEN*

Praised by critics far and wide as Big Bear Lake's finest restaurant, the **Iron Squirrel** is a class act indeed. It's quite a delight to find escargots, duckling in orange sauce, and scrumptious dessert pastries at a restaurant deep in the mountains. But here it is, a fine Continental dining room. Dinner only. ~ 646 Pine Knot Boulevard, Big Bear Lake; 909-866-9121. MODERATE TO DELUXE.

Steak is the order of the day at **Stillwell's**, an exquisite restaurant located in the Northwood Resort. Adorned with stenciled leaf murals, antler chandeliers, and old photos of Big Bear Valley, this dining room recalls the glorious season of autumn. Three gourmet chefs preside over the menu, which includes fresh pastas, vegetarian entrées, homemade soups, and salads. ~ 40650 Village Drive, Big Bear Lake; 909-866-3121, fax 909-878-3242; www.north woodsresort.com, e-mail stillwells@northwoodsresort.com. DELUXE TO ULTRA-DELUXE.

Lake Arrowhead Village, a mock mountain chalet shopping complex, contains dozens of shops. Located directly on Lake Arrow-

SHOPPING

head, the mall includes boutiques, galleries, sporting goods stores, and sundries shops. ~ Route 189 at Route 173, Lake Arrowhead.

At **Big Bear Lake** the stores are concentrated along Pine Knot Avenue and Big Bear Boulevard (Route 18). Here you'll find crafts shops and knickknack stores. My favorite is a must-see destination called **Sugarloaf Cordwood Co.** The chain-saw carvings of bears and Indians are as big as totem poles, and the shop is cluttered with thousands of ingenious carvings. ~ 42193 Big Bear Boulevard, Big Bear Lake; 909-866-2220.

NIGHTLIFE   There are a few lounges around Lake Arrowhead and Big Bear Lake, particularly at the **Lake Arrowhead Resort**, but most are little more than pool-table bars. Their coffeehouse offers live jazz on weekends. ~ Route 189, Lake Arrowhead; 909-336-1511; www.laresort.com.

Ballroom, swing, and polka describes the music and the setting at **Defazio's.** This cowboy bar kicks up live entertainment Friday night and Sunday afternoon. Cover. ~ 28314 Winchester Road, Winchester; 909-926-1057.

PARKS   **SAN BERNARDINO NATIONAL FOREST** The most popular national forest in the country, this 670,000-acre park encompasses Lake Arrowhead, Big Bear Lake, and a half-dozen ski areas. It's divided into two sections, one covering the San Bernardino Mountains and the eastern section of the San Gabriel Mountains, the other extending across the San Jacinto Mountains. Topographically, the preserve reaches from desert to mountains, Joshua trees to Jeffrey pines. There are six peaks over 10,000 feet high, four wilderness areas, and 538 miles of hiking trails (as well as a 193-mile section of the Pacific Crest Trail). The park's lakes and 110 miles of streams teem with trout, crappie, bluegill, and smallmouth bass. Skiers, anglers, and boaters will also find complete amenities. Facilities include picnic areas, restrooms, and showers. Day-use fee, $5. ~ Off Route 18 north of San Bernardino is the main highway through the national forest's northern section. Routes 74 and 243, between Hemet and Palm Springs, lead through the southern portion; 909-382-2600, fax 909-383-5770; www.bigbeardiscoverycenter.org.

The Milky Way will provide most of your evening entertainment in the San Bernardino Mountains.

▲ There are 47 campgrounds including 45 sites with hookups. Campgrounds have developed tent/RV sites; $16 to $20 per night for developed sites, $34 to $48 per night for sites with hookups. Reservations: 877-444-6777.

SILVERWOOD LAKE STATE RECREATION AREA A 976-acre lake and 13 miles of hiking trails make this park a prime destination. It's located at 3355 feet elevation in the San Bernardino Mountains. Except for the recreation area and marina, Silverwood remains undeveloped, a great place to swim and fish. Almost 130 species of birds have been spotted here; coyotes, bobcats, and black bears range the forested slopes that encircle the lake. Trout, bass, bluegill, crappie, and catfish inhabit the lake. There are restrooms, picnic areas, a snack bar, a store, boat rentals, and lifeguards. Day-use fee, $3. ~ Route 138, about 30 miles north of San Bernardino; 760-389-2303.

▲ There are 136 tent/RV sites (no hookups); $8 per night. Reservations required: 800-444-7275.

Extending south from the San Bernardino Mountains, California's Inland Empire encompasses the cities of San Bernardino, Redlands, and Riverside. Once a cattle-ranching region and later a prime citrus-growing area, this interior belt continues being developed at a mind-boggling rate. The Inland Empire stretches over a wide area—it's not really feasible to see everything in just a day or two without spending most of your time in in the car.

Inland Empire

The region does provide several possibilities: you can tour the San Bernardino Mountains, seek out sites in Riverside and Redlands, or continue farther south to the Murrieta Hot Springs and the pine forests of Mt. San Jacinto.

Blessed with water from Big Bear Lake, the town of **Redlands** became a prime citrus-growing region during the 1880s. By the turn of the 20th century wealthy Easterners seeking mild winters began building mansions amid the orange groves. Today the town numbers about 350 period homes, from tiny California-style bungalows to gaudy Victorian estates.

SIGHTS

Among the most spectacular is **Kimberly Crest**, constructed in 1897. An overweening assemblage of turrets, gables, arches, and fountains, this hilltop château is surrounded by five acres of Italian gardens. The grounds are open daily and there are tours of the house every Thursday through Sunday from 1 to 4 p.m. Closed August. Admission. ~ 1325 Prospect Drive, Redlands; 909-792-2111, fax 909-798-1716; www.kimberlycrest.org.

Redlands also takes pride in its public buildings. Several brick stores line Orange Street (just north of Redlands Boulevard), a commercial strip highlighted by the Grecian-style **Santa Fe Railroad Station**.

The **A. K. Smiley Public Library** is a Moorish structure dramatized by carved sandstone friezes, stained-glass windows, and elaborate woodwork. ~ 125 West Vine Street, Redlands; 909-798-7565; www.akspl.org, e-mail admin@akspl.org.

Behind this 1898 edifice stands the **Lincoln Memorial Shrine**, a noteworthy museum devoted to Abraham Lincoln. Built of polished limestone in 1932, the octagonal building displays marvelous WPA-type murals. Closed Monday.

San Bernardino County Museum, one of the region's major cultural and natural history facilities, has three floors of changing exhibits. There's an anthropology and history hall with Indian artifacts and covered wagons, plus an excellent mineral collection, fossils, North American mammals, and fine arts. It also features the third-largest bird egg collection in North America, and a kid-friendly exploration station. Around the grounds you'll find orange groves and antique mining equipment as well as odds and ends from the golden age of the railroad. Closed Monday. Admission. ~ 2024 Orange Tree Lane, Redlands; 909-307-2669, fax 909-307-0539; www.sbcountymuseum.org, e-mail museum@ sbcounty.gov.

Whitewashed adobe buildings surround a tranquil courtyard at **Asistencia Misión de San Gabriel**. Built in 1830 as an outpost of the San Gabriel Mission, the entire site was used during later years as a rancho. The tree-shaded plaza is a wonderful place to sit and ponder; to divert your attention, there are two small museums re-creating the era of padres and pioneers. Closed Sunday, Monday, a week in December, and during the summer; call ahead. ~ 26930 Barton Road, Redlands; 909-793-5402.

The **Yucaipa Adobe** in neighboring Yucaipa dates to 1842. As the oldest standing two-story adobe in San Bernardino County, the house is a showcase of artifacts from the era. With overhanging trees and rusting farm implements, the surrounding yard is another throwback to California's colonial era. Closed Sunday and Monday. ~ 32183 Kentucky Street, Yucaipa; 909-795-3485.

HIDDEN ▶ A **country drive** out on Oak Glen Road will carry you past orange groves and into apple country. Orchards, blossoming each spring and heavy with fruit in autumn, blanket the landscape. Between Yucaipa and Cherry Valley the road winds through foothills, passing cider mills and roadside stands.

Imaginative but often overlooked, the **Edward–Dean Museum and Gardens** has a rare selection of fine furniture, porcelain, and crystal. The museum has gathered one of the country's best collections of Far Eastern bronzes. The beautifully landscaped grounds are also a pleasure to visit. Open Friday through Sunday, or by appointment. Admission. ~ 9401 Oak Glen Road, Cherry Valley; 909-845-2626, fax 909-845-2628; www.edward-deanmuseum.org, e-mail soonloves@aol.com.

Two cities, **San Bernardino** and **Riverside**, dominate the Inland Empire. While the former has few noteworthy attractions, the latter provides visitors with several opportunities. Riverside's chief landmark is 1337-foot **Mount Rubidoux**, a rocky prominence on the west side of town. Capped by a memorial cross and peace tower, the cactus-coated hill affords a full-circle vista of the Inland Valley. A narrow thoroughfare, Mount Rubidoux Drive, corkscrews to the summit. (Cars are no longer allowed on Mount Rubidoux Drive but you can walk all the way up to the top.)

Pride of the city is the **Riverside County Court House,** a beaux-arts beauty built in 1903. The community also boasts several museums. ~ 4050 Main Street, Riverside.

The **Riverside Art Museum**, set in a 1929 Mediterranean-style building designed by Julia Morgan, hosts changing exhibits and special events. Closed Sunday. Admission. ~ 3425 Mission Inn Avenue, Riverside; 909-826-7111, fax 909-684-7332; www. riversideartmuseum.org, e-mail ram@riversideartmuseum.org.

At the nearby **Riverside Municipal Museum**, housed in the equally inviting 1912 Post Office building, cultural exhibits portray American Indian crafts and trace the history of citrus growing in the region. Among the natural-history displays are fossils, minerals, and dioramas illustrating local animal life in its native habitat. Closed Monday. ~ 3580 Mission Inn Avenue, Riverside; 909-826-5273; www.riversideca.gov/museum.

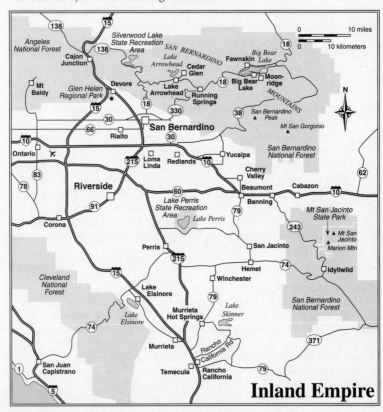

Inland Empire

The **Mission Inn,** one of California's most famous hotels, dates to the 1880s when Frank Miller began expanding his family's adobe house to accommodate guests. The home eventually became a palace with room keys, sprawling across an entire city block and entertaining four United States presidents. (Teddy Roosevelt helped Miller dedicate the structure in 1902, the Nixons were wed here, and the Reagans honeymooned here.) Built in Mission Revival fashion, with Moorish and Oriental elements, Miller's dream became a labyrinth of alcoves and art galleries, balconies and terraces, and patios. More than a hotel, the building incorporates a museum displaying an extensive collection of artifacts from around the world, including Craftsman-period furniture and Tiffany stained glass. But really, the entire building is an antique-filled museum. You can arrange a docent-guided walking tour (fee) by calling the Mission Inn Foundation at 909-788-9556. ~ 3649 Mission Inn Avenue, Riverside; 909-784-0300, fax 909-683-1342; www.missioninn.com, e-mail sales@missioninn.com.

If you tour the campus of the **University of California at Riverside,** located at the east end of University Avenue, be sure to take in the **Botanic Gardens.** Extending across 39 acres of rugged terrain, it contains cactus, rose, and iris gardens as well as a fruit orchard. The preserve specializes in plants from California, Australia, and southern Africa. ~ 909-787-4650; www.gardens.ucr.edu.

Down in **Perris,** a town better known as a center for hot-air ballooning, the **Orange Empire Railway Museum** displays freight and passenger cars, cabooses, and trolleys. A kind of junkyard for trains, this outdoor museum also contains a station house and several antique buildings. The facility is rather disorganized, however, with exhibits scattered across a sprawling railyard. On weekends and minor holidays, when they muster enough volunteers, the museum provides train and trolley rides. Admission for rides and on special-event days. ~ 2201 South A Street, Perris; 909-657-2605 or 909-943-3020; www.oerm.org.

The 19th-century town of **San Jacinto,** rapidly developing in all directions, preserves its heritage along Main Street, where falsefront buildings line several blocks.

FOLKLORIC THEATER

Hemet is home to the **Ramona,** an annual re-enactment of Helen Hunt Jackson's fabled love story of an Indian maiden. The Ramona Bowl, a natural amphitheater where the play is presented, is set in the foothills of Mt. San Jacinto and utilizes the rocky terrain as its stage. ~ 27400 Ramona Bowl Road, Hemet; 909-658-3111, 800-645-4465, fax 909-658-2695; www. ramonabowl.com, e-mail ramona@ramonabowl.com.

The American Indians portrayed in the Ramona Pageant (see "Folkloric Theater" sidebar) once occupied the entire area. An outstanding example of their artistry is evident at the **Maze Stone**   ◄ *HIDDEN* outside Hemet. This large, perfectly preserved pictograph, carved into a hillside boulder, presents a detailed labyrinth. To get there, take Route 74 about five miles west from Hemet; turn north on California Avenue; turn left on Tres Cerritos Avenue and follow for two and two-tenths miles; then turn right on Reinhardt Canyon Road.

A geologic hot spot, the Inland Empire contains some of California's finest spas. At **Glen Ivy Hot Springs Spa** you can down a platter of nachos from the snack bar while relaxing in a jacuzzi, sauna, or mineral pool. Get a massage or a sea kelp wrap, or head for the favorite spot—one for which Glen Ivy has gained its nickname—the red clay mud bath. Be sure to try the Grotto, an underground body moisturizing treatment. ~ 25000 Glen Ivy Road, Corona; 909-277-3529, 800-454-8772, fax 909-277-1202; www.glenivy.com, e-mail info@glenivy.com.

Like many towns in transition throughout the Inland Empire, **Temecula** is an Old West community that is simply exploding with development. Falsefront stores still line Front and Main streets, with wooden sidewalks leading to antique stores. And the **Temecula Valley Museum**, located in Sam Hicks Monument Park, preserves the village's early history. Among the displays are Indian artifacts, a diorama of the town, and antique machinery. Closed Monday. ~ Sam Hicks Monument Park, 28314 Mercedes Street, Temecula; 909-694-6450, fax 909-506-6871; www.city oftemecula.org.

Travel east from Temecula along Rancho California Road and you'll discover more than a dozen vineyards. **Callaway Coastal Winery**, largest of the lot, produces premium wines and offers free tours of its facilities. ~ 32720 Rancho California Road; 909-676-4001; www.callawaycoastal.com. At **Mount Palomar Winery** there are shady picnic areas amid 100 acres of vineyards as well as a full-service Mediterranean deli. ~ 33820 Rancho California Road; 909-676-5047; www.mountpalomar.com, e-mail mtpalomar@earthlink.net. **Maurice Carrie Vineyard and Winery**, with 113 acres and a contemporary tasting room, offers free tastings. Most of the other local wineries now charge a minimal tasting fee. ~ 34225 Rancho California Road; 909-676-1711; www.mauricecarriewinery.com, e-mail mcvrwinery@aol.com. **Thornton Winery**, in addition to the winery tour (weekends only), offers a champagne bar where, for a fee, you can sample a variety of champagnes, freshly baked breads, and goat cheese inside or on a patio overlooking its 20 acres of vineyards. ~ 32575 Rancho California Road; 909-699-0099, fax 909-699-5536; www.thorntonwine.com, e-mail info@thorntonwine.com.

LODGING Other than being the second largest city in the Inland Empire, San Bernardino has little to recommend it. Since the intersection of Routes 10 and 215 lies along the edge of town, many desert travelers use San Bernardino as a jumping-off point, though few remain more than one night. One of the most convenient motel strips is Hospitality Lane, a frontage road adjacent to Route 10. **La Quinta Inn San Bernardino**, a representative sample, has 153 units. ~ 205 East Hospitality Lane, San Bernardino; 909-888-7571, 800-531-5900, fax 909-884-3864. MODERATE.

Innkeeper Don Wilcott runs a very special establishment in Redlands. **The Edwards Mansion**, a stunning 1890 Victorian with three and a half acres of beautiful grounds, is a popular spot for weddings and special occasions. It's run as a bed and breakfast, but there are only two guest accommodations, replete with private patio and outdoor jacuzzi. ~ 2064 Orange Tree Lane, Redlands; 909-793-2031, fax 909-793-5269; www.edwards mansion.com. ULTRA-DELUXE.

The **Mission Inn** is the region's most luxurious hotel and one of the most famous hostelries in the country. Originally constructed in the 19th century, the hotel has been completely renovated to preserve its elegant and original design. A veritable palace, the Mission Inn features an arched entranceway that extends a full city block, Oriental gardens, and a cloister complete with music room and museum. The rotunda curves upward to a gallery where there are now meeting rooms and retail outlets. There are 239 rooms, an outdoor pool, a health club, a massage room, three restaurants, and two lounges. ~ 3649 Mission Inn Avenue, Riverside; 909-784-0300, 800-843-7755, fax 909-683-1342; www. missioninn.com. ULTRA-DELUXE.

If you want to indulge in the spa treatments at Glen Ivy Hot Springs Spa, be sure to spend the night at the **Ayres Inn**. The place offers French-country atmosphere in the Low Desert. There are 102 guest rooms decorated with four-poster beds and colorful prints. Guests have access to the pool and jacuzzi. A complimentary breakfast buffet is offered every morning. ~ 2260 Griffin Way, Corona; 909-734-2140, 800-448-8810, fax 909-734-4056; www.ayrescoronaeast.com, e-mail lewing@ayreshotel.com. MODERATE.

At long last there's a proper bed and breakfast in the scenic Temecula Valley wine country. **Loma Vista Bed and Breakfast** is a classy, Mission-style hilltop home overlooking vineyards. It offers a choice of ten spacious designer rooms, each done in a different decorative motif. Guests share a lovely living room with a fireplace and take breakfast family-style in a formal dining room. An outdoor hot tub and complimentary wine and cheese round out the experience. ~ 33350 La Serena Way, Temecula; 909-676-7047, fax 909-676-0077. MODERATE TO ULTRA-DELUXE.

Known mostly as a golf resort, **Temecula Creek Inn** offers a heavily wooded, rustic setting for its six lodge-like buildings. All of the 130 rooms and junior suites—which are large and comfortable—have golf-course views and amenities like terry robes and coffee makers. A restaurant on the premises looks out over the golf course. ~ 44501 Rainbow Canyon Road, Temecula; 909-694-1000, 800-962-7335, fax 909-676-8961; www.temecula creekinn.com. DELUXE.

DINING

If you're in San Bernardino, check out **GuadalaHarry's**, a hacienda-style Mexican restaurant. With its brilliantly colored walls, interior balcony, and serape decor, the place evokes a sense of the high life in Old Mexico. Despite the ironwork and handcarved beams, this multichambered establishment is reasonably priced. The menu presents a medley of *chimichanga* and taco dishes as well as *favoritos Mexicanos* like fajitas and flautas. ~ 280 East Hospitality Lane, San Bernardino; 909-889-8555, fax 909-885-8372. BUDGET TO MODERATE.

Café Champagne is ideally located overlooking the vineyards at the Thornton Winery. The elegant California-style decor makes this the perfect spot to sip champagne or wine. Entrée choices vary but typically include meat, seafood, and poultry dishes. ~ 32575 Rancho California Road, Temecula; 909-699-0088, fax 909-699-5536; www.thorntonwine.com. DELUXE TO ULTRA-DELUXE.

Despite its shopping-center location, which is really a shame considering all those lovely vineyards right down the road, **Baily's** offers one of the more sophisticated dining experiences in Temecula. Tequila shrimp flambéed tableside and filet mignon grilled with a rich demi-glaze are typical of the California-Continental menu that changes weekly. No lunch Saturday through Thursday. ~ 27644 Ynez Road, Temecula; 909-676-9567,

WINE IN THE DESERT

The Temecula Valley is not where most people would expect to find award-winning wineries. But the valley is actually a prime winegrowing region whose 18 or so wineries benefit from well-drained soil and a gap in the South Coast mountain range, which lets cool afternoon breezes from the ocean sweep across the hillside vineyards. The valley's 1500-foot elevation also helps, making for cooler summer nights. Many of the wineries offer special wine-tasting dinners and other events. See page 478 for some of the best wineries. For more information on Temecula's wineries, contact the **Temecula Valley Winegrowers Association**. ~ P.O. Box 1601, Temecula, CA 92513; 800-801-9463; www.temeculawines. org, e-mail postmaster@temeculawines.org.

fax 909-676-0257; www.baily.com, e-mail baily@baily.com. MO-
DERATE TO ULTRA-DELUXE.

NIGHTLIFE   Big-name rock and pop acts play at **Hyundai Pavilion**, an outdoor arena in a natural setting. Closed in winter. ~ Glen Helen
Regional Park, Devore; 909-886-8742.

PARKS   **GLEN HELEN REGIONAL PARK** 🏃 🚴 ⛵ 🎣 There are 500
acres of shady groves and chaparral-coated hills here at the foot
of the San Bernardino Mountains. Two lakes stocked with trout
and catfish, a nature trail through a marsh, and ample playground and picnic areas are among the features. Facilities include
restrooms, showers, paddle boat rentals, and a waterslide. Day-use
fee, $5. ~ 2555 Glen Helen Parkway, Devore (near the intersec-
tion of Routes 15 and 215); 909-880-2522, fax 909-887-1359.

▲ There are 60 tent sites; $10 per night. Camping is also
available at **Yucaipa Regional Park** (33900 Oak Glen Road, Yucaipa; 909-790-3127, fax 909-790-3121), which has 9 tent sites
and 26 RV sites (full hookups); $22 per night for RV sites, $13 per
night for tent sites.

LAKE PERRIS STATE RECREATION AREA 🏃 🚴 🐎 ⛵ 🏊 🎣
🚣 🛶 🚤 Another of the Inland Empire's attractive lakes,
Perris is bounded by the Russell Mountains and Bernasconi Hills.
It features rock-climbing areas, a sandy beach for swimming,
boat rentals, and a ten-mile bike trail around the lake. More than
100 bird species have been spotted here, including ducks and
geese, and the eastern shore is open seasonally to hunters. Everything from lizards to mule deer inhabits the surrounding sage
scrub countryside. Facilities here include picnic areas, restrooms,
showers, lifeguards, and a marina. If you fish, try for bass, trout,
catfish, and bluegill. Day-use fee, $8. ~ 17801 Lake Perris Drive,
Perris; 909-940-5603, fax 909-657-2736.

▲ There are 177 tent sites and 254 RV sites with hookups;
$20 per night for RV sites, $14 per night for tent sites.

AUTHOR FAVORITE

Ask for a table in the vault at **The Bank** and withdraw
your favorite Mexican dishes. Housed in the 1913 First National Bank
of Temecula building, this is the town's most unusual restaurant. The enchiladas, quesadillas, fajitas, and tacos, served at lunch and dinner, make
it the area's favorite Mexican eatery. ~ 28645 Front Street, Temecula;
909-676-6160, fax 909-676-8075. BUDGET TO MODERATE.

▼▼▼▼▼▼▼▼▼▼
Idyllwild

Bordering the Inland Empire to the east are the San Jacinto Mountains, a spectacular chain of 10,000-foot peaks
dividing the region from Palm Springs and the Low Desert.
Routes 243 and 74 climb into this alpine environment from the
north and west respectively.

SIGHTS

At the center of the chain sits the mile-high town of **Idyllwild**.
Tucked beneath bald granite peaks, this pine-tufted community
is surrounded by San Bernardino National Forest. Once inhabited
by Cahuilla Indians, the area now is a major tourist destination.
In addition to restaurants and shops, Idyllwild has a host of secluded cabins for rent. For information on trails and campgrounds
throughout the region, stop by the **Idyllwild County Park Nature
Center.** ~ 25225 Route 243, one mile north of Idyllwild; 909-
659-3850, fax 909-659-3106; www.idyllwildnaturecenter.net.

LODGING

Strawberry Creek Inn is a rambling old mountain home nestled
among the pines and oaks of the San Jacinto Mountains. Country-
decorated and carefully maintained, it offers a cozy, cabin-in-the-
woods atmosphere within walking distance from Idyllwild's busy
village center. Guests can choose from several original rooms in
the main house or newer ones in an added wing at the rear. A
full gourmet breakfast is served in a bright, cheery wraparound
dining porch. ~ 26370 Route 243; 909-659-3202, 800-262-
8969, fax 909-659-4707; www.strawberrycreekinn.com. MOD-
ERATE TO ULTRA-DELUXE.

A place with a name like **Knotty Pine Cabins** could easily de-
volve into a self-parody. But there they are, eight woodframe
cabins nestled in a conifer grove. Nicely secluded yet still within
walking distance of town, the units feature fireplaces, knotty-
pine walls, and homespun decorations. Some offer a living room,
bedroom, and kitchen, and price in the moderate to deluxe
range; one cabin, the "Sleepy Pine," is a single room without
kitchen at a budget price. ~ 54340 Pine Crest Drive; 909-659-
2933. BUDGET TO DELUXE.

You can also rent houses and cabins in Idyllwild through a
local agency, **Idyllwild Muirs Mountain Vacation Rentals**. Closed
Sunday. ~ 54440 North Circle Drive, Idyllwild; 909-659-4145,
877-270-3285, fax 909-659-4485; www.idyllwildcabins.com.

DINING

The local gathering place up in Idyllwild is **JC's Red Kettle**.
Homey as a log cabin, it's a knotty-pine café with lace curtains.
Breakfast items fill about half the menu and include "old-fashioned oatmeal," omelettes, and biscuits with gravy. Completing
the daily offerings are soups, salads, hamburgers, pastas, and
sandwiches. No dinner. ~ 54220 North Circle Drive; 909-659-
4063. BUDGET.

Among Idyllwild's finest restaurants is **Restaurant Gastrognome**, a pretty woodframe place with a stone fireplace and beam ceiling. The selections are diverse, the portions plentiful, and the food delicious. Beef tournedos, Australian lobster, and rack of lamb head the menu; also included are calamari and a variety of other seafood, pasta dishes, and fresh fish. No lunch on Monday. ~ 54381 Ridgeview Drive; 909-659-5055, fax 909-659-5719; www.thegnome.com. MODERATE TO ULTRA-DELUXE.

SHOPPING Idyllwild offers numerous arts-and-crafts shops. Several country roads near the village center are dotted with cabins converted into small stores.

Oakwood Village is a collection of nine such small shops and galleries typifying the local arts and crafts scene. You'll find hand-carved wooden lamps, sculpture, and oils and watercolors, all from local artists. ~ 54425 North Circle Drive, Idyllwild.

The Ice House, by contrast, demonstrates the elite influence of Palm Springs filtering into this remote mountain town. Elegant cut glass and crystal objets d'art fill the shelves along with throws and gifts. ~ 54245 North Circle Drive, Idyllwild; 909-659-5458.

PARKS **MOUNT SAN JACINTO STATE PARK** 🚶 🚲 🏇 Extending from Idyllwild in the west to Palm Springs in the east, this magnificent preserve encompasses a broad swath of the San Jacinto Mountains. It features mountain meadows and subalpine forests as well as granite peaks 10,000 feet high. The park covers about 14,000 acres, most of which constitute a wilderness area. Facilities include picnic areas, restrooms, and showers. Day-use fee, $5. ~ Route 243; the park can also be reached via the aerial tramway in Palm Springs; 909-659-2607 or 760-327-0222 (district office), fax 909-659-4769; www.sanjac.statepark.org.

Tahquitz Rock, looming 1000 feet above Idyllwild, is Southern California's tallest rock formation.

▲ About 125 sites are spread out over several campgrounds and hike-in camps and include 23 RV sites without hookups. Camping costs $14 to $19 per night, depending on site and location. There is also camping at **Idyllwild County Park** (909-659-2656).

Palm Springs Area

Take a desert landscape thatched with palm trees, add a 10,000-foot mountain to shade it from the sun, then place an ancient mineral spring deep beneath the ground. What you have is a recipe for Palm Springs. It's a spot where the average daily temperature swings from an invigorating 55° to a toasty 85°.

Little wonder that the town represents the nation's desert showplace, one of the few Western locales where winter brings the best weather. A fashionable health spa and celebrity playground, Palm Springs is the ultimate destination for sunning, swimming, and slumming. Many attractions close or have limited hours during the hot summer months, so it's advisable to call in advance.

To direct you, divert you, and help you determine an itinerary for touring the town, there are two local agencies. You may try the **Palm Springs Desert Resorts**, which is closed on weekends. ~ Atrium Building, Route 111, Rancho Mirage; 760-770-9000, 800-417-3529, fax 760-770-9001; www.palmspringsusa.com. Printed information and friendly advice is also available at the **Palm Springs Chamber of Commerce**. Closed Saturday and Sunday. ~ 190 West Amado Road, Palm Springs; 760-325-1577, fax 760-325-8549; www.pschamber.org, e-mail pschamber@pschamber.org.

SIGHTS

They'll inevitably point you toward the **Palm Springs Desert Museum**, one of California's great regional art centers. Contained in a dynamic and contemporary structure with stone facade, the museum combines desert art, culture, and natural history. There are dioramas illustrating local animal life, a wing devoted to Death Valley, exhibits of basketry by indigenous Cahuilla Indians, and stark black-and-white photos of the American West. Set against the mountains in an exclusive section of Palm Springs, the complex includes works of contemporary art as well as a section devoted to Western American art. The most appealing places of all are the sculpture gardens—lovely, restful plots with splashing fountains and native palms. There's also a 22,000-square-foot addition housing a lecture hall, a theater, and an education center. Closed Monday. Admission. ~ 101 Museum Drive, Palm Springs; 760-325-7186, fax 760-327-5069; www.psmuseum.org, e-mail info@psmuseum.org.

A few blocks to the east is Palm Canyon Drive, site of the **Palm Springs Walk of Stars**. In the style of Hollywood's Walk of Fame, gold stars embedded in granite memorialize celebrities such as Sophia Loren, Elvis Presley, Marilyn Monroe, and William Powell. ~ On Palm Canyon Drive, between Alejo Road and Tahquitz Canyon Way.

To learn about the early inhabitants of Palm Springs, visit the tiny **Agua Caliente Cultural Museum**. Changing exhibits illustrate the history and culture of the Agua Caliente Indians with photographs and artifacts. Closed Monday and Tuesday. ~ 219 South Palm Canyon Drive, Palm Springs; 760-323-0151, fax 760-322-7724; www.accmuseum.org, e-mail accmuseum@acc museum.org.

If it's local history you're after, the **Village Green Heritage Center** will do quite nicely. Located in a small downtown park are three historic buildings. ~ 221 South Palm Canyon Drive, Palm Springs.

In the **McCallum Adobe Museum** (760-323-8297), you'll find tools, fashions, children's toys, paintings, and books from Palm Springs' early years. Constructed in 1884, the town's oldest building, it's also filled with photos of Hollywood stars, including one of Groucho Marx without his trademark moustache. Admission.

Neighboring on the old McCallum place is **Cornelia White House** (760-323-8297), the 1893 home of a pioneer woman. Fabricated from railroad ties, it displays 20th-century appurtenances, including a wrought-iron wood stove and Palm Springs' first telephone. Both museums are closed from mid-October to May and Monday and Tuesday. Admission.

Had Cornelia lived longer, she could have patronized **Ruddy's General Store Museum** (760-327-2156). A re-creation of a 1930s-era general store, this marvelous museum is literally lined with tins of Chase & Sanborn coffee, boxes of Rinso Detergent, and an entire wall of apothecary jars. One of the most complete collections of its kind, it contains an inventory of over 6000 items, almost all filled with their original contents. The store has penny gumball machines, nickel candy bars, and, yes, Prince Albert in a can. Open weekends only during the summer and Thursday through Sunday the rest of the year. Admission.

One of the most luxuriant labyrinths you will ever traverse is a place called the **Moorten Botanical Garden**. The result of a 50-year effort by the Moorten family, this living monument to the desert displays over 3000 varieties of desert plants. There are prickly pears, agaves, and a cactarium with a desert's worth of cacti in a single greenhouse. It's an enchanted garden, inhabited by birds and turtles, dotted with petrified trees, and filled with dinosaur fossils. Closed Wednesday. Admission. ~ 1701 South Palm Canyon Drive, Palm Springs; 760-327-6555.

Renowned as a retreat for millionaires and movie stars, Palm Springs for centuries was the private domain of the Agua Caliente Indians. A band of the Cahuilla Indian group, the Agua Calientes roamed the territory, seeking out the cool canyons of the San Jacinto Mountains in summer, then descending during winter months to the warmth and healing mineral springs of the desert floor.

HIDDEN ►

Among the most scenic parcels are the **Indian Canyons**, a string of four lush mountain valleys that reach from desert bottom-lands deep into the San Jacinto Mountains. Visitors can spend the day hiking, exploring, and picnicking in these preserves:

Andreas Canyon, a spectacular mountain gorge, contains Indian rock art as well as mortar holes left by Indian women pounding beans and acorns into meal. A stream tumbles through the valley, cutting the canyon walls and watering the 150 plant species that parallel its course. From here a one-mile trail leads to **Murray Canyon**, where more than 750 palm trees cluster around deep pools and small waterfalls. Mountain sheep and wild ponies roam this remote chasm.

Just three miles north of Palm Canyon, the once litter-filled and graffiti-covered **Tahquitz Canyon** has been restored to its natural state through the joint efforts of the Agua Caliente tribe and the city of Palm Springs. Part of the Agua Caliente Reservation, the canyon features a spectacular 60-foot waterfall, ancient petroglyphs and irrigation systems, and an abundance of native flora and fauna. Two-hour ranger-led tours begin at the visitors center. Hours and tour schedules vary; call ahead for details. Admission. ~ 500 West Mesquite Boulevard; 760-416-7044; www.tahquitzcanyon.com.

Palm Canyon stretches for 15 miles and contains more than 3000 Washingtonia palm trees, some as old as 2000 years. An island of palms in a desert sea, it displays exotic rock formations and mountain pools. Admission. ~ Four miles south of Palm Springs, off South Palm Canyon Road; 760-325-3400, 800-790-3398, fax 760-325-0593; www.aguacaliente.org.

If hiking 14 miles up Palm Canyon is really a bit much, you can soar into the San Jacinto Mountains on the **Palm Springs Aerial Tramway**. Climbing at a teeth-clattering 50-degree angle and ascending more than a mile to 8516 feet elevation, this mountain shuttle makes Disney's Space Mountain seem like a cakewalk. The rotating tramcars, offering 360-degree views, are just icing on

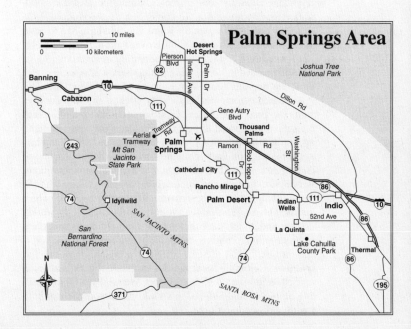

the cake. Admission. ~ Tramway Road, Palm Springs; 760-325-1391; www.pstramway.com, e-mail pstramway@pstramway.com.

The reward for those white knuckles is a view of the Coachella Valley from Joshua Tree to the Salton Sea. On a clear day you might not see forever, but you will spot a mountain peak near Las Vegas, 175 miles away.

In addition to the usual snack bar/souvenir shop amenities, there are several trails at the top, including a three-quarter-mile nature loop. The nearby **ranger station**, which serves this section of Mount San Jacinto State Park, has information on longer hikes. From mid-November to mid-April, snow permitting, the Nordic Ski Center is open for cross-country skiing. ~ 760-327-0222.

South of Palm Springs lie **Rancho Mirage** and **Palm Desert**, two extraordinarily wealthy bedroom communities. Parked in the middle of the desert, these havens for the rich and retired display so many country clubs, palm trees, and landscaped estates as to create a kind of release from reality. They name streets after people like Bob Hope and Frank Sinatra and use water everywhere—for fountains, cascades, golf greens—in a splendid display of excess.

The ultimate expression of this profligacy is **Marriott's Desert Springs Resort and Spa**, a 400-acre resort with hanging gardens, five-tiered waterfalls, and a lagoon with gondolas. There are lovely crystalline lakes and one of the swimming pools is a 12,000-square-foot extravaganza. To combine such unrestrained decadence with so much water, the Romans would have had to build Venice. ~ 74-855 Country Club Drive, Palm Desert; 760-341-2211, fax 760-341-1872; www.desertspringsresort.com.

Aptly named indeed is **The Living Desert**, a 1200-acre nature park that presents a raw and realistic picture of desert life. This grand outdoor zoo contains giraffes, gazelles, and Arabian oryx from the deserts of Africa. Lizards, rattlesnakes, and screech owls inhabit a special display that simulates the desert at night; and a walk-through aviary houses finches, green herons, and hermit thrushes. The Eagle Canyon section, a wildlife exhibit and endangered species breeding center, is home to mountain lions, wolves, and golden eagles, among other animals. Village WaTuTu features leopards, camels, hyenas, and a "petting Kraal." There are also botanical gardens with vegetation from eight of the world's deserts, and hiking trails that wind for more than six miles into nearby foothills. Ponds re-create life at a desert oasis, and a special tortoise exhibit presents some of the region's most familiar creatures. Culturally speaking, this exceptional park is an oasis in itself. Admission. ~ 47-900 Portola Avenue, Palm Desert; 760-346-5694, fax 760-568-9685; www.livingdesert.org, e-mail information@livingdesert.org.

For an overview of the entire area, head up Route 74 on the **Palms to Pines Tour**, which will carry you high into the Santa Rosa Mountains. Desert ironwood trees and creosote bushes front the road, giving way at higher elevations to manzanita and mountain mahogany. As the highway climbs to lofty heights, dramatic vistas of the Coachella Valley open to view. If you're ambitious, it's possible to connect with Routes 243, 10, and 111 on a 130-mile loop trip through the San Jacinto Mountains and back to Palm Springs.

You can take a 20-minute mule ride (summer only) around the slopes of Mt. San Jacinto before descending on the Palm Springs Aerial Tramway.

Indio may be flat, dry, and barren, but it has one homegrown product that puts the place on everyone's map—dates. The only region in the U.S. where the fruit is grown, Indio boasts 3000 acres of date palms. Tall, stately trees with fan-shaped fronds, they transform a bland agricultural town into an attractive oasis.

At **Shield's Date Gardens** they serve date shakes and date ice cream. Unfortunately, the most exciting thing about their movie, *The Romance and Sex Life of the Date*, is the title. ~ 80-225 Route 111, Indio; 760-347-0996, 800-414-2555, fax 760-342-3288; www.shieldsdates.com, e-mail shieldate@aol.com.

If you still haven't had your fill, the **Coachella Valley Museum and Cultural Center** features displays on local agriculture, including the date industry. This small regional showplace also contains an Indian room with artifacts from the Cahuilla tribe and a collection of heirlooms donated by local residents. Closed Monday and Tuesday, and from mid-June to mid-September. Admission. ~ 82-616 Miles Avenue, Indio; 760-342-6651, fax 760-863-5232; www.coachellavalleymuseum.org.

LODGING

Travelers interested in rubbing elbows with show-biz types should consider the elegant little **Ingleside Inn**. Garbo slept here, they say, and Sinatra, Schwarzeneger, and Shields. And why not? The double rooms, villas, and minisuites are cozy, charming, and laden with unusual antiques. Extras include fireplaces, private steambaths, and terraces, but everyone gets the same attentive service here. ~ 200 West Ramon Road, Palm Springs; 760-325-0046, 800-772-6655, fax 760-325-0710; www.inglesideinn.com, e-mail contact@inglesideinn.com. MODERATE TO ULTRA-DELUXE.

Ballantines Hotel, a '50s-themed complex, has 14 rooms surrounding a pool. The interior patio has a blue astroturf sun deck, and the different theme rooms—such as the Marilyn Monroe and the Jaspar Johns—which contain period furniture by Eames, Miller, and Bertoin. The suites and rooms are very spacious; most have dressing areas and some are equipped with kitchens. Adults preferred. ~ 1420 North Indian Canyon Drive, Palm Springs; 760-320-1178, 800-780-3464, fax 760-320-5308; www.ballantines hotels.com, e-mail info@ballantineshotels.com. ULTRA-DELUXE.

With only eight exquisitely furnished rooms, **The Willows** is an exclusive retreat into privilege and class. Located in the historic section of Palm Springs, this handsomely restored 1924 Italianate-style villa features a frescoed ceiling in the dining room, a garden waterfall, fireplaces, pillowed stone floors, antiques, clawfoot bathtubs, and pedestal sinks. The inn attracts a diverse and well-traveled clientele. Complimentary gourmet breakfast and evening wine reception are included. Closed July and August. ~ 412 West Tahquitz Canyon Way, Palm Springs; 760-320-0771, 800-966-9597, fax 760-320-0780; www.thewillowspalmsprings.com, e-mail innkeeper@thewillowspalmsprings.com. ULTRA-DELUXE.

The private villas at **La Mancha Private Villas and Spa Resort** are the last word in romantic escapism. Spanish-Moroccan architecture, high arched windows, and massive ceiling beams give the 50 accommodations an almost castlelike ambience. All the villas have private courtyards; many have private pools. Spa and in-room dining are among the amenities. ~ 444 North Avenida Caballeros, Palm Springs; 760-323-1773, 866-673-7501, fax 760-323-5928; www.la-mancha.com, e-mail reservations@la-mancha.com. DELUXE TO ULTRA-DELUXE.

HIDDEN ► In a small personalized hotel like **Desert House Inn** it's rare to find yourself in the hands of seasoned, professional hotelieres. But here's an exception. Before purchasing this charming six-room inn and remodeling it, Doug and Donna Mannoff had long careers in the hotel business. This one is a labor of love and it shows. You'll find four studios with kitchenettes, and two rooms with refrigerators; five rooms sit poolside. If you can muster the energy to leave the pool and sun deck, you'll find yourself within walking distance of some of the city's finest restaurants. ~ 200 South Cahuilla Road, Palm Springs; 800-549-9230, fax 760-325-6736; www.deserthouseinn.com, e-mail info@deserthouseinn.com. MODERATE TO ULTRA-DELUXE.

Casa Cody Hotel bills itself as "a country bed and breakfast inn." The second oldest hostelry in Palm Springs, Casa Cody has

AUTHOR FAVORITE

The retro scene reaches its zenith in Palm Springs at the ten-room **Orbit In**, a truly classic modern hotel. Built in 1957, it has been restored beyond its original sleek-lined beauty. The rooms feature classic furniture and art (originals, not reproductions) from the giants of the period: Eames, Niguchi, and Bertioa. Some splendid details include saltwater pools, outdoor cooling misters, DSL data ports, cruiser bikes, and spa services. It's a time trip. ~ 562 West Arenas Boulevard, Palm Springs; 760-323-3585, 877-996-7248, fax 760-323-3599; www.orbitin.com, e-mail mail@orbitin.com. DELUXE TO ULTRA-DELUXE.

a hideaway feel that recalls the early gentility of Palm Springs. Its 23 guest rooms have been refurbished in a Southwest-chic decor. All but two have kitchens and some have fireplaces. A 1910 two-bedroom adobe, where Charlie Chaplin once stayed, is also available. Breakfast is served poolside. ~ 175 South Cahuilla Road, Palm Springs; 760-320-9346, 800-231-2639, fax 760-325-8610; www.casacody.com, e-mail casacody@aol.com. MODERATE TO ULTRA-DELUXE.

With its overweening wealth, Palm Springs inevitably possesses numerous luxury resorts. Unlike many, **Villa Royale Inn** displays its richness in an understated, personalized fashion. Every room of this walled-in complex follows an individual theme, reflecting the art and culture of a different European country. Many have kitchens, fireplaces, and private patios. Covering more than three acres, the inn's grounds are a series of interior courtyards framed by pillars and planted in bougainvillea. Amid brick footpaths and asymmetrical gardens are two swimming pools, jacuzzis, and a restaurant. The complimentary breakfast is cooked to order, and served alfresco. ~ 1620 Indian Trail, Palm Springs; 760-327-2314, 800-245-2314, fax 760-322-3794; www.villaroyale.com, e-mail info@villaroyale.com. DELUXE TO ULTRA-DELUXE.

The hot mineral pools that the Agua Caliente Indians originally discovered are today part of the **Spa Resort Casino**. Bubbling from the ground at 106° and containing 32 trace minerals, the waters made Palm Springs famous. They have also made the Spa a unique resort. On the grounds are two Roman-style tubs, an outside swimming pool, and spa facilities including inhalation rooms, dry saunas, and mineral baths. The entire hotel is lavishly appointed with desert-colored carpets and contemporary decor. A pictorial history of the Agua Caliente tribe adorns the lobby walls. Guest rooms are equally fashionable. There's a casino on the premises. ~ 100 North Indian Canyon Drive, Palm Springs; 760-325-1461, 800-854-1279, fax 760-325-3344; www.spare sortcasino.com, e-mail hotel@srcmail.net. ULTRA-DELUXE.

If you listen to their publicity agents, many resorts are destinations unto themselves, providing everything a traveler could possibly desire. **Two Bunch Palms** is an entire oasis unto itself, a world of hot mineral baths surrounded by ancient palm trees. This exclusive 45-acre retreat, with its guarded entrance, serves as a hideaway for Hollywood celebrities. They've been visiting since the 1930s, when mobster Al Capone reputedly built the place. According to local lore, he turned this desert retreat into a fortress, constructing a stone house with a lookout turret and secret escape tunnel. The gangster's gambling casino has given way to a gourmet restaurant and his ultra-secure hideout has become an informal resort. Guests soak in the hot mineral pool, utilize a spa facility with saunas and massage therapists, and wander an estate that includes lawns, tennis courts, swimming pool, nude sunbathing areas, and koi ponds. Closed the last week of August. ~ 67-425 Two Bunch Palms Trail, Desert Hot Springs; 760-329-8791, 800-472-4334, fax 760-329-1317; www.twobunchpalms. com, e-mail whiteowl@twobunchpalms.com. ULTRA-DELUXE.

Guests at any of the 240-plus accommodations at **The Lodge at Rancho Mirage** have only to open the French doors to their patio or balcony to enjoy a commanding view of the entire Palm Springs area. Located on a 650-foot-high plateau in the Santa Rosa Mountain foothills, this is a 24-acre hotel and tennis resort. Fine artwork, custom fabrics, antiques, crown moldings, and luxury-level amenities are standard in the rooms; the suites are truly elegant. ~ 68-900 Frank Sinatra Drive, Rancho Mirage; 760-321-8282, 800-367-7625, fax 760-321-8997; www.rockresorts.com, e-mail reservationsrm@rockresorts.com. MODERATE TO ULTRA-DELUXE.

DINING

A spacious hacienda with murals, fountains, and inlaid tile, **Las Casuelas Terraza** is a classic Mexican dining room. Pass through the archways and you'll discover hanging plants and exquisite wrought-iron decorations throughout. The outdoor patio features a palapa bar, a stage, and a dancing area. A step above other Mexican restaurants, the establishment serves *pollo asado* (marinated chicken), *pescado greco* (fish filet in garlic and wine), and *camarones florencio* (shrimp in salsa), as well as the standard south-of-the-border entrées. ~ 222 South Palm Canyon Drive, Palm Springs; 760-325-2794, fax 760-327-4174; www.lascasuelaster raza.com. MODERATE.

For entertainment with your dinner, make reservations at **Moody Productions**. You'll dine at Livreri's Italian restaurant and choose from a bill of fare including osso buco, angelhair primavera, or shrimp scampi. An ensemble with five vocalists and a pianist will perform "A Swingin' Salute to Sinatra" and, at the conclusion of this festive but relaxed evening, the waiter will present you with an extravagant dinner tab. Closed Sunday through

AUTHOR FAVORITE

If you do nothing but admire the stained glass at **Lyon's English Grille**, it will prove worth the price of admission. This grand British dining room also displays a museum-quality collection of plates, Toby jugs, and art pieces from Olde England. The bill of fare at this enchanting establishment includes steak-and-kidney pie, braised lamb shank, roast duckling, prime rib, calf's liver, and fresh seafood. Dinner only. Closed July and August. ~ 233 East Palm Canyon Drive, Palm Springs; 760-327-1551, fax 760-322-9833. MODERATE TO ULTRA-DELUXE.

Friday. ~ 350 South Indian Canyon Drive, Palm Springs; 760-323-1806, 800-422-9394, fax 760-323-2909. ULTRA-DELUXE.

Melvyn's is one of those famous establishments with as many awards on the wall as items on the menu. Among the toniest addresses in town, it's a classic Continental restaurant complete with mirrors, crystal chandeliers, and wooden upholstered chairs. Celebrities have frequented the place for years. Among its other attributes is an inventory of entrées that features Maryland crab cakes, grilled fish, and châteaubriand. Sunday brunch is also served. ~ 200 West Ramon Road, in the Ingleside Inn, Palm Springs; 760-325-0046, 800-772-6655; www.inglesideinn.com, e-mail contact@inglesideinn.com. DELUXE TO ULTRA-DELUXE.

Le Vallauris is an enclave of Mediterranean cuisine and decor just off the main drag. A piano bar sets the tone in this converted private residence for rich dishes such as duck foie gras and roasted rack of lamb. A garden of ficus trees and blooming cyclamen warm up this attractive two-room restaurant. ~ 385 West Tahquitz Canyon Way, Palm Springs; 760-325-5059; www.levallauris.com, e-mail vallauris@aol.com. ULTRA-DELUXE.

Kam Lum, a Chinese eatery set in a mini-mall, serves Cantonese dishes such as orange beef and shrimp with lobster sauce, as well as a dozen specialty dishes. Closed Monday. ~ 66610 8th Street, Desert Hot Springs; 760-251-1244. BUDGET.

El Gallito Restaurant is a cheap, funky, bare-bones Mexican restaurant with good food at even better prices. There are piñatas and hokey paintings on the walls and some talented people back in the kitchen. The crowd is local, and the menu is solid and predictable. Closed Monday and the month of August. ~ 68-820 Grove Street, Cathedral City; 760-328-7794. BUDGET.   ◄ HIDDEN

Everybody's favorite lunch counter is **Louise's Pantry**, a landmark café so popular with the local gentry that people are inevitably lined up outside the door. This is a plastic-and-formica eatery providing standard American fare. Settle into a booth, pull up a counter stool, or relax on the patio and dine on meatloaf, pork chops, or filet of sole. Breakfast and lunch only. ~ 44491 Town Center Way, Palm Desert; 760-346-9320; e-mail mrspehney@aol.com. BUDGET TO MODERATE.   ◄ HIDDEN

The Inn on El Paseo is a little old-fashioned, which might be the reason it's so popular with local residents. White walls, flowery curtains, and oak booths are a trademark here. The cuisine, accordingly, is American, with such entrées as fresh salmon, beef medallions, and rack of lamb. ~ 73-445 El Paseo, Palm Desert; 760-340-1236, fax 760-340-2624. MODERATE TO DELUXE.

Palm Canyon Drive, the Main Street of Palm Springs, contains the region's greatest concentration of shops. There are almost as many signature stores as palm trees along this swank boulevard. The center within the center is **Desert Fashion Plaza**, a stone-   **SHOPPING** floor-and-splashing-fountain labyrinth, which wends past jewelers, designer boutiques, and department stores. Under renovation until fall 2004. ~ Between Tahquitz Way and Amado Road, Palm Springs.

Adagio Galleries down the street has a fine collection of Latin American and Southwestern art. The inventory includes oil paintings, pastels, and bronze as well as sculptures and ceramics. Closed in August and on Tuesday. ~ 193 South Palm Canyon Drive, Palm Springs; 760-320-2230; www.adagiogalleries.com.

The region's most elegant stores line El Paseo, a multiblock extravaganza that runs through the heart of Palm Desert. Among the galleries lining this well-heeled boulevard, is **San Soucie Art Glass Studios**. More of a shop than a gallery, San Soucie's master craftsmen have been turning out custom-designed sandblasted carved glass art since 1976. Pick up a set of glass doors, etched windows, mirrors, tables, or sculptures. Closed Sunday; open Saturday by appointment. ~ 73-890 El Paseo, Palm Desert; 760-340-3000, fax 760-340-3305; www.sanssoucie.com.

Stop by **Plaza Gifts**, the gift shop at the Living Desert. They have an excellent collection of books, prints, and gift items, all relating to the desert. Call ahead for hours. ~ 47-900 Portola Avenue, Palm Desert; 760-346-5694; www.livingdesert.org.

Cathedral City has several shops that will delight any budget-minded shopper. At **Little Baja** you will find Mexican pottery, wall masks, statuary, and pre-Columbian idols. ~ 34-750 Date Palm Drive, Cathedral City; 760-328-3708.

NIGHTLIFE   A growing Palm Springs tradition of recent vintage is **Villagefest**, a weekly night street fair on Palm Canyon Drive that features food booths, live music, and 150 artists and craftspersons. The fair takes place every Thursday evening throughout the year.

The center of action in downtown Palm Springs is **Zeldaz**, a rocking disco with video screens, two dancefloors, and eight bars. Contests punctuate sets of deejay music. Closed Monday and Tuesday during winter, and Sunday through Monday during summer. Cover. ~ 169 North Indian Canyon Drive, Palm Springs; 760-325-2375; www.zeldaznightclub.com.

Sunday's comedy night at Zeldaz is always good for a laugh.

The place to view and be viewed in this celebrity-conscious town is **Melvyn's**. The lounge at this fashionable Continental restaurant offers piano bar music and a small dancefloor. A jazz jam is held every Sunday. ~ Ingleside Inn, 200 West Ramon Road, Palm Springs; 760-325-0046; www.inglesideinn.com.

Over at the Wyndham Palm Springs Hotel, **The Lobby Bar** is a pleasant spot for a quiet drink. ~ 888 East Tahquitz Way, Palm Springs; 760-322-6000.

State-of-the-art and ultra-fashionable, the **McCallum Theatre for the Performing Arts** represents the desert showplace for Broadway touring companies, symphonies, dramas, and concerts. This 1127-seat theater is the cultural capital of the Palm Springs area. ~ 73-000 Fred Waring Drive, Palm Desert; 760-340-2787 (box office), fax 760-341-9508; www.mccallumtheatre.com.

LAKE CAHUILLA COUNTY PARK   **PARKS**
Stark is the word for this place. It's a manmade lake with dirt banks, very little vegetation, and bald mountains looming in every direction. One section of the park has been landscaped with lawns and palm trees; the rest is as dusty as the surrounding desert. Since the lake is stocked with trout, bluegill, and catfish, most people come to fish, swim, or camp. The park offers picnic areas, a swimming pool, lifeguards, a playground, restrooms, and showers. From May through September, the park is only open Friday through Monday. Day-use fee, $2. ~ 58-075 Jefferson Street, La Quinta; 760-564-4712, fax 760-564-2506.

There are 65 RV sites, all with hookups, and 85 primitive sites; $16 for hookups, $12 for primitive sites. This park is locked at 10 p.m., so campers need to obtain keys from the camp manager. Reservations: 800-234-7275.

Gay travelers are heartily welcomed in this desert resort community. Since the first exclusively gay resort opened in

Palm Springs Gay Scene

the 1970s, Palm Springs has grown to be a popular gay getaway. Today the lively scene is as much a part of Palm Springs as are golf courses; there are over two dozen gay resorts as well as numerous restaurants, nightspots, and shops, owned by gays and catering to gay visitors.

Much of the scene revolves around the resorts, so selecting one that reflects your personal taste is an important part of planning your trip. Once you arrive you'll need a car to get to all the hot spots, but finding your way around is easy. Most visitors overlook the fact that having a car provides the opportunity to enjoy the wilderness areas around Palm Springs, and while I don't recommend you try to reenact the hiking scene from *The Adventures of Priscilla, Queen of the Desert*, I do suggest you consider escaping town for a picnic and a stroll on a desert trail.

With almost 30 resorts and hotels serving a gay clientele, Palm   **LODGING**
Springs is a major vacation destination for both gay men and women. Lodgings range from small bed-and-breakfast inns to deluxe resorts that serve singles, couples, or a mix of both.

The **Tortuga Del Sol** offers a variety of one- and two-bedroom suites and studios, some with full kitchens or kitchenettes.

Tastefully appointed, these guest rooms boast brilliantly colored walls and furniture with Southwestern wood accents. The resort affords complete privacy and allows nude sunbathing. The grounds have a poolside misting system and outdoor *chimeneas*. Men only. ~ 715 East San Lorenzo Road, Palm Springs; 760-416-3111, 888-541-3777; www.tortugadelsol.com, e-mail palm-springs@tortugadelsol.com. MODERATE TO ULTRA-DELUXE.

Harlow Club Hotel bills itself as "a civilized Eden." Surrounded by tropical gardens, it features Spanish-style 1930s-era bungalows. The 15 guest rooms, designed in award-winning style, include fireplaces and private patios. There's also a gymnasium, spa, and rooftop sundeck for guests. Breakfast and lunch are included in the price. ~ 175 East El Alameda, Palm Springs; 760-323-3977, 888-547-7881; www.theharlow.com, e-mail info@theharlow.com. DELUXE TO ULTRA-DELUXE.

Debuting in 1975 as Palm Springs' original gay resort, **El Mirasol Villas** has deluxe bungalows in a garden setting. This stylish resort has suites and studios with custom furnishings, wet bars, kitchens, and poolside patios, two clothing-optional heated pools, a steam room, and a jacuzzi/spa with outdoor shower. The outdoor misting system provides relief from the heat. Complimentary breakfast and Saturday barbecue are served poolside. ~ 525 Warm Sands Drive, Palms Springs; 760-327-5913, 800-327-2985; www.elmirasol.com, e-mail elmirasolps@aol.com. MODERATE TO ULTRA-DELUXE.

Part of El Mirasol Villas was built in the '40s by Howard Hughes for Elizabeth Taylor's mum, so the story goes.

Spread across two acres, **The Hacienda** is an upscale retreat with ten rooms and suites. Along with two pools and a jacuzzi, there are gardens, trees, and grassy areas at this refined getaway. ~ 586 Warm Sands Drive, Palm Springs; 760-327-8111, 800-359-2007, fax 760-778-7890; www.thehacienda.com, e-mail info@thehacienda.com. ULTRA-DELUXE.

The **Chaps Inn** is a male-only resort catering to the leather and bare crowd. Most of its ten rooms have full kitchens or kitchenettes, and some have private patios. The pool, spa, and steam room are clothing-optional. Continental breakfast is included. ~ 312 Camino Monte Vista, Palm Springs; 760-327-8222, 800-445-8916, fax 760-325-7734; www.chapsinn.com, e-mail chapsinn@aol.com. MODERATE.

Terrazzo offers 12 air-conditioned rooms decorated in a Southwestern style. All units feature microwaves and refrigerators, as well as French doors overlooking a swimming pool and garden. Enjoy an expanded continental breakfast in the morning. A catered lunch is also included. ~ 1600 East Palm Canyon Drive, Palm Springs; 760-778-5883, 866-837-7996, fax 760-416-2200; www.terrazzo-ps.com, e-mail info@terrazzo-ps.com. DELUXE TO ULTRA-DELUXE.

Chestnutz, a luxury resort for men, serves a complimentary full breakfast and evening wine and hors d'oeuvres to its boarders. Its 12 rooms are individually decorated, with both queen- and king-size beds available. The king suites are very cozy; they feature private patios and full kitchens. There are some nice touches here such as welcome baskets, nightly turndown service, and free local phone calls. A misting system over the pool and jacuzzi keeps things cool, as does the clothing-optional rule. ~ 641 San Lorenzo Road, Palm Springs; 760-325-5269, 800-621-6973, fax 760-320-9535; www.chestnutz.com, e-mail chestnutzps@aol.com. MODERATE TO ULTRA-DELUXE.

DINING

The **Rainbow Cactus Restaurant** has a large gay clientele and keeps it loyal with good homecooking: chicken and dumplings, liver and onions, and New York steak. Lunch consists of soups, salads, and sandwiches. A piano bar swings into action at night. Brunch on Sunday. ~ 212 South Indian Canyon Drive, Palm Springs; 760-325-3868; www.rainbowcactus.com. MODERATE.

With mauve brocade booths and a giant granite slab for a bar, gay-owned **Shame on the Moon** is both elegant and modern. Despite its debonair standards, "desert-casual" wear is heartily welcomed. Diners may feast on the special dinner entrées whipped up each evening, usually Continental dishes ranging from baked filet of salmon with a fresh horseradish crust to sautéed calf's liver. Dinner only. Closed mid-July to mid-August. ~ 69-950 Frank Sinatra Drive, Rancho Mirage; 760-324-5515, fax 760-770-4654; www.shameonthemoon.com, e-mail shameonthemoon@aol.com. MODERATE TO DELUXE.

SHOPPING

R & R Menswear stocks contemporary, stylish clothing for the guy on the go. Beach wear, sports jackets, active wear, and club-geared garb can all be found here at moderate prices. ~ 333 North Palm Canyon Drive, Palm Springs; 760-320-3007.

For all things aloe, visit **Palm Springs Aloe People**. This store carries a large line of skin moisturizers, tanning products, body scrubs, masks, and bath and shower gels. ~ 243 South Indian Canyon, Palm Springs; 760-320-3007.

For novelty gifts and gags, try **Paper Lilli**. ~ 114 North Palm Canyon Drive, Palm Springs; 760-327-3373.

NIGHTLIFE

The friendly atmosphere of **Streetbar** explains why it's so popular among the locals and tourists. Although the clientele is primarily men, women also receive a hearty welcome. If you happen to be here on the right day at the right time, you might catch a drag show or a diva captivating the crowd. Otherwise, take a seat inside or on the outdoor patio, have a drink, and relax. ~ 224 East Arenas Road, Palm Springs; 760-320-1266.

The Tool Shed is a spirited watering hole/leather bar where the guys pass the time by downing a few drinks and playing a little eight-ball. ~ 600 East Sunny Dunes Road, Palm Springs; 760-320-3299; www.toolshed-ps.com, e-mail info@toolshed-ps.com.

Located in the Villa Resort, the **Dates Bar** features live music and comedy acts on Friday and Saturday nights. The rest of the week, it's a great place for a quiet drink. ~ 67-670 Carey Road, Palm Springs; 760-328-7211.

Badlands, a mellow neighborhood bar catering to a gay and lesbian clientele, is a good first stop for advice on the best local hot spots. ~ 200 South Indian Canyon Drive, Palm Springs; 760-778-4326.

The **Village Pub**, a favorite haunt of Palm Springs locals, both gay and straight, has live entertainment every afternoon and evening. Check out the upstairs area, where there are pool tables, couches, big-screen TVs, and patrons smoking premium cigars from the pub's humidor. ~ 266 South Palm Canyon Drive, Palm Springs; 760-323-3265; www.villagepubpalmsprings.com.

A number of alternative lifestyle establishments are springing up south of Palm Springs in Cathedral City.

Check out **Ground Zero**, a club for gay men offering karaoke, dancing, and pool tournaments. ~ 36737 Cathedral Canyon Drive, Cathedral City; 909-321-0031. The **Poolside Bar** in the Desert Palms Inn features nightly entertainment ranging from cabaret-style productions to local acts. Occasional cover. ~ 67-580 East Palm Canyon Drive, Cathedral City; 760-324-3000; www.desert palmsinn.com.

▼▼▼▼▼▼▼▼▼▼▼▼▼
Joshua Tree National Park Area

It's only about 50 miles from Palm Springs to Joshua Tree, but in the course of the journey you will pass from the heart of California's hot, windblown Low Desert to the edge of its rugged and diverse High Desert. In the course of this transition, the road rises from 400 feet above sea level to over 4000 feet. Even more dramatic is the change in the flora and fauna as you pass from one biological zone to another.

SIGHTS

No, that's not a hallucination on Route 10 west of Palm Springs. Those really are dinosaurs at **Dinosaur Delights** looming above the highway. Or dinosaur replicas anyway: an *Apatosaurus* 45 feet high and 150 feet long, and his companion, a *Tyrannosaurus rex* that stands 65 feet high. Each weighs more than 40 tons and has interior viewing platforms. The *Apatosaurus* even contains a gift shop. ~ 50-800 Seminole Drive, Cabazon; 909-849-8309, fax 760-849-5900.

Bridging the gap between the High and Low desert areas is **Big Morongo Canyon Wildlife Preserve**, a 29,000-acre facility

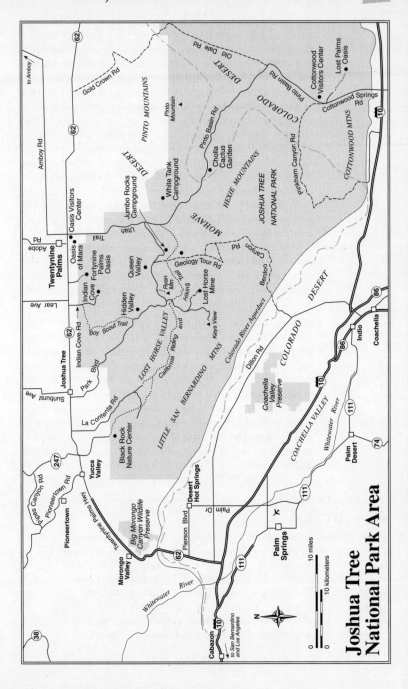

Joshua Tree National Park Area

managed by the Bureau of Land Management. This oasis, with several springs and one of the region's few year-round streams, features several nature trails, including a full-access boardwalk that wends through marshes and streamside woodlands. Bobcat and bighorn sheep inhabit the area, which is also prime bird-watching territory. The bird population here is about 100 times as plentiful as elsewhere in the desert. Varying from a cottonwood-rimmed stream to desert washes, the canyon is a place of rare beauty. ~ Located on East Drive, Morongo Valley; 760-363-7190, fax 760-363-1180; www.bigmorongo.org.

In addition to dramatic rock formations, the town of Yucca Valley, a stopover on the way to Joshua Tree, possesses two points of interest. **Desert Christ Park**, at the north end of Mohawk Trail, created by one man during the last nine years of his life, portrays several biblical scenes. Among the outsize sculptures are a 16-ton statue of Christ and a tableau of the Last Supper.

The town's **Hi-Desert Nature Museum** exhibits fossils, rocks, minerals, and Indian artifacts. They also have an interactive kids corner, and a small zoo with desert animals and reptiles. Closed Monday. ~ 57116 Twentynine Palms Highway, Yucca Valley; 760-369-7212, fax 760-369-1605; e-mail museum@yucca-valley.org.

JOSHUA TREE NATIONAL PARK   One of the great inland destinations, **Joshua Tree National Park** is an awesome 794,000-acre sanctuary straddling California's High and Low deserts. Its northern region, of greater interest to visitors, rests at about 4000 feet elevation in the Mojave. To the south, where Joshua trees give way to scrub vegetation, lies the arid Colorado Desert. Admission.

The main entrance to the park, off Route 62 in Twentynine Palms, leads to the **Oasis Visitors Center**, a full-facility stop with park exhibits. The best place to chart a course through the park, it rests in the **Oasis of Mara**, a grove of palms once used by Indians and prospectors. Day-use fee, $10 (good for seven consecutive days). ~ 760-367-5500, fax 760-367-6392; www.nps.gov/jotr.

FICTIONAL GHOST TOWN

Fiction, it seems, has become reality in **Pioneertown**. This unusual hamlet was built in 1947 as a film set for Westerns. Somehow the producers never managed to start the cameras rolling and the place became an ersatz ghost town. Then people began moving in, converting falsefront buildings into a general store, post office, private homes, and even a bowling alley. Today several of the old raw wood structures survive and you can tour the neighborhood, exploring a fictional ghost town that returned to life. ~ Located four miles northwest of Yucca Valley on Pioneertown Road.

Black Rock Nature Center, featuring a ranger station and small exhibit, lies about 30 miles farther west of the Oasis Visitors Center. Closed June through September. ~ 760-365-9585, fax 760-228-9100; www.nps.gov/jotr.

As you proceed south and west into the heart of the park, weathered granite, smoothed by the elements, rises in fields of massive boulders. In the foreground, Joshua trees, their branches like arms raised heavenward, stand against a cobalt sky. Many of the rocks are carved and hollowed to create skulls, arches, and whatever shapes the imagination can conjure. With such an abundance of rock, it's no wonder that Joshua Tree is one of the world's top rock-climbing destinations. Especially in winter, you'll see lizard-people all over the park, scaling sheer faces with impossible grace.

The Joshua trees that complement this eerie landscape are giant yucca plants, members of the agave family, which grow to heights of almost 50 feet. They were named in the 1850s by Mormon pioneers, who saw in the stark, angular trees the figure of the prophet Joshua pointing them farther westward.

West of Jumbo Rocks Campground, **Geology Tour Road**, a dirt track (four-wheel-drive vehicles recommended), leads for nine miles past unusual rock sculptures, alluvial fans, and desert washes. **Squaw Tank**, an ancient Indian campsite, contains Indian bedrock mortars and a concrete dam built by ranchers early in the 20th century. A pamphlet available from the information centers will also help locate petroglyphs, mine shafts, and magnificent mountain vistas.

A paved route from the main roadway deadends at **Keys View**. The finest panorama in the park, it sweeps from 11,485-foot Mt. San Gorgonio across the San Jacinto Mountains to the Salton Sea, and takes in Palm Springs, the Colorado River Aqueduct, and Indio. The full sweep of the Coachella Valley lies before you, a dusty brown basin painted green with golf courses and palm groves.

Desert Queen Ranch, one of the few outposts of civilization in Joshua Tree, was built early in the 20th century by William F. Keys, a former sheriff, prospector, and Rough Rider. On a ranger-led tour you can visit this ghost village complete with ranch house, school, corral, and barn. Admission.

The unique transition zone between the Mojave and Colorado deserts becomes evident when you proceed toward the southern gateway to the park. As the elevation descends and temperatures rise, plant life becomes sparser.

Yet here, too, the inherent beauty of the park is overwhelming. **Cholla Cactus Garden**, a forest of cactus that is a pure delight to walk through, is one of Joshua Tree's prettiest places. With their soft, bristly branches, these Bigelow cactus live in a region that rarely receives more than four inches of rain a year.

Beyond this natural garden the road passes through a landscape of long, lithe ocotillo plants. Then you'll journey past the parched, dust-blown Pinto Basin to the **Cottonwood Visitors Center**, the southern gateway to Joshua Tree National Park.

LODGING   A desert traveler could not ask for more than a rustic family inn in a palm oasis. Located in a natural setting within eyeshot of Joshua Tree National Park headquarters, **29 Palms Inn** has 12 adobe cottages and four renovated old frame cottages. With fireplaces, country decor, and sturdy old furniture, they bear personalized names like "Ghost Flower" and "Fiddle Neck." This marvelous inn, encompassing 70 acres, was founded in 1928 and has been in the same family for four generations. (Be aware that some readers have complained of poor service.) Amenities include a heated pool, restaurant, and lounge. Continental breakfast is served. ~ 73950 Inn Avenue, Twentynine Palms; 760-367-3505, fax 760-367-4425; www.29palmsinn.com, e-mail 29palmsinn@ eee.org. MODERATE.

DINING   Near the northern entrance to Joshua Tree National Park, **29 Palms Inn** is a homespun restaurant with a friendly staff, local art, and family photos on the walls. Situated in a rustic hotel, it serves American cuisine such as fresh grilled seafood, steaks, vegetarian offerings from their own garden, and several daily specials. Sunday brunch is available. ~ 73950 Inn Avenue, Twentynine Palms; 760-367-3505, fax 760-367-4425; www.29palmsinn. com, e-mail 29palmsinn@eee.org. MODERATE TO DELUXE.

PARKS   **JOSHUA TREE NATIONAL PARK** 🏃 🚲 Covering 794,000 acres, most of it wilderness, this famous park lies on the border of California's High and Low deserts. It possesses characteristics of both the Mojave and Colorado deserts, ranging from Joshua tree forests at 4000 feet to ocotillo and cholla cactus at lower elevations. The park's granite hills offer sport for rock climbers, while its miles of hiking trails attract day-hikers and wilderness enthusiasts alike. The desert life includes tarantulas, roadrunners, sidewinders, golden eagles, and coyotes, but it is the desert plants that make the sanctuary truly special. Facilities include picnic areas, restrooms, and museums; there are three information centers. Entrance fee, $10 per car for seven days. ~ Entrances are located off Route 62 in Joshua Tree and Twentynine Palms and off Route 10, 27 miles east of Indio; 760-367-5500, fax 760-367-6392.

In 1857, the first transcontinental mail service passed through the Box Canyon region; soon afterwards the Butterfield Overland Stage Line began transporting passengers.

▲ There are five primitive campgrounds; $5 per night. (Bring your own water and firewood.) The two developed campgrounds, Black Rock and Cottonwood, cost $10 per night; no hookups are available but RVs may use any of the sites. Indian Cove and Black Rock Canyon sites can be reserved by calling 800-365-2267. All vehicles must pay the $10 park entrance fee.

The largest state facility in the United States, Anza–Borrego Desert State Park, which extends across a broad swath of the Colorado Desert, reaches almost to the Mexican frontier. Within its borders lie desert sinks, sculpted rocks, and multicolored badlands. Bighorn sheep roam the mountains and desert life abounds in the lowlands.

Anza–Borrego Desert State Park

Borrego Springs, the only sizeable town in the entire preserve, contains an excellent **visitors center**. Here are nature trails, a cactus garden, and a small museum with displays and a slide show. Open weekends only from June through September. ~ End of West Palm Canyon Drive; 760-767-5311, fax 760-767-3427; www. anzaborrego.statepark.org, e-mail cddhq@parks.ca.gov.

SIGHTS

For a **vantage point** overlooking this magnificent territory, follow Route S22 west toward Culp Valley. Sharply ascending into the mountains, the road looks out across the Borrego Badlands to the Salton Sea. To the north rise the Santa Rosa Mountains and in the south, deep brown against the blue sky, are the Vallecito Mountains.

Font's Point, one of the park's most popular vistas, will provide a close-up view of the Borrego Badlands. A truly spectacular spot, it overlooks rock formations painted brilliant colors and chiseled by wind and water. This heavily eroded area reveals remnants of the prehistoric Colorado River delta. To reach Font's Point, follow Route S22 for about 12 miles east from Borrego Springs, then turn south for four miles onto a marked road. This rough, sandy track lies at the bottom of a wash, so take care not to become mired in the sand.

The entire stretch of Route S22 from Borrego Springs east to the Salton Sea is nicknamed **Erosion Road**. Along its 30-mile length are countless sandstone hills, brilliant red in color and carved into myriad shapes. Many are banded with sedimentary layers containing marine fossils.

Perhaps one even contains the lost gold mine of "Pegleg" Smith. Thomas Long "Pegleg" Smith, it seems, was a prospector with a talent for tall tales. The nickname, he claimed, resulted from an 1827 Indian battle from which he emerged missing one leg. A few years later Pegleg passed through California, discovering a small amount of gold, which in the alembic of his imagination was eventually transformed into an entire mine.

Even a prospector needs a public relations man. Pegleg's publicity agent came along a century later when Harry Oliver, a

Hollywood director, created the **Pegleg Monument**. Drawing a circle on the ground, Oliver urged everyone hoping to discover Pegleg's lost gold mine to fill the area with rocks. Today the monument is a huge pile of stones to which you are obliged to contribute. Good luck! ~ Route S22 and Henderson Canyon Road, eight miles east of Borrego Springs.

HIDDEN ▶ Along the eastern border of the park, near Ocotillo Wells, lie the **Split Mountain/Fish Creek**. Sculpted by water, these heights have been transformed into a variety of textures and compositions. Each level presents a different color, as if the hills had been deposited layer by layer from on high. To get there, follow Split Mountain Road south from Route 78 for 12 miles; turn right onto the road to Fish Creek campground and follow it for about two and one-half miles (until it becomes impassable). When the road is in good condition, you can drive right into the gap in the mountain created by geologic forces.

South of Borrego Springs, Route S3 traverses Yaqui Pass. From the roadside (near the 2.0 mile sign), a .25-mile trail leads to **Kenyon Overlook**, with views of Sunset Mountain and surrounding canyons.

Farther south in Anza–Borrego, Route S2 parallels the historic Southern Emigrant Trail. At **Box Canyon Monument**, a path leads to a point overlooking the old trail. It was here in 1847 that the Mormon Battalion hewed a track wide enough for wagons. ~ Nine miles south of Scissors Crossing.

The **Vallecito Stage Station**, built in 1852, served the Butterfield and other lines for years. Today an adobe reconstruction of the building stands in Vallecito County Park. With its plentiful water supply, this site was also an important campground for the gold prospectors coming overland to Northern California mines in 1849. ~ Route S2, 19 miles south of Scissors Crossing, four miles north of Agua Caliente.

For a dramatic idea of the terrain confronting these pioneers, continue to **Carrizo Badlands Overlook**. In all directions from this windswept plateau, the landscape is an inhospitable mix of mountain peaks and sandy washes. Heavy erosion has worked its magic here, creating stone sculptures and hills banded with color. ~ Route S2, 36 miles south of Scissors Crossing.

LODGING Anza–Borrego's premier hostelry is **La Casa del Zorro**, a desert hideaway in a garden setting. Spread across 48 acres, the resort is a collection of Spanish-style buildings positioned around several swimming pools and jacuzzis. There are tennis courts, a fitness center, a restaurant, and a cozy lounge. The Southwestern-theme lobby contains spacious sitting rooms finished with washed pine. Guest rooms vary from small traditional motel rooms to lavish suites and casitas with fireplaces, private patios, and desert

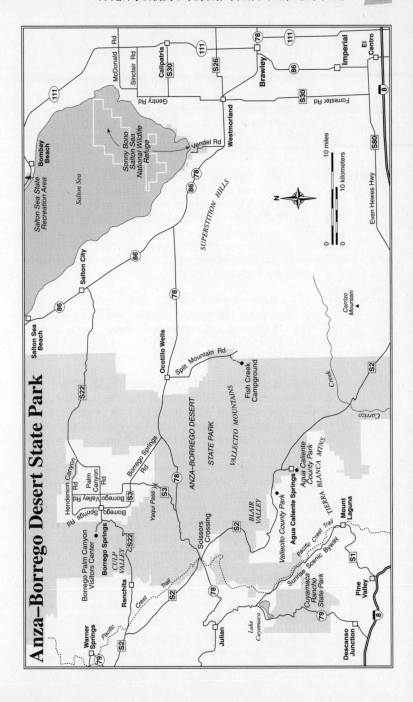

Anza–Borrego Desert State Park

accoutrements. Most have a private pool or spa. ~ 3845 Yaqui Pass Road, Borrego Springs; 760-767-5323, 800-824-1884, fax 760-767-5963; www.lacasadelzorro.com, e-mail reservations@la casadelzorro.com. ULTRA-DELUXE.

The **Oasis Motel** is a small, seven-unit establishment. Set amid palm trees and offering views of the mountains, it has rooms with or without kitchens. There is a pool and a jacuzzi. Closed July and August. ~ 366 Palm Canyon Drive (West Route S22), Borrego Springs; 760-767-5409, fax 760-767-0968; www.oasismotelbor rego.com, e-mail oasismotel@aol.com. MODERATE.

DINING

With whitewashed walls, *viga* ceilings, and candle sconces, the din-ing room at **La Casa del Zorro** is Southwestern in atmosphere. Part of a lavish resort complex, the restaurant serves three meals daily, offering guests a traditional selection of dishes. Among the entrées are veal chops, prime rib, and rack of lamb. ~ 3845 Yaqui Pass Road, Borrego Springs; 760-767-5323, fax 760-767-5963; www.lacasadelzorro.com, e-mail reservations@lacasadelzorro. com. DELUXE TO ULTRA-DELUXE.

NIGHTLIFE

For live music in Borrego Springs, check out the scene at La Casa del Zorro's **Fox Den Pub**. Overlooking the hotel's swimming pool and featuring a dancefloor and fireplace, this evening re-treat is a special place. ~ 3845 Yaqui Pass Road, Borrego Springs; 760-767-5323; www.lacasadelzorro.com.

PARKS

ANZA–BORREGO DESERT STATE PARK 🏃 🚲 🏇 Spreading across more than 600,000 acres of the Colorado Desert, this dusty behemoth is the largest state park in the contiguous United States. It's a tumbling region of jagged mountains, hidden springs, and deep sandstone canyons. The tree life ranges from palms at sea level to pines at 6000 feet. Hiking trails lead along the desert floor, through multihued valleys, and up into the mountains. You'll find a museum, a visitors center, picnic areas, restrooms, and showers. Day-use fee, $5. ~ Routes 78 and S22 lead into the park from both the east and west; 760-767-5311, fax 760-767-3427; www.anzaborrego.statepark.org, e-mail cddhq@parks.ca.gov.

▲ In the Borrego Palm Canyon Campground there are 52 RV sites with hookups and 65 developed tent sites; in Tamarisk Grove Campground there are 27 tent sites; in Bow Willow there are 16 primitive sites; and in Vern Whitaker Horse Camp there are 9 sites with corrals. Camping costs $16 to $22 per night for sites with hookups, $10 per night for all other sites. Call 800-444-7275 for reservations.

AGUA CALIENTE COUNTY PARK 🏃 🚲 🛶 Surrounded by Anza–Borrego Desert State Park, this scenic desert reserve meas-

The Salton Sea

One of California's strangest formations lies deep in the southern section of the state, just 30 miles from the Mexican border. Situated 234 feet below sea level, directly atop the San Andreas Fault, the area has been periodically flooded by the Colorado River for eons. From six million until two million years ago forests covered the hillsides and local hollows were filled with lakes and streams. But as the region became increasingly arid, the lakes dried up, and for two million years the basin was desert.

Then in 1905 the irrigation system for the Imperial Valley went amok, the Colorado River overflowed its banks, and a flood two years in duration inundated the land. The Salton Sea was reborn.

California's largest lake, it continues even today to grow from agricultural runoff. As you approach it from the north, this vast sea resembles the ocean itself. Lying at the confluence of the Imperial and Coachella valleys, one of the lushest agricultural regions in the world, the Salton Sea possesses rare beauty. Along its northwest shore on Route 86, rows of date palms run to the water's edge and citrus orchards create a brilliant green landscape backdropped by chocolate-brown mountains. Other sections of shore, given over to trailer parks, mud flats, and alkali deposits, are astonishingly ugly.

The best place to fish and enjoy sandy beaches is at the **Salton Sea State Recreation Area**. Long and narrow, this amazing park extends for 18 miles along the northeast shore. Since the lake represents California's richest inland fishery, there are great opportunities to fish for sargo, tilapia, corbina, and gulf croaker. Birdwatchers also flock here, and birdwatching tours are offered December through February. The best places to birdwatch are at Sneaker Beach, the marshes around Salt Creek Campground, and between the campgrounds at park headquarters and Mecca Beach. Swimming is popular at each of the park's five campgrounds, but is best at Mecca Beach. Admission. ~ Route 111; 760-393-3052, fax 760-393-2466; www.saltonsea.statepark.org.

Farther south lies the **Sonny Bono Salton Sea National Wildlife Refuge**. This is a prime avian habitat: over 400 bird species have been sighted here, including stilts, pintails, and the endangered Yuma clapper rail and brown pelican. The rising of sea level has diminished the park's land area from 35,000 to 10,000 acres, but you're still liable to see great blue herons wading along the shore and snow geese arriving for the winter. ~ Entrances from Sinclair Road northwest of Calipatria and Vendel Road northwest of Westmorland; 760-348-5278, fax 760-348-7245; www.saltonsea.fws.gov.

ures 910 acres. It's located at 1300 feet elevation on the eastern slope of the Tierra Blanca Mountains. The greatest attraction here is the system of natural waters—four springs, one cool and pure, the others warm and sulfurous, percolate to the surface. As a result, the park has two pools—an outdoor wading area and an indoor pool complete with jacuzzi jets. The park offers picnic areas, restrooms, a store, and hiking trails. Parking fee, $2. ~ Located on Route S2, 23 miles south of Scissors Crossing; 858-565-3600, fax 858-495-5841; e-mail ask parks.luc@sdcounty.ca.gov.

> Because of present-day evaporation as well as minerals left by earlier seas, the Salton Sea is ten percent saltier than the Pacific.

▲ There are 93 sites with hookups ($18 per night) and 34 developed tent sites ($14 per night). Camping is also permitted at nearby **Vallecito County Park** (858-565-3600), four miles north of Agua Caliente. Vallecito has 45 developed tent/RV sites (no hookups); $12 per night. Closed Memorial Day through Labor Day.

Outdoor Adventures

SPORT-FISHING

Lakes in the Inland Empire and Low Desert areas offer a variety of fishing opportunities. Alpine Trout Lakes, Silverwood Lake State Recreation Area, Lake Perris State Recreation Area, Lake Arrowhead, Big Bear Lake, and the Salton Sea are stocked with an assortment of fish, including trout, bass, catfish, bluegill, corbina, croaker, sargo, and tilapia.

Big Bear Marina has fishing boats, pontoon boats, canoes, and kayaks. Closed in the winter. ~ Lakeview Drive, Big Bear; 909-866-3218, fax 909-866-3846; www.bigbearmarina.com. To spend your day idling away on the water looking for bear and deer, contact **Pleasure Point Marina**, which rents canoes, pedal boats, fishing boats, and pontoons. Closed November through April. ~ 603 Landlock Landing Road, South Shore, Big Bear Lake; 909-866-2455; www.pleasurepointbbl.com.

WATER SPORTS

For boating and canoeing trips on mountain lakes, try **Pine Knot Landing**, which rents pontoons, canoes, and fishing boats. Closed November to April. ~ 439 Pine Knot Avenue, Big Bear Lake; 909-866-2628; www.pineknotlanding.com. **Pleasure Point Marina** has boat rentals. Closed November through April. ~ 603 Landlock Landing Road, South Shore, Big Bear Lake; 909-866-2455; www.pleasurepointbbl.com.

RIDING STABLES

In Palm Springs, **Smoke Tree Stables** offers one-hour, two-hour, and custom-catered guided rides through stunning desert terrain. No credit cards. Closed July and August. ~ 2500 Toledo Avenue; 760-327-1372. **Covered Wagon Tours** hosts two-hour pioneer-style desert tours on mule-drawn wagons, leading through the natural desert environs of Coachella Valley Preserve. A barbecue follows. Reservations required. Closed June through September. ~ La Quinta; 760-347-2161; www.coveredwagontours.com.

For unmatched views of open desert terrain, call **Sunrise Balloons**, operating since 1976. Hour to hour-and-a-half-long rides with a continental breakfast brunch on board take off from November through March in Palm Springs, where citrus and date groves abound, and in Borrego Springs, where badlands and the Anza–Borrego Desert State Park are the backdrop; and year-round in Temecula, with views of rolling hills and wine country. ~ 800-548-9912; www.sunriseballoons.com. **Desert Balloon Charters** offers two hour-long rides a day from late September through May. ~ La Quinta; 760-346-8575. In Temecula, **A Grape Escape Balloon Adventures** offers morning balloon rides above the wine country vineyards, and sunrise rides over the Temecula Valley. All flights include champagne and a continental breakfast. ~ Murietta; 909-698-9772; www.hotairtours.com.

BALLOON RIDES

Skiing in the desert? Yes, even Palm Springs, California's vaunted warm-weather hideaway, gives spa-goers a chance to challenge the surrounding slopes. The Palm Springs Aerial Tramway carries desert dwellers to over 8000 feet in **Mount San Jacinto State Park**, where an adventure center rents cross-country gear, and two loop trails circle through backcountry wilderness. Permit required and obtainable at the ranger station. ~ 760-327-6002 (adventure center), 909-659-2607 (park information).

For more information on skiing in Southern California, see "Skiing the Southland" in Chapter Eight.

SKIING

With more than 85 golf courses, it's no surprise that Palm Springs is known as the Golf Capital of the World. Though other Low Desert communities may not be bursting with greens quite in the same way, they still have an impressive share. Courses here rent both clubs and carts; most feature driving ranges and 18 holes.

GOLF

SAN BERNARDINO MOUNTAINS Golfers can visit **El Rancho Verde Country Club**, which has a mostly flat course studded with eucalyptus trees. ~ Country Club Drive, Rialto; 909-875-5346. For outstanding views of the San Bernardino Mountains, go to the public **Shandin Hills Golf Club**. The course's 15th hole sits over water. ~ 3380 North Little Mountain Drive, San Bernardino; 909-886-0669. Around Big Bear Lake you'll have to settle for the nine-hole, public **Big Bear Mountain Golf Course**. ~ 43101 Goldmine Drive, Moonridge; 909-585-8002.

PALM SPRINGS AREA The **Tahquitz Creek Resort**, which is open to the public, has two 18-hole courses. The 17th hole of this Ted Robinson–designed green boasts waterfalls. Cart is included. ~ 1885 Golf Club Drive, Palm Springs; 760-328-1005. **Mesquite**

Golf and Country Club has a course surrounded by mesquite trees and featuring spectacular mountain views. Cart is included. ~ 2700 East Mesquite Avenue, Palm Springs; 760-323-1502.

The semiprivate **Desert Falls Country Club** is dotted with majestic palm trees. ~ 1111 Desert Falls Parkway, Palm Desert; 760-340-5646. At the semiprivate **Oasis Country Club** the playing field meanders around 22 lakes and ponds. ~ 42-330 Casbah Way, Palm Desert; 760-345-2715. To play with palm trees swaying in the breeze, visit the semiprivate **Palm Desert Resort Country Club**. ~ 77-333 Country Club Drive, Palm Desert; 760-345-2791. Surrounded by mature olive and eucalyptus trees, the semiprivate **Palm Date Country Club** was designed by Ted Robinson. Closed October. ~ 36-200 Date Palm Drive, Cathedral City; 760-328-1315.

The **Indio Golf Club** is a flat, public course with the longest par 3 in the nation. ~ 83-040 Avenue 42, Indio; 760-347-9156.

TENNIS   Around Big Bear Lake, there are several public courts at **Meadow Park**. ~ Park Avenue. For more information, call the park district at 909-866-0130.

Demuth Park offers four lighted courts. ~ 4365 Mesquite Avenue, Palm Springs; 760-323-8272. **Wardman Park** features two lighted public courts. ~ 66150 8th Street, Desert Hot Springs. In Indio, there are two lighted courts at **South Jackson Park**. ~ Jackson Street and Date Avenue. You can also try the four lighted courts at **Miles Avenue Park**. ~ Miles Avenue. **Indio High School** has ten lighted courts. ~ Avenue 46 and Clinton Avenue.

Also, check local papers for information on weekly events and activities sponsored by private clubs.

BIKING   Cycling is popular throughout the Inland Empire and Low Desert. There's mountain riding in the San Bernardino Mountains, desert cycling around Palm Springs, Joshua Tree, and Anza–Borrego, and recreational riding in the regional park areas.

Many of the regional and national parks listed in the "Parks" sections of this chapter have miles of bicycle trails, including **Silver-**

AUTHOR FAVORITE

Golfers in Palm Springs will think they have died and gone to heaven. Mild weather year-round has attracted professionals and amateurs alike, including Bob Hope, Arnold Palmer, and former President Dwight Eisenhower. (Eisenhower actually recorded his only hole-in-one at a Palm Springs facility.) This desert oasis is chockablock with courses open to the public; see above for a select list of golf greens.

wood Lake State Recreation Area and **Lake Perris State Recreation Area.** Riding in Anza–Borrego and Joshua Tree is also very good.

Mountain riding is popular around **Lake Arrowhead** and **Big Bear Lake,** especially on forest service roads. The north shore of Big Bear Lake is a popular route, as is **Skyline Drive** (Route 2N10), a graded road that travels past Snow Summit to the Goldmine Ski area. **Snow Summit** sells all-day passes that allow mountain bikers access to the ski lift and a honeycomb of mountain trails. Passes are available at Team Big Bear at Snow Summit (see "Bike Rentals" below). Another graded thoroughfare, **Sand Canyon Road** (Route 2N27) in the Moonridge district, is also a lovely ride.

Thirty-five miles of bike routes encircle **Palm Springs.** Popular riding spots include the luxurious residential neighborhoods, the Mesquite Country Club area, the Indian Canyons, and around the local parks. A notable trail is the ten-mile long **White Water Wash,** which begins in Palm Springs and extends into Palm Desert. Check with bike-rental shops for more tour information.

Bike Rentals   For bike rentals, as well as maps and information on mountain biking throughout the San Bernardinos, stop in at **Big Bear Bikes.** Bike tours are available. ~ 41810 Big Bear Boulevard, Big Bear Lake; 909-866-2224. For competitive mountain-bike racing, call **Team Big Bear.** Rental bikes come equipped with helmets, and you can stop by for a fix-up if need be. Closed November to mid-May. ~ 880 Summit Boulevard, Big Bear Lake; 909-866-4565; www.teambigbear.com. **Skyline Ski and Sports** offers rentals and repairs. ~ 653 Pine Knot Boulevard, Big Bear Lake; 909-866-3501. For four-and-a-half-hour guided bike tours to Indian Canyon, call **Big Horn Bike Adventures.** Rentals include mountain bikes, cruisers, and tandems. Closed Wednesday. ~ 302 North Palm Canyon, Palm Springs; 760-325-3367.

All distances listed for trails are one way unless otherwise noted.   **HIKING**

SAN BERNARDINO MOUNTAINS   Hikers will delight in the San Bernardino Mountains trails, with their sweeping views of valleys and surrounding peaks.

Pacific Crest Trail covers the entire length of the chain. It passes through pine forests, overlooks Big Bear Lake, and continues on to Lake Arrowhead before turning north toward Deep Creek.

Just above Mount Baldy Village, **Icehouse Canyon to Cucamonga Peak via Icehouse Saddle Trail** (7.3 miles) is an arduous hike through subalpine wilderness to an 8859-foot summit. The views are worth the struggle.

Another ascent, **San Bernardino Peak Trail** (8 miles) leads up the jagged slope of its 10,624-foot namesake, providing breathtaking vistas.

Serious hikers should not miss **Mt. San Gorgonio Trail** (7.5 miles). The highest peak in this range, 11,499-foot Mt. San Gorgonio, presents an extraordinary challenge. The trail leads through meadows and past lakes to a summit high above the world.

The strenuous **Siberia Creek Trail** (7 miles) passes the largest known lodgepole pine, Champion Lodgepole, then continues through coniferous forest to the edge of a picturesque meadow. Here the route crosses Siberia Creek and descends Lookout Mountain to Siberia Creek Group Camp.

Near Lake Arrowhead, **Heaps Peak Arboretum Trail** (1 mile) offers a loop tour through deciduous and coniferous forests.

IDYLLWILD   Rising high above the desert, the 10,000-foot **San Jacinto Mountains** present endless alpine hiking opportunities.

From Idyllwild County Park Visitors Center, **Deer Springs Trail** (3.3 miles) crosses Marion Ridge and travels past oak and pine forests to Suicide Rock (7510 feet), a granite monolith that offers spectacular views.

From Mountain Station at the top of the Palm Springs Aerial Tramway, there's an exhilarating hike along **Mt. San Jacinto Trail** (6 miles) to the 10,804-foot summit. A shorter, two-and-a-half-mile trek leads through pine and white fir forest to Round Valley.

If these don't interest you, there are 54 miles of trails to choose from atop Mt. San Jacinto. Remember to bring extra clothes, food, and water with you. To hike in the Mt. San Jacinto wilderness, you must have a permit. Self-issuing day permits are available at the ranger station, about a quarter-mile from the tram station on the mountain. Overnight permits may be arranged in advance by mail (send a self-addressed, stamped envelope to Mt. San Jacinto State Park, P.O. Box 308, Idyllwild, CA 92549). For recorded weather information, call 760-327-0222. For other information about hiking in the park, call the ranger station in Idyllwild at 909-659-2607; www.sanjac.statepark.org.

PALM SPRINGS AREA   For those uninterested in playing golf or lolling about in swimming pools, the desert environs of Palm Springs offer numerous hiking adventures.

In Palm Springs, the **Museum Trail** (1 mile) ascends the mountain behind the Palm Springs Desert Museum. Markers along this nature trail describe the plant life and other features of the terrain.

In **Palm Canyon**, an easy-to-difficult trail begins at the Trading Post and descends into the canyon and through the largest stand of fan palms in the world. The well-traveled trail winds back and forth across the stream. You can hike distances of a half-mile to 13 miles, and explore the 3200-foot ridges that overlook the canyon. Other trails in the canyons include the moderate **Fern Canyon Trail** (2.5 miles) and **Victor Trail** (2.5 miles), as well as the strenuous **Maynard Mine Trail** (4 miles) in Andreas Canyon. You can buy a map of hiking trails through the canyons at the Trading Post.

For very informative guided hikes through the Indian Canyons and elsewhere in the Palm Springs area, of varying degrees of difficulty, contact **Desert Safari**, next to the Trading Post in Palm Canyon. ~ 760-770-9191.

For a splendid view of Palm Springs and the Coachella Valley, climb the **Shannon Trail** (3.5 miles), a steep hike that ascends 1522-foot Smoke Tree Mountain.

At the eastern end of the Living Desert Reserve sits **Eisenhower Mountain Trail** (3 miles). The path carries across a wash and up the mountain slope for sweeping views of the Coachella Valley.

Bear Creek Canyon Trail (2 miles), located near La Quinta, also probes a desert valley. In the spring after rains this lovely area is alive with golden poppies and a bubbling creek.

Another vantage point is reached via **Edom Hill Trail** (3 miles). In the center of the Coachella Valley, this 1610-foot promontory offers panoramic views of Mt. San Jacinto, Mt. San Gorgonio, and the Salton Sea.

In Mecca Hills, **Painted Canyon Trail** (3 miles) explores a beautifully sculpted canyon.

JOSHUA TREE NATIONAL PARK AREA Joshua Tree National Park is an area where the High Desert meets the Low Desert, providing marvelous hikes through both environments.

Ryan Mountain Trail (1.5 miles) is a prime place to view both the Joshua trees and granite outcroppings for which the park is renowned. This difficult trail, which leads to the top of Mt. Ryan (5470 feet), also offers views of several valleys.

Another sweeping vista is reached along **Mastodon Peak Trail** (1.5 miles). Atop the 3371-foot promontory, the Hexie Mountains, Pinto Basin, and the Salton Sea extend before you.

Hidden Valley Trail (1-mile loop), beginning near Hidden Valley Campground, is a twisting loop through boulder-strewn desert to a legendary cattle rustler's hideout.

From Canyon Road, **Fortynine Palms Oasis Trail** (1.5 miles) is a moderate hike to a refreshing desert oasis. Near Cottonwood Visitors Center, **Lost Palms Oasis Trail** (3.75 miles) leads through a canyon to another oasis, which sports the largest group of fan palms in the park.

Lost Horse Mine Trail (2 miles) takes you to an old gold mine. It's a moderately strenuous hike that should be avoided in hot weather—there is no shade or water en route. A less taxing trip for anyone intent on exploring abandoned diggings is the **Desert Queen Mine Trail** (.2-mile overlook), located north from Geology Tour Road (a four-wheel drive is recommended).

The **Cottonwood to Morton Mill Trail** (.5 mile) leads to a gold-refining mill.

More than 150 bird species have been sighted at Anza–Borrego Desert State Park.

For the hearty hiker, **Boy Scout Trail** (8 miles) leaves from Indian Cove and traverses the western edge of Wonderland of Rocks.

Ideal for families, **Arch Rock Nature Trail** (.3-mile loop) in White Tank Campground wanders through intriguing rock formations while interpreting the geology of the region.

ANZA–BORREGO DESERT STATE PARK An arid landscape filled with desert wonders awaits hikers in Anza–Borrego. As with all desert hiking, you'll need plenty of water, protection from the sun, and a map of the area.

The most popular trail in Anza–Borrego Desert State Park is the **Borrego Palm Canyon Nature Trail** (1.5 miles). This short route leads to a palm grove and cool stream. If you're in good shape, you can continue up the canyon on **Borrego Palm Canyon Trail** (1.5 miles). There's a lot of boulder hopping, but the rewards are a palm-studded and colorful route.

In the Split Mountain area, rare elephant trees are the highlight of **Elephant Trees Discovery Loop Trail** (1.5 miles roundtrip).

A steep climb along **Marshal South Home Trail** (1 mile) leads to ruins of a writer's home on top of Ghost Mountain. The trailhead is in the Blair Valley area. Also in Blair Valley, **Morteros Trail** (.5 mile roundtrip) leads to a field of large granite boulders used by Indians as bedrock mortars.

Nearby **Pictograph Trail** (2 miles roundtrip) guides you to rocks painted by Diegueño Indians, then continues to a vista point above Vallecito Valley.

California Riding and Hiking Trail (6 miles) courses down a chaparral-covered mountain to the desert below. Lovely views of the Borrego Desert are seen from the ridge between Hellhole and Dry canyons. The trailhead is in the Culp Valley camp area.

From the Bow Willow area, **Mountain Palm Springs Canyon, North Fork** (1.3 miles) leads to a natural bowl ringed with more than 100 palm trees. **Mountain Palm Springs Canyon, South Fork** (1.5 miles) explores a pygmy palm grove and stand of elephant trees.

▼▼▼▼▼▼▼▼▼▼▼▼
Transportation

CAR

Route 10, the San Bernardino Freeway, travels east from Los Angeles through the heart of the Inland Empire and Low Desert. Near San Bernardino you can pick up **Route 18** (Rim of the World Drive), which runs along the entire length of the San Bernardino Mountains.

Farther east, **Route 62** departs Route 10 and leads northeast to Joshua Tree National Park, while **Route 111** courses southeast through Palm Springs and down to the Salton Sea.

From San Diego, **Route 8** goes east along the southern fringes of the Low Desert near the Mexican border. The main roads in Anza–Borrego Desert State Park are **Routes S22** and **78**, which travel east and west through the preserve.

Ontario International Airport and **Palm Springs International Airport** serve this region. Alaska Airlines, America West Airlines, American Airlines, Continental, Delta, Frontier Airlines, Northwest, Southwest Airlines, and United Airlines fly into Ontario.

Carriers into Palm Springs International Airport include Alaska Airlines, America West, American Airlines, American Eagle, Continental, Delta, Northwest and United Airlines.

AIR

Greyhound Bus Lines (800-231-2222; www.greyhound.com) offers service to San Bernardino at 596 North G Street, 909-884-4796; Riverside at 3911 University Avenue, 909-686-2345; Perris at 412 4th Street, 909-657-7813; Palm Springs at 311 North Indian Avenue, 760-325-2053; and Indio at 45-525 Oasis Street, 760-347-5888.

BUS

Amtrak (800-872-7245; www.amtrak.com) has one passenger train to San Bernardino, the "Southwest Chief." The "Sunset Limited" stops at the railroad platform on Jackson Street in Palm Springs. From here, Greyhound Bus Lines connects to Palm Springs. ~ 1170 West 3rd Street, San Bernardino; 909-884-1307.

TRAIN

Located at Ontario International Airport are the following rental agencies: **Avis Rent A Car** (800-331-1212), **Budget Rent A Car** (800-527-0700), **Hertz Rent A Car** (800-654-3131), and **National Car Rental** (800-227-7368).

Alamo Rent A Car (800-327-9633) and **Thrifty Car Rental** (800-367-2277), located outside the airport, have pickup service.

Several agencies are located at the Palm Springs terminal: **Avis Rent A Car** (800-331-1212), **Budget Rent A Car** (800-527-0700), **Dollar Rent A Car** (800-800-4000), **Hertz Rent A Car** (800-654-3131), and **National Car Rental** (800-227-7368). If you're looking for a jeep, contact **Aztec Rent A Car**. ~ 477 South Palm Canyon Drive; 760-325-2294; www.azteccarrentals.com.

CAR RENTALS

For local bus service in San Bernardino, Redlands and points in between call **OmniTrans**. ~ 909-379-7100; www.omnitrans.org. Riverside is served by the **Riverside Transit Agency**. ~ 909-682-1234; www.riversidetransit.com.

In the Palm Springs area, **Sun Bus** carries passengers to destinations throughout the Coachella Valley. ~ 760-343-3451; www.sunline.org.

PUBLIC TRANSIT

Strangely enough, Palm Springs no longer has a taxi cab company, but it does have more than a dozen limousine services for those who want to go out for the evening in style, among them **Red Carpet Limousine**. ~ 38471 Bel Air Drive; 760-325-4116. There's also **Palm Springs Limousine Services**. ~ 255 North El Cielo Road; 760-320-0044.

TAXIS

EIGHT

High Desert

Picture an endless expanse of basin and range, desert and mountain, a realm guarded by the sharp teeth of the Sierra Nevada and the gaping maw of Death Valley. California may be known for glittering cities and postcard beaches, but along its southeastern shoulder the Golden State unveils a different face entirely. Here the Mojave Desert reaches from Los Angeles County across an awesome swath of territory to Arizona and Nevada.

The sky in these parts is immense, and the landscape is so broad that mountains are like islands on its surface. The Mojave is a region of ancient lakebeds and crystalline sinks, ghost towns and deserted mines. When Jedediah Smith, one of the West's great explorers, trekked through in 1826, he declared the desert "a country of starvation."

Even today it seems desolate and unyielding. Winters are cold here, the summers hot. Rainfall, which dwindles from six inches in the western Mojave to less than two inches around Death Valley, comes only during winter. But plants proliferate and the area is alive with reptiles and small mammals—and, increasingly, people. Edwards Air Force Base and the NASA space shuttle make the Mojave a strategic aerospace center. Its western reaches around Antelope Valley are rapidly filling with developments spilling over from the Los Angeles Basin.

Foreign and unforgiving though it might be, the Mojave Desert has always possessed particular importance in the history of California. In 1774, Yuma Indians guided Juan Bautista de Anza and other Spanish explorers through this wasteland. By 1831 the vital Santa Fe Trail was open from Santa Fe to Los Angeles. Later in the century the U.S. Army converted other Indian paths into roads, opening them to wagon trains and stage coaches.

The land Jedediah Smith labeled "a complete barrens" proved rich in minerals. For four decades beginning in the 1870s, the Mojave was a major thoroughfare for 20-mule teams laden with borax and miners weighted down with gold, silver, zinc, and tungsten. The towns of Mojave and Barstow became important railroad centers; even now they remain essential crossroads, oases with amenities.

At the northern edge of the Mojave, in a land the Indians knew as "Tomesha" or "ground on fire," lies Death Valley. Measuring 120 miles long and varying in width from four to sixteen miles, it is among the hottest places on earth, second only to the Sahara. During summer the *average* daily high temperature is 116°.

This long narrow valley is itself only a small part of Death Valley National Park. In 1995, Death Valley was "upgraded" from a national monument to a national park, affording it a higher degree of protection and an additional 1.3 million acres. The 3.3 million-acre park is now the largest in the continental United States.

A museum without air conditioning, Death Valley is a giant geology lab displaying salt beds, sand dunes, and an 11,000-foot elevation climb. Its multitiered hills contain layers that are windows on the history of the earth. One level holds Indian arrowheads, another Ice Age fish, and beneath these deposits lies Precambrian rock.

At the end of the Pleistocene, when warming temperatures melted glaciers atop the Sierra Nevada, this desiccated domain was covered by a vast inland sea. Today mud playas and the shadows of ancient shores are all that remain. Instead of water, the lowlands are filling with rock debris from the neighboring Black and Panamint mountains.

One of the most hauntingly beautiful places in the world, Death Valley received its ominous name in 1849 when a party of pioneers, intent on following a shortcut to the gold fields, crossed the wasteland, barely escaping with their lives. Later, prospectors stayed to work the territory, discovering rich borax deposits during the 1880s and providing the region with a home industry.

Testament to the diversity of the High Desert, Death Valley contains the lowest spot in the contiguous U.S. (Badwater, 282 feet below sea level), yet rests within 60 miles of the highest place (Mt. Whitney, 14,495 feet above sea level). Its snow-rimmed neighbor, the Sierra Nevada, is the largest single mountain range in the country, a solitary block of earth 430 miles long and 80 miles wide. A mere child in the long count of geologic history, the Sierra Nevada rose from the earth's surface a few million years back and did not reach its present form until 750,000 years ago. During the Pleistocene epoch, glaciers spread across the land, grinding and cutting at the mountains. They carved river valleys and deep canyons, and sculpted bald domes, fluted cliffs, and stone towers.

The glaciers left a landscape dominated by ragged peaks where streams number in the thousands and canyons plunge 5000 feet. There are cliffs sheer as glass that compete with the sky for dominance. It is, as an early pioneer described it, a "land of fire and ice."

On the western flank of this massive range lie Sequoia and Kings Canyon national parks. Within eyeshot of the brine pools and scrub growth of Death Valley, they contain more than 1000 glacial lakes and boast rich stands of giant sequoia trees, the largest living things on earth.

Unlike its western face, which slopes gently down into California's verdant Central Valley, the eastern wall of the Sierra Nevada falls away in a furious succession of granite cliffs to the alkali floor of the Owens Valley.

Folded between three mountain ranges, with 14,000-foot peaks on either side, the long, slender Owens Valley was discovered by Joseph Walker in 1834. Indians had occupied the territory for perhaps 40,000 years, even during the period up to 10,000 years ago when the canyon floor was an immense lake. Paiutes later dominated the region, subsisting on rabbits, birds, and nuts, and perfecting the art of basket weaving.

During the 1860s gold and silver miners flooded the area, discovering rich deposits in Cerro Gordo, Darwin, and elsewhere. By the turn of the century, Owens Valley was a prime ranch and farm region planted in corn, wheat, and alfalfa. A population of 4500 settlers lived in an area dominated by Owens Lake, a 30-foot-deep lake that stretched across 100 square miles.

Then in 1905 agents from water-hungry Los Angeles began buying up lands and riparian rights. Two years later Los Angeles voters passed a multimillion-dollar aqueduct bond. When the 223-mile conduit was completed in 1913, the destruction of Owens Valley commenced. Over the next few decades, as Los Angeles systematically drained the basin, trees withered, ranchers sold out, and farms went unwatered. Outraged residents rebelled, dynamiting the water works and pleading their case in Washington.

Today bristlecone pines, the oldest living things on earth, still occupy the nearby White Mountains, as they have for 4000 years. The Mammoth Lakes region to the north, with its alpine forests and glacial lakes, remains a favorite ski area. But Owens Valley itself is a dusty testament to the needs of a distant metropolis. A place of unconquerable beauty, bounded by granite mountains and visited with hot winds, it has in the end become a manmade extension of the great Mojave Desert.

▼▼▼▼▼▼▼▼▼▼
Mojave Desert

Stretching from Los Angeles County all the way to Arizona and Nevada, the Mojave Desert is a region of daunting distance. Sightseeing this open range means driving hundreds of miles between points of interest. As a result, the descriptions below are organized by geographic region, some covering extremely extensive areas.

Bakersfield actually lies west of the Mojave but incorporates much of its history and culture. Antelope Valley sits in the desert's western corner just south of the town of Mojave. The "Barstow area" extends south from the town of Barstow for 35 miles and east for over 100 miles. Death Valley, actually part of the Mojave Desert, is treated as a separate destination.

SIGHTS   **BAKERSFIELD AREA** Up in Grapevine Canyon, where Tejon Pass cuts a notch in the Tehachapi Mountains, the U.S. Army built an outpost in 1854 to patrol American Indian tribes on the Sebastian Indian Reservation. At **Fort Tejon State Historic Park**, a few restored and reconstructed adobe structures stand, set against a backdrop of curving mountains. Once headquarters for the First Dragoons, horse-mounted troops that controlled all of Southern California, this mountain outpost was the center of the effort to secure this region as part of the United States. Today there is little to see here, though mock re-enactments of 1850s military life and Civil War battles are staged on the first and third Sunday of each month, April through October. Admission. ~ Route 5, Lebec; 661-248-6692, fax 661-248-8373; www.cal-parks.ca.gov.

Pride of Bakersfield is the **Kern County Museum**, a reconstructed town dating to the late 19th century. Dotted across the 56-acre grounds are about five dozen Western structures, each depicting life on the early frontier. There are watchmaker and dressmaker shops, and a log cabin complete with photographs of Abe Lincoln over the fireplace. You can step up to the Fellows Hotel, visit old Mr. Pinckney's house, and tour the railway station. An excellent outdoor museum, the town contains everything from caboose to calaboose and features an adjacent museum that re-creates the history of the region's vital history and culture. Admission. ~ 3801 Chester Avenue, Bakersfield; 661-852-5000, fax 661-322-6415; www.kcmuseum.org, e-mail caenriquez @kern.org.

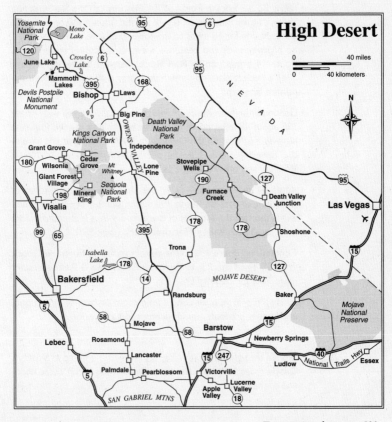

Text continued on page 522.

Three-day Weekend

Owens Valley and Death Valley

It's quite common to see sports car clubs, large groups of motorcyclists, and other serious road warriors in Death Valley, and this excursion will show you why. It involves almost 600 miles of driving, more than half of it on two-lane blacktop, spread over three days—a bit much if you have a backseat full of kids, but a fantastic scenic journey for lovers of the open road.

DAY 1
- Eat a big breakfast or pack some munchables to eat on the road; you won't find much in the way of food along today's travel route.

- Taking Route 5 north from Los Angeles through the San Fernando Valley, exit northbound on Route 14, the Antelope Valley Freeway, and continue for 68 miles to the town of Mojave, where the divided highway ends and becomes a two-lane route. Farther along, Route 14 brings you to **Red Rock Canyon State Park** (page 524), a perfect place to stretch your legs with a hike through the painted landscape.

- Continue north on Route 14, which eventually merges with Route 395 about 49 miles north of Mojave, becoming a divided four-lane highway that runs up the **Owens Valley** (page 540) at the base of the towering Sierra Nevada, offering nonstop views of Mount Whitney and other majestic peaks.

- After 41 miles of freeway, at the almost nonexistent town of Olancha exit east on Route 190, which skirts a dry lake bed and winds through the foothills of the dust-dry Inyo Mountains before entering **Death Valley National Park** (page 555).

- Continue on Route 190 to the visitors center at **Furnace Creek** (page 557) and check in to **Furnace Creek Inn & Ranch Resort** (page 561) for two nights.

- Taking a nap in your air-conditioned room or basking by the pool until dinner probably sounds pretty good about now.

DAY 2
- Explore the sights of Death Valley, starting with a drive up to **Scotty's Castle** (page 559) and **Ubehebe Crater** (page 559) at the north end of the park.

- Returning to the resort, enjoy a relaxing midday break before setting out to see other park highlights including **Zabriskie Point** (page 558) and **Dante's View** (page 558).

- Try out at least one of the unpaved backcountry roads that lead to Death Valley's hidden scenic treasures.

DAY 3 • After checking out of Furnace Creek Inn, drive south through the park on Route 178, with a detour along **Artist Drive** (page 557) and a short sidetrip to **Natural Bridge** (page 557).

- Where Route 178 intersects Route 127 near the southeast corner of the park, turn south (right) to follow Route 127 over Ibex Pass and continue for 56 miles, joining Route 15 southbound at Baker.

- It's about 160 miles back to Los Angeles via Routes 15 and 10. You may wish to take a break at the touristy **Calico Ghost Town San Bernardino Regional Park** (page 526) east of Barstow or, if time permits, get off Route 5 on Route 138 and follow scenic Route 2, the Angeles Crest Highway, for 60 miles over the San Gabriel Mountains and through Angeles National Forest, descending into Glendale.

ANTELOPE VALLEY For Angelenos, the Mojave Desert begins in **Antelope Valley** on the far side of the San Gabriel Mountains. Here urbanization has sprawled over the hills to create Palmdale and Lancaster, towns long on aerospace and short on soul.

Backed against the mountains are several natural attractions that make this western corner of the Mojave a dramatic intro-

HIDDEN ▶

duction to the desert. The first is a scenic drive into the **Juniper Hills** (go south from the town of Pearblossom along 106th Street East and Juniper Road). Climbing to 4600 feet, this loop trades the Joshua trees of the valley floor for higher-elevation piñon and juniper trees and provides endless views across a multihued desert.

Connect with Route N6 and you'll arrive at **Devil's Punchbowl County Natural Area.** This wedge-shaped canyon, paralleled on two fronts by earthquake faults, has been crushed between opposing geologic forces. On either side sedimentary rocks have been thrust upward to create vertical walls reaching up to 300 feet that are folding in upon each other like the pages of a closing book. Hiking trails lead through these angular sandstone slabs, passing stands of juniper, piñon, and manzanita. A nature center has live animal displays that include birds of prey and insects. Tours of the San Andreas Fault are conducted on Sunday; call for hours or to make an appointment. ~ 28000 Devil's Punchbowl Road, Pearblossom; 661-944-2743, fax 661-944-6924.

Unique is too timid a term to describe the **Antelope Valley Indian Museum.** Located on a prehistoric trade route, the museum houses artifacts that were bartered from the California coastal islands to the Southwestern desert. With displays of stone, shell, and bone tools, kachina dolls, and basketry, the museum offers a cross section of American Indian life in California. But the truly impressive element is the museum building itself. Built directly into the rocks that backdrop the complex, it's a chalet-style house with two gabled turrets and seven different roof levels. Constructed in the 1930s as a private home, the facility contains walls of wood and natural bedrock. One room has a rock floor with huge boulders rising in the center. These natural formations combine with brilliant murals and colorfully painted ceilings to create a striking desert setting. Call for tour reservations. Closed Monday through Friday and June to mid-September. Admission. ~ 15701 East Avenue M, Lancaster; 661-942-3055, fax 661-940-7327; www.calparksmojave.com.

On the other side of Lancaster's sprawling metropolis, about 14 miles away, is the **Antelope Valley California Poppy Reserve.** From mid-March to mid-May, when California's state flower blooms, these slopes are transformed into a wildflower wonderland. In addition to the bright-hued countryside, there is an architecturally noteworthy visitors center, with three sides built into the earth for insulation against desert extremes. The visitors center is open mid-

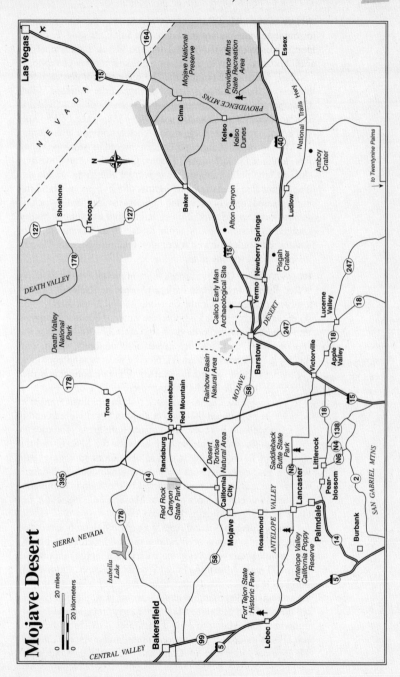

Mojave Desert

March to early May. Ranger-led walks start at the visitors center on Saturday and Sunday at 11 a.m. and 1 p.m. Parking fee during poppy season. ~ 15101 West Lancaster Road, Lancaster; 661-724-1180, fax 661-940-7327; www.calparksmojave.com/poppy.

To find out if the poppies are blooming and for general information on the Antelope Valley area, contact the **Antelope Valley Chamber of Commerce**. Closed Saturday and Sunday. ~ 554 West Lancaster Boulevard, Lancaster; 661-948-4518, fax 661-949-1212; www.lancasterchamber.org, e-mail lcoc@lancasterchamber.org.

Most of the gold mines that once flowered in Antelope Valley have long since died. **Burton's Tropico Gold Mine**, shut down and closed to the public, can still be seen from afar in its hillside setting. Amid slag heaps and the detritus of a bygone era stand the mining buildings. Formerly one of Southern California's richest strikes, it is now a cluster of tin structures and woodframe houses ravaged by desert wind. ~ From Route 14 in Rosamond, take Rosamond Boulevard west four miles, then turn right on Mojave Tropico Road for one mile.

MOJAVE AREA   One of nature's most impressive desert displays is **Red Rock Canyon State Park**, a photogenic badlands that resembles a miniature Grand Canyon. As you enter through the sheer-walled gorge that leads into the valley, the landscape opens into a succession of accordion-pleated cliffs. Eroded by water, the rockfaces are carved into minarets, spires, and crenelated towers. Nearby walls of sandstone have been formed by weather to create columnar structures resembling stalagmites.

The opening scenes of the 1993 hit *Jurassic Park* were filmed at Red Rock Canyon State Park.

This 27,500-acre park rests in a biologic transition zone between the Mojave and the Sierra Nevada and is alive with flora and fauna from both areas. The canyon also sits on a geologic cusp between the Mojave and the Great Basin, making it a kind of outdoor museum. Little wonder that everyone from early American Indians to modern-day movie makers has been attracted to the region. Admission. ~ Route 14 about 20 miles north of Mojave; 661-942-0662, fax 661-940-7327; www.calparksmojave.com.

Desert Tortoise Natural Area is a unique habitat housing one of the largest known concentrations of desert tortoises. This 40-square-mile preserve serves as sanctuary for a reptile that can live up to 100 years. Measuring only 15 inches, the desert tortoise digs burrows that are often 10 feet long. Since they hibernate in winter and stay underground to avoid summer heat, the best time to see them is from March to May in the early morning and late afternoon. From March to May a naturalist is on duty; there are several self-guided loop trails, restrooms, and a visitors center. ~ Three miles northeast of California City along Randsburg-

Mojave Road (graded). For more information, contact the Desert Tortoise Preserve Committee at 4067 Mission Inn Avenue, Riverside, CA 92501, or call the Bureau of Land Management at 760-384-5400, fax 760-384-5499; www.tortoisetracks.org.

The "living ghost town" of **Randsburg,** as well as neighboring **Johannesburg** and **Red Mountain,** is rich in minerals and history. Together these frontier communities formed a mining district that boomed first from gold deposits, then tungsten and silver. Of course that was a century ago, but today Randsburg still retains an aura of the 1890s. Many of the houses in town are stripped of paint and seem ready to fall to the next desert wind; others are restored and occupied. There's a gravity-feed gas pump, wooden sidewalk, and an outhouse with a crescent moon carved in the door. You'll pass a white-steepled church and a succession of tin-roof stores whose signs have long since faded into indecipherable blurs.

The **Randsburg General Store** still has its antique soda fountain and grizzled clientele. And over at the **Desert Museum** (Butte Avenue) you can view such mining-era artifacts as a miniature five-ton steam locomotive (which seems more like a toy train for big kids than a real machine). The museum is open weekends, and by appointment. ~ 35 Butte Avenue, Randsburg; 760-374-2111.

BARSTOW AREA Crossroads of the Mojave is the sun-baked community of **Barstow.** An important railroad town, Barstow is the converging point for the Union Pacific and Santa Fe railways. It's also the intersection of Routes 58, 15, and 40, which together cover much of the California desert.

You'll find the **California State Welcome Center** tucked away in the Tanger Outlet Center. There are pamphlets, maps, and an information desk. ~ 2796 Tanger Way, Suite 100, Barstow; 760-253-4782, fax 760-253-4814; www.visitmojavedesert.com, e-mail contact@visitmojavedesert.com.

The nearby **Mojave River Valley Museum** has a more complete collection of artifacts and memorabilia. Dedicated to the preservation of local history and culture, it contains discoveries from the Calico Early Man Site and specimens of desert minerals and gems. There is also a display depicting the recent advent of the space industry. ~ 270 East Virginia Way, Barstow; 760-256-5452; www.wemweb.com/mrvm.

Surprisingly, just a few miles from the drab streets of Barstow you'll discover folded and faulted mountains that are layer cakes of color. Drive out to **Rainbow Basin Natural Area** and encounter a deep canyon surrounded by striped cliffs of sedimentary rock. Rich in fossil deposits, the adjacent hills were created over eons and contain the remains of mastodons, rhinos, and camel-type creatures.

Even more impressive is the bald beauty of the place. These are hills the color of dawn built in a myriad of shapes that change character with the light. The three-mile road that loops through this rock preserve passes zebra-striped buttes, boulders formed into fists, and tortuously twisted formations. To explore the basin from Barstow follow Irwin Road north for five miles from Route 58, then turn left on Fossil Bed Road for three miles to the loop drive.

The commercial outlets are as numerous as the memories at **Calico Ghost Town San Bernardino Regional Park**. This old mining center has been transformed into a kind of windblown theme park complete with narrow-gauge railroad rides and a hall of illusions. Native charm endures despite it all. There are stone houses built into the surrounding mountain and woodframe stores bent with time. Mining paraphernalia lies scattered everywhere; and the town's cemetery and open mines remain prime exploring sites. Camping is permitted. Admission. ~ Ghost Town Road, ten miles northeast of Barstow; 760-254-2122, fax 760-254-2047; www.calicotown.com, e-mail calico@mscomm.com.

Perhaps 200,000 years before Calico Ghost Town was even conceived, hunters roamed the **Calico Early Man Archaeological Site**. Back in those Pleistocene times the landscape was lush with junipers, live oaks, and pines. The climate was temperate and a large body of water, Lake Manix, attracted mammoths, sloths, and saber-toothed cats.

This scientifically important site was a tool factory where early man rendered local deposits of chert and chalcedony into choppers, picks, and scrapers. Directed for several years by Dr. Lewis S. B. Leakey, famed discoverer of Africa's Olduvai Gorge, the site is so ancient it upset earlier theories that man was in the New World for only 10,000 or 20,000 years. In fact Calico Early Man might not have been a *Homo sapiens* at all, but a now-extinct species such as *Homo erectus* or *Homo sapiens neandertalensis*.

Today, either on a guided or self-guided tour, you can view the archaeological pits, see early stone tools, and wander back in your mind to an age of ice when the desert was in bloom. To get your body to the place from which your mind can wander, take Route 15 for about 15 miles northeast from Barstow, get off at the Minneola exit, and follow the signs north about 2.5 miles.

COLORFUL CALICO

It was 1881 when prospectors struck it rich and Calico boomed to life with over 20 saloons, a temperance society, and its own Chinatown. More than $86 million in gold, silver, and other minerals was mined from the multi-hued "calico" mountains before the town went bust. Eventually Walter Knott, of Knott's Berry Farm fame, restored the ramshackle town and turned it over to the local government.

Closed Monday and Tuesday; guided tours offered Wednesday through Sunday. For information, call the Bureau of Land Management. Admission. ~ 760-252-6000, fax 760-252-6098; www.ca.blm.gov/barstow.

North of the San Bernardino Mountains, where the hills descend to meet the Mojave Desert, lie the **Lucerne Valley** and the **Apple Valley**. Characterized by dry lake beds and granite heights, the region is 35 miles south of Barstow.

Victorville, the chief town hereabouts, is known primarily as a stop along Route 15, the golden road that whisks Angelenos to the promised land of Las Vegas.

Two long, lonesome highways, Routes 40 and 15, travel east from Barstow deep into the desert. Along Route 40, which tracks east toward Arizona and New Mexico, chocolate brown mountains crowd the horizon in every direction.

Along Route 40 about 35 miles from Barstow, **Pisgah Crater**, a 250-foot cinder cone, rises to the south. Another young volcano, **Amboy Crater**, lies along old Route 66 (National Trails Highway), which diverts from Route 40 in Ludlow. A curving black figure against a mountain backdrop, the volcano is surrounded by a vast lava field. To the southeast this lava flow gives way to **Bristol Dry Lake**, an ancient freshwater lake that now supports an extensive chloride works.

The vast area between Routes 40 and 15, east of Barstow and west of Needles, appears to the interstate traveler to offer very little, but the **Mojave National Preserve** easily rivals Death Valley, Anza–Borrego, and Joshua Tree for desert beauty. In the heart of the scenic area is **Hole-in-the-Wall**, where volcanic rock solidified into all sorts of unusual formations, ideal for rock scrambling and framing funny pictures. ~ To reach Hole-in-the-Wall campground, take Route 40 east from Barstow for 100 miles, go ten miles north on Essex Road, then turn right onto the Black Canyon Road fork and follow it ten miles; 760-733-4040, fax 760-733-4027; www. nps.gov/moja.

◄ HIDDEN

From Hole-in-the-Wall, you can make a circle tour of other highlights of the area. First, go north on Black Canyon Road to Midhills, where juniper and piñons provide shade and relief from the prevailing scrub of the desert. Then turn left on Cedar Canyon Road, and left again on the paved Kelso-Cima Road. This leads to **Kelso Depot**, a surprisingly gracious, abandoned Spanish-style train depot that may one day be restored as a visitors center.

Then continue to the marked turnoff for **Kelso Dunes**. A three-mile approach road leads to the tallest dunes in the California desert. An intriguing phenomenon here results from the wind, which shifts around the dunes in circular fashion, causing the tall grasses to etch round tracks in the sand with their tips. If you hike the dunes, watch for these telltale marks and for the lizards

◄ HIDDEN

inhabiting this forlorn but beautiful spot. ~ To get there from Route 40, travel 80 miles east of Barstow, then go north 15 miles on Kelbaker Road; turn left onto a marked road (just past the power line). This rough dirt road leads three miles to a parking lot.

From Kelso Dunes, return to Kelbaker Road, go south to Route 40, and once again take the Essex Road exit. This time stay on Essex Road and go 16 miles northwest to **Providence Mountains State Recreation Area**. This island of state land within the Scenic Area rests sidesaddle on the slopes of a rugged mountain. From the visitors center, perched at 4300 feet, you can gaze across 300 square miles of desert to mountains 125 miles away in Arizona. Buttes, dunes, and broad desert valleys extend in a 180° panorama.

HIDDEN ▶

The park's most remarkable feature, however, lies not upon the earth but within it. Carved deep into the Providence Mountains are the **Mitchell Caverns**, limestone caves filled with elaborate rock formations. For about 500 years the Chemehuevi Indians used the caverns, blackening the walls with campfires. Touring El Pakiva and Tecopa caves, you'll see delicate stalactites and monstrous stalagmites in a natural cathedral. Cavern tours are scheduled weekdays at 1:30 p.m. and on weekends and holidays at 10 a.m., 1:30 p.m., and 3 p.m.; from Labor Day to Memorial Day, only the 1:30 p.m. weekend tour is offered. Admission. ~ To reach the park take Route 40 east from Barstow for 100 miles, then go 16 miles northwest on Essex Road; 760-928-2586.

LODGING

Towns in the Mojave Desert are little more than corridors for cars. Lined with neon, they resound with the shudder and drone of passing trucks. The larger communities have standard motel accommodations, catering to truck drivers, desert rats, and itinerant salesmen. Bed-and-breakfast inns, it seems, are rare as rain out here.

The crossroads town of Barstow, where Routes 58, 14, and 40 converge, is a neon enclave. Here the sleeper's strip lies along Main Street, where you'll find the **American Inn**, which has a pool and a cluster of adequately appointed rooms. ~ 1350 West Main Street, Barstow; 760-256-8921, fax 760-256-5829; www. americaninnbarstow.com. BUDGET.

The nicest place in town is **Ramada Inn Barstow**, a 148-unit hotel with adjoining restaurant, pool, and jacuzzi. Ultramodern in design, it's clean to the point of being sterile. Rooms are finished in blond woods and nicely appointed. They are fairly spacious, well-carpeted, and include room service. The ample lobby area is decorated with fabric paintings and furnished with plump, irresistible armchairs. ~ 1511 East Main Street, Barstow; 760-256-5673, 800-272-6232, fax 760-256-5917; www.ramadabar stow.com. MODERATE.

Named after the quirky movie that was filmed here, the **Bagdad**
Café is decorated with pictures of the stars and scenes from the
movie. Souvenir T-shirts are on sale, but the eatery hasn't gone
highfalutin' on us. It serves good-quality, no-nonsense grub: hamburgers, chicken-fried steak, and made-before-your-eyes milk-
shakes. ~ 46548 National Trails Highway/Old Route 66, New-
berry Springs; 760-257-3101. BUDGET.

Chain restaurants and fast-food outlets proliferate throughout Antelope Valley. In Lancaster, the largest town in this western Mojave region, you'll encounter **Marie Callender's**, a sterile
brass-and-hardwood-style restaurant known more for its homemade pies than gourmet dinners. The menu includes fresh pasta
dishes as well as vegetable casserole, meatloaf, hamburgers, and
chicken dishes. ~ 1649 West Avenue K, Lancaster; 661-945-6958,
fax 661-945-5366. BUDGET TO MODERATE.

Idle Spurs Steak House is Barstow's gathering place, a common denominator destination for locals and outlanders alike. A
Texas-size establishment with a lounge and two dining rooms, it's
Southwestern in style. The menu is a reasonably priced steak-and-
seafood affair with prime rib, pork ribs, chicken, scallops, lobster, and halibut. No lunch on the weekend. ~ 690 Old Route 58,
Barstow; 760-256-8888; www.idlespurssteakhouse.com, e-mail
idlespurs@gte.com. MODERATE TO DELUXE.

When in doubt, cover all bases: that seems to be the motto at
Canton Restaurant. Ostensibly a Chinese restaurant, it offers egg
rolls, sweet and sour pork, *chow yuk*, and other Asian standards.
But the switch-hitting eatery also serves breakfast all day and
prepares sandwiches, steaks, rainbow trout, fried scallops, and
fried chicken on toast. On toast? Closed on Monday and the last
two weeks in December. ~ 1300 West Main Street, Barstow;
760-256-9565. BUDGET TO MODERATE.

Somehow the desert seems an unlikely place to find fine art and
contemporary fashions. There are stores in Mojave and Barstow,
but most serve the local populace.

AUTHOR FAVORITE

The year-round Christmas lights add to the local color at **Peggy**
Sue's Nifty 50's Diner, a jukebox and soda-fountain joint that serves
burgers, sandwiches, and all-American lunches and dinners. Meatloaf,
honey-dipped chicken, roast beef, and chicken-fried steak are specialties.
For decor there are photos of '50s celebrities as well as period pieces
from the early era of rock-and-roll. ~ Yermo and Ghost Town roads,
Yermo; 760-254-3370, fax 760-254-3155. BUDGET.

Calico Ghost Town, a kind of antique theme park in the mountains ten miles northeast of Barstow, has several shops. These are located in the town's 1880s-era buildings and include a confectionery, spice shop, pottery store, and rock shop. The Old West town also features the obligatory general store, which in this case generally sells tourist items. ~ Ghost Town Road; 760-254-2122; www.calicotown.com, e-mail calico@mscomm.com.

NIGHTLIFE   Out in the railroad town of Barstow, the **Idle Spurs Steak House** features a dancefloor; a live band performs about twice a month, and people sometimes dance to recorded music. ~ 690 Old Route 58, Barstow; 760-256-8888.

PARKS   **SADDLEBACK BUTTE STATE PARK** 🚶🐎 Sprinkled with Joshua trees and backdropped by its 3651-foot namesake, this desert facility gazes out toward distant mountains. Roadrunners, desert tortoises, kit fox, and rattlesnakes inhabit these 2900 acres. Trails lead up the granite butte and through the state park. There are picnic areas here. Day-use fee, $3. ~ Located on East Avenue J, 17 miles east of Lancaster; 661-942-0662, fax 661-940-7327.

▲ There are 50 tent/RV sites (no hookups); $9 per night.

RED ROCK CANYON STATE PARK 🚶🚴🐎 This 28,000-acre facility, situated amid sculpted cliffs, is a major sightseeing destination. Its deposits of red sandstone, white clay, lava, and pink tuff have been uplifted and then eroded to create a dramatic landscape. Joshua trees, desert holly, and creosote bushes abound and wildlife is plentiful. The Visitors Center (closed weekdays and all summer) displays wildlife and geology as well as gold mining, American Indian, and film histories. Day-use fee, $3. ~ Route 14, about 25 miles north of Mojave; 661-942-0662, fax 661-940-7327; www.calparksmojave.com.

▲ There are 50 family campsites. Tent/RV sites are available (no hookups); $9 per night.

MOJAVE NARROWS REGIONAL PARK 🚶🚴🐎⚓ Sitting astride an old riverbed, this 880-acre park boasts two lakes and an intaglio of waterways. There are broad meadows and stately stands of willow and cottonwood. Renowned for its fishing (permits are required and can be obtained at park), the park also offers riding stables and hiking trails. Facilities include restrooms, picnic areas, a snack bar, and a bait shop. Day-use fee, $3 per vehicle, $1 walk-in. ~ From Route 15, take the Bear Valley Road exit east and turn left on Ridgecrest, which turns into Yates Road. Located at 18000 Yates Road, Victorville; 760-245-2226, fax 760-245-7887.

▲ There are 38 sites with hookups and 50 tent sites; $17 for hookups, $10 for tent sites.

MOJAVE NATIONAL PRESERVE 🏃 Featuring volcanic rock formations, a variety of cacti, and shady groves of juniper and piñons, this remote area showcases the diverse beauty of the desert. People come here primarily for the camping. The petroglyph-covered rock walls of Hole-in-the-Wall campground open up into Box Canyon with great views of Wild Horse Mesa. The Midhills campground is surrounded by trees and populated by bobcats, coyotes, and foxes. Hiking trails wind through both campgrounds. Stock up before you arrive—restaurants and groceries are dozens of miles away. See the "Mojave Desert" sights section above for more details. ~ From Barstow take Route 40 east for 100 miles, go eight miles north on Essex Road, then another eight miles on Black Canyon Road. Continue past Hole-in-the-Wall campground to reach Midhills campground; 760-255-8801; www.nps.gov/moja.

The Mojave Desert is home to the Mojave Green Rattlesnake, whose venom is the most potent of any North American rattler.

▲ Each campground has from 25 to 35 tent/RV sites (no hookups); $12 per night.

PROVIDENCE MOUNTAINS STATE RECREATION AREA 🏃 This 5900-acre park, set on a mountain slope overlooking a vast desert panorama, is remarkably beautiful. Hiking trails lead into the hills; and Mitchell Caverns, a series of spectacular limestone formations, provide sightseeing opportunities. You have to go with a guide to see Mitchell Caverns (closed weekdays during summer; for more information, call 760-928-2586). Bighorn sheep, wild burros, coyotes, and bobcats traverse the area and yucca and cacti cover the hillsides. You'll find restrooms and a picnic area. As with the Mojave National Preserve, restaurants and groceries are dozens of miles away. See the "Mojave Desert" sightseeing section above for further details. Day-use fee, $3. ~ From Barstow go east on Route 40 for 115 miles, then northwest on Essex Road for 16 miles; 661-942-0662, fax 661-940-7327.

▲ There are six tent/RV sites (no hookups); $10 per night.

AFTON CANYON 🏃 🚲 🐎 One of the rare places in the Mojave Desert to have year-round running water, this valley has been carved for millennia by the Mojave River. The result is a remarkable series of eroded cliffs, brilliantly colored and reminiscent of the Grand Canyon. There are remote gorges to explore and ancient Indian trails nearby. The railroad runs through the center of this scenic wonder, with a steel trestle crossing one span. The place also has limited off-road-vehicle access, so in some places you have to weigh the beauty against the intrusions. There are pit toilets and picnic areas. ~ From Barstow take Route 15 east for 38 miles, then go south for three miles on Afton Road; 760-252-6000.

▲ There are 22 tent/RV campsites with primitive facilities (no hookups); $6 per night.

▼▼▼▼▼▼▼▼▼▼▼▼▼▼▼▼▼

Sequoia & Kings Canyon

Two of California's finest parks, Sequoia and Kings Canyon, lie next to each other along the western slopes of the Sierra Nevada range. Encompassing 14,000-foot peaks, alpine lakes, and stands of giant sequoia trees, they provide a lush counterpoint to the flat, dry Mojave. These natural wonders provide a stunning landscape where the mountains extend into the sky, and the sky knows no limit.

SIGHTS

SEQUOIA NATIONAL PARK Prelude to the park is the drive to Mineral King, a remote mountain hamlet that boomed as a silver mining center during the 1870s and quickly went bust. The 25-mile Mineral King Road, branching from Route 198 a few miles before the park entrance, leads to a remote and particularly pretty section of Sequoia National Park. (Mineral King Road is usually closed in winter.)

Though paved along most stretches, the road winds through the mountains in maddening fashion, tracing the random course of the Kaweah River. En route are sharp canyons, switchbacks that jackknife above sheer cliffs, and a lone arched bridge.

Mule deer and black bear inhabit the region. Along the precipitous slopes ponderosa pines and quaking aspens give way to white fir, incense cedar, and sequoia. At **Atwell Mill**, a late-19th-century logging center, there are Indian bedrock mortars as well as an old steam engine. Here you'll also see the ever-present sequoia stumps that are a legacy of the logging era. Farther along lies **Mineral King**, a mountain village studded with numerous cabins, each braced against the winter wind by the chimney stem of a woodburning stove.

HIDDEN ►

At **Mineral King** there's a campground (Cold Springs), ranger station, a cluster of cozy private cottages, and a lovely subalpine meadow. All around are the mountains, rock-ribbed ranges that leap up and outward from the town, leaving far behind on their shoulders waterfalls, talus slides, and rivers that are silver pennants fluttering down the canyons. And everywhere there are hiking trails, which radiate from Mineral King like spokes from a hub.

Generals Highway, the road through Sequoia and Kings Canyon, is a continuation of Route 198, which enters the park at Ash Mountain. The nearby **Foothill Visitors Center** (559-565-3134) provides maps, books, and information, but your symbolic entrance into this world of granite mountains and giant trees comes a few miles beyond as you reach **Tunnel Rock**. The roadway, cut from a monstrous boulder, once served as a portal to the park.

At **Hospital Rock**, a granite outcropping near the turnoff to Buckeye Flats Campground, there are pictographs from an early tribe of Indians. These painted designs, red stains against gray rock, were a vital element in local American Indian culture. Of a more

practical nature are the nearby mortar holes, ground into the re-
sistant bedrock by Indian women pounding acorns into meal.

Generals Highway is menacingly steep, ascending 4700 feet
in 16 miles between Ash Mountain and Giant Forest, and numbering in its serpentine course some 230 curves. Each switchback
reveals a succession of ridges folded against one another. Domes
and spires of granite dominate the horizon; from the valleys stands
of conifers run along the hillsides, vaulting upward and then falling
back just short of the peaks. As you ascend into the heart of the
park, this mix of scrub vegetation and tall pine surrenders to
stately groves of sequoia. Generals Highway is usually closed for
road cleanup after snowstorms from November through April. The
11-mile section of Generals Highway between Potwisha Campground and Giant Forest Village is not recommended for vehicles over 22 feet long. Instead, take Route 180 from the north.

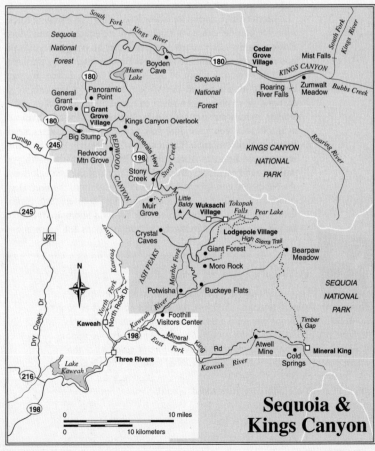

Sequoia &
Kings Canyon

Round Meadow is a flowering glade with a one-mile loop trail that passes regal stands of sequoia.

Starting at the village, Crescent Meadow Road curves through the woods past several points of interest. **Auto Log**, a giant tree that fell in 1917, has been dug out to form a driveway. If for some unspeakable reason you long to wheel your car onto a sequoia, this is your only chance. The **Parker Group**, a pretty grove of sequoias, lies farther up the road, as does **Tunnel Log**, a felled sequoia under which you can drive (having already driven *over* another of the brutes).

From here, noble explorers, it's on to **Crescent Meadow**, a wetland surrounded by sequoia trees and filled (in spring and summer) with wildflowers. Continue four-fifths of a mile along the meadow trail and you'll arrive at **Tharp's Log**, a fallen hollow sequoia that was converted into a log cabin (in the literal sense of the term).

A fork from Crescent Meadow Road runs past **Hanging Rock**, a granite boulder poised uneasily above a deep chasm, and **Moro Rock**, where a steep quarter-mile staircase ascends a magnificent dome. The views from this 6725-foot summit reach along the Great Western Divide, a chain of 12,000-foot peaks. In the dizzying depths 4000 feet below, the Middle Fork of the Kaweah River carves a stone channel en route to the San Joaquin Valley.

In the summer months one-hour tours of **Crystal Caves** are available, but you must first buy tickets at either Lodgepole or Foothills Visitors Center. The hike down to these beautiful caverns is steep and requires sturdy shoes. Once beneath the earth you will encounter temperatures of 48°, so bring along extra clothing.

Next, you can follow Generals Highway up to the central attraction of the entire park. Surrounded by conifers that appear little more than children, stands the **General Sherman Tree**. The largest living thing on earth, this leviathan weighs 1385 tons, meas-

sights

AUTHOR FAVORITE

From Grant Grove a mountain road corkscrews up to **Panoramic Point**. Situated at 7520 feet, this lookout could just as soon be at sea level considering the peaks that rise above it. Stretched along the horizon in a kind of granite amphitheater is a line of bald domes, cresting at 13,000- and 14,000-foot heights. Each bears a name resonant of the simple poetry of stone—Kettle Dome, Marble Mountain, Eagle Peaks, and Thunder Mountain. Cradled beneath them, an aquamarine glint in a forest of green, is Hume Lake. Roads leading to Panoramic Point close in winter.

ures 102 feet around, and rises 275 feet high. About 2100 years old, the tree is as tall as a 27-story building. Even statistics so overwhelming fall short in conveying the magnificence of this colossus.

To truly appreciate the General Sherman Tree, stand for a few minutes in his lengthy shadow and then explore the adjacent **Congress Trail.** This two-mile self-guided loop passes several awesome stands of sequoias, including one grove named for the United States Senate and another honoring the House of Representatives.

Generals Highway climbs and weaves from Sequoia to Kings Canyon. There are groves of the big trees along the way, as well as broad vistas of the Sierra Nevada mountains. At **Lodgepole Visitors Center** you can gain your bearings at the information desk and watch a slide show on the region. ~ Located on Generals Highway two miles north of General Sherman Tree; 559-565-3782; www.nps.gov/seki.

KINGS CANYON NATIONAL PARK   Near the park entrance, **Big Stump Trail,** a one-and-one-half mile nature loop, demonstrates some of the natural and manmade disasters that can befall giant trees. Within its narrow ambit the path crosses a sequoia scarred by lightning, another shattered into unusable pieces by clumsy loggers, and a third sequoia that was reduced to sawdust piles big as giant anthills. The most striking specimen is the Mark Twain Stump, a 24-foot-wide behemoth felled as a display piece for the American Museum of Natural History in New York City.

Headquarters in Kings Canyon National Park for sightseers, rangers, hikers, and assorted others is **Grant Grove.** This mountain village, a few miles from the park entrance, offers a small grocery, restaurant, lodge, and gift shop. The **Grant Grove Visitor Center** provides information, maps, books, and wilderness permits. There is also a small museum dedicated to the sequoia tree. ~ 559-565-4307; www.nps.gov/seki.

Pride of the park is the **General Grant Grove,** a forest of giants dating back more than 2000 years. Here a short loop leads past a **twin sister sequoia** (on the left at the end of the parking lot), formed when two trunks grew from a single base. Nearby lies the **Fallen Monarch,** the proverbial tree that crashed in the forest when there was no one around to record its demise. A 120-foot-long hollow log, it has served as a loggers' shelter, saloon, and stable. Today this natural tunnel makes a unique corridor for inquisitive hikers.

The Civil War is still being fought here in Grant Grove. Among these sentinel-straight sequoias is the **Robert E. Lee Tree,** rising 254 feet above the forest floor. The **General Grant Tree** is a gnarly giant tattooed with woodpecker holes and adorned with thick, stubby branches that twist upward. Proclaimed the Nation's Christmas Tree, it is the site of special services every year. Needless to say, the General Grant outstrips its Confederate counterpart, topping out at 267 feet and boasting a diameter (40 feet) greater than any other sequoia tree.

In the shadow of this leviathan sits the **Gamlin Cabin**, a log house built in 1872 by an early settler. Looking as sturdy as the trees around it, the structure was used at one time by U.S. Cavalry patrols.

Follow Route 180 from Grant Grove down into Kings Canyon itself. Along this 35-mile mountain road, which twists and curves as it descends the canyon walls, are countless vista points. You can peer down sharp rockfaces, gaze out at massive ridges, and take in the rivers which rumble into the San Joaquin Valley.

A side road diverges to **Hume Lake**, a small mountain lake that reflects in its glassy surface the faces of surrounding peaks. Then Route 180 (usually closed from November through April) descends through lofty mountains that break the sunlight into shafts and splinters. As you spiral farther and farther into this shadowy canyon, the granite walls edge closer and climb more steeply. Eventually the landscape narrows to a sharp defile and then re-opens to reveal a tumbling river strewn with boulders, the South Fork of the Kings River.

Here, where road meets river, sits **Boyden Cave**. Formed over a 300,000-year period, this marble cave descends past rock pools, massive stalagmites, cave pearls, and ornate stalactites. Among these marvelous underground formations are sights named Upside Down City, The Wedding Cake, Christmas Tree Room, and the Drapery Room. Closed November through April. Admission. ~ 209-736-2708, fax 209-736-0330; www.caverntours.com, e-mail caverns@caverntours.com.

Route 180 continues along the river past **Cedar Grove**, where civilization rises in the form of a lodge with grocery store and snack bar. Upstream from Cedar Grove is Kings Canyon itself. Just beyond Cedar Grove lies **Roaring River Falls**, a cascade that rolls down from the mountains, crashes through a granite chasm, and debouches into an emerald pool.

Nearby **Zumwalt Meadow** is awash with color in spring when the wildflowers bloom. Follow the self-guided nature trail. Here, deep in the canyon, you will find the river loud in your ears. Sounds echo off the surrounding walls, ricocheting upward along flinty rockfaces and vertiginous cliffs. Comparable to Yosemite in grandeur, the valley is more than 8000 feet beneath the surrounding mountains, one of the deepest canyons in the United States.

LODGING   Accommodations in both Sequoia and Kings Canyon national parks fall into several categories. At Grant Grove in Kings Canyon, there are "rustic cabins," available only in summer, which lack bathrooms, kitchens, and decoration, utilize oil or wood stoves, have both hard and canvas roofs, and price in the budget range.

Both parks also offer "motel rooms." Tabbed in the moderate category, they are roadside-style accommodations with veneer furniture, wall-to-wall carpeting, decorative appointments, and private baths. The central reservation number to most facilities is 559-452-1081, 866-522-6966, fax 559-335-5507; www.sequoia-kingscanyon.com.

Stony Creek, located on Generals Highway between Sequoia and Kings Canyon, features a lodge with motel-type accommodations. There's a dining room, gas station and gift shop/market here, as well as a lobby with stone fireplace. Closed in winter. ~ 559-452-1081, 866-522-6966, fax 559-335-5507; www.sequoia-kingscanyon.com. DELUXE.

Grant Grove Lodge, the central facility in Kings Canyon National Park, sits in a village that features a restaurant, grocery store, a gift shop, and an information center. Facilities at Grant Grove include rustic and developed cabins. ~ 559-452-1081, 866-522-6966, fax 559-335-5507; www.sequoia-kingscanyon.com. BUDGET TO DELUXE.

> Remember when planning your vacation, large sections of Sequoia and Kings Canyon are closed during the winter.

Also at Grant Grove and under the same management, the **John Muir Lodge** offers 30 modern rooms and suites in a two-story pine building with sweeping porches and a beamed lobby warmed by a big stone fireplace. ~ 559-452-1081, 866-522-6966, fax 559-335-5507; www.sequoia-kingscanyon.com. DELUXE TO ULTRA-DELUXE.

Cedar Grove, located on Route 180 deep within Kings Canyon, is a mountain lodge idyllically set in a grove of tall trees beside a river. There are motel rooms here, as well as a café, market, and gift shop. Closed in winter. ~ 559-452-1081, 866-522-6966, fax 559-335-5507; www.sequoia-kingscanyon.com. MODERATE.

Sequoia National Park's **Bearpaw Meadow Backcountry Camp** offers canvas cabins. Extremely popular, this mountain hideaway lies at the end of an 11-mile trail along which guests hike in. The accommodations include breakfast and dinner. Closed Labor Day to mid-June. ~ 888-252-5757, fax 559-454-0952; www.visit sequoia.com, e-mail sequoiacom@dncinc.com. ULTRA-DELUXE.

◄ HIDDEN

For a full-facility mountain resort, you'll be hard pressed to find anything quite like **Montecito Sequoia Lodge.** Located at 7500 feet elevation along Generals Highway between Sequoia and Kings Canyon national parks, it's a family vacation camp with rustic cabins and a lodge. The complex rests next to a lake on 15 acres and offers a pool, tennis courts, basketball, volleyball, canoeing, waterskiing, archery, horseback riding, and cross-country skiing, snowshoeing, and tubing in the winter. There's a dining room with a stone fireplace, an ample recreation room, and a bar. Lodging includes three meals a day, plus drinks and snacks. ~

559-565-3388, 800-227-9900, fax 559-565-3223; www.mslodge.
com, e-mail info@mslodge.com. DELUXE.

On the road down into Kings Canyon, surrounded by roughhewn mountains, lies **Kings Canyon Lodge**. This way station, with
its homemade bar and grill and gravity-feed gas pumps, contains
a cluster of simple woodframe cottages. They are basic accommodations, with knotty-pine walls and uninspired furnishings.
Located just off the highway, some have kitchen facilities. Closed
November to mid-April. ~ 67751 Route 180; 559-335-2405.
MODERATE.

Also serving the national parks are several affordable motels
in the nearby town of Three Rivers. Located along Route 198
within a few miles of Sequoia National Park is the **Lazy J Ranch
Motel**, an 18-unit facility with plain rooms; some rooms come with
kitchens and fireplaces, and there are individual housekeeping
cottages. There's a pool and access to the nearby river. ~ 39625
Sierra Drive, Three Rivers; 559-561-4449, 888-315-2378, fax
559-561-4889; www.bvilazyj.com, e-mail lazyj@inreach.com.
MODERATE TO DELUXE.

Nearby, **The River Inn & Cabins** has standard rooms at reasonable prices. There are fully equipped riverside cabins with
knotty pine walls and barbecues across the way. ~ 45176 Sierra
Drive, Three Rivers; 559-561-4367. MODERATE TO ULTRA-DELUXE.

DINING

You can scale granite cliffs in Sequoia and Kings Canyon, shoot
whitewater rapids, and return unscathed. What will kill you is
the food. Nowhere is the "good enough for government work"
philosophy more closely followed than in the kitchens of these
national parks.

The **Grant Grove Restaurant** is located at Grant Grove Village,
adjacent to the information center. A simple mountain eatery, the
restaurant offers a menu of soups, salads, and sandwiches. Daily
specials may feature such entrées as ravioli, fettuccine, fish and
chips, and steak. ~ 559-452-1081, 866-522-6966, fax 559-335-
5507; www.sequoia-kingscanyon.com. BUDGET TO MODERATE.

The decor consists of stuffed game animals and wilderness
photos. The bar is hewn from pine, and the dining room is filled
with oilcloth tables. Otherwise **Kings Canyon Lodge**, set deep in
the mountains, is just your average backcountry café. The menu
features standard breakfast fare and sandwiches and hamburgers
for lunch and dinner. Closed November to mid-April. ~ 67751
Route 180; 559-335-2405. BUDGET.

PARKS

SEQUOIA AND KINGS CANYON NATIONAL PARKS 🕴 🐎 🚵
🏊 ⛵ These adjoining facilities, together covering more than
850,000 acres, are discussed at length elsewhere in this chapter.
For wilderness enthusiasts they offer 800 miles of trails, 14,500-

foot peaks, and opportunities for cross-country skiing and horseback riding. There are streams and lakes throughout both parks, and some trout pools. Fishing licenses are required. Swimming is permitted in certain spots, but do not take any chances when the river is high. Facilities include restrooms, picnic areas, restaurants, cabins, and museums. ~ Route 198 leads into Sequoia from the southwest and Route 180 (Generals Highway) enters Kings Canyon from the Northwest; 559-565-3341, fax 559-565-3730; www.nps.gov/seki.

> Feeling lucky? There's recreational gold-panning at Blue Canyon and Duff Creek in Sierra National Forest. Bring your own equipment.

▲ In the two parks, there's camping in 14 campgrounds that offer 550 sites in Sequoia and 750 sites in Kings Canyon, most of which are closed in winter. Prices range from $12 to $18 per night; RV sites are available (no hookups). Reservations are required for Lodgepole Campground (the largest of the campgrounds with 204 sites) and Dorst Campground; call 800-365-2267. All others are on a first-come, first-served basis. Wilderness camping is very popular. Lodgepole Campground is located four miles north of Wuksachi Lodge.

SEQUOIA NATIONAL FOREST/GIANT SEQUOIA NATIONAL MONUMENT 🚶🚴🏇🎿🏠🚡⛷🛶🚣�ship🛥🔦 Located at the southern edge of the Sierra Nevada, this facility boasts more than 38 sequoia groves. It also includes several resort spots like Kern Canyon, popular with weekend refugees from Los Angeles. Climbing from 1000 to 12,000 feet, the forest contains six wilderness areas. About 1200 miles of streams and rivers and more than a dozen high-country lakes offer ample opportunities to drop a line or raft the rapids. Day-use fee for some picnic areas, $5. ~ Access is via Routes 178, 155, 180, and 190; 559-784-1500, fax 559-781-4744.

▲ There are 50 campgrounds with about 1300 sites; $8 to $20 per night. Most campgrounds accommodate RVs (no hookups).

SIERRA NATIONAL FOREST 🚶🚴🏇🎿🏠🚡⛷🛶🚣�ship🔦 Tucked between Kings Canyon and Yosemite national parks, this 1,300,000-acre forest climbs from 1000 to 14,000 feet elevation and ranges from rolling chaparral country to bald peaks. There are two groves of sequoias and 1100 miles of trails. More than one-half of the forest is wilderness. About 1200 miles of streams and more than 1000 lakes (including Bass Lake) provide excellent trout, bass, and kokanee salmon fishing. ~ Access is via Routes 168 and 41; 559-297-0706, fax 559-294-4809; www.fs.fed.us/r5/sierra.

▲ There are 59 campgrounds, most of which are closed in winter; free to $17 per night. RV sites are available in some campgrounds (no hookups). You can make reservations at about one-third of the sites (877-444-6777). In addition to developed campgrounds, dispersed and primitive camping are allowed with the appropriate permits.

Owens Valley

The backbone of the Eastern Sierra is Route 395, which runs north past black lava hills, red cinder cones, and other volcanic outcroppings. The land all about is a morass of sand divided in random fashion by arroyos, a dust bowl with a rim of mountains. This is the Owens Valley, bled dry by Los Angeles, which diverted its once plentiful water. Today only the mountains remain—to the east the Inyos, Panamints, and Whites, in the west the Sierra Nevada. From them the valley, victimized by a metropolis hundreds of miles away, derives its identity and maintains its dignity.

SIGHTS

At **Fossil Falls,** 20,000-year-old lava flows have solidified to create dramatic cascades of black rock. ~ On Route 395 for three miles north of Little Lake; go east one-half mile on Cinder Road; turn right on the dirt road and proceed three-quarters of a mile to a parking lot; hike one-quarter mile to the falls; a second set of falls lies several hundred yards farther south.

Route 395 continues past miles of sage brush in a landscape that is broken only occasionally by a solitary and spindly cactus. **Owens Lake Bed,** once part of a rich string of intermountain lakes, stretches for miles to the west—a dry, salt-caked expanse.

To understand the allure of Owens Valley, stop by the **Eastern Sierra InterAgency Visitor Center.** A valuable resource, the information center has a good selection of maps and pamphlets and an excellent collection of books on California's mountain and desert regions. ~ Junction of Routes 395 and 136; 760-876-6222, fax 760-876-6234.

In the neon town of **Lone Pine** you can pick up **Whitney Portal Road** (one of America's greatest byways), which climbs from 4000 to 8300 feet elevation in its 13-mile course. Passing streams shaded by cottonwood trees, it cuts through the **Alabama Hills,** a unique formation of weathered granite whose reddish colors contrast brilliantly with the gray backdrop of the Sierra Nevada.

Then Whitney Portal Road rides out of this rolling range land, trading the soft contours of the Alabamas for the cold granite world of the Sierra Nevada. These latter mountains are young (geologically) and roughhewn, with adze-like slopes that lift away from the road in vertical lunges. Far from embracing admirers, the surrounding heights seem to dare people to ascend them. Even the pine trees, which grow in crowded groves along the early slopes, quit the climb half way up.

When the road itself quits at Whitney Portal, base camp for climbers, you find above you **Mount Whitney,** at 14,496 feet the tallest mountain in the contiguous United States. In the giant's

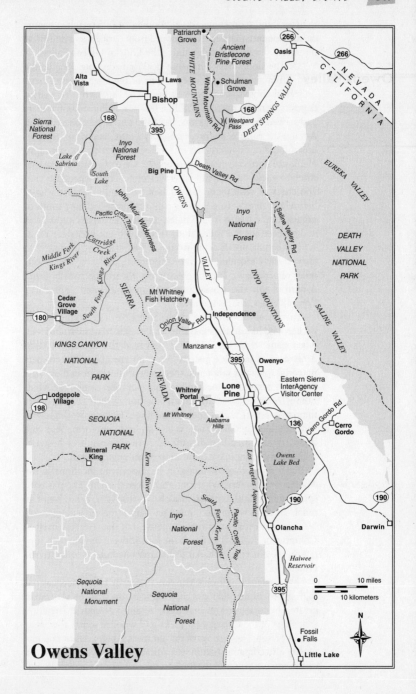

Patriarch Grove

WHITE MOUNTAINS

Ancient Bristlecone Pine Forest

266

266

Oasis

NEVADA

CALIFORNIA

Alta Vista

Laws

White Mountain Rd

Schulman Grove

DEEP SPRINGS VALLEY

Bishop

168

395

Westgard Pass

168

Sierra National Forest

Inyo National Forest

EUREKA VALLEY

Lake Sabrina

South Lake

Big Pine

Death Valley Rd

OWENS

Inyo National Forest

DEATH VALLEY NATIONAL PARK

John Muir Wilderness

Pacific Crest Trail

Saline Valley Rd

Cartridge Creek

Middle Fork Kings River

South Fork Kings River

SIERRA

VALLEY

INYO MOUNTAINS

SALINE VALLEY

Cedar Grove Village

Mt Whitney Fish Hatchery

180

Onion Valley Rd

Independence

KINGS CANYON NATIONAL PARK

Manzanar

395

Owenyo

Eastern Sierra InterAgency Visitor Center

Lodgepole Village

198

NEVADA

Whitney Portal

Lone Pine

Cerro Gordo Rd

SEQUOIA

Mt Whitney

Alabama Hills

136

Cerro Gordo

NATIONAL

Owens Lake Bed

PARK

Mineral King

Kern River

South Fork Kern River

Pacific Crest Trail

Los Angeles Aqueduct

190

190

Inyo National Forest

Olancha

Darwin

Haiwee Reservoir

Sequoia National Monument

Sequoia National Forest

0   10 miles

0   10 kilometers

395

N

Fossil Falls

Little Lake

Owens Valley

shadow stand six other peaks, all topping 14,000 feet. It is a scene of unpronounceable beauty, fashioned from dark chasms and stone minarets, almost two miles above the floor of Owens Valley.

On the slopes of a 9000-foot peak outside Lone Pine lie the rusting remains of **Cerro Gordo**. One of the High Desert's best-preserved ghost towns, its story begins in 1865 when rich silver deposits were discovered. Within a few years almost 2000 miners had arrived, hauling out as much as 5300 tons of bullion each year. Among the ruins is a store, two-story house, and other tumble-down buildings constructed in 1871. Later structures, dating to 1916, are dotted around the property. Cerro Gordo is now privately owned, but the public is welcome. The owners ask that you check in with them at their home to sign a liability waiver before entering. ~ To get there, pick up Route 136 just south of Lone Pine and follow it 12.5 miles; turn left on Cerro Gordo Road and proceed for five miles along this graded but *very* steep road.

Proceeding north along Route 395 from Lone Pine (particularly in early morning and late afternoon), pull over about four miles outside town and gaze eastward toward the river bottom. A herd of **tule elk**, whose ancestors once inhabited California's Central Valley, roams the area.

Farther outside town, with the Sierra Nevada looming in the background like an impenetrable wall, stands **Manzanar**. In 1942, when panic over Pearl Harbor pervaded the country, 10,000 Americans of Japanese ancestry were interned here. Perceived as potential spies and saboteurs, they were uprooted from their West Coast homes and "relocated" to concentration camps like Manzanar. Today little remains to commemorate their tragedy other than two security checkpoint buildings, fashioned, almost insultingly, like pagodas. There is also a plaque imploring that "the injustices and humiliation suffered here as a result of hysteria, racism, and economic exploitation never emerge again."

HIDDEN ►   Even more overwhelming in its moral ramifications is the **Manzanar cemetery**, where internees were buried. The place inspires sadness and remorse, and also a sense of terror. It is not so much the stark white monument set against the unyielding Sierra Nevada that evokes this final response, but the cemetery itself. ~ Continue on Route 395 north for four-fifths of a mile, then turn left on the dirt road; when it forks after one mile, bear left to the cemetery.

The **Eastern California Museum** in nearby Independence contains photographs and news clips retracing the story of Manzanar, created by former Manzanar internee Shiro Nomura. There are snapshots of the tarpaper barracks and wooden sentry towers as well as personal belongings of the internees. This excellent regional facility also contains such Indian artifacts as arrowheads, baskets, and beadwork. Tools of the trade from cowboy days include brand-

ing irons, a mule pack canteen, leather chaps, and even a spit-
toon. The antique telephones and accordion cameras of the region's
more genteel set are also presented. Out back, a few of the town's
original buildings—weather-beaten, woodframe structures—still
stand. Closed Tuesday. ~ 155 Grant Street, Independence; 760-
878-0258, fax 760-878-0412; e-mail ecmuseum@usamedia.tv.

The **Mount Whitney Fish Hatchery** raises brood stock (egg-
producing) trout. The resultant fingerlings are used for stocking
backcountry streams, making this area one of the most popular
freshwater fishing regions in the state. Breeding rainbow, brook,
brown, and golden trout, the facility offers an opportunity to
watch gamefish hatching and to glimpse fat but spirited adult
fish. The building alone, a stone structure with Tudor flourishes
and a red tile roof, built in 1916, makes the visit worthwhile. ~
Off Route 395 about one mile north of Independence; 760-878-
2272, fax 760-878-2284; e-mail mountwhitneyhatchery@ca.gov.

East of the little town of Big Pine, Route 168 connects with
a side road that leads up into the White Mountains. Climb this
backcountry byway and a dazzling 180-degree **mountain panorama** of the Sierra Nevada Mountain Range will open to view.
The mountains seem to wrap around you, forming an amphitheater of stone and snow. Within this ring of 13,000-foot peaks
rests **Palisade Glacier**, the southernmost glacier in North America.
For more information, contact the White Mountains Ranger Station. ~ 760-873-2500.

Then the road ascends to over 10,000 feet elevation and—in
a kind of high altitude riddle—enters a territory where the living
reside next to the dead and the dead are often half alive. The
denizens of this mysterious locale are over 4000 years old, the
world's most ancient living things, dating back to the days of the
Egyptian pyramids.

The site is an **Ancient Bristlecone Pine Forest**, where short,
stunted trees with needles like fox tails grow on an icy, wind-
blown landscape. Sculpted by the elements, they resemble living

COWBOY COUNTRY

If the Alabama Hills seem a bit too familiar, little wonder: they have served
as the setting for countless Westerns. At one time they were almost as
important to the movie industry as the Hollywood Hills. Hopalong
Cassidy, Gene Autry, and the Lone Ranger all rode this range. For a close-
up of cowboy country, turn right on Movie Road. A network of dirt
roads leads past **Movie Flat**, where many sequences were shot, then
continues into this badlands of humpbacked boulders. ~ On Movie
Road, off Whitney Portal Road three miles from Route 395.

driftwood; many of the trees are partially dead, sustained by a thin strip of bark that protects tissues carrying water and nutrients.

In the forest's **Schulman Grove**, where the oldest trees survive, you can follow a one-mile loop trail past Pine Alpha, a 4300-year-old tree. Here you will also find the **Edmond P. Schulman Visitors Center** (open mid-May through October), which has outdoor exhibits, a bookstore, a small theater with educational film, and demonstrative trails on the region's natural history. Picnic areas and restrooms are also available. From here a dirt road, which is sometimes closed due to weather, continues for 12 miles along the lip of the world, through a lunar landscape, and past ever-thinning forest to the **Patriarch Grove**, a second stand of bristlecones located at 11,000 feet. ~ For recorded information on the Bristlecone Forest, call 760-873-2500.

Bishop is one of those towns that exist not in and for themselves but for what is around them. The **Bishop Area Chamber of Commerce and Visitors Bureau** serves as the local information center, a good place to plan an exploration of the area. ~ 690 North Main Street, Bishop; 760-873-8405, 888-395-3952, fax 760-873-6999; www.bishopvisitor.com, e-mail info@bishopvisitor.com.

Route 168 buzzes west from Bishop for about 20 miles into the high country of the Sierra Nevada. Here **Lake Sabrina** and **South Lake**, favored fishing holes, are like crystal inlaid in a setting of granite.

Directly north of Bishop, the **Volcanic Tablelands** rise above the valley floor, ascending to 7912-foot Casa Diablo Mountain. Built from a series of lava flows, this sparse plateau is cut by sharp, narrow canyons. Gleaming red against the gray walls of the Sierra Nevada and White Mountains, it's a desolate but enchanting region, particularly pretty around dawn and dusk. ~ Pick up Five Bridges Road at the north end of Bishop and take it to the end, where it continues as Casa Diablo Road, a dirt road that climbs all the way to Casa Diablo Mountain.

The nearby town of **Laws**, a major railroad stop during the 1880s, is re-created at the **Laws Railroad Museum and Historical**

AUTHOR FAVORITE

sights

Dedicated to American Indian traditions, the **Owens Valley Paiute Shoshone Indian Cultural Center** has outstanding displays of basketry, leathercrafts, and beadwork. There are also showcases filled with petroglyphs and arrowheads. Centerpiece of the showroom is a circular house of cane, in the traditional style of Owens Valley tribes. Closed weekends. ~ 2300 West Line Street, Bishop; 760-873-4478.

Site. Combining the town's original buildings with antique structures relocated from other parts of the valley, it conveys an atmosphere of the Old West.

The general store is here with its lard buckets and spice canisters; tumblers still turn in the mailbox locks at the post office; and the surgical tools in the doctor's office look as threatening as they did back when. In addition, the original Bishop Catholic Church has been converted into a library, museum, and art gallery, and the Wells Fargo office now displays rock crystals and Indian artifacts.

But the centerpiece of the exhibit is still the railroad yard. Here the station, with its waiting room, telegraph office, and loading dock, has been nicely preserved. Resting just down the track is old Southern Pacific Engine Number Nine, with a line of freight cars and a bell whose clangs still echo across the valley. Please call ahead before visiting to ensure that staff will be on hand. ~ Route 6 about four miles northeast of Bishop; 760-873-5950.

Artifacts of a much earlier era, **Indian petroglyphs**, lie off the beaten track north of Laws. Etched into volcanic rocks, these ancient drawings portray people, deer, snakes, and insects. Possibly left by ancestors of local Paiutes, the figures carry significant symbolic meaning. Since they occur along old deer trails, one theory holds they were intended to bring the blessing of good hunting. Another theory maintains that these figures are the work of shamans, representing communication with the spirit world. Closed weekends during winter. For maps and directions to the petroglyphs, contact the Bureau of Land Management at the Inyo National Forest. ~ 798 North Main Street, Bishop; 760-873-2503.

◀ HIDDEN

The neon strip along Route 395 serves as motel row in Lone Pine. Several resting places line the highway, each providing adequate accommodations. The **Dow Villa Hotel and Motel** features a modern motel attached to a 1920s-era hotel. The complex includes a lobby, pool, and spa. Rooms in the hotel are time-worn but tidy; the motel rooms are more modern and very comfortable. ~ 310 South Main Street, Lone Pine; 760-876-5521, 800-824-9317, fax 760-876-5643; www.dowvillamotel.com, e-mail dow villa@qnet.com. BUDGET TO DELUXE.

LODGING

Another important find is **Winnedumah Hotel**, an imposing two-story edifice across the street from the Inyo County Court House on Route 395 in Independence. Built in 1927, its spacious lobby greets guests with a stone fireplace, beam ceiling, and cozy armchairs. The accommodations are bright, friendly rooms with quilts and original furnishings. Breakfast is complimentary. ~ 211 North Edward Street, Independence; 760-878-2040, fax 760-878-2833; www.winnedumah.com, e-mail winnedumah@ qnet.com. MODERATE.

Bishop also has its share of roadside motels, strung like lights along Route 395. **Bishop Motel 6** is a two-story complex with a pool. Two of the 52 units have kitchenettes; each room is spacious, carpeted, and well maintained. ~ 1005 North Main Street, Bishop; 760-873-8426, 800-466-8356, fax 760-873-8060. MODERATE.

HIDDEN ▶

Up at 8500 feet elevation, socked in by mountains and graced with a stream and natural pond, is **Cardinal Village Resort**. Part of an old mining claim, this retreat consists of a cluster of cabins dating to 1906. Attractive houses, they combine such old-fashioned amenities as wooden counters with newfangled conveniences like tile baths. Blended into the nearby aspen grove are the general store and restaurant as well as a lodge complete with stone fireplace. All units contain kitchens. Reservations are necessary in winter. ~ Route 168 about 16 miles west of Bishop; 760-873-4789, fax 769-873-8857; www.cardinalvillageresort.com, e-mail info@cardinalvillageresort.com. MODERATE TO DELUXE.

DINING

Dining on the east side of the Sierra Nevada is as grand a gourmet experience as in Sequoia and Kings Canyon. Somehow the love of the good life in this area has never been translated to the dinner table. All the towns located along Route 395 are lined with restaurants, but most are cafés unworthy of note.

The vivid-red hue of Owens Lake is caused by the billions of resident halobacteria, microscopic, salt-loving organisms.

At **The Seasons**, the atmosphere is decidedly rustic. Landscape paintings by local artists line the walls, imparting a mountain-country flavor. The menu includes rack of lamb with fresh rosemary, grilled chicken breast with a tropical fruit sauce, and filet mignon with green peppercorn sauce. If you're otherwise inclined, they offer steak and seafood entrées plus some pasta dishes. Dinner only. Closed Sunday from November to April ~ 206 South Main Street, Lone Pine; 760-876-8927; www.seasonsrestaurantusa. com. MODERATE TO ULTRA-DELUXE.

Over at **Margie's Merry-Go-Round** they specialize in steaks, pork chops, barbecue dishes, and grilled seafood. This small, friendly restaurant attracts a local crowd. Dinner only. Closed Tuesday in winter. ~ 212 South Main Street, Lone Pine; 760-876-4115. MODERATE.

HIDDEN ▶

If local crowds are any indication, **Bishop Grill** is the best place in Bishop to eat. It's certainly the cheapest: the low budget prices at this café are vintage 1960s. The cuisine is straight Americana, from the hamburgers to the ham dinners to the pork chops. Meat and potato entrées extend to steak and chicken-fried steak. ~ 281 North Main Street, Bishop; 760-873-7248. BUDGET.

Then there's the place that offers the world's strangest Sunday champagne brunch special—all the Chinese food you can eat. Hopefully you won't be stopping at **Imperial Gourmet Chinese**

Restaurant on your way to church. Instead I recommend lunch and dinner, when you'll find enough Asian atmosphere and a variety of Chinese dishes for an enjoyable meal. ~ 785 North Main Street, #K, Bishop; 760-872-1144, fax 760-872-1145. BUDGET TO MODERATE.

In sharp contrast to the dust-blown basin of Owens Valley is the green Mammoth Lakes region. Here on the eastern face of the Sierra Nevada, volcanoes and earthquakes have wracked the region, leaving a legacy of lakes.

Mammoth Lakes

Among the most lovely lakes in the region is **Convict Lake**, a mountain jewel formed by receding glaciers. Bounded by precipitous cliffs and multihued rocks, the lake was the scene of a famous 1871 gun battle between a sheriff's posse and a band of fugitives. ~ Convict Lake Road about two miles west of Route 395.

SIGHTS

Hot Creek, a beautiful stream set deep in a rock-rimmed canyon, is one of Mammoth Lakes most deceptive and alluring spots. One section, peaceful as a babbling brook, is popular with fly fishermen. Farther downstream, there are hot springs that warm the water to perfect spa temperatures. Then, within a 100 yards of this pool, the creek erupts in low geysers and dramatic steam vents. Light concentrations of chemicals and dangers of scalding prompted local authorities to post "swimming not recommended" signs. Visitors, however, generally ignore them, opting to soak in the emerald moss-filled creek. Vapors percolate from gray mud holes and pungent bubbles rise out of the depths. ~ Located six miles south of Mammoth Lakes. From Route 395 turn east on Hot Creek Hatchery Road next to Mammoth–Yosemite Airport and follow the signs for three and a half miles to the parking lot; its a short hike down to the creek.

◄ HIDDEN

The **Mammoth Visitors Center** has information on hiking, camping, and other outdoor activities. In addition, they provide information on local hotels, restaurants, and other amenities. ~ Route 203, one block from Mammoth Lakes; 760-924-5500; www.visitmammoth.com.

A thumbnail introduction to the history of this former mining region awaits along Old Mammoth Road. Back in 1878, after gold and silver were uncovered, Mammoth City developed into a boom town with 22 saloons, two breweries, 13 stores, and two newspapers. The place went bust within a year, but a few artifacts from the glory days remain.

From July through September the **Mammoth Museum**, housed in a log cabin, traces the region's story from the days of mining and ranching to the current era. ~ 100 College Parkway; 760-932-6592. About a mile from the top of Old Mammoth Road, the grave of one Mrs. J. E. Townsend, deceased 1882, rests in a shaded grove. Farther along, across from a state historical marker, are the remains of a log cabin and the ill-fated mine.

Lake Mary Road climbs past a chain of beautiful glacial lakes. **Twin Lakes**, a wasp-waisted body of water that was once two separate lakes, sits in a granite bowl. Just beyond here a half-mile trail leads to **Panorama Dome**, a volcanic rock with outstanding views of the surrounding lakes and the White Mountains.

The loop around **Lake Mary**, largest of this glacial group, diverts to **Lake George**, a crystal pool dominated by a single granite shaft. During early summer, meadows along the nearby hiking trails are filled with flowers.

Spilling down from **Lake Mamie** are the **Twin Falls**, which cascade 300 feet along a granite bed into Twin Lakes. **Horseshoe Lake**, the only lake where swimming is permitted, sits near the top of the road at 8950 feet elevation. To explore the alpine waters that rest beyond Horseshoe Lake, you'll have to don hiking boots.

A number of sights lie along Minaret Road (Route 203), which ascends from the town of Mammoth Lakes into the mountains. Unsettling evidence of Mammoth Lakes' dramatic geology lies along the sharp walls of the **earthquake fault**. A nature trail wends along the sides of this fracture, where the earth has opened to create a deep fissure. The rocks on either side fit perfectly into their counterparts, providing a graphic illustration of how an earthquake can split the globe like a ripe fruit.

Minaret Vista, with its views of the Ansel Adams Wilderness, is otherworldly. The San Joaquin River winds through the deep canyon below; and the stark peaks of the Ritter Range loom above, a setting in which the top of the world seems to have been ripped away, leaving a jagged line of needle-point peaks and razor-edge ridges.

But enough mere beauty. At **Devils Postpile National Monument**, where Route 203 reveals its final surprise, physical beauty is combined with the magic of geology. Here layer on layer of angular shafts, some vertical, others twisted into curving forms, create a 60-foot-high cliff with smooth-sided columns.

Volcanic forces molded this rare formation when surface cracks appeared during the cooling of molten lava. The surface breaks extended vertically through the rock, creating the polygonal posts. Then glaciers flowed over the fractured mass 10,000 years ago, polishing the tops of the posts and leaving a geometric surface resembling a tile floor (which can be viewed from atop Devils Postpile).

Along the trail at the bottom you can gaze at this unique wall of pillars, some of which curve toward the mountain, seeming to support the posts behind, while others lean free and appear about to collapse. Directly below them, like splinters from a magnificent sculpture, lie piles of fallen columns.

Mammoth Scenic Loop, branching from Minaret Road one mile outside Mammoth Lakes, contains within its ambit several points of interest. **Inyo Craters** is a string of the southernmost volcanic cavities created by violent eruptions. Part of the volcanic ridge that runs between Mammoth Mountain and Mono Lake, these craters and their lakes are mere babies in geologic terms, dating back perhaps 1500 years. ~ One mile down a dirt side road and one-quarter mile up a trail.

En route to June Lake, another string of glacial lakes, the local geology shows another of its many faces. **Obsidian Dome** is a glass

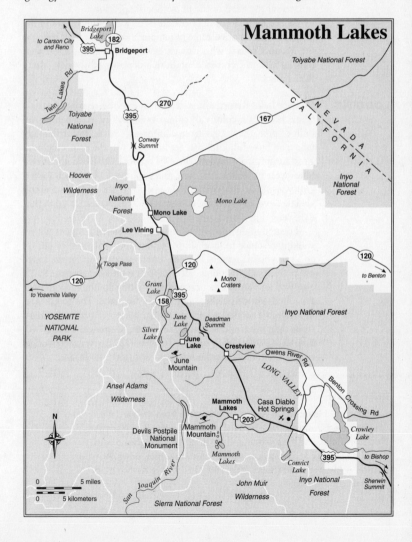

Mammoth Lakes

mountain composed entirely of obsidian. This black volcanic glass, created during the cooling of molten lava, was used by local Indians to fashion arrowheads. ~ Follow Route 395 about 11 miles north of Mammoth Lakes, then turn west for one and a half miles on Glass Flow Road.

June Lake Loop (Route 158), a mountain road 15 miles north of Mammoth Lakes, curves past June Lake and three other pools. Each is an alpine beauty, a shimmering blue lake bounded by forest and lofty peaks. Popular for fishing, camping, and hiking, the region is also crowded with skiers in winter. June Mountain is situated at the head of the horseshoe-shaped loop.

As the loop closes upon Route 395, with Mono Lake in the distance, a series of volcanic mountains rise in the east. These are the **Mono Craters**, which reach elevations of about 2700 feet. Built of lava, the craters contain rich deposits of obsidian along their flanks.

LODGING   **Convict Lake Resort**, situated near one of the region's prettiest lakes, features a colony of cabins bounded by an aspen grove. Built of pine, they range from comfortably rustic to surprisingly fancy; all have full kitchens. Set at 7600 feet, the resort includes a restaurant, store, and marina. ~ Convict Lake Road about two miles west of Route 395, nine miles south of Mammoth Lakes; 760-934-3800, 800-992-2260, fax 760-923-8139; www.convictlake.com, e-mail info@convictlake.com. MODERATE TO ULTRA-DELUXE.

Located in downtown Mammoth, the **Sierra Lodge** is within walking distance to local shops, restaurants, and, best of all, ski and snowboard rentals. A sleek, contemporary affair, the lodge offers 36 spacious rooms, all equipped with kitchenettes. You'll also find an outdoor jacuzzi and an inviting common room with a vaulted wooden ceiling and a cozy fireplace. The free Mammoth shuttle service, which transports you to all major ski areas, stops right out front. ~ 3540 Main Street, Mammoth Lakes; 760-934-8881, 800-356-5711, fax 760-934-7231; www.sierralodge.com, e-mail info@sierralodge.com. MODERATE TO DELUXE.

RIDE HIGH

At Mammoth Mountain Ski Resort farther uphill from the earthquake fault, you can take a **gondola ride** to the 11,053-foot summit of Mammoth Mountain. Of course if it's winter and the area has been graced with the white powder for which locals pray, you can ski back down. Admission. ~ Minaret Road (Route 203); 760-934-2571; www.mammoth mountain.com.

Mammoth Mountain Inn is a modern hotel with a distinct rustic-mountain atmosphere. Located across the road from Mammoth Mountain Ski Area, the inn is primarily a ski lodge, but its easy proximity to Devils Postpile and other natural features makes it popular year-round. There are restaurants, lounges, spas, a heated outdoor pool, and shops here, as well as a wood-and-stone lobby, which is decorated with antler chandeliers. The hotel rooms are deluxe to ultra-deluxe. Condos, with kitchen facilities, are ultra-deluxe during peak periods. ~ Minaret Road, Mammoth Lakes; 760-934-2581, 800-626-6684, fax 760-934-0701; www.mammothmountain.com, e-mail mcv@mammothmtn.com. DELUXE TO ULTRA-DELUXE.

One of the prettiest and most secluded spots in Mammoth Lakes is **Tamarack Lodge and Resort**. A classic mountain lodge with split log walls and stone fireplace, it sits on Twin Lakes in the shadow of the mountains. The lobby is a cheery alpine room inevitably filled with guests warming themselves by a fire. There are small rooms (with shared and private baths) in the lodge, sentimentally decorated and paneled in knotty pine. More than 25 cabins, ranging from studios to three-bedroom extravaganzas, also dot the six-acre grounds. While these are traditional wood-frame structures, the interiors of many are modern in design with wall-to-wall carpeting, stall showers, and contemporary kitchens. Most offer partial views of the lake. Located at 8600 feet, the resort is in a major Nordic ski area, with trails radiating in all directions. It also features a lakefront restaurant. Depending on the season, lodge rooms with shared baths are budget to moderate; cabins range from moderate to ultra-deluxe, also depending on the season. ~ Twin Lakes Road, just off Lake Mary Road, Mammoth Lakes; 760-934-2442, 800-626-6684, fax 760-934-2281; www.tamaracklodge.com. DELUXE TO ULTRA-DELUXE.

For information on the Mammoth Lakes area, including lodging referrals, contact the **Mammoth Lakes Visitors Bureau**. ~ 760-934-2712, 888-466-2666, fax 760-934-7066; www.visitmammoth.com, e-mail info@visitmammoth.com.

Over in June Lake, **Big Rock Resort** has eight cabin units. These are attractive duplexes with kitchens and knotty-pine interiors. Some have fireplaces. Nicely situated on the lake, the complex includes a tackle shop and marina. It's a convenient locale if you want to fish, swim, boat, or gaze out at the mountains. Closed in November. ~ 1 Big Rock Road, June Lake; 760-648-7717, 800-769-9831, fax 760-648-1067; www.junelake.com, e-mail bigrock@gte.net. MODERATE TO ULTRA-DELUXE.

One of the area's prime dining rooms is not on Mammoth Lakes at all, but a few miles south near a neighboring lake. **The Restaurant at Convict Lake** is a plush but rustic place. A fireplace

DINING

with copper hood dominates the main room and the adjoining lounge has a wood-burning stove. But the menu is the true drawing card at this critically acclaimed establishment. The chef prepares a California cuisine–style menu of rack of lamb, beef Wellington, duck breast sauté, homemade gravlox, stuffed chicken breast, and a nightly fresh fish special like salmon. Lunch in the summer under the aspen trees. Dinner only in the winter. ~ Convict Lake Road about two miles west of Route 395, Mammoth Lakes; 760-934-3803, 800-992-2260, fax 760-923-8139; www.convictlake.com, e-mail info@convictlake.com. MODERATE TO ULTRA-DELUXE.

At Rainbow Falls the San Joaquin River plunges 100 feet over volcanic rock to an alpine pool, creating multihued patterns in the mist. This spot is particularly pretty in the afternoon. ~ Off Reds Meadow and along a 1.3-mile trail.

Shogun Japanese Restaurant may be parked in a shopping mall, but it still provides marvelous views of the mountains. Equipped with a sushi bar and adjoining lounge, the restaurant features sukiyaki, *tonkatsu*, tempura, and teriyaki dishes. Dinner only. ~ Sierra Centre Mall, Old Mammoth Road, Mammoth Lakes; 760-934-3970. MODERATE.

Matsu Restaurant is a small wood-paneled place offering an Asian grab bag. The entrées cover a lot of geography, ranging from Filipino-style *pansit* (shrimp and pork sautéed with onions and noodles) to teriyaki dishes from Hawaii to Chinese courses like sweet-and-sour chicken. No lunch on Sunday. ~ 3711 Main Street, Mammoth Lakes; 760-934-8277. MODERATE.

Pine plank walls and hand-stitched decorations make **La Sierra's Mexican-American-Italian Grille and Cantina** a charming spot for a meal. They prepare a full array of dishes from south of the border and some Italian and American food. The restaurant serves lunch and dinner, with a champagne brunch on Sunday during football season. No lunch on weekends. ~ 3789 Route 203, Mammoth Lakes; phone/fax 760-934-5420. BUDGET TO MODERATE.

With its German alpine atmosphere, the **Austria Hof Restaurant** is a congenial dining spot. The Continental dinner menu begins with ahi tournedo on crispy wontons, tomato and basil bruschetta, and potato pancakes. Among the entrées are more than a dozen dishes—rack of lamb, Angus beef rib eye, blackened salmon, and Old World specialties like wienerschnitzel and bratwurst. Add a wine list plus dessert tray and you have an excellent opportunity to feast. No lunch. Closed in spring and fall. ~ 924 Canyon Boulevard, Mammoth Lakes; 760-934-2764. MODERATE TO DELUXE.

HIDDEN ▶   Informal, inexpensive café dining is the specialty of the house at **Blondie's Kitchen and Waffle Shop**. Famous for its waffles and homemade specialties, this unassuming spot is favored by a local crowd. Breakfast, served all day, includes granola and oatmeal, omelettes, *machacas* (shredded beef and eggs), and blueberry pancakes. Lunch features cheeseburgers, a "veggie" sandwich with cream cheese, avocado, and sprouts, plus burritos and homemade soup. No dinner. ~ 3599 Main Street, Mammoth Lakes; 760-934-4048; e-mail koni@gte.net. BUDGET.

It's a far stretch from the sea, but **Ocean Harvest Restaurant** has an impressive selection of broiled seafood dishes. This establishment also offers steaks, chicken dishes, and baby back ribs in a comfortable setting. Dinner only. Closed the first two weeks of June, and from mid-October to mid-November. ~ Corner of Old Mammoth and Sierra Nevada roads, Mammoth Lakes; 760-934-8539, fax 760-934-8530; www.oceanharvestrestaurant.com, e-mail oharvest@yahoo.com. MODERATE.

The **Sierra Inn Restaurant,** near the center of town in June Lake, performs double duty. Part of the complex is a coffee shop serving standard breakfast, lunch, and dinner items. In the evening the dining room opens, providing fresh seafood dishes as well as steaks, lasagna, pizza, and chicken dinners. With a high-beamed ceiling and full lounge, the dining room overlooks June Lake. Dinner only from April to November. Closed from November to mid-December and for one week in April. ~ 2588 Route 158, June Lake; 760-648-7774. BUDGET TO DELUXE.

Who would have guessed that a place called **Carson Peak Inn** would be right there at the base of Carson Peak offering spectacular views of the mountain? In addition to plate-glass vistas this restaurant serves up steaks and seafood as well as pork ribs and vegetarian dishes. Dinner only. ~ Two miles west of June Lake on Route 158; 760-648-7575, fax 760-648-7020. MODERATE TO ULTRA-DELUXE.

NIGHTLIFE

In Mammoth Lakes, where the ski crowd livens up the territory, there are several nightspots worthy of note. During summer and winter, the bar at **Slocums Italian American Grill** is a popular watering hole. ~ Main Street (Route 203); 760-934-7647.

There's dancing to live bands nightly at **La Sierra's Mexican-American-Italian Grille and Cantina**. This club has one of the largest dancefloors in town. Cover for live music. ~ 3789 Route 203, Mammoth Lakes; 760-934-8083.

Whiskey Creek features bands from the Los Angeles and San Diego areas. Live music is available on Friday and Saturday nights. Cover. ~ 23 Lake Mary Road, Mammoth Lakes; 760-934-2555.

For a quiet drink and a view of June Lake, try the lounge at **Sierra Inn Restaurant** near the center of town in June Lake. ~ 2588 Route 158, June Lake; 760-648-7774.

PARKS

INYO NATIONAL FOREST 🚶 🚴 🐎 🎿 ⛺ 🎣 ⛷ 🛶 This sprawling giant encompasses the high-country crest of the Sierra and plunges 150 miles into the eastern Sierra region. It contains within its domain the Ansel Adams Wilderness (formerly Minarets Wilderness), Mammoth Lakes, the John Muir Wilderness, Devils Postpile, the White Mountains, Mono Lake, the Ancient Bristlecone Forest, and Mount Whitney. Numbering 400 lakes and 150 streams, it is traversed by 1273 miles of trails, including the John Muir Trail. There's excellent angling in trout streams and well-stocked lakes. ~ Access points are generally located off Route 395 in the Owens Valley and Mammoth Lakes areas; 760-873-2400, fax 760-873-2958.

▲ Camping is permitted in 73 campgrounds; most take RVs (no hookups) and most are closed in winter. The majority of the sites are available on a walk-in basis. Reservations: 877-444-6777. Prices range from $11 to $15 per night.

▼▼▼▼▼▼▼▼▼▼▼▼▼
Death Valley Area

Set between the lofty Black and Panamint ranges, Death Valley is a place renowned for exquisite but merciless terrain. A region of vast distances (the national park is half as large as Delaware) and plentiful plant life (over 900 plant species subsist here, 22 of them growing only in this area), Death Valley holds a magician's bag of surprises.

SIGHTS

BAKER TO DEATH VALLEY AREA A fitting prelude to dusty, desiccated Death Valley lies along the southern gateway to this fabled destination. Here, stretching north along Route 127 from the town of Baker, is a chain of **dry lakes**. Once part of Lake Mojave, an ancient body of water that drained over 3500 square miles, they are now flat expanses baked white in the sun. Silver Dry Lake, which appears to the west four miles outside Baker, was an Indian habitat over 10,000 years ago.

To the east rise the Silurian Hills, backdropped by the Kingston Range. If there is a snow-domed mountain in the far distance, it's probably 11,918-foot Charleston Peak, 60 miles away in Nevada. Those pretty white hills with the soft curves are the Dumont Dunes, 30 miles north of Baker.

Beyond Ibex Pass, as the road descends into another ancient lake bed, you'll pass **Tecopa Lake Badlands**, where erosion has carved fascinating formations from soft sedimentary rock.

A side road leads several miles to **Tecopa Hot Springs**, rich mineral baths once used by Paiute Indians. Today this natural resource has been transformed into a bizarre tourist attraction.

If there is a last outpost before the world ends, this will be the place. A white mineral patina covers the ground everywhere, as if salt had been shaken across the entire desert. Water sits in stagnant pools. Wherever you look—backgrounded by rugged, stark, glorious mountains—there are trailers. Many trailers, metal refuges against the Mojave sun, painted white like the earth and equipped with satellite dishes. In a kind of desert monopoly game, if you collect enough mobile homes you can hang a sign out front and call it a motel.

The species that inhabits these tin domiciles is on permanent vacation. This is, after all, a health resort; people walk about clad in bathrobes. They wander from the private baths at the trailer parks and "motels" to the public baths, which, in the single saving grace to this surreal enclave, are free. ~ 760-852-4264, fax 760-852-4243.

DEATH VALLEY NATIONAL PARK   Better times lie ahead. Picking up Route 178 as it leads into Death Valley National Park (ad-

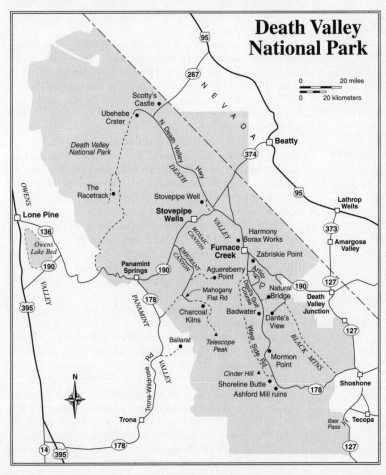

mission) and maintaining a steady composure despite the raw landscape and signs that threaten "No Roadside Services Next 72 Miles," you will enter the most famous desert in the United States.

Due to the extreme summer temperatures (average July highs of 115° and up to the 120s!), travel to the valley is not recommended in summer months. The best time to see the park is from November through April. In late February and March (average highs of 72°, dropping to a cool 45° average at night) the desert comes alive with the spring blossoms of Death Valley sage, rock *mimulus*, and Panamint daisies if sufficient winter rains fall.

Crossing two low-lying mountain passes as it travels west, Route 178 (Badwater Road) turns north upon reaching the floor of Death Valley. Within a couple miles lie the ruins of **Ashford Mill**, built during World War I when gold mining enjoyed a comeback. The skeletons of a few buildings are all that remain of that early dream.

A nearby vista point overlooks **Shoreline Butte**, a curving hill marked by a succession of horizontal lines. Clearly visible to the naked eye, they trace the ancient shorelines of Lake Manly, which covered the valley to a depth of 600 feet and stretched for 90 miles. Formed perhaps 75,000 years ago when Pleistocene glaciers atop the Sierra Nevada began melting, the lake dried up about 10,000 years ago.

For a close-up of a cinder cone, follow nearby West Side Road, a graded thoroughfare, downhill for two miles. That reddish-black mound on your left is **Cinder Hill**, residue from an ancient volcano. Though West Side Road is usually open to all vehicles, it's a good idea to check with the visitors center regarding any restrictions.

The main highway continues through the heart of the region to **Mormon Point**. From here northward Death Valley is one huge salt flat. As you traverse this expanse, notice how the Black Mountains to the east turn from dark colors to reddish hues as gray Precambrian rocks give way to younger volcanic and sedimentary deposits.

Then continue on to that place you've been reading about since third-grade geography, **Badwater**, 282 feet below sea level, the lowest point in the western hemisphere. Legend has it the place got its name from a surveyor whose mule refused to drink here, inspiring him to scratch "bad water" on the map he was charting.

Take a stroll out onto the salt flats and you'll find that the crystals are joined into a white carpet which extends for miles. Despite the brackish environment the pool itself supports water snails and other invertebrates. Salt grass, pickleweed, and desert holly also endure here. Out on the flats you can gaze west at 11,049-foot **Telescope Peak** across the valley. Then be sure to glance back at the cliff to the west of the road. There high in the rocks above you a lone sign marks "Sea Level."

The water that carved **Natural Bridge** was quite unlike those stagnant pools on the valley floor. Indeed, it cascaded from the mountains in torrents, punched a hole in the underlying rock, and etched this 50-foot-high arch. Behind the bridge, you can still see the lip of this ancient waterfall. Also notice the formations along the canyon walls that were left by evaporating water and bear a startling resemblance to dripping wax. ~ Off Route 178 about two miles along a bumpy gravel road and up a half-mile trail.

Another dirt side road travels one mile to the **Devil's Golf Course**. Rather than a sand hazard, this flat expanse is one huge salt trap, complete with salt towers, pinnacles, and brine pools. The salt deposits here are three to five feet thick. They were formed by a small lake that evaporated perhaps 2000 years ago; below them earlier deposits from larger lakes reach over 1000 feet beneath the surface.

> The sodium chloride at Devil's Golf Course is 95 percent pure, comparable to table salt.

Artist Drive, a nine-mile route through the Black Mountains, is one of Southern California's most magnificent roads. The hills all around are splashed with color— soft pastels, striking reds, creamy browns—and rise to sharp cliffs. En route at **Artists Palette**, the hills are colored so vividly they seem to pulsate. It's a spot admired by photographers from around the world, a place where the rainbow meets the badlands.

If you'd like a scientific explanation for all this beauty—the artistic medium is oxidation: chloride deposits create the green hues, manganese oxides form the blacks, and the reds, yellows, and oranges are shades of iron oxide. These contrasting colors are most spectacular during late afternoon.

Up in **Golden Canyon**, erosion has chiseled chasms into the bright yellow walls of a narrow gorge. Climb the three-quarter-mile trail and you arrive in a natural amphitheater, named for the iridescent quality of the canyon walls, which are the embodiment of sunlight.

In this entire land of natural wonders the only major center of civilization is **Furnace Creek**, where a gas station, campground, restaurants, and two hotels create a welcome oasis. The **Furnace Creek Visitors Center** is a good resource for information and maps. It houses a museum re-creating the history of American Indians and early prospectors. There are also mineral displays, descriptions of Death Valley flora and fauna, and an oversize relief map of the valley. ~ 760-786-2331, fax 760-786-3246; www.nps.gov/deva.

The nearby **Borax Museum** features the oldest house in Death Valley, a sturdy 1883 structure built by a borax miner. There's also a wonderful collection of stage coaches as well as a huge Rube Goldbergesque contraption once used to extract gold deposits from rock. ~ Furnace Creek Ranch; 760-786-2345, fax 760-786-2185.

While the yellow metal symbolizes the romance of desert prospecting, the lowly borax mineral proved of much greater value to Death Valley miners. Important as a cleaning agent, the white crystal was first discovered in 1881. Eventually it inspired its own romantic images, with 20-mule teams hauling 20-ton wagonloads across 160 miles of desert to the railhead in Mojave.

A two-and-a-half-mile trail climbs from Golden Canyon to **Zabriskie Point**, but most folks follow Route 190, which leads southeast from Furnace Creek. In any case, everyone inevitably arrives at this place, as though it were a point of pilgrimage for paying homage to nature.

What else can a mortal do, confronted with beauty of this magnitude? In the east amber-hued hills roll like waves toward the horizon. To the west lies a badlands, burnished by blown sand to fierce reds and soft pastels. All around, the landscape resembles a sea gone mad, waves of sand breaking in every direction, with a stone tsunami, Manly Beacon, high above the combers, poised to crash into Death Valley.

Prosaic though it sounds, these mustard-colored hills are dry mud, lake-bed sediments deposited 2 to 12 million years ago, then uplifted to their present height. In the early morning and late afternoon, when the place is suffused with color, Zabriskie Point demonstrates that humble origins are of little consequence.

For a close-up view of those mud hills, follow the nearby dirt road through **Twenty Mule Team Canyon**. It winds almost three miles through a former borax-mining region.

Then to get above it all, venture on to **Dante's View**, a 5475-foot perch with a 360-degree vista. From this vantage point, the salt flats and trapped pools of Death Valley are like a bleak watercolor. Though the Panamint Mountains wall off the western horizon, a steep half-mile trail (up the knoll north of the parking lot) leads to a point where you can gaze beyond them to Badwater and the snow-thatched Sierra Nevada.

R.I.P.

One person found neither well nor stovepipe at Stovepipe Well. **Val Nolan's grave**, a simple resting place within crawling distance of the well, consists of a pile of stones and a wooden marker. Carved into the grave is an epitaph that graphically reveals Val Nolan's last days: "A Victim of the Elements."

Backtracking to Furnace Creek, Route 190 proceeds north toward the upper end of Death Valley. The history of the region's most valuable mineral is further revealed at the **Harmony Borax Works**. Surrounded by the ruins of Death Valley's most successful borax plant is an original 20-mule team rig.

At the very end of Death Valley, when you've gone as far north as you can without bumping fenders with the Nevada border, you'll find the strangest feature in the entire park—a castle in the desert. It's a place called **Scotty's Castle**, though Scotty never owned it. In fact Scotty swindled the fellow who did own it, then became his lifelong friend. Sound preposterous? Perhaps.

It seems that one Walter "Death Valley Scotty" Scott, a former trick rider in Buffalo Bill's Wild West Show, once convinced a Chicago millionaire, one Albert Johnson, to invest in a nonexistent gold mine. Johnson traveled west to see the mine, discovered that the dry desert clime helped his fragile health, forgave Scotty, and decided during the 1920s to build a mansion in the sand.

The result was a $2 million Moorish castle, a wonderfully ridiculous building with wrought-iron detailing, inlaid tile, carved-beam ceilings, expensive antiques, and nothing for miles around. Scotty, the greatest story teller in Death Valley history, told everyone it was his castle. Hence the name. Somehow it reminds me of Hearst Castle in San Simeon, a place too gaudy to appreciate but too outrageous to ignore. Admission.

Ubehebe Crater, eight miles from Scotty's lair, is another of the park's natural wonders. One-half mile in diameter and reaching a depth of 500 feet, this magnificent landmark was created by a single explosion. The force of the volcanic steam scattered debris over a six-square-mile area and blew the crater walls so clean that one side retains its original sedimentary colors.

◀ *HIDDEN*

From the crater a winding gravel road leads 27 miles to **The Racetrack**, another of nature's magic acts. This two-mile mud playa, set at the bottom of a dry lake, is oval shaped like a racecourse. In fact an outcropping at the north end of the valley is dubbed The Grandstand. The racers, oddly enough, are rocks, ranging in size from pebbles to boulders. Pushed by heavy winds across the mud-slick surface, they leave long, faint tracks that reveal the distances they have "raced." Though the road to The Racetrack is usually open to all vehicles, it's a good idea to check with the visitors center for any restrictions.

Stovepipe Wells, Death Valley's other village, is even smaller than Furnace Creek. A motel, restaurant, store, gas station, and campground comprise the entire town. It was near here at **Burned Wagons Point** that a desperate party of '49ers killed their oxen and dried the meat by burning their wagons. Stop by the Stovepipe Wells Ranger Station for directions to the point. ~ 760-786-2342, fax 760-786-2111; www.nps.gov/deva.

Six miles east of Stovepipe, a graded road departs Route 190 and travels four miles past **sand dunes** before joining North Death Valley Highway, the road to Scotty's Castle. The highest dunes are more than 100 feet, and take decep-

Whether Ubehebe Crater dates back 10,000 years or is only a few hundred years old is currently being debated by geologists. They do agree that other nearby craters have been formed in the last few centuries.

tively long to reach. Alive with greenery, they support many plant species, including creosote bushes, mesquite, and pickleweed. Coyotes hunt prey in these undulating sand-hills and there are kit fox, lizards, kangaroo rats, and beetles. All of these creatures leave their fascinating tracks in the sand, making the dunes a paradise for children and wildlife lovers, as well as photographers.

Farther along rests the old **Stovepipe Well** from which the village derived its name. Used by prospectors crossing Death Valley, the well was fitted with a tall stovepipe so travelers could see it even when sand blanketed the area.

DEATH VALLEY TO TRONA AREA Stovepipe Wells marks the western gateway to Death Valley. From here Route 190 travels out of the valley southwest through Towne Pass in the Panamint Range. An alternative route leaving the park is Trona–Wildrose Road that winds south through Emigrant Canyon. This route, leading to Trona, passes several intriguing spots.

Aguereberry Point, a 6433-foot overlook, lies at the end of a six-mile-long side road. From atop this crag you gaze back at Death Valley and enjoy a circular view of the Black Mountains and the Sierra Nevada. (Despite a sign advising four-wheel drive, the road is graded and usually passable by two-wheel-drive vehicles. It's advisable to inquire about road conditions at the ranger station.)

Another detour onto **Mahogany Flat Road** (partially paved) leads seven miles to a startling site. As you round a bend, ten bee-hives, 25 feet high, line the road. At least they look like beehives; in fact these stone-sided cones are **Charcoal Kilns**, used to create fuel for nearby silver smelters.

Meanwhile, Trona–Wildrose Road descends into the **Panamint Valley**, a sun-parched plain bounded by the Panamint and Argus ranges. Here another side road cuts east for four miles to

HIDDEN ► **Ballarat**, a ghost town dating to 1897. The wood and adobe ruins are remnants of a mining supply center that flourished until 1905. In its heyday this desolate spot boasted a stagecoach stop, three general stores, a school, Wells Fargo office, and hotel.

LODGING Near the southeast corner of Death Valley, in the postage-stamp town of Shoshone, the **Shoshone Inn** has standard motel rooms. There is a tree-shaded courtyard, a nearby swimming pool, museum, gas station, restaurant and bar. The Shoshone is conveniently placed for exploring the southern stretches of Death Valley. ~ Route 127, Shoshone; 760-852-4335, fax 760-852-4107; e-mail shoshonevillage@shoshone.net. BUDGET.

The main lodging in Death Valley is at **Furnace Creek Inn & Ranch Resort**, which consists of two adjacent, formerly separate properties that share facilities but offer different qualities of rooms. The 224-unit "ranch" sprawls across several acres. In addition to three restaurants, a saloon, and a general store, it has a swimming pool, riding stable, golf course, tennis courts, and playground. Guest accommodations include duplex "cabins," fully furnished but lacking extra amenities, and standard rooms, which are plusher, more spacious, and feature televisions and refrigerators. The posher "inn" is a 66-room Moorish-style stone and adobe building set high on the hillside, surrounded by flowering gardens. Palm trees shade the grounds, and a stream feed three koi ponds. It has a restaurant, a swank lobby, tennis courts, and a spring-fed swimming pool. Guest rooms, priced in the ultra-deluxe range, are trimly appointed and quite comfortably furnished, with such features as tile baths with brass fittings. The "inn" is closed May to October. ~ Route 190, Furnace Creek; 760-786-2345, 800-236-7916, fax 760-786-9098; www.furnacecreekresort.com. MODERATE TO ULTRA-DELUXE.

Stovepipe Wells Village is an attractive 83-unit motel about 25 miles up the road. With a pool, lounge, restaurant, general store and gas station, it's as well-equipped as you could expect. If your heroes have always been cowboys, you'll sleep well here; some of the rooms are decorated Western-style with oxen yokes attached to the headboards and steer heads carved into the light fixtures. ~ Stovepipe Wells; 760-786-2387, fax 760-786-2389; www.stovepipewells.com. MODERATE.

DINING

Not far from the southern entrance to Death Valley, there's a café where water is served in Mason jars. The **J & R's Crowbar Cafe & Saloon** offers sandwiches, Mexican dishes, and standards such as steak, pork chops, fried chicken, and trout filet. ~ Shoshone; 760-852-4180. MODERATE.

Eat heartily because the next facilities are 72 miles away in Furnace Creek off Route 190. Here you'll find three full-service restaurants open to the public, all of which can be reached at 760-786-2345.

The biggest meals in all of Death Valley can be found at the **Wrangler Buffet** at Furnace Creek Ranch. Open for breakfast and lunch, this steam-tray emporium serves an all-you-can-eat buffet of American food classics. Atmosphere is nonexistent and the food has invariably been warming for hours before it hits your plate, but oh, that bountiful salad bar! In the evening, the Wrangler

Buffet becomes the **Wrangler Steak House**, serving steak, chicken, and seafood entrées. ~ MODERATE TO ULTRA-DELUXE.

The **49er Café** next door has omelettes, hot sandwiches, hamburgers, and a selection of dinners ranging from pork chops and steak to calf's liver. With woodplank walls and ranch atmosphere, it's a good place for a reasonably priced meal. ~ MODERATE.

At **The Inn Dining Room**, candlelight and a beamed ceiling create a more formal atmosphere. It's a five-course meal, and the menu is fixed-price. You can choose from among nearly 40 entrées. The breakfast menu is standard. There is a dress code for dinner from October to mid-May. ~ ULTRA-DELUXE.

In Stovepipe Wells you'll spot the spacious **Tollroad Restaurant,** embellished with Indian rugs and paintings of the Old West. The cuisine matches the ambience, an all-American menu featuring filet mignon, chicken, steak, and ribs. ~ Route 190, Stovepipe Wells; 760-786-2604, fax 760-786-2389. MODERATE TO DELUXE.

NIGHTLIFE In Death Valley, the Furnace Creek Inn includes the **Lobby Lounge** among its elegant facilities. It's a lovely spot to enjoy a quiet evening. ~ Furnace Creek; 760-786-2345; www.furnace creekresort.com.

The **Badwater Saloon** in Stovepipe Wells also hosts jukebox dancing. With Western-style decor and a dancefloor, it's a night owl's oasis. ~ Stovepipe Wells; 760-786-2608.

PARKS **DEATH VALLEY NATIONAL PARK** 🚶 🚲 Extending across more than three million acres and rising from below sea level to over 11,000 feet, this park is a land unto itself, varied and full of possibility. It contains 550 square miles of salt flats, 30 square miles of sand dunes, and several mountain ranges. Death Valley itself covers only a small part of the facility.

In addition to standard sightseeing spots there are hiking trails and 300 miles of jeep tracks leading to obscure high-desert lo-

AUTHOR FAVORITE

The best entertainment for many miles is at the **Amargosa Opera House.** This amazing show is the creation of Marta Bucket, who performs dance pantomimes in a theater that she herself decorated with colorful murals. Performances run every Saturday from October through January, and every Saturday and Monday from February through April. Internationally renowned, she's extremely popular, so call for reservations. ~ Death Valley Junction; 760-852-4441, fax 760-852-4138; www.amargosa-opera-house.com, e-mail amargosa@kay-net.com.

cales. Almost 350 bird species migrate through here, together with desert tortoises, rattlesnakes, mountain lions, bobcats, mule deer, and bighorn sheep. There's a visitors center and museum, as well as hotels, restaurants, picnic areas, restrooms, and limited groceries. For complete information see the "Sights" and "Hiking" sections in this chapter. Day-use fee, $10. ~ Located in the northern Mojave Desert along Routes 178 and 190. Furnace Creek Campground is located one-quarter of a mile north of the Furnace Creek Visitors Center. Mesquite Springs Campground is at the north end of the desert near Scotty's Castle; 760-786-3200, fax 760-786-3283; www.nps.gov/deva.

▲ Camping is permitted in nine campgrounds. Furnace Creek has 136 tent/RV sites (no hookups); $10 to $16 per night. Located at about 2500 feet, Mesquite Springs (open year-round) has 30 tent/RV sites; $10 per night. Three low-elevation facilities are open from October to April; two other low-elevation campgrounds and three high-elevation campgrounds are open from March to November.

Outdoor Adventures

The Kern and Kings rivers in Sequoia and Kings Canyon national parks offer trout fishing. The Mammoth Lakes area is also an angler's delight.

FISHING

OWENS VALLEY   Lake Sabrina is stocked with rainbow, brook, and brown trout. The **Lake Sabrina Boat Landing** rents 12- to 14-foot boats to anglers who'd like to try their luck. ~ Bishop Creek, Bishop; 760-873-7425.

MAMMOTH LAKES   For fishing-gear rentals, tackle, and friendly information, contact **Ernie's Tackle and Ski Shop**. They can arrange trips on June, Gull, Silver, Grant, and Crowley lakes. Ernie takes you out on a fishing boat; the trip lasts six hours. ~ 2604 Route 158, June Lake; 760-648-7756.

Bass, catfish, crappie, bluegill, and trout can all be found in Lake Kaweah, depending on the season. **Kaweah Marina** rents fishing and patio boats and jet skis. Bait and tackle are also available. ~ 34467 Sierra Drive, Lemon Cove; 559-597-2526. **June Lake Marina** has 50 boats to rent, including 14-foot Valcos and 16-foot Gregors. Closed November through March. ~ End of Brenner Street, June Lake; 760-648-7726; www.junelakemarina.com.

RIVER RUNNING

Shooting the rapids on the Kern and Kings rivers is great sport. Several California tour companies offer exciting adventures on rubber rafts; some offer kayaking.

Sierra South runs Class II and III rapids on the Kern River in both rafts and kayaks. Trips last from one hour to a full day. They also offer paddling lessons on Lake Isabella. ~ 11300 Kern-

Text continued on page 566.

Ski the
Southland

As a travel destination, Southern California offers everything. Even during winter, when rain spatters the coast and fog invades the valleys, the Southland has one more treat in its bottomless bag—snow.

No sooner has the white powder settled than skiers from around the world beeline to the region's high-altitude resort areas. They come to schuss through fir forests in the San Gabriel Mountains, challenge the runs above San Bernardino, and breathe the beauty of Mammoth Lakes at Christmas. The season begins in late fall and sometimes lasts until May. During those frosty months, dozens of alpine areas offer both downhill and cross-country skiing.

One of Southern California's most popular ski destinations is **Mt. Baldy**, a 10,064-foot peak just 45 minutes from Los Angeles. With a vertical drop of 2100 feet, the facility provides 26 runs, four lifts, a lodge, a rental lodge, and a ski school. ~ 909-981-3344, fax 909-982-4874; www.mtbaldy.com.

The neighboring San Bernardino Mountains, which rise to over 11,000 feet, offer several alpine ski areas. These resorts are located along Route 18 between Lake Arrowhead and Big Bear Lake. Most ski areas rent equipment and offer lessons.

The first of these, **Snow Summit Mountain Resort**, has a family park for easy skiing, complete with its own lift. With a base elevation of 7000 feet, the resort's runs (10 percent beginner, 65 percent intermediate, and 25 percent advanced) are served by 11 lifts. For snowboarders, there is a freestyle park with a half-pipe. ~ 909-866-5766, fax 909-866-3201; www.snowsummit.com, e-mail info@snowsummit.com.

Big Bear Mountain Resorts feature four peaks of ski runs, including Bear Peak, the steepest and highest in Southern California. Twenty-three lifts allow you to experience 400 skiable acres. Half the runs are intermediate and the other half are evenly divided between beginner and advanced. They also have four terrain parks and a test center where you can try out the latest ski and snowboard models. ~ 909-866-5766, 800-232-7686, fax 909-866-3201; www.bearmountainresorts.com.

Downhill skiers are kept happy at the **Snow Valley Mountain Resort**, which is at a base elevation of 6800 feet. The runs are about evenly split for beginning, intermediate, and advanced skiers. For snowboarders, the designated park features hits, spines, and tabletops. Night skiing is offered Friday and Saturday evenings, depending on the weather. ~ 909-867-2751, fax 909-867-7687; www.snow-valley.com, e-mail info@snow-valley.com.

If you prefer a base of operations from which to experience the wild, several Nordic ski centers operate in Sequoia and Kings Canyon national parks. The **Giant Forest** and **Lodgepole/Wolverton** sections of Sequoia, for instance, feature 35 miles of trails. Nearby **Wuksachi Lodge** rents cross-country skis and snowshoes. ~ 559-565-3301.

Grant Grove in Kings Canyon National Park has five marked trails that vary in difficulty. Like Sequoia National Park, Kings Canyon sits amid a network of High Sierra cross-country trails. More than 75 miles of these alpine paths extend in every direction, leading through forests of giant sequoia trees. There are frozen lakes to explore, extraordinary mountain vistas, and secluded warming huts. For rentals, contact **Grant Grove Market**. ~ 559-335-2665; www.sequoia-kingscanyon.com.

Near Palm Springs, cross-country skiing is possible at **Mount San Jacinto State Park**. The Palm Springs Aerial Tramway whisks visitors up to Mountain Station at an elevation of 8516 feet. Behind the station, the Adventure Center in Long Valley rents cross-country skis and snowshoes. More than 50 miles of ungroomed backcountry wilderness and subalpine forest await both beginning and advanced skiers. ~ 760-325-1391, 888-515-8726 (ski conditions); www.pstramway.com.

For Angelenos, the Mammoth/June Lakes region represents skier heaven. Located high in the Sierra Nevada chain, about 300 miles from the streets of Los Angeles, **Mammoth Mountain** is one of the largest ski areas in the United States. A major center for both alpine and Nordic skiers, it boasts mountain lodges, craggy peaks, and enough white powder to create an aura of the Alps right here in sun-drenched Southern California. With 30 lifts, there are plenty of runs to keep downhillers and boarders busy (30 percent beginner, 40 percent intermediate, and 30 percent advanced). The terrain park has a half-pipe. Weekend skiing is offered on several runs. ~ 760-934-2571, 800-626-6684; www.mammothmountain.com.

ville Road, Kernville; 760-376-3745; www.sierrasouth.com. **Whitewater Voyages** books trips on the Kern that last from one hour to three days. They raft Class III, IV, and V rapids. Closed October through May. ~ 5225 San Pablo Dam Road, El Sobrante, CA 94803; 510-222-5994; www.whitewatervoyages.com.

Zephyr Whitewater Expeditions takes on the Class III rapids of the Kings, Tuolumne, and Merced rivers. Trips last from a half-day to five days. All meals are included. ~ P.O. Box 510, Columbia, CA 95310; 209-532-6249, 800-431-3636; www. zrafting.com.

BALLOON RIDES

Soaring in a hot-air balloon is all part of a day's work at **Mammoth Balloon Adventures**. Watch the sun come up over the mountains on the Sierra sunrise flight. Reservations are required. ~ Mammoth Lakes; 760-937-8787; www.mammothballoonadventures.com.

RIDING STABLES & PACK TOURS

Out here in the High Desert you can saddle up and ride into the American past.

MOJAVE DESERT   **Mojave Narrows Riding Stables** take you on a one-hour ride along the Mojave River and around the woods in the area. Closed Monday during summer and weekdays during winter. ~ Phone/fax 760-244-1644.

SEQUOIA AND KINGS CANYON   **Grant Grove** in Kings Canyon National Park offers one- to two-hour trips through the Giant Sequoia redwoods. Closed October through April. ~ 559-335-9292. Also in Kings Canyon, **Cedar Grove Pack Station** occasionally leads one-hour to full-day rides. Their specialty is overnight trips through Kings River and Canyon backcountry. Closed November through April. ~ 559-565-3464.

Pack trips in the Sierra Nevada often combine horseback riding with fishing expeditions. If you prefer something less adventurous, most outfits offer full-day or half-day excursions as well as longer treks. Keep in mind that most pack stations close in winter, so call in advance. **Bishop Pack Outfitters** offers horse and cattle drives, as well as four- to six-day pack trips into the John Muir Wilderness or the Sequoia and Kings national parks. Closed November through May. ~ 247 Cataract Road, Aspendell; 760-873-4785.

MAMMOTH LAKES   **Red's Meadow Resort Pack Train** leads treks through the Yosemite high country, Ansel Adams, John Muir, and Minaret Wilderness. You can ride a horse or hike; pack mules carry all the gear. Closed September through May. ~ Mammoth Lakes; 760-934-2345. **Frontier Pack Train** gives pack tours in the Ansel Adams Wilderness near June Lake. Closed October through May. ~ June Lake; 760-648-7701 in summer, 760-873-7971 in winter; www.frontierpacktrain.com.

DEATH VALLEY AREA In Death Valley, **Furnace Creek Ranch** offers wagon rides and winter carriage rides. ~ 760-786-2345; www.furnacecreekresort.com.

The desert may be one huge sand trap, but golf enthusiasts won't find many greens in these parts.

GOLF

MOJAVE DESERT The 18-hole **Green Tree Golf Course** is a challenging par 72. ~ 14144 Green Tree Boulevard, Victorville; 760-245-4860. In Mojave, try the nine holes at the **Camelot Golf Course**. The holes are played twice; the course is par 72. ~ Camelot Boulevard, Mojave; 661-824-4107.

SEQUOIA AND KINGS CANYON The public **Three Rivers Golf Course** has nine holes. ~ 41117 Sierra Drive, Three Rivers; 559-561-3133.

OWENS VALLEY **Mount Whitney Golf Course**'s nine holes can be played once or twice; the views of Mount Whitney are stunning. ~ Route 395, south of Lone Pine; 760-876-5795. **Bishop Country Club** has a fun 18-hole course with tree-lined fairways and water at every hole. ~ South Route 395, Bishop; 760-873-5828.

DEATH VALLEY AREA Tee off 214 feet below sea level at the **Furnace Creek Golf Course**. Designed by Perry Dye, the 18-hole, par-70 course is built on rolling hills; there is water at nine of the holes. ~ Route 190, Death Valley; 760-786-2301; www.furnace creekresort.com.

The Eastern Sierra is a prime place for mountain biking.

BIKING

MAMMOTH LAKES In Mammoth Lakes, the **Mammoth Scenic Loop** (off of Minaret Road) offers a lovely, though hilly, overview of this majestic area. Another picturesque ride is the **June Lake Loop** (Route 158), an easy 16-mile route around the base of the mountains and along the lake shore. The **Mammoth Mountain**

CRAZY FOR CROSS-COUNTRY

The demanding Nordic-style skiing is popular around the state. It's the adventurer's way to explore the slopes—fill a daypack, strap on skis, and take off across the mountains. In the pack are extra clothes, food, water, flashlight, knife, map, compass, blanket, matches, equipment repair tools, and a first-aid kit. Unrestricted by ski lifts and marked runs, cross-country skiers venture everywhere that geography and gravity permit. Their sport is tantamount to hiking on skis, with the entire expanse of the mountain range their domain. Some skiers disappear into the wilderness for days on end, emerging only when supplies run low. See "Ski the Southland" for more information on Nordic skiing.

Ski Area is a mountain-bike mecca in summer. Riders can take the gondola to the top of the mountain and descend on the ski area's extensive service roads. For experienced bike riders, the road from **Tom's Place** to **Rock Creek Winter Lodge** is nine miles of uphill pedaling through a stunning canyon. Think of the fun you'll have coming back.

DEATH VALLEY AREA **Death Valley** may seem like the last place to ride a bicycle, but it's actually quite pleasant from October through April. The main road in the park is paved and there's little traffic in the early morning and late afternoon. The paved roads to Badwater and Scotty's Castle are also low-traffic options. The side roads to some of the sights are dirt or gravel, however, and require a mountain bike.

Furnace Creek is a good starting point: it's an easy ride from here to Badwater and Artist Drive, though the latter destination requires uphill pedaling. For an even more challenging ride you can venture up, up, uphill to Dante's View; plan on an all-day effort and bring provisions (especially water!).

Excellent mountain biking can be found in most of the canyons off the West Side Road—they'll all be challenging uphills for as long as you can stand it, and downhill thrills on the way out. If you have two cars—or a big thumb and a nice smile—you can ride Titus Canyon, one way downhill; it's a stunning run through a deep gorge that is, in places, hardly wide enough for a car.

Bike Rentals and Tours **Mammoth Sporting Goods** is a full-service shop that rents mountain bikes, children's bikes, and trailers. The staff is extremely knowledgeable about trails in the area; they even have a map to help you find those hidden locales. ~ Old Mammoth Road; 760-934-3239. **Footloose** rents mountain and children's bikes during the summer. ~ 3043 Main Street, Mammoth Lakes; 760-934-2400; www.footloosesports.com.

HIKING   All distances listed for hiking trails are one way unless otherwise noted.

SEQUOIA AND KINGS CANYON Sequoia and Kings Canyon national parks offer miles of serene trails amid towering sequoia trees and tumbling waterfalls.

Mist Falls Trail (4.5 miles), near Zumwalt Meadow, leads north past a massive stone face called The Sphinx, then continues on toward its namesake, a cascade so light it resembles mist.

A moderate hike along **Sugarbowl–Redwood Canyon–Hart Tree Loop Trail** (6 miles) takes you through some of the most beautiful country in Grant Grove. Beginning on Sugarbowl Trail, then connecting with Redwood Canyon Trail and Hart Tree Trail, the loop passes the 209-foot Hart Tree. The trailhead is located at Redwood Saddle. (Check ahead with the ranger, the area is sometimes closed.)

For a 360-degree view of the Sierra Crest, Kings Canyon, and the sequoias of Redwood Canyon, hike **Buena Vista Peak** (1 mile), one of the highest points west of Generals Highway. (The trailhead is south of Kings Canyon Overlook.)

Another majestic view lies along **Little Baldy Trail** (1.7 miles). From here on a clear day you can see the San Joaquin Valley. Begin this trail at Little Baldy Saddle, located 11 miles north of Giant Forest Village on Generals Highway.

The ever-popular **Muir Grove Trail** (2 miles), which begins near Dorst campground, contains magnificent sequoias in a lovely setting.

An easy hike along the **Tokopah Falls Trail** (1.7 miles) leads through Tokopah Valley, where the Marble Fork of the Kaweah River flows between soaring granite cliffs. The trailhead is located at Lodgepole campground.

From the same campground, **Pear Lake Trail** (6.7 miles), a moderate climb, carries past Emerald Lake and through an area rich in wildlife and wildflowers to Pear Lake. The trail ends in a granite-bound basin amid a dozen tiny lakes and crystal creeks.

Of the many trails crossing Mineral King, several offer day-excursions. **Tar Gap Trail** (2.2 miles), rising quickly from Cold Spring campground, crosses several creeks and provides views of Sawtooth Peak, Empire Mountain, and Timber Gap.

Timber Gap Trail (2.2 miles), which begins near the end of the road in Mineral King, passes through a red fir forest, crosses a summit, then dips into the flower-strewn meadows of Timber Gap Creek.

> As tempting as mountain waters look, don't drink from them unless you have brought water-purification equipment: the intestinal parasite *Giardia* is widespread in this area.

Sawtooth Pass Trail (5.5 miles), beginning at the same trailhead as Timber Gap, follows Monarch Creek upward through manzanita cover to Groundhog Meadow. Here Monarch Lakes Trail continues across the creek and zigzags up through open pine and fir stands to Monarch Lakes.

From the road's end in Mineral King, **Eagle Lake Trail** (3.4 miles) follows Eagle Creek through fragrant sagebrush and colorful wildflowers. The path ascends 2000 feet before reaching Eagle Lake, which nestles below White Chief Peak in a granite bowl.

OWENS VALLEY   The Sierra Nevada offer the finest hiking in California, attracting adventurers from all over the world. Along Route 395 in the Owens Valley, roads leading to major trailheads branch off in nearly every town.

Sparkling lakes, wildflowers, cascades, and encircling peaks await when you climb the **Kearsarge Pass to Flower Lake Trail** (2.5 miles). The trailhead is at the end of Onion Valley Road, outside the town of Independence.

West of Bishop, Lake Sabrina and South Lake are important trailheads for serious backpackers. Backdropped by glacier-bearing peaks, **South Lake to Treasure Lakes Trail** (5 miles) climbs 1000 feet through mixed coniferous forest to the south fork of Bishop Creek.

Lake Sabrina to Dingleberry Lake Trail (5 miles) ascends 1500 feet to an alpine lake and presents a panorama of lakes, forests, and lofty Sierra crests.

MAMMOTH AND JUNE LAKES The Mammoth and June lakes region is a key entranceway to the Ansel Adams (formerly Minarets) and John Muir wilderness areas. From here there is easy access to the **Pacific Crest** and **John Muir trails**. The John Muir Trail, which extends from Lake Tahoe to Mount Whitney, is a 200-mile-long portion of the Pacific Crest Trail. (Permits are required for these wilderness areas and should be obtained well in advance.)

Day-hikes up Coldwater Creek and Mammoth Creek from Lake Mary offer great outings. Try **Mammoth Creek to Duck Lake Trail** (5 miles), with its many lakes, vistas, and flowering meadows. Duck Lake is an ideal trout-fishing spot.

An easy hike along **Mammoth Rock Trail** (3 miles) leads east past its namesake, a fossil-embedded marble and limestone monolith. The trail, which begins from Old Mammoth Road, also skirts the largest Jeffrey pine forest in the world.

It's a beautiful hike along the **Sherwin Creek Canyon Trail** (2.5 miles) to the five small Sherwin Lakes. Switchbacks ease the 800 foot climb. Once here, you can ascend farther along **Valentine Lake Trail** (5 miles) to a forest-fringed lake squeezed into a glaciated cirque. Sherwin Creek Canyon trailhead is located one mile west of Sherwin Creek campground.

Lake George to Crystal Lake Trail (1.5 miles) treks through mountain hemlock to a serene lake at the base of Crystal Crag. For sweeping views, continue up to the top on **Mammoth Crest Trail** (3 miles).

You'll experience a touch of wilderness with little effort along **Lake George–Lake Barrett–T. J. Loop Trail** (1.5 miles). It starts at Lake George campground and follows the lake shore before veering uphill through flowering meadows and stands of alder and pine.

From the June Lake Loop, **Agnew Lake Trail** (2 miles) departs near Silver Lake and rises 1300 feet to a picnic area and cold mountain lake.

Another hike leaving the Silver Lake area is **Fern Creek Trail** (1.5 miles), which climbs nearly 2000 feet en route to Fern Lake. A branch trail travels another three miles to Yost Lake.

Convict Creek Trail (10 miles) is a long but rewarding trek from Convict Lake past three alpine lakes, well-stocked with fish, over a 10,000-foot ridge. The trail then switchbacks down to Laurel Canyon Road.

Horseshoe Lake to Reds Meadow Trail (6.5 miles) passes through pine-hemlock forest, skirts McCloud Lake, and crosses the Sierra Crest. The trail then descends to the old John Muir Trail, where a side trip leads to Red Cones, a formation of geologically young cinder cones. The main trail continues through red-fir forests to Reds Meadow campground with its refreshing hot springs.

DEATH VALLEY AREA   Rugged hiking in the desert and mountains is a favorite sport around Death Valley. Special precautions, however, must be taken throughout this area: be sure to carry plenty of water; watch for rattlesnakes; do not enter mine shafts and tunnels; and avoid desert hiking between May and October. Maps of more than 20 hiking trails are available at the visitors center.

The **Salt Creek Interpretive Trail** (.5 mile), 12 miles north of Furnace Creek, provides a glimpse of the salt-tolerant grasses and rare pupfish of Salt Creek. Arriving at dawn you will see the tracks left by numerous nocturnal animals.

West of Stovepipe Wells Village, a short dirt road heads south to **Mosaic Canyon Trail** (2 miles). Formed by a fault zone, the canyon's walls are polished by wind and water. The multicolored rock debris deposited here gives the canyon its name.

For a view from the highest peak for miles around, park your car at Mahogany Flat and climb **Telescope Peak Trail** (7 miles). Summer and fall are the best seasons for this moderate ascent. Once atop this 11,049-foot peak you can gaze east across Death Valley and west to the Sierra Nevada. Note: If you do not have a high-clearance vehicle, you will have to hike an additional mile and a half to the trailhead.

A less ambitious trip is up **Wildrose Peak Trail** (4 miles) from Charcoal Kilns. Here you'll find wide vistas and a variety of animals and plants, including bristlecone pines.

Hikers who are history buffs or ghost town enthusiasts should consider a journey to **Panamint City** (5 miles), a once-booming

AUTHOR FAVORITE

The most famous climb in the Sierra is along **Mount Whitney Trail** (11 miles) to the 14,496-summit. The lure of ascending the highest peak in the "lower 48" is irresistible to many. Camping is permitted at Outpost Camp (3.5 miles) and Trail Camp (6 miles). Spots are assigned by lottery only. ~ Contact the Mount Whitney Ranger Station, 640 South Main Street, Lone Pine; 760-876-6200.

mining center dating from the 1870s. Located on the west side of the Panamint range at the top of Surprise Canyon, the remains of the town include a brick chimney several stories high—part of the original lumber mill—plus several cabins, some of which date from later booms in the 1920s and 1930s. To reach the mouth of Surprise Canyon, take the Trona–Wildrose Road to Ballarat Road. After passing through the ghost town of Ballarat, take the second turnoff on your right—the road should be in noticeably better shape than the others along this stretch—and follow it up the large alluvial fan as far as you can. Park at the encampment of trailers, where you'll see forbidding signs inaccurately admonishing hikers that Panamint City is "ten miles on foot"; these are the work of modern-day prospectors who try to dissuade others from exploring the canyon.

The hike up Surprise Canyon is wonderful, wild, and may be a little wet, depending on the time of year. Some climbing is involved in the lower section, where the canyon is steep and narrow; above the narrows it's a four-wheel-drive road all the way. Above Panamint City, the trail continues up to Panamint Pass, from which you can view Death Valley and Johnson Canyon. Carrying a topographic map is a good idea during any hike in Death Valley, and is essential if you intend to continue above Panamint City.

▼▼▼▼▼▼▼▼▼▼

Transportation

CAR

The California desert is a region of Texas-style proportions. In this chapter it is divided into several large slices —the Mojave Desert, Sequoia and Kings Canyon national parks, Owens Valley, Mammoth Lakes, and Death Valley.

In crossing the Mojave Desert, **Route 58** leads from Bakersfield to Barstow, the hub of this entire area. From here **Route 40** travels east to Arizona and **Route 15** buzzes northeast toward Las Vegas.

Two highways lead into Sequoia and Kings Canyon national parks, which are located on the western slopes of the Sierra Ne-

◆◆◆

DESERT DRIVING

There are several important points to remember when driving in the desert. Stay on the main roads unless you have inquired about the conditions of side roads. Turn back if a road becomes too difficult to navigate. Be sure to keep your radiator and gas tank filled and make sure the cooling system is in good condition. Also, carry spare water, food, and gas in your vehicle. If stranded in the summer heat, do not leave the shade of your car. Happy trails!

vada: **Route 198** from Visalia and **Route 180** from Fresno. The **Generals Highway,** generally closed in winter, connects the parks.

From Route 15, **Route 127** proceeds north and links with **Route 178** and **Route 190,** which wind through Death Valley National Park.

Route 395, the desert's major north–south thoroughfare, runs the entire length of the Owens Valley, then continues north to Mammoth Lakes.

Airports in these areas are rare and regularly scheduled flights are even scarcer. A few small airlines provide flights from various California locations. For air travel to Sequoia and Kings Canyon national parks you'll have to fly into Fresno, then pick up ground transportation.

AIR

Alaska Airlines, Allegiant Airlines, America West Airlines, American Airlines, Continental Airlines, Delta Air Lines, Hawaiian Airlines, Horizon Air, Northwest Airlines, Skywest Airlines, and United Airlines all fly into **Fresno Yosemite International Airport.** ~ www.flyfresno.org.

For information about charter service, contact **Mammoth Yosemite Airport Information** (760-934-3825).

Death Valley visitors usually fly to Las Vegas, then drive from there.

For ground transportation from the Amtrak and Greyhound stations from Merced to Yosemite, call **VIA.** ~ 800-369-7275.

Bus service here is almost as scarce as air transportation. To visit Owens Valley and the Mammoth Lakes area, try **Greyhound Bus Lines,** which stops in Mammoth Lakes (Mammoth Tavern Road). ~ 800-231-2222.

BUS

The nearest **Amtrak** station servicing Sequoia and Kings Canyon is in Fresno, 65 miles west of the parks. From here you'll have to hike, hitch, or rent a car.

TRAIN

For service to Death Valley, the closest city is Barstow, a stop for the "Southwest Chief."

For car rentals at the Fresno airport, contact **Avis Rent A Car** (800-331-1212), **Budget Rent A Car** (800-527-0700), **Dollar Rent A Car** (866-434-2226), **Hertz Rent A Car** (800-654-3131), or **National Car Rental** (800-227-7368).

CAR RENTALS

In Barstow, call **Avis Rent A Car** (800-331-1212). There's a **You Save Auto Rental** (760-872-1070) in Bishop. Around Mammoth Lakes, try **You Save Auto Rental** (800-207-2681) or **Mammoth Car Rental** (760-934-8111).

Index

A. K. Smiley Public Library, 475
Abalone Cove Shoreline Park, 177–78
Above the Fold, 64
Ackerman Student Union (UCLA), 115
Adamson House, 204
Adventures at Sea gondola cruises, 248
African American Firefighter Museum, 46
Afton Canyon, 531
Agua Caliente County Park, 506, 508
Agua Caliente Cultural Museum, 485
Aguereberry Point, 560
Ah Louis Store, 440
Ahmanson Theatre, 24; nightlife, 35, 36
Air and Space Gallery (California Science Center), 44
Air travel. See Transportation *in regional chapters*
Airport in the Sky, 215, 231–32; dining, 220
Airport Road (Avalon), 215
Alabama Hills, 540
Alamitos Peninsula, 171
Albinger Archaeological Museum, 398–99
Aliso Creek Beach Park, 70
Allen (Gracie) home, 108
Alto Nido Apartments, 75
Amboy Crater, 527
Amtrak. See Transportation *in regional chapters*
Anacapa Island, 402–403
Anaheim: dining, 287; lodging, 283–86; nightlife, 290; shopping, 289; sights, 282. See also Disneyland
Anaheim Museum, 282
Ancient Bristlecone Pine Forest, 543–44
Anderton Court, 106
Andreas Canyon, 486
Andree Clark Bird Refuge, 416
Andrés Pico Adobe, 127
Angeles National Forest, 144, 149
Angelino Heights, 50–51
Angels Flight (railway), 27
Angelus Temple, 50
Antelope Valley area: sights, 522, 524
Antelope Valley California Poppy Reserve, 522, 524
Antelope Valley Indian Museum, 522
Anza–Borrego Desert State Park, 328, 503–506, 508; camping, 508; dining, 506; lodging, 504, 506; map, 505; nightlife, 506; parks, 506, 508; sights, 503–504; visitor information, 503
Apple Valley, 527

Aquarium of the Pacific, 165–66
Arboretum of Los Angeles County, 142
Arcadia: dining, 146; nightlife, 148; shopping, 148; sights, 142–43
Arch Cove, 269
ARCO Plaza, 28; shopping, 32
Argyle Hotel, 92; lodging, 93
Arrowhead Queen (paddlewheeler), 468
Arroyo Burro Beach Park, 430
Arroyo Terrace (Pasadena), 140
Art Center College of Design, 140
Artist Drive (Death Valley), 557
Artists Palette, 557
Ashford Mill, 556
Asistencia Misión de San Gabriel, 476
Atwell Mill, 532
Autry Museum of Western Heritage, 55
Avalon: dining, 219–20; lodging, 216–19; map, 213; nightlife, 222; shopping, 220, 222; sights, 212, 214
Avalon Casino, 214; nightlife, 222
Avalon Pleasure Pier, 212
Avenues of Art and Design, 90–91
Ávila Adobe, 40
Avila Beach (town): sights, 438

Bacall (Lauren) home, 118
Backesto Building, 364–65
Backside Rincon (Bates Beach), 427–28
Badwater (lowest point), 556
Bakersfield area: sights, 519
Balboa Beach, 255
Balboa Island: lodging, 251; shopping, 254; sights, 246
Balboa Island Ferry, 246, 248
Balboa Park, 357–62; dining, 361–62; lodging, 360–61; nightlife, 362; shopping, 362; sights, 357–60; visitor information, 358
Balboa Pavilion, 246; dining, 252; shopping, 253
Balboa Peninsula, 246, 248–49; lodging, 250
Balboa Pier, 248–49; dining, 252; lodging, 250–51; nightlife, 254
Ball (Lucille) home, 109
Ballarat (ghost town), 560
Ballard: sights, 432
Ballard School, 432
Balloon rides, 384, 509, 566
Banco Popular building, 27
Barnsdall Arts Center Gallery, 72
Barnsdall Park, 72

Lodging Index

Dining Index

HIDDEN GUIDES

Adventure travel or a relaxing vacation?—"Hidden" guidebooks are the only travel books in the business to provide detailed information on both. Aimed at environmentally aware travelers, our motto is "Where Vacations Meet Adventures." These books combine details on unique hotels, restaurants and sightseeing with information on camping, sports and hiking for the outdoor enthusiast.

THE NEW KEY GUIDES

Based on the concept of ecotourism, The New Key Guides are dedicated to the preservation of Central America's rare and endangered species, architecture and archaeology. Filled with helpful tips, they give travelers everything they need to know about these exotic destinations.

PARADISE FAMILY GUIDES

Ideal for families traveling with kids of any age—toddlers to teenagers—Paradise Family Guides offer a blend of travel information unlike any other guides to the Hawaiian islands. With vacation ideas and tropical adventures that are sure to satisfy both action-hungry youngsters and relaxation-seeking parents, these guides meet the specific needs of each and every family member.

Ulysses Press books are available at bookstores everywhere. If any of the following titles are unavailable at your local bookstore, ask the bookseller to order them.

You can also order books directly from Ulysses Press
P.O. Box 3440, Berkeley, CA 94703
800-377-2542 or 510-601-8301
fax: 510-601-8307
www.ulyssespress.com
e-mail: ulysses@ulyssespress.com

HIDDEN GUIDEBOOKS

____ Hidden Arizona, $16.95
____ Hidden Bahamas, $14.95
____ Hidden Baja, $14.95
____ Hidden Belize, $15.95
____ Hidden Big Island of Hawaii, $13.95
____ Hidden Boston & Cape Cod, $14.95
____ Hidden British Columbia, $18.95
____ Hidden Cancún & the Yucatán, $16.95
____ Hidden Carolinas, $17.95
____ Hidden Coast of California, $18.95
____ Hidden Colorado, $15.95
____ Hidden Disneyland, $13.95
____ Hidden Florida, $18.95
____ Hidden Florida Keys & Everglades, $13.95
____ Hidden Georgia, $16.95
____ Hidden Guatemala, $16.95
____ Hidden Hawaii, $18.95
____ Hidden Idaho, $14.95

____ Hidden Kauai, $13.95
____ Hidden Maui, $13.95
____ Hidden Montana, $15.95
____ Hidden New England, $18.95
____ Hidden New Mexico, $15.95
____ Hidden Oahu, $13.95
____ Hidden Oregon, $15.95
____ Hidden Pacific Northwest, $18.95
____ Hidden Salt Lake City, $14.95
____ Hidden San Francisco & Northern California, $18.95
____ Hidden Southern California, $18.95
____ Hidden Southwest, $19.95
____ Hidden Tahiti, $17.95
____ Hidden Tennessee, $16.95
____ Hidden Utah, $16.95
____ Hidden Walt Disney World, $13.95
____ Hidden Washington, $15.95
____ Hidden Wine Country, $13.95
____ Hidden Wyoming, $15.95

THE NEW KEY GUIDEBOOKS

____ The New Key to Costa Rica, $18.95

____ The New Key to Ecuador and the Galápagos, $17.95

PARADISE FAMILY GUIDES

____ Paradise Family Guides: Kaua'i, $16.95
____ Paradise Family Guides: Maui, $16.95

____ Paradise Family Guides: Big Island of Hawai'i, $16.95

Mark the book(s) you're ordering and enter the total cost here ➭ [   ]

California residents add 8.25% sales tax here ➭ [   ]

Shipping, check box for your preferred method and enter cost here ➭ [   ]

❑ BOOK RATE   **FREE! FREE! FREE!**

❑ PRIORITY MAIL/UPS GROUND   cost of postage

❑ UPS OVERNIGHT OR 2-DAY AIR   cost of postage

Billing, enter total amount due here and check method of payment ➭ [   ]

❑ CHECK   ❑ MONEY ORDER

❑ VISA/MASTERCARD _____ EXP. DATE _____

NAME _____ PHONE _____

ADDRESS _____

CITY _____ STATE _____ ZIP _____

MONEY-BACK GUARANTEE ON DIRECT ORDERS PLACED THROUGH ULYSSES PRESS.

ABOUT THE AUTHOR

RAY RIEGERT is the author of nine travel books, including *Hidden San Francisco & Northern California*. His most popular work, *Hidden Hawaii*, won the coveted Lowell Thomas Travel Journalism Award for Best Guidebook as well as a similar award from the Hawaii Visitors Bureau. In addition to his role as publisher of Ulysses Press, he has written for the *Chicago Tribune*, *San Francisco Chronicle* and *Travel & Leisure*. A member of the Society of American Travel Writers, he lives in the San Francisco Bay area with his wife, co-publisher Leslie Henriques, and their son Keith and daughter Alice.